DISCOUNTING
FOR TIME AND RISK
IN ENERGY POLICY

With comments by

Robert Dorfman
Martin S. Feldstein
Tjalling C. Koopmans
Hayne E. Leland
Talbot Page
Mark Sharefkin
Robert Smiley
James L. Sweeney
Daniel Usher

DISCOUNTING
FOR TIME AND RISK
IN ENERGY POLICY

Robert C. Lind
Kenneth J. Arrow • Gordon R. Corey
Partha Dasgupta • Amartya K. Sen
Thomas Stauffer • Joseph E. Stiglitz
J. A. Stockfisch • Robert Wilson

Published by Resources for the Future, Inc., Washington, D.C.

Distributed by The Johns Hopkins University Press, Baltimore and London

Published by Resources for the Future, Inc., 1755 Massachusetts Avenue, N.W.,
Washington, D.C. 20036
Distributed by The Johns Hopkins University Press, Baltimore, Maryland 21218
The Johns Hopkins Press, Ltd., London

Library of Congress Cataloging in Publication Data
Main entry under title:

Discounting for time and risk in energy policy.

  Includes index.
  1. Energy development—United States—Cost
effectiveness—Addresses, essays, lectures. 2. Energy
development—Social aspects—United States—Addresses,
essays, lectures. 3. Energy policy—United States—
Addresses, essays, lectures. I. Lind, Robert C.
II. Resources for the Future.
HD9502.U52D57   1982   333.79'0973   81-47619
ISBN 0-8018-2709-4

Resources for the Future is a nonprofit organization for research and education in the development, conservation, and use of natural resources, including the quality of the environment. It was established in 1952 with the cooperation of the Ford Foundation. Grants for research are accepted from government and private sources only on the condition that RFF shall be solely responsible for the conduct of the research and free to make its results available to the public. Most of the work of Resources for the Future is carried out by its resident staff; part is supported by grants to universities and other nonprofit organizations. Unless otherwise stated, interpretations and conclusions in RFF publications are those of the authors; the organization takes responsibility for the selection of significant subjects for study, the competence of the researchers, and their freedom of inquiry.

This book was edited by F. R. Ruskin and designed by Elsa B. Williams. The index was prepared by Florence Robinson.

Contents

Foreword

This volume is the result of six years of planning, research, and writing, including a conference held on March 4 and 5, 1977. The conference brought together academics, government officials, and representatives of industry to discuss the rate of discount that should be used to evaluate national energy options and policies. The motivation for this effort was, in large part, a response to (1) the determination by energy modelers that their findings were quite sensitive to the discount rate used and (2) the belief that if economic models were to provide a useful tool for choosing among our energy options, it was imperative that an appropriate rate of discount be specified.

In addition, there was a more general concern. Some people working in the energy field believed that the standard method of investment analysis, in which benefits and costs are forecast into the future and then discounted to their present value, might not be appropriate for evaluating many energy policy decisions, particularly those in which benefits and costs are expected in the distant future. These critics noted that some major energy-related research and development projects are expected to produce benefits no sooner than thirty or forty years hence, and that with almost any positive rate of discount, their benefits do not appear to justify their cost. Nevertheless, they believed such research and development is critical to assure energy supplies for the future.

Similarly, others were concerned that some environmental costs that would occur in the distant future would be given almost no weight in the standard benefit–cost formulation because such costs, discounted to the present by the use of almost any discount rate, would be infinitesimal. The case of nuclear waste is a particularly striking example because the costs might not occur for several thousand years. The question was raised: Are we not shortchanging future generations if we evaluate energy options by discounting future costs and benefits?

These concerns led Martin Greenberger, of the Electric Power Research Institute (EPRI), to propose a project in which the foremost experts on the question of the appropriate rate of discount would be commissioned to write papers on the methodology underlying the use of a discount rate in the evaluation of energy-related investments and policies. The objectives of the project were to present the commissioned papers at a conference and to produce a conference volume that would (1) lay out and resolve the basic conceptual issues, (2) provide the basic methodology for determining the appropriate discount rate for energy policy decisions, (3) provide a recommendation of a discount rate, or at least present a recommended procedure for computing the appropriate discount rate, and (4) influence government policy with regard to the choice of the discount rate and the evaluation of energy policy. A further objective was to make these results accessible to energy modelers and policy analysts who are not economists. Meeting these objectives would require that this volume be written in a style such that technically trained professionals, for example, energy modelers from the fields of engineering and operations research, or policy makers, could follow the line of argument and comprehend the results.

With these objectives in mind, Greenberger contacted Resources for the Future (RFF) to discuss the possibility of sponsoring the conference jointly with the Electric Power Research Institute and later publishing the volume of conference papers. Robert Lind, of Cornell University, was selected to be the project leader. He had contributed importantly to the literature and had previously worked with RFF. His responsibilities would be planning the conference, selecting topics for inclusion, finding appropriate authors and discussants, and editing the final volume. Late in the spring of 1976, EPRI and RFF agreed to sponsor the project jointly, and Lind agreed to manage it.

It was clear from the beginning that the project objectives were extremely ambitious. No doubt it was unrealistic to believe that all of the objectives could be achieved with a single volume of papers. There was no consensus within the economics profession on the question of the appropriate rate of discount for use in evaluating government energy projects or, for that matter, any other government projects. A long history of debate on this issue in the context of water resources projects and the scores of papers on the subject over the past twenty years had not resolved the issue. Therefore, it seemed probable that a conference would not produce a consensus.

Certainly the task was not simply one of providing a synthesis of the opinions of experts. To solve the problem would require extension of the existing theory and a major effort to integrate the development of various conceptual issues into an overall methodology for choosing a discount rate and for evaluating government projects and policies.

Further, even if some agreement could be reached on the theoretical issues, translating the theoretical framework into estimation of a defensible number to be used as the discount rate would not be a trivial problem. That is, even if there were agreement on the appropriate rate of discount from a conceptual standpoint, the problem of how to measure it empirically would remain. Another problem would be the difficulty of writing a paper that treats the technical issues adequately and extends the state of an art in as complex a field as the evaluation of investment decisions and, at the same time, is accessible to a wide audience.

Despite these difficulties, papers and comments were commissioned on the major issues that were identified during the months of discussion and planning that preceded the conference. Lind was assisted by an RFF advisory committee and drew upon other sources of advice as well. He was successful in assembling a group of contributors that included some of the world's foremost economists.

When the initial drafts of the papers became available at the conference, it was clear from the reaction of the participants that most of the papers would be accessible to only a relatively small group of economists even though they provided excellent technical assessments of the state of knowledge as well as a number of major theoretical contributions. This simply demonstrated the problem of trying to meet the ambitious objectives of the project in a single volume of papers. Further, no single paper provided a complete basis for determining the appropriate rate of discount or presented and defended a complete methodology for selecting a rate of discount that could be used in energy policy decisions under various conditions.

Two options were available. One was to publish the papers as they were, recognizing that they were a substantial contribution to the literature on this subject and that the volume would be of major scholarly value. Another option was to write additional material, drawing on findings of these papers, attempting to lay out the conceptual issues for a wider audience, and developing a methodology that would give specific guidance on the appropriate methods of evaluating energy policy decisions.

The second course was chosen and Robert Lind accepted the responsibility of adding four additional chapters to the book for the purpose of achieving these broader goals. The first three chapters and the final chapter of the book are the result of this work. The first chapter is an introduction to the discount rate issue in connection with energy decisions and relates the current controversy over the discount rate to the earlier literature on the selection of discount rates in the analysis of water resources projects. It also introduces the authors and commissioned papers and shows how they fit into the plan for the conference and this volume.

The second chapter develops systematically the issues that have been central to the controversy over discount rates and, in the process, develops a method for analyzing social investment decisions. That method equates the social rate of discount with the rate of time preference in social investments and also accounts for the opportunity cost of capital by making adjustments in the benefits and the costs. In this way, it is possible to specify a single rate of discount for evaluating social investment decisions and to develop an analytical procedure that takes into account the opportunity costs of these investments and the associated risks.

This analytical procedure draws on ideas presented in the papers contained in this volume, and it also draws heavily on other literature in the field. However, it was not possible to develop a procedure for analyzing social investment and make recommendations based solely on the existing literature. Therefore, Lind's role in the production of this volume became far more than that of an editor. Rather this volume is in large part a report on the findings of Lind's own research that grew out of his attempt to meet the original objectives of the project. I believe that Lind has broken new ground by bringing together various elements of the theoretical and the applied literature. The second chapter advances our theoretical insights while promising to yield significant practical benefits.

The third chapter is an overview of the commissioned papers, the comments, and the major findings. Its purpose is to acquaint the reader with the papers and to make the most important findings accessible to a wider audience than would be willing or able to read the full technical discussions.

In the final chapter, Lind presents an approach for analyzing alternative energy investments, including the treatment of the discount rate for different types of energy projects and policies. He draws heavily on the analytical procedure established in the second chapter and on his work as a consultant to the U.S. Department of Energy.

Because of the way in which the volume evolved, it was not possible to develop a way of analyzing policy and to propose policy recommendations that would command a consensus of the contributing authors, and there was no attempt to do so. The work presented in the final chapter is solely Lind's responsibility, although he sought comment and criticism from the authors, the discussants, and a wide audience working in the energy field.

Finally, it is interesting to note that, despite the six years that have passed since the inception of the project, the issue of the discount rate in energy planning is as important and troublesome to energy analysts and policy makers today as it was then. As this was written, the Department of Energy was reviewing the appropriateness of using the 10 percent real rate of discount mandated by the Office of Management and Budget (OMB) in the context of solar energy. Economists at OMB and the Council of Economic Advisors were also considering this issue.

The papers contained in the volume have been made available to a large number of analysts and others before publication. Many of the findings have found their way into the Department of Energy's analysis of the discount rate issue and elsewhere through the work of Lind and others. Thus the work of the authors and discussants has already influenced the ongoing policy debate on planning for energy alternatives. This volume will not be the final word, but I believe it is the latest word on this complex subject. It not only aids understanding but it also assists with the development of policy.

Emery N. Castle
President
Resources for the Future

March 1982

Acknowledgments

The objective and history of this volume have been ably described by Emery Castle in the foreword. Therefore, I simply want to thank the many people who have contributed to the book for their help and for their patience. I especially want to thank Martin Greenberger for conceiving of the book, the Electric Power Research Institute for supporting it, and Resources for the Future for undertaking the project. I owe a very special debt of gratitude to Emery Castle, president of Resources for the Future, for his steadfast support in the long and sometimes frustrating process of bringing the volume to print.

I am grateful to the authors and discussants for their help and their patience in this process, particularly to those who met the deadlines, but suffered the delays. I also wish to thank Martin Bailey, John Krutilla, and an anonymous reviewer for their work which contributed significantly to the volume as a whole and in particular to my chapters, and to thank my colleague Henry Wan for his careful review and insightful comments on several chapters. I am very grateful for the painstaking work of F. R. Ruskin, the editor, who made the book more readable, and to Sally Skillings, the managing editor at Resources for the Future, who moved the manuscript through the publications process.

March 1982

Robert C. Lind

DISCOUNTING
FOR TIME AND RISK
IN ENERGY POLICY

1

*Robert C. Lind**

Introduction

Not since the late 1950s and 1960s, when the economic evaluation of federal water projects centered on the selection of discount rates to be used in policy analysis, has this issue been as important as it is now in connection with national energy policy. Development of our nation's options for new energy supplies and for conservation requires large investments now that will produce benefits well into the future. To evaluate these options we must weigh the future benefits against the present costs. Therefore, the weight we give to benefits and costs at different times is critical and is determined by the discount rate that we use. The higher the discount rate, the lower we value future benefits and costs as compared with present ones.

Energy research and development projects costing billions of dollars may not begin to produce benefits for twenty to thirty years, and these benefits may then accrue over one or more centuries. To compare these benefits and costs over time, the standard analytical procedure is to discount them to their present values. Their sum, the net present value of the project, is the critical measure of a project's economic value. In investments that will produce large benefits or costs well into the future, the discount rate used in the calculation of present values strongly affects these totals.

If the discount rate is as high as 10 percent, the present values of costs and benefits in the future become insignificant compared with those of the present. For example, the present value of $1,000 of benefits fifty years hence is worth $8.52 if discounted at 10 percent, $87.20 if discounted at 5 percent, and $371.53 if discounted at 2 percent. Therefore, if we use a discount rate of 10 percent rather than 2 percent, we reduce the present value of benefits and costs fifty years hence by more than a factor of 40. The implication of this basic arithmetic is nowhere more apparent than in the evaluations of the U.S. liquid metal fast breeder reactor program. The net present value of the benefits from breeder development as estimated by the Energy Research and Development Administration (1975) falls from $46.8 billion to $16 billion when the discount rate is raised from 7.5 percent to 10

---

* Graduate School of Business and Public Administration, Cornell University.

percent.[1] Not only are the benefits and costs of many energy policy options highly sensitive to the discount rate, but whether the net benefits are positive or negative depends critically on the discount rate; small variations in that rate will often tip the balance.

Even the sensitivity of the present value of the net benefits of many energy policy options would not pose such a serious analytical problem if there were agreement that the appropriate discount rate lay within relatively narrow bounds. Unfortunately, there is no such agreement, and rates of 2 percent and 10 percent both lie within the range of rates that have been proposed and defended for evaluating energy policy decisions. Furthermore, different studies of alternative energy technologies use widely varying discount rates. In evaluation of the breeder reactor alone, Manne and Richels (1978) use 5 percent and 10 percent; Stauffer, Wycoff, and Palmer (1975, p. 6), 6 percent; the Energy Research and Development Administration, 7.5 percent and 10 percent; and Chow (1975) recommends a procedure for determining the appropriate rate that in one particular case results in a rate of 10.07 percent.

To put the discount rate issue in perspective, it is useful to compare today's analytical debates, accepted wisdom, and positions on energy policy with those twenty years ago on water resource policy. In many ways the present debate is a replay or at least a continuation of the previous one, but there are some new elements and fundamental differences that are peculiar to energy.

The basic similarity is that energy projects, like water projects, require initial investments that produce benefits well into the future. Therefore, with energy projects, as with water projects, the discount rate is critical to three major dimensions of energy policy evaluation. First, it is a major determinant of whether a project is economically efficient, that is, whether the net present value of benefits is positive. This is a critical test of whether we should invest in a project. A second, closely related point is that the discount rate is a major determinant of the relative value of competing projects. Because funds are limited, we may have to choose among competing energy technologies, and this choice will depend on which have the highest net present value. Third, the discount rate is a major determinant of the optimal timing of projects. For example, should we proceed now to develop a technology such as the breeder, or should we postpone its development?

With energy projects, as with water projects, sometimes even a small change in the discount rate will make a significant difference in the evaluation of a project's economic potential. Sometimes the evaluation will not be as sensitive to the discount rate. There are times when an analyst needs to be able to specify the rate of discount with precision, and other times when, if

---

[1] For a table showing the effect of using different discount rates in AEC and ERDA studies of the breeder, see Chow (1977, p. 553).

the discount rate lies within a fairly broad range of values, the economic evaluation of the investment decision remains unchanged.

One technique that has long been used to resolve policy disputes arising over the selection of a discount rate is to test the sensitivity of a particular policy to the discount rate. However, in many other cases, either it may not be practical to test for sensitivity (because of the cost of energy model runs, for example), or the benefits of the policy may be found to be highly sensitive to the discount rate that is used. In these cases, greater resolution of the discount rate issue is required if benefit–cost studies and energy models that incorporate a discount rate are to be useful in choosing among alternative energy policies. Therefore, the energy modeling community, like the water policy community before it, has been one of the groups most interested in resolving the discount rate issue and, in particular, in developing a defensible discount rate that can be used in economic and energy models and in energy policy analysis.

In many economic and energy models, a discount rate enters in two ways. First, analysts use a discount rate to calculate the net present value of national economic benefits for alternative energy policies or investments. To compute the social value of these benefits from a national perspective, one must discount using the appropriate rate for such a calculation, that is, the "social rate" of discount. Second, these models sometimes use a discount rate in order to simulate private sector investment behavior. The models predict which investments will be made in the private sector, evaluating private investment alternatives by means of a discount rate equal to the required rate of return on investment in the private sector. One of the big open questions in the controversy over discount rates is whether the social rate should be the same as the required rate of return on private investment.

This volume will primarily address the question of the appropriate rate of discount for evaluating the present value of benefits from a national or social perspective. That is, it focuses on the question of the social rate of discount. There are several reasons for examining this rate as opposed to the appropriate rates for use by utilities or oil companies. First, the federal government will play a major role in making energy policy and will probably be one of the major supporters of energy research and development. In making public policy decisions on the development of the breeder reactor, the mandating of coal conversion, the setting of energy efficiency standards, and the regulation of utilities, many individuals in government will want to know the net present value of alternative policies from a national or social viewpoint. The social rate of discount is relevant to this calculation.

A second reason for considering the social rate of discount is that, despite its importance for energy policy, there is no agreement on how this rate should be determined nor on what the correct rate should be. By contrast, firms and individuals will make their decisions on the basis of the rates of return and rates of interest prevailing in the market place. When compared with determination of the social rate, determination of rates that should be used by private firms in making their own decisions, while subject to some controversy, is relatively straightforward. However, determination of a defensible rate of discount for use in computation of the present value of net national economic benefits has caused considerable difficulty for energy modelers and policy analysts. Hence, it is the focus of this volume.

Before exploring various dimensions and issues associated with the social rate of discount, it is useful to consider how the discount rate has been handled in examples of energy models and benefit–cost studies of energy options. The modeling group for the study by the National Research Council's Committee on Nuclear and Alternative Energy Systems (CONAES) used an average pretax rate of 13 percent as the required rate of return on private investment, and they used 6 percent to discount national economic benefits (National Academy of Sciences, 1978). The 6-percent rate is considered to represent the after-tax rate of return on private investment. From the CONAES project followed the Energy Modeling Forum (EMF), sponsored by the Electric Power Research Institute (EPRI). In five of the first six energy models that were developed under its aegis, one or two discount rates enter as important parameters.[2] Because of practical limitations on the number of scenarios that could be considered in the studies based on these models, sensitivity testing was not generally performed to determine whether the discount rate assumptions that these models incorporate have a significant effect on the policy-relevant outputs of the models. However, the perceived dependence of the model results on the assumed discount rates coupled with the absence of a clear-cut choice of values for these parameters has frequently been cited as a major potential limitation by energy modelers (Hogan and coauthors, 1979).

To see the variety of discount rate assumptions that are built into EMF models alone, consider that the report of the first EMF study, *Energy and the Economy* (EMF, 1977), follows the CONAES practice of using discount rates of 13 percent and 6 percent to represent the required rate of return on private investment and the social rate of discount. The second EMF study report, *Coal in Transition* (EMF, 1978), incorporates only one rate, namely, 13 percent, as the required private sector rate of return. The third EMF study report, *Electric Load Forecasting* (EMF, 1979), uses different discount rates for different regions. A 1980 EMF working paper, *World Oil Study Design* (EMF, 1980b) uses a uniform rate of discount of 5 percent, and *U.S. Oil and Gas Supply* (EMF, 1980a) incorporates a required rate of return for the oil and gas industry of 8 percent. However, in this last case, the results were

---

[2] Information regarding discount rates and how they are used in various studies of the Energy Modeling Forum was supplied by John P. Weyant, deputy director, in a letter dated April 17, 1980.

tested for sensitivity, and changing the discount rate from 8 percent to 16 percent reduced the 1995 projection of conventional crude oil production from 9.5 million barrels a day to 4 million barrels a day.

The report of another study that does limited testing of the results for changes in the discount rate is "A Decision Analysis of the U.S. Breeder Reactor Program" by Manne and Richels (1978). They compute the present value of national economic benefits from alternative breeder reactor programs using 5 percent and 10 percent as discount rates. They state: "Since both breeder and reprocessing benefits accrue almost entirely post-2000, their present value is quite sensitive to the choice of a public discount rate. (This comment holds not only for the breeder but also for fusion, solar electric, and virtually any other phenomenon of the 21st century!)''

Because the choice of the discount rate can influence strongly which public policies can be supported by benefit–cost analysis and which cannot, it is a matter of concern to politicians as well as policy analysts. The choice of the discount rate for evaluating public choices is itself a public policy decision that in most cases will be politically determined. While philosophers, economists, and financial analysts may debate the appropriateness of one rate as opposed to another for public policy decisions, and while their arguments may well be influential, the final choice will often be determined politically. It will depend not only on the merits of the supporting economic arguments but also on the policy implications of one choice versus another and on the political strength of forces in support of those implications.

For example, under the Nixon administration, the Office of Management and Budget (OMB) in March 1972 directed most federal agencies to apply a 10 percent real rate of discount when calculating the present value of the costs and benefits of federal projects (OMB, 1972). Previously there had been a wide range of practices with regard to discounting and discount rates used by federal agencies, as reported by the comptroller general to the Joint Economic Committee in 1968, and some agencies did not use discounting at all. The comptroller general's report states:

> A divergence of opinion on discounting is reflected in agency practices. Some agencies use the Treasury cost of borrowing money as the discount rate while others use a rate based on the return on investment in the private sector of the economy. Still others employ different criteria to determine the agencies discount rate and agency borrowing cost. The agencies included in our survey used discount rates which vary over an extremely wide range—from about 3 to 12 percent.
>
> Within each school of thought there are important differences of opinion. Of those agencies which tie the discount rate to Treasury borrowing costs, one uses the estimated cost of new money to the Treasury, another uses the average cost of money to the Treasury, others use the cost prescribed by Senate Document 97 (about 3.2 percent at the time of our review).

One of those agencies which would tie the discount rate to the rate of return in the private sector uses a rate of return on a safe investment and a slightly higher rate (3 percent and 5 percent) while another uses for some programs the rate representative of average capital returns in the private sector (presumed to be 12 percent) and for some programs permits the analyst to determine the rate on the basis of his judgment as to the nature of the program and the kind of analysis considered most meaningful.

Views are equally disparate in those agencies which report that discounting was not used in their analyses of individual programs for support of their fiscal year 1969 budget decisions. At one extreme is the view that decisions on programs should be made on the basis of first year costs and benefits—a procedure which implies a discount rate of 100 percent, since the future is ignored. At the other extreme is the view that decisions should be based on total undiscounted costs and benefits—a procedure which implies a discount rate of zero, since costs and benefits applicable to, say, the 20th year are treated as being as important as current costs and benefits (U.S. Congress, 1968, pp. 11–12).

The directive in OMB Circular A–94 raised the discount rate used by most agencies to 10 percent and made it consistent across agencies. One exception, however, was the rate used to evaluate water resources projects. Congress resisted the move to raise the discount rate to 10 percent for water projects by refusing to abandon use of the formula set forth in Senate Document 97 (U.S. Congress, 1962). Raising the discount rate for water projects would have had adverse implications for public works projects; that is, many fewer would have met the benefit–cost test. Finally, Congress itself wrote into law the formula that determines the discount rate to be used in evaluating water projects in Section 80–A of the Water Resources Development Act of 1974 (Public Law 93–251). The prescribed discount rate for use in evaluating water projects has been consistently below the 10 percent rate for other agencies including energy agencies.

Those supporting the 10 percent rate, which was believed to approximate the marginal real rate of return on capital in the private sector, argued that to achieve greater overall economic efficiency, the rate of return in the public sector should be the same as in the private sector. Perhaps a more important argument for this change, however, was that the administration in power favored reduced government spending and fewer government projects. With a higher rate of discount, fewer government projects would pass the test of economic efficiency. Consequently, it was easier for the administration to make the case that they should not be funded.

It is instructive to look at how the political interests of different groups would be affected by a high versus a low discount rate in evaluation of both water and energy policies. Those groups favoring regional development, particularly in the West and South, supported large-scale, government-supported water projects and generally argued for lower discount rates. Their counterparts today are groups favoring an expanded role for government in implementing a national energy policy and groups favoring expanded government funding for research and development projects for new energy-producing and energy-conserving technologies; for example, the breeder reactor, solar and fusion power, and alternative propulsion systems. Similarly, now as in the 1950s and 1960s, those who favor cuts in government spending and less direct government involvement in the economy tend to support a higher rate.

Two other groups have a stake in the choice of the discount rate that is used in evaluating public investments and public policies. They are the environmentalists and the private, investor-owned utilities. The situation of the environmentalists with respect to the discount rate, as they have come to realize, is complicated by the fact that in some cases a higher rate leads to policy conclusions that are consistent with their goals, and in some cases it does not. With regard to water resources, for example, environmentalists saw the requirement of a high rate of discount for use in evaluating water projects as a way of slowing development and preserving natural areas. The result was that the environmentalist groups found themselves in coalition with fiscal conservatives in support of a high rate of discount and fewer federal water projects.

However, a high discount rate cuts the other way in energy and minerals policy. The economic case for rapid development and exploitation of our mineral and fossil fuel resources is enhanced by the use of a high discount rate. This is because the higher the discount rate, the lower the value that these resources will have if left for future development. Another example in which a higher discount rate goes against the environmentalists' position is the case of nuclear waste or any other case in which environmental pollutants may pose a potential threat to the environment well into the future. To the extent that these long-term costs are quantified and incorporated into a benefit–cost analysis, the higher the rate of discount, the less important these costs will appear.

In the case of nuclear waste, where the costs of contamination might accrue several thousand years from now, any positive rate of discount, when compounded over that period, would be sufficient to render the present value of even catastrophic costs to future generations relatively insignificant in terms of their present value. Also, a higher rate of discount goes against the development of new solar and conservation technologies and favors greater reliance on fossil fuels, which have adverse environmental consequences. Therefore, when considering water resources, the environmentalists generally find that they agree with the policy implications of using a high discount rate, whereas in the field of energy and resource policy, they do not.

Private utilities have long supported the requirement that public investments, particularly public power projects, earn the same rate of return as private sector investments and that the return for public utilities be computed on the basis of the private sector cost of capital. The reason is simple: in many areas, private, investor-owned power companies are in direct competition with government-owned facilities. If the government computes its cost of producing power using a cost of capital below the private cost of capital, the government appears more efficient and able to produce power more cheaply than a private utility can. The government also appears to have lower capital costs even though in terms of the opportunity cost of the capital resources required, both the public and private power facilities require identical capital faculties.

Therefore, the choice of the rate of discount that is used to evaluate alternatives in water resources policy, energy policy, or public policy in general has critical implications for the federal budget, for regional development, for technological choices, for the environment, and for the size of government. That is, the choice of the discount rate affects issues important to thousands of special interest groups, from the nuclear lobby to the Sierra Club. It is much more than a technical matter of interest only to economists and policy analysts. It embodies the values on which we make social choices that affect the state of our economy and our environment.

In the large private sector of the U.S. economy, prices, including interest rates, are determined by the market; the effective rates of discount governing the investment decisions of private firms and the consumption and savings decisions of individuals are the rates of return and the rates of interest that prevail in the market. This raises a number of fundamental questions. Do market rates of interest or rates of return bear any relation to the rate of discount that is appropriate for evaluating alternative public policies? In particular, should public investments be required to earn the same rate of return as private investments so that the rate of discount for public investments equals the rate of return in the private sector? Or are there considerations that would justify a different (and in particular, a lower) rate of discount for evaluating investments in public projects or for analyzing public policy choices in general?

Further, to the extent that differences in the riskiness of private sector investments are reflected in differences in rates of return on these investments, should differences in the riskiness of public investments be reflected in differences in the discount rates used to evaluate their benefits and costs? That is, should riskier public investments be required to earn the same higher rate of return that private investors demand from riskier investments? These were the basic questions that were at the center of the controversy over the discount rate in the 1950s and 1960s as it pertained to the development of criteria for evaluating water resource projects.

Although many economists agreed that, in an idealized economy with perfectly competitive and complete markets, the rate of return in the private sectors should be the same and should equal the market rate of interest, once one moved from this idealized economy to an economy in which the allocation of resources was distorted by taxes, credit restrictions, and numerous other market imperfections, there was sharp disagreement about the appropriate rate of discount for evaluating public investment and public policy decisions.

On the one hand, there were economists who held that the required rate of return should be the same in the public sector as in the private sector to ensure that public investments with low rates of return would not displace private investments with higher rates of return. On the other hand, there were economists who argued that distortions in the market cause the rate of return on private capital to be higher than the rate that should be used to evaluate public investments. This second group took the position that a lower rate equal to the consumption rate of interest, that is, the rate at which consumers are willing to trade consumption now for consumption in the future, should be used by the government in benefit–cost calculations. A third position was that the rate used to evaluate public investments should be a weighted average of the private rate of return and the consumption rate of interest.

Similarly, there were economists who argued that discount rates used to evaluate public investments should be adjusted upward to account for the riskiness of each project in exactly the way that such an adjustment is made in the private sector. Others argued that no such risk adjustment should be made in public investments. Finally, there were economists who held that there was no relation between the rate of discount that was appropriate for evaluating public investment or public policy decisions and rates of return on private investment or market rates of interest. These positions will be developed more fully in the next chapter; however, they are stated here to illustrate that there was neither a consensus in the late 1960s about how the discount rate should be determined in theory nor a consensus on a specific number. Individuals had their own beliefs about what the appropriate rate should be, but the numbers varied greatly.

For example, Resources for the Future sponsored a conference in 1966 on the appropriate rate of discount for evaluating water projects. The foremost economists and water policy analysts from across the country were invited. After most of a day of debate without agreement on the conceptual basis for the choice of the discount rate, one of the conference's organizers posed the question, If you had to pick a single number, what would be your personal estimate of the appropriate rate? The answers ranged from a low of 2 to 4 percent, based on the real rate of return on long-term government bonds, to 20 percent, based on the interest rate for short-term consumer credit.[3] It is

---

[3] I was writing my dissertation while in residence at RFF and attended this conference.

not surprising, therefore, that the comptroller general found federal agencies using a wide range of discount rates supported by an equally wide range of theories. This situation simply reflected the lack of a consensus.

In the decade between that conference and this one, scores of scholarly papers were written on the discount rate. These papers have advanced our understanding of the conceptual issues that underlie the evaluation of public investment and policy decisions, and in particular, the selection of the appropriate rate for discounting social benefits and costs. Nevertheless, at the time of this conference, the profession was no closer to agreement on the theory, on a procedure for computing the discount rate, or on a rate itself than it was in 1966. If anything, the work of the last decade showed that the issue is even more complex than we had thought and that the range of disagreement, not to say confusion, is as great as before.

A graduate course in benefit–cost analysis in 1966, while revealing no agreement on the appropriate rate of discount, would have presented a number of issues upon which there was a fair amount of agreement. Although economists could not agree on the correct rate, they generally did agree that whatever the correct rate was, this rate should be used to evaluate all public projects and policies, with the exception of possible adjustments for differences in risk. Today, as we see in this volume, the advances in theory have led to the belief that perhaps different rates are appropriate for different projects and policies.

Further, one would have learned that the discount rate should not be affected by macroeconomic considerations such as unemployed resources, the level of the national debt, or the method of financing the project, for example, the sale of bonds, an income tax, a corporate profits tax, the printing of money, or some combination of these methods. The accepted doctrine was to separate macroeconomic considerations of stabilization from benefit–cost analysis by assuming that monetary and fiscal policy would keep the economy fully employed. To the extent that resources were unemployed, they were to be accounted for by adjustments in the cost of employing those resources; for example, the cost of using unemployed labor on public works projects in Appalachia would not be counted as a cost in the benefit–cost analysis even though this labor was paid the going wage rate. However, as we see from the papers in this volume, these simplifying procedures to isolate the problems of macroeconomic policy from the microeconomic aspects of public resource allocation (benefit–cost analysis) cannot be maintained. Macroeconomic policy does in fact have a powerful effect on questions pertaining to efficient resource allocation and, in particular, to the choice of the discount rate.

Finally, in the controversy over high versus low discount rates, there was more or less agreement that the appropriate discount rate for public projects probably lay between the rate of return on private capital at the upper end and the consumption rate of interest on the lower end, with the proponents of a weighted-average rate placing it somewhere in the middle. In this volume, Joseph Stiglitz demonstrates that in some cases the appropriate rate may even lie outside of these bounds.

We have learned that to properly analyze and evaluate the economic effects of public investments or public policy decisions in an economy with many market distortions requires a great deal more information about the economy and its structure and about the economic instruments used to implement a public investment or public policy than we previously believed necessary. As if these added considerations did not sufficiently complicate the mission of reaching agreement on a discount rate for analyzing alternative energy options, there are several additional complicating issues that arise in energy policy that did not arise to the same degree in connection with water resources.

We have finite supplies of fossil fuels and at some point we will have to switch to alternative sources of energy to support future generations. If we are to have new sources of energy in place for future generations, we must begin to do the necessary research and development. If we do not, future generations may have a markedly reduced standard of living because past generations depleted the resource base without providing a substitute. However, research and development on technologies that will not be used for many years may not appear justified economically, given that the benefits that accrue many years in the future have a low present value. Proponents of such research and development question the wisdom of postponing or failing to undertake such research on the basis of benefit–cost calculations, which appear to them to assign too little weight to the welfare of future generations.

We are considering energy options that may impose catastrophic environmental costs in the distant future. A striking case in point is nuclear power and the problem of nuclear waste disposal. Suppose that we could put the waste in containers that would safely last two thousand years but then might release the waste into the environment raising the possibility of large-scale contamination. In this case, the potential costs to future generations would begin thousands, not just hundreds, of years in the future. Discounting those costs at any positive rate would make them appear minuscule.

There are many who share the concern that it is not appropriate to choose a nuclear option on the basis of a benefit–cost calculation that places a very low weight on possible catastrophic consequences in the future. They have a similar concern about a policy of not pushing ahead on the research and development that will provide future generations with a safe, economical, and environmentally sound energy option. They question the efficacy of an evaluation procedure that appears, from their perspective, to disregard the interests of future generations and lead to the adoption of unwise policies.

They raise two basic questions. First, if we discount benefits and costs at a positive rate, are we not putting less value on the welfare of future generations than our own? Or, put differently, if we were egalitarian among generations living now and in the future, wouldn't this require that we use a zero rate of discount in benefit–cost analysis? This position accepts the benefit–cost framework, but argues for a zero discount rate on the grounds of intergenerational equity.

The second question is more fundamental and goes to the philosophical foundation of benefit–cost analysis, which applies utilitarian principles to the analysis of public investment and public policy. This practice has been extended and elaborated upon in modern welfare economics. Benefit–cost analysis fits within the utilitarian tradition because benefits and costs to different individuals living at different times are measured, assigned weights with respect to time (discounted to their present value), and added together. The decision rule is to accept the policy or project that produces the highest total without regard for the distribution of benefits and costs among individuals or among generations. An extension of this procedure, which is used in the theory of optimal economic growth, is to convert benefits and costs into units of utility and then to select the policy that maximizes the discounted sum of utilities over time.

Whichever procedure is used, the same fundamental question remains: Is this method of analysis sufficiently robust, with respect to capturing the important dimensions of resource allocation across generations, to be used as a basis for such decisions? One frequent criticism of this application of the utilitarian criteria and of discounting, in particular, is that it ignores fundamental questions of fairness among generations.

If there is some merit in this criticism of the benefit–cost approach to analysis of public investment and public policy, do we need to develop totally new criteria or can we salvage the benefit–cost framework by imposing some additional constraints upon it or by adding elements to the decision criterion, for example, a system of generational rights that must be satisfied by any acceptable policy? Because of the general interest in, and sympathy for, the positions stated above by a respected group of economists as well as a much larger group of people who are not economists, it is important in any discussion of the discount rate in energy policy to consider the distribution of benefits and costs.

Although there has in the past been discussion of whether discounting at a high rate would result in too little investment and thereby unfairly reduce the wealth of future generations, the climate for this discussion twenty years ago was very different from what it is now. In the first place, the choice was between relatively more consumption immediately and relatively less con-sumption in the future whereas the choice now may be between more consumption today and catastrophic costs for the future. Similarly, twenty years ago our forecast of the prosperity of future generations was much brighter. After all, technical progress had produced a rising standard of living over the past hundred years, and each successive generation had been richer than the previous one. The energy crisis, the development of major environmental problems, and the potential for shortages of other natural resources have dampened our optimism about the prospects of future generations. We no longer believe that they, necessarily, will be wealthier than we are. Twenty years ago we simply were not considering issues such as nuclear waste or a critical shortage of energy and the untold harm they might cause to future generations.

A final difference between policies governing federal water projects and energy policy is that the water projects were undertaken by the government; the decision regarding the initial investment and the operation of the facility were under the direct control of the government. A decision could be based on the benefit–cost criterion incorporating the rate of discount that was appropriate from the public policy perspective, and once made, a decision could be implemented directly. This is not the case with energy policy. Most energy is produced and delivered to the consumer by private, investor-owned companies. These companies compete in the same markets for capital, face market prices including market rates of interest, and have to be able to offer their investors the prospect of a competitive rate of return. Within the constraints placed upon them by market forces and by government regulations, they attempt to maximize their net worth for the benefit of their shareholders.

Under these circumstances it will be the firm's cost of capital and institutional constraints that will determine the firm's investment behavior. This is why in many energy economic models the private rate is used in simulations of private investment behavior while another rate is used to compute net economic benefits. Similarly, personal decisions about consumption and saving will be determined by the prices and interest rates in the market. If the government analyzes a policy using a discount rate that is appropriate from a public perspective but that does not correspond to the governing market rate, then individuals and firms will not behave in a manner consistent with that policy unless some action is taken to alter their incentives or to make consistent behavior mandatory.

A case in point is that of a national policy of converting to coal-based power. Unless it is required by law or unless the incentives are structured to make conversion to coal the option that maximizes the net worth of a firm, the policy will not be carried out. To determine the appropriate incentives or the appropriate regulation, one needs to know what firms and households are doing, how this compares with the desired policy, and what incentives or regulations would bring about the desired change. How do regulated utilities make investment decisions? What discount rates do they use? Do these practices lead to investments consistent with the criterion of maximizing the present value of net social benefits?

At the time of the conference, the state of economic theory pertaining to the discount rate had advanced in that it provided insights into the complexity of this issue, but still it did not provide the policy analyst with a procedure for choosing a defensible rate. It showed him more potential pitfalls but without showing him how to avoid them. The old controversies were not resolved but, rather, were complicated. New issues had been piled on top of the old, and there was confusion, or at least a marked lack of consensus, about what rate should be used in benefit–cost analyses of the nation's energy options. Benefit–cost studies of alternative energy policies were being performed using a range of discount rates. In some studies a number of rates were used and sensitivity testing was performed, leaving the final choice of a discount rate to someone else.

To address the new issues as well as the old, unresolved issues pertaining to the discount rate and energy policy, the conference brought together a distinguished group of authors and discussants. The old controversies about the appropriate rules for public investment decisions and, in particular, the questions about the appropriate discount rate in an economy distorted by taxes, constraints on government, business, and individuals, and other market distortions were by no means settled. Should the rate of discount used in evaluating public investment be the real rate of return on private capital or should it be the consumption rate of interest? Should the rate of discount for public projects be some weighted average of these two rates? If so, how should the weights be determined? These and other, related questions had to be addressed if issues pertaining to the discount rate in energy planning were to be resolved.

These issues are discussed in this volume by Kenneth Arrow of Harvard, and more recently Stanford, and by Joseph Stiglitz of Oxford, and more recently Princeton. Arrow, a pioneering contributor to the literature on the discount rate, extends the theory by building on his previous work. Stiglitz sets forth systematically many of the results pertaining to decision rules for social investment and their implications for the discount rate—rules he had derived in his extensive work on benefit–cost analysis and economic planning. In addition, Martin Feldstein of Harvard and Daniel Usher of Queens, important contributors to this literature in their own right, served as discussants.

Risk and how it should or should not be reflected in the discount rate is a part of all discussions of the discount rate for public as well as private investments. Recent developments in finance and economics have demonstrated that in many cases what is most relevant for determining the riskiness of an investment project is the covariance of its return with the returns to the economy as a whole and not the variance of its own return. This is true both from the standpoint of the nation as a whole and from the standpoint of individual investors, provided that they have access to fairly complete markets for risk, such as the securities markets. The discussions of the risks associated with new energy technologies have not always reflected this result. The development of an energy technology with very uncertain future returns may not constitute a risky project. If it will have a high payoff under just those conditions when the rest of the economy will do poorly, it will reduce the overall variability of national income and therefore reduce risk. Such an investment has the characteristics of insurance.

This issue and many others that relate to risk, uncertainty, and discounting are addressed by Robert Wilson of Stanford, whose paper lays out the basic issues pertaining to risk and discounting and develops an approach to the treatment of risk in evaluating major energy projects. In addition, Hayne Leland of the University of California at Berkeley, whose work is in the area of finance and the economics of uncertainty, commented on the issue of risk and discounting.

The conference also was intended to address the question of whether discounting at a positive rate is equivalent to giving less weight to the welfare of future generations. More generally, the conference sought to investigate how the consumption by future generations would be affected by an economic system in which consumption and investment decisions over time accord with the maximization of the sum of the discounted utilities of all generations. Conference organizers also wanted to be fully responsive to questions about the appropriateness of present value criteria for analyzing such issues as nuclear waste disposal and the exhaustion of nonrenewable resources without providing for substitutes. Does the utilitarian formulation of the objective function, namely, the discounted sum of net benefits or of utilities over time, provide the appropriate basis for making these decisions that will have a profound effect on the well-being of future generations?

Two additional papers answer these questions. Partha Dasgupta of the London School of Economics, a leading expert on the economics of depletable resources, uses the framework of optimal economic growth to analyze the implications of positive-rate discounting for the consumption and welfare of future generations. He clarifies, among other things, the distinction between the discounting of units of "utility" or "felicity" and the discounting of units of consumption and shows the relation between these two concepts. This distinction has been the source of much confusion among analysts who are not fully conversant with the literature on optimal economic growth. He also explores the role of research and development in a model of optimal economic growth.

The discussants for the Dasgupta paper were three noted economists— Tjalling Koopmans of Yale, Robert Dorfman of Harvard, and James Sweeney of Stanford—and a physicist from Resources for the Future, Mark Sharefkin, who has worked extensively on environmental policy issues, including the ethical issues associated with intergenerational effects.

The second paper is by Amartya K. Sen, then of the London School of Economics and more recently of Oxford University. Sen, who is noted for his work in welfare economics, was asked (1) to summarize the lines of argument that support the conclusion that market-determined rates of interest or rates of return bear no necessary relation to the discount rate that should be used in evaluating public investments or policies and (2) to address the question of whether the utilitarian foundations of welfare economics that underlie benefit–cost techniques are an adequate basis for making some of the critical choices facing society as part of the energy crisis. The discussants of Sen's paper were again Dorfman and Sharefkin, who were joined by Talbot Page of Resources for the Future.

Although the conference was convened in the belief that a better understanding of the theoretical foundations of benefit–cost analysis and of the implications of discounting was important for clarifying some misconceptions and that a review of these foundations might modify the use of these techniques and the interpretation of their results, many also believe it was highly unlikely that the techniques of benefit–cost analysis would be abandoned altogether. Therefore, after such a reexamination, the problem of establishing a number for the discount rate would remain. Even if the conference were to resolve all the theoretical issues, there still was the question of how to measure or compute the discount rate. If, for example, the theory indicates that the rate of discount should equal the marginal rate of return on private capital or the consumption rate of interest, then how can these magnitudes be measured empirically? Or if the theory says that the appropriate discount rate is a weighted average of the two, how are the weights to be determined? Any attempt at providing practical guidance on the choice of the discount rate must address the measurement issue.

It was difficult to commission papers on measurement before the theoretical results were in. However, two rates discussed in the literature have been such prominent contenders for the appropriate discount rate or a component of it that it was fairly safe to address the issue of their measurement. These two rates are the marginal pretax rate of return on private capital and the consumption rate of interest.

One approach to measuring the marginal rate of return on private capital is to use accounting data to measure the average rate of return on private capital. The proponents of this approach argue that the average and marginal rates of return will be approximately equal. One leading proponent of the position that the rate of discount for public investments should be the same as for private investments and that the marginal rate of return on capital can be estimated from accounting data by measuring the average rate of return on capital is Jacob Stockfisch. Stockfisch contributed a paper laying out the theory upon which measurement of the return on private capital is based and providing his latest estimates of these returns.

A second approach to the measurement of the rate of return on marginal investments in the private sector and of the consumption rate of interest is to estimate from interest rates observed in the market, for example, the rate of interest on long-term government bonds. Economic theory tells us that firms will undertake investment projects up to the point at which, for the marginal project, the before-tax rate of return just equals their cost of capital, which is determined by some mix of the cost of debt and equity financing. If we could estimate the cost of capital for firms in the private sector from financial data, this would provide us with an estimate of the before-tax rate of return in the private sector. It should be evident to anyone familiar with the cost of capital that, except in special cases, this is not an easy route to the measurement of the marginal rate of return on investment in the private sector.

Similarly, on the basis of economic theory, we can conclude that in equilibrium, the consumption rate of interest for an individual will equal the after-tax rate of interest earned on savings or the after-tax rate of interest to be paid on debt. If we could determine this rate from financial data, we would know the individual's consumption rate of interest. Clearly this approach also presents some problems that will be discussed later.

Another matter deserving detailed attention is the question of how one might measure the marginal rate of return on capital and the consumption rate of interest using financial data, and in particular, how one would adjust market data to correct for the effects of expected inflation that are reflected in market rates of interest. Unfortunately, the potential contributors of papers on that question either thought that the problem was too difficult or that only negative results could be obtained or they wanted to write an additional theoretical paper and then address the measurement issues only in the context of their theory. The conference organizers were unable to define a set of topics that were acceptable to a potential contributor and that fit the plan for the book.

Within the energy-producing sector of the economy, there is one industry that stands out because of its institutional diversity, namely, the electric power industry. In 1970, that industry in the contiguous United States included nearly 3,500 systems, which varied greatly in size, type of ownership, and range of function. Within the electric power industry, there are basically four types of utility companies: (1) investor-owned companies, (2) nonfederal public agencies, (3) cooperatives, and (4) federal agencies. Each of these has a different form of organization, different objectives, and different taxes and faces different regulations. However, it will be the totality of the decisions by these diverse units that will determine the configuration of the electric power industry over the next two decades and into the twenty-first century. These enterprises will determine the choice of technology and the level of generating capacity.

Therefore, one important question is, How do the various segments of the industry make capital investment decisions? Do they use discounted cash-flow procedures, and if so, what discount rates do they use? This was the question posed to Gordon R. Corey, vice chairman of the Commonwealth Edison Company, who agreed to provide a survey and an interpretation of industry practice from the point of view of a participant in the industry. Robert Smiley of Cornell, former director of research of the New York Public Service Commission, was selected as the discussant.

In addition, it was important to analyze the investment decision process used by investor-owned, regulated utility companies and to compare the results of these procedures with the results that would be obtained from an ideal social benefit–cost analysis using the appropriate rate of discount. This task was undertaken by Thomas Stauffer of Harvard, who has worked extensively with the utility industry.

Originally Corey and Stauffer, who had worked together closely on projects in the past, were to combine their contributions in one paper. However, it soon became apparent that it was more appropriate to divide their contribution, one part dealing with industry practice and one dealing with the analysis of industry practice as it pertains to investor-owned utilities as compared with an idealized benefit–cost procedure.

In summary, this volume addresses the unresolved issues pertaining to the choice of the discount rate to be used in benefit–cost evaluation of public investments and public policies in a market economy with many distortions. It analyzes the question of risk and discounting in connection with energy policy, and it addresses the issues of whether discounting at a positive rate implies intergenerational inequity and whether the benefit–cost framework is sufficiently robust to be used as the basis for choosing between alternatives that may have far-reaching consequences. It addresses the practical problems associated with trying to estimate the appropriate rate of discount, and finally it evaluates the discounting practices within the electric power industry.

References

Chow, B. G. 1975. *The Liquid Metal Fast Breeder Reactor: An Economic Analysis* (Washington, D.C., American Enterprise Institute for Public Policy Research, December) pp. 21–27.

————. 1977. "The Economic Issues of the Fast Breeder Reactor Program," *Science* (February 11).

Energy Modeling Forum. 1977. *Energy and the Economy,* EMF Report Number 1, two volumes (Stanford University, Stanford, California, September).

————. 1978. *Coal in Transition: 1980–2000,* EMF Report Number 2, three volumes (Stanford University, Stanford, California, September).

————. 1979. *Electric Load Forecasting: Probing the Issues with Models,* two volumes (Stanford University, Stanford, California, April).

————. 1980a. *U.S. Oil and Gas Supply,* EMF Working Paper 5.4 (Stanford University, Stanford, California, March).

————. 1980b. *World Oil Study Design,* EMF Working Paper 6.1 (Stanford University, Stanford, California, March).

Hogan, W. W., T. R. Eck, J. Paddock, and G. Kaufman. 1979. *Limitations of the Models Participating in the Energy Modeling Forum's U.S. Oil and Gas Supply Study,* EMF Working Paper 5.7 (November).

Manne, A. S., and R. G. Richels. 1978. "A Decision Analysis of the U.S. Breeder Reactor Program," *Energy* vol. 3, pp. 747–767.

National Academy of Sciences. 1978. *Energy Modeling for an Uncertain Future,* Study of Nuclear and Alternative Energy Systems. Supporting Paper 2, The Report of the Modeling Resource Group Synthesis Panel of the Committee on Nuclear and Alternative Energy Systems, National Research Council (Washington, NAS).

Stauffer, T. R., H. L. Wycoff, and R. S. Palmer. 1975. "The Liquid Metal Fast Breeder Reactor: An Assessment of Economic Incentives" (Chicago, Breeder Reactor Corporation, March 7).

U.S. Congress. 1968. "Survey of Use by Federal Agencies of the Discount Technique in Evaluating Future Programs." Report to Joint Economic Committee by the Comptroller General of the United States, January 29, 1968.

U.S. Congress, Senate. 1962. *Policies, Standards, and Procedures in the Formulation, Evaluation, and Review of Plans for Use and Development of Water and Related Land Resources,* Report by the President's Water Resources Council, S. Doc. 97, 87 Cong. 2 sess. (Washington, GPO).

U.S. Energy Research and Development Administration. 1975. *Final Environmental Statement, Liquid Metal Fast Breeder Reactor Program,* ERDA-1535 (Washington, GPO).

U.S. Office of Management and Budget, Executive Office of the President. 1972. *Circular No. A–94* (Revised) To the Heads of Executive Department and Establishments, Subject: Discount Rates to Be Used in Evaluating Time Distributed Costs and Benefits (Washington, OMB, March 27, 1972).

2

Robert C. Lind

A Primer on the Major Issues Relating to the Discount Rate for Evaluating National Energy Options

Introduction

The purpose of this chapter is to introduce the reader to the central issues in the controversy over the choice of the discount rate for evaluating federal energy projects and policies and to develop a way to make specific recommendations on the selection of this rate and on procedures for evaluating federal policies and projects. The question of what rate of discount is appropriate for use in the evaluation of federal projects, that is, what is the social rate of discount, is complex and continues to be the subject of controversy among professional economists. This chapter is an attempt to lay out the major elements of the controversy in a manner that will make it accessible to readers with some knowledge of economics, but who are not professional economists, and to professional economists who have not followed the literature on this issue. The exposition relies largely on simple numerical examples, and the reader need not be familiar with the mathematical techniques employed in much of the recent literature on this subject. The reader who is conversant with the literature may also benefit from an organized review of the issues and have an interest in the analytical method that is developed to provide guidance to policy makers on the choice of the discount rate.

   Five concepts are central to the discussion of the choice of the social rate of discount, which is the rate that should be used to compute the present values of benefits and costs of public investments and public policies if decisions based on these benefit–cost analyses are to be optimal; that is, benefit–cost analysis using the social rate of discount will direct policy makers to the correct decision from a social perspective. These concepts are (1) the social rate of time preference, which is the rate at which society is willing to exchange consumption now for consumption in the future; (2) the consumption rate of interest, which is the rate at which individual consumers are willing to exchange consumption now for consumption in the future; (3) the marginal rate of return on investment in the private sector; (4) the opportunity cost of a public investment, that is, the value of the private consumption and investment forgone as a result of that investment; and (5) risk, which is related to the degree to which variation in the outcome of a public project will affect variation in the payoff from the nation's total assets. These concepts will be introduced and discussed as issues pertaining to the choice of the social rate of discount are developed.

Several conclusions are presented in this chapter. First, if one were to establish the social rate of discount so that it properly reflected the differences in the opportunity costs and riskiness of different projects and so that it properly reflected the social rate of time preference as well, one would have to set a different rate for almost every project, and the choice of the social discount rate for each project would depend upon many things. There would be no single rate that could be applied to government projects such as the 10 percent real rate of discount now required by the Office of Management and Budget for the evaluation of most federal projects.

Second, it can be demonstrated that the appropriate adjustments for risk and the opportunity cost of capital frequently cannot be made correctly by a straightforward adjustment in the discount rate. Third, if the social discount rate were set equal to the social rate of time preference in a riskless world, then the opportunity cost and risk associated with a public investment could alternatively be accounted for by making the appropriate adjustments in the benefits and costs rather than further adjustments in the social rate of discount. We develop a way of dealing with all the complex issues relating to the social rate of discount and the evaluation of public investments that is conceptually correct and lends itself to practical implementation.

The following section on the choice of a discount rate in the absence of market distortions and risk sets the stage for the subsequent discussion and the development of the overall approach by analyzing the question of the social rate of discount in an idealized economy that satisfies the conditions of perfect competition in a world of certainty. We demonstrate that in such an economy social rate of time preference will equal the opportunity cost of capital measured by the marginal return on private investment and the consumption rate of interest and that both rates will equal the market rate of interest. Therefore, the market rate of interest should be used as the discount rate for evaluating public as well as private investment decisions and, by definition, is equal to the social rate of discount.

The problem of the choice of the discount rate is then made more complicated by introducing corporate and personal income taxes. Under these conditions, the consumption rate of interest and the social rate of time preference will, in many cases, be less than the opportunity cost of capital.

The problem of selecting the appropriate social rate of discount is discussed in light of how economists first attempted to cope with these complications. The section discussing the choice of the discount rate when there is continuous reinvestment addresses further developments in the analysis of the public investment criteria. Such analysis considers the social rate of discount as part of the theory of optimal economic growth, and the social rate of discount is derived as part of the solution to the optimization problem.

The section presenting the "framework of analysis" that is adopted as the basis for policy recommendations lays out an approach to the analysis of public investments that equates the social rate of discount and the social rate of time preference. The opportunity cost of financing public investments is accounted for by adjusting benefits and costs to reflect both the positive and the negative effects of the public investment on formation of private capital. This adjustment is made using the concept of the shadow price of private capital formation. This theoretical framework provides the basis for the policy recommendations on the choice of the discount rate and on the investment criteria developed in the final chapter of the book.

The discussion of market rates in relation to benefit–cost analysis considers alternative lines of argument that lead to the conclusion that the social rate of discount may neither equal nor bear any systematic relation to market rates of interest, market rates of return, or market behavior by individuals. These lines of argument lead to the conclusion that the social rate of discount should be determined politically. Issues related to the distribution of benefits and costs of public investments among individuals of one generation and among generations are central to these lines of argument and are discussed in this section.

In the section that addresses the relationship between risk and the rate of discount for public investment decisions, the concept of risk is discussed briefly and some of the major analytical results pertaining to risk and the discount rate are set forth. Several conclusions emerge from this discussion. The first is that considerations of risk may be important for many public investment decisions and, in these cases, it is appropriate to make adjustments for risk, taking into account many of the same factors that an individual would consider in evaluating risky private investments. However, a second conclusion is that in general it is not theoretically correct to adjust for risk by adjusting the discount rate used in capital budgeting decisions. This is true for public sector benefit–cost analyses and for private sector capital budgeting decisions, although there are cases in which such an adjustment will lead to approximately correct results. Thirdly, we conclude that for reasons including data problems, it is extremely difficult to predict the statistical relationship between the returns to future energy investments and returns to other investments in the economy, and therefore that only the crudest measures of risk can be developed for major energy investments.

Finally, such crude analyses indicate that energy investment may, in fact, not be risky when risk is properly defined, but rather that it provides the nation with insurance. We discuss the theoretical and practical problems of making adjustments in the discount rate to take account of risk and consider alternative approaches to these problems in the implementation of benefit–cost analyses.

The section entitled "Problems of Measurement" addresses the question of how one might measure or determine the social rate of time preference and the shadow price of capital. Numbers that are important for the estimation of the social rate of time preference and the shadow price of capital include the marginal rate of return on private capital and the consumption rate of interest. We discuss some of the problems of how these variables can be measured from accounting data and from market data. Finally, estimates are developed and examined in light of the theory and the existing data.

The section on implementation of benefit–cost analysis discusses some of the characteristics that any practical "solution" to the question of the social rate of discount must have if benefit–cost analysis is to be a useful tool for public sector decision making. In particular, whatever procedure is adopted, it must be simple enough that the users can apply it, and it must not be subject to the discretion of the analyst to the extent that he can obtain any desired answer by manipulating the methodology. In short, it must be usable, and it also must be specific enough so that it cannot be easily manipulated.

Furthermore, benefit–cost analysis need not and cannot provide precise answers to policy questions. Rather it is a procedure that can provide a crude but highly useful picture of the relative merits of alternative policies. It therefore can be used to identify those investments that are either very good or very bad. Benefit–cost analysis also organizes data that bear on policy decisions and does so in a way that educates us about the important elements of a problem and allows us to test the sensitivity of the decisions to changes in those elements.

The final section summarizes the position that we adopt on the selection of the discount rate and the evaluation of public investment decisions and discusses needs for future research. This position forms the basis for the policy analysis and recommendations developed in the final chapter on the evaluation of various types of energy investments and policies.

The Rate of Discount for Government Projects in a Competitive Economy Without Market Distortions and Without Risk

Many of the issues related to the choice of a discount rate for public as well as private investments can best be understood by starting with the analysis of the conditions of market equilibrium in an ideal economy and, in particular, of the significance of the equilibrium rate of interest in such an economy. Suppose there were an economy that met the conditions of perfect competition, and further, suppose that in this economy there were complete certainty, no transaction costs, no taxes, and no restrictions on credit. In such an economy, equilibrium prices would represent the true value of each commodity traded in the market in the sense that the price of each factor of production would equal the opportunity cost of using that factor in an alternative way, and the price of each consumption good would equal the amount consumers would be willing to pay for an additional unit of that good. Further, individuals and firms would be able to borrow or lend all they would choose to at the market rate of interest, subject only to the constraint that, in borrowing, their future earnings or their wealth would be sufficient to pay off their debts, including accumulated interest. The rate of interest would be determined so that the supply of loanable funds would equal the demand.

In such an economy, the rate of interest would be important from the standpoint of making intertemporal economic choices for two reasons. First, it would represent the cost of capital for firms, so they would choose to make investments with positive present values when computed using the market rate of interest. As a result, the marginal or break-even investment for firms would be those with a present value of zero, and, therefore, the rate of return on these marginal investments would equal the rate of interest.

Second, consumers could adjust their consumption over time to best meet their needs by borrowing and lending at the market rate denoted by i. Since the opportunity to borrow or lend at the rate i would mean they could trade $1 of consumption today for $(1 + i)$ of consumption a year from now, people would adjust their patterns of consumption so that, at the margin, they would be indifferent to giving up an additional $1 of consumption now for $(1 + i)$ of consumption a year hence. More generally, they would be indifferent to choosing between $1 of consumption today and $(1 + i)^n$ consumption n years hence. Since every person in the economy could borrow and lend at the same rate i, this indifference would be true for everyone. The rate of interest at which people are indifferent to exchanging consumption now for consumption in the future is sometimes called their marginal rate of time preference or their consumption rate of interest.

In our idealized economy, the consumption rate of interest for individuals and the marginal rate of return on investment in the economy would be equal to the market rate of interest i. This equality is a necessary condition for efficient intertemporal allocation of resources. To understand this condition, suppose that there were one-year investments that would yield a rate of return of 20 percent; that is, a $1 investment today would yield $1.20 in a year. Further, suppose the consumption rates of interest for all individuals were 10 percent; that is, individuals would be willing to trade $1 of consumption now for $1.10 a year from now. Clearly, by saving an additional $1 and investing it at a 20 percent rate of return, consumers can trade $1 now for $1.20 a year hence, and, therefore, will be better off because they would willingly have traded $1 of present consumption for an amount of consumption greater than or equal to $1.10 one year from now. If an allocation of resources is such that a change in the allocation can make all or some people better off while making none worse off, it is by definition not efficient, or not Pareto optimal. As long as the consumption rate of interest and the rate of return that can be earned on the marginal investment in the economy are unequal, resources are not allocated optimally. If the consumption rate of interest is below the rate of return that can be earned on the marginal investment, saving and investment should be increased; if the converse is true, saving and investment should be reduced. Only when the two are equal will it be true that the intertemporal allocation of resources cannot be further improved by reallocation of resources over time.

Again, consider an equilibrium in our idealized economy in which the consumption rate of interest for everyone and the rate of return on the marginal investment are equal to the market rate of interest. Suppose we introduce a public sector into our economy and contemplate withdrawing resources from the private sector of the economy to be invested in the public sector. For simplicity, assume we were considering a public investment with an initial resource of C that would produce benefits one year from now with a value B_1, which represents the total of what people, as citizens, would be willing to pay to have these benefits. The critical questions are: Should we undertake this investment? What criterion should we use to decide?

If we undertake the public investment, we have to give up either present consumption or private investment or some combination of the two that adds up to the cost of the project. First, suppose the project were totally financed at the expense of private consumption. Then, individuals collectively would be trading C of present consumption for B_1 of consumption a year hence. Because their consumption rate of interest would be i, they would prefer to undertake the public investment only if $B_1 > C(1 + i)$, or equivalently, if $\dfrac{B_1}{(1 + i)} - C > 0$; that is, they would apply a present value criterion using i as the interest rate in the present value calculation.

Next, suppose the cost of the public investment comes at the expense of an equal amount of a marginal investment that can earn a rate of return of i; that is, a marginal one-year private investment of C will pay $C(1 + i)$ in a year. Clearly, the public investment should be adopted in this case if $B_1 > C(1 + i)$. Again, this is equivalent to using a present value criterion for the public investment with i as the rate of interest. It follows that since the criterion is the same whether the public investment displaces consumption or private investment, the criterion holds when the public investment displaces some combination of the two.

More generally, it can be shown that in an economy without constraints on the allocation of resources, namely, on what types of investments are made in the public sector, or without market distortions that cause the consumption rate of interest for individuals to differ from the marginal rate of return on private investment, both public and private investments should meet the same present value test, where the interest rate used in these calculations is the market rate. Put differently, at the margin, investments in both the public and private sectors should earn the same rate of return, namely, a rate of return equal to the market rate of interest. This basic result, which commands widespread agreement among economists, is clearly stated by Arrow (1966, p. 25).

> Thus, the optimal discount rule for public investment is that it uses the rates of return to private capital. But this is only valid in the context of a more inclusive policy in which aggregate capital is being adjusted to a long-run position where the natural rate of interest is governing. . . . A perfectly competitive capital market will achieve this optimum.

We have implicitly assumed in the foregoing discussion that if individuals' marginal rates of time preference for privately produced consumption equal the market rate of interest i, then this same rate of time preference should be applied to benefits and costs in the public sector. Where the marginal rates of time preference are the same for everyone, there is a strong case for the position that the social rate of time preference (that is, the rate at which society, through government action, is willing to trade benefits and costs today for benefits and costs in the future) should be the same as rates that govern the investment behavior of individuals. This position is widely, though not universally, accepted. We will discuss some alternative positions later, but it is important to note this fundamental proposition.

A second point worth noting here is that in the perfectly competitive economy we have been analyzing, the social rate of time preference, measured by the consumption rate of interest, and the opportunity cost of private capital, measured by the marginal rate of return on private investment, both equal the market rate of interest. Whether one takes the position that the opportunity cost of capital is the appropriate rate of discount to use in evaluating public projects or that the social rate of time preference is the appropriate rate, one reaches the same conclusion, namely, to use the market rate of interest. However, once one leaves the conditions of this ideal economy, these two measures diverge and, for reasons to be discussed, the social rate of time preference is probably significantly lower than the rate of return on the marginal private investment. This divergence is one of the major sources of the controversy over the discount rate.

A world in which the allocation of resources is fully optimal is frequently referred to by economists as a "first-best" world; a world in which there are market imperfections and constraints imposed on the economy that cause the allocation of resources to be suboptimal is called a "second-best" world. It is well known that economic policies and, in particular, public investment decision rules that may be appropriate when resources in the economy are allocated optimally may not be appropriate when resources are not allocated optimally. The rules that apply for a first-best world generally are not appropriate for a second-best world. Which rules should apply in a second-best world depends upon the types of market imperfections and constraints that are the cause of the misallocation as well as upon the nature of the misallocation. This often makes the analysis of economic policy in a second-best world a difficult and elusive task. In referring to the problem of determining the appropriate rate of discount for public investment decisions, Baumol (1978) comments that "we find ourselves forced to hunt for a solution in the dark jungles of the second best."

The Basic Problem of the "Second Best" As It Applies to the Rate of Discount for Public Investments

The problem that Baumol describes can be seen as follows. Suppose we retain all of the assumptions about our idealized economy, except that we introduce both a corporate profits tax and a personal income tax. For simplicity, assume the corporate profits tax rate is 50 percent, that the personal income tax rate is 25 percent, that all investment is undertaken by corporations, that all investment is funded with equity capital, and that all after-tax profits are paid to shareholders as dividends that are subject to the personal income tax. Further suppose that the after-tax rate of return required by investors is 6 percent; that is, 6 percent is their consumption rate of interest. In order to have the shareholders earn this rate of return after taxes, the corporation has to earn a pretax rate of return of 16 percent. This can be seen as follows. If the corporation earns a 16 percent pretax rate of return, half of that goes to pay the corporation's income tax, leaving 8 percent to be paid in dividends to the stockholders. However, the stockholder has to pay an additional 25 percent of that dividend in personal income tax, which means that his after-tax rate of return on his investment is 6 percent.

Under these circumstances, corporations will have to pay a dividend that will yield a 6 percent after-tax return on investment, which is what the investor requires for the use of his money, but in order to pay such a return, the corporation must undertake investments with at least a 16 percent rate of return. Therefore, in equilibrium, the marginal investment will yield 16 percent. At the same time, the individual who is saving through investment in the capital market will invest up to the point at which his consumption rate of interest is 6 percent, that is, his after-tax rate of return. Thus, the marginal rate of return on investments in the economy will be 16 percent, and the social rate of time preference as determined by individuals' consumption rates of interest will be 6 percent. We have demonstrated that this situation is not consistent with an optimal allocation of resources. In this situation, people would be better off by saving more and investing in any investment yielding more than a 6 percent rate of return. The problem is that the corporate income tax and the personal income tax distort incentives in such a way that people will not make these investments because their after-tax rate of return will not be sufficient to meet the required 6 percent rate.

Clearly, in the real world, the situation is even more complex. Individuals have different marginal tax rates; corporations pay the corporate income tax while unincorporated businesses do not; different people face different borrowing and lending rates. These complicating factors mean that, in equilibrium, the rates of return that will be earned on the marginal investments will be different for different firms and that the after-tax rates of return that people can earn on their savings, to which they equate their consumption rate of interest, will vary greatly among individuals. The person accumulating savings in a savings account will have one rate, say an after-tax rate of 4 percent, whereas someone borrowing on a Mastercharge account may be paying an after-tax rate of 12 percent. We will return to discuss these complicating factors as they bear on what we can infer from observed market rates of return and market rates of interest with respect to the rate of interest that should be used in evaluating public investment decisions. The essential point, however, is that the corporate income tax and the personal income tax create a significant differential between the pretax rate of return that can be earned on the marginal investment in the economy and the after-tax rate of return that individuals can earn on their savings, which equals their consumption rate of interest.

Suppose we again set aside the many complicating factors and consider an economy in which, in equilibrium, the consumption rate of interest is 6 percent for everyone, so that the social rate of time preference is 6 percent, and the rate of return available on the marginal investment is 16 percent. Again, consider the questions of undertaking a one-year public investment with initial cost C producing benefits B_1 at the end of one year. As before, first suppose the resources for the public investment were to be drawn entirely from private consumption. Therefore, the effect of the investment would be to exchange C worth of private consumption today for B_1 of publicly provided consumption a year from now. In order to abstract from questions pertaining to the distribution of income that might be associated with such an investment, assume that all individuals would share equally in the costs and the benefits. Since the consumption rate of interest is assumed to be 6 percent for everyone, the investment will make people better off if

$B_1 > (1.06)C$, or equivalently, $\dfrac{B_1}{1.06} - C > 0$, that is, if the present value of benefits calculated at 6 percent, the consumption rate of interest, is greater than the cost.

Suppose, on the other hand, the resources for the public investment were to be withdrawn from marginal private investments yielding 16 percent. Such a private investment produces $C(1.16) worth of consumption benefits in one year. Of this return of 16 percent, 6 percent goes to the private sector as dividends and 10 percent goes to the government in the personal and corporate income taxes. The implicit assumption here is that the government's share of the return goes into individual consumption in the form of publicly provided goods and services. Abstracting from the problems of any income redistribution, it is clear the public investment should be undertaken in this case if $B_1 > C(1.16)$, or equivalently, if $\dfrac{B_1}{1.16} - C > 0$, that is, if the present value of the benefits exceeds the cost when computed using an interest rate equal to the rate of return on the marginal private investment. Therefore, depending on where the resources for the public investment are drawn, the criterion for acceptance differs and, more specifically, the discount rate in one case should be the social rate of time preference, and in the other case, it should be the marginal rate of return in the private sector.

One might object, however, and argue that the marginal rate of return on private and public investments should be the same in all cases and that, even in the first case, in which all resources for the public investment were drawn from private consumption, the government should invest in private sector investments that would yield 16 percent to maximize the return to its citizens. This line of argument would certainly be correct if that option were open to the government. However, in the United States there are well-defined areas of activity reserved for the private and public sectors. Significant areas of economic activity are reserved for private enterprise, and we do not allow our government to invest in such industries as steel, oil, plastics, that is, industries that are typically thought of as being in the private sector. This is what would be required if the government were to undertake the relatively high-return investments available at the margin in the private sector. In fact, the set of investments that are considered appropriate for the government is a very limited subset of all investments, and many of these will yield less than the marginal rate of return in the private sector.[1]

---

[1] It is important to point out that the lines between the activities of the private and public sectors in mixed economies are not always so firmly drawn. In some mixed economies the government may have open to it the same set of investment opportunities that are open to the private sector. This significantly changes the problem of choosing the appropriate discount rate. Clearly, it is this latter situation that Harberger (1973, p. 71) has in mind when he states in an essay, "On Discount Rates of Cost–Benefit Analysis,"

> In the calculation of the appropriate rate of discount to be applied in India under any given set of assumptions, I have tried to estimate what would be the marginal productivity of capital in the private sector of the Indian economy under these assumptions.

One might argue that, while it is appropriate to reserve certain areas of economic activity for private enterprise and to preclude the government from making investments in these areas, it is still inappropriate to use a lower discount rate for evaluating public investments than is used for evaluating private investments. The argument is that if society wishes to increase total investment, it should not do so by undertaking low-return public investments, but rather it should stimulate more higher-yield private investment. The problem with this policy suggestion is, How would it be implemented? One approach would be to subsidize private investment. However, if we subsidized private investment to the point that all of the distortionary effects of the personal and corporate income taxes were removed, this would require the expenditure of vast amounts of revenue and would substantially negate the revenue-producing characteristics of the personal and corporate income taxes.

We might be better off abolishing these taxes and replacing them with others that would raise the necessary revenues without distorting the inter-temporal allocation of resources by creating a gap between the before-tax and after-tax rates of return on investment. Two taxes that are often proposed as alternatives for accomplishing this are a value-added tax and a consumption tax. Another alternative would be to abolish the corporate income tax and exclude earnings from capital investment, that is, dividends, interest, and the like, from taxable personal income. These options certainly deserve serious consideration and have distinct advantages. However, as long as we have the present tax system, there will remain a gap between the rate of return on private investment and the social rate of time preference measured by individuals' consumption rates of interest. This gap will result in an intertemporal misallocation of resources.

Much of the analysis that follows takes the present tax system and the resulting distortions in resource allocation as a starting point. This is not to imply that the optimal policy is to avoid changing the system of taxation to correct for the distortions caused by the present system. It might well be. This would remove much of the case for using a lower rate of discount for evaluating public investments and policies than is used for evaluating private investments. However, the present system of corporate and personal income taxes has been in effect for some time and a major change to some other system, such as a value-added tax or a consumption tax, does not appear likely in the near future. Until such a change occurs, we continue to be faced with the need to evaluate public investments and policies in an economy with the distortions caused by our present tax system.

To summarize, the case for using a lower rate of interest for evaluating public investments that displace consumption than for those that displace

---

I justify this approach by noting that if a government wishes to use a certain amount of its financial resources to provide benefits (via investment) for future generations, among the avenues open to it are investments in industrial establishments, similar in nature to those already existing in the private sector.

private investment and the case for the adoption of public investments that yield a rate of return that is lower than the marginal rate of return in the private sector is based on (1) the fact that corporate and personal income taxes cause a divergence between the consumption rate of interest and the marginal rate of return in the private sector; (2) the fact that the federal government is constrained as to the investments it can undertake; and (3) the fact that we do not have effective, politically acceptable policies for increasing private investment to optimal levels.

It is interesting to note that in the area of electric power generation, the line between the private and public roles is not clearly defined and in some of the battles between public and private power advocates over the choice between public or private provision of power, the advocates of public power have argued that they could provide power more cheaply because their cost of capital would be lower. A primary reason for this is the structure of the tax laws. In fact, this argument, if pushed to its extreme, can be used to support the case for socialism on the grounds that a private market economy, given these distortions, will produce too little saving and investment. One response to this line of argument, designed to limit the encroachment of public enterprise into the private sector, has been to propose that the rate of interest used to discount public costs and benefits should be required to be the same as that in the private sector. This was one motivating factor in the Office of Management and Budget directive, issued during the Nixon administration, that the discount rate for evaluating public projects was to be 10 percent in constant dollars.

A discussion of the merits of the case for socialism versus a mixed economy with a large private market sector and of the case for a larger rather than a smaller federal sector is well beyond the scope of this paper. Whatever the merits of each alternative, discussion of the discount rate certainly is not central to the resolution of these issues, and decisions regarding activities appropriate to the public and the private sectors should not be linked to the choice of the discount rate to be used in discounting public investments.

Again, let us return to our second-best world, where the consumption rate of interest is 6 percent and the marginal rate of return on private investment is 16 percent. Recognizing that the appropriate decision rule will depend on where the resources to finance public investment are drawn, a number of economists have attempted to determine the appropriate rate of discount for public investment decisions and the opportunity cost of public investment by analyzing the effects of financing public investment on current private consumption and current private investment. The idea underlying this work is that the social rate of discount should reflect both the consumption rate of interest insofar as consumption is displaced and the marginal rate of return on private investment insofar as private investment is displaced. Therefore, it has been argued that the social rate of discount should be a weighted average of the two rates, the weights being established in proportion to the percentage of the public investment drawn from consumption and from private investment (Krutilla and Eckstein, 1958; Harberger, 1968; Haveman, 1969; Sandmo and Drèze, 1971). This is, in essence, the same as evaluating that part of the private investment which comes out of consumption on the basis of the consumption rate of interest and that which comes out of investment on the basis of the marginal rate of return in the private sector.

This position is best summarized in a paper by Haveman (1969, p. 950), in which he traces the development of this argument and then estimates the social rate of discount on the basis of a weighted average formula for 1966, which is 7 percent. He states,

> Accepting the proposition that efficient public expenditures must demonstrate a social rate of return at least as great as that of the alternative spending that is sacrificed, this position argues that federal public expenditures are paid for by the taxes through which they are financed. Hence it is the private spending displaced by these taxes which represents the opportunity cost of the public expenditure. . . . Because the incidence of federal taxes falls on both consumers and businesses, both consumption spending and investment spending get displaced. Hence the private sector interest rates relating to both borrowing-saving–borrowing-consuming decisions (rate of time preference) and business investment borrowing decisions (rates of return before taxes) must be reflected in the social opportunity cost rate of discount. Empiric estimation of this rate requires that the relevant bundle of federal taxes be traced to its source in the various subsectors of the household and business sectors. The observed interest rates in each of these subsectors must then be weighted by the relative amounts of spending displaced in each by the imposition of federal taxes. The social discount rate then appears as the weighted rate of return on private sector spending displaced through the taxes implicit in a public investment expenditure.

If in our example the tax levied to finance a public investment were to reduce private investment by 20 percent and consumption by 80 percent of the total of the public investment, then the appropriate social rate of discount, according to this position, would be $(0.8)(0.06) + (0.2)(0.16) = 0.08$. Implicit in the entire line of argument to this point has been the assumption that the economy remains fully employed so that a public investment will necessarily divert resources from the private sector to the public sector. This assumption was believed to eliminate the need to consider the macroeconomic consequences of public investment on the level of GNP and employment on the one hand, or on the rate of inflation on the other. We will consider the appropriateness of this assumption later in more detail.

There are other economists, notably Harberger and Stockfisch, who have argued that public investment displaces private investment and that the pretax private rate of return should also be the rate of return required on public investments. Stockfisch (1967, 1969) asserts simply that public investment displaces private investment and he then calculates the weighted average of rates of return for the corporate sector and for the unincorporated business sector as a basis for determining the social rate of discount. Harberger (1968), while adopting the weighted-average approach to the social rate of discount, has argued that, at the margin, increases in public investment result in increases in the deficits that are financed by government borrowing. He argues further that the financing of this additional debt will result in the crowding out of an equal amount of private investment. In this case he would conclude that, in making public investment decisions, we should adopt the private rate of return as the rate for discounting benefits and costs.

Harberger's position has not gained widespread acceptance among economists, who dismiss it by arguing that while it may hold in the very short run, surely it does not in the long run. This position is well stated by Haveman (1969, p. 951).

> The argument . . . that public investments are financed through borrowing so that the opportunities foregone are those private investments squeezed out by the resulting capital market restriction can also be questioned. While the capital market may well be the short-run sponge for the federal budget, absorbing any given year's surplus and financing any given year's deficit, marginal dollars of expenditure over the longer run are financed by increments to public tax revenue.

However, a strong case can be made for Harberger's position, which has not been given sufficient attention. First, it is clear that the federal government has operated with deficits of tens of billions of dollars for a significant period of time so that even major changes in expenditure levels, holding taxes constant, would fall within this margin. Second, changes in the tax structure are made relatively infrequently, largely because of the many difficulties of formulating legislation and obtaining political support to change tax laws. Major tax changes occur infrequently, although minor changes may occur somewhat more frequently. The rationale for such tax revisions is, for the most part, not related to being able to support more or less public expenditure, but rather to achieving overall stabilization of the economy, promoting social equity, or remedying the effects of taxation on economic incentives and productivity. There have been only a few cases in which changes in the level of government spending have been clearly related to proposed changes in taxes. For example, the enormous increase in government expenditures for the Vietnam War led finally to a proposal for a tax increase to stem the destabilizing inflationary forces that the war expenditures created.

However, normally the tax structure is taken as given and expenditures are adjusted at the margin in response to perceived national needs and the requirements of economic stabilization. Under these conditions, marginal increases or decreases in public investment will result in corresponding changes in the deficit. The effect of financing these public investments, however, will be a one-to-one displacement of private investment only if (1) resources are fully employed, (2) consumption is unaffected by changes in the interest rate, and (3) the monetary authority adjusts the money supply to keep the money market and the market for goods in equilibrium at the full-employment level of GNP, given the higher interest rates. The way that crowding-out would occur is that the Treasury Department would go into the capital market to sell bonds and thereby drive up the rate of interest to the point at which private investment would be reduced by the amount of the government borrowing. Note that if consumption as well as investment is sensitive to the interest rate, the impact will be both on investment and consumption.

Empirical evidence suggests that consumption is not very sensitive to changes in the interest rate so that, as a first approximation, the one-to-one displacement of private investment by public investment may be defensible. However, a more serious objection is that at least part of the increase in aggregate demand will be met by increased production from unemployed resources if they exist. On the other hand, if resources are fully employed and the Federal Reserve System increases the money supply, increased inflation will lead to the displacement of both consumption and investment.

In general, if one takes the position that taxes are fixed and changes in expenditures are matched by changes in the deficit—and this is often a defensible description of how the system works in the United States—then it is not appropriate to assume the economy is necessarily fully employed, that banks have no excess reserves, and that the Federal Reserve System will hold the money supply constant, given changes in the deficit.

This points out what we believe to be two major areas of advancement in the analysis of the criteria for public investment decisions. First, one cannot reasonably divorce the analysis of public investments from macro-economic considerations because the financing of public investments has different impacts on the economy depending on the state of the economy, including the monetary system. Second, and perhaps even more important, the choice of criteria by which to evaluate public investments in a second-best world depends critically on how one believes the economic and political system works, because this determines the impacts that public investment will have on the economy. More analysis of these issues is needed, and more debate should take place on the assumptions and models of the economy that are appropriate as a basis for the analysis of public investment criteria and the social rate of discount. We will return to this line of argument later in this chapter.

The Rate of Discount in a Second-Best World with Continuous Reinvestment

The next major development in the theory of public investment decisions—in particular, a development pertaining to the choice of the discount rate to be used when evaluating public investments—was Arrow's (1966; Arrow and Kurz, 1970) observation that an investment made in either the private or the public sector affects not only the levels of present investment and present consumption but the levels of investment and consumption at all points of time in the future.

For example, if we invest $1.00 today, that investment will yield $1.10 of income a year hence, and that income will be divided between consumption and investment in some proportion. Further, the returns from that part which will be invested a year hence will affect the level of consumption and investment in the subsequent year, and this process repeats itself through time. The significance of this example for the analysis of public investment decisions is that to compute the opportunity cost of a public investment, it is not sufficient to identify and measure the initial impact of a public investment on current consumption and current private investment, but rather, one must take into account the entire stream of consequences that this investment has on future investment and consumption. Similarly, it follows that the beneficial impacts of the public investment are not the benefits of the investment alone, but depend upon the entire stream of consequences for future consumption and investment resulting from these benefits. For example, if $1.00 of a public investment produces $1.10 of benefits a year hence, and if as a result of these benefits private investment will be increased, there will be an infinite stream of consequences from the private investment and reinvestment stimulated by the public investment.

Arrow's position was that to evaluate a public investment decision, one has to take into account the entire stream of effects associated with both the financing of the project and the outputs of the project. Further, he has pointed out that in order to trace this stream of effects through time, one has to know not only what the government's economic policy is at the present time but what government policies will be in the future as well. Therefore, his discussion of decision rules for choosing public investment is in terms of formulating optimal government policies that should be adhered to over time.

Obviously, the observation that public investment decisions will result in an infinite stream of consequences for both consumption and private investment greatly complicates the problem of evaluation. To cope with this complexity, Arrow formulated the problem of the appropriate decision rule for public investment and, in particular, the problem of the choice of the discount rate in terms of the theory of optimal economic growth. According to Arrow (1966, pp. 14, 15),

Public investment policy by definition involves a commitment over time, and, as modern economic theory makes clear, must be judged in the context of a growing economy. Fundamentally, growth here means increases in population and technical knowledge, though the course of capital accumulation also enters as both cause and effect. . . . Explicit introduction of a growth model will clarify much of the current discussion of the effect of time patterns of return on the choice among projects. Much effort . . . has gone into explicit consideration of the so-called "throw off." But this discussion has been unnecessarily complicated.

In the optimal growth formulation, the objective of economic policy is to maximize the equation

$$V = \int_0^\infty e^{-\delta t} U(c(t)) dt \tag{1}$$

where $c(t)$ = consumption at each point in time
    $U(c(t))$ = social utility derived from consumption at time t
    $e^{-\delta t}$ = discount factor determined by δ, the rate of discount applied to units of utility

In other words, the objective is to maximize the discounted sum of social utility from consumption over time, subject to constraints placed on the economy by its population, its production possibilities, its investment possibilities, and its structure, including such characteristics as market imperfections and restrictions on the set of investments that are permitted by the public sector.

Notice that in this formulation of the objective function, it is only the stream of consumption that ultimately counts. Investment is simply a means of transforming potential consumption at one point in time into consumption at another point in time. Therefore, in comparing two situations, one with and one without a particular public investment, we need only compare the streams of consumption over time associated with these two situations. More specifically, we need only compare the sum of the discounted utilities, or equivalently, the present values of the consumption streams discounted at the appropriate consumption rate of interest. At this point it is important to note, especially for the reader who is not familiar with the theory of optimal economic growth, that the discount rate δ that is used to discount utilities over time is not the same as the discount rate that applies to consumption, that is, the consumption rate of interest, although the two rates are closely related. More will be said about this distinction.

The use of the optimal growth theory has many methodological advantages. First, this theory allows for explicit analysis of the effects of an investment and subsequent reinvestment through time. Second, it makes clear that our ultimate concern is to choose the best feasible consumption stream. Third, it sets up the public investment problem as an explicit optimization problem defined on consumption streams; this allows us to use the tools of dynamic optimization to derive the optimal policy or decision rule. Fourth, as used by Arrow (1966; Arrow and Kurz, 1970), it makes clear that monetary and fiscal policy are an integral part of the public investment problem. These are important advantages.

However, there are some disadvantages as well. First, in order to make the analysis tractable, we have to deal with a highly simplified economy, for example, an economy with one individual or a number of identical individuals who live forever. The range of real-world complexities that we can introduce and still have a manageable problem with results that are easily interpreted is, in practice, limited. Second, and probably more important, the results that can be obtained from deriving the optimal policy generally are results in which the discount rate converges to some variable, for example, the natural rate of interest, when the economy reaches a steady state. It is only then that one can draw strong conclusions about the discount rate for public investments. However, there is a serious question as to whether it is appropriate to base our public investment policy and, in particular, our choice of a rate of discount on analytical results that apply only in an economy that has reached a steady state.

Third, the statement of the solution of the optimal policy—in particular, the derivation of the appropriate rate of discount—is often extremely difficult to interpret in a way that allows one to estimate its value from observable data for our economy. Finally, it is often difficult to judge whether a particular, highly simplified model of the economy has captured all the essential elements of the real economy that are important to the results. For example, do the results change if one assumes overlapping generations rather than a single consumer who lives forever? It is not clear that they do not. For all of these reasons, we do not believe this approach alone will ultimately provide the operational basis for the choice of a rate of discount to be used in public investment decisions, although this type of analysis is highly instructive and has been critical in developing insights into the problem.

Those insights may have provided a basis for obtaining an operational solution to the problem of analyzing public investment decisions and, in particular, of choosing the appropriate rate of discount. First, there is a growing consensus among the economic theorists who have addressed this issue that public investment decisions should be based on an analysis of the total effects of that investment on the consumption streams of the economy. That analysis should consider positive as well as negative effects on both publicly and privately provided consumption. Second, given this starting point, if we trace all of the effects of a public investment on consumption streams, then it follows that in evaluating these we should use as the discount rate the social rate of time preference, whether determined on the basis of individuals' consumption rates of interest or on some other bases.

Thus, there is a growing consensus that if we can display the alternative consumption streams that will obtain with and without a public investment, then the appropriate rate of discount is the social rate of time preference. However, we have not yet solved our problem because tracing all of the consumption effects is by no means a simple matter. In particular, there is the problem of capturing the negative and positive consumption effects associated with a public investment when it displaces or stimulates a private investment over time.

A Framework of Analysis that Separates the Issues of Time Preference and the Opportunity Cost of Public Investment

In this section we develop a framework of analysis that separates consideration of social time preference from consideration of the effects of a public investment on private capital formation and the opportunity cost of displacing private investment. The social rate of discount is set equal to the social rate of time preference and the effects on private capital formation are accounted for using the concept of the "shadow price" of capital.

This approach was first set out by Eckstein in 1958 and more recently by Diamond (1968) and Feldstein (1970). It was then systematically developed by Bradford (1975). The shadow price of capital is simply the present value of the future stream of consumption benefits associated with $1 of private investment discounted at the social rate of time preference.

The concept of a shadow price of private capital can be easily understood in terms of a simple example. Suppose, as in our previous examples, the rate of return earned on a marginal investment in the private sector is 16 percent, whereas the social rate of time preference is 6 percent. Further suppose that we are considering a one-year public investment that costs $1 and yields benefits of B_1 a year hence, which would be entirely consumed, and that this public investment will displace a one-year private investment that will yield $1.16. For the purpose of simplifying this example, we will assume that the yield from the private investment would also be entirely consumed. The assumption that the yield from both the private and public investment would be consumed simplifies the problem in that we do not need to consider the effects of the reinvestment and reinvestment of the return accruing in one year on consumption in all subsequent years.

To summarize, the situation that we are considering is whether to make a $1 public investment that will displace a $1 private investment that will yield \$1.16 a year hence. The consumption streams produced by these two investments are summarized below.

Investment	Consumption	
	t_0	t_1
Public	0	B_1
Private	0	1.16

Clearly, we should only undertake the public investment if $B_1 \geq 1.16$. We could obtain this result by using 16 percent in discounting the public investment. Another way to look at this problem is that the present value of the future consumption provided by the private investment is $\dfrac{1.16}{1.06}$ when discounted at the social rate of time preference, that is, this is the shadow price of the dollar of private investment displaced by the public investment. Therefore, it is appropriate to treat $\dfrac{1.16}{1.06}$ as the opportunity cost, measured in terms of the present value of future consumption forgone, of the public investment. Following this line of reasoning, we should therefore require that the present value of future benefits exceed this cost; that is, $\dfrac{B_1}{1.06} > \dfrac{1.16}{1.06}$, which is equivalent to $B_1 > 1.16$.

In this example we get the correct result whether we use the rate of return on private investment as the interest rate or we compute the shadow price of private capital and discount at the consumption rate of interest. However, this result does not hold in general. Suppose that we alter the problem so that while the public investment still displaces \$1 of private investment that will yield \$1.16 of consumption a year hence, the public investment will yield benefits of B_1 and B_2 over two years. Then the criterion of discounting benefits at the consumption rate of interest and comparing their present value with the shadow price yields the inequality

$$\frac{B_1}{1.06} + \frac{B_2}{(1.06)^2} \geq \frac{1.16}{1.06} \tag{2}$$

if we use the shadow price approach as opposed to

$$\frac{B_1}{1.16} + \frac{B_2}{(1.16)^2} \geq 1,$$

which is the appropriate inequality if benefits are discounted at the rate of return on the private investment and compared with initial cost. Although this example incorporates the unrealistic assumption that both the earnings and the return of the initial capital (depreciation) are consumed, it is clear that these two criteria are not the same. It should be stated, however, that the appropriate treatment of the reinvestment of depreciation is an important consideration that will be addressed later.

Using a shadow price to account for effects on private capital formation and then discounting at the social rate of time preference yields results substantially different than those from discounting public investments using the rate of return on private capital in some important cases. In particular, when the benefits from an investment accrue far into the future, as is true of many energy investments, using a discount rate equal to the marginal return on private capital, as opposed to taking the opportunity cost of capital displacement into account through the shadow price on capital and then discounting at the social rate of time preference, improperly biases the evaluation against projects that pay out over a long period of time.

This also demonstrates that the corporation income tax, the personal income tax, and the resulting wedge they drive between the marginal rate of return on private investment and the social rate of time preference cause private investment decisions to be biased against long-term investments when judged from a social perspective. This is one reason why the government may have to become involved with energy investment where many of the benefits will occur well into the future. Thus, not only does the wedge between the marginal rate of return on private investment and the social rate of time preference cause underinvestment, it also creates a bias toward short-term projects.

If one accepts the argument that the appropriate way to look at public investment decisions is to trace the impacts on consumption over time and then to discount at the social rate of time preference (and there is a growing acceptance of this position), then the appropriate procedure is to compute the shadow price of capital and to multiply the costs of public investment that represent a displacement of private capital by this shadow price to obtain the true opportunity cost in terms of consumption. The procedure in benefit–cost analysis should be to multiply project costs, to the extent that they represent a displacement of private capital, by this shadow price of private capital and to add these costs to those that represent a displacement of present consumption to obtain the project's consumption costs in each year. A similar adjustment has to be made on the benefit side, and the adjusted stream of benefits and costs should then be discounted at the social rate of discount. To make this procedure operational, we need to be able to compute the shadow price on private capital, to estimate the share of each dollar of project costs that comes from displaced private investment and consumption, and to estimate the impact that future benefits from the project will have on private investment.

This approach is more fully developed in Bradford's article entitled "Constraints on Government Investment Opportunities and the Choice of Discount Rate," in which he lays out a simple framework for analyzing public investment decisions involving private investments that produce an infinite stream of future consumption and public investments that influence future private investment (Bradford, 1975). He then uses this framework to analyze many of the subtle issues pertaining to the criterion for public investments by using the concept of a shadow price for private investment. He computes this shadow price under various sets of assumptions about the social rate of time preference, the marginal rate of return on private investment, and the marginal propensity to save. The remainder of this section draws heavily on the framework developed by Bradford and on recent extensions and modifications of his results (Lind, 1981).

Following Bradford, suppose that all investments, private or public, are one year in duration and earn rates of return, respectively, of r and ρ; that is, \$1 of private investment will yield $\$1 + r$ a year later and \$1 of public investment will yield $\$1 + \rho$ a year later. Further suppose that the social rate of time preference is i, and let the shadow price of private capital, that is, the present value of the consumption stream produced by \$1 of private investment computed using the social rate of time preference as the discount rate, be represented by v. We will discuss the computation of v later, but generally we will assume that $r > i$, so that $v > 1$.

Before proceeding, we need several more definitions. Let a be the amount by which private capital formation is decreased by an additional \$1 of public investment. If we assume that resources are fully employed so that \$1 of public expenditure requires the withdrawal of \$1 of resources from the private sector, then $(1 - a)$ is the corresponding decrease in private consumption as a result of \$1 of public expenditure. Further, let α denote the amount of private capital formation that would result from \$1 worth of output or benefits from a public project; for example, if the benefit produced by the development of a new energy technology took the form of lower energy costs in the future, α would represent the amount of increased private investment that would take place as a result of every \$1 of savings in energy costs. To complete the notation, let s represent the marginal propensity to save. Bradford made all of the above variables time dependent, but we have assumed that they remain constant through time to simplify the presentation.

We now employ the basic calculus set out by Bradford to obtain an insight into the appropriate decision rule for public investments by considering a \$1 public investment. The cost of that investment in terms of the present value of forgone consumption is $(1 - a)$, the current consumption that is forgone, plus av, the amount of forgone private investment multiplied by the shadow price of capital, for a total cost of $(1 - a + av)$. The return from the investment is $(1 + \rho)$, of which $(1 - \alpha)$ will be consumed and α will go into the new private capital formation. Therefore, the value of the returns from the investment one year hence in terms of consumption is $(1 + \rho)(1 - \alpha + \alpha v)$. Its present value is $\dfrac{1 + \rho}{1 + i}(1 - \alpha + \alpha v)$, discounting at the social rate of time preference. Therefore, the present value of net benefits is given by

$$-(1 - a + av) + \frac{1 + \rho}{1 + i}(1 - \alpha + \alpha v) \tag{3}$$

By rearranging terms, the present value of net benefits is positive if and only if

$$\frac{1 + \rho}{1 + i} > \frac{1 + a(v - 1)}{1 + \alpha(v - 1)} \tag{4}$$

Therefore, whether a public investment should be undertaken depends critically on the values of a, α, and v, as well as on ρ and i.

Bradford (1975) determines what value of ρ, the rate of return on the public investment, would be required for the inequality in (4) to hold under different assumed values for a and α. He demonstrates that the required rate of return α ranges from less than i for $a = 0$, $\alpha = 1$ to greater than r for $a = 1$, $\alpha = 0$. Put differently, if a public investment does not displace private capital, and, at the same time, the output of the public investment goes entirely into private investment, then the required rate of return is less than the social rate of time preference because of the stimulation of subsequent private investment. On the other hand, if the public investment totally displaces private capital and does not stimulate any future private capital formation, then the required rate of return for the public investment will be higher than the rate of return earned on private investments. Clearly, given this situation, we must carefully analyze the question of the appropriate values of a and α.

The expression for the present value of net benefits (3) can be used to illustrate two approaches to the determination of the social rate of discount. First, and the approach that by far has been used most by economists who have addressed the question of the social rate of discount, is to derive the conditions for the optimal decision and then to ask what discount rate will yield the optimal decision if applied to the benefits and costs. In this case one would set the social rate of discount equal to the value of ρ for which the inequality in expression (4) is satisfied. Clearly, in this example the social rate of discount would range from less than i to more than r, and it would depend on the values of i, v, a, and α. Therefore, different projects might have to be evaluated using different discount rates because the nature of their benefits and costs might be such that the values of a and α would differ or their financing might differ in a way that would yield different values for a and α.

In the case of differences in financing, the evaluation of the same project might require a different rate of discount depending on how it is financed. More will be said about the factors that might affect the values of a and α and result in their taking on different values for different projects. However, one thing is certain: If we adopt the approach outlined above for determining the social rate of discount, there will be no single social rate of discount but, rather, different rates for different projects and different rates for the same project depending on how it is financed or on the state of the economy when it is implemented. Stiglitz demonstrates this effect on the social rate of discount in a wide range of examples in a paper in this volume.

The social rate of discount is so highly variable in the simple example that we have constructed because public investment will produce quite different effects on private capital formation now and in the future depending on what the investment is and how it is financed. Solving for the optimum and then choosing the discount rate that, when applied to benefits and costs, will direct the decision maker to that optimum means that all the complexity of the effects of the public investment on private capital formation as well as the weights determined by the social rate of time preference have to be captured in a single number, the discount rate for that project. If we also attempt to account for risk by adjusting the discount rate, we further complicate the determination of the appropriate discount rate.

This approach to the evaluation of public investment decisions in practice attempts to account for too many dimensions of the evaluation problem through adjustments in the discount rate. To use the selection of the discount rate to address the complex differences among public investments or public policies with respect to their impact on private capital formation and with respect to risk can only confuse the analysis of those important issues.

An alternative approach, which we adopt here following Bradford, is to let the discount rate in the social benefit–cost analysis be the social rate of time preference. We then address issues pertaining to private capital displacement or stimulation directly for each investment through the analysis of a, α, and v. Using this analysis we adjust benefits and costs at each point in time so that they are expressed in terms of consumption equivalents, which can appropriately be discounted using the social rate of time preference.

Note that this latter approach requires no more information and one less step than the previously described approach. One must know i, r, a, α and v as before, but one need not compute the break-even rate of return for ρ. In this second approach, there is a single social rate of discount equal to the social rate of time preference, and the analysis is properly focused on the effect of the project on private capital formation through a and α and on the value of \$1 of private investment, in units of consumption, namely, the shadow price of capital represented by v. We believe that by adopting this approach, we can develop a procedure that is workable in practice, that helps clarify the issues, and that is methodologically correct for performing benefit–cost analyses of public policy alternatives.

Return to inequality (4) and consider several special cases. In one case, Bradford sets $a = \alpha = s$. Clearly, in this case the inequality (4) holds if $\rho > i$; that is, the decision rule for public investments would be to undertake public investments with a rate of return greater than the social rate of time preference. This could be achieved by evaluating public investments at the discount rate i. This is the basic result derived by Arrow (1966). The rationale for setting $a = \alpha$ is that in a model of the economy in which individuals save a fixed proportion s of their disposable income and public expenditures are financed by taxes, \$1 of public expenditure will reduce private saving and investment by s. Similarly, \$1 of future public output, if it is considered part of individuals' disposable income, will increase private saving and investment by s.

However, an asymmetry in this line of argument, if corrected, changes the result so that the required rate of return on public investment is r, not i (Lind, 1981). The line of reasoning here is as follows. If individuals save a fixed percentage of their disposable income, which they perceive to include publicly produced benefits, and if the government increases their taxes by \$1 to invest it on their behalf, rational individuals will perceive this as saving by the government on their behalf and, therefore, this public saving will displace an equal amount of private saving and investment. If we assume that individuals treat the output of public projects as if it were disposable income, then it is appropriate for them to consider public investment as if it were saving and investment on their behalf. Given these symmetrical assumptions about individuals' saving behavior, $a = 1$, $\alpha = s$ and from statement (4) it can be demonstrated that the inequality holds if $\rho \geq r$ (Lind, 1981). Under the first approach to determining the social rate of discount, the rate would be i if $a = \alpha$ and r if $a = 1$ and $\alpha = s$. Under the approach we adopt here, the social rate of discount would be i in both cases, but the benefits and costs in units of consumption would be different depending on the values of a and v.

This discussion illustrates three important points. First, determining the effects of a public investment on private capital formation, both positive and negative, is critical to the evaluation of a public investment decision. Second, these effects along with the value of v determine the opportunity costs or benefits of public expenditures related to private investment. Finally, the values of a and α may differ depending on the nature of a public expenditure and the form of the output it produces. For example, the benefits from a cost-reducing energy technology may affect future private saving decisions, while benefits from risk reduction as a result of the strategic petroleum reserve may not.

The procedure for evaluating the benefits and costs of a public investment using the approach developed by Bradford (1975) would be as follows. First, we would separate the benefits and costs that have an effect on outlays by the federal treasury from those that do not. Benefits and costs that affect federal outlays may have a different impact on private capital formation than those that do not because costs or benefits that require government expenditure or that produce revenue have an impact on the government's need to raise revenue. Therefore let e_t, $t = 1, \ldots, T$, be the government's net costs or revenues from a project over its lifetime T. Then e_t would include outlays for resources required by the project as well as any revenues or savings to the government that might be produced by the project. Let b_t, $t = 0, \ldots, T$, represent all other benefits and costs not represented by payments to or from the federal treasury. For example, b_t might include the benefits from lower fuel prices produced by a coal liquefaction plant as well as environmental costs produced by the project. Then to obtain value of e_t in terms of consumption at time t, one would adjust for the effects on capital formation and multiply e_t by $\epsilon = (1 - a + av)$. Similarly, one would multiply b_t by $\beta = (1 - \alpha + \alpha v)$. Then one would compute the present value of these streams as the summation

$$\sum_{t=0}^{T} \frac{1}{(1 + i)^t} (\beta b_t - \epsilon e_t) \geq 0 \tag{5}$$

Unless otherwise stated, the summations in this section are taken from $t = 0$ to T. Clearly, if $\alpha = a$ then $\beta = \epsilon$ and the criterion embodied in (4) is equivalent to

$$\sum_{t=0}^{T} \frac{1}{(1 + i)^t} (b_t - e_t) \geq 0 \tag{6}$$

which is simply the present value of unadjusted benefits and costs discounted at the social rate of time preference.

There are a number of extremely important cases in which the criterion expressed in (6) is appropriate. These cases will be analyzed in some detail in the concluding chapter of the book for their application to energy investments. One such case is the comparison of two alternative government outlays that produce the same benefits, for example, a standard cost-effectiveness analysis in which all of the costs are reflected by government expenditures. An example of this case would be the decision by the government whether to install solar or conventional heating units on its buildings or to buy or lease a given piece of equipment. In the example of the solar heating units, the government will heat its buildings in any event; the question is whether to spend more now on the more expensive solar capital equipment in return for future government savings on fuel costs. This is a problem in cost minimization, and the government should choose the lesser of

$$\epsilon\left(\sum \frac{e_t^c}{(1 + i)^t}\right) \quad \text{or} \quad \epsilon\left(\sum \frac{e_t^s}{(1 + i)^t}\right) \tag{7}$$

where the superscript c denotes the conventional heating technology and s denotes the solar technology. Clearly, one should discount the alternative costs at the social rate of time preference because the adjustment factor ϵ applies equally to all costs and, therefore, does not affect the decision. This problem can be turned into a benefit–cost problem by counting the benefits as savings in fuel costs, but this is simply represented by the statement

$$\epsilon\left(\sum \frac{e_t^c - e_t^s}{(1 + i)^t}\right) \geq 0 \tag{8}$$

which is identical to minimization of the present value of costs discounted at the social rate of time preference. It should be noted that this line of argument applies to all government programs in which the problem is to choose the least-cost solution.

It is important again to emphasize that if $\alpha = a$, then the social rate of time preference should be used to discount the benefits and costs of public investment, and the value of v, the shadow price of capital, is not a factor in determining whether net benefits are positive. This is because $\beta = (1 - \alpha + \alpha v)$ and $\epsilon = (1 - a + av)$, and when $\alpha = a$, then $\beta = \epsilon$. Therefore,

$$\sum \frac{\beta b_t - \epsilon e_t}{(1 + i)^t} = \beta\left(\sum \frac{b_t - e_t}{(1 + i)^t}\right) \geq 0 \tag{9}$$

only if

$$\sum \frac{b_t - e_t}{(1 + i)^t} \geq 0 \tag{10}$$

However, the magnitude of v does affect the magnitude of β and ϵ, which in turn are factors that determine the magnitude of net benefits.

The case in which $\alpha = a$ is the generalized case of Arrow's result. It can be interpreted as follows. If the effect on private capital formation of a unit of a project's benefits or costs that goes to the federal treasury is the same as that of a unit of the benefits or costs that accrue directly to the private sector, then the correct decision rule will be to discount benefits and costs to their present value using the social rate of time preference even though these benefits and costs have not been adjusted to their consumption value equivalents. The reason is that under these conditions all benefits and costs are adjusted by multiplication by a positive constant.

Bradford differentiates between benefits and costs that go to the federal treasury and those that accrue directly to the private sector. However, to capture the effects of a public investment, one may need further classifications of benefits and costs accruing to the private sector. For example, $1 of benefits in the form of increased income will in general have a different impact on individual savings and investment than $1 worth of benefits from the greater security provided by a weapons system. Similarly, $1 of direct cost associated with an expenditure for an emission-control device for one's car will probably have a different effect on savings and investment than $1 of cost in the form of increased air pollution. Although this complicates the analysis, it does not change the basic format of the approach.

If v lies close to 1, then β and ϵ will lie close to 1. Under these conditions the impact on net benefits of the effect of the public investment on private capital formation will be small. Bradford develops the infinite series that represents v and then calculates v for various values of s, r, and i, which are the parameters that determine the value of v. He finds that, for a wide range of values for s, r, and i, v lies in the interval $(0.84, 1.19)$ and concludes that the effects of a public investment on private capital formation are not likely to be very important in any case, and that one probably gets a reasonable approximation of the present value of net benefits by discounting benefits and costs at the social rate of time preference. He arrives at this result by rewriting equation (8) as

$$\sum \frac{b^t - \epsilon/\beta e^t}{(1 + i)^t} \geq 0 \tag{11}$$

and demonstrates that ϵ/β lies in the interval $[1/v, v]$, which for $v = 1.19$ becomes $0.84 < \epsilon/\beta < 1.19$. In other words, in his most extreme cases, one would multiply government expenditures associated with a public investment by 0.84 or 1.19.

However, the low values that Bradford obtains for v are critically dependent on two assumptions: (1) depreciation or the return of capital from private investment is not reinvested but simply treated as any other component of current income and (2) all investments are one year in duration and the principal and interest are returned at the end of each year. Neither of these assumptions is appropriate, and when the necessary corrections are made in Bradford's model, the shadow price of capital is substantially greater than unity (Lind, 1981).

To understand the reason for this, let us begin with Bradford's equation for v based on the assumption that \$1 of investment will yield \$$(1 + r)$ of income in one year and that, of this income, $(1 - s)(1 + r)$ is consumed and $s(1 + r)$ is saved and reinvested. The reinvested portion earns a rate of return r. Again the principal plus the return on the principal are returned a year later, at which time $(1 - s)$ of it is consumed and s of it is saved and invested. This pattern repeats itself indefinitely. If one takes the stream of consumption generated by this process and discounts it at the social rate of time preference i, one gets the series

$$v = (1 - s)\,\gamma \sum_{t=0}^{\infty}(s\gamma)^t \quad \text{where } \gamma = \frac{1 + r}{1 + i} \tag{12}$$

If $s\gamma < 1$, which is required for convergence, then according to Bradford (1975),

$$v = \frac{(1 - s)\gamma}{1 - s\gamma} \tag{13}$$

In equations (12) and (13) Bradford assumes that of the initial capital and the interest that are returned each year, a portion $(1 - s)$ is consumed and the remaining fraction s is reinvested, where s is the marginal propensity to save. This assumes that people or corporations treat the return of capital or depreciation in the same way they treat the earnings on that capital. Bradford then goes on to compute the shadow price of capital for different values of r and i, assuming values for s of $0.1, 0.2$, and 0.3. He finds that, for these values of s and for a wide range of values of r and i, the value for v ranges from 0.96 to 1.19.

However, if we assume that investors treat the return of capital not as current income but as part of their original wealth, then, in the aggregate, it is appropriate to assume that this portion of the payout of an investment will be saved and reinvested. Consider a firm that makes an investment; part of the payout from that investment will be depreciation, which is treated differently than the part that is profit. Firms typically invest more than the capital returned through depreciation; that is, net investment is positive. From an individual's standpoint, if he or she puts \$1 in a savings account that yields interest of \$$r$ after one year, only the \$$r$ is counted as part of current income, not \$$(1 + r)$, of which \$1 represents past savings.

Returning to Bradford's equation for computing the shadow price of capital, if we assume the initial \$1 of private capital is reinvested each year along with the fraction s of the return \$$r$, which is the portion representing current income that is saved, then the fraction of the total return that is reinvested each year is $z = \dfrac{1 + rs}{1 + r}$ and not s. Therefore, if $r = 0.10$ and s

$= 0.2$, the fraction reinvested would be $\dfrac{1.02}{1.10} = 0.93$ not 0.2. This makes a very significant difference in the results. Table 2-1 summarizes Bradford's computation for v, given various values of r, i, and s. In brackets above each of the values of v computed by Bradford is the corresponding value for v assuming that the return of capital is reinvested each year along with a fraction s of the return on that capital. The results change dramatically when the returned capital is fully reinvested. For every pair of values of r and i such that $r > i$, the new value of v is substantially higher than the value computed by Bradford (1975) and in several cases the series in equation (12) does not converge, meaning that the shadow price of capital is infinite.

This discussion also brings out an important difference between private and public investment. In the case of a private investment the investor in most cases can identify the return of capital and distinguish it from the return on that capital so that only the latter will be treated as current income. It is reasonable to assume that, at least in the aggregate, depreciation will be fully reinvested. In the case of a public investment this is not necessarily so. The benefits may accrue to people in the form of increased income or in the form of nonmonetary amenities, such as security and clean air, that may not be reflected in changes in individual savings and investment decisions. Benefits may also accrue to the government itself in the form of revenue or future cost savings. Therefore, the consumption–reinvestment pattern resulting from $1 of private investment will be very different from the pattern resulting from $1 of public investment. In general it is correct to evaluate only a public investment that displaces private investment dollar for dollar, using the rate of return on the private investment if the pattern of reinvestment of the returns for the public investment is the same as for the private investment (Lind, 1981). In general the two reinvestment patterns will not be the same. The implication is that even where a public investment displaces private investment on a one-to-one basis, it is not correct to evaluate the public investment using the rate of return on private investment as the discount rate.

Table 2-1. The Shadow Price of Private Capital Under a Range of Assumptions About Parameter Values

r		$s = .10$			$s = .20$			$s = .30$	
i $r =$	0.05	0.10	0.15	0.05	0.10	0.15	0.05	0.10	0.15
	(3)	(9)	(27)	(4)	(∞)	(∞)	(7)	(∞)	(∞)
0.02	1.03	1.09	1.14	1.04	1.10	1.16	1.04	1.12	1.19
	(1.00)	(2.25)	(3.86)	(1.00)	(2.67)	(6)	(1.00)	(3.5)	(21.0)
0.05	1.00	1.05	1.11	1.00	1.06	1.12	1.00	1.07	1.14
	(0.60)	(1.29)	(2.07)	(0.57)	(1.33)	(2.4)	(0.53)	(1.4)	(3)
0.08	0.97	1.02	1.07	0.97	1.02	1.08	0.96	1.03	1.10

Source: Bradford (1975).

The second reason that Bradford obtained such low values for v is that he assumes that all capital and interest are returned each year. This assumption is useful in simplifying the presentation of the basic concepts but is clearly unrealistic and distorts the computation of v. Most capital investments return the principal and the return on that principal over a much longer period of time, and this will increase the value of r.

To see this again, consider the series in equation (12), which was based on the assumption that the principal plus the return on the investment would be returned in one year. To see the critical importance of this assumption for the numerical results that Bradford obtains pertaining to v, suppose instead that the principal and earned interest are returned in ten years. In that case, equation (12) becomes

$$v = (1 - s)\gamma^{10} \sum_{t=0}^{\infty} (s\gamma^{10})^t \tag{14}$$

where γ^{10} replaces γ and where the condition for convergence is that $s\gamma^{10} < 1$, in which case

$$v = \frac{(1 - s)\gamma^{10}}{1 - s\gamma^{10}} \tag{15}$$

Even assuming that depreciation is treated as ordinary income, this difference will, in general, lead to a significant increase in the value of v.

A brief discussion of the arithmetic of the shadow price of capital will clarify how these differences arise. Suppose one were to invest $1 in the private sector and continue to reinvest the principal and interest so that the value of the initial investment grows at the exponential rate r. After n years, the present value of the accumulated capital, when discounted at the social rate of time preference, would be $\left(\dfrac{1 + r}{1 + i}\right)^n$. Clearly, if $r > i$, then as n increases, the present value of the accumulated capital, in terms of consumption, increases and in the limit goes to infinity. Therefore, if public investment displaces $1 worth of private capital that would have been continuously reinvested along with the accrued interest, then the social cost of displacing that investment in terms of the present value of future consumption forgone at $t = \infty$ would be infinite.

The reason that, in general, the social cost of displacing a unit of private capital is not infinite, given realistic values for r, i, and s, is that when the principal and accrued return on private investment are returned to the economy, only a fraction of the return is reinvested; the rest is consumed. The sooner the principal and earnings are returned, the sooner a large fraction of the earnings will be consumed. Now, consider the case of a $1 private investment in which the principal and the accumulated interest are returned to the economy after ten years. Since this investment must earn a rate of return r, the investment will pay back $(1 + r)^{10}$. This is equivalent to a series of one-year investments in which the entire capital and accrued earnings are reinvested for ten years. Therefore, if the capital has a longer life, it is as if the principal plus the return were being continuously reinvested for that period so that the present value of the investment will grow much more before part of it is actually consumed.

For example, Bradford computes the shadow price of capital to be 1.10 for $r = 0.10$, $i = 0.02$, and $s = 0.2$ for the case in which all capital is returned each year and both the principal and interest are treated as ordinary income. If, however, the initial capital plus the accrued interest does not become available for ten years as in the previous example, the shadow price of capital would be 3.04, assuming $r = 0.10$, $i = 0.02$, and $s = 0.2$, and if the capital plus the accrued interest were not returned for twenty years, the value of the shadow price of capital would be 53.29.

Clearly, the assumption that all capital is returned each year is unrealistic, but it is equally unrealistic to assume that the invested capital and the accrued interest are returned in a lump sum after any fixed period of time. Generally, an investment pays out over its entire economic life which, in the case of buildings, may be more than fifty years. Also, different investments will have their payouts distributed differently over their economic lives. The question for the analysis of the shadow price of capital is, What is the economic life and pattern of payout of the typical private investment that might be either displaced or stimulated by public expenditures or publicly produced benefits?

One approach to the calculation of the shadow price of capital takes into account that the capital and accumulated interest are returned over the entire life of the investment (Lind, 1981). For simplicity, this approach employs the assumption that in each year of the life of an investment it pays out an equal amount. For example, for a $10 investment with a ten-year life earning a 10 percent rate of return, the yearly cash flow generated by this investment would be $1.60, that is, the yearly payment of an annuity with a present value of $10 computed at 10 percent. Clearly, this is not the pattern of returns for every investment, but it is probably a reasonably good first approximation of the pattern of returns from a portfolio of investments. We can now show how the fact that investments typically tie up substantial amounts of capital for significant periods of time and the fact that depreciation is fully reinvested affect the shadow price of private capital formation.

Consider $1 of investment in the economy in a capital asset with a life of N years. Assuming the rate of return on this investment is r, and that it pays out uniformly over N years, then the payment in each year will be

$A = \dfrac{r}{1 - (1 + r)^{-N}}$, that is, an annuity for N years with a present value of $1 discounted at r. Therefore, $1 of investment today will produce a stream of N equal payments of A. Of these payments, individuals will reinvest zA and consume $(1 - z)A$, and the investment zA associated with the first payment will in turn result in a series of N payments, zA^2, starting the following year. The reinvestment rate z equals $\dfrac{D + (A - D)s}{A}$; that is, z is that fraction of the payment A that represents depreciation D plus the fraction of the earnings $(A - D)$ that is saved. Now consider the first payment A from the investment. Following that payment will be a sequence of payments N payments equal to zA^2. Each of these will generate N more payments of z^2A^3. The first terms of the series generated by this process are shown below:

$$t = 0 \quad 1 \quad 2 \quad 3 \quad \ldots \quad N \quad N+1 \quad N+2 \quad N+3 \quad \ldots \quad 2N$$
$$A \quad A \quad A \qquad A$$

N rows $\begin{cases} zA^2 \ldots \ldots \ldots zA^2 \\ \quad zA^2 \ldots \ldots \ldots \ldots zA^2 \\ \qquad \qquad \cdot \\ \qquad \qquad \cdot \\ \qquad \qquad \cdot \\ \quad\quad\quad zA^2 \ldots \ldots \ldots \ldots zA^2 \end{cases}$

Each generates a new N period annuity equal to the payment multiplied by zA. The ultimate objective is to obtain an expression for the present value of consumption streams generated by the $1 of investment and discounted at the rate i, but since $(1 - z)$ of every payment is consumed, one need only find the present value of the payment streams and multiply by $(1 - z)$.

Now let x be the expression that, when multiplied by a single payment of an N-period annuity, gives the present value of the annuity discounted at the rate i. Now if we return to the series of payments generated by $1 of investment, careful consideration will reveal that the present value of this series of terms can be represented by the following equation (Lind, 1981).[2]

---

[2] One can see the idea behind the proof as follows. The first row in table 2-1 is an n-year annuity of payments A. Ax is the present value of this annuity discounted at i. Proceeding in this manner we can collapse the terms in the next N rows to their present values as of $t - 1$, where t is the time of the first payment, by multiplying by x. After performing this operation we still have annuity of N payments of zA^2x starting at $t = 1$. Multiplying by x again we get zA^2x^2 as the present value, discounted at the rate i, of the terms in these N rows. The following blocks of terms will be of the form z^2A^3 and, following the same procedure, the present value of these terms is $z^2A^3x^3$. This process continues to repeat itself. Therefore, the present value of the sum of all these terms is the sum $Ax \sum_{t=0}^{\infty} (Axz)^t$.

$$(Ax) \sum_{t=0}^{\infty} (Axz)^t = Ax \frac{1}{1 - Axz} \text{ if } Axz < 1 \tag{16}$$

Therefore, $v = Ax(1 - z) \dfrac{1}{1 - Axz}$. Note that for $r = i$, $Ax = 1$, and $v = 1$.

When one allows for the reinvestment of depreciation and for the fact that the returns to an investment will be spread over the life of that investment, the value for the shadow price of capital rises somewhat above the values for v in table 2-1, which were calculated assuming a one-year investment life but full reinvestment of depreciation. For example, assuming that the life of the average capital investment is fifteen years, that $r = 0.10$, $i = 0.05$, and $s = 0.2$, the value of v, computed using the formulation above, is 3.09, whereas the values for v, as shown in table 2-1, are 1.06 using Bradford's assumptions and 2.67 allowing for reinvestment of depreciation with a one-year investment life.

The purpose of this discussion is not to resolve the issue of the appropriate value of the shadow price on private capital formation; the purpose is to demonstrate that, in some cases, the shadow price of private capital may be a significantly large number so that in cases where $\alpha \neq a$, β may differ significantly from ϵ. From the previous inequality $1/v < \epsilon/\beta < v$, it follows that if the life of the typical investment is fifteen years, then for $i = 0.05$, $r = 0.10$ and $s = 0.2$, $v = 3.09$ and $0.32 < \epsilon/\beta < 3.09$. Therefore, the impacts of a public investment on private capital formation may be highly significant for evaluating its benefits and costs.

It should be pointed out that the approach of using the shadow price of capital to account for the costs or benefits associated with the displacement or stimulation, respectively, of private investment resulting from a public expenditure, and of using the social rate of time preference as the discount rate does not automatically lead to the justification of increased government expenditure. This approach does correct the biases against public investments as opposed to public programs that consume resources today and provide no future benefits, and it corrects for biases against long-term investments. Several numerical examples will help clarify these points.

First, for purposes of the examples, assume that the shadow price of capital is 4, and further assume that all marginal public expenditure is financed by government debt that crowds out private investment on a one-to-one basis. Now, consider the addition of a new regulatory program to enforce laws requiring the lowering of thermostats or an increase in welfare expenditures to offset the rising costs of energy. These programs consume resources at the present time, but they do not stimulate any investment now or in the future. In evaluating these programs, we should multiply the costs to the government by 4 to get the true social costs. Even if we assumed these marginal expenditures were financed by increased taxes and that the marginal propensity to save was 0.2, then $a = 0.2$ and $\epsilon = 1.6$ so that the social costs are 60 percent greater than the costs to the government.

Now, consider an energy investment that will produce benefits in thirty years. The present value of $1,000 of benefits thirty years hence is $57.31 when discounted at 10 percent and $231.37 when discounted at 5 percent, that is, 4.03 times greater when discounted at 5 percent. Therefore, in the case of this hypothetical energy investment, the economic evaluation will be more favorable if we multiply its costs by 4, assuming the displacement of private investment equal to the total cost, and discount the benefits at 5 percent than if we simply discount the benefits at 10 percent. If, in addition, we take into account that the accrual of the benefits of the energy investment thirty years in the future may stimulate some private investment at that time, the economic evaluation will be even more favorable.

The system of economic evaluation that is currently being used by the federal government, namely, benefit–cost analysis using a discount rate of 10 percent in constant dollars, will (if 10 percent is above the social rate of time preference) lead to a systematic underestimation of the costs of government programs that involve current consumption and will incorrectly bias the analysis against government expenditures that will produce benefits that will flow back into the economy in the future. The approach presented here extends the approach developed by Bradford and remedies these problems. By using the concept of the shadow price of capital, we can separate the issues of social rate of time preference and the opportunity cost of private capital displacement. Further, this approach provides us with a conceptual basis for correctly calculating the opportunity cost of private capital displacement for all public expenditure programs, not just public investments. These costs are likely to be much less significant for public investments that stimulate future private investment than for public consumption expenditures that displace private investment but do not stimulate any investment (Lind, 1981).

Why Market Rates May Be Inappropriate for Social Benefit–Cost Analysis

Before turning to the issues pertaining to risk and the social rate of discount, it is important to mention a thread of the literature that maintains that observed market rates of return and market rates of interest are simply irrelevant for determining the social rate of discount. Most economists who have analyzed the discount rate for social benefit–cost analysis have concluded that there is some systematic relationship between this rate and rates of interests or rates of return in the private sector. Others, however, have argued that private rates of return and private rates of interest determined by the market bear no systematic relationship to the discount rate that should be used in social benefit–cost analysis. One line of argument that leads to this conclusion is based on a concept of the state as an entity with an existence and objectives totally separate from, and independent of, its individual citizens. Put differently, under such a theory the state is the guardian of the national interest, which goes beyond the interests and the preferences of the individual citizens of that state. The state may have separate objectives and embody values that differ from those of its individual members.

Under such a theory of the state, the preferences of individual citizens are not necessarily relevant to or related to those of the state. Therefore, individual time preferences such as are measured by the consumption rate of interest and revealed in the market are not relevant to social decisions. The social rate of time preference under such a theory would be politically determined on the basis of the politically determined goals. However, even under such a theory of the state, individual time preferences may be irrelevant to the determination of social time preference, but the decision makers for the government would have to be concerned about the displacement effects of their policy decisions on private investment if there were a private sector in the economy. And to this extent, the rate of return on private investments, if it differed from the politically determined social rate of time preference, should be taken into account even though the weight given to consumption at different points in time would be determined politically.

In most of the debate the participants have accepted the proposition that individual preferences are relevant to social choices and that the government's actions should be responsive to the preferences of its citizens. However, even accepting the relevance of individual preferences, one may come to the conclusion that the discount rate for social benefit–cost analysis need not bear any systematic relationship to market rates of return or interest. Those who adopt this position essentially argue that for one or more reasons private citizens prefer that their government use a different discount rate in evaluating public policies and social choices than they use in evaluating their own savings and investment decisions. What are the reason for this apparent inconsistency?

One argument is that a person's preferences as citizen voter and as private consumer are separate and not necessarily consistent. Although one can certainly find examples of inconsistent individual behavior, this line of argument is not particularly compelling; it leaves open the question of how one would go about ascertaining the individual's time preferences for public projects. Clearly, one would have to look to some political process to establish the social rate of time preference.

A second argument is that while people may appear to exhibit one set of preferences in their private lives and another in their role as citizen voters, this behavior is not inconsistent because the economic choices that they make as citizen voters and as private individuals are fundamentally different. It is argued that the government, in making public investments and public policy decisions, is the guardian of future generations as well as the servant of the present one. Therefore, citizens in their role as voters reflect their concern for this responsibility, whereas in their private economic decisions they do not, except possibly through their concern for their immediate heirs. Pushed further, the argument is that a discount rate that is lower than the market rate is appropriate because it increases the weight given to the benefits and costs of future generations.

Certainly, the use of a lower discount rate in the case of energy favors greater investment and therefore the formation of a greater capital stock for the future. It favors the development of new energy technologies and it favors less rapid development or exploitation of our natural resources, including fuel resources. Further, it gives greater weight to long-run environmental costs that might be associated with current programs for energy production. However, if we accept the fact that the government is the guardian of future generations and that in our role as citizen voters we should be concerned about the future, the question remains whether we can effectively exercise our role as guardian through changes in the discount rate or within the framework of the benefit–cost approach. We will not try to answer this question here because it is addressed in the papers and the discussion in this volume.[3] This question has become of much greater interest in connection with the analysis of energy policy than it has been in the past because of our ever-increasing pessimism about the economy and the environment of the future.

There is also another line of argument, which depends on distributional considerations, that explains why individuals may want the government to use a rate of discount for evaluating public investment decisions that differs from market rates. This argument is that public and private investments are essentially different in that they have different distributions of benefits and costs; individuals place different weights on their own consumption vis-à-vis the consumption of other people, so that the alternatives they see in a private investment decision are different from those that they see in a public investment decision.

There are two essential elements to this line of argument. The first is that individuals derive utility from the consumption of other people as well as from their own consumption; that is, there are consumption externalities, but individuals give a different weight to a unit of consumption benefits that goes to themselves than they do to a unit of consumption benefits that goes to their heirs or that goes to the public at large now or in the future. The

---

[3] A. Sen, "Approaches to the Choice of Discount Rates for Social Benefit–Cost Analysis," chapter 9 in this volume; comments on this paper by M. Sharefkin, R. Dorfman, and T. Page.

second part of the argument hinges on the fact that if individuals can undertake an investment in cooperation with others, then the cost of a public investment to any one individual will be only his share of that investment, whereas the benefit to him may be the same as if he had paid the entire cost, for example, investment in low-income housing.

Taken together, this means that the benefits and the costs associated with a unit of public investment will in general be distributed very differently among oneself, one's heirs, and the public at large. Since these benefits and costs are given different weights by the individual, depending on the beneficiary, it follows that from an individual's point of view, the choice between one dollar of private investment today and the benefits of that investment one year hence differs from the choice between one dollar of public investment and one dollar of publicly produced benefits a year hence. Under these circumstances, it can be shown that an individual may want the government to use a different discount rate for evaluating public investments than he would use to evaluate his private investment opportunities.

Furthermore, it can be shown that the optimal rate of discount for public projects may differ from individual to individual and it may be higher or lower than the private rate that governs each of those individuals' private investment decisions. Therefore, under these circumstances, the appropriate rate for discounting benefits and costs of public investments depends not only on the rate of time preference of different individuals and the rates of return on private investment; it depends also on how the benefits and costs of both public and private investments are distributed among the population and how individuals weigh the benefits and costs accruing to different individuals at different times.

Given this framework of analysis and the assumptions that are embodied in it, even the simplest case in which everyone has identical preferences and is identical in all other respects will yield a different rate of discount that is appropriate for evaluating virtually every public investment decision, depending on the distribution of its benefits and costs. These rates will not in general bear any systematic relationship to any market rates. If people differ, of course, no one will agree on the appropriate rates to be used in social decision making.

There are, however, special cases in which the market rate and the rate for public projects will be the same. This topic has received a great deal of attention in the literature. We will not develop the argument more fully here or cite the literature because this is done very incisively by Sen in this volume.

If one adopts the position that the appropriate rate of discount for evaluating benefits and costs over time from a public perspective is unrelated to private rates for whatever reason, then the discount rate must be chosen on the basis of a political process and based on political goals. However, not using the private rate of return to evaluate public investment decisions because one wishes to weigh benefits and costs on a different basis leaves the following problem. After the appropriate social rate has been chosen, one must still account for the effects of public investments and public policies on the formation or displacement of private capital. In terms of our earlier discussion, the arguments discussed here are essentially for a social rate of time preference that is different from the rates of return or rates of interest observed in the market. If one uses the social rate of time preference as the rate of discount for social benefit–costs analysis, one has to use some mechanism, such as the shadow price on capital, to reflect the effects of the policy on private capital formation. One of the advantages of the approach using the shadow price of capital is that it provides a methodology for accounting for displacement effects when the social rate of time preference is politically determined.

Risk in the Discount Rate for Public Investment Decisions

The relationship between risk and the rate of return on investment has been one of the major topics of modern finance, and it also has comprised a significant part of the debate on the social rate of discount. In relation to public investment decisions, the controversy has been between those who have argued that the government should use a risk-free rate of discount in its computation of the present value of benefits and costs and those who have argued that, for risky public projects, a higher rate of return should be required and therefore a higher rate of discount should be applied, just as it is in the private sector. In general, the proponents of the latter position have also argued that the rate of return on public investments should be identical to the rate of return on private investments of comparable riskiness. The literature that addresses risk and the rate of return on public investments draws upon the theory of economic markets under uncertainty and upon the literature of modern finance, primarily the capital asset pricing model (CAPM) and its extensions, which both have the same theoretical roots, namely the expected utility theorem as developed by Von Neuman and Morganstern and the theory, as developed by Arrow (1964) and Debreu (1959), of complete markets for claims contingent on states of the world.

A comprehensive review of the literature on investment and the treatment of uncertainty and risk in the valuation of assets is well beyond the scope of this chapter. We shall neither attempt to develop the fundamental aspects of the theory nor to summarize fully developments in the theory relating to this topic. This would require a review of the theory of decision making under uncertainty, the theory of economic markets in a world of uncertainty, and the rapidly growing body of theory in modern finance. Robert Wilson provides a clear development of these theoretical issues later in this volume.

The more limited objectives here are, first, to state some well-known results of the theory of economics and finance in an attempt to clear up some common misconceptions about the nature of risk and, second, to demonstrate that there is not necessarily a simple adjustment in the discount rate that can correct for risk. A third objective is to state the basic result of the CAPM and to use this result to demonstrate that those who have argued that the rate of return in the public sector should be adjusted for risk in the same way as it is in the private sector and those who have argued that the rate of discount in the public sector should be the risk-free rate do not have a fundamental disagreement in the theory but simply a disagreement over the appropriate assumptions to apply to investments in the public sector as compared with the private sector. The critical question is whether returns in the public sector can be treated as if they are independent of returns in the economy as a whole or whether they are correlated with returns in the economy in the same way that returns from many private investments are.

A fourth objective is to investigate whether recent multiperiod extensions of the CAPM and their application to capital budgeting problems provide a basis for determining the appropriate correction in the discount rate to be used for public investment decisions. We examine whether the state of the theory is adequate for this task and, if it is, whether it would be possible to estimate the necessary parameters empirically. Finally, we summarize the basic conclusions on the state of the art in economics and finance as they pertain to risk and the social rate of discount.

Among professionals who are not familiar with the modern literature in finance or with modern developments in the theory of markets under uncertainty, there are many misconceptions about risk. Many consider any investment that has an uncertain return to be risky. They would be right if that investment were the only one in an individual's portfolio, or from the national point of view, if that investment produced a major fraction of the national income. However, from the point of view of an individual, one is not primarily interested in the variability of the return on a single particular investment but, rather, the variability of the return on the total portfolio of assets that produces one's income. From a national point of view, the variability of total national income is of interest. One is interested only in the variability of any single component of a portfolio insofar as it affects the variability of the total portfolio. The recognition of this fact is central to the analysis of risk.

The concept of risk in investment can best be understood in terms of insurance. Consider, for example, the individual who buys fire insurance. His purchase constitutes an investment with an uncertain return. The investment pays zero if his house does not burn down, but it pays off an amount equal to the value of the house if the house does burn down. Does the purchase of the insurance increase the risk to a homeowner and thereby constitute a risky investment? Clearly, the answer is that it does not; it reduces the risk to the homeowner because, by adding the asset of insurance to a portfolio containing an asset of a house, the value of that portfolio becomes certain and equal to the value of the house less the insurance premium.

Notice that because of the risk premium charged by the insurance company and because of transaction costs, the price of the policy must exceed the expected value of fire losses. Therefore, when a person buys fire insurance, he or she is making an investment with an uncertain payoff and a negative expected rate of return. However, one may be willing to undertake such an investment in order to reduce the variability of one's total portfolio. This example brings out two points. First, the riskiness of an investment, as seen from the point of view of the nation as a whole or from the point of view of an individual, depends not on the variability of the outcome of that investment itself but on how that asset will affect that variability of the total portfolio.

A second point that is illustrated by this example is that an individual may alter the composition of the assets in his or her portfolio by buying insurance or by diversifying the portfolio through investment in the securities markets. For example, although there are no complete markets for risk, as are envisioned in the idealized models developed by Arrow and Debreu, in which one can insure or hedge against every contingency, still there are substantial markets in which one can trade claims against future income in order to reduce the overall variability of one's income and insure against certain contingencies.[4] These markets include the insurance and securities markets, and, although by no means complete, they are substantial and have an important bearing on how the riskiness of an individual project should be considered. An investment financed by one person might be quite risky from that individual's point of view but might not be very risky if the ownership can be spread over a large number of people who have diversified portfolios of assets.

Therefore, the question of the riskiness of an asset from an individual perspective depends on how the addition of the asset or source of income affects the overall variability of income from the total portfolio. This variability will in general depend both on the variance of the return to that asset and the covariance of its return with the return to the total portfolio. This relationship is thoroughly developed by Wilson in this volume. The riskiness of an asset will also depend critically on the opportunities the individual investor has to diversify his or her portfolio through the securities markets and to insure against undesirable contingencies. If the securities and insurance

[4] See R. Wilson, "Risk Measurement of Public Projects," chapter 6 in this volume.

markets are fairly complete and efficient, then the individual can greatly reduce his or her risk through diversification in these markets.

Now consider an asset (investment) that is a relatively small fraction of the total portfolio of assets in the total economy. For an individual who is well diversified in the sense that his or her portfolio consists of a small share of many assets in the total national portfolio, the risk associated with the addition of this asset is only slightly affected by its own variance. The investor's risk is primarily dependent upon the covariance of the return to this asset with the returns to the total portfolio of assets in the economy. If the covariance is positive, adding this asset increases the variability of the investor's portfolio and therefore adds to the risk, if it is negative it reduces the risk, and if it is zero the risk is unchanged. If this asset constitutes a very small fraction of the total portfolio, the importance of the variance in the risk of a diversified portfolio will be very small. This is the idea underlying the CAPM in modern finance, in which the riskiness of an asset is measured by the covariance of its return with the return to the total market portfolio.

The riskiness of a public investment that constitutes a small fraction of national income from a national economic perspective depends on the covariance of its returns with national income, provided the risk can be efficiently distributed. Whether such risk will be efficiently distributed depends in part on whether the benefits and costs of the public investment are widely distributed or whether they constitute a significant fraction of the portfolios of some of the people affected by the project. If they do, their variation may constitute a significant risk to these people. However, assuming such risk can be efficiently distributed, then from the standpoint of the nation, a public investment will involve some risk if it has a positive covariance with national income. If, on the other hand, the covariance between the returns to the investment and national income is zero, then from the standpoint of the nation as a whole the risk is minimal. Alternatively, if the covariance between the returns to a public investment and national income is negative, then from a national perspective the investment has the characteristic of insurance. When other investments that make up national income will earn a lower return, this investment will earn a higher return and, therefore, will stabilize the total level of national income.

This observation is extremely important in analyzing risk, particularly risk associated with research and development projects for new energy technologies. From the standpoint of someone looking at an investment in the research and development of a new technology, there are many sources of uncertainty about what the ultimate return to this investment will be. The first question might be, What is the likelihood that this investment will be technically viable? For example, what is the likelihood that we will ever develop a commercially viable fusion process? In general, with a process such as fusion, there is a range of possible technical outcomes to which we assign different subjective probabilities.

If we could determine what the payoff would be if each of those outcomes occurred, we could compute the expected value of the investment and we could also compute the variance of that investment. Although we would be able to evaluate its expected payoff, we could not evaluate the risk associated with the investment unless we could somehow determine the covariance between the returns to fusion and the returns in the economy as a whole. However, it is unrealistic to believe that the payoff resulting from any one technical outcome will be clearly determined in advance. In fact, the payoff from any technical outcome will depend on a whole variety of contingencies and, therefore, will be a random variable itself. For example, the payoff to fusion will depend very critically upon its cost and therefore upon the price of energy produced by this technique as opposed to energy produced by other techniques. It will also depend upon the demand for electricity, and that is a function of a large number of variables. In general, predicting how the payoff of a technology, if successful, will vary in relation to other components of national income in the future will be highly speculative at best.

However, in the case of research and development on new energy technologies we might speculate that the higher energy prices are in the future, the greater the return to these investments will be. Furthermore, our energy–economic models predict that higher energy costs will result in a lower GNP. Therefore there can be a reasonable presumption that the payoff from energy research and development will correlate negatively with GNP in recessions that are caused by increases in energy prices. In these situations such investments would have the characteristic of insurance from a national standpoint. If the return to energy investments were in fact negatively correlated with the return to other investments, they would not constitute risky projects but would be insurance policies for the future. If this were the case, rather than reducing the value of net benefits to reflect the cost of risk, the value of net benefits should be increased by the amount of their insurance value. This concept and line of argument will be developed further.

Another observation is that although the analysis of the alternative technical outcomes is crucial to determining the expected payoff from the technology, insofar as the technical uncertainties are independent of other economic developments that are likely to affect the future price and cost of energy, these technical uncertainties contribute little if anything to the riskiness of the project as seen from a national perspective. Clearly an evaluation procedure that discounts future benefits and costs at a higher rate of interest because of their uncertainty would be in error.

There is a second popular misconception that sometimes creeps even into professional discussions of risk and investment. It is that when evaluating an investment with uncertain returns over time, one can appropriately adjust for the riskiness of the investment in the analysis of the present value of its returns by simply adjusting the discount rate or required rate of return. More specifically, it is argued that for riskier investments, the appropriate adjustment for risk is made by raising the discount rate used to calculate the present value of the investment. The situation is much more complex and, in general, neither proposition is true except under specific conditions or when an investment pays out in one period. In computing the present value of an investment that pays out over a number of periods, one generally cannot adjust for the risk associated with returns at different times by adjusting the discount rate, nor can one always capture the desired effect of increased riskiness by simply increasing the discount rate and applying it to expected future returns. This can be demonstrated with the help of a simple model.

Before turning to this model, it is important to point out that the perpetuation of this misconception appears to come about in two ways. First, there is a common belief that people prefer an investment with certain rather than risky returns if two investments have the same expected return. Therefore, if people are to undertake investments with risky returns, they will have to have the prospect of earning a high expected return. From this it follows that if we compute the rate of return earned on risky assets, it will be higher than on assets that earn a certain return. So far there is no problem with this formulation.

The error comes if we conclude that the appropriate way to account for the complex time–risk relationship in a multiperiod investment, whether private or public, is to adjust the discount rate used in the present value calculations. Except under special circumstances, there is no well-defined way to adjust the discount rate such that it will make the appropriate adjustment for risk in the present value of uncertain future benefits and costs in each period. The one case in which the appropriate adjustment for risk can be made by raising the discount rate is that of a one-period investment that has a positive expected return. This happens to be the case, however, for which the CAPM was first developed and for which many analyses are carried out, and these results are sometimes loosely extrapolated to investments that have benefits and costs in two or more future periods.

Consider the following simplified example of a multiperiod benefit–cost evaluation. We will begin with the case of a \$1 investment with a return one period later represented by a random variable X_1 with a mean $\overline{X}_1$. We know from expected utility theory that a risk-averse individual will value the uncertain return less than a certain return equal to $\overline{X}_1$ because of the risk. However, there is some certain amount $X_1^* < \overline{X}_1$ so that the individual will be indifferent between the uncertain return represented by X_1 and the certain return X_1^*. X_1^* is the certainty equivalent of X_1.[5] The difference, $\overline{X}_1 - X_1^*$, is the risk adjustment that must be made in the expected value of X_1 to obtain the certainty equivalent.

[5] This is explained in some detail by Wilson in chapter 6 in this volume.

Now suppose that the individual undertaking this investment can borrow and lend at the rate r, the risk-free rate. Then the individual will undertake the investment if

$$-1 + \frac{X_1^*}{1 + r} > 0 \tag{17}$$

that is, if the present value of the certainty equivalent of that investment minus the cost of investment is positive when computed at the rate r. However, suppose that we wanted to discount the expected return $\overline{X}_1$ directly. Clearly, it would be inappropriate to apply the discount rate r to $\overline{X}_1$. Can we adjust r to r' so that the criterion

$$-1 + \frac{\overline{X}_1}{1 + r'} > 0 \equiv -1 + \frac{X_1^*}{1 + r} > 0 \tag{18}$$

Clearly, we can do this by determining r' such that

$$\frac{\overline{X}_1}{1 + r'} = \frac{X_1^*}{1 + r} \quad \text{or} \quad \frac{X_1^*}{\overline{X}_1} = \frac{1 + r}{1 + r'} \tag{19}$$

Now consider another \$1 investment with a return two periods hence. This return is represented by the random variable X_2 with mean $\overline{X}_2$ and a certainty equivalent of X_2^*. Now the individual following the previous line of argument will choose this investment if

$$-1 + \frac{X_2^*}{(1 + r)^2} > 0 \quad \text{or if} \quad -1 + \frac{\overline{X}_2}{(1 + r'')^2} > 0 \tag{20}$$

where r'' satisfies the relationship

$$\frac{X_2^*}{\overline{X}_2} = \frac{(1 + r)^2}{(1 + r'')^2} \tag{21}$$

However, r'', which is the appropriate risk-adjusted rate for discounting the mean value of returns in period two, will equal r' if and only if

$$\left(\frac{X_1^*}{\overline{X}_1}\right)^2 = \frac{X_2^*}{\overline{X}_2} \tag{22}$$

More generally, to be able to make one adjustment in r that, when applied to the expected returns in each period, will appropriately adjust the present value of these expected returns for risk, the following relationship

$$\left(\frac{X_1^*}{\overline{X}_1}\right)^n = \frac{X_n^*}{\overline{X}_n} \tag{23}$$

must hold for every period, that is, for all values of n. Clearly, this requires risk to be such that the ratio of the certainty equivalent of returns to the expected value of returns decreases in a well-specified way over time.

In general this will not be the case. For most investments the risk-adjusted rate of discount r' that will produce the correct risk-adjusted present value for returns in period 1 will not be the same as the risk-adjusted rate r^n that will produce the correct risk-adjusted present value of returns in period n.

There may be some rate $\bar{r}$ such that

$$\sum_{t=1}^{T} \frac{X_t^*}{(1+r)^t} = \sum_{t=1}^{T} \frac{\overline{X}_t}{(1+\bar{r})^t} \tag{24}$$

that is, such that the present value of the stream of the certainty equivalent returns when discounted at the risk-free rate r and the present value of the expected returns discounted at the rate $\bar{r}$ would be equivalent. However,

$$\frac{X_t^*}{(1+r)^t} \neq \frac{\overline{X}_t}{(1+\bar{r})^t} \quad \text{for } t = 1, \ldots, T \tag{25}$$

that is, the present value of expected returns in each period computed using $\bar{r}$ would not equal the present value of returns correctly adjusted for risk, but the totals would be the same. However, there is no way to estimate $\bar{r}$ without going through the exercise of computing the expected returns and their certainty equivalents for each period and then solving an equation such as (22) except under some specialized conditions that we will discuss. It is easier and more straightforward to compute the present value of the certainty equivalents using a risk-free rate and thereby avoid the extra step of solving a difficult polynomial equation.

In the previous example, the expected future returns were assumed to be positive. By raising the interest rate used to discount those returns, we could lower the present value of the future expected return to make it equivalent to the present value of the certainty equivalent return discounted using a risk-free rate. Now suppose that we were considering an investment in which the expected value of the return in some period t was negative, that is, $X_t < 0$. In this case $X_t^* < \overline{X}_t$, but $|X_t^*| > |\overline{X}_t|$. Therefore, if we were to discount the certainty equivalent of these costs at the rate r and then choose r' such that

$$\frac{\overline{X}_t}{(1 + r')^t} = \frac{X_t^*}{(1 + r)^t} \tag{26}$$

we would have to choose $r' < r$; that is, when one has negative returns, the direction of the appropriate adjustment in the discount rate to account for risk is to lower the rate. An increase in the discount rate diminishes the present value of future costs, whereas a decrease in the discount rate increases the present value of these costs. It follows that no single correction in the discount rate can be made to reflect risk correctly at every point in time if the expected values of returns are positive in some periods and negative in others.

The foregoing discussion illustrates that, except in one special case, no single adjustment can be made in the discount rate to adjust for risk the present value of expected returns in each period. There may be some value for $\bar{r}$ that will give the correct valuation when used to discount the expected returns $\overline{X}_t$, but in this example there is no easy way to compute it. However, a significant part of the work in modern finance has been directed to solving exactly this problem of finding a measure of risk and relating it to a risk-adjusted rate of return. This work has been associated with the development of the CAPM.

There is one very important case in which the appropriate risk adjustment can be made and can be measured from market data. This is the case of a one-period investment for which the degree of risk can be measured by the covariance of its return with the return to a portfolio consisting of all assets; that is, in the case of a stock, its risk would be measured by the covariance of its return to the market portfolio consisting of all stocks. This is the special case for which the CAPM was initially developed. The CAPM provides a theoretical basis for relating the required rate of return on an asset to the riskiness of that asset.[6]

The CAPM has been extended to multiple time periods, and in some versions of the model trading takes place on a continuous basis and in others it takes place at discrete intervals. We will discuss some of the extensions of the basic model shortly and examine their implications for the treatment of risk in public investment decisions. However, much of the controversy to date can be clarified in terms of the simple one-period CAPM. Given this model, there is a well-defined relationship between the required rate of return on an asset and the riskiness of that asset measured in terms of its covariance with the market portfolio. This model demonstrates that when returns to an

---

[6] For an excellent but introductory discussion of the CAPM by one of its originators, see Sharp (1978).

asset are positively correlated with the market portfolio, the required rate of return is greater than the risk-free rate; when the returns are uncorrelated, the required rate of return is the risk-free rate; and when the returns are negatively correlated, the required rate of return is less than the risk-free rate. Using these basic results, we can clarify much of the controversy between those who have argued that risky public investments should be required to earn the same rate of return as risky private investments, including a premium to account for risk, and those who have argued that a risk-free rate should be used to evaluate public investments.

Before turning to this discussion, it is important to state the basic result of the CAPM, which was initially developed for a single period and pertained to the decision of an individual to buy a stock and to hold it for one period. The return on that stock was compared with the return from the stock market as a whole. Under the idealized conditions specified in the CAPM, the expected risk-adjusted rate of return on a stock in an efficient market will satisfy the equation

$$\overline{R}_i = r + \beta_{im}[\overline{R}_m - r] \tag{27}$$

where $\overline{R}_i$ is the expected rate of return on the stock in question, r is the risk-free interest rate,

$$\beta_{im} = \frac{Cov\,[R_i - r, R_m - r]}{Var\,[R_m - r]} \tag{28}$$

is a measure of the risk, and $\overline{R}_m$ is the expected rate of return on a portfolio consisting of all stocks in the market (Sharp, 1978). Notice that if the returns to a particular investment are independent of the returns to the market portfolio, then $\beta_{im} = 0$ and it follows that $\overline{R}_i = r$; that is, the required expected rate of return on that investment should equal the risk-free rate r. The rate r is generally considered to be the rate of return on Treasury bills. If there is a negative correlation between R_i and R_m, then the investment denoted by i provides insurance against fluctuations in the market rate of return, and $\beta_{im} < 0$. Therefore, the required rate of return, as evaluated by such an efficient stock market, would be lower than the risk-free rate of interest.

We can now use the results of the CAPM to clarify the controversy between those who have argued that risky public investments should be required to earn the same rate of return as risky private investments, including a premium to account for risk, and those who have argued that a risk-free rate should be used to evaluate public investments. Proponents of the first position have argued that the discount rates used to evaluate risky public investments should be the same discount rates, based on the cost of capital, that are used to evaluate comparable investments in the private sector. On the other side of this controversy is a group of economists who have argued that the government is somehow in a better position to bear risk than is a private firm and, therefore, that no premium for risk should be charged against public investments and that a risk-free rate of discount should be used in evaluating public investment projects.

In the 1960s, the leading proponent of the position that public projects should earn the same risk-adjusted rate of return as comparable private projects was Hirshleifer (1965), who presented this position using a simplified state-preference model of the economy. More recently, the same conclusion has been presented in a paper by Sandmo (1972). Bailey and Jensen (1972) have worked out a detailed description how such an adjustment might be made in connection with a theoretical model developed by Harberger.

The proponents of using a riskless rate included Arrow, Samuelson, and Vickery among others; this position was most rigorously developed in a paper by Arrow and Lind in 1970. Their results demonstrated that under the conditions assumed in their model, it was appropriate to discount the expected value of the benefits of a public project at a rate of discount equal to the risk-free rate of return in the market. The question then is, Are these positions compatible or incompatible? If they are incompatible, which one is correct?

The results derived by Arrow and Lind on the one hand and those obtained by Hirshleifer, Sandmo, and Bailey and Jensen on the other, are not necessarily incompatible; however, this fact is not generally understood even though it was pointed out in the paper by Bailey and Jensen. Given the assumptions that Arrow and Lind make about the returns to public investments, it follows that if private investors were considering investments with identical returns, both the government and private investors should evaluate these investments using a risk-free rate of discount. The controversy arises because of differences regarding the appropriate assumptions about returns from public as opposed to private investments. To understand the relationship between the two positions in this controversy it is instructive to interpret the Arrow–Lind results in terms of the CAPM.

The first of the two theorems in the Arrow–Lind paper demonstrates that, in an economy characterized by complete markets for claims contingent upon states of the world, the appropriate rate of discount for public investment decisions would be the risk-free rate of interest, provided that the distribution of returns to the investment being evaluated were statistically independent of returns to the economy as a whole (Arrow and Lind, 1970; Wilson, this volume). If one interprets the model correctly, however, one sees that this would be the rate of discount that would be used also by private firms for evaluating investments with returns that were statistically independent of t⁺ⱼ returns to the economy as a whole.

In terms of the simple CAPM, in which the returns to an investment are statistically independent of the returns to all other investments, the covariance of these returns with the returns to the rest of the economy is zero. In other words, this is an investment with a beta coefficient of zero. It essentially has zero market risk and, according to the CAPM, it should earn a rate of return equal to the risk-free rate of return, which, for practical purposes, is generally assumed to be the rate of return on Treasury bills. Therefore, the first Arrow–Lind theorem may be interpreted as giving results for an n-period economy under uncertainty that are analogous to those of the CAPM for an investment with a beta coefficient of zero. Because of the independence of the return, the cost of the risk associated with such an investment can be almost eliminated through diversification, provided the investment is a relatively small proportion of the total economy.

Other authors have concluded that investments in the public sector should be required to earn a risk-adjusted rate of return and therefore should be evaluated using a rate of discount that reflects the risk of a comparable private project. This view is not necessarily inconsistent with the Arrow–Lind results because, for investments that are statistically independent, the risk-adjusted rate should be the risk-free rate of return for both private and public investments.

The second of the two primary Arrow–Lind theorems demonstrates that if the government undertakes a risky investment and spreads it over a large number of people so that each one holds a small share of that investment, the effect is to substantially reduce the cost of the risk—reducing the cost to zero in the limit—even though the risk would not be optimally allocated among individuals as it would be in an economy with complete markets for claims contingent upon states of the world. Again, as Arrow and Lind pointed out, this theorem holds as well for a private investment as for a public investment if the private investment can be diversified among a large number of shareholders even though there are neither complete nor perfect markets for risk.

Therefore, the critical question is, What is the nature of the correlation between returns from public projects and the level of national income as a whole or the returns from all other projects in the economy? Clearly this will vary from project to project. As we have suggested previously, the returns from energy research and development in the future may be negatively correlated with the returns to all other investments so that public investments in this case would have the effect of insurance. If we were to account for this insurance effect by altering the rate of discount, we should use a lower rate of discount than the risk-free rate, not a higher one.

Bailey and Jensen (1972) argue that the returns to most public investments will be correlated with returns to investments in the private sector because the demand for the output of public investments will rise and fall with the business cycle just as it does for goods in the private sector. Therefore, they argue that a risk-adjusted rate should be used to evaluate public investments, and they derive the formula for computing such a rate based on the framework of the capital asset pricing model. Bailey and Jensen analyze the one-period case and derive the appropriate risk-adjusted rate for evaluating a public investment. One important question that this procedure raises is whether it is appropriate to derive the risk-adjusted rate of return for returns in one period and then use that rate to discount the returns over the life of the investment in the standard discounted net-benefit calculation. We will return to this question shortly.

Clearly, if one were to derive a risk adjustment it would be necessary to determine the covariance between the returns of a public investment and the returns to an appropriately chosen portfolio of assets. The covariance of the returns to an asset is usually measured with respect to the stock market portfolio or the level of national income that represents the return to all economic activity. Later in this volume we will discuss further the interesting question of what portfolio of assets is the proper one for comparison in determining the level of risk of a particular public investment. Whatever the appropriate portfolio is, clearly one of the major problems in most public investments will be determining the degree of correlation between the returns to the public investment and returns to another portfolio. The problem is that most publicly produced goods and services are not sold in the market and that we cannot observe all of the benefits and costs in each year. Developing the appropriate data for determining their risk would be a monumental task. We will discuss this problem further in the section on measurement.

Before discussing the extensions of the CAPM and whether or not it provides a basis for determining a risk-adjusted rate of discount that should be used in evaluating public investment decisions, let us consider the question of whether the discount rate used for public investment should be a risk-adjusted rate or whether it should be a risk-free rate. And further, let us consider whether the risk-adjusted rate should be the same as the risk-adjusted rate used by firms in evaluating private investment decisions. The CAPM provides us with a framework for answering these questions.

The answer to the first question is that it should be a risk-adjusted rate. The government, in evaluating public investments, should reflect the riskiness of the investment in the same way as individuals in the society would reflect that risk in their own private investment decisions. On the other hand, it does not necessarily follow that the risk-adjusted rate that should be used for public investments should be the same as the risk-adjusted rate used by firms in making investment decisions. The distinction between the individual citizen as an investor choosing a portfolio of assets and the firm making capital investment decisions is critical here, and this distinction is sometimes lost in the discussion of the discount rate issue.

It is basic to the benefit–cost methodology that the benefits and costs to society as a whole are computed as the sum of the benefits and costs to individual members of that society as evaluated by them. Therefore, if a public investment produces a stream of net returns to an individual, the present value of that stream of net benefits from the standpoint of that individual will reflect any adjustment that that individual makes because the stream of benefits is uncertain. Furthermore, if the individual is consistent, he will place the same value on the returns from a public project as he would on an identical stream of returns from a private project. Therefore, the individual would discount the future stream of returns from the public investment at the same rate as he would an identical future stream of returns from a private investment so that they would have the same present value.

To the extent that these returns are correlated with other components of the individual's income, a risk-averse individual will discount them for risk. Therefore, because it is basic to the benefit–cost approach that individual valuations be used to measure the present values of benefits and costs, and because these individual valuations will reflect any adjustment for risk, it is appropriate to adjust for risk in computing present values of benefits and costs when evaluating public investment decisions. Furthermore, the adjustment for risk should be the same in evaluating public investments from the individual standpoint as for evaluating an identical private investment from the individual's point of view, for example, an asset with identical properties that he or she might buy in the private market. If markets for risk are efficient, then for public and private investments with returns that are uncorrelated with national income, the required rate of return should be the risk-free rate.

This does not imply that the appropriate risk-adjusted rate for evaluating the benefits and costs of public projects should be the same risk-adjusted rate that private firms might use in making capital budgeting decisions. First, as we have discussed at length, there is a divergence between the before-tax rate of return a firm must earn to yield the after-tax rate required by the investor. This is true of risk-adjusted rates of return as well as risk-free rates of return. Second, the managers of firms may make investment decisions that exhibit more risk aversion than is in the interest of the stockholders. This is because the stockholders view the risk of the company in relation to a diversified portfolio of assets, whereas the careers of the managers are highly correlated with the outcomes of the ventures of their particular companies. One argument against this reasoning is that managers must behave in the interest of the stockholders. If they do not, the value of the stock of the company will be lower than it could be and they would face the threat of being replaced in a takeover. However, takeover bids are costly and time-consuming, and recent evidence indicates that the threat of a takeover does not place tight constraints on managerial discretion (Smiley, 1976).

The test of whether firms behave in a manner that is inconsistent with the interest of their shareholders in perfect risk markets or whether they exhibit this risk aversion because risk markets are far from perfect would be whether firms discount investment opportunities in which the returns are statistically independent of other returns in the economy, for example, a zero-beta project, at a rate that would yield an after-tax rate of return to the investor equal to the risk-free rate. Bailey and Jensen (1972) point out that "Arrow erroneously concludes . . . that the performance of the risk market is far from perfect since . . . perfect markets would eliminate risk to the firm and we know this elimination has not occurred." The appropriate test is whether it has occurred for investments whose returns are uncorrelated with national income.

If one takes the Treasury bill rate to be the risk-free rate over the period from 1926 to 1978, the average real rate of return on Treasury bills was zero (Ibbotson and Sinquefield, 1979). In other words, investors were willing to accept a rate of return equal to the rate of inflation, which over this period averaged 2.5 percent. If the corporate income tax were 50 percent, this would mean that if markets for risk were perfect, the discount rate used by firms to evaluate investments with returns that were uncorrelated with national income should, on average, have been 5 percent. Although this is the appropriate restatement of Arrow's test, it is difficult to carry out this test this empirically because the returns to individual investments are generally buried in the returns to a firm and it is also difficult to identify particular investments that have returns that are not correlated with other components of national income.

Although this issue is important for the question of whether firms are more averse to risk and require higher rates of return on investments than is socially optimal, it is not particularly important for the analysis of risk in social benefit–cost analysis. What is relevant for evaluating individual benefits and costs is how individuals value the returns from assets with different degrees of risk. We can determine this from market data; however, we have to adjust these data to obtain the rate of return after personal income tax. First, let us consider the risk-free rate of return represented by Treasury bills, which has averaged 2.5 percent over the period 1926–1978 (Ibbotson and Sinquefield, 1979). If we conservatively assume the average taxpayer has a marginal income tax rate of 20 percent, then the nominal after-tax rate of return on a risk-free asset has been 2 percent and the real after-tax rate of return has been − 0.5 percent, so that individuals have accepted a real return of − 0.5 percent on a risk-free investment.

Now consider the average returns to common stocks, that is, the market portfolio with a beta coefficient of unity. The average nominal rate of return has been 8.9 percent (Ibbotson and Sinquefield, 1979). Again assuming a marginal personal income tax rate of 20 percent, the nominal after-tax rate of return has been 7.1 percent and the real after-tax rate of return has been 4.6 percent. Therefore, over the period 1926–1978, the average real rate of return required by a taxpayer with a marginal income tax rate of 20 percent has been -0.5 percent for an asset with $\beta = 0$ and 4.6 percent for an asset with $\beta = 1$. These are the after-tax, risk-adjusted consumption rates of interest. For individuals in a marginal tax bracket of 30 percent, the respective real after-tax rates of return have been -0.75 percent and 4.23 percent.

Of course, the foregoing analysis implicitly assumes that expected inflation, on average, equaled actual inflation. The conclusion that the risk-adjusted consumption rates of interest equal actual after-tax rates of interest has to be modified if actual inflation has systematically exceeded expected inflation. Then the estimates of the real risk-adjusted consumption rates of interest would have to be raised by the amount of this difference because decisions to save and invest, from which we can draw inferences about the consumption rate of interest, are based on expected inflation, not actual inflation. More will be said about this in the section on measurement. We have chosen to present data for a fifty-year period rather than for the last ten or fifteen years because this latter period has been characterized by high inflation and a very poor performance by the market portfolio. Over the last ten to fifteen years, rates of return on the market portfolio have been extremely low.

What is instructive from these data is that typical risk-adjusted, after-tax, real rates of return on assets—including rates of return on assets that are essentially risk-free and rates of return on the market portfolio—during the period 1926–1978 have ranged from -1 percent to 6 percent. This can be used to narrow the range of the risk-adjusted rates of discount that people use to evaluate after-tax cash flows from private investments and net benefits from public investments.

An important question is whether it is appropriate to use the risk-adjusted discount rate estimated on the basis of a single investment period in computing the present value of a multiperiod investment. Put differently, if one starts with the CAPM, under what conditions is it valid to discount cash flows (or net benefits) over several periods at a single risk-adjusted rate to determine the present or market value of an asset? This question is an extension of the question, Can a single adjustment in the discount rate be made to account for risk in a present value calculation when the conditions of the CAPM are met? This topic has been central to modern finance and has been addressed in various forms by a number of authors, and a full review of this literature is well beyond the scope of this chapter. The results of a recent paper by Myers and Turnbull (1977) are instructive and both encouraging and discouraging. The authors derived and presented expressions for the market value of a long-lived capital investment project, assuming the CAPM holds in each period. They then used these expressions to investigate the determinates of the beta coefficient for the project and to evaluate whether traditional capital budgeting procedures based on a discounted cash flow formula and the opportunity cost of capital are valid. They reported as follows (p. 331):

> The good news is that it is possible to value capital investments using relatively simple formulas derived from the CAPM. Also, the traditional procedures give close-to-correct answers, provided that the right asset beta is used to calculate the discount rate.
>
> The bad news is that the right asset beta depends on project life, the growth trend of expected cash flows, and other variables which are not usually considered important in assessing business risk. Moreover, for growth firms the right discount rate cannot be inferred from the observed systematic risk of the firm's stock, even if the firm invests only in projects of a single risk class. The reason is that growth opportunities affect observed systematic risk.

It is interesting to note that Myers and Turnbull found that except for cases in which cash flows follow a pure random walk or in which $T = 1$ or infinity, there is no risk-adjusted interest rate that can be plugged into the equation for present value that will give the correct answer, just as was the case in the simple example we presented earlier. However, they found that if one calculates the single-period required rate of return $R = r + \beta[E(R_m) - r]$ and plugs it into the equation for present value, this yields a present value that is approximately correct. Therefore, using the required rate of return for one period as the discount rate yields a good approximation of the present or market value of the stream of returns. What is more troublesome is that it may be difficult to determine the appropriate beta for the investment.

The literature in modern finance has made a number of advances with regard to the CAPM and one, in particular, bears mentioning in connection with the discussion of risk and public investment criteria. As has been mentioned, the model has been extended to multiple time periods assuming either discrete or continuous trading. One of the most interesting developments was Merton's (1975) multiperiod CAPM with multiple sources of risk and corresponding multiple beta coefficients. He pointed out that, in addition to market risk, the risk an individual perceives may be associated with uncertainty about (1) his future tastes, (2) the future menu of consumption goods, (3) the future relative prices of these goods, (4) his future labor income, (5) future values of nonhuman assets, (6) future interest range, and (7) has age at death. Merton derived this model for continuous time and derived an equation, which is analogous to that for the simple CAPM, for the required rate of return on an asset. Certainly a substantial part of the risk in energy investments is associated with possible changes in relative prices of goods, changes in the menu of goods (for example, big cars may not be manufactured in the future), uncertainty about future investment opportunities, as well as uncertainty about one's income.

The literature of modern finance and its extensions of the CAPM have not provided a totally satisfactory method for determining an appropriate risk-adjusted discount rate that can be applied to the expected value of future benefits and costs to calculate the present value of net economic benefits. The problems are both theoretical and empirical. First, the theory shows that it may not be possible on the basis of the CAPM to determine such a risk-adjusted discount rate, although it may be possible to find one that gives a good approximate answer. The second source of problems is empirical. How would one estimate the appropriate beta coefficient for a public investment project with an uncertain stream of future returns? This is a problem for capital budgeting decisions in the private sector as well as for public investment decisions.

Finally, there is little data about costs and benefits from past public projects; such data could be used to evaluate how the returns from these projects have varied over time and how they correlate with fluctuations in national income. Developing a data base that would enable us to estimate the correlation between the returns to specific types of projects and the national income would be a monumental, if not impossible, task. Probably the best that one can do is to consider the nature of a public investment and to ask, as Bailey and Jensen (1972) do, whether its returns are likely to be highly correlated, uncorrelated, or negatively correlated with those of the economy as a whole. Then one can use a real after-tax, risk-adjusted rate of return for the market portfolio in the first case, the real after-tax Treasury bill rate in the second case, and a still lower rate in the third case. From our previous discussion these rates appear to range between − 1 percent and 6 percent.

However, historical data on rates of return show that the real after-tax rates of return required by individuals on assets ranging from relatively safe assets such as Treasury bills to the stock market portfolio have been under 6 percent and that the required real rate of return on a safe asset such as Treasury bills has been near zero. This suggests that whatever the risk-adjusted real rate of discount for evaluating public projects should be, it very probably is in the range zero to 6 percent as opposed to the range 10 to 15 percent. This assumes, of course, that we are equating the social rate of discount with the social rate of time preference as determined by the risk-adjusted consumption rate of interest. The opportunity cost of capital displacement caused by a public investment still must be accounted for through a shadow price on capital. The risk-adjusted consumption rates of interest would be applied only to streams of benefits and costs adjusted to their consumption equivalents.

There are several practical approaches to the treatment of risk in benefit–cost analysis. The first, and the one that is conceptually superior and fits most nicely into the framework developed here, would be to use a risk-free rate of discount and to adjust benefits and costs for risk using techniques such as those developed by Wilson. The problem with this approach is that it is difficult to implement. A second approach would be to use a risk-free rate and then perform a sensitivity analysis using rates up to 6 percent, which might be interpreted as an upper bound on the after-tax rate of return required by investors on the market portfolio. A third, and related, approach would be for some special cases in which it can be argued that certain public investments have returns that are either uncorrelated or negatively correlated with returns to the total portfolio. In these cases one would discount at a risk-free rate and argue that, if using this rate does anything, it understates the present value of the project. Finally, one can argue that, unless there is substantial evidence to the contrary, the returns associated with public projects should be assumed to be highly correlated with returns to the economy as a whole. Therefore, as a first approximation, the after-tax rate of return on the market portfolio should be used to discount benefits and costs for both time and risk. For reasons to be discussed in the next section, we shall assume that this rate is 4.6 percent.

Sometimes more than one of these four approaches may be appropriate for public policy analysis. Clearly, when leaving the realm of theory and needing to develop procedures to improve decision making about public or private investments, one must be pragmatic and accept approximation. The case of adjustments for risk is no exception.

Problems of Measurement

Whatever theory we use for the social rate of discount, there is still the problem of computing the appropriate number or numbers for the discount rate, given the underlying conditions in the economy and the procedures we adopt. This task is by no means trivial. As we have seen, the major contenders for the social rate of discount are the marginal rate of return on private capital, the consumption rate of interest taken as a measure of the social rate of time preference, a weighted average of the consumption rate of interest and the marginal rate of return on private capital, and a social rate of time preference revealed through the political process. Finally, the procedure that we adopt is to set the social rate of discount equal to the social rate of time preference as revealed by individuals' consumption rates of interest and to use a shadow price on capital to convert capital displaced or stimulated by a public investment into its consumption equivalent.

This shadow price of capital in turn requires that we have estimates of the marginal propensity to save, the marginal rate of return on private capital, the social rate of time preference measured by the consumption rate of interest or by some other means, and the length of life of the "typical" private investment. In addition, this approach requires that we be able to estimate the displacement and stimulative effects of the public investment on private capital formation. Further, if we are to account appropriately for any systematic risk of public investments, we must either develop a procedure to adjust the discount rate for risk or a procedure for estimating the risk adjustment that should be made in the value of expected benefits and costs. Clearly, it is not a trivial task to estimate all the required parameters for the approach that we adopt here in using a shadow price on capital and equating the social rate of discount to the social rate of time preference however it is measured. One can see in advance that approximation is going to be essential.

Consider first the measurement of the marginal rate of return on investment in the private sector. One approach that has been used to measure the marginal rate of return on capital has been to use aggregate accounting data and to compute the rate of return on private capital by computing the relationship between the value of capital assets and the before-tax earnings of those assets. This procedure is carried out on a year-by-year basis, and in order to arrive at an estimate of the real before-tax rate of return on private capital, an adjustment is made to account for the effects of inflation. This is the basic approach used by Stockfisch (1967), Nordhaus (1974), and by Holland and Myers (1979). Up until the 1970s, when inflation rates increased substantially, estimates of the real rate of return despite some differences in how these rates were measured had been in the range of 10 to 15 percent.

The development of measures of rates of return from aggregate accounting data is associated with many technical problems, such as possible biases created by depreciation rules, differences in the adjustment for inflation, and the differences in the tax treatment of incorporated and unincorporated businesses. Different writers have analyzed the rates of return in different sectors of the economy and formed averages in different ways. Nevertheless, the basic technique provides a reasonably accurate measure of the average real rate of return on private capital. Differences in procedures with regard to depreciation and the like appear to have relatively little effect on the results. The major problem with this number is that it is the average rate of return on private capital and not the marginal rate of return on private capital. The marginal rate of return is what we wish to measure because it is the marginal investment that will be displaced if private investment is crowded out by a public investment and it is marginal investment that will be stimulated in the future if more funds are invested in the private sector.

If we believe that the schedule for the marginal efficiency of capital slopes downward, then the average rate of return on investment will be above the marginal rate of return, and there is no easy way of estimating the difference between the average and marginal rates of return on private capital. Those who argue that the marginal rate will be closely approximated by the average rate appeal to the fact that when capital stocks are adjusted optimally in a perfectly competitive economy, then, in equilibrium, the marginal rate of return to each factor of production will be equal to the average rate of return. Put differently, at the point of equilibrium, there will be constant returns to scale to all factors including capital. However, if other factors of production are fixed, such as population, it is not true that as we increase the capital level of investment that the marginal rate of return will remain constant over any significant range. In fact, in all macroeconomic analyses, we assume that the marginal efficiency of capital slopes downward at any time.

A further problem is that the average rate of return to capital in the economy as a whole, based on accounting figures, reflects returns for risk. When we allow risks to enter the picture, then the concept of a marginal rate of return on capital becomes more complex and we have to talk about a marginal rate of return on investments that in some sense are equally risky. Therefore, in equilibrium, the marginal rates of return on investments of one risk class may be 13 percent, and that of investments in another may be 10 percent, while the rate of return may be the same for all of these marginal investments after appropriate adjustments are made for risk.

A second approach for determining the marginal rate of return on private investment would be to try to compute the cost of capital to firms and then to argue that firms will invest up to the point at which the return of the marginal investment is equal to their cost of capital. Computing a weighted average cost of capital for an average firm in the economy would be a Herculean task, but it could possibly be done. However, the theory of modern finance tells us that this old model of investment behavior by the firm is incorrect. The modern position is that the present value of the stream of returns produced by an asset should be valued in a way that depends only on the stream of cash flows generated by the investment. This would mean that every firm, regardless of its debt–equity ratio, its profits at the time, or its alternative opportunities, should place the same value on investment with cash flows that are identically distributed. The theory tells us that this procedure, and only this procedure, will maximize the net worth of the firm from the standpoint of the shareholder, who is assumed to hold a diversified portfolio of assets.

This position is clearly developed in "Corporate Investment Decisions" by Traynor and Black (1976).

> We have made two simple assumptions: that corporate investment decisions should be made from the stockholder's point of view and that the stockholder is only interested in the pattern of cash flows that result from the decision. From these assumptions it follows that after the cash flows are estimated, decisions should be made without reference to the company making them. In deciding on a project, the profitability of current company products is not important, and the company's tentative capital or cash budget is not important.

They go on to state:

> The present value method with risk-adjusted discount rates is incomplete
> because we do not know how to measure the risk of a project or how
> to choose a risk discount rate based on this. In looking for a way to
> measure risk and a way to discount it, we will find a new method for
> making corporate investment decisions that is equivalent to the present
> value method with risk-adjusted discount rates only in special circum-
> stances.

Their position is that there may not be a well-defined risk-adjusted rate
of discount for use in capital budgeting decisions by firms and, even if there
is, we do not know how to measure the risk or to define the relationship
between this measure of risk and the risk-adjusted rate of discount. This
position is consistent with the results obtained by Myers and Turnbull (1977).
It leads to the conclusion that there may not be a well-defined marginal rate
of return on private capital except for risk-free investments in which the
appropriate pretax rate of return would be the rate of return that would yield
an after-tax rate of return on equity equal to the rate of return on a riskless
asset. However, even here, the concept of being "riskless" is not without
ambiguity. Keeping in mind the major sources of risk enumerated by Merton,
one might ask, riskless in what sense or in terms of what portfolio of assets?
These issues are not of great importance if we have complete markets for
goods and services contingent on the state of the world; however, they do
complicate the task of defining and measuring a marginal rate of return on
capital in the private sector of an economy that does not closely approximate
this ideal.

Another problem is that it appears that in making capital budgeting
decisions, most firms do not follow procedures that are consistent with those
that are advocated in the theory of modern finance. It is not clear that
investment decisions are in fact made only from the point of view of the
stockholder, nor is it clear that investments are made without regard to the
current conditions of the company making the investment and the alternatives
that they have open to them. The reason that investments may not be made
in the interest of stockholders is, as previously stated, that the interests of
the managers and their perception of risk may differ from those of the
shareholders. And secondly, most investors or shareholders would say that
a company's investment should bear some relation to the current state of the
company. Traynor and Black (1976) discussed three current approaches used
by corporate managers in making capital budgeting decisions. The first
approach is to use the criterion that a project should be accepted if it will
increase the corporation's book rate of return and rejected if it does not. The
second approach involves ranking proposed investments according to their
payback periods, and the third technique is to rank projects by their internal
rates of return.

This third approach is divided into three variants. The first is to use the corporation's book rate of return as the discount rate. The second variant is to use the corporation's cost of capital as the discount rate. The third variant uses a discount rate that reflects the riskiness of the cash flows in the project. Traynor and Black demonstrated that each of these approaches is flawed in one way or another. Nevertheless, it is clear that in many investment decisions, corporate planners do consider the cost of capital in capital budgeting decisions, they do look at the payback period, and they do sometimes assign set target rates of return for acceptable projects.

The truth is that capital budgeting decisions in the private sector are made on consideration of a number of types of calculations, and there generally is no fine adjustment for risk in the discount rate used in present value calculations. What we observe in terms of the portfolio of projects that are undertaken is the product of a wide variety of decisions based on many factors. Probably only in the management of portfolios of market assets is the riskiness of each individual asset carefully measured and related to its rate of return, and this has been a relatively recent development.

In practice, capital investment projects, whether in the public sector or the private sector, can be evaluated only in a very rough-and-ready fashion. In most cases, it is not possible to estimate the distribution of returns to a potential project with sufficient accuracy to develop reliable estimates of their variance and their covariance with other portfolios of assets or to allow one to make fine adjustments for risk, even if that were a conceptually satisfactory method of proceeding.

Therefore, the situation we find ourselves in with regard to the measuring of the rate of return on private investment that would be displaced by increased public expenditure is that if we increase government borrowing and if this drives up the rate of interest, then some set of projects in the private sector will be displaced. The displaced projects will have different internal rates of return, depending in some way on their degree of riskiness, and the average rate of return of these displaced projects will be less than the average for all projects.

In general the estimates of the rates of return on private capital, after adjustment for inflation, are in the neighborhood of 10 percent to 15 percent on an average annual basis. Therefore, the rates of return on the marginal projects that would be crowded out by private investments are probably in the neighborhood of 10 percent, although this is clearly a matter of judgment; one could just as easily defend 11 percent or 9 percent.

However, as we shall demonstrate, the precise measurement of the marginal rate of return is not important for the computation of the shadow price of capital. This is because if the pretax rate of return for the marginal investment is less than the average, the after-tax rate of return on the marginal investment also will be less than the average after-tax rate of return. As will

be demonstrated, it is the ratio of the before- and after-tax rates that is critical
to the value of the shadow price of capital.

Now consider the consumption rate of interest and its use in measuring
the social rate of time preference. Clearly, the concept of the consumption
rate of interest applies to the individual and is defined as being the same as
the individual's marginal rate of time preference. We can infer the magnitude
of an individual's consumption rate of interest by looking at his after-tax
borrowing or lending rates of interest. From the assumption that the individual
will adjust his borrowing and lending to a point that maximizes his utility,
we can infer that the rate at which he is willing to trade consumption today
for consumption in the future will just equal his borrowing or lending rate
of interest, whichever is applicable. However, individuals are in different
marginal tax brackets, have different opportunities to borrow and invest, and
have different asset positions, so that for some the operative rate will be the
after-tax borrowing rate, whereas for others the operative rate will be the
after-tax rate of return on their savings and investment. For these reasons,
almost everyone will have a different consumption rate of interest. This is
unlike the very tidy case in which there was one rate of interest in the
economy and all individuals could borrow and lend at that rate and therefore
had the same consumption rate of interest.

The situation is complicated further by the individual who has a
mortgage on his house at one rate, a savings account that pays another rate,
is borrowing on his Mastercharge account at a third rate, and is investing in
a pension plan that earns a return at a fourth rate. Although this apparent
anomaly usually can be explained on the grounds of transaction costs,
considerations of liquidity, and differences in tax treatment, from the practical
standpoint of determining the individual's marginal rate of time preference,
there is the question of which rate is the appropriate one.

The approach we adopt here to circumvent the seemingly messy and
insurmountable practical problems of determining different rates for different
people is to observe that most people over their working lifetime do save
and invest in a variety of assets, including passbook savings accounts, money-
market accounts, and various forms of mutual funds. Certainly this saving
takes place both through an individual's making direct investments and
through institutionalized insurance plans to which an individual contributes.
Therefore, for the society as a whole, we should be able to get some idea of
the range in which the marginal rates of time preference lie by looking at
the rates of return on the savings instruments that individuals have available
to them.

It is highly instructive to return to the earlier observation that over the
period from 1926 to 1978, the real after-tax rate of return from holding
Treasury bills for an individual in a 20 percent tax bracket was, on average,
negative, and the real after-tax rate of return on holding a mutual fund made

up of the market portfolio was 4.6 percent. The real rate of return on most other instruments available to individual investors would be less than 4.6 percent. For individuals in a higher marginal tax bracket, corresponding real rates of return are lower.

What this says is that individuals at the margin have been willing to invest in assets earning a zero or negative return for relatively safe assets and a real rate of return of less than 6 percent for the market portfolio. If we look at the data for the past ten years, these rates are even lower. However, during the last ten years there have been rapid increases in the rate of inflation, and this presents some problems for interpreting market data in terms of individuals' consumption rates of interest.

The problem is that expected inflation may not equal actual inflation, or more accurately, expected inflation on average may not equal actual inflation. One can understand this problem as follows. Suppose an individual requires a real rate of return of 2 percent on an investment. Then if the individual expects the inflation rate to be 6 percent, he will demand a rate of return in nominal dollars of approximately 8 percent so that he will maintain the real value of his assets and earn the required rate of return over and above that. Therefore, interest rates will reflect both a component representing the expected rate of inflation plus the component representing the required real rate of return. Since the individual is looking ahead when he makes the investment, it will be his expected rate of inflation that governs the rate of interest or the rate of return that he will accept.

Now suppose an individual demanding a 2 percent real rate of return on his investment invests in an asset that pays an 8 percent rate of return and suppose that instead of the 6 percent inflation rate that he expected, the rate of inflation is 8 percent. Then the actual rate of return on his investment will be zero. When we compute real rates of return, we don't subtract expected inflation because we cannot observe that, but instead we subtract actual inflation. To the extent that the individual's expectation of inflation is less than the actual inflation, his marginal rate of time preference will be above the observed real rate of return in the market. On the other hand, to the extent that expected inflation is greater than actual inflation, the observed rate of return will be greater than his marginal rate of time preference. Therefore, if on average the individual predicts inflation correctly, then inflation does not cause any problems with regard to our inferences about his marginal rate of time preference based on average observed real rates of return over time.

However, if the individual systematically underestimates the rate of inflation, as he might do in a period of rapidly rising rates of inflation, then actual real rates of return will understate his marginal rate of time preference. There is some reason to believe that this in fact is what has happened over the past ten years as inflation rates have escalated. There is some evidence that individuals predict inflation on the basis of past inflation rates and that they adjust their expectations fairly quickly. Therefore, the fact that real rates of return on almost all financial assets were negative for some periods in the 1970s does not necessarily imply that individuals' marginal rates of time preference were negative over these periods.

The data for the last fifty years suggest that the required real rate of return on a relatively safe asset such as Treasury bills or long-term government bonds, which have slightly more risk related to changes in the rate of interest, is near zero and that the required rate of return on the market portfolio is 4 percent to 6 percent. This is also true in the period from 1946 through 1976. One can infer from such data that whatever the adjustment for risk, the marginal rates of time preference exhibited by individuals range from zero to 6 percent and may even be negative but certainly are not in the range from 10 percent to 15 percent. Therefore, the discount rate applied to the benefits and costs, adjusted to their consumption equivalent, of a public project should be less than 6 percent.

One can also conclude that for investments that do not have systematic risk or those with returns that are negatively correlated with national income and therefore provide an element of insurance, the rate of discount should be closer to zero than to 6 percent. Although one cannot refine these inferences much further, the fact that the social rate of time preference appears to be in the range from zero to 6 percent instead of 10 percent to 15 percent clearly is significant.

Before turning to the question of the shadow price of capital and how it might be estimated, it is important to remind the reader that the low real rates of discount that we are talking about do not necessarily mean using low nominal rates of discount or return. While the reader is certainly at least intellectually aware of this fact, in these times of high rates of inflation, it is sometimes psychologically difficult to think in terms of low rates of return. We have trouble thinking about 1 and 2 percent rates of return when the prime lending rate is 20 percent, even though we know that when the prime rate first went to a record high of 20 percent in 1980, the monthly inflation rate adjusted to a yearly average was about 18 percent so that the real rate of return was slightly less than 2 percent.

To calculate the shadow price of capital, one needs to know four parameters: (1) the social rate of time preference, (2) the marginal rate of return on investments in the private sector, (3) the marginal propensity to save, and (4) the economic life of the private capital investment that will be displaced or stimulated as a result of a public investment or expenditure. Consider first the length of life of a representative unit of capital equipment. Clearly, different capital assets will have different economic lives, but we can estimate the average life of the capital stock by the ratio of the initial book value of assets to the depreciation of these assets in a particular year. If all firms used strict straight-line depreciation for tax purposes, this would give us the appropriate measure of the average life of capital equipment. Unfortunately, many investments are depreciated more rapidly in the early stages of their life than in later stages. This would present no problem if the percentage of the total capital that was new was the same as that which was old, because while depreciation of new capital would be higher than the amount that would be charged under straight-line depreciation methods, depreciation of older capital would be lower. A bias creeps into the analysis, however, because as the capital stock is growing, a greater percentage of the capital is in the early stages of its useful life rather than in the later stages. As a rough measure, this gives a reasonable estimate of the average life of a piece of capital equipment. Using corporate income tax data, we can determine both the book value of corporate assets and depreciation. Using such data for 1973, 1974, and 1975, we estimate that the average life of such an asset is approximately 15 years (U.S. Department of the Treasury, 1973; 1974; 1975).

We will assume throughout the remainder of this discussion that marginal propensity to save is 0.2, which is less than the short-run marginal propensity to save out of disposable income and greater than estimates—by Friedman and others—of the long-run marginal propensity to save, which equals the average propensity to save. The higher the marginal propensity to save, the higher will be the shadow price of capital because more of the capital that is invested will be reinvested. However, our estimates of the shadow price of capital are not highly sensitive to small variations in the savings rate.

Given that the average life of an investment is 15 years and given an assumed marginal propensity to consume of 0.2, then using values for r ranging from 10 percent to 15 percent and values for i ranging from 1 percent to 6 percent, the shadow price of capital ranges from 2.09 for $r = 0.10$ and $i = 0.06$ to infinity for values of r at the high end of the range and values of i at the low end. This, however, is not as serious as it might at first appear. Values for r that are in the 10 percent to 15 percent range represent the average rate of return on what for practical purposes makes up the market portfolio. Investments of this type, on average, have the same risk as the market portfolio and their average rate of return reflects this risk. At the same time, the after-tax rate of return to the market portfolio has been in the neighborhood of 4 percent to 6 percent. The real after-tax rates of return of zero to 2 percent are the rates on safe assets, and the pretax rate of return on such an asset would certainly be well below 10 percent if capital markets worked efficiently. The problem from an empirical standpoint is that it is difficult to identify riskless capital projects and to measure their real rates of return from accounting data, as we can for all corporate investments.

In the case of corporate investments, Holland and Myers (1979) estimate that the real rate of return on capital in the period from 1946 to 1976 has been 12.41 percent and that the real after-tax rate of return to claimants on this income, taking into account both personal and corporate income taxes, has been 5.77 percent; that is, 54 percent of the pretax return went to taxes, leaving 46 percent as the after-tax return to the claimants on that income. Using 12.41 percent for r and 5.77 percent for i, we get a shadow price for capital equal to 3.79. It turns out that the shadow price of capital is primarily determined by the ratio of r to i. Suppose we believe that as a result of the corporate and personal income taxes, the after-tax rate is 46 percent, on average, of the pretax rate. Then for values of r ranging from 5 percent to 15 percent and the corresponding values of i ranging from 2.3 percent to 6.9 percent, the shadow price of capital ranges from 3.41 for $r = 5$ percent and $i = 2.3$ percent to 3.89 for $r = 15$ percent and $i = 6.9$ percent. Table 2-2 shows the values for the shadow price of capital, assuming that the after-tax rate of return, which we equate with i, is 40 percent, 46 percent, and 50 percent, respectively, of the before-tax rate of return r, which varies from 5 percent to 15 percent.

If corporate and personal income taxes take 60 percent of pretax income, the shadow price of capital is about 5. If such taxes take 54 percent of pretax earnings, as they have on average in the period 1946–1976, the shadow price of capital given today's tax laws is approximately 3.8. Finally, if personal and corporate income taxes claim about 50 percent of pretax earnings, the shadow price of capital is about 3. It is interesting to note that for the assumptions about discount rates used in the CONAES study (National Academy of Sciences, 1978) ($r = 13$ percent, $i = 6$ percent), the shadow price would be 3.84; for the assumptions used in the Manne–Richels study of the breeder ($r = 12$ percent, $i = 5$ percent), the shadow price of capital would be 4.81.

We will use 3.8 as a first approximation of the shadow price of capital based on a real after-tax rate of return on the assets of nonfinancial corporations that is 46 percent of the real pretax rate of return, including both the corporation income tax and personal income taxes (Holland and Myers, 1979). However, as the real after-tax rate of return on the market portfolio, we shall use 4.6 percent and not 5.77 percent as estimated by Holland and Myers. There are two reasons for this. First, this appears to be more consistent with the long-term data cited earlier on stock market returns, and second, there is some evidence that real rates of return on corporate investment were

Table 2-2. The Shadow Price of Capital Given Alternative Assumptions Regarding r, i, and the Relationship Between Pretax and After-tax Earnings

$r = 5\%$		$r = 10\%$		$r = 15\%$	
$i = 2\%$	4.59	$i = 4\%$	5.29	$i = 6\%$	5.48
$i = 2.3\%$	3.41	$i = 4.6\%$	3.67	$i = 6.9\%$	3.89
$i = 2.5\%$	2.90	$i = 5\%$	3.09	$i = 7.5\%$	3.26

declining in the 1960s and 1970s. For example, the real rate of return from 1973 to 1976 on the assets of nonfinancial corporations was 9.4 percent before taxes and 5.6 percent after taxes, not including personal income taxes (Holland and Myers, 1979). If, including personal income taxes, the rate of return after all taxes was 46 percent of the pretax rate of return, the real after-tax rate would be 4.32 percent. Although 4.6 percent is not a perfect risk-adjusted measure of the real rate of time preference for returns that are highly correlated with the market portfolio, it is probably a good first approximation.

We will also use 1 percent as a first approximation of the real rate of time preference associated with a safe asset such as U.S. Treasury bills and 2 percent as the real rate of time preference on safe long-term assets such as long-term U.S. government bonds, with which the primary risk is a change in interest rates. These rates are a percent or two higher than the historical after-tax real rates of return on these assets and therefore are likely to be in error on the high side, if at all.

Clearly, more work needs to be done to test and refine these estimates. The concept of the shadow price of capital, its use in benefit–cost analysis, and its estimation are in their infancy. At the same time, on the basis of assumptions, estimates, and measured rates of return that are well accepted, the numbers that we have adopted here are robust and not highly sensitive to changes in the underlying assumptions. Also, the data on after-tax rates return to a variety of assets strongly suggest that individual rates of time preference range from zero to 6 percent.

Practical Implementation of Benefit–Cost Analysis in Public Policy Decisions

One might emerge from the preceding section on measurement with a sense of despair because precise measurement of the social rate of time preference, the marginal rate of return on private capital, and the shadow price on capital is probably impossible. From this, one might conclude that the discount rate issue is so fraught with difficulties that it cannot be resolved sufficiently to enable benefit–cost calculations to be a useful guide in making public decisions. In fact, if one were to evaluate the accuracy of all the numbers that go into benefit–cost analyses, one would see that the estimates of benefits and costs are subject to large margins of error as well. While all of this is true, it does not mean that benefit–cost analysis cannot be exceedingly useful in public investment and policy analysis. This is because of the way benefit–cost analysis is generally used in the policy process. One does not need pinpoint accuracy; usually ballpark accuracy is sufficient. The role of benefit–cost analysis in the policy process is not to provide us with a decision but, rather, to help us identify those projects that might be uneconomical and, similarly, to help identify those projects that are clearly in the public interest. If we do our job well in performing benefit–cost analyses, we can often eliminate from consideration the worst 20 percent of the projects that are being proposed as well as identify and make the case for those projects that are clearly of great economic benefit. These are the projects in which mistakes are most costly. For those projects in which the benefits and costs are balanced, the cost of a wrong decision is not likely to be great.

Furthermore, when there is not a clear and demonstrable economic advantage to one decision as opposed to another, it is perhaps appropriate that the decision be made on political grounds, which will take into account the many intangible factors that did not enter the benefit–cost calculation. Therefore, although we cannot make precise measurements of the benefits and costs and we may be able to make only a rough approximation of the social rate of time preference, one should not conclude that the crudeness of our measurements eliminates their usefulness.

In addition, the very process of going through a benefit–cost analysis helps to educate decision makers about the alternatives and about what the benefits and costs would be under various assumptions. This may well contribute to more informed decision making on their part.

In short, benefit–cost analysis is not a precise tool but, rather, is a crude tool that can identify projects that are clearly losers or winners. It also is a process that improves decision making by informing decision makers as to the important elements in a public investment or policy decision.

Many of the applications of benefit–cost analysis will be carried out by professional analysts who are operating more or less in isolation and who have greater or lesser ability and training in economics. Therefore, if analyses to evaluate governmental policies are to be at all comparable, there must be clear instructions to the analysts about what discount rate to use or how to compute the appropriate rate of discount for different projects. This is true also for the measurement of benefits and costs of similar projects. The analyst simply cannot have discretion in the choice of the discount rate. If he did, studies of similar projects would not be comparable because different discount rates would be used. Further, having such discretion would enable the analyst to manipulate the choice of the rate so as to influence the results, and this would make analysis less credible. If we are to use benefit–cost analysis as a tool in the policy process and in particular to use it in government agencies, we must specify either a discount rate or a procedure for computing the discount rate that can be easily followed.

One possibility for establishing guidelines for benefit–cost analyses would be to have an office of the federal government, such as the Office of Management and Budget, take the lead in defining the assumptions and procedures that are to be used in benefit–cost studies. Such an office might

well have an advisory group of professional economists and policy analysts
who would assist in defining procedures and specifying critical assumptions
and parameter values. Such an office might actually carry out or commission
benefit–cost studies of major projects, such as development of the breeder,
synfuels, or an all-nuclear navy. In the final chapter of this volume, we set
forth the kind of instructions on the discount rate, the shadow price of capital,
and assumptions and procedures that should be used in benefit–cost studies
of energy options.

Summary and Conclusion

The approach that we adopt for performing benefit–cost analyses of public
investments and policies, particularly energy investments and energy policies,
is to equate the social rate of discount with the social rate of time preference
as determined by consumption rates of interest and estimated on the basis of
the returns on market instruments that are available to investors. We also
account for the effects of public investments and policies on private capital
formation by directly analyzing the magnitude of these effects and then
converting them to their consumption equivalents through the use of a shadow
price on capital. On the basis of the calculations made in the previous section,
we estimate that, as a first approximation, the shadow price of capital is 3.8.

On the basis of data on after-tax rates of return, we have taken 4.6
percent to be the approximate risk-adjusted real rate of time preference that
should apply to projects with the same risk as the market portfolio. Unless
a strong argument can be made that the benefits and costs of a public
investment or policy will not be highly correlated with the returns to the
market portfolio, this should be the discount rate applied to the benefits and
costs. On the basis of data on rates of return on Treasury bills, we assume
1 percent is the real rate of time preference on safe investments and that 2
percent is the real rate of time preference associated with a safe long-term
asset such as long-term government bonds, for which the primary risk is a
shift in the level of interest rates. This last point is important in considering
energy policy and investments. If the payoff to energy projects were
uncorrelated with the return on the market portfolio, 2 percent would be the
appropriate rate for discounting the net benefits of energy investments because
such investments would be riskless except for the risk of interest rate changes.

We have argued that when energy prices rise, the return to energy
investments will go up while the return to investments in general will go
down. In other situations the returns to energy investments will move up and
down with the business cycle so that they will be correlated with returns to
other investments. Therefore, we can tentatively conclude that the correlation
between returns to most energy investments and the returns to the market

portfolio is less than one and perhaps zero or negative. If the correlation is between zero and one, then the appropriate real risk-adjusted rate of discount is in the range from 2 percent to 4.6 percent. This conclusion is itself significant in that this range is substantially lower than the 6 percent to 10 percent range that has been commonly used in the literature on energy policy. It is important to emphasize, however, that this rate applies to benefits and costs adjusted for their impact on private investment.

The approach adopted here is more in the tradition of partial-equilibrium analysis than of general-equilibrium analysis. Although it takes into account the effects of decisions through time, it is not fully dynamic. It is designed to display the most important effects of a public policy or investment decision through time and to evaluate these effects, but it is not designed as a method for determining optimal policies over time. The decision to adopt a more partial form of analysis was deliberate and relates to the two main reasons that partial-equilibrium analysis forms the basis for most applied economics. The reasons are, first, that one can obtain results that are specific enough to be applicable to actual data, and second, that for many complex problems partial-equilibrium analysis is a better tool than general-equilibrium analysis for understanding the major first-order effects.

This does not mean that we do not derive important insights from fully dynamic general-equilibrium models, which can be used to identify optimal policies. The approach we adopt has been strongly influenced by the treatment of investment and reinvestment in the optimal growth formulation of the public investment problem. What the more general and fully dynamic formulations of the problem do not do is provide an analytical method that can be clearly stated to and understood by a competent policy analyst with economic training. The method we adopt for performing benefit–cost analysis must also be such that it can be applied with some confidence that we have captured at least the major effects, or benefits and costs, of a policy based on data. There is no doubt that to use the benefit–cost methodology in the policy process, we have to give up elegance, generality, and to some degree the pursuit of optimality.

Again, for reasons related to the practical application of the result, we have chosen to use the social rate of time preference as the discount rate and to account for the impacts of a public investment or policy on private capital formation, adjusting the benefits and costs by using the shadow price for capital. The effects that are accounted for by the model that has been adopted are those that relate to the direct displacement or stimulation of private investment. This approach is different from the approach adopted by both Arrow and Stiglitz in this volume. They attempt to infer the social rate of discount from the optimal policy. The practical problem with that approach is that in a second-best world, where different projects may be undertaken under various sets of conditions and where risk is taken into account, it may well turn out that every project will require a different discount rate.

This situation simply is not consistent with the practical requirements for the use of benefit–cost analysis. Every analyst in performing a benefit–cost analysis would have to specify a set of assumptions about the underlying structure of the economy, the constraints on government action, and the nature of the investment. From these assumptions he would derive the appropriate rate of discount by means of formulas such as those set out by Stiglitz in the paper in this volume. This runs contrary to the practical demands of a solution to the discount rate problem. Although the procedure we develop as an alternative is not simple, we attempt to set forth a workable set of instructions for its use, and these are presented in the final chapter of this volume.

The approach adopted here separates the questions of time preference from the question of opportunity cost in terms of capital displacement and from the question of risk. We contend that these are the three major factors that come into play in choosing the appropriate rate of discount for use in benefit–cost analysis. In this way we can focus the analysis on capital displacement or risk and then analyze them separately from the issue of time preference. One of the reasons for the confusion in the discount rate controversy is that various analysts have come up with different and seemingly contradictory answers on the basis of analyses that are technically correct but that differ in their assumptions about the underlying structure of the economy and the constraints on government. These differences tend to get buried when we try to account for capital displacement and other effects as well as risk in the selection of the discount rate.

Nevertheless, the choice of the approach we have adopted is not without its difficulties. The only distortionary effect that it takes into account is the direct effect on the formation of private capital. While we believe this to be the most important effect that we need to consider, it is, as Stiglitz points out, certainly not the only one. Similarly, this approach to public investment analysis has all the pitfalls associated with partial analyses. It does not consider fully all the dynamic effects, nor does it consider the full range of effects at any point in time. The justification for such an approach is that one can capture the most important effects and measure their impact over time. If we can achieve this objective and have an analytical method that we can use in the practical application of benefit–cost analysis, then we have a useful tool for policy analysis. The practical requirements are that it be simple enough to be explained and applied, specific enough that the results are not subject to the discretion of the analyst through manipulation of the assumptions, and specific enough that the results of different analyses performed by different people will be comparable.

One of the major problems with the approach that we have adopted is that we do not fully understand the impact of public investment decisions on private capital formation. We do not understand how alternative methods of financing affect private capital formation, and we do not fully understand how government investments affect the savings and investment decisions of individuals. Nevertheless, we will demonstrate in the final chapter of the book that satisfactory first approximations can be obtained for a number of cases.

Certainly more research is needed on the ways in which public investment, public expenditure in general, and the financing of these expenditures affect private savings and investment. However, events within the field of economics as well as the intense political interest in this subject suggest that this topic will be carefully studied.

References

Arrow, K. J. 1964. "The Role of Securities in the Optimal Allocation of Risk-Bearing," *Review of Economic Studies* vol. 31 (April) pp. 91–96.

———. 1966. "Discounting and Public Investment Criteria," in A. V. Kneese and S. C. Smith, eds., *Water Research* (Baltimore, Johns Hopkins University Press for Resources for the Future).

———, and M. Kurz. 1970. *Public Investment, the Rate of Return, and Optimal Fiscal Policy* (Baltimore, Johns Hopkins University Press for Resources for the Future).

———, and R. C. Lind. 1970. "Uncertainty and the Evaluation of Public Investment Decisions," *American Economic Review* vol. 60 (June) pp. 364–378.

Bailey, M. J., and M. C. Jensen. 1972. "Risk and the Discount Rate for Public Investment," in M. C. Jensen, ed., *Studies in the Theory of Capital Markets* (New York, Praeger) pp. 269–293.

Baumol, W. J. 1978. "On the Social Rate of Discount," *American Economic Review* (September) pp. 788–802.

Bradford, D. F. 1975. "Constraints on Government Investment Opportunities and the Choice of Discount Rate," *American Economic Review* vol. 65, pp. 887–895.

Debreu, G. 1959. *Theory of Value* (New York, Wiley).

Diamond, P. 1968. "The Opportunity Cost of Public Investment: Comment," *Quarterly Journal of Economics* (November) pp. 686–688.

Eckstein, O. 1958. *Water Resource Development: The Economics of Project Evaluation* (Cambridge, Mass., Harvard University Press).

Feldstein, M. S. 1970. "Financing in the Evaluation of Public Expenditure," Discussion Paper No. 132 (Harvard Institute for Economic Research, August).

Harberger, A. C. 1968a. "Economic Analysis of Public Investment Decisions: Interest Rate Policy and Discounting Analysis," Hearings before the Subcommittee on Economy in Government, Joint Economic Committee, U.S. Congress, July 31, 1968 (Washington, GPO) pp. 57–65.

————. 1968b. "On Measuring the Social Opportunity Cost of Public Funds," in *Proceedings of the Committee on Water Resources and Economic Development of the West: The Discount Rate in Public Investment Evaluation* (Denver, Western Agricultural Economic Research Council).

————. 1973. *Project Evaluation: Collected Essays* (Chicago, Markham).

Haveman, R. H. 1969. "The Opportunity Cost of Displaced Private Spending and the Social Discount Rate," *Water Resources Research* vol. 5, no. 5 (Richmond, Va., American Geophysical Union, October).

Hirshleifer, J. 1965. "Investment Decision Under Uncertainty: Choice-Theoretic Approaches," *Quarterly Journal of Economics* vol. 79 (November) pp. 509–536.

————. 1966. "Investment Decision Under Uncertainty: Applications of the State-Preference Approach," *Quarterly Journal of Economics* vol. 80 (May) pp. 252–277.

Holland, D. M., and S. Myers. 1979. "Trends in Corporate Profitability and Capital Costs," in R. Lindsay, ed., *The Nation's Capital Needs* (New York, Committee for Economic Development) pp. 103–189.

Ibbotson, R. G., and R. A. Sinquefield. 1979. "Stocks, Bonds, Bills and Inflation: Updates," *Financial Analysts Journal* (July–August).

Krutilla, J. V., and O. Eckstein. 1958. *Multiple Purpose River Development* (Baltimore, Johns Hopkins University Press for Resources for the Future).

Lind, R. C. 1981. "The Social Rate of Discount, The Shadow Price of Private Capital Formation, and The Opportunity Cost of Public Programs," unpublished paper.

Merton, R. C. 1975. "Theory of Finance from the Perspective of Continuous Time," *Journal of Financial and Quantitative Analysis* (November).

Myers, S. C., and Turnbull S. M. 1977. "Capital Budgeting and the Capital Asset Pricing Model: Good News and Bad News," *Journal of Finance* (May) pp. 321–333.

National Academy of Sciences. 1978. *Energy Modeling for an Uncertain Future,* Study of Nuclear and Alternative Energy Systems. Supporting Paper 2, The Report of the Modeling Resource Group Synthesis Panel of the Committee on Nuclear and Alternative Energy Systems, National Research Council (Washington, NAS).

Nordhaus, W. D. 1974. "The Falling Share of Profits," *Brookings Papers on Economic Activity* vol. 2, pp. 169–208.

Sandmo, A. 1972. Discount Rates for Public Investment Under Uncertainty," *International Economic Review* vol. 13 (June).

————, and J. H. Drèze. 1971. "Discount Rates for Public Investments in Closed and Open Economies," *Economica* vol. 38 (November) pp. 395–412.

Sharp, W. F. 1978. *Investments* (Englewood Cliffs, N.J., Prentice–Hall).

Smiley, R. 1976. "Tender Offers, Transaction Costs and the Theory of the Firm," *Review of Economics and Statistics* (February).

Stockfisch, J. 1967. "The Planning–Programming–Budgeting System: Progress and Potentials," Hearings before the Subcommittee on Economy in Government, Joint Economic Committee, U.S. Congress (Washington, GPO, September) pp. 133–143.

————. 1969. "Measuring the Opportunity Cost of Government Investment," Research Paper 490, Institute for Defense Analysis (March).

Traynor, J. L., and F. Black. 1976. "Corporate Investment Decisions," in S. C. Meyers, ed., *Modern Development in Financial Management* (New York, Praeger) pp. 310–327.

U.S. Department of the Treasury, Internal Revenue Service. 1973. *Corporation Income Tax Returns: Statistics of Income* (Washington, GPO).
————. 1974. *Corporation Income Tax Returns: Statistics of Income* (Washington, GPO).
————. 1975. *Corporation Income Tax Returns: Statistics of Income* (Washington, GPO).

3

Robert C. Lind

A Reader's Guide to the Papers
in this Volume

Introduction

The purpose of this chapter is to guide the reader in approaching the papers and discussion in this volume. Because readers differ in their economics training, mathematical skills, and interests, this chapter provides information about the technical difficulty of each paper and discussion, the issues that are treated, and the conclusions. This overview is not a substitute for the papers themselves. Most of the authors, even those whose papers are highly technical, have attempted to state their assumptions, lay out the problems they address, and state their conclusions for a general audience of economists and policy analysts. Therefore, even if one cannot follow the full technical argument presented in these papers, there is much to be gained from reading them, skipping the technical details, and focusing on those parts that deal with the assumptions, issues, and conclusions.

In addition to providing an overview of the papers and discussion, we also attempt to show how each of the papers in this volume relates to the literature on the discount rate as described in chapter 2 and how it relates to the analytical method developed in chapter 2. Further, wherever possible, we point to the origins of that analytical method in the material in this volume, although it would be impossible to acknowledge the full debt that we owe to the authors and discussants.

"The Rate of Discount on Public Investments with Imperfect Capital Markets"

The lead paper is by Kenneth J. Arrow, who has been one of the most important and prolific contributors to the discussion of the social rate of discount and public investment criteria over the last twenty years. His paper represents a continuation of this work and of his association with Resources for the Future. The introductory pages of Arrow's paper contain an interesting review of the development of this work, beginning with the publication of "Discounting and Public Investment Criteria" in 1966 and continuing through the publication of his book with Mordecai Kurz, *Public Investment, the Rate of Return, and Optimal Fiscal Policy,* in 1970.

One of the major contributions of Arrow's work has been his formulation of the problem of public investment criteria, and in particular the question of the appropriate rate of discount in relation to optimal economic growth. He views the problem as one of choosing the optimal public investment policy. The selection of the discount rate is a part of this problem and is made by solving for the optimal policy. A second significant contribution of this work has been that Arrow has treated the financing of public investment, and monetary and fiscal policy in general, as an integral part of the analysis of public investment decisions. He demonstrates that the optimal policy and the appropriate rate of discount are in many cases dependent upon the method of financing and upon macroeconomic policies in general.

Arrow's paper continues in this tradition. It formulates the problem as a general optimization problem and solves for the discount rate by solving for the optimal policy. In addition, it ignores issues of intergenerational equity by assuming that there is one consumer and that this consumer has the same time horizon as the government, which in this case is infinite. Arrow assumes that government investment produces its benefits through its effect on the productivity of private capital. An example would be research and development expenditures by the government on new energy technologies that would produce benefits to the consumer indirectly through the private sector's investment in these technologies.

There are two new dimensions to this work. First, the model is set up so that individuals take public investments and the anticipated consumption that they will produce into account when determining their optimal consumption–savings plans. Second, Arrow focuses on the effects of financing public investment by means of a corporate income tax. The effect of adding these new dimensions to the problem is to change the results of his previous analysis. Arrow says: "The conclusion of the earlier models, that the rate of return on public investment should equal the fully optimal rate even if private investment does not receive it, is no longer necessarily valid."[1]

Speaking of his conclusions he says, "Probably the most striking, to me, though others would regard it as obvious, is the conclusion that there is a strong case for equating the rate of discount in the public sector to that in the private sector to the extent that public investment is financed by taxes on profits. However, as should have been clear all along, if public investment

---

[1] K. J. Arrow, "The Rate of Discount on Public Investments with Imperfect Capital Markets," chapter 4 in this volume.

is financed partly through nondistortive taxes, the public rate moves to the utility discount rate, that is, in the long run, the public rate moves to consumer's rate, and indeed more rapidly than in proportion to the proportion of nondistortive taxes.''[2] The social rate of discount associated with the optimal policy is indeed a weighted average of the consumer's rate of interest and the rate of return on private capital, but the weights are not established in strict proportion to the funds financed through nondistortive as opposed to distortive taxes. These results hold when the economy reaches a long-run steady state.

A further conclusion is that, in the steady state, the discount rates depend on the initial level of the public debt if borrowing is being permitted. One possible interpretation of this result is that if a public debt exists, then the rate of taxation or the rate of borrowing required to pay the interest on the debt or repay part of the principal is set by this initial level of debt. This has an effect on the behavior of the economic system in that it determines how much money has to be raised through taxation or borrowing, both of which cause distortions, to fund a certain level of public investment.

While the paper by Arrow is highly mathematical and very technical, it is written in such a way that someone who cannot follow the technical details can benefit greatly by reading through those sections that are not highly technical.

The first discussion of Arrow's work is by Martin S. Feldstein, who makes three suggestions for extending Arrow's analysis. First, he suggests that the model be extended to consider government investments that not only produce benefits by enhancing the productivity of private capital but also provide services directly to the consumer. Feldstein says, "The special form of Arrow's analysis implies that the output resulting from the public investment will always be divided between consumption and investment in the same way as other private income. More realistically, some public expenditures induce added personal saving, while others reduce such saving.''[3] As a result, Feldstein argues that ''it is generally necessary to have both a shadow price per dollar of public funds spent on the activity (to reflect the excess burden in raising the revenue) and a discount rate for comparing costs and consumption benefits at different times.''[4] He goes on to state that Arrow's special case of a single year's public expenditure that produces only concurrent consumption benefits "disguises the general need for a shadow price because of the implicit assumption about the private saving induced by the public project.''[5] The use of the shadow price along with a separate discount rate for comparing consumption costs and benefits at different times is central to

[2] Ibid.

[3] M. S. Feldstein, comment on Arrow's "The Rate of Discount on Public Investments with Imperfect Capital Markets," in this volume.

[4] Ibid.

[5] Ibid.

the approach we develop in chapter 2, in which the work of Feldstein, one of the early advocates of this approach, is cited.

The second extension that Feldstein suggests is that the government be allowed to charge for services because they have a major impact on the financing requirements and therefore on the problem of the distortionary effects of tax or debt financing that might be associated with a public investment. Feldstein's third suggestion is that the "infinite life" assumption used in Arrow's model be evaluated by formulating the same problem in a model that assumes overlapping generations. Feldstein's comments are relatively short and easily accessible to all readers.

The second comment is by Daniel Usher, and although it concerns primarily the paper by Arrow, it addresses issues raised also in the paper by Stiglitz. Usher points out that unless we can resolve the problem of the discount rate for public investment decisions, economists are not going to be able to provide much guidance in the area of public investment decisions. He observes that we are in the confusing position of having different theorists writing on these issues and obtaining what seem to be essentially different results that cannot easily be compared. He says, "Comparison of the Stiglitz and Arrow prescriptions is made doubly difficult by the contrast in their styles of analysis. Stiglitz looks directly at marginal decisions in the public sector and adjusts private costs and benefits by multipliers alleged to reflect distortions in the economy. Arrow treats the derivation of a rule for public sector investment as an 'agency problem' in which the public sector determines the whole time path of investment with due regard to the response of the private sector both to the investment itself and to the taxes and bonds through which it is financed."[6] In the context of these remarks, it should be emphasized that the approach we adopt and develop in chapter 2 is much more closely related to that of Stiglitz than that of Arrow, although we have been strongly influenced by both authors.

Usher then undertakes a simplified and concise two-period analysis of the issues that relate to the papers of both Arrow and Stiglitz. This analysis can be easily understood by a reader with a knowledge of basic economic theory. Usher focuses on the indirect effects and the indirect costs of public investments. "The distinction made here is, following Stiglitz, between the direct and indirect effects of a public project," Usher says. "Stiglitz's argument is that, though the use rate [consumption rate] of interest is always appropriate in comparing total effects of a project, the response of the private sector is more often than not such that the opportunity cost rate is appropriate when only the direct effects can be observed."[7]

[6] D. Usher, comment on Arrow's "The Rate of Discount on Public Investments with Imperfect Capital Markets," in this volume.
[7] Ibid.

Usher analyzes in some detail three sources of indirect effects, which he calls the demand effect, the tax effect, and the substitution effect. He discusses also a number of indirect costs that are not covered by those three effects of public investments. Finally, he discusses the need to define clearly the public and private domains of the economy and argues that this process of definition should be independent of the issue of the discount rate.

"The Rate of Discount for Benefit–Cost Analysis and the Theory of the Second Best"

The paper by Joseph E. Stiglitz addresses the general question of how to perform benefit–cost analyses in an economy that is nonoptimal, that is, in the world of the second best. He says that "intrinsically, benefit–cost analysis is concerned with second-best situations."[8] In this sense the paper by Stiglitz is similar to the paper by Arrow. However, rather than focus on the analysis of one particular source of distortion, Stiglitz attempts to put forth a general methodology for performing benefit–cost analysis under different distortional situations. In particular, he applies this analysis to the choice of the rate of discount. He says: "I hope that use of explicit but simple models of the economy, in which the appropriateness of alternative second-best constraints can be discussed, will eliminate much of the controversy over the choice of a discount rate for use in benefit–cost analysis."[9]

Stiglitz's paper contains an excellent discussion of what one would need to know to analyze a public investment decision, and in particular, the appropriate social rate of discount in an economy that is nonoptimal. He states that it is necessary to explore constraints upon government action in order to determine the relationship between the total effects of a government investment or policy and the direct effects. To determine this relationship Stiglitz states that "one needs to have a theory of the structure of the economy, including statements about governmental behavior."[10] He continues: "Although a full-blown theory of government and a fully specified model of our economy are probably beyond what we can expect soon, we can specify scenarios about government policy (for instance, how it responds to any balance-of-payments deficit resulting from undertaking a project) and make reasonable assumptions about the structure of the economy to reach some conclusions for broad classes of public projects."[11]

[8] J. E. Stiglitz, "The Rate of Discount for Benefit–Cost Analysis and the Theory of the Second Best," chapter 5 in this volume.
[9] Ibid.
[10] Ibid.
[11] Ibid.

Stiglitz contends that the conventional views on the social rate of discount are incorrect. He states:

Thus, the three major "extreme views" hold that . . .

$\rho = r$, the social rate of discount should equal
the producer's rate of interest;
$\rho = i$, the social rate of discount should equal
the consumer's rate of interest; and
$\rho = \delta$, the social rate of discount should equal
the social rate of time preference.

In addition to these extreme views, there is the more common, eclectic view that it should be a weighted average of the producer's and consumer's rates of interest.

Our analysis casts doubt on the *general* validity of any of these simplistic approaches; we identify some important cases in which, for instance, the social rate of discount may not lie between the producer's and consumer's rates of interest. We find other cases in which, even in the long run, the social rate of discount is not equal to the pure social rate of time preference."[12]

However, this conclusion is based on the assumption that we cannot measure all of the direct and indirect effects of a project or policy on the consumption streams within the economy. Stiglitz says, "If we could always calculate the total effects, there is a trivial sense in which we would always wish to use the social rate of time preference for evaluating the benefits and costs accruing in different periods. The problem is that we normally do not calculate total effects and there is no reason to believe that the total effects are simply proportional to the direct effects."[13]

Therefore, Stiglitz abandons the approach of attempting to estimate the total effects of a program or policy and using the social rate of time preference as the discount rate. Rather, he attempts to solve for the optimal policy in a particular situation and then to find the rate of discount that will lead to that optimum, given the constraints on government and the intergenerational structure of the economy. In this sense his approach is like that of Arrow. He then presents a series of simple models, with which he is able to derive precise formulas for determining the appropriate social rate of discount for that particular problem. He states, "Our analysis shows that one must specify what one thinks are the critical sources of market imperfection; then one can infer the correct rate of discount to use."[14]

The remainder of the Stiglitz paper is a discussion of six important reasons why market rates of interest for private consumption goods might

[12] Ibid.
[13] Ibid.
[14] Ibid.

not be appropriate for evaluating public projects. The first reason cited is that the outputs of public projects are often public consumption goods and that the marginal rate of substitution between consumption of public goods at different dates will in general differ systematically from the marginal rate of substitution between private goods at those same dates. The second and third reasons he discusses arise from limitations on the set of taxes that government can impose, and in general, this relates to the fact that imposition of nonoptimal taxes may have an impact on the formation of private capital. The fourth reason is that there are constraints on savings; the fifth is that public investment has an effect on unemployment; and the final reason is that there are imperfections in the markets for risk.

We shall attempt neither to summarize all of the results that Stiglitz obtains nor to restate all of the model variations that he presents. There are simply too many models, too many variations, and too many results, and they are well stated in the paper itself. In fact, the assumptions used in one particular model yield so many different results that Stiglitz has put them in a table to reduce the possibility for confusion.

We can, however, explore briefly the relationship between the results in Stiglitz's paper and the analytical method adopted in chapter 2. First, in chapter 2 we attempt to translate all the effects of a public investment or a public policy decision into its effects on the streams of consumption so that we are able to apply the social rate of time preference as the discount rate, which is measured by the consumption rate of interest. This is done by applying a shadow price to benefits and costs reflecting private capital formation that is either displaced or stimulated as a result of the policy. This is consistent with the principles Stiglitz sets forth if not the practice he adopts. However, he rejects the approach presented in chapter 2 on the grounds that it will be extremely difficult to compute the direct effects of a public investment or policy, and even if one could, he says, there is the problem of determining the appropriate social rate of time preference.

We adopted that particular approach after reading the paper by Stiglitz and seeing the array of results that one gets under different conditions. The alternative adopted in chapter 2 is simpler in many ways than the alternative proposed by Stiglitz, which is to try to specify all of the underlying conditions in the economy and then to determine the rate of discount on the basis of those conditions. It appears from Stiglitz's results that his approach would yield a different rate of discount for every project and would grant the analyst a great deal of discretion over the choice of assumptions about the structure of the economy. It is our belief that, as a practical matter, the approach that he proposes is not workable. Furthermore, while we agree that we may not be able to capture all of the effects of a public investment on the consumption streams in the economy, we believe that by using the concept of the shadow price of capital and by analyzing directly the impact of public expenditures and the associated benefit and cost flows on private investment, we can capture the major impacts.

For the student of public finance and of public policy analysis, as well as the person interested in the application of benefit–cost analysis, the paper by Stiglitz is particularly significant in that it lays out the problems of public policy analysis in a second-best world and develops economic models for some of the most important market imperfections. For the most part the paper is easy to read, and even where the economic analysis is largely mathematical, the reader can gain a great deal by reading the text only. The paper is a very important synthesis of previously uncollected work that Stiglitz and others have done on public investment criteria.

"Risk Measurement of Public Projects"

Robert Wilson's paper provides a comprehensive discussion of risk and the role of risk and uncertainty in the evaluation of public investment and policy decisions with particular emphasis on the relationship between the treatment of risk and the rate of discount. The paper includes everything from a definition of risk and the development of formulas for the measurement of risk to a discussion of how risk can be accounted for in the practical application of benefit–cost analysis.

In many ways a discussion of Wilson's paper in this chapter is redundant in that Wilson provides the reader with a summary at the beginning of his paper and an introduction to the topics covered in each of the subsequent sections. Nevertheless, it is perhaps useful to repeat, for emphasis, some of Wilson's important conclusions.

The first is that capital markets and insurance markets are critical to the attainment of an efficient allocation of risk and to the analysis of risk in connection with public investment and policy decisions. The second is that a key factor in the analysis of risk is the rate at which the riskiness of a project is eliminated. The third conclusion, one that is stressed in chapter 2, is that it is generally inaccurate to use a risk-adjusted interest rate to account for risk. Often a risk-adjusted interest rate biases the evaluation against long-lived investments. The fourth conclusion is that the major component of the risk premium is due not to the variation in a project's outcome in isolation but to its correlation with other projects or with other sources of national income. Wilson points out that if this correlation is sufficiently negative, then the charge for risk is actually negative. Put differently, if one were to account for risk by changing the required rate of return on the investment, then the appropriate action would be to lower, rather than to raise, the required rate of return on such investments. The final conclusion is that the evaluation of the risk of public projects is parallel to the evaluation of the risk of private projects with two major exceptions that stem from the effects of taxes and of consumer surplus.

The first major section of the paper is a survey of the principles of risk measurement in a static context in which time plays no essential role. The material in this section constitutes a clear review of the concepts of risk, risk aversion, and the benefits from risk sharing. The material is well known but is explained by Wilson in a manner that is accessible to anyone who has a basic understanding of probability theory and can follow the formulation in terms of certain well-known utility functions.

A second section of the paper is a detailed analysis of risk measurement in a dynamic context in which the problem of solving for the joint time–risk relationship is a central issue. Wilson analyzes the question of the sequential resolution of uncertainty and of the value of early resolution of uncertainty. This latter analysis, unlike that presented in the discussion of static risk measurement, is largely original work. In a third section Wilson provides an introduction to the evaluation of risk from stock market data. Finally he discusses various sources of risk and lists the pitfalls to be avoided in the application of risk measurement.

The paper by Wilson addresses various topics discussed in the section on risk in chapter 2. However, it does not address the literature on risk and the rate of discount for public investment decisions, nor does it address the empirical evidence on risk and rates of return in the private sector. Also, in chapter 2 we are able to cite some results that were published in the literature on finance at about the same time as Wilson's paper was completed and therefore were not available to him.

However, the paper by Wilson provides a much more complete discussion of the technical foundations of risk measurement, risk sharing, and the theory of capital markets than we attempt in chapter 2. Further, the discussion of the sequential resolution of risk and the importance of early resolution of uncertainty to the analysis of public policy is uniquely treated by Wilson. This timely discussion bears on the evaluation of major research and development projects, such as the continuation of the breeder reactor or the development of synfuel technologies, in which there is a high degree of uncertainty. The analysis of the value of the early resolution of uncertainty is extremely important in the context of energy investments and energy policy.

Wilson's paper can be read by people with greatly differing technical abilities. However, the paper is ideally suited for the economist, systems analyst, or policy analyst who knows some economics as well as basic probability theory but who is not fully conversant with the literature dealing with the economics of uncertainty, decision analysis, and modern finance. It will serve both as a primer for those wishing to get a better grasp of the subject of risk as it pertains to analysis of public investment and as a contribution to the state of the art pertaining to the sequential resolution of risk and the value of information.

Hayne Leland's discussion of Wilson's paper extends and clarifies a number of aspects of the measurement of risk and the pricing of risk in public projects. First, Leland demonstrates that it is "covariance rather than variance" that is the relevant measure of project risk.[15] In his discussion of the choice of the appropriate portfolio with which to compare the returns of public projects, he concludes that the covariance should be computed with respect to the market portfolio and he cites the literature to support that conclusion. The framework of analysis that Leland uses is essentially that of the capital asset pricing model. He uses this framework to develop expressions for measuring the price of risk associated with a project.

Leland then analyzes several propositions within Wilson's paper. The first proposition is that market prices of a risky project undervalue the project's benefits because market prices do not include the consumer's surplus. Leland states that this proposition depends on whether the project in question is already included in the market portfolio. He argues that if the project is not already included in the market portfolio, the predicted market price will in fact overvalue the project's certainty equivalent. However, Leland concludes that for all but very large projects, the estimated market price will provide a good estimate of the true certainty equivalent.

Finally, Leland discusses Wilson's contention that if individuals have logarithmic, or power, utility functions as opposed to exponential utility functions, there are no gains from risk sharing. Leland demonstrates that this is true only when the individuals that would be sharing the risky asset have no other sources of income. Typically, however, individuals would have substantial sources of income other than the risky asset in question, so that this asset would be a small fraction of their total portfolio. In that case, there will be gains from risk sharing and the risk premium will approach zero as the number of people sharing the risk becomes large.

"Measuring the Social Rate of Return on Private Investment"

J. A. Stockfisch discusses the relationship between the social rate of discount and the rate of return on private investment in the economy and then develops measures of the rate of return on private capital from basic accounting data. The first section of his paper is a brief discussion of the controversy over the social rate of discount; in particular, it is an elaboration of the position

---

[15] H. E. Leland, "On Wilson's Risk Measurement of Public Projects," chapter 6 in this volume.

that the rate of return on private capital is the appropriate rate of discount for public-sector decision making.

The second section of the paper sets out the neoclassical, static model that provides the theoretical underpinnings of the measurement technique that Stockfisch uses to estimate the rate of return on private capital. In this section, he discusses some of the methodological difficulties, such as the fact that one is actually measuring the average rate of return on private capital, whereas ideally one would want to measure the marginal return on private capital. He also discusses some of the difficulties of using accounting data, such as problems associated with the treatment of depreciation.

In the third section of the paper, he develops the estimates of the rate of return on private-sector capital investment in the United States from 1961 to 1971. He compares these estimates with those by John A. Gorman and he discusses the data on which the estimates are based. The final section contains his concluding remarks.

As discussed in chapter 2, the paper by Stockfisch is representative of studies in which an attempt was made to use accounting data to estimate the average real rate of return on capital assets in the private sector. It is written in such a way that any student of economics with a basic understanding of price theory should be able to follow the argument without difficulty. The value of this paper is that it provides both an empirical estimate of the rate of return in the private sector and an excellent statement of one of the major positions in the controversy over the discount rate.

"Resource Depletion, Research and Development, and the Social Rate of Discount"

One of the major questions that arose repeatedly in the months we were planning the conference is whether or not discounting at a positive rate implies that we are somehow shortchanging future generations. A second question is whether the utilitarian framework, which serves as the philosophical underpinning of benefit–cost analysis, adequately reflects the interests of future generations. To some extent the first question reflects a confusion between the utility or felicity rate of discount and the consumption rate of interest or consumption rate of discount, which is the discount rate one would apply to consumption streams in benefit–cost analysis. However, the fundamental question about discounting and the appropriateness of benefit–cost analysis required that we look systematically at the implications of a positive rate of discount and of the utilitarian framework. We therefore asked Partha Dasgupta to formulate this problem as it relates to optimal economic growth.

The resulting paper provides a number of useful insights. In the first two sections, he develops the analytical framework of optimal economic growth as it applies to this problem. Although these sections contain material that is well known to economists who are familiar with the theory of optimal economic growth, they present a useful introduction to the subject for the economist who does not work in this area or for the systems analyst or policy analyst.

In the third section, Dasgupta uses the general framework of optimal economic growth to analyze the question of optimal resource depletion. He derives the relationship between the consumption rate of discount and the utility or felicity rate of discount. The consumption rate of discount equals the utility rate of discount plus the elasticity of marginal utility times the percentage rate of growth in consumption. As long as consumption is not constant, the consumption rate of discount need not equal the utility rate of discount; if consumption is growing, the consumption rate of interest will be positive even when the utility rate of discount is zero. From this it follows that simply because we weigh the consumption of different generations differently by discounting at a positive consumption rate of discount, we are not necessarily placing a lower value on units of welfare, as measured by utility, for one generation as compared with another.

To analyze the question of the optimal depletion of a depletable resource, Dasgupta changes the underlying production function of the economy to a function not of capital and labor, which is the normal formulation, but of capital and the depletable resource, in this case energy. He then analyzes the optimal consumption path given this production function, the capital stock, and the stock of the depletable resource. He formulates the general problem and then, to obtain more specific results, considers the class of production functions that have a constant elasticity of substitution between factors of production. The first question he raises is whether the feasible consumption path can be bounded away from zero or whether it must tend to zero in the long run. He finds that it is possible to have a feasible consumption path that is bounded away from zero.

Dasgupta defines $\overline{C}_{max}$ as the maximum constant consumption level that the economy is capable of sustaining, given the limited natural resource. He then asks the question, Is there some utility or felicity rate of discount such that the maximum constant consumption path is the one that is in fact the optimal program? Put differently, the concept of a maximum constant consumption level is analogous to the concept of a maximum sustainable yield in the case of a renewable resource in the sense that it is the maximum level of consumption that we can sustain indefinitely. Then, presumably, if we were to give equal weight to the welfare of all generations, this would be the level of consumption we would choose for each generation, and therefore it would be the optimal program.

What Dasgupta finds is that a positive utility or felicity rate of discount, no matter how small, implies that it is optimal to allow the economy to decay in the long run even though it is feasible to avoid such a decay in consumption by choosing another policy. He then investigates the optimal program in the case in which the utility rate of discount is zero. He finds that the optimal program may not be well defined in that the integral of utility is infinite. In those cases in which it is well defined, he finds the optimal consumption policy is monotonically increasing over time with consumption at time zero being below the maximum sustainable level of consumption and with consumption in future periods rising monotonically.

These results are somewhat disturbing because, given the way the problem was formulated, the criteria for maximizing discounted utility seem to imply choice of consumption paths that are inconsistent with intergenerational equity. This apparent inconsistency holds whether one chooses a positive discount rate or a zero rate. In the first case consumption goes to zero as time goes to infinity, and in the second case, consumption increases over time. Under no circumstances is consumption the same for each generation—the result that one would intuitively consider to be equitable.

In his analysis of the optimal level of research and development consistent with optimal economic growth, Dasgupta essentially considers research and development that might result in a technological breakthrough, such as a clean breeder reactor or a commercial controlled-fusion technology, that will provide a source of energy for all future time. He concludes from this analysis that, even if individuals are risk averse, they will always undertake some research and development simply because it has the property of insurance. A second result is that, if this is true, the utility or felicity rate of discount should be raised in analyses of research and development programs.

Although much of Dasgupta's paper is highly technical, he puts his findings in a concluding section that is accessible to a much wider audience so that the reader who cannot follow the technical development should read the first several sections of the paper and the conclusion.

As one might expect, given the topic and results, Dasgupta's paper prompted considerable comment. Although the format of the conference provided for discussion of the papers, and authors had an opportunity to incorporate and respond to comments in revising their papers, the format did not allow authors separate replies to comments. We have decided that it is neither appropriate nor feasible to attempt to summarize the authors' responses to comments. We do, however, attempt to direct the reader to other publications in which the authors have dealt with the subject of the controversy more fully. The revised version of Dasgupta's paper in this volume contains a number of footnotes (10, 11, and 16) that address some of the major issues raised by the discussants.

The comment on Dasgupta's paper by Robert Dorfman, Tjalling Koopmans, James Sweeney, and Mark Sharefkin falls into two categories. The first includes extension of the analysis by changing various assumptions and investigating the corresponding changes in the results of the analysis. The second category of comment includes concerns about drawing conclusions for important practical policy issues from the results of simple models such as Dasgupta has used. These concerns arise because the assumptions that go into the models, the functional forms of the models, or factors that have been left out of the models may invalidate the results. The discussants share a common concern that one has to be very careful in basing conclusions about the real world on such models, although all would agree that such models can be highly instructive.

The comment by Sweeney addresses three issues: (1) how an assumption of continuous technical progress influences the results that Dasgupta obtains for a world in which resources are finite and depletable; (2) caveats about the conclusions based on empirical observations that are inconsistent with the underlying assumptions about the form of the model that Dasgupta employs; and (3) the relationship between the rate of discount that should be used to evaluate investment decisions under uncertainty in a world of depletable resources and the decision about research and development. Sweeney shows that when one introduces the assumption of continuous technical progress, it is possible to have a positive utility rate of discount and not have the optimal consumption path go to zero over time. He also finds that, given the extensions of Dasgupta's model including technical change, the optimal consumption path may be the maximum rate of sustained consumption. With these extensions he finds that whether "the economy grows or declines is not dependent upon the depreciation rate for capital, nor is the question dependent upon the elasticity of marginal felicity."[16] He finds further that only a relatively small rate of technical progress is needed to insure against doom in the economy.

Sweeney considers a number of empirical relationships in energy technology and points out that these are not totally consistent with the model that Dasgupta uses. First, he points out that in Dasgupta's model there is one depletable natural resource, namely energy, without a backup technology. When the scarce resource is used up, that is the end. He points out that in the world as we know it, there are backup technologies and that as opposed to exhausting a finite resource, the question of depletion is really one of increasing scarcity associated with rising energy costs. This is a point that Dorfman also makes.

Sweeney points out that the elasticity of substitution between energy and other inputs in the U.S. economy is much smaller than that implied by the Cobb–Douglas production function that Dasgupta uses to obtain many of the results in his paper. This means that Dasgupta assumes a form of the production function that implies that capital can be much more readily

---

[16] J. L. Sweeney, "Resource Depletion, Research and Development, and the Social Rate of Discount: A Commentary and Extension," at the end of chapter 8 in this volume.

substituted for energy than seems to be the case. For this reason, the analysis by Dasgupta may be overoptimistic. Sweeney then discusses in some detail the analysis of the relationship Dasgupta draws between the rate of return and the risk premium associated with research and development projects.

Dorfman begins in this way:

> I am persuaded that we cannot give reliable advice about any . . . practical problem involving nonrenewable resources until we have gotten to the bottom of the issues that Dasgupta deals with. Is a positive "pure rate of impatience" morally defensible? What are its consequences? Whatever the rate of impatience, what principles are there to determine the efficient rate of use of nonrenewable resources? As long as such questions are obscure, there will be no sound, generally accepted criteria for discussing the pros and cons of practical decisions or resolving practical debates.
>
> Work such as this, then, establishes the foundations for practical decisions.[17]

However, beyond this acceptance of the importance of the problem and the general framework of analysis, Dorfman raises a number of concerns about the Dasgupta paper. First, he is concerned about the neglect of depreciation. Second, he is particularly concerned about Dasgupta's assumption "that the exhaustible resources can be extracted costlessly."[18] Dorfman's concern here is essentially equivalent to that expressed by Sweeney, namely, that we don't live in a world of exhaustible resources in that we have virtually inexhaustible sources of supply but at an ever-increasing cost. The question then is not one of using up all the resources, but one of using up so much of the relatively inexpensive resources that we are left with only extremely costly alternatives. The final concern that Dorfman raises is with the particular probability model that Dasgupta uses in the last section of his paper, in which he discusses research and development of new energy technologies.

Sharefkin commends Dasgupta for his ambitious attempt to clarify the role of the discount rate in the context of the allocation of exhaustible resources over time as this is central to the energy debate. He says, "many staples of the energy debate—'discounting is unfair to future generations,' for example—are based in part upon simple and remediable confusion. But only in part. Although Dasgupta's paper dispels some of that confusion, it is less successful at identifying the substantive questions posed by more 'sympathetic' reading of such statements."[19] Sharefkin goes on to point out some of the important problems.

---

[17] R. Dorfman, comment on "Resource Depletion, Research and Development, and the Social Rate of Discount," a comment on Dasgupta's chapter in this volume.

[18] Ibid.

[19] M. Sharefkin, comment on "Resource Depletion, Research and Development, and the Social Rate of Discount," a comment on Dasgupta's chapter in this volume.

The comment by Koopmans is essentially a word of caution to all energy modelers about using highly aggregated models to draw practical conclusions about energy policy. Koopmans' comments apply not only to the paper by Dasgupta but to all attempts to use highly simplified economic models to characterize major social choices. It was the feeling of participants at the conference that Koopmans' comments constituted a very important and wise admonition. Rather than attempt to summarize his remarks, we encourage every reader who is interested in the use of energy models to read Koopmans' comments.

"Approaches to the Choice of Discount Rates for Social Benefit–Cost Analysis"

The paper by Amartya Sen may be considered in two parts. The first part is a discussion of the economics literature supporting the conclusion that the social rate of discount may differ substantially from private market rates of interest or market rates of return for reasons of externality or distributional differences, broadly defined. This conclusion is discussed in the section on market rates in relation to benefit–cost analysis in chapter 2 of this volume, and Sen's paper draws together the pertinent literature. Sen's paper is an important contribution in that he is able to integrate very incisively and efficiently a large body of material and, at the same time, present the arguments in a manner that can easily be followed by anyone with some training in welfare economics.

With his section on social welfare functionals and discounting, Sen introduces another question that is central to this volume, namely, whether the utilitarian framework is sufficiently robust to be used to answer questions about intergenerational equity. In particular, he addresses carefully the question of whether utilitarianism as it is embodied in modern welfare economics takes into account all relevant considerations. He begins this analysis by examining the principles underlying standard welfare economics. He concludes that standard welfare economics is inadequate since its informational structure simply does not permit incorporating such considerations as liberty, rights, or entitlements. He goes on to discuss these shortcomings in terms of an example involving torture and to apply his conclusions to the problem of environmental pollution. Without doubt, this section of Sen's paper stimulated some of the most spirited discussion at the conference. It is not highly technical and should be read by anyone with even a moderate interest in welfare economics.

Sen finally rejects the utilitarian framework of welfare economics as an inadquate basis for social judgments that involve questions of intergenerational equity. He concludes that the "parsimonious informational structure on which the market operates (the adequacy of which under certain circumstances has been shown for the attainment of certain efficiency results, for example, Pareto optimality, being in the core) is in fact quite inadequate to sustain ethical analysis involving equity or liberty or even utilitarianism.''[20]

Sen's paper addresses an extremely important subject and it is highly provocative. It is also somewhat technical in that to read and understand much of the paper, one needs a foundation in welfare economics and a familiarity with the terminology and notation used in that field. Therefore, Sen's paper is likely to be most interesting and accessible to economists and philosophers who have a particular interest in welfare economics and ethics. To a large extent, the comments by Robert Dorfman, Mark Sharefkin, and Talbot Page are also highly technical. Their comments are difficult to summarize as they contain a number of extensions and technical interpretations of Sen's results.

Perhaps the most easily stated comment is that by Dorfman, who contends that Sen's conclusion that welfarism does not incorporate such concerns as liberty or entitlement results from his failure to recognize that these concerns enter the individual welfare functions that go into the overall social ranking. Sen strongly disagreed with this and other comments, arguing that the importance of such considerations as liberty cannot be judged exclusively by their utility consequences, and the rub lies there rather than in any alleged assumption of independence of utility from liberty. Instead of trying to reproduce fully Sen's responses to the comments, we refer the reader to a subsequent publication in which Sen develops many of the points on which there was contention.[21]

We advise the reader to sample the two parts of Sen's paper. We believe that if one reads nothing else, one should read the later sections of the paper, skipping over the highly technical parts and concentrating on the issues that Sen raises and the conclusions that he draws.

"Investment Decision Making in the Electric Power Industry"

A major portion of the energy produced in the future will be produced by regulated private utilities and various forms of public utilities. To a large extent they will choose the technologies for the production of electric power, and it will be their rules of investment decision that determine what the electric power industry looks like in the twenty-first century. Therefore it is

[20] A. Sen, "Approaches to the Choice of Discount Rates for Social Benefit–Cost Analysis," chapter 9 in this volume.

[21] A. Sen, "Personal Utilities and Public Judgments: Or What's Wrong with Welfare Economics," *Economic Journal* vol. 89 (1979), and "Utilitarianism and Welfarism," *Journal of Philosophy* vol. 76 (1979).

extremely important that we grasp how decisions are made in that industry. Gordon R. Corey, vice chairman of Commonwealth Edison Company at the time of the conference, provides us with a very interesting paper on this subject. It is based on his years of experience as an executive in a major investor-owner utility and on a survey of utility companies. Corey's paper reports the findings of the survey, which he conducted in preparation for the conference, and includes his own interpretation of what is happening in the industry with regard to investment decisions and discounting.

Just as with the paper by Robert Wilson, a detailed discussion of Corey's paper in this chapter is unnecessary because he provides an excellent introduction and summary. Rather than reproduce it, we note that Corey's paper differs from the others in the volume in both tone and subject matter. Corey is a businessman and not an academic, although he has a deep knowledge of, and keen interest in, the theory of investment and finance. He focuses on what he considers the most important practical aspects of utility decisions. These aspects include the effect of taxes and inflation on investment decisions. His discussion of risk differs considerably from the discussion one would hear from an academic in finance. The paper by Corey should be read by anyone with an interest in utility practice, particularly the practice of making investment decisions.

Robert Smiley, commenting on Corey's paper, says that within the academic literature there has been very little attention paid to corporate investment practices from the point of view of corporate officers and little attention to the objectives stated by these corporate officers. For the most part, the academic community in finance has relied totally on the assumption that firms maximize shareholder wealth and then has used this premise to develop models that have been tested on the basis of security market data.

Smiley begins with a theoretical inquiry into the objectives of utilities and discusses Corey's statement of these objectives in light of the theory of modern finance. He notes that there are two basic differences between regulated utilities and unregulated firms. First, regulated utilities are legally required to meet all demands for service, except possibly in an emergency. Second, regulated firms are not free to set prices as their unregulated counterparts are. He contends that the most appropriate objective would seem to be the maximization of the market value of the firm, subject to these constraints.

Smiley uses this contention to discuss Corey's finding that the solution most often sought in utility investment analysis is the minimization of revenue requirements. He also discusses Corey's treatment of the well-known Averch–Johnson proposition, which is that regulated, investor-owned utilities will tend to be more capital-intensive than is economically efficient. The paper by Smiley is a relatively straightforward application of the theory of modern economics and modern finance to the statements about utility decision making by a seasoned utility executive. Smiley brings to the discussion his considerable experience at the New York State Public Service Commission. Therefore, the interplay between the businessman Corey and the academic Smiley, who is a sympathetic commentator, makes for interesting reading. Both Corey and Smiley are easily read and should be read carefully by anyone who is interested in the theory and practice of utility decision making.

"The Social Efficiency of Electric Utility Decision Criteria"

Thomas Stauffer investigates whether taxpaying, investor-owned, regulated electric utilities are biased against capital-intensive options and in favor of fuel-intensive technology for electricity generation. He finds that they are so inclined but that the relative efficiency losses are small. He finds that for tax-exempt public utilities, on the other hand, there is a distinct bias in favor of capital-intensive options leading to very large efficiency losses.

To obtain these results, Stauffer essentially takes the decision criteria set forth by Gordon Corey and sets up a model of a utility's decision making, incorporating all of the financial details, such as income taxes, property taxes, depreciation, and the utility's cost of capital. He then investigates the investment decisions of a utility that uses this decision rule, given reasonable values for the parameters that go into the decision. He compares the behavior of the utility with the behavior that would be optimal from a social point of view, given the social rate of discount, and taking into account the resulting displacement effects on private capital formation. To a large extent, Stauffer attempts to apply the kind of decision method and the ideas of the model developed in chapter 2 to analyze decisions of utilities from the point of view of social efficiency.

Stauffer has accurately captured the decision process or rules followed by regulated utilities and in so doing has described not only the electric utilities but many other regulated utilities that produce a significant fraction of national output. Therefore Stauffer's analysis goes beyond the electric power industry. Some of his assumptions may be questionable—for example, the assumption that increases in operating costs fall on consumption as opposed to being divided between consumption and investment. Nevertheless, the work that Stauffer has done is a useful beginning in the evaluation of the performance of regulated utilities from the point of view of social efficiency. Stauffer's paper is largely technical and requires some mathematical sophistication to follow. However, the introduction and the conclusion state the problem and summarize the results.

References

Arrow, K. J. 1966. "Discounting and Public Investment Criteria," in A. V. Kneese and S. C. Smith, eds., *Water Research* (Baltimore, Johns Hopkins University Press for Resources for the Future).

———, and M. Kurz. 1970. *Public Investment, the Rate of Return, and Optimal Fiscal Policy* (Baltimore, Johns Hopkins University Press for Resources for the Future).

Sen, A. K. 1979a. "Personal Utilities and Public Judgments: Or What's Wrong with Welfare Economics," *Economic Journal* vol. 89.

———. 1979b. "Utilitarianism and Welfarism," *Journal of Philosophy* vol. 76.

4

Kenneth J. Arrow*

The Rate of Discount
on Public Investments
with Imperfect Capital Markets

Introduction

This paper is a continuation and extension of an earlier association with
Resources for the Future. Mordecai Kurz and I developed a general approach
to the determination of optimal policy for public investment and, in particular,
the determination of the rate of discount to be used for it (Arrow and Kurz,
1970).

Our attempt was to draw upon and refine commonly accepted principles
and to present them in a consistent synthesis, through which a number of
disputes either disappeared or could be stated more clearly. We interpreted
the concept of public investment to include the investment aspect of the
provision of inappropriable public goods. That is, public capital is capital
whose use was not reimbursed on the market. Examples would be the capital
aspects of national defense or research and development, as in the breeder
reactor. (We did include the possibility that the government was reimbursed
at least in part for the use of the public capital [see Arrow and Kurz, 1970,
chapter VI, section 8, and all of the first-best analysis in chapter VIII].
However, most of the specific problems of public investment remain if the
provision of public goods is not determined by the market; in that case, the
charge for the use of public capital is essentially a lump-sum tax with no
intertemporal allocative significance.)

A second condition we felt important for a model of public investment
was a recognition that a given act of investment was part of a continuing
stream of investment activities, public and private, and that future investments
would be made under the same sort of rules as present investments. Previous
analyses have implicitly assumed that the returns from public investment

* Department of Economics, Stanford University.

were either entirely consumed or were divided between public or private investment in exogenously given proportions. We argued that whatever principles were used in allocating national income among consumption, private investment, and public investment today should also be assumed to prevail in the future. In particular, if choice was governed by some kind of optimization principle, the problem became one in dynamic programming or control theory, in which current and future public and private investment were simultaneously determined (Arrow and Kurz, 1970, chapter I, section 3).

Specific results depend upon the exact nature of the model. Kurz and I followed the usual practice of ignoring intragenerational distribution. This practice is certainly contestable; it is based on the assumption that public investment is not a useful mechanism for income redistribution, partly because of its limited scope and partly because many forms of public investment are more or less neutral distributively. We therefore assumed a single consumer in each time period.

For convenience, we also assumed that utilities in successive time periods were additive and therefore, by the usual arguments, that the government maximized a sum of discounted utilities. Intergenerational equity was implicit in the choice of the discount rate for utility. I will discuss the choice of utility discount rate presently.

Kurz and I distinguished between a *fully optimal* policy, which assumes a single agent who makes all decisions on consumption and on public and private investment, and a policy in which the government chooses directly public investment, taxes, and government borrowing but decisions on consumption, private investment, and purchase of government bonds are made by private consumers and producers. The latter are assumed to take the government's decisions as given. The choice of government decisions must then be optimal, taking account of the repercussions on private decisions. It may be that the fully optimal policy is controllable in the sense that the government, by suitable choice of its instruments over time, can cause the economy to follow the fully optimal path. Alternatively, the fully optimal policy may not be controllable, in which case the government should maximize the criterion function insofar as it is able, that is, seek a second-best policy.

If the private sector is making its own decisions, then assumptions have to be made about its behavior. For the productive sector, competitive behavior is assumed, so that the marginal productivity of private capital is equated to the appropriate market rate of interest. The model of the consumer is more controversial. We assumed that the consumer has the same infinite time horizon as the government and therefore, like the government, maximizes a sum of discounted utilities.

The assumption of an infinite time horizon for the consumer strikes many as absurd, and a favorite alternative is that of overlapping generations (see Pestieau, 1974, for example). In the simplest form of this model, each consumer maximizes utility over his or her lifetime. If it is further assumed that the government has some definite policy goals that embrace all future consumer–citizens, then there is inevitably a divergence between private and social benefits. As soon as it is granted that individuals have some concern about their heirs, the divergence is definitely mitigated. In the present study, in which I wish to concentrate on the efficiency problems created by taxation, it is best to avoid the complication of diverging private and social benefits.

Kurz and I indeed allowed both the discount rate for utility and the utility function itself to differ between the consumer and the government. However, we did not examine the possible explanations for these divergences as Amartya K. Sen has done so well in his paper in this volume. In fact, to sharpen the results, in this paper I have assumed the identity of utility functions and discount rates between the consumer and the government.

In particular, the present model and that of Arrow and Kurz (1970, chapter VIII) differ in assumptions and conclusions from the fixed-saving-ratio model studied by Arrow (1966) and Arrow and Kurz (1970, chapter VI), and also, in a generalized form, by Bradford (1975). Individual consumers in those studies were assumed to behave myopically; in particular, they were assumed to be unaware of the public investment and its consequences. Hence, the future income from public investment did not enter into their savings decisions. Otherwise, it might be held that public and private investment would be alternative ways of providing future income for the individual. In the present model, all future incomes, including private returns from public investment, are anticipated. The conclusion of the earlier models, that the rate of return on public investment should equal the fully optimal rate even if private investment does not receive it, is no longer necessarily valid.

The last essential element of the model is specification of the role of public capital in the economic system. In our book, Kurz and I assumed that both private output and utility were dependent in part on public capital. In the present paper, I will simplify by ignoring the possible dependence of private utility on the stock of public capital. The public capital considered here, then, is an intermediate good, for example, research and development or highways, that increases private productivity. The utility of the consumer depends only on consumption, and the government's aim is to maximize consumer welfare.

Given the essential structure of the model, the variations possible are in the range of government instruments. Since I will continue to assume that government investment is a decision variable of the government, the only variations are in the methods of financing. Kurz and I explored a number of financing methods with a view to finding combinations of instruments that would permit achievement of the fully optimal model (Arrow and Kurz, 1970, chapter VIII). Here, emphasis will be placed on financing government investment through taxes on profits. Since consumers and firms are facing different rates of return, there is presumptive evidence of inefficiency, which has been strongly argued by many authors and perhaps most vigorously by Harberger (1974).

In this paper, then, I study the second-best policies, where public investment is wholly or partly financed by profits taxes, both with and without the additional possibility of financing by borrowing. I concentrate on the steady-state solutions and study the relations among the rates of return on public and private capital and the rates that would obtain in a fully optimal policy. Are the first two rates necessarily equal even if the policy is not fully optimal? Or is the rate of return on public investment equal to the fully optimal rate even when the private rate is not?

The Behavior of the Consumer

Let

$C(t)$ = consumption at time t

$U(C)$ = instantaneous utility (or felicity) of consumption at rate c

ρ = rate of discount of utility by consumer

Then the consumer seeks to choose his consumption path to maximize

$$\int_0^\infty e^{-\rho t} U[C(t)] \, dt \tag{1}$$

subject to budgetary constraints. At any moment, his income is derived from two sources—interest on previously accumulated wealth and noninterest income, which includes both wages and pure profits.

Let

$A(t)$ = wealth at time t

$r(t)$ = interest rate to consumer at time t

$W(t)$ = noninterest income of consumer at time t

Note that $r(t)$ is the interest received by the consumer and hence is free of taxes. The consumer is assumed to take $r(t)$ and $W(t)$ as given; the latter implies in particular that the supply of labor is fixed.

The accumulation of wealth is governed by the differential equation

$$\dot{A}(t) = r(t) A(t) + W(t) - C(t) \tag{2}$$

where the dot denotes differentiation with respect to time. The constraint (2) is relevant because it is required that $A^\infty \geq 0$ (the superscript ∞ refers to the limit as t approaches infinity, that is, the steady-state value), or equivalently, that $A(t) \geq 0$ for all t.

Such dynamic optimization problems can be solved by means of the calculus of variations or Pontryagin's maximum principle (Arrow and Kurz, 1970, chapter II). Introduce the current-value Hamiltonian

$$H = U(C) + q \, (r \, A + W - C) \tag{3}$$

where

q = shadow price of wealth (dual variable).

Then C, the sole instrument in this problem, is to be chosen at any instant of time to maximize H, while q evolves according to the differential equation

$$\dot{q} = \rho \, q - (\partial H / \partial A) = (\rho - r)q \tag{4}$$

Since C maximizes H, we must have

$$U'(C) = q \tag{5}$$

Equations (2)–(5), together with the initial value of wealth, $A(0)$, and an appropriate initial value for the dual variable, $q(0)$, define the optimal paths of A, q, and C.

(The investment decisions A of all individuals do, of course, affect the rate of return r as will be seen in the following section, but in a competitive world, each individual takes r as given.)

The consumer is embedded in a complete economic system. We assume that the economy will approach a steady state such that $W(t) \rightarrow W^{\infty}$ and $r(t) \rightarrow r^{\infty}$ and that consumption in such a world will also converge to a steady state, so that $C(t) \rightarrow C^{\infty}$ and $A(t) \rightarrow A^{\infty}$. From equation (4), this is possible only if $r(t)$ approaches ρ. Thus, even though the consumer regards $r(t)$ as given, it must be consistent with consumers' behavior achieving a steady state consistent with the equation[1]

$$r^{\infty} = \rho \tag{6}$$

---

[1] Since the condition holds in the steady state for any possible production function, it can be said that the supply of capital is perfectly elastic in the long run. This restrictive conclusion is an implication of the sum-of-discounted-utilities criterion (1).

Optimal Government Policy: Profits Taxes and Borrowing

I assume that public investment is financed by profits taxes and borrowing. At this stage, I do not consider the effects of growth, but it is easy to do so, as will be seen later in the section dealing with growth.

To be precise, I assume that taxes fall on interest income, since the purpose of the investigation is to study the effects of a divergence between the cost of capital to firms and that to consumers. The private sector's wealth consists of private capital and government bonds. For the bonds, however, interest taxes could as well be thought of as deducted in advance, so that the rate of interest is the post-tax rate $r(t)$. Finally, in a deterministic model, the rate of interest is known, so that a tax on interest income is equivalent to a tax on private capital. This statement gives rise to slightly simpler formulas and will be followed here. Note that, optimally, the tax varies with time.

Let
$Y(t)$ = total output
$K_p(t)$ = private capital
$K_g(t)$ = public capital

Under the assumption of full employment and constant population, output is a function of the two kinds of capital; the role of public capital is to increase output.

$$Y = F(K_p, K_g) \tag{7}$$

where the production function F has the usual concavity conditions. (Since the labor force is assumed constant and is omitted, the function F will in general not have constant returns.)

Let
$I_p(t)$ = private investment
$I_g(t)$ = public investment

Then, by definition,

$$Y(t) = C(t) + I_p(t) + I_g(t) \tag{8}$$
$$\dot{K}_p = I_p \tag{9}$$
$$\dot{K}_g = I_g \tag{10}$$

Finally, let

$x(t)$ = tax rate on capital
$B(t)$ = government debt

Then, private profit-maximizing investment satisfies the condition

$$F_p [K_p(t), K_g(t)] = r(t) + x(t) \tag{11}$$

where $F_p = \partial F/\partial K_p$

The government balance equation is

$$\dot{B} = r(t) B(t) + I_g(t) - x(t) K_p(t) \tag{12}$$

Properly interpreted, equation (12) is equivalent to an equation for the consumer's accumulation of wealth. For $A = K_p + B$, while W (private noninterest income) $= Y - rK_p - xK_p$, so that

$$\dot{A} = rA + W - C = r(K_p + B) + Y - rK_p - xK_p - C$$
$$= rB + C + I_p + I_g - C - xK_p = rB + I_p + I_g - xK_p$$

while $\dot{A} = \dot{K}_p + \dot{B} = I_p + \dot{B}$. (Use has been made of equations (2), (8), and (9).)

The instruments that govern the system are the two kinds of investment I_p and I_g, the tax rate x, the consumption C, and the rate of interest r. Of course, the government cannot choose them arbitrarily, since it must take account of restrictions, both those imposed by technology, as in equations (7) and (8), and those imposed by the decentralized nature of the system, namely, equation (11) and the determination of consumption as a result of a long-term optimization by the consumer. The government cannot influence the latter at any moment of time, though it can do so through its partial control of future income and therefore wealth.

The state of the system at any moment is determined by the stocks of the two kinds of capital K_p and K_g, the shadow price q of private wealth, and the stock of bonds B. Consumption C is determined by q through equation (5); we can therefore eliminate C by solving equation (5) for $C = C(q)$. The government can choose x and I_g; its choice of x determines r, by equation (11), since the marginal productivity of private capital, F_p, is determined by state variables. If we eliminate Y from equations (7) and (8), we have

$$F(K_p, K_g) = C(q) + I_p + I_g \tag{13}$$

so that I_p is determined by the government's choice of I_g, given the state variables K_p, K_g, and q.

Equivalently and more symmetrically, we can say that the government can choose the four instruments, I_p, I_g, x, and r, subject to the two constraints, equations (13) and (11).

As stated in the section on consumer behavior, the government's objective function is the same as the consumer's, namely,

$$\int_0^\infty e^{-\rho t} U[C(t)]\, dt \tag{1}$$

If we substitute $C = C(q)$ and then write

$$V(q) = U[C(q)],$$

the government's maximand becomes

$$\int_0^\infty e^{-\rho t} V[q(t)]\, dt \tag{14}$$

There are four state variables, namely, K_p, K_g, q, and B, evolving according to the equations

$$\dot{K}_p = I_p \tag{9}$$
$$\dot{K}_g = I_g \tag{10}$$
$$\dot{q} = (\rho - r)q \tag{4}$$
$$\dot{B} = rB + I_g - xK_p \tag{12}$$

Hence, the current-value Hamiltonian is given by

$$H = V(q) + p_1 I_p + p_2 I_g + p_3 (\rho - r)q \\ + p_4(rB + I_g - x K_p) \tag{15}$$

where $p_1, p_2, p_3,$ and p_4 are the shadow prices of $K_p, K_g, q,$ and B, respectively. (It may seem odd to have a shadow price for q, which is itself a shadow price; but from the social viewpoint it is one of the variables that define the state of the system, and a change in its initial value will affect the value of the maximand if an optimal policy is pursued.)

At any time, H is to be maximized with respect to the four instruments $I_p, I_g, x,$ and r, subject to the constraints

$$F(K_p, K_g) - C(q) - I_p - I_g = 0 \tag{13}$$

and

$$F_p(K_p, K_g) - r - x = 0 \tag{11}$$

As usual in constrained maximization problems, it is convenient to introduce Lagrange parameters λ_1 for equation (13) and λ_2 for equation (11) and find the values of the instruments yielding zero values for the partial derivatives of the Lagrangian

$$
\begin{aligned}
L = H &+ \lambda_1[F(K_p, K_g) - C(q) - I_p - I_g] \\
&+ \lambda_2[F_p(K_p, K_g) - r - x]
\end{aligned}
\tag{16}
$$

The four equations so obtained, together with equations (13) and (11), determine the values of the instruments and the Lagrange parameters as functions of the state variables and their duals (p_1, p_2, p_3, p_4). The dual variables evolve according to differential equations analogous to equation (4) above. In general, if z is any state variable and p is the corresponding dual variable (the shadow price of that state variable), then

$$
\dot{p} = \rho\, p - (\partial L/\partial z)
\tag{17}
$$

There are four dual variables and four corresponding differential equations. Together with the four primal equations (9), (10), (4), and (12), they constitute a complete system of differential equations when the instruments have been solved for in terms of the state and dual variables.[2]

In studying the steady state, we can confine ourselves to points of rest for the system of differential equations. These are defined by setting all time derivatives equal to zero in the primal equations (9), (10), (4), and (5) and in the four dual equations of the form of equation (17). If we add to these the constraint equations (13) and (11) and the four equations found by setting the derivatives of L with respect to the four instruments equal to zero in equation (16), we have fourteen equations altogether.

But in fact *the steady-state equilibrium is underdetermined*. Two of the fourteen equations are the same. We have seen that the steady-state equation for q, the consumer's shadow price of private wealth, reduces to

$$
r^{\infty} = \rho
\tag{6}
$$

so that the consumer rate of interest approaches the utility rate of interest asymptotically. But now let us consider the steady state of the equation for the dual variable to B, the stock of government bonds. Equation (17) shows that if p is the variable dual to a state variable z, then

$$
\rho\, p^{\infty} - L_z^{\infty} = 0
\tag{18}
$$

---

[2] We have not rigorously shown either that an optimal solution exists or that it has a steady state. Rather, we are examining the consequences of making these assumptions.

In particular, let z be the state variable B, so that p is p_4. From equations (16) and (15)

$$L_B = H_B = p_4 \, r$$

so that equation (18) becomes

$$\rho \, p_4^\infty - r^\infty \, p_4^\infty = 0$$

and therefore this condition is the same as equation (6).[3] Hence, there are (at most) thirteen equations for the fourteen unknowns defining the steady state.

Thus, there is a one-dimensional infinity of possible steady states. One way of interpreting this is to say that the steady state is not independent of the initial conditions. Other things being equal, the steady state will depend on the initial value of government debt. Intuitively, the equation (12) determining government borrowing is unstable; a higher government debt implies more interest payments, hence more borrowing, therefore more debt, and so forth. This instability can be offset only if a higher initial government debt implies a change in the target to which the system is going.

It is natural to index the one-dimensional infinity of steady states by the (asymptotic) tax rate x^∞. For each value of x^∞, then, there is a steady-state value for each of the other variables of the system, including in particular the two kinds of public capital.

In the steady state, by definition, public capital formation $\dot{K}_g$ is zero, so that $I_g = 0$, by equation (10). Similarly, government debt B is constant, so that $\dot{B} = 0$. Hence, from equations (12) and (6)

$$B^\infty / K_p^\infty = x^\infty / \rho \tag{19}$$

Thus, the alternative steady states could also be indexed by the ratio of government debt to private capital. As is obvious, the steady state corresponding to $x^\infty = 0$ is that which would have occurred under a fully optimal policy. There would then be no government debt in the limit. However, this policy would be feasible only for a specific value of initial debt.[4]

---

[3] In fact, a stronger conclusion follows. If we look at the differential equation for p_4, that is, equation (17) with $z = B$ and $p = p_4$, we see that

$$\dot{p}_4 = (\rho - r)p_4$$

which has the same form as equation (4). Hence, p_4/q is a constant.

[4] This is, in effect, what was proved in Arrow and Kurz (1970, Proposition VIII.4); indeed, for that initial value of government debt, no taxes at all would be needed; the initial debt would have to be negative if there were to be positive government investment.

How does this cast light on the rates of return to public and private investment, at least in the steady state? We already know that the rate of return to private investment is given by equation (11); in the steady state,

$$F_p^\infty = \rho + x^\infty \tag{20}$$

where x^∞ is determined essentially by the initial debt level. How does this compare with the rate of return on public investment in the steady state? The following can be shown (see appendix, section 1):

$$F_g^\infty = \frac{K_p^\infty (x^\infty F_{pg}^\infty + \rho F_{pp}^\infty)}{K_p^\infty F_{pp}^\infty + x^\infty} \tag{21}$$

It is interesting to note that the appropriate rate of discount for public investment is related to the rate of diminishing returns to private capital and to the complementarity or substitutability between public and private capital. However, equation (21) is not an expression that yields a value of F_g^∞, the steady-state public discount rate, because both sides of the equation depend on the steady-state values for public and private capital, K_p^∞ and K_g^∞. Rather, equations (20) and (21) form a pair of simultaneous equations to determine asymptotic capital values for any given x^∞. Note that these values do not depend on the shape of the utility function.

One can use equations (20) and (21) to gain some idea of when the public rate of discount is equal either to the private rate or to ρ, the same rate as in the fully optimal policy. It can quickly be seen that if $x^\infty = 0$, then both private and public discount rates are equal to the utility discount rate ρ.

The greatest insight seems to be obtained by considering specific utility functions.

Consider the Cobb–Douglas case, for example.
Let

$$F(K_p, K_g) = A K_p^\alpha K_g^\beta, \quad \alpha + \beta < 1 \tag{22}$$

Then, since F_p is homogeneous of degree $\alpha - 1$ in K_p, and F_g is homogeneous of degree α in K_p

$$K_p^\infty F_{pp}^\infty = -(1 - \alpha) F_p^\infty, \quad K_p^\infty F_{pg}^\infty = \alpha F_g^\infty \tag{23}$$

Substitute equation (20) into the first half of equation (23), then substitute into equation (21), and solve for F_g^∞:

$$F_g^\infty = \rho + x^\infty = F_p^\infty$$

If output is a Cobb–Douglas function of private and public capital for fixed labor supply, then in any steady state the public and private rates of discount are equal, regardless of the level of taxation of profits or capital.

This result, however, does not hold for other classes of production functions. If the production function has a constant elasticity of substitution different from one among the three inputs (private capital, public capital, and labor), then it can never be true that the steady-state discount rates for public and private capital will be equal. The discount rate for public capital will be less than that of private capital if and only if $(1 - \sigma)x^{\infty} > 0$, where σ is the elasticity of substitution. There will be one tax rate (other than zero) for which the discount rate for public capital will be the rate of discount of utility (see appendix, section 1).[5,6]

Financing with Some Nondistortive Taxes

The previous results, in particular the apparent close tie between the discount rates on the two kinds of capital, assumed that financing of public investment was either through taxes on private capital or through borrowing, which also competes with private capital formation. Clearly, if financing through lump-sum or other nondistortive taxes and borrowing were permitted, a fully optimal policy would be achievable. Let us assume instead that the proportion of taxes collectible in a nondistortive way (for example, taxes on wages if the supply of labor is inelastic or taxes on consumption) is arbitrarily restricted. Let

μ = ratio of nondistortive to total taxes

We assume that taxes on capital or profits are the only distortive taxes. Then total taxes are $[1/(1 - \mu)]$ capital taxes. The only equation in the previous model that is affected is equation (12), which governs the rate of government bond increase:

$$\dot{B} = rB + I_g - x K_p/(1 - \mu) \tag{24}$$

[5] I am indebted to John Conlisk, University of California at San Diego, for the observations on the constant elasticity of substitution (CES) production function.

[6] P. M. Pestieau (1974) has studied optimal discount rates for public investment in a model somewhat resembling the above. He has argued that when borrowing is permitted, the public and private rates should be equal (equation (32), p. 231). I am unable to reproduce his argument. In any case his model differs in several relevant respects, most noticeably that instead of a single consumer, he has an infinite stream of overlapping generations. However, I think the most important difference for the present purpose is that the use of government capital is charged for at its marginal product. If, as is assumed here, government capital is used free, then Pestieau's model leads to quite different conclusions.

The conclusion about the infinite multiplicity of steady-state solutions is unchanged. As before, equation (20) still holds at the steady state. However, equation (21) is somewhat altered (appendix, section 2).

$$F_g^\infty = \frac{K_p^\infty (x^\infty F_{pg}^\infty + \rho F_{pp}^\infty) + \rho \mu x^\infty}{K_p^\infty F_{pp}^\infty + x^\infty} \tag{25}$$

To get some insight into equation (25), one must first find the steady state of equation (24)

$$x^\infty = (1 - \mu) \rho B^\infty / K_p^\infty \tag{26}$$

If we index the alternative steady states by the ratio B^∞ / K_p^∞, then for any fixed alternative, x^∞ approaches zero as μ approaches 1, so that the fully optimal policy is approached.

As before, we may get some feeling for the meaning of equations (20) and (25) by considering equation (22), the Cobb–Douglas case. Substitute equations (20) and (23) into equation (25), and solve for F_g^∞.

$$F_g^\infty = \rho + x^\infty [1 - \mu/(1 - \alpha)]$$
$$= \nu\rho + (1 - \nu) F_p^\infty, \text{ where } \nu = \mu/(1 - \alpha)$$

With a Cobb–Douglas function, the steady-state public discount rate is a weighted average of the utility discount rate and the private discount rate, but the weight on the utility discount rate is greater than the share of nondistortive taxes in total taxes. Indeed, if the nondistortive share and the elasticity of output with respect to private capital are sufficiently high, the public discount rate may be less than the utility discount rate.

Thus, the correct average is *not* weighted by tax shares as is frequently suggested (for example, see Eckstein, 1958, pp. 98–99).

The Effect of Growth

If we assume for convenience that the felicity function $U(C)$ is homogeneous of some degree (less than one, to preserve concavity), then, as is well known, the previous results hold with some reinterpretation of symbols (Arrow and Kurz, 1970, sections I.5, III.1–2). I will discuss here only the case of constant population with exponential labor-augmenting technological progress. Assume

$$U(C) \text{ homogeneous of degree } 1 - \sigma, \sigma > 0 \tag{27}$$

$$\tau = \text{constant rate of labor-augmenting technological progress} \quad (28)$$

Then the natural rate of growth of the system is τ. For each magnitude (consumption, capital, and so forth), denoted by a capital letter, let the corresponding magnitude per effective worker be denoted by the corresponding small letter. Thus

$$c(t) = e^{-\tau t}C(t), \quad k_p(t) = e^{-\tau t}K_p(t), \quad i_p(t) = e^{-\tau t}I_p(t)$$

and so forth.

From equation (27)

$$e^{-\rho t}U[C(t)] = e^{-\rho t}U[e^{\tau t}c(t)] = e^{-\rho t}e^{\tau(1-\sigma)t}U[c(t)] = e^{-(\omega-\tau)t}U[c(t)]$$

where $\omega = \rho + \sigma\tau$

Thus, the maximand (1) for both consumer and government can be written

$$\int_0^\infty e^{-(\omega-\tau)t}U[c(t)]\, dt \quad (29)$$

For the consumer, the accumulation equation (2) becomes, when written in intensive form (that is, per effective worker)

$$\dot{a} = (r - \tau)\,a + w - c \quad (30)$$

Comparison with the original system equations (1)–(2) shows that we have replaced capital letters by small letters, ρ by $\omega - \tau$, and r by $r - \tau$. Therefore we have

$$U'(c) = q \quad (31)$$

and

$$\dot{q} = [(\omega - \tau) - (r - \tau)]q = (\omega - r)q \quad (32)$$

The dual variable q is now the shadow price of wealth per effective worker. For this system to have a steady state requires now that

$$r^\infty = \omega \quad (33)$$

Given this behavior on the part of the consumer, the government is to maximize equation (29). If we solve for $c = c(q)$ in equation (31), substitute into $U(c)$, and let

$$V(q) = U[c(q)]$$

the government's maximand then has the form of equation (14), with ρ replaced by $\omega - \tau$.

The differential equations governing the state of the system are, in intensive units, equation (32) and the following analogues of equations (9), (10), and (12), respectively:

$$\dot{k}_p = i_p - \tau k_p \tag{34}$$
$$\dot{k}_g = i_g - \tau k_g \tag{35}$$
$$\dot{b} = (r - \tau)b + i_g - xk_p \tag{36}$$

Note that if we have constant returns to scale jointly in effective labor and the two kinds of capital, $F(k_p, k_g)$ is the output per effective worker. Hence, the constraint (13), expressing the equality of output and demand, remains essentially unchanged:

$$F(k_p, k_g) - c(q) - i_p - i_g = 0 \tag{37}$$

Finally, since F_p is homogeneous of degree 0 in the three factors, the profit-maximizing condition (11) is unchanged:

$$F_p(k_p, k_g) - r - x = 0 \tag{11}$$

The new optimization is very similar to the old: small letters replace large ones, ρ is replaced by $\omega - \tau$, and equations (34)–(36) have extra terms of the form $-\tau z$, where z is a state variable. Without writing out the easily verifiable details, we can see that if z is any of the state variables k_p, k_g, or b, and p is the corresponding dual variable, then L_z is changed by a term $-\tau p$, so that the differential equation governing the dual variable becomes

$$\dot{p} = (\omega - \tau)p - (L_z^0 - \tau p) = \omega p - L_z^0 \tag{38}$$

following equation (17). (Here, L_z^0 means $\partial L/\partial z$ as it would have been calculated from the model without growth, but with intensive magnitudes substituted for extensive ones.) In particular, for $z = b$, let p_4 be the corresponding dual variable; then the equation is exactly the same as equation (32) for q, and as before, the equations defining the stationary state contain two identical equations. Hence, the indeterminacy of the steady state remains.

It is easy to see that the analysis leading to equations (20) and (21) is unchanged, with ω replacing ρ everywhere.

Optimal Policy without Borrowing

We now modify the previous analysis to assume that there is no existing debt and no borrowing. We will continue to assume growth but not lump-sum taxes. The extension to the case in which some nondistortive taxes are permitted follows easily along the lines of the previous section on financing with nondistortive taxes.

The consumer model is unchanged from that of the section on the effect of growth, so that equation (32) continues to be a differential equation for a state variable q. The bond equation now disappears, or more exactly, it remains valid with $b = \dot{b} = 0$, so that

$$i_g = xk_p$$

If we substitute this equation into equations (35) and (37) and then eliminate i_p between the new equations (37) and (34), we have the following differential equations for k_p and k_g:

$$\dot{k}_p = F(k_p, k_g) - (x + \tau)k_p - c(q) \tag{39}$$

$$\dot{k}_g = xk_p - \tau k_g \tag{40}$$

The maximand remains as shown in equation (14), except that ρ is replaced by $\omega - \tau$. The constraints are the differential equations (32), (39), and (40) and equation (11). Even in the absence of government borrowing, r can be regarded as an instrument; this convention merely reflects the fact that the instrument x determines r through equation (11). The current-value Hamiltonian is

$$\begin{aligned}
H = {}& V(q) + p_1[F(k_p, k_g) - (x + \tau)k_p - c(q)] \\
& + p_2(xk_p - \tau k_g) + p_3(\omega - r)q
\end{aligned} \tag{41}$$

to be maximized at any moment with respect to the instruments r and x, subject to the constraint (11), so that the Lagrangian is

$$L = H + \lambda[F_p(k_p, k_g) - r - x] \tag{42}$$

Since equation (11) is still valid, the steady-state rate of private discount still satisfies the condition

$$F_p^{\infty} = \omega + x^{\infty} \tag{20}$$

What may be more surprising is that the public discount rate also satisfies the same relation as before

$$F_g^{\infty} = \frac{k_p^{\infty}(x^{\infty}F_{pg}^{\infty} + \omega F_{pp}^{\infty})}{k_p^{\infty}F_{pp}^{\infty} + x^{\infty}} \tag{21}$$

with, of course, ρ replaced by $\omega = \rho + \sigma\tau$, as shown in section 3 of the appendix.

We do not, however, have any indeterminacy as to the steady state. From equation (40) it follows that the condition for k_g to be stationary is that

$$x^{\infty}k_p^{\infty} - \tau k_g^{\infty} = 0 \tag{43}$$

Equations (20), (21), and (43) constitute three equations in the three unknowns k_p^{∞}, k_g^{∞}, and x^{∞}.

Since equations (20) and (21) are still valid, all the remarks made at the end of the section on optimal government policy still hold. In particular, for a Cobb–Douglas function, we have necessary equality of the two rates of discount. If there is no growth, $\tau = 0$, then $x^{\infty} = 0$ and there is no distortion in the limit.

Conclusions

It would be nice if more definite conclusions could be drawn, but that is too much to ask. Probably the most striking, to me, though others would regard it as obvious, is the conclusion that there is a strong case for equating the rate of discount in the public sector to that in the private sector to the extent that public investment is financed by taxes on profits. However, as should have been clear all along, if public investment is financed partly through nondistortive taxes, the public rate moves to the utility discount rate, that is, in the long run, the public rate moves to the consumer's rate, and indeed more rapidly than in proportion to the proportion of nondistortive taxes.

The other conclusion, at the moment more interesting intellectually than practically, is the dependence of steady-state rates on the initial public debt if borrowing is permitted.

Appendix 4-A

1. Profits Taxes and Borrowing

In this section, I will derive equation (21) of the text and also discuss the steady-state discount rates when the social production function has a constant elasticity of substitution.

Of the fourteen equations defining the steady state, we need only five here. First, we must have $\partial L/\partial n = 0$ for any instrument n, where L is the Lagrangian (16). Let n be I_p, I_g, and x. From equations (16) and (15), we have

$$p_1 - \lambda_1 = 0 \tag{A.1}$$
$$p_2 + p_4 - \lambda_1 = 0 \tag{A.2}$$
$$-K_p p_4 - \lambda_2 = 0 \tag{A.3}$$

Now consider the stationary values of the dual variables p_1 and p_2. Apply equation (18) to the state variables K_p and K_g.

$$\rho p_1^\infty + x^\infty p_4^\infty - F_p^\infty \lambda_1^\infty - F_{pp}^\infty \lambda_2^\infty = 0 \tag{A.4}$$
$$\rho p_2^\infty - F_g^\infty \lambda_1^\infty - F_{pg}^\infty \lambda_2^\infty = 0 \tag{A.5}$$

Equations (A.1–3) hold everywhere and in particular in the limit. We can consider equations (A.1–5) to be a set of simultaneous linear equations in the variables p_1^∞, p_2^∞, p_4^∞, λ_1^∞, λ_2^∞. Since the equations are homogeneous, they have a nonzero solution only if their determinant vanishes. (Clearly, not all of these variables can vanish at infinity, for that would mean, in particular, that there was no scarcity of capital.)

After some simplification, the statement that the determinant is zero can be written

$$K_p^\infty (F_p^\infty F_{pg}^\infty - F_g^\infty F_{pp}^\infty + \rho F_{pp}^\infty - \rho F_{pg}^\infty) \\ + (-x^\infty F_g^\infty - \rho F_p^\infty + \rho x^\infty + \rho^2) = 0 \tag{A.6}$$

Now substitute for F_p^∞ from equation (20); that is, let

$$F_p^\infty = \rho + x^\infty$$

then collect the terms in F_g^∞, and solve for F_g^∞. This yields equation (21) of the text.

Suppose that the production function has a constant state of elasticity with constant returns to scale in all three factors (public capital, private capital, and labor). Set the labor force equal to 1. Then

$$F(K_p, K_g) = (\alpha K_p^{-\theta} + \beta K_g^{-\theta} + \gamma)^{-1/\theta}$$

In what follows, we omit the superscript ∞ for ease in reading. Let

$$w = F_p, z = (\alpha/\beta)(K_g/K_p)^{1+\theta}$$

The elasticity of substitution between any two factors is

$$\sigma = 1/(1 + \theta)$$

After a little manipulation, we find

$$K_p F_{pp} = \frac{\alpha^\sigma w^{2-\sigma} - w}{\sigma}, K_p F_{pg} = \frac{\alpha^\sigma w^{2-\sigma}}{\sigma z}, F_g = w/z$$

If we substitute these into the basic equation (21), we find

$$\frac{w}{z} = \frac{\rho(\alpha^\sigma w^{2-\sigma} - w) + x\alpha^\sigma w^{2-\sigma}(1/z)}{\alpha^\sigma w^{2-\sigma} - w + \sigma x}$$

Clear fractions, transpose terms in which z does not appear to the left-hand side, and simplify. Thus

$$(w - x)\alpha^\sigma w^{2-\sigma} - w(w - \sigma x) = \rho(\alpha^\sigma w^{2-\sigma} - w)z$$

But equation (20) can be written, $w = \rho + x$, so that $w - x = \rho$ and $w - \sigma x = \rho + (1 - \sigma)x$. Then solve for z.

$$z = 1 - \frac{w(1 - \sigma)x}{\rho(\alpha^\sigma w^{2-\sigma} - w)} \tag{A.7}$$

Since $F_p = w$ and $F_g = w/z$, $F_g < F_p$ if and only if $z > 1$. Note that

$$\rho(\alpha^\sigma w^{2-\sigma} - w) = \rho\sigma K_p F_{pp} < 0$$

Hence, $F_g < F_p$ if and only if $(1 - \sigma)x > 0$, as asserted in the text.

It can also be shown that there is a value of x for which $F_g = \rho$, the value at the fully optimal solution, with x, in general, not equal to zero. The statement $F_g = \rho$ is equivalent to $z = w/\rho$. Substitute for z in equation (A.7), and then let $w = \rho + x$ on the left-hand side. The equation holds when $x = 0$; if both sides are divided by x, the equation also holds if

$$w = (\sigma a^{-\sigma})^{1/(1-\sigma)}$$

or, since $w = \rho + x$, if

$$x = (\sigma\alpha^{-\sigma})^{1/(1-\sigma)} - \rho$$

2. Financing with Some Nondistortive Taxes

Since the only change from the previous model is the modification in the bond equation, which now takes the form of equation (24), the Hamiltonian is altered only in that a term $-p_4 x K_p$ is replaced by the term $-p_4 x K_p/(1-\mu)$. It follows that the differentiation of the Lagrangian with respect to I_p and I_g is unaltered, and equations (A.1–2) still hold. In differentiation with respect to x, however, there is an alteration, and equation (A.3) is replaced by

$$-[K_p/(1-\mu)]p_4 - \lambda_2 = 0 \tag{A.8}$$

Similarly, the stationariness of p_1, which is derived from the differentiation of the Hamiltonian with respect to K_p, has a slightly different form; equation (A.4) is replaced by

$$\rho p_1^\infty + [x^\infty/(1-\mu)]p_4^\infty - F_p^\infty\lambda_1 - F_{pp}^\infty\lambda_2 = 0 \tag{A.9}$$

The system of linear equations (A.1), (A.2), (A.8), (A.9), and (A.5) is exactly the same as the system (A.1–5), except that K_p^∞ and x^∞ have been replaced respectively by $K_p^\infty/(1-\mu)$ and $x^\infty/(1-\mu)$. Therefore, equation (A.6) holds with these replacements. If we then substitute from equation (20) and solve for F_g^∞, we derive equation (25).

3. Financing without Borrowing

For the case of financing without borrowing, we write the stationarity conditions for p_1 and p_2 and the equation obtained by setting $L_x = 0$.
From equations (41) and (42), stationariness in p_1 requires that

$$(\omega - \tau)p_1^\infty - [F_p^\infty - (x^\infty + \tau)]\,p_1^\infty - x^\infty p_2^\infty - F_{pp}^\infty\lambda^\infty = 0$$

If the terms in p_1^∞ are collected and then the stationary version of profit maximization, equation (20), is used, the equation simplifies to

$$-x^\infty p_2^\infty - F_{pp}^\infty \lambda^\infty = 0 \tag{A.10}$$

Stationariness of p_2 entails

$$(\omega - \tau)p_2^\infty - F_g^\infty p_1^\infty + \tau p_2^\infty - F_{pg}^\infty \lambda^\infty = 0$$

or, after collecting terms in p_2,

$$-F_g^\infty p_1^\infty + \omega p_2^\infty - F_{pg}^\infty \lambda^\infty = 0 \tag{A.11}$$

The equation $L_x = 0$ becomes, at the stationary solution,

$$-k_p^\infty p_1^\infty + k_p^\infty p_2^\infty - \lambda^\infty = 0 \tag{A.12}$$

The equations (A.10–12) constitute three homogeneous linear equations in three unknowns, p_1^∞, p_2^∞, and λ^∞; they must have a nonzero solution, so their determinant must vanish. But this yields equation (21), with K_p^∞ replaced by k_p^∞ and ρ by ω.

References

Arrow, K. J. 1966. "Discounting and Public Investment," in A. V. Kneese and S. C. Smith, eds., *Water Research* (Baltimore, Johns Hopkins University Press for Resources for the Future) pp. 13–32.
———, and M. Kurz. 1970. *Public Investment, the Rate of Return, and Optimal Fiscal Policy* (Baltimore, Johns Hopkins University Press for Resources for the Future).
Bradford, D. F. 1975. "Constraints on Government Investment Opportunities and the Choice of Discount Rate," *American Economic Review* vol. 65, pp. 887–895.
Diamond, P., and J. Mirrlees. 1971. "Optimal Taxation and Public Production, I and II," *American Economic Review* vol. 61 (March and June) pp. 8–27 and 261–278.
Eckstein, O. 1958. *Water Resource Development* (Cambridge, Mass., Harvard University Press).

Harberger, A. C. 1974. "Discussion: Professor Arrow on the Social Discount Rate," in G. G. Somers and W. D. Wood, eds., *Cost–Benefit Analysis of Manpower Policies* (Kingston, Ontario, Industrial Relations Centre, Queen's University) pp. 76–88.

Pestieau, P. M. 1974. "Optimal Taxation and Discounting for Public Investment in a Growth Setting," *Journal of Public Economics* vol. 3, pp. 217–235.

*Martin S. Feldstein**

Comment

Kenneth Arrow has given us a valuable extension of his earlier research on the optimal level of public investment. The current study is particularly important because it explores the significance of distortionary taxes on capital income and the interaction of such taxes with finance through public debt. Any student of the problem of optimal discount rates and public investment will benefit from a careful study of this paper.

In this comment, I want to suggest three directions in which I believe Arrow's analysis can usefully be extended. Although I cannot present any specific results for these extensions, I believe that considering these suggestions can in itself clarify the meaning and applicability of Arrow's analysis.

First, it should be noted that Arrow's criterion is limited to government investments that are intended to increase private income. It would be good to have a more general public expenditure analysis that would be applicable to the much wider class of public expenditures (including but not limited to investments in the conventional sense of the word) that produce consumer services directly. The special form of Arrow's analysis implies that the output resulting from the public investment will always be divided between consumption and investment in the same way as other private income. More realistically, some public expenditures induce added personal saving, while others reduce such saving. The appropriate criterion of expenditure for this wider class of projects cannot be stated as a required rate of return.

It is generally necessary to have both a shadow price per dollar of public funds spent on the activity (to reflect the excess burden in raising revenue) and a discount rate for comparing costs and consumption benefits at different times. In the special case of a single year's government expenditure that produces only concurrent consumption benefits, only a shadow price for transferred funds is required since no future costs or benefits need be discounted. Arrow's special case disguises the general need for a shadow

* Harvard University and the National Bureau of Economic Research.
Author's note. I am grateful to the National Science Foundation for financial support.

price because of the implicit assumption about the private saving induced by the public project.

A second important extension would be to allow the government to receive some sales revenue from its investment. Selling the output to consumers or to industry changes the financing mix and therefore alters the appropriate criteria of an acceptable expenditure. As Diamond and Mirrlees (1971) have shown, if this is carried to the extreme of allowing the government to set optimal prices and levy optimal excise taxes on all goods, public investment should earn the same return as private investments. Arrow has examined a different extreme assumption and his conclusion should be understood as applying to this special case. More generally, any arbitrary sales revenue changes the financing of the project, and this in turn changes the relevant criterion of choice.

Finally, Arrow's assumption that individuals adjust their consumption rationally is clearly an improvement over the arbitrary "fixed propensity to save" models that have characterized much of the previous literature on public investment criteria. In considering the implications of Arrow's analysis, however, it is good to bear in mind that his individuals live forever. Individuals therefore take into account the indefinite ramifications of their actions and adjust their current consumption to changes in taxes and income that will occur in the very distant future. This "infinite life" assumption clearly has important implications for the effect of government debt. It also affects the participation of individuals in the process of private capital accumulation. Because of the special results that will follow from the "infinite life" assumption, it would be desirable to examine an alternative model based on overlapping generations.

These three suggestions are not intended as criticisms of Arrow's paper, but as ways of extending his analyses to deal with a much richer collection of applications. I anticipate that this paper will provide a valuable framework within which such extensions can be developed.

Reference

Diamond, P., and J. Mirrlees. 1971. "Optimal Taxation and Public Production, I and II," *American Economic Review* vol. 61 (March and June) pp. 8–27 and 261–278.

Daniel Usher*

Comment

Economic theory is not going to be much help to those who have to choose a rate of discount for public sector projects until it is resolved how to proceed when the use rate differs from the opportunity cost rate in the private sector. Neither rate by itself may be sufficient. Perhaps a weighted average is called for. Perhaps there is a general rule that favors one or another of these rates depending on the circumstances. But theory will not, and ought not, constitute a guide to practice in this instance until the issue is resolved. Reduced to the simplest terms, the problem is this: Suppose the corporation income tax is 50 percent, the before-tax rate of return in the private sector is 16 percent, and (we are ignoring bonds) the after-tax rate is 8 percent. The 16 percent rate is what we are calling the opportunity cost rate of interest; the 8 percent rate is what we are calling the use rate of interest. The problem is whether the cut-off point for public investment should be 16 percent, 8 percent, something in between, or perhaps even a rate outside of these limits.

We find ourselves in the unfortunate position in which the two theorists who address the problem have derived what appear to be different and uncomparable rules for discounting in the public sector. Stiglitz argues that the appropriate rate depends critically on the reason why use rates and opportunity rates differ in the private sector, and that, while we cannot say in general what rate is appropriate for public sector projects, we can often infer the correct rate once the source of the distortion is identified. Arrow recommends that (1) if public capital is financed by taxes on private capital, the rate of discount should be more or less than the opportunity cost rate according as the elasticity of substitution between private and public capital is greater or less than unity, and that (2) if public capital is financed partly through a distortionary tax and partly through a nondistortionary tax, the rate of discount in the public sector should normally lie between the opportunity cost rate and the use rate, approaching the latter as the share of nondistortionary taxes approaches zero. Comparison of the Stiglitz and Arrow prescriptions is made doubly difficult by the contrast in their styles of analysis. Stiglitz

* Queen's University, Kingston, Ontario, Canada.

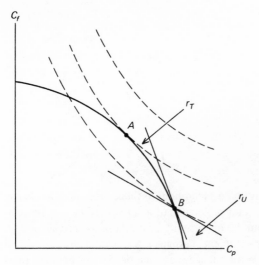

Figure 4-1

looks directly at marginal decisions in the public sector and adjusts private costs and benefits by multipliers alleged to reflect distortions in the economy. Arrow treats the derivation of a rule for public sector investment as an "agency problem" in which the public sector determines the whole time path of investment with due regard to the response of the private sector both to the investment itself and to the taxes or bonds through which it is financed.

The most useful task I can perform in discussing Arrow's paper is to try to simplify the analysis, to show what forces interact there even if I cannot show their relative importance in the determination of the discount rate for public projects, and to give the reader a sense of the meaning of his results. I should confess at once that I do not follow Arrow's mathematics in detail. Though I think I understand what Arrow is doing, I cannot check his computations and would not be able to spot a mistake; I take it on faith that Arrow's conclusions follow from his premises.

The simplification is to reduce history to two time periods, present and future, where future is understood to be a perpetuity rather than a single year. This simplification, originally introduced into economics by Irving Fisher, has the great advantage that it permits representation of the problem of intertemporal resource allocation on a two-dimensional diagram, an advantage purchased at the cost of having to abstract from all changes occurring after the end of the present year.

This two-period economy is represented in figure 4-1. Present consumption C_p is indicated on the horizontal axis, and future consumption C_f is indicated on the vertical axis. The unbroken curve is a production possibility curve of present and future consumption. Because future consumption is looked upon as a perpetuity, we can represent the opportunity cost rate of interest r_T at any combination of C_p and C_f along the curve as the slope of the curve at that point. The broken curves are a set of indifference curves of a "representative consumer" for present and future consumption. Slopes of indifference curves at any combination of C_p and C_f can be thought of as use rates of interest r_U.

In the absence of distortions, the consumer would choose the point A, corresponding to the greatest attainable utility at the given technology and characterized by the property that $r_U = r_T$. If the corporation income tax, or some other distorting influence, has placed a wedge between the use rate and the opportunity cost rate so that $r_T = r_U + X$ (Arrow's equation (11) with different symbols) where X is a measure of the size of the distortion, then the economy chooses a mix of present and future consumption represented by the point B at which utility is less than it is technically constrained to be. In our example $r_T = 16$ percent, $r_U = 8$ percent, and $X = 0.5r_T$. The model is exactly analogous to the standard analysis of the loss of consumer's surplus resulting from an excise tax; the corporation income tax is being treated like an excise tax on future consumption.

A public project can be looked upon as a shift in the economy from an initial point B to a new point E, representing an increase in future consumption ΔC_f and a corresponding decrease in present consumption ΔC_p. By definition the project is beneficial if E is on a higher indifference curve than B. It may be seen at once from figure 4-1 that, for a small project, this condition is met if

$$\frac{\Delta C_f}{\Delta C_p} > r_U$$

regardless of whether the point E lies above or below the original production possibility curve. The effects of several alternative projects are illustrated in figure 4-2, which reproduces and extends the section of figure 4-1 in the vicinity of the point B. The project terminating at E^1 is harmful because E^1 is below the tangent to the indifference curve through B, but the remaining projects are beneficial, even the project terminating at E^2, which takes the economy below the original production possibility curve.

Does that settle the issue? Does simple analysis show that public projects ought to be discounted at a use rate of interest regardless of whether there is a distortion of the sort depicted in figure 4-2?

Yes, it does if ΔC_p and ΔC_f can be interpreted broadly enough to include all the effects of a project upon the economy, including those effects that flow from the response of the rest of the economy, private and public sectors alike, to the existence of the project. The problem is that a government department, such as an electricity authority, cannot reasonably be expected

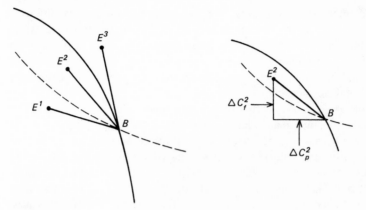

Figure 4-2

to anticipate all the effects of a project it may undertake. What we are seeking is a rule for balancing those costs and benefits that a private electricity company would take into account if the project were in the private sector. We want a discount rate for the costs and benefits that the electricity authority can control. Consider a project that costs $100 and generates $10 worth of electricity each year forever. At a use rate of 8 percent, the project would have a positive present value of $25 and would seem worth doing. But suppose $100 extra expenditure on public power would cause the private sector to reduce its expenditures by $60, and suppose private sector investment earns 16 percent, of which half is paid out in tax. Discounted at 8 percent, the present value of the stream of benefits and costs of an investment of $60 yielding 16 percent is $60 $\left(\dfrac{60 \times 0.16}{0.08} - 60 \right)$, so that the net loss to society from undertaking the project is $35, even though the project itself has a positive present value.

The distinction made here is, following Stiglitz, between the direct and indirect effects of a public project. Stiglitz's argument is that, though the use rate of interest is always appropriate in comparing total effects of a project, the response of the private sector is more often than not such that the opportunity cost rate is appropriate when only the direct effects can be observed.

The magnitudes ΔC_p and ΔC_f can be decomposed into the investment's direct effects ΔC_{pd} and ΔC_{fd}, which the agency undertaking the investment can control, and the indirect effects ΔC_{pi} and ΔC_{fi}, embodying the economy's response to the existence of the project. The two effects are illustrated in figure 4-3, which reproduces and extends a portion of figure 4-2. The economy begins at point B. The direct effects of the investment bring

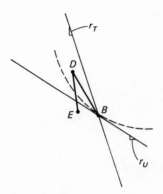
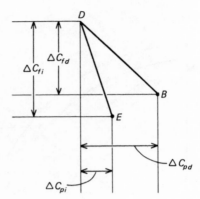

Figure 4-3

the economy to the point D, and the response of the private sector brings the economy from point D to the point E, so that the total effect of the investment is to move the economy from B to E.

Thus we find ourselves in a situation in which

1. We apply the use rate of interest if we know the full effects ΔC_p and ΔC_f of the project.
2. We have reason to believe that there are indirect effects of investment in excess of what the public authority can control.
3. It is often alleged that the indirect effects are usually perverse, so that a cut-off rate of return on public projects in excess of the use rate of interest would seem to be warranted.
4. It is difficult to quantify indirect effects.

To carry the analysis further and, in particular, to assess the allegation that the indirect effects of investment normally would warrant evaluation of direct effects alone by the opportunity cost rate of interest, we must model the response of the private sector to public investment. This I shall try to do under three headings: *demand effect, tax effect,* and *substitution effect.* Though Arrow does not identify these effects explicitly, they are all present in his model and his results can be interpreted as a working out of their joint implications for the choice of a discount rate.

Within the context of this simple model, it is best to look upon the response of the private sector to public sector investment as a shift along the new production possibility curve through the point D. In discussing the demand and tax effects, we shall suppose for convenience that the new production possibility curve is of the same shape as the old one; the substitution effect will be a consequence of the twisting of the curve in a manner I will explain later.

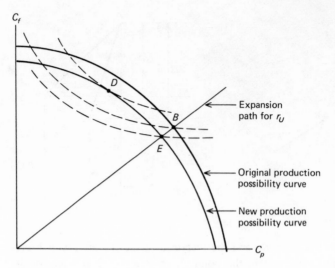

Figure 4-4

The demand effect is the tendency of the private sector to preserve the proportion between C_f and C_p, regardless of the share of investment undertaken by the private sector. Consider the public investment illustrated in figure 4-4 where the direct effect is to bring the economy to a point D that is below the production possibility curve but on a higher indifference curve than that passing through the original point B. As before, the opportunity cost rate of interest is greater than the use rate of interest at point B because of a distortion that the public sector cannot correct. The distortion constrains the economy to adhere to the equation $r_T = r_U + X$. But this equation is no longer true at point D, and the response of the private sector will be to alter the rate of private investment until the equality is restored. What happens depends critically upon the shape of the new production possibility curve. If, as we are assuming, the new curve is of the same shape as the old one and therefore uniformly below it, the economy must necessarily move to a point E on the expansion path of r_U passing through the point B, in which case the representative consumer is necessarily worse off than he was before. The demand effect, taken by itself, is such as to render public investment harmful if its rate of return does not exceed the opportunity cost rate of return in the private sector.

The tax effect makes matters even worse. In discussing the demand effect, we have supposed that X is constant; but as X is a reflection of the tax system and as the extra public investment requires an increase in public revenue that can only be gotten by increasing tax rates, there is a presumption that the distortion will grow and that X will increase in the process. This is not absolutely necessary. New taxes could, in principle, be levied in such a

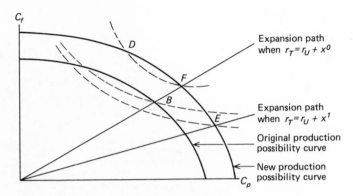

Figure 4-5

way as to reduce the distortion. The assertion that extra tax results in extra distortion rests on the presumption that if the extra tax could be levied in such a way as to remove the initial distortion, there would be no distortion in the first place because the government would from the beginning have levied taxes in a nondistortionary way. The existence of a distortion implies a constraint upon the government in the taxes it can levy. As public expenditure increases, the government has to rely on progressively more distortive taxes to raise the required tax revenue.

The tax effect is illustrated in figure 4-5. Consider a public project that passes Stiglitz's test—that is, a project for which the rate of return on the primary costs and benefits is in excess of r_T —and suppose that one of the secondary effects is to increase X from X^0 to X^1. The primary effect of the investment is to shift the production possibility outward bringing the economy to a point D. The secondary effect, according to the preceding argument, takes the economy to a point F on the expansion path of r_U *if X remains unchanged.* But X does not remain unchanged. It increases as tax rates increase to pay for the extra public expenditure, and this increase forces the economy down the new production possibility curve to a point E, which could be better than point B but could just as easily be worse as shown in the figure. In this case, even the opportunity cost rate of interest may not be high enough. An extra premium should be added, its size dependent on the magnitude of the change in X brought about by the increase in tax rates to finance the increase in public expenditure. The rule is that the greater the marginal distortion in the tax structure, the higher the appropriate rate of interest for public projects.

The substitution effect is a systematic twisting of the production possibility curve as a result of investment in the public sector. Here it is necessary to take account of a distinction that we have so far been able to avoid between public and private types of capital goods. The technology in

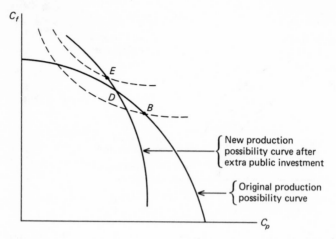

Figure 4-6

Arrow's model is represented by a production function $Y = F(k_p, k_g)$, where k_p is capital in the private sector, k_g is capital in the public sector, and Y is output that may equally well be consumed, transformed into k_p, or transformed into k_g according to the equation $y = C + k_p + k_g$. Consequently, in our simple two-period world, we have to differentiate between two concepts of the production possibility curve: (1) the relation between C_p and C_f when *both* k_p and k_g are varied optimally and (2) the relation between C_p and C_f when k_g is fixed and only k_p is variable. Because we are concerned with the reaction of the private sector, it is the latter concept with which we are concerned. The production possibility curves we have drawn are those for the private sector, and we portray the effects of public sector investment as shifts in these production possibility curves.

Such shifts will not normally be uniformly inward or uniformly outward as we have supposed in discussing the demand and tax effects. In particular, in the Cobb–Douglas case that Arrow considers in deriving the result that the opportunity cost rate of interest is the appropriate rate for public sector investment, an increase in k_g raises the rate of return to k_p (that is, $\dfrac{\partial}{\partial k_g}\left(\dfrac{\partial Y}{\partial k_p}\right) > 0$), which implies that there must be a clockwise rotation of the production possibility curve as shown in figure 4-6. And if the rotation is sufficiently large, the indirect effect of the public investment might be northwest rather than southeast along the new production possibility curve, leading the economy to a point E that is even better than the point D.

An example that seems to fit Arrow's model rather well is this: Public investment consists in the draining of a swamp to create land suitable for habitation and for agriculture. Once the land itself is developed, there will be a flurry of private investment in residential and industrial construction on the new territory, for the rate of return there will be abnormally high. One might object to this example, on the grounds that the relevant consideration is not the complementarity between land clearance and construction but the substitutability between public and private clearance of the land. Why, after all, could not land clearance be left to the private sector? I do not propose to try to answer this question, for that would open up the whole subject of how we draw the line between public and private sectors. There are many well-known reasons for putting certain activities in the public sector. Among those reasons are natural monopoly, the inevitable imperfection of property rights on large and conspicuous projects, and the cost of collection of rents on certain types of investments. It is sufficient to observe that, in practice, certain types of projects will be undertaken in the public sector if they are to be undertaken at all, and that such projects may be complements rather than substitutes for private investment.

The simple economics of the substitution effect is that whenever there is a distortion in the market for private investment such that less investment is forthcoming than is warranted to maximize utility of the representative consumer, there is a case for (1) requiring a high rate of return on public investments if public and private investments are substitutes in the sense that extra public investment lowers the rate of return to private investment, and (2) requiring a low rate of return on public investment if public and private investments are complements in the sense that extra public investment raises the rate of return to private investment. The example of the electricity authority at the beginning of my remarks illustrates the first case; the example of the draining of the swamp illustrates the second.

In Arrow's model, public and private capital could, in principle, be substitutes or complements depending on the form of the production function $Y = F(k_p, k_g)$. They are, in fact, complementary in Arrow's analysis where F is a Cobb–Douglas function. They would tend to be substitutes (in the sense that more k_g lowers the rate of return to k_p) if there were decreasing returns to scale in k_p and k_g together. This would be the case if labor were an argument in the production function—that is, if the production function were of the form $Y = F(L, k_g, k_p)$ where L is worker-hours of labor and there were constant returns to scale in L, k_g, and k_p altogether—or if the elasticity of substitution σ between k_p and k_g were considerably greater than 1. This last condition comes out clearly in Arrow's appendix, where it is shown that $\dfrac{\partial F}{\partial k_g} < r_T$ if and only if $(1 - \sigma)X > 0$.

Though the demand effects and tax effects of public investment are quite general, applying more or less in the same way to all investments in the public sector, the substitution effect is necessarily project specific. Some projects in the public sector tend to eliminate similar projects in the private sector, while others tend to create new opportunities for investment. Thus, the theory cannot lay down general prescriptions about rates of discount for the public sector other than the one prescription that is too general to be of much use, namely, that the use rate of interest is the appropriate rate of discount when all effects, no matter how far-reaching, of the investment on present and future consumption are taken into account. Perhaps there is after all no practical alternative to the discounting of all of the effects of public investments at the use rate of interest. One can at least see why the search for "the" rate of discount on public projects has proved to be such an intractable problem.

Finally, I would like to touch upon two issues that were not raised in Arrow's paper but have a distinct bearing on the applicability of his results. The first has to do with the concept of cost of a public-sector project. It is natural for the agency undertaking the project to measure cost as the amount of money it has to spend—on research, surveys, and construction—to reap the benefits of the project. But there are indirect costs that should be considered, too. There is the marginal cost of collecting the extra tax, the extra cost to taxpayers of tax avoidance, and the administrative overhead of the whole government in the process of deciding whether to undertake the project or not. Above all, there is the extra distortion in the private sector attendant on the increase in tax rates that the extra project requires. This last consideration is similar to the tax effect of an increase in public investment, but it is not identical; the tax effect was defined as an influence on the rate of discount, while the indirect cost of public projects is proportional to expenditure and independent of the durability of the project. Consider a project intended to produce "instant" electricity in the sense that the electricity generator lasts for one week only and then disintegrates. Suppose that the value of the electricity generated is $1.01 per $1.00 of cost. Would it be worth our while to produce electricity in this way? If we looked only at the shadow rate of interest, the answer has to be yes, because the durability of the project is so short that the rate of discount, no matter what rate we choose within the limits we have been talking about, has too small an impact on the present value of the benefits to affect the worth of the project significantly. But if the marginal social cost of getting funds into the public sector were as little as 2 percent—I think, though I cannot justify my view, that the cost is more like 25 cents on the dollar—the project would not on balance be worthwhile. The distinction being made here is between the social rate of discount and the shadow price of getting funds into the public sector. Costs need to be augmented to account for the shadow price of public funds before a discount rate can legitimately be applied.

There is, however, an important exception that may have particular relevance for power projects as opposed to other sorts of public investments. Just as a premium should be applied to the use of public funds in a project, so too should a premium be applied to public revenue generated by the project because each dollar of revenue replaces a dollar of tax for any given amount of public expenditure in the year the revenue accrues. The premium should therefore be applied to benefits as well as to cost whenever benefits accrue as public revenue; the premium should be applied to cost alone whenever benefits accrue directly to consumers. Investment in power generation is an example of the first kind if there is no element of subsidy in the pricing policy; road construction is an example of the second kind except where the cost is covered by a toll on road use.

The other issue I wish to address has to do with the setting of the agenda. Public-sector projects may be selected in two ways. The public sector may choose to undertake all projects, regardless of content, where the present value of benefits exceeds the present value of costs, with due allowance in the assessment of costs and benefits for the reaction of the private sector. Or there may first be established an agenda of the kinds of activities and industries to be undertaken in the public sector. The usual rules of benefit–cost analysis would then be applied to projects on the agenda, but no project off the agenda would be undertaken in the public sector, regardless of the expected rate of return. To assume with Arrow that $Y = F(k_g, k_p)$ is to assume this problem away because k_g cannot be produced in the private sector and k_p cannot be produced in the public sector no matter what the rates of return. Though this is a reasonable assumption to make within the context of Arrow's model, it should be recognized that it does not take into account that people do choose whether schools, hospitals, or steel mills belong in one sector or another. The questions I am raising are whether that choice comes before benefit–cost analysis or is incidental to it, whether benefit–cost criteria should be applied everywhere impartially or to a limited class of projects, and whether a sharp line need be drawn between public and private sectors. It is at least arguable that an agenda is unnecessary. A government may invest in pipelines but not in farm machinery because it judges that the indirect effects, particularly the substitution effect, of the investment in farm machinery would be such that the present value of the investment would, all things considered, be negative, while the indirect effects of the pipelines might on balance be favorable. No prior agenda is required for decisions of this kind.

The case for the establishment of a fixed agenda has to do with the influence of public investment criteria upon the competitive economy and with the impact of changes in economic organization on government and society as a whole. It is an essential characteristic of the competitive economy that society says to businessmen, "You are free to go off and make as much money as you can, provided you do not violate certain rules—you must not steal, lie, monopolize, cheat on your income tax, and so on." The absence of a fixed agenda imparts a certain ambiguity to the rules of the game. No business can be quite sure that it will not at some time have to face the competition of a public enterprise that may be unconstrained by normal considerations of profitability. The competitive economy may, therefore, work less well when there is no agenda than it would otherwise, or resources that would otherwise be used productively might be diverted to assuring that public activity benefits this or that region, firm, or community. This phenomenon, difficult though it may be to quantify, is surely real and may be observed in countries where the agenda is not well defined.

5

*Joseph E. Stiglitz**

The Rate of Discount for
Benefit–Cost Analysis and the
Theory of the Second Best

Introduction

In this paper I wish to present a way of thinking about what the rate of discount ought to be for evaluating projects within the public sector. The conclusion of my analysis is that there is not a convincing case that the social rate of time preference ought to be used. Nor is there a convincing case that the marginal rate of transformation in the private sector ought to be used. Neither of these rates is, in general, appropriate; indeed, the appropriate rate of discount may not even lie between the two.

Interest in the problems of benefit–cost analysis arises from the belief that in a variety of circumstances one does not want to use market prices for evaluating a project; implicitly, there is some market failure, which leads market prices not to reflect social evaluations. Thus, intrinsically, benefit–cost analysis is concerned with second-best situations. We assume, for one reason or the other, that the failure giving rise to a discrepancy between market prices and social evaluations cannot be attacked directly.

It seems fundamental that the first stage in any analysis of the relation between market prices and shadow prices is the analysis of the structure of the economy and the constraints on government that lead to the persistence of a nonoptimality. That is, we must begin with an explanation of why market prices do not reflect social evaluations and of why the given set of distortions cannot be better corrected by government policy.

I hope to show that use of explicit but simple models of the economy, in which the appropriateness of alternative second-best constraints can be discussed, will eliminate much of the controversy over the choice of a discount rate for use in benefit–cost analysis.

In the remainder of this introduction, I wish to summarize the results of the paper. First, however, it may be useful to review certain terms that will be used throughout the analysis.

We consider a project that has net consumption benefits of ΔC_1, $\Delta C_2, \ldots, \Delta C_t, \ldots$ at each date; ΔC_t could easily be a vector, but it is convenient for the moment to think of it as a single commodity. We wish to know whether the project should be undertaken. We cannot simply add $\Delta C_1 + \Delta C_2 + \ldots + \Delta C_t + \ldots$ because consumption at one date is a different commodity from consumption at another date. Rather, we normally assign less weight to future benefits and costs than to present benefits and costs. We form the weighted sum

$$\sum v_t C_t$$

If the economy is in some kind of long-run steady state, we have

$$v_t = \left(\frac{1}{1 + \rho} \right)^t$$

We refer to $\dfrac{1}{1 + \rho}$ as the *social discount factor*. It is more convenient, however, to express our results in terms of ρ. This is called the social *rate of discount*.

There are some analysts who believe that the social discount factor ought to be equal to *consumers' marginal rate of substitution,* the amount of income they require at time t to compensate for a decrease in income at $t + 1$. If there are perfect capital markets, this will be equal to

$$\frac{1}{1 + i}$$

where i is the *consumer rate of interest,* the real rate at which individuals can borrow and lend.

There are others who believe that the social discount factor ought to be equal to producers' marginal rate of transformation, the inverse of the increase in output next period generated by an increase in input this period. If firms can borrow and lend at the rate r, then the producers' marginal rate of transformation will be equal to $1 + r$. We refer to r as the *producer* rate of interest.

Finally, there are those analysts who postulate a social welfare function, of the form

$$\sum_t U(C_t) \frac{1}{(1 + \delta)^t} \tag{1}$$

(where C_t is total consumption at time t and δ is the rate at which future utility is discounted). They believe that the social discount factor should not be the individual consumer's marginal rate of substitution but the social marginal rate of substitution defined by the welfare function (1). Thus, they believe that the social rate of time discount should equal the *social rate of time preference*

$$\frac{\dfrac{U'(C_t)}{U'(C_{t+1})} - 1}{1 + \delta}$$

In the steady state, in which $C_t = C_{t+1}$, this is equal to δ, which is referred to as the *social rate of pure time preference*.

Thus, the three major "extreme views" hold that (dropping for the moment the t subscripts)

$\rho = r$, the social rate of discount should equal the producer rate of interest;

$\rho = i$, the social rate of discount should equal the consumer rate of interest; and

$\rho = \delta$, the social rate of discount should equal the social rate of time preference

In addition to these extreme views, there is the more common, eclectic view that it should be a weighted average of the producer and consumer rates of interest.

Our analysis casts doubt on the *general* validity of any of these simplistic approaches; we identify some important cases in which, for instance, the social rate of discount may not lie between the producer and consumer rates of interest. We find other cases in which, even in the long run, the social rate of discount is not equal to the pure social rate of time preference. These results should not, however, be looked upon as simply negative results, contradicting so much of the conventional wisdom. For in each of the models we present, we are able to derive precise formulas determining the appropriate social rate of discount. Our analysis shows that one must specify what one thinks are the critical sources of market imperfection; then one can infer the correct rate of discount to use.

In this paper, I shall discuss briefly six important reasons that market rates of interest for private consumption goods might not be appropriate for evaluating public projects.

The first is that the outputs of public projects are often public consumption goods, and the marginal rate of substitution between the consumption of public goods at different dates will in general differ systematically from the marginal rate of substitution of private goods at different dates. I shall argue that this systematic difference implies that the discount rate that should be used for public consumption ought to differ (perhaps by a considerable amount) from that for private goods.[1]

The second and third reasons arise from limitations on the set of taxes that the government can impose. If the government must raise revenue through distortionary taxation, then in general it will be desirable to impose an interest income tax. But if the government produces only private goods, and there are no other constraints on taxation, then the discount rate that should be used is equal to the marginal rate of transformation in the private sector. I shall show that, in effect, under these circumstances a unit of public investment displaces exactly a unit of private investment.

On the other hand, if the government produces public capital goods, and if some part of the returns to the public capital goods are appropriated by private firms and are not taxed away, then an increase in public investment will in general displace some private investment. Accordingly, the social rate of discount will not in general be equal to the private return to capital. The precise relationship between the rate of discount and the producer rate of interest, the rate of social time preference and the consumer rate of interest depends critically on the constraints that are imposed on the government. Specifically, the relationship depends on the government's ability to (1) impose a 100 percent tax on profits, (2) control the real debt supply freely, and (3) differentiate tax rates among individuals and across classes of income. If the government cannot control the real debt supply, the social rate of discount, though equal to the social rate of time preference, will not in general be equal to the producer rate of interest, and indeed, will not necessarily lie between the producer and the consumer rates of interest.

---

[1] Here, as elsewhere, we have to be careful about specifying precisely what it is that is being discounted. Assume, for instance, that we are evaluating an aircraft carrier, and for simplicity, assume its performance characteristics are identical for N years, after which it falls apart (the conventional one-hoss shay assumption). Assume that we can ascertain the value, say in terms of forgone consumption today, of the services of the aircraft carrier this year. Assume, moreover, there is no technological change, so we can avoid the problem of obsolescence. How do we discount the future output of each of the next N years (assumed to be identical)?

One reader of an earlier draft suggested that it is benefits that should be discounted, not outputs. But then, how are we to evaluate these benefits? If we evaluate them using their net marginal change in social utility, we have simply begged the question, for then we need no discount factor at all.

For a more extensive discussion of these issues, the reader is referred to the discussion of problems of evaluation later in this chapter.

If the government cannot impose a 100 percent tax on profits, then in general, the social rate of discount will not be equal to the social rate of time preference but all projects within the public sector should use the same rate of discount.

If the government has constraints on its ability to differentiate the tax rates imposed on different kinds of income, then different projects within the public sector should have different rates of discount. The distributional impact of various projects needs to be taken into account. Thus, the Diamond–Mirrlees result, seeming to reverse the long-standing presumption that within public projects, distributional effects need not be taken into account, is seen to be very special—a consequence of the extremely strong assumptions concerning the government's taxing powers.

One of the more widely discussed explanations for why the social rate of time discount ought to differ from market rates of interest is that there are constraints on savings. I shall attempt to show that the case for such a constraint is far from persuasive. Indeed, I shall argue that, if there is a constraint on savings, the effect is not that too little savings occurs but that the level of consumption is less than is socially desirable. If this argument is accepted, it implies that the rate of discount to be used in public projects exceeds the private return to capital.

The fifth explanation for the use of social rates of discount that differ from market rates of interest relates to unemployment and the indirect effect of public expenditure on unemployment. This provides an argument for using social rates of time discount differing from market rates of interest only if the unemployment rate is changing. But if the unemployment rate is changing, inputs and outputs need to be valued with different rates of discount.

The final explanation I shall discuss for the use of social rates of discount differing from market rates is concerned with the imperfections in the risk markets. I will show that there may be a discrepancy between the marginal rates of transformation and substitution in the private sector (even in the absence of taxation) and that the social rate of discount lies between the two.

This paper focuses on a centralized governmental structure. There is a single decision-making unit, which sets all taxes, controls monetary policy, and allocates all public expenditures. It calculates shadow prices, including the social rate of discount, which it transmits to project managers, who use these prices to decide whether to accept or reject various projects.

Most governmental structures are not this centralized; those people who make decisions concerning monetary policy may be different from those who make decisions about taxation, and there may be yet a third group of decision makers allocating revenues among alternative projects. These different decision makers may have different objective functions, there may be limited coordination between them, and the relationship between their objectives and the preferences of the populace may be very weak. In such a situation, should a project manager use the project to pursue his own social goals if there are agencies of the government that are better suited to pursue those goals, but do not? To what extent should he take into account the consequences of his actions on other agencies and their responses to his actions? These are important questions, but I shall not be able to deal with them here. At the same time, it should be emphasized that these may be central questions in the political debate about the appropriate rate of discount. If the intertemporal distribution of income is inappropriate, I shall argue that there are better instruments for correcting the distribution than distorting the choice of projects. But if those people who have control of these instruments refuse to use them, what is the project manager to do? Should it be assumed that these better instruments are not used because there is some not usually recognized constraint on their use and, hence, that what would appear to be a better instrument is not really available? Or should it be assumed that there is not social consensus concerning the social goal in question, and that "direct instruments" are not used because to do so would require a clearer statement of social objectives or, indeed, that those people who control these direct instruments have different judgments concerning social objectives? If that is the case, is it appropriate for the project manager to attempt to use the instruments he controls (project selection) to pursue his interpretation of social objectives? Unfortunately, the approach taken in this paper casts little light on these important questions.

The Nature of the Problem and the Approach

Any project can be viewed as a perturbation of the economy from what it would have been had some other project been undertaken instead. To determine whether the project should be undertaken, we first need to look at the levels of consumption of all commodities by all individuals at all dates under the two different situations. If all individuals are better off with the project than without it, then clearly it should be adopted (if we adopt an individualistic social welfare function). If all individuals are worse off, then clearly it should not be adopted. If some individuals are better off and others are worse off, whether we should adopt it or not depends critically on how we weight the gains and losses of different individuals.

Although this is obviously the "correct" procedure to follow in evaluating projects, it is not a practical one; the problem of benefit–cost analysis is simply whether we can find reasonable shortcuts. In particular, we are presumed to have good information concerning the direct costs and benefits of a project, that is, its inputs and its outputs. The question is, Is there any simple way of relating the total effects, that is, the total changes in the vectors of consumption, to the direct effects? Then, having calculated the total effects, is there any way of relating the relative evaluations of different effects to market prices? For instance, if consumers are not rationed in the market, it is reasonable to assume that their relative evaluation of different commodities is equal to the relative (consumer) prices. If all total effects were simply proportional (say by a factor k) to the direct effects, then the net social benefit of the project would be simply k times the net benefit of the project, evaluated using consumer prices.

To ascertain the relationship between the total effects and the direct effects, one needs to have a theory of the structure of the economy, including statements about governmental behavior. Although a full-blown theory of government and a fully specified model of our economy are probably beyond what we can expect soon, we can specify scenarios about government policy (for instance, how it responds to any balance-of-payments deficit resulting from undertaking the project) and make reasonable assumptions about the structure of the economy to reach some conclusions for broad classes of public projects.[2]

In the first-best world, in which there are no distortions and there is lump-sum redistributive taxation, then, with an individualistic welfare function, there exists a general result relating direct and total effects: If the project is "profitable" on the basis of its direct effects using market prices, it is socially desirable. Thus the problem of finding the correct shadow prices (including the social rate of discount) for benefit–cost analysis arises from the existence of market imperfections and failures. The problem concerns situations in which one cannot necessarily infer social desirability on the basis of the profitability of the project.

The question of the appropriate rate of discount for public projects is simply a question of how we evaluate outputs and inputs at different dates. If we could always calculate the total effects, there is a trivial sense in which we would always wish to use the social rate of time preference for evaluating the benefits and costs accruing in different periods. The problem is that we normally do not calculate total effects and there is no reason to believe that

---

[2] This approach was first developed, in the context of the question of shadow foreign exchange rates, by Blitzer, Dasgupta, and Stiglitz (1981).

The critical effect of constraints on government policy on the shadow prices used in the public sector had earlier been brought out by Boiteux (1956), Stiglitz and Dasgupta (1971), Dasgupta and Stiglitz (1974). Indeed, in his classic paper, Boiteux established that shadow prices in the public sector should equal those in the private sector only under special conditions.

The critical role of assumptions concerning the structure of the economy in determining shadow prices has been emphasized by the author in a series of papers on the shadow price of labor in less developed countries (Stiglitz, 1974, 1977). It was shown that an implicit assumption in most of the benefit–cost analyses (for example, Little and Mirrlees, 1968) was that there was no migration from the rural to the urban sector, at least no migration induced by additional jobs within the urban sector. If there were such migration, then the shadow wage would, in general, be larger than if there were none; indeed, if migration continued until the expected wages in the urban sector equaled the rural wage, which was fixed, then the shadow wage in the urban sector was equal to the market wage.

the total effects are simply proportional to the direct effects. Indeed, if the ratio of total effects to direct effects systematically changes over time, then we would not wish to use the social rate of time discount in evaluating a project when looking only at direct costs and benefits.

Even if we could calculate the total effects, saying that we should use the social rate of time discount may not be very helpful. Who is to determine the social rate of time discount? And how is the social rate of time discount related to observed (consumer and producer) market rates of interest?

Thus the analysis of the social rate of discount needs to focus on the intertemporal structure of the economy; that is, the analysis should focus on the constraints on individual and governmental behavior and how these constraints are changing over time. This, as I have suggested, is the focus of this paper.

An example may help clarify the issue. Consider a simple project costing I today and yielding a benefit B in private consumption goods in the next period. To raise the revenue for the project, bonds will have to be floated, taxes will have to be raised, or money must be printed. The "indirect effects" for each of these ways of financing the project may be quite different. The complete specification of the project ought to include all of the perturbations to which it gives rise. Assume, for instance, that the government raises the revenue by floating bonds and that, as a consequence, $I less of private investment has occurred. The private investment yielded a return of r (the before-tax marginal rate of return), and hence the loss in consumption next period from the reduction in private investment is $(1 + r)I$. The total change in consumption during the first period is zero and during the second period, $B - (1 + r)I$. Hence, the project should be undertaken only if

$$\frac{B}{I} > 1 + r \tag{2}$$

the return on the project exceeds the *producer* rate of interest. But note that there is no intertemporal evaluation involved in this project. The question is simply, What is the effect on consumption in the second period?

In contrast, had the project been financed out of taxation in such a way that consumption during the first period had been reduced (but private investment had been unchanged), then the project would have lowered consumption during the first period by I and raised it in the second period by B. Assume that we use an individual's own marginal (relative) evaluations of consumption in each period. Clearly, then the project should be undertaken only if

$$\frac{B}{I} > \text{marginal rate of substitution} \tag{3}$$

If there is a perfect capital market, the marginal rate of substitution will be equal to the consumer (after-tax) rate of interest.

Thus, we have determined, under two different hypotheses concerning the total effects of the project, that we should either use the consumer or the producer rate of interest. Clearly, as we have stated the problem, the decision depends on what the public project displaces; but this is just another way of saying that it depends on the relationship between the total effects and the direct effects.

A two-period model, however, really cannot provide an adequate framework within which to analyze the problem of intertemporal evaluation of different projects. A two-period model cannot distinguish between situations in which the shadow price on investment in the public sector differs from the market price on investment and situations in which the relative social evaluation of consumption at different dates in the future differs from the market rate of interest. To see this most clearly, return to the first example, in which the public investment is financed by bonds and displaces private investment, and assume that both the private project and the public project yield returns over two periods. Thus, if the investment occurs at time 0, and we denote the output of the public project in the two periods by C_1^g and C_2^g and the output of the private project by C_1^p and C_2^p, then the net changes in consumption are $C_1^g - C_1^p$ and $C_2^g - C_2^p$. If i is the after-tax return (the marginal rate of substitution), the project should be undertaken only if

$$C_1^g - C_1^p + \frac{C_2^g - C_2^p}{1 + i} > 0 \tag{4}$$

where, for the marginal project in the private sector costing I,

$$I = \frac{C_1^p}{1 + r} + \frac{C_2^p}{(1 + r)^2} \tag{5}$$

Rewriting equation (4), we require

$$\frac{C_1^g}{1 + i} + \frac{C_2^g}{(1 + i)^2}$$
$$> I + C_1^p \left(\frac{1}{1 + i} - \frac{1}{1 + r} \right) + C_2^p \left(\frac{1}{(1 + i)^2} - \frac{1}{(1 + r)^2} \right) \tag{6}$$

The left-hand side of the equation gives the present discounted value of benefits using the consumer rate of interest. Different public projects with the same displacement effect can be ranked simply by their present discounted value, using consumers' marginal rates of substitution. But the criterion for

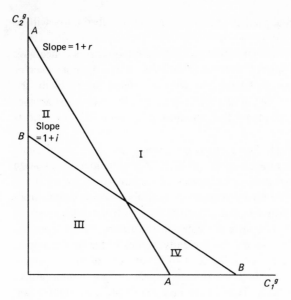

Figure 5-1

accepting the project is not just a benefit–cost ratio exceeding unity. There is, in effect, a shadow price on investment, caused by the divergence between the producer and the consumer rates of interest.

Figure 5-1 illustrates how using the producer rate of interest—even when there is complete displacement of private production—leads to incorrect decisions. The line *BB* is the locus of points at which equation (6) is satisfied, while line *AA* provides the acceptance criterion using the producer's rate of interest, that is,

$$C_1^g - C_1^p + \frac{C_2^g - C_2^p}{1 + r} > 0 \tag{7}$$

Thus in region I, both criteria lead to acceptance of the project, while in region III both lead to rejection. Using the producer's rate of interest in region II leads to rejection when the project should have been accepted; the converse occurs in region IV.

Most of this paper is, in fact, concerned with the relationship between the direct effects and the total effects of a project and with exploring simple models in which the relationship between the two classes of effects can be easily calculated.

However, as we noted in the previous section, there are two aspects of benefit–cost analysis—first, calculating the total effects, and second, *evaluating* them. The first calculation requires a specification of the structure of the economy, the responses of firms and individuals to the particular project, and the constraints on individual and government behavior. The evaluation entails somewhat different considerations and is the focus of the next section.

Problems of Evaluation

In this section, we assume that we have (somehow) correctly calculated all the effects, direct and indirect, of the project. As I suggested earlier, there is a trivial sense in which we can now say, "evaluate the projects' total effects using relative marginal social evaluations." Though correct, this evaluation is relatively uninformative. What we would like to know is, Is there any systematic relationship between market prices and this marginal social evaluation? In the first-best world, with an individualistic social welfare function and optimal lump-sum redistributive taxes, the answer is, generally, yes. Prices will reflect relative marginal social valuations. Thus a project is desirable if its net present discounted value is positive. In the second-best situations with which we are concerned, there are at least three reasons that using market prices to evaluate total effects may not be appropriate:

1. Individuals may be constrained in their purchases or sales, and thus prices are not equal to marginal rates of substitution. For instance, if there is involuntary unemployment, the marginal rate of substitution between leisure and consumption goods is not necessarily equal to the real wage. If individuals are constrained in borrowing, then the marginal rate of substitution between consumption today and consumption tomorrow may not be equal to the market rate of interest.

2. There does not exist optimal-lump sum redistribution, so that the distributional consequences of projects have to be taken into account. The marginal social utility of an increase in consumption to one individual may not be the same as that to another. There are two distinct aspects of this situation: intratemporal redistribution, that is, the effects on different groups at a particular date, and intergenerational distribution, that is, the effects on the relative welfare of different generations. For instance, the question of whether the savings rate is optimal is really a question of whether the distribution of income among different generations is optimal. Thus, questions of what rate of discount should be used for public projects almost inevitably will involve some discussion of these distributional issues, although there is at least one important situation in which, even in the absence of optimal redistribution taxes, the distributional implications of a project can be ignored. (See the section on optimally chosen taxes, below.)

3. The output of the project may be a pure public good, for which there are no market prices. The question is, Is it reasonable to use, for evaluating public consumption at different dates, the same discount rate one uses for evaluating private consumption at different dates? What I wish to show here is that the answer to this question is no.

More formally, assume we have a social welfare function of the form

$$W = \int U(c_t, g_t, N_t)e^{-\delta t}\,dt \tag{8}$$

where c_t = per capita private consumption at time t

g_t = public goods consumption at time t

N_t = population at time t

δ = pure rate of (utility) time preference

That is, we have assumed that there is intertemporal separability of utility and that the instantaneous utility at each date is a function of the level of public goods, private goods, and the size of the population at that date. There is considerable controversy about the appropriate specification of the social welfare function; the precise specification may affect the relationship between the intertemporal marginal rate of substitution for public goods and for private goods.

Assume there are no constraints on the allocation of output between public goods expenditure and private goods expenditure, that is, if Q is total output, we have

$$Q = pg + cN$$

where p is the marginal rate of transformation between public and private goods (assumed to be given at each date but changing over time). Then, if the allocation between private and public goods has no effect on total output (this is a pure consumption good) and no effect on the size of the population, optimality requires

$$\frac{NU_g}{U_c} = p \tag{9}$$

which is equivalent to the familiar condition that the sum of the marginal rates of substitution equal the marginal rate of transformation.[3]

---

[3] It is not even always the case that, with a separable utility function, we can use a myopic decision rule for the allocation of public consumption goods as in equation (9). For instance,

Differentiating equation (9) logarithmically, we obtain

$$\frac{d\ln U_c}{dt} = n + \frac{d\ln U_g}{dt} - \alpha \qquad (10)$$

where $\alpha = \dfrac{\dot{p}}{p}$, the rate of change of the marginal rate of transformation, and

$$n = \frac{d\ln N}{dt}, \text{ the rate of change of population}$$

The left-hand side of equation (10) is the marginal rate of substitution between consumption of private goods at different dates, while $n + \dfrac{d\ln U_g}{dt}$ is the corresponding marginal rate of substitution for public goods. Clearly, the two rates are the same if and only if the marginal rate of transformation remains unchanged, that is, if relative prices of public and private goods remain unchanged. Notice that what is relevant is really the marginal economic rate of transformation; that is, if distortionary taxation is required to raise the revenue for financing the public good, it is the total amount of private goods that have to be forgone to increase public expenditure by a unit that is relevant to the public investment decision. This might change even if the marginal physical rate of transformation remained unchanged (see Stiglitz and Dasgupta, 1971).

Thus, even if all the consequences of the project being undertaken can be calculated, and even if there is complete agreement on the use of an individualistic social welfare function for evaluating projects, there can still be disagreement concerning the relationship between market prices and social evaluations.

However, most of the debate about the appropriate rate of discount arises not from these considerations but, rather, from incomplete specification of the structure of the economy and the constraints on the behavior of various agents within it. These are the questions to which we turn in the following sections.

---

if, as in the section on public capital goods, the government is restricted in imposing lump-sum taxes and does not have complete control over private capital supply (for example, it does not have complete freedom in its debt policy), then changing the level of consumption goods at any date may affect the level of savings, and hence the level of (private) capital at subsequent dates. These ''dynamic'' effects need to be taken into account and would lead to a modification in equation (9).

Tax-Induced Distortions

Introduction

The question of what rate of discount to use for benefit–cost analysis is often presented as, Should we use the producer rate of interest or the consumer rate of interest? The examples we have already given suggest that this way of looking at the question is oversimplified. Indeed, this way of posing the question suggests that if there were no difference between the producer and the consumer rates of interest, there would be no problem. In fact, I shall show that this is not the case.

First, however, we turn to the analysis of the consequences of the major alleged source of distortion between consumer and producer rates of interest—the interest income tax.

Does the Corporation Tax Introduce a Distortion?

There are two questions to be addressed in an examination of the effects of the corporation tax. First, is there an important wedge imposed by the tax structure between the marginal rate of substitution and the marginal rate of transformation, that is, between consumer and producer rates of interest? There is undoubtedly a wedge, but how important it is is another matter. I have suggested that, because of the interest deductibility provision, the corporation tax can best be viewed as a tax on pure profits (Stiglitz, 1973; 1976); the marginal cost of capital to the firm is the before-tax rate of interest.[4] Moreover, because of the special provisions for pension funds and the special treatment of capital gains, a large fraction of interest income is exempt from taxation. Of course not all returns to capital receive such favorable treatment, so the wedge cannot be neglected.

Second, if there is a wedge, what implications does it have for the prices to be used in benefit–cost analysis? The answer depends in part on how the tax rate is determined.

I shall present two important cases in which, despite distortionary taxation, we can see that the correct rate of discount to use is the producer rate of interest. The cases, though important, are still special. In the following discussion of optimally chosen taxes, we see that, in general, with governmental budget constraints and distortionary taxation, the appropriate rate of discount need not even fall between the producer and consumer market rates of interest.

---

[4] Indeed, under certain circumstances it can be established that the cost of capital is less than the before-tax rate of interest. If the firm does not invest the funds, it will distribute them and they will be immediately subjected to taxation. If the firm invests them, the taxes can, in effect, be permanently postponed.

Optimally Chosen Taxes

First, consider the case in which all tax rates are optimally chosen, there are no untaxed profits or rents, and there is no exogenously imposed budgetary constraint for the public sector. Then an immediate application of the theory of optimal taxation and production (see Diamond and Mirrlees, 1971) is that producer prices, that is, marginal rates of transformation, ought to be used in benefit–cost analysis.

There are two alternative intuitive explanations of this result. Assume that government controlled all of production. Then it obviously would want to be productively efficient; by the usual theorems, this would imply the same marginal rates of transformation in all producing units in the economy. Now, assume that some of the firms are called private but that they have no profits because they are constant returns to scale or because their profits are fully taxed away. Obviously, calling them private makes no difference; the equilibrium will be sustained if the "private firms" face relative producer prices equal to the marginal rates of transformation in the optimal allocation. For a formalization of this interpretation, see Stiglitz and Dasgupta (1971).

Alternatively, we can approach the problem using the concept of "displacement" introduced earlier. We know that, for each commodity

$$q_i = p_i + \tau_i$$

the consumer price q_i is equal to the producer price p_i plus the (specific) tax τ_i. In our optimal-tax problem, it is usual to take q, the set of consumer prices, as one set of control variables. Having chosen the optimal q, we then choose the level of private and public production, subject of course to the feasibility constraint. In this formulation, once q is chosen, consumption levels are fixed; hence, a unit of public investment must exactly displace a unit of private investment.

Fixed Tax Rates

The same line of reasoning leads to another result. So long as the interest income tax rate (and all other tax rates) are fixed and unaffected by the project undertaken, and so long as the country involved is small and able to borrow and lend at the international market rate of interest (or so long as the production technology is a hyperplane), then it is producer prices, or international interest rates, that should be used for benefit–cost analysis. Again, the argument can be put simply. Assume we had a representati·ᵥ individual with an indirect utility function

$$V(q, Y)$$

where q represents the consumer price vector of dated commodities—so (q_{t+1}/q_t) equals $1/1+i$, where i is the consumer rate of interest—and Y represents the total value of the individual's endowment.

$$Y = \sum p_t Y_t$$

where p_t represents the producer price vector of dated commodities Y_t. With fixed taxes, for a small price taking country, p and hence q are given and utility depends simply on Y. Maximizing Y maximizes welfare, and it is clear that in evaluating income we should use producer prices. For other applications of this kind of result, see Dasgupta and Stiglitz (1974), and Blitzer, Dasgupta, and Stiglitz (1981).

These are the two conditions in which producer prices, or before-tax rates of interest, *clearly* should be used to evaluate projects. Note that these results hold for a quite general model, for example, a model including growth or many commodities.

But when the conditions assumed are not satisfied, the calculation of shadow prices becomes far more complicated. A full catalog of the possible ways in which these conditions might not be satisfied would be laborious; we choose to mention here only those conditions that appear to be the most important.

Budgetary Constraints, Nonoptimally Chosen Taxes, and Finite Supply Elasticities

Assume that the magnitude of the tax distortion is fixed at τ and assume that there are profits taxes at the rate τ_c. For simplicity (the results can easily be generalized), we employ a partial-equilibrium analysis; we assume demand and supply functions are functions only of the price in that market. Let z be the purchase of the good by the government and x be the purchase by consumers. As before, let q be the consumer price, p be the producer price, and τ be the commodity tax, so $q = p + \tau$. Let $\mathcal{D}(q)$ and $\mathcal{S}(p)$ be the demand and supply functions, respectively. Let μ be the shadow price associated with government revenue. Then, market clearing requires[5]

$$\mathcal{D}(p + \tau) + z = \mathcal{S}(p) \tag{11}$$

from which we can immediately calculate the effect of an increase in the government's purchase of z.

$$\frac{dp}{dz} = \frac{1}{\mathcal{S}' - \mathcal{D}'} = \frac{p/x}{\left(\dfrac{x + z}{x}\right)\epsilon + \left(\dfrac{p}{p + t}\right)\eta} \tag{12}$$

---

[5] If we drop the assumption of separability of demand and supply functions, we can reinterpret equation (11) as a set of vector equations.

where $x \equiv \mathcal{D}(q)$, private consumption

$\eta = -\mathcal{D}'q/x$, elasticity of demand

$\epsilon = \mathcal{S}'p/\mathcal{S}$, elasticity of supply

Let γ equal the fraction of the good consumed in the private household sector:

$$\gamma = \frac{x}{x + z}$$

Then we can rewrite equation (12) as

$$\frac{dp}{dz} = \frac{1/x}{\eta/q + \epsilon/\gamma p} \tag{12'}$$

The representative individual's indirect utility function can be written as

$$V[p + \tau, \pi(p)(1 - \tau_c)] \tag{13}$$

where π is the profits generated by a profit-maximizing firm when the price of its output is p. Hence, the effect that an increase in z has on utility can be written as

$$\frac{dp}{dz}[V_q + V_y(1 - \tau_c)\pi_p] = V_y\{-x + (1 - \tau_c)(x + z)\}\frac{dp}{dz} \tag{14}$$

where $V_q = -V_yx$ and $\pi_p = x + z$.

The government's budget is also affected by the increase in z. Besides the direct cost of z, there is an increase in costs of earlier purchases of z

$$z\frac{dp}{dz}$$

and a loss of tax revenue from the excise tax

$$\frac{d\tau\mathcal{D}(q)}{dz} = -\frac{\tau}{q}\eta\frac{xdp}{dz} \tag{15}$$

and finally, a gain in tax revenue from the increased profits of the firm

$$\frac{d\tau_c\pi(p)}{dz} = \tau_c(x + z)\frac{dp}{dz} \tag{16}$$

Thus, the total effect that an increase in z has on welfare is given by

$$
-(1 + \rho) = \frac{dp}{dz} \left\{ V_y[z(1 - \tau_c) - \tau_c x] \right.
$$
$$
\left. + \mu \left[-z - \frac{\tau x}{p + \tau} \eta + \tau_c(x + z) \right] \right\} - \mu p \quad (17)
$$

where $1 + \rho$ represents the shadow price of the given good and μ is the shadow price associated with government revenue. Then, using equation (12'), we obtain

$$
1 + \rho = \frac{\mu(\eta + \epsilon/\gamma)}{\eta/q + (\epsilon/\gamma p)} \left[1 + \frac{\mu - V_y}{\mu} \left(\frac{1 - \gamma - \tau_c}{\epsilon + \gamma \eta} \right) \right] \quad (18)
$$

Equation (18) provides a general formula from which a number of special cases may be identified:

1. If there are infinite supply elasticities, relative shadow prices are just equal to relative producer prices, as we asserted earlier.
   Take the limit of the right-hand side of equation (18) as $\epsilon \to \infty$ to obtain
   (provided $\dfrac{\mu - V_y}{\mu}$ is bounded)

$$
1 + \rho = \mu p
$$

Relative shadow prices for commodities i and j are

$$
\frac{1 + \rho_i}{1 + \rho_j} = \frac{p_i}{p_j}
$$

that is, equal relative producer prices, as asserted.[6]

2. If there are no profits tax and no government consumption, or purchases, of the given good, that is, $1 - \gamma = \tau_c = 0$, or if there is no budgetary constraint, in the sense that a dollar in the public sector has the same value as a dollar in the private or consumer sector, that is, $\mu = V_y$, then shadow prices are just a weighted harmonic average of p and q, that is, of producer and consumer prices.
   Thus, the relative shadow price of commodities i and j is given by

$$
\frac{1 + \rho_i}{1 + \rho_j} = \frac{\lambda_j/q_j + (1 - \lambda_j)/p_j}{\lambda_i/q_i + (1 - \lambda_i)/p_i}
$$

where $\lambda_i = \eta_i/(\eta_i + \epsilon_i/\gamma_i)$

[6] This assumes the same kind of analysis can be applied to each market separately.

3. If there is a budgetary constraint ($\mu > V_y$), then the shadow price need not lie between the producer and consumer prices. Because of the budget constraint on the public sector, we have to value resources used in the public sector more highly; but because of their indirect effects on profits, different commodities may have different budgetary implications.

4. The effect of the budgetary constraint is dominant if $\tau = 0$, that is, $p = q$. Then, again from equation (18)

$$\frac{(1 + \rho_i)/p_i}{(1 + \rho_j)/p_j} = 1 + \left(\frac{\mu - V_y}{\mu}\right)\left(\frac{1 - \gamma_i - \tau_c}{\epsilon_i + \gamma_i \eta_i}\right) \bigg/ 1 + \left(\frac{\mu - V_y}{\mu}\right)\left(\frac{1 - \gamma_j - \tau_c}{\epsilon_j + \gamma_j \eta_j}\right)$$

If there is a fixed *ad valorem* tax, we obtain[7]

$$1 + \rho = \mu\left\{\bar{p} + \frac{\mu - V_y}{\mu}\frac{p}{\epsilon + \gamma\eta}[(1 - \gamma) - \gamma\tau - \tau_c]\right\}$$

where $\bar{p} = \dfrac{p\epsilon/\gamma + q\eta}{\epsilon/\gamma + \eta}$

Again, without a budgetary constraint, the shadow price is just a weighted average of the consumer and producer prices. With a budgetary constraint, the shadow price may not be between the two; for example if $p = q$

[7] Instead of equation (12') we have

$$\frac{dp}{dz} = \frac{1}{\mathcal{S}' - \mathcal{D}'(1 = \tau)} = \frac{p/x}{\epsilon/\gamma + \eta} \tag{12''}$$

Instead of equation (14) we obtain

$$\frac{dp}{dz}\{(1 = \tau)V_q + V_y(1 - \tau_c)\pi_p\} = \frac{dp}{dz}V_y\{-\tau x - x + (1 - \tau_c)(x + z)\} \tag{14'}$$

and instead of equation (15) we have

$$\frac{d\,\tau p\,\mathcal{D}(q)}{dz} = \tau x\frac{dp}{dz}(1 - \eta) \tag{15'}$$

Hence equation (17) becomes

$$- (1 + \rho) = \frac{dp}{dz}\{V_y[z(1 - \tau_c) - (\tau_c + \tau)x] \tag{17'}$$
$$+ \mu[-z + \tau x(1 - \eta) + \tau_c(x + z)]\} - \mu p$$

or

$$1 + \rho = p\mu\left[1 + \frac{\tau\eta}{\epsilon/\gamma + \eta} - \frac{\mu - V_y}{(\epsilon/\gamma + \eta)\mu}\left(\tau + \tau_c - \frac{(1 - \gamma)}{\gamma}(1 - \tau_c)\right)\right]$$

$$\frac{1 + \rho_i}{1 + \rho_j} = \frac{p_i}{p_j} \frac{1 + \dfrac{\mu - V_y}{\mu}(1 - \gamma_i - \tau_c - \tau_i\gamma_i)/(\epsilon_i + \gamma_i\eta_i)}{1 + \dfrac{\mu - V_y}{\mu}(1 - \gamma_j - \tau_c - \tau_j\gamma_j)/(\epsilon_j + \gamma_j\eta_j)}$$

The application of these results to discounting for public projects is immediate if we interpret τ_c as the corporate profits tax rate and τ as the tax on consumption in the second period.

Alternatively, if we have an interest income tax we need to interpret x as savings, so η is the interest elasticity of the supply of savings by individuals and ϵ is the interest elasticity of the demand for savings, or investment, by firms.

The Fundamental Non-Decentralizability Theorem

One of the interesting implications of the above analysis is that it may not be optimal to leave the determination of the correct set of shadow prices, including the social rate of time discount, to decentralized units. There are two reasons for this. Assume we divide the economy into a large number of subunits; then the elasticity of supply facing each subunit would be infinite, that is, each would be a price taker. This implies, using the results of the previous discussion of budgetary constraints, that the social rate of discount should be the producer rate of interest or, more generally, that producer prices should be used. But if the decision is made centrally, then, except under the stringent conditions noted in the preceding discussion, producer prices should not be used.

Moreover, even if larger units are used, so that the elasticity of supply is finite, each of the subunits would have to be instructed to take into account its effect on the tax revenues of all other subunits; the correct determination of its shadow prices cannot depend simply on its own demand and supply functions and tax rates. This presents serious problems for the determination of shadow prices in noncentralized economies.

Savings Constraints[8]

Introduction

Traditional discussions of the choice of the correct social rate of discount have focused on constraints on savings. I find most of the arguments that the savings rate is too low unpersuasive; indeed, I shall argue that, if

[8] This section owes much to David Bevan and John Flemming.

anything, there is some presumption that to the extent there is a deviation between socially desirable savings and market savings, the social rate of discount ought to exceed the market rate of interest.

We need to ask three questions:

1. What can the government do that individuals cannot do?
2. What can the government do that individuals cannot (or will not) undo?
3. If there are arguments that the social rate of time discount is not equal to the market rate of interest, is there any reason to believe that the appropriate remedy can, or ought to, involve an alteration in the choice of techniques in public projects?

In the subsequent discussion, we shall consider these questions.

The Problem of Intertemporal Redistribution

So far we have treated the goods "consumption today" versus "consumption tomorrow" just like any other two goods and have adapted the standard theory of the second best to the problems at hand. There are, however, some peculiar features of our intertemporal problem to which some special attention should be devoted; in particular, it should be noted that the individuals who consume goods on different dates are different individuals. Thus, the problem of intertemporal allocation is essentially a problem of the distribution of income across generations.

The rate of interest has two effects. It affects the allocation of consumption over the lifetime of an individual, and it affects the allocation of consumption among generations. The modeling we have done so far has treated the problem as if there were a single generation. So long as each generation considers the utility of the next generation entering its utility function, and so long as there are some bequests (that is, there is some altruism), then the above analysis is applicable. Any attempt by the government to alter the intergenerational distribution of income by lump-sum transfers will be offset by a change in bequests. Hence, to alter the intergenerational distribution of income, the government would have to introduce distortionary measures. There is no reason, in such a context, that concern for future generations ought to enter more strongly into the social welfare function than it does in the individual's own utility function.

There is an asymmetry, however. The present generation might like to increase its consumption at the expense of future generations but cannot so long as negative bequests are not allowed. Thus, it is conceivable that the present generation will attempt to use public means to increase its consumption in excess of its lifetime earnings, for example, by an unfunded social security scheme.

In short, if individuals would like to save more for future generations, they can do so; if they would like to borrow from future generations, they might not be able to. Thus, there is no natural constraint that would lead to too little savings, but there may be a constraint that could lead to excessive savings.

An objection may be raised to this argument. So long as children are earning income at the same time as their parents are alive, the children could transfer income to their parents, and in many cultures they do. Again, if the family has optimized its intergenerational family welfare, any lump-sum redistribution on the part of the government will be undone by the individuals.

The analysis, however, is not necessarily perfectly symmetric; we could postulate utility functions of the form

$$V^t = V(c_t, V^{t+1}, V^{t+2}, \ldots)$$

where V^t is the tth generation's utility, which depends on the welfare of descendants but not antecedents. Children may show no altruism toward their parents even though the parents show altruism toward their children. Thus, one generation may be able to redistribute toward itself from succeeding generations only by coercion, that is, taxation.

Even if there were perfect symmetry in the utility function between antecedents and descendants, there still may be constraints on the private transfer of income, or wealth, among generations. These constraints follow from the fact that perfect annuity, rental, and mortgage markets do not exist. (The analysis of Rothschild and Stiglitz (1976) provides an argument for why, with imperfect information, one should not expect to find perfect annuity, rental, and mortgage markets.)

The consequence of this, and the unpredictable timing of death, is that individuals may leave more to their heirs than they would have left had there been perfect markets. In the limit, if there had been no bequest motive, they would have left nothing. Accordingly, if the government leaves more to one's heirs in the form of public projects, it is likely that the government's action will not be completely undone. But at the same time, the presumption is that one's heirs are already, on average, better off than they would have been with perfect markets, and hence the presumption is that the social rate of discount is greater than the market rate of interest.[9]

In short, if individuals are concerned for their descendants, and if the government's attitudes toward intergenerational distribution are identical to those of the representative individual within his or her own family, then:

1. There is no convincing case that the savings rate is too low;

---

[9] The importance of these considerations for the distribution of wealth has also been emphasized in recent work by Flemming (1976) and Bevan and Stiglitz (1979).

2. Because of certain market imperfections, there is some presumption that the savings rate is too high; and

3. Except in those cases in which the savings rate is too high, any attempt by the government to redistribute income to future generations by nondistortionary means will be undone by changes in individual actions.

However, we must enter an important caveat to the above analysis. The presumption that future generations will be better off than the present one, though certainly consistent with the history of the past few hundred years, ignores certain critical aspects of the energy and environmental problem. The essence of the argument that there is a long-term energy and resource problem and that there are likely to be serious long-term environmental problems is that the future will be less prosperous than the present. The critical issue, as has been discussed elsewhere (Solow, 1974; Stiglitz, 1979) is whether capital accumulation and technical change can offset the decreasing stock of natural resources and prevent environmental problems from becoming more serious. This remains a moot question.

It is apparent, however, that, aside from the unintentional positive bequests to heirs, there are probably unintended negative bequests in the form of nuclear wastes, lower air quality, and general environmental degradation. Although this may redress the balance, it does so in an extremely inefficient way. (See the discussion below on alternative instruments for changing the intergenerational distribution of income.)

Plausibility of the Existence of a Savings Constraint

There is, of course, in this argument one crucial assumption: individual and public attitudes toward intergenerational equity are at least roughly congruent. There is an alternative assumption that is, in my judgment, at least equally plausible as a working hypothesis: individuals have no altruistic feelings toward their descendants. In this case, the problem of redistribution across generations is identical to that of redistribution within a generation. Although private charity does exist, it is not so great that there is any presumption that public transfers will be offset significantly by a change in private transfers.

If we take this view, there is no more reason to believe that the distribution of income among generations is socially desirable than there is to believe that the intragenerational distribution of income resulting from the competitive process is socially optimal. But recognizing this, we need to ask, Is it likely that the market economy yields an intergenerational distribution of income which excessively favors the present generation or excessively disfavors it? There are strong reasons to believe, if the experience of the last hundred years is any guide, that the benefits of technical change will so improve the standards of living of our descendants that, under reasonable sets of value judgments, our present savings rate is probably too high. These benefits of technical change more than offset the disadvantages we bequeath to future generations in the form of a smaller stock of natural resources (see Stiglitz, 1979).

More formally, we ask, For what ethical beliefs about the optimal intergenerational distribution of income would the present savings rate be significantly too low? That is, we postulate that we wish to maximize a social welfare function of the form

$$\int_0^\infty U(c)e^{(n-\delta)t}\,dt$$

and we assume we have complete control of the economy. What would this imply about the long-run rate of interest, or social rate of discount for public projects? And how does this contrast with the long-run rate of interest that would emerge in a market economy with a savings rate of the kind ordinarily observed?

It is well known that the economy will converge to a steady state in which the long-term rate of interest r^* is equal to the rate of growth divided by the savings-to-profit ratio s, that is,

$$r^* = \frac{n+\lambda}{s}$$

where n = rate of growth of population and λ is the rate of technical change.

On the other hand, the long-run social rate of time preference ρ is given by

$$\frac{-d\ln U'(c)e^{-\delta t}}{dt} = \frac{-U''c}{U'}\left(\frac{\dot{c}}{c}\right) + \delta$$

$$= \nu\lambda + \delta$$

where $\nu = -U''c/U'$

Hence $r^* \gtreqless \rho$ as $\nu\lambda + \delta \lesseqgtr \dfrac{n+\lambda}{s}$

$$\text{or}\quad s \lesseqgtr \frac{n+\lambda}{\nu\lambda+\delta}$$

Assume, for instance, that the elasticity of marginal utility is approximately -2 (see Stern, 1977, for an extensive discussion of arguments for alternative values of the elasticity of marginal utility), the rate of labor augmenting technical progress is 2 percent, and the rate of population growth is 1 percent. Assume that $\delta = 3$ percent. Then, if the savings-to-profit ratio is, say, 0.8, the long-run rate of interest is 3.75 percent, while the long-run social rate of discount is 7 percent.

There is no presumption that the market rate of interest will be greater than the long-run social rate of discount for reasonable values of the parameters.

Alternative Instruments for Changing the Intergenerational Distribution of Income

Finally, even if we were convinced that the social rate of discount is less than the market rate of interest, a question would remain. Why does not the government directly attack the problem, by using, for example, monetary–debt policy or social security policy to change the intergenerational distribution of income? Why should the government approach the problem of altering the intergenerational distribution of income in such a piecemeal way by affecting particular public projects? One needs to identify economic or political constraints, binding on a more general policy of intergenerational redistribution, that are not binding on the choice of technique for a public project. One obvious reason for pursuing intergenerational redistribution through public projects rather than by implementing a general policy of redistribution is that the redistribution through public projects is less open, less public, and therefore less subjected to the same kinds of political pressures than a clearly articulated redistributional policy. However, this seems to be a questionable basis for public policy in a democratic society.

An alternative explanation, based on constraints facing the government in its tax and debt policy, is discussed in the next section.

Public Capital Goods, Distortionary Taxation, and the Intergenerational Distribution of Income

The preceding section argued that there is no convincing case for the existence of a savings constraint, at least not in a developed economy such as the United States. On the other hand, the market obviously will provide an insufficient supply of pure public goods, including pure public capital goods. The government must necessarily be involved in deciding how much of these goods to produce. Because the revenues for these public capital goods are generally raised at least partially by distortionary taxation, the problem of the second best is unavoidable. Moreover, since the benefits accrue over time to different generations, we inevitably face a problem of intergenerational distribution. We explicitly assume that the individuals are nonaltruistic, that is, they care only for their own consumption. Thus, to decide on the level of public goods to be produced, we need to introduce a social welfare function. We postulate that we are concerned with maximizing the expression

$$\sum_{t}\sum_{j}U_t^j\left(\frac{1}{1+\delta}\right)^t \qquad (19)$$

where U_t^j is the utility of the jth individual in the tth generation, and δ is the pure social rate of time preference; that is, if $\delta > 0$, we weight future generations' utility less than that of the present generation. If $\delta = 0$, we simply add the individual, unweighted utilities. If the horizon is infinite, this criterion may not be well defined, but there are standard techniques for handling this difficulty. Expression (19) is just a weighted sum. As Ramsey argued, there is no convincing reason for setting $\delta > 0$ (except, perhaps, that associated with the probability of the world ending in finite time). Although I find the arguments against discounting persuasive, I shall continue the analysis without restricting δ to be zero.

The problem now is a standard *indirect* control problem. The government wishes to choose, at each date, for the instruments under its control (taxes, investments in public goods, levels of debt, etc.) a set of levels that are feasible, satisfy the government's budgetary constraints, and optimize social welfare. The government does not directly control private capital accumulation or labor supply, but its decisions affect private decisions, and the government must take that into account. We assume that the government does this. The solution to this problem yields, at each date, a set of shadow prices from which we can calculate the appropriate rate of discount to use at each date for each kind of expenditure.

Our problem is to find a simple way of characterizing the solution to this complicated indirect control problem, a characterization that provides some insight into the relationship between the rate of discount to use on public projects and market rates of interest.

We can obtain a fairly complete characterization of the steady-state equilibrium of the economy. Under quite weak conditions, the economy will eventually converge to a balanced-growth path. In the balanced-growth path, we can make strong statements about the relationship between the rate of discount for public projects and market rates of interest. The relationship, as

I suggested in the introduction, depends critically on the set of instruments available to the government.[10]

The Basic Model

The particular model (formulated by Pestieau) that has been examined in some detail is the following.[11] We assume each generation lives for two periods but works only in the first and that each generation saves in the first to provide for its retirement. Thus we have a utility function of the form

$$U_t = U_t(C_{1t}, C_{2t}, L_t) \tag{20}$$

where C_{1t} is the tth generation's consumption in the first period of life

C_{2t} is the tth generation's consumption in the second period of life

L_t is the tth generation's supply of labor

If there are different individuals alive in each generation, we simply add superscript j's to all variables. For this part of the analysis, we simplify by assuming all individuals are identical. For simplicity we assume the size of the population is fixed, and for the moment we normalize it to unity.

Each generation earns a wage w_t and can invest savings at an interest rate i_t. The individual chooses (C_{1t}, C_{2t}, L_t) to maximize his utility subject to the budget constraint

---

[10] It is important to recognize that the way we have formulated the problem is not equivalent to asking what is the best steady state, that is, the steady state that maximizes utility. One can show that, in general, unless the discount rate is zero, the two formulations yield quite different results. The best steady state question is not a meaningful question, since one cannot go from one steady state to another without cost, and one must evaluate the utility levels of intervening generations. (See Stiglitz, 1970, and Atkinson and Stiglitz, 1980.)

[11] The model is an extension of Samuelson's consumption loan life-cycle model. The first application of the life-cycle model to the problem of determining the social rate of discount is contained in Diamond (1974), but no clear results are obtained.

The result contained in equation (32), that even with a full set of excise taxes we do not want the return on private and public capital to be equal, is contained in Pestieau's paper, as is the result on the effect of government debt.

The generalization of Pestieau's results to diverse consumers is contained in Stiglitz (1978); this also contains a more detailed discussion of the role of restricted taxation. The formulation presented here follows that of Stiglitz (1978).

The pioneering work of Arrow (1966) and Arrow and Kurz (1970) analyzes the problem of the choice of discount rates as a control problem. However, it differs in several important ways from Pestieau's treatment. First, savings are arbitrarily given and not related directly to the utility function of consumers. Second, labor supply is inelastic. Third, there is no explicit treatment of different generations. The result is that there is no clear connection between the social welfare function and consumers' preferences, and there exists the possibility of nondistortionary taxation. The modeling of both the structure of the economy and the nature of the second-best constraints is less persuasive than that of Pestieau and the extensions presented here.

$$C_{2t} = (1+i_t)(w_t L_t + I_t - C_{1t}) \tag{21}$$

where I_t is a lump-sum transfer, or tax, to the tth generation. For most of the analysis, we assume $I_t = 0$, that is, lump-sum taxes, or transfers, are not feasible.

The solution to the individual's maximization problem yields his labor supply

$$L_t = L_t(w_t, i_t, I_t) \tag{22a}$$

and his first-period consumption

$$C_{1t} = C_{1t}(w_t, i_t, I_t) \tag{22b}$$

from which we can immediately calculate the value of his savings S_t, which is given by

$$S_t = S_t(w_t, i_t, I_t) = w_t L_t + I_t - C_{1t} \tag{22c}$$

The level of utility attained by the individual will thus be a function of the wage, the interest rate, and his exogenous income (lump-sum transfers). This is given by the indirect utility function

$$V_t = V_t(w_t, i_t, I_t) \tag{23}$$

We describe the production possibilities of the economy by an aggregate production function of the form

$$Y_t = F(K_t, G_t, L_t) \tag{24}$$

where G_t is the supply of the public capital good
$\quad\quad K_t$ is the supply of the private capital good
$\quad\quad L_t$ is the *aggregate* supply of labor

We assume F has constant or decreasing returns to scale in the private factors (K,L) but may exhibit increasing returns in all three factors together.[12]

The aggregate labor supply L_t is given by the solution to the utility maximization problem stated in equation (22a). The determination of K_t, however, is somewhat more complicated. The solution to the individual's

---

[12] When the government can impose 100 percent rent or profits taxes, in order for distortionary taxation to be required to finance the public good, there will, in general, have to be increasing returns to scale.

utility maximization problem gives a value to total savings. To relate K_t to S_t, we have to make specific assumptions concerning depreciation and the existence of alternative stores of value. The simplest depreciation assumption is that all capital lives for only one period. Then, if there exists no alternative store of value,

$$S_t = K_{t+1} \tag{25}$$

Output is allocated to three uses: consumption, public investment, and private investment. We simplify the analysis by assuming that

$$Y_t = C_{1t} + C_{2t-1} + K_{t+1} + G_{t+1} \tag{26}$$

That is, we assume the production possibilities schedule is a hyperplane.

We are now prepared to formalize our maximization problem. We wish to maximize the present discounted value of social welfare

$$\max \sum_{t=0}^{\infty} V_t \frac{1}{(1 + \delta)^t} \tag{27}$$

subject to the national income constraint

$$F(K_t, G_t, L_t) = C_{1t} + C_{2t-1} + G_{t+1} + K_{t+1} \tag{28}$$

where $K_{t+1} = S_t$, and where S_t is given by equation (22c) and L_t is a function of the wage rate and the consumer rate of interest given by equation (22a). The instruments available to the government are the wage rate, the consumer interest rate, and the expenditures on public investment goods. There are numerous other equivalent formulations; this one is particularly simple to work with, as will be evident shortly. Note that in this formulation we do not treat the level of taxation as a control variable, but it is implicitly defined in the solution. From equation (25) we will be able to find the level of capital in each period, and from equation (22a) we can find the labor supply. This, combined with knowledge of G_t gives us

$$1 + r_t = F_1(K_{t+1}, G_{t+1}, L_{t+1})$$

where r is the producer rate of interest. From this expression we can easily calculate the producer rate of interest. Since we know the consumer rate of interest, the difference between the consumer and the producer rates of interest is simply the interest income tax. Similarly we calculate F_3 and the difference between that and the wage is the wage tax.

By directly substituting equations (25) and (26) into equation (28), we can obtain a simple formulation of the Lagrangian for our maximization problem.

$$\mathcal{L}_1 = \sum_t \left(V_t \frac{1}{(1 + \delta)^t} \right) + \sum \lambda_t [F(S_{t-1}, G_t, L_t)$$
$$- C_{1t} - C_{2t-1} - S_t - G_{t+1}] \quad (29)$$

An immediate result is that, in the steady state

$$\lambda_{t+1} = \frac{\lambda_t}{1 + \delta} \quad (30)$$

and, differentiating equation (29) with respect to G_t, we have

$$\lambda_{t+1} F_2 = \lambda_t \quad (31)$$

Combining equations (30) and (31) we obtain

$$F_2 = 1 + \delta \quad (32)$$

Equation (32) tells us that, in the steady state, the marginal return to public investment, F_2, should be equal to $1 + \delta$; that is, the social rate of discount is equal to the pure rate of social time preference. The relationship between F_2 and the market rates of interest, however, is not so obvious. After some manipulation of the first-order conditions, it can be shown that (see Pestieau, 1974)

$$1 + \delta \equiv F_2 = \frac{F_1(1 - \epsilon_i) + (1 + i)\epsilon_i}{1 - \dfrac{t_w}{w} \epsilon_w} \quad (33)$$

where $\epsilon_w = \left(\dfrac{dL}{dw} \right)_{\bar{U}} \dfrac{w}{L}$ = total compensated variation elasticity of labor

$\epsilon_i = \left(\dfrac{dC_2}{di} \right)_{\bar{U}} \dfrac{i}{C_2}$ = total compensated variation elasticity of second-period consumption

That is, $\left(\dfrac{dL}{dw} \right)_{\bar{U}} = \dfrac{\partial L}{\partial w} - \dfrac{Lr^2}{C_2} \left(\dfrac{\partial L}{\partial i} \right)$

$\left(\dfrac{\partial C_2}{\partial i} \right)_{\bar{U}} = \dfrac{\partial C_2}{\partial i} - \dfrac{C_2}{L \cdot i^2} \left(\dfrac{\partial C_2}{\partial w} \right)$

where t_w is the tax on wages.

If there were no tax on wages, the social rate of discount would be simply a weighted average of producer and consumer interest rates. But closer inspection shows that ρ does not have to lie between the two market rates, because of the wage tax and because ϵ_i is not constrained to lie in the interval $(0, 1)$.

Restrictions on Profits Taxes

The above formulation includes the assumption that the implicit returns to the pure public capital good were appropriated by the government, that is, there were 100 percent pure profits taxes. If such taxes are not levied, firms will have an equity value E_t given by

$$E_t = \frac{(F - F_1 K_{t+1} - F_3 L_{t+1})(1 - \tau_c)}{1 + i_t} + \frac{E_{t+1}}{1 + i_t} - \frac{\tau_g(E_{t+1} - E_t)}{1 + i_t} \quad (34)$$

where τ_c is the total tax on rents, that is, corporation profits tax plus personal income tax, and τ_g is the capital gains tax. F is output, F_1 is the producer rate of interest, and hence $F_1 K$ is payment to capital owners, or bond holders. Similarly, F_3 equals the wage that the firm pays, so $F_3 L$ is total wage payment. The expression $F - F_1 K - F_3 L$ thus represents the profits of the producing sector. The amount that individuals would be willing to pay (in the aggregate) for the equity in the producing sector at the end of period t is the rent they will receive during period $t + 1$ discounted back to t at the consumer rate of interest, plus what they can sell the equity for at the end of the period (after taxes). Equation (34) defines a difference equation for E as a function of the control variables $\{i, w, G\}$, which we write (in backward form) as

$$E_\tau = \varphi[E_{\tau+1}, G_{\tau+1}, S_\tau(i_\tau, w_\tau), w_{\tau+1}, i_{\tau+1}, i_\tau] \quad (34')$$

Clearly, now there are two stores of values, capital and equity, and we need to replace equation (25) with

$$S_{t-1} = K_t + E_{t-1} \quad (25')$$

Using equation (25') we obtain a new Lagrangian

$$\mathcal{L}_2 = \sum_\tau V_t \frac{1}{(1 + \delta)^t} + \sum \lambda_t [F(S_{t-1} - E_{t-1}, G_t, L_t) \\ - C_{1t} - C_{2t-1} - S_t + E_t - G_{t+1}] + \sum Z_\tau (E_\tau - \varphi) \quad (29')$$

where Z_τ is the Lagrange multiplier associated with constraint (34'), from which we immediately derive, for the steady state,

$$F_2 - (1 + \delta) = [F_1 - (1 + \delta)] \frac{\varphi_G}{1 - \varphi_E/(1 + \delta)} \tag{35}$$

The right-hand side represents the displacement effect, the reduction in private investment induced by the increase in equity values from an increase in public capital.

The social rate of discount should be equal to the pure rate of time preference δ if and only if either

1. The private rate of return is also equal to the pure rate of time preference, a first-best situation that is not very interesting in our present context, or
2. There is no displacement effect, a situation that is equivalent to assuming that the public investment good has no effect on private profits that are not taxed away. This, too, is an unlikely situation. Indeed, if the effect on private profits is large, so that, for example,

$$\frac{\varphi_G}{1 - \varphi_E/(1 + \delta)} = 1$$

the social rate of discount equals the private return to capital. For reasons that we shall set out shortly, we believe there is some presumption that the effect on equity values is smaller, with the result that the social rate of discount lies between $1 + \delta$ and F_1.

It may be useful to consider two polar cases. First, assume the production function has constant returns in K and L, the private factors; then $E = 0$ and there is no displacement effect.

With $\tau_g = 1$ and constant returns to scale in all factors,

$$E_t = \frac{F_2 G_{t+1}(1 - \tau_c)}{i}$$

and

$$\frac{\varphi_G}{1 - \varphi_E/(1 + \delta)} = \frac{(F_{22}G + F_2)(1 - \tau_c)}{i}$$

Hence

$$\frac{F_2 - (1 + \delta)}{F_2} = [F_1 - (1 + \delta)] \frac{(1 - \tau_c)}{i} \left(1 + \frac{F_{22}G}{F_2} \right) \tag{36}$$

Hence, provided $-1 < \dfrac{F_{22}G}{F_2} < 0$, either both F_1 and F_2 are less than

$1 + \delta$, or both are greater than $1 + \delta$. But F_2 may be greater or less than F_1. With a Cobb–Douglas production function with the share of G being α_2,

$$\frac{F_2 - (1 + \delta)}{F_2} = \frac{[F_1 - (1 + \delta)]}{F_1} \frac{(1 + i)}{i} \alpha_2$$

Hence, if $i > \alpha_2/(1 - \alpha_2)$, either

$$F_1 < F_2 < (1 + \delta) \text{ or } F_1 > F_2 > (1 + \delta)$$

if $i < \alpha_2/(1 - \alpha_2)$

$$F_2 > F_1 > (1 + \delta) \text{ or } F_2 > F_1 > (1 + \delta)$$

while if $i = \alpha_2/(1 - \alpha_2)$

$$F_1 = F_2$$

On the Selection of Appropriate Constraints in Second-Best Tax Models

The model I have described imposes one constraint on the behavior of the government which I think is at least questionable; on the other hand, it ignores a number of other constraints, the effects of which ought to be taken into account. The questionable constraint is that the government must raise all the revenues for the public good by taxation; it cannot use debt. Obviously governments do use debt. Therefore, at first sight, this would appear to be an extremely artificial constraint. However, few governments have deliberately used debt policy to effect an intergenerational redistribution of income—an essential element in our analysis. Rather, debt and monetary policy are more a part of stabilization and balance-of-payments policy than they are of intergenerational redistribution policy.

The constraints we should have taken into account involve the ability of the government to impose an unrestricted set of taxes, except for lump-sum taxes and 100 percent profits taxes. In particular, the above analysis requires that we be able to tax labor and capital at different rates, which is difficult within the unincorporated sector, and, even more important, that we be able to tax every kind of labor at different rates, clearly an absurd assumption.

In the following discussion, I show how the model may be modified to handle these cases.

Taxation Constraints

First, assume we do not have complete control over all wage and interest income taxes; that is, we impose constraints, such as a requirement that the ratio of the after-tax wage to the marginal product be the same for all individuals. Then our new Lagrangian becomes

$$\mathscr{L}_3 = \sum_t \left(\sum_j V_t^j \frac{1}{(1 + \delta)^t} \right) + \sum_t \lambda_t [F(K_t, G_t, L_t)$$
$$- C_{1t} - C_{2t-1} - K_{t+1} - G_{t+1}]$$
$$+ \sum_t \sum_j \mu_{tj} \left(\frac{F_L^j}{F_L^0} - \frac{w^j}{w^0} \right)$$

(29'')

where $C_{1t} = \sum C_{1t}^j$, aggregate first-period consumption
  $C_{2t} = \sum C_{2t}^j$, aggregate second-period consumption
  $L_t = \sum L_t^j$, aggregate labor supply
and where F_L^j = marginal product of the jth type of labor

Hence, instead of equation (35), we obtain (assuming for simplicity a 100 percent pure profits tax)

$$F_2 - (1 + \delta) = \sum_j \left(\frac{\mu_{tj}}{\lambda} \right) \frac{d(F_L^j/F_L^0)}{dG}$$

(32')

Even with a 100 percent profits tax, the social rate of time discount equals the pure rate of social time preference if and only if public expenditures have no distributive effects.

Debt

Assume the government can control the real money supply. Equation (25) becomes

$$S_{t-1} = E_{t-1} + K_t + M_{t-1}$$

(25'')

where M_{t-1} is the real money supply. Then from our Lagrangian, we obtain

$$F_1 - (1 + \delta) = \sum \left(\frac{\mu_{tj}}{\lambda} \right) \frac{d(F_L^j/F_L^0)}{dK}$$

(37)

If there are no distributive effects of capital, or if there are no constraints on redistribution, then the private return on capital is equal to the pure rate of social time preference. Thus we obtain the result referred to earlier in the discussion of alternative instruments for changing the intergenerational distribution of income, that is, with appropriate monetary policy and in the absence of problems concerning *intragenerational* distribution, the rate of discount should equal the producer's market rate of interest. In general, the discount rate will not be equal to the consumer's market rate of interest because of the necessity of taxing interest income.

With constraints on the government's ability to tax different groups at different rates, the appropriate rate of discount to use will depend on the distributional impact of the particular project. Different types of projects will have different distributional effects, and hence should use different discount rates. Production efficiency is not desirable, and the "distribution branches" and the "allocation branches" of the public sector cannot be separated.

Further Constraints

The implications of other constraints may be analyzed similarly. Assume, for instance, that the government cannot choose the tax rate but can decide only how much of tax revenue to spend on public (production) goods or on social security (lump-sum payments to the aged). Then, instead of the Lagrangian given by equation (29''), we have

$$\mathcal{L}_4 = \mathcal{L}_1 + \sum_t \mu_{3t}[w - (1 - \tau)F_3] \\ + \sum_t \mu_{1t}[(1 + i) - (1 - \tau)F_1] \tag{29'''}$$

where $V = V(w, i, I)$; I is the lump-sum transfer ($I > 0$); L_t, C_{1t}, and C_{2t} are all functions of I; and τ is the tax rate, which is assumed to be fixed.

Again for simplicity, we assume the government imposes a 100 percent tax on pure profits, so there are no equities. The government budget constraint is thus[13]

$$\frac{I_{t-1}}{1 + i} + G_t = \tau F + (1 - \tau) F_2 G$$

Then, differentiating equation (29''') with respect to G, we obtain, letting b_τ be the Lagrange multiplier associated with the government's budget constraint,

$$F_2 - (1 + \delta) \\ = \frac{(1 - \tau)}{\lambda} [\mu_3 F_{32} + \mu_1 F_{12}] + b[F_2 + (1 - \tau)F_{22}G - 1]$$

[13] The lump-sum payment is made to the aged. The term I is the value of that lump-sum payment in the first period of the individual's life. See the discussion on the selection of appropriate constraints in second-best tax models.

The deviation between the social discount rate and the pure rate of time preference depends on the complementarity of the public good with labor and private capital; it also depends on the effect of social security on private savings.[14]

Comparison of Results with Standard "Efficiency" Results

There are two reasons for the difference between these results and those in the section on tax-induced distortions. That section suggested that the economy ought to be productively efficient and hence $F_1 = F_2$. First, the result of the desirability of productive efficiency of the economy required having only one restriction on the set of taxes that could be imposed, that is, there could be no lump-sum taxes. In Stiglitz and Dasgupta (1971) it is shown that if any restriction is imposed, production efficiency is, in general, not desirable.

Second, the Diamond–Mirrlees efficiency result required that the government be able to produce or purchase all commodities. In our first model, the government is not allowed to sell bonds, which are one of the "commodities" in our economy. We already showed how the ability to sell bonds led the economy to a situation in which

$$1 + \rho = F_1 = F_2 = (1 + \delta)$$

That is, the economy is productively efficient, and both the private and public rates of return are equal to the pure rate of time preference. As we noted earlier, without debt the amount of private capital is completely determined by consumers' savings decisions. Although the government can affect those decisions by altering wages w and interest rates i, it cannot alter consumers' savings decisions by any production or purchase decision.

Conclusion

In this section we have analyzed the implications of a variety of restrictions on the set of instruments available to the government within a context in which the intergenerational distribution of welfare is explicitly taken into account.

In the first-best situation, in which the government has complete control over all taxes, including lump-sum taxes, there is obviously no question. The social rate of discount should equal the pure rate of social time preference, which in turn equals the private producer rate of interest, which in turn equals the consumer rate of interest.

[14] This affects the value of b.

Table 5-1. Implications of Various Constraints on the Determination of the Social Rate of Discount

Constraints:

	A:	No lump-sum individual tax
	B:	100 percent pure profits tax not allowed
	C:	Restrictions on government's control of real money supply (debt)
	D:	Restrictions on the government's ability to differentiate tax rates (e.g., different types of labor must be taxed at the same rate)
	E:	Restrictions on the government's ability to choose the tax rate

First-Best (no restriction): $\rho = i = r = \delta$

Second-Best (one restriction): A $\rho = r = \delta \neq i$

Third-Best (two restrictions):

A, B	$\rho = r = \delta \neq i$
A, C	$\rho = \delta$, ρ need not lie between i and r
A, D or E	$\rho \neq \delta, r \neq \delta$

Fourth-Best (three restrictions):

A, B, C	either $\delta < \rho < r$ or $r < \rho < \delta$
A, B, D or E ⎫	ρ need not lie between i and r, or r and δ; different ρ for
A, C, D or E ⎭	different projects

Fifth-Best (four restrictions):

A, B, C, D or E	ρ need not lie between i and r or r and δ; different ρ for different projects

In the second-best situation where the government can impose 100 percent taxes on profits and use debt policy but can impose only interest income and wage taxes on individuals, with different rates for different individuals, it is still true that the social rate of discount is equal to the pure rate of social time preference, which in turn is equal to the private producer rate of interest. The economy is (in a particular sense) productively efficient, but the social rate of discount will not, in general, equal the consumer rate of interest.

The third-best situation in which the government cannot impose 100 percent taxes on profits (we have imposed *two* constraints on the government) turns out to be equivalent to the second-best situation. The social rate of discount is equal to the pure rate of time preference, which equals the private producer's rate of interest. However, the third-best situation in which the government cannot freely control debt, that is, the real money supply, but can impose 100 percent taxes on profits, is markedly different. The social rate of time discount is equal to the pure rate of social time preference. It is not, however, in general equal to either the consumer or the producer rate of interest, nor does it necessarily lie between the two.

In the third-best situation in which the government can freely control debt (the real money supply), can impose 100 percent taxes on profits, but cannot impose lump-sum individual taxes and cannot differentiate the tax rate (for example, between skilled and unskilled laborers), in general, the social rate of discount will be different from project to project. For any particular project, the social rate of discount may be either larger or smaller than the pure rate of social time preference, and the private producer's rate of interest may be either larger or smaller than the pure rate of social time preference or the social rate of discount.

In the fourth-best situation, in which three constraints are imposed on the government, and the fifth-best situation, in which four constraints are imposed, similar results obtain. Since it is precisely these situations that appear to be relevant, the search for a single social rate of discount would seem to have been a misdirected effort. Rather, the questions should have been, What are the determinants of the social rate of discount? What are the characteristics of the project and the constraints on government action that affect the determination of the social rate of discount?

The results of this section are summarized in table 5-1.

A Simple Example

In this section, I illustrate some of the results of the previous example by examining in detail a particularly simple example. I assume that individuals have a logarithmic utility function of the form

$$U = a \ln (1 - L) + \ln C_1 + \frac{1}{1 + d} \ln C_2 \qquad (38)$$

All individuals are considered identical.

For simplicity, I assume that the social welfare function entails no discounting and that the government thus simply maximizes long-run, or steady-state, utility.[15]

The production function is of the form

$$Y = K^{\alpha_1} G^{\alpha_2} L^{\alpha_3} \text{ with } \alpha_1 + \alpha_3 \leq 1 \qquad (39)$$

From equation (39) we can easily derive the savings and labor supply equations. Let

$$Y = wL + I, \text{ the individual's income}$$

---

[15] If an optimum exists to our control problem, it will converge to the steady state, which maximizes long-run (steady-state) utility. There may exist no optimum to the problem posed in the previous section when the pure rate of social time preference is zero.

Then

$$C_1 = \frac{1 + d}{2 + d} Y \tag{40a}$$

$$C_2 = \frac{(1 + i)Y}{2 + d} \tag{40b}$$

$$L = \frac{(2 + d)/(1 + d) - al/w}{a + (2 + d)/(1 + d)} \tag{40c}$$

If $I = 0$, $Y = w\bar{L}$

where $\bar{L} = \dfrac{(2 + d)/(1 + d)}{a + (2 + d)/(1 + d)}$

$$S = \frac{Y}{2 + d} \tag{40d}$$

Note that $\bar{L}$ does not depend at all on the wage rate or the interest rate.

The indirect utility function can now be written as (if $I = 0$)

$$V = \left[a \ln (1 - \bar{L}) + \ln \left(\frac{1 + d}{2 + d} \right) + \frac{2 + d}{1 + d} \ln \bar{L} \right. \tag{41}$$
$$\left. + \frac{1}{1 + d} \ln \frac{1}{2 + d} \right] + \left(\frac{2 + d}{1 + d} \right) \ln w + \frac{1}{1 + d} \ln (1 + i)$$

Note that the terms within the brackets are all fixed, independent of the government's actions.

The feasibility constraint can be written in a slightly different way for this special example. If τ_1 is the tax rate on private capital and τ_3 is the tax rate on labor, and if there are 100 percent taxes on profit, then

$$G = \tau_1 F_1 K + \tau_3 F_3 L + F - F_1 K - F_3 L$$

or, using well-known properties of the production function given by equation (39), we obtain

$$\frac{G}{F} = \tau_1 \alpha_1 + \tau_3 \alpha_3 + (1 - \alpha_1 - \alpha_3) \tag{42}$$

Similarly, from equation (40d)

$$K = \frac{w\bar{L}}{2 + d} = \frac{\alpha_3 F}{2 + d} \tag{43}$$

Thus, we can write aggregate output as a function of the tax rates

$$\begin{aligned}
F &= \left(\frac{\alpha_3}{2 + d}\right)^{\alpha_1} F^{\alpha_1} [1 - \alpha_1(1 - \tau_1) - \alpha_3(1 - \tau_3)]^{\alpha_2} F^{\alpha_2} L^{\alpha_3} \\
&= [1 - \alpha_1(1 - \tau_1) - \alpha_3(1 - \tau_3)]^{\alpha_2/1 - \alpha_1 - \alpha_2} \kappa
\end{aligned} \tag{44}$$

where $\kappa = \left[\left(\dfrac{\alpha_3}{2 + d}\right)^{\alpha_1} \bar{L}^{\alpha_3}\right]^{1/1 - \alpha_1 - \alpha_2}$

Thus, since

$$\begin{aligned}
w &= F_3(1 - \tau_3) \\
&= \frac{\alpha_3}{\bar{L}} F(1 - \tau_3)
\end{aligned} \tag{45a}$$

and

$$\begin{aligned}
1 + i &= F_1(1 - \tau_1) \\
&= \frac{\alpha_1}{K} F(1 - \tau_1) \\
&= \frac{\alpha_1(2 + d)}{\alpha_3}(1 - \tau_1)
\end{aligned} \tag{45b}$$

maximizing V is equivalent to maximizing the expression

$$(2 + d)[\ln F + \ln(1 - \tau_3)] + \ln(1 - \tau_1) \tag{46}$$

which, using equation (44), is equivalent to maximizing the expression

$$(2 + d)\left[\frac{\alpha_2 \ln[1 - \alpha_1(1 - \tau_1)\alpha_3(1 - \tau_3)]}{1 - \alpha_1 - \alpha_2} + \ln(1 - \tau_3)\right] + \ln(1 - \tau_1) \tag{47}$$

Differentiating,

$$\frac{\alpha_2}{1 - \alpha_1 - \alpha_2} \frac{(2 + d)\alpha_1}{1 - (1 - \tau_1)\alpha_1 - (1 - \tau_3)\alpha_3} = \frac{1}{1 - \tau_1} \tag{48a}$$

$$\frac{\alpha_1}{1 - \alpha_1 - \alpha_2} \frac{\alpha_3}{1 - (1 - \tau_1)\alpha_1 - (1 - \tau_3)\alpha_3} = \frac{1}{1 - \tau_3} \tag{48b}$$

Dividing equation (48a) by equation (48b) we obtain

$$\frac{1 - \tau_3}{1 - \tau_1} = \frac{(2 + d)\alpha_2}{\alpha_3} \tag{49}$$

Substituting back into expression (48a) we obtain

$$\frac{\alpha_2}{1 - \alpha_1 - \alpha_2} \frac{(2 + d)\alpha_1}{1 - \alpha_1(1 - \tau_1)(3 + d)} = \frac{1}{1 - \tau_1}$$

or

$$1 - \tau_1 = \frac{1}{\dfrac{\alpha_2\alpha_1(2 + d)}{1 - \alpha_1 - \alpha_2} + \alpha_1(3 + d)}$$

$$= \frac{1 - \alpha_1 - \alpha_2}{-\alpha_1\alpha_2 + (3 + d)(1 - \alpha_1)\alpha_1} \tag{50}$$

Hence, using equation (42) and the fact that $F_2 = \dfrac{\alpha_2 F}{G}$, we have

$$F_2 = \alpha_2/[1 - (1 - \tau_1)\alpha_1 - (1 - \tau_3)\alpha_3]$$

$$= \frac{(3 + d)(1 - \alpha_1) - \alpha_2}{2 + d} \tag{51}$$

which should be contrasted with the producer rate of interest

$$F_1 = \frac{\alpha_1(2 + d)}{\alpha_3} \tag{52}$$

and the consumer rate of interest

$$1 + i = F_1(1 - \tau_1) = \frac{(2 + d)(1 - \alpha_1 - \alpha_2)}{\alpha_3[(3 + d)(1 - \alpha_1) - \alpha_2]} \tag{53}$$

The contrast between r, i, and ρ can be seen most easily by fixing α_1, α_2, and α_3 and viewing them as functions of $2 + d$:

$$1 + \rho = F_2 = \frac{1 - \alpha_1 - \alpha_2}{2 + d} + 1 - \alpha_1 \tag{54a}$$

$$1 + r = F_1 = \frac{\alpha_1}{\alpha_3}(2 + d) \tag{54b}$$

$$1 + i = F_1(1 - \tau_1) = \frac{1}{\alpha_3\left(\dfrac{1}{2 + d} + \dfrac{1 - \alpha_1}{1 - \alpha_1 - \alpha_2}\right)} \tag{54c}$$

In figure 5-2, $1 + \rho$, $1 + i$, and $1 + r$ are plotted as functions of d, for the case in which $\alpha_1 = \alpha_2 = 0.25$, $\alpha_3 = 0.75$. It is apparent that F_2 will not in general equal F_1; neither F_2 nor F_1 will in general equal unity, the pure social time preference factor.

This example is particularly useful for introducing constraints. Assume, for instance, that there is only a wage tax, no interest income tax. Then we obtain the optimal tax rate as

$$\frac{\alpha_2}{1 - \alpha_1 - \alpha_2}\left(\frac{\alpha_3}{1 - \alpha_1 - (1 - \tau_3)\alpha_3}\right) = \frac{1}{1 - \tau_3} \tag{55}$$

or

$$1 - \tau_3 = \frac{1 - \alpha_1}{\dfrac{\alpha_2\alpha_3}{1 - \alpha_1 - \alpha_2} + \alpha_3} \tag{56}$$

$$= \frac{1 - \alpha_1 - \alpha_2}{\alpha_3}$$

so

$$F_2 = \alpha_2/[1 - \alpha_1 - (1 - \alpha_1 - \alpha_2)] \tag{57}$$
$$= 1$$

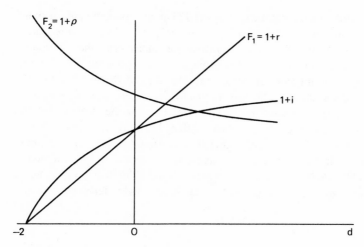

Figure 5-2

The rate of discount is equal to the pure rate of social time preference for all values of the parameters.

These calculations show that given assumptions about technology, savings functions, labor supply functions, and so forth, and about the constraints on the government, the precise value of the social discount rate can easily be calculated. The attempts to find simple answers, however, of the form, "the social rate of discount is equal to the producer rate of interest" seem doomed to failure, even under quite strong assumptions.

Market Disequilibria

A major reason that market prices might not reflect social values is that the *equilibrium* assumptions, under which the two are the same, are not satisfied. The prevalence of unemployment equilibria is evidence that the competitive equilibrium model is deficient in some important respects. Whether this has an important effect on the appropriate rate of discount for benefit–cost analysis is not obvious, but it is clear that arguments based on a competitive equilibrium model are, at least, suspect.

In a disequilibrium situation, the analysis of the effect of an increased expenditure on one commodity requires a detailed specification of how the government and economy respond to the new situation. Some examples may help illustrate the point. Assume we have a situation in which the price in some market is fixed below the market clearing price. There must, in effect, be rationing in this market. Now an increase in government demand for the commodity shifts the demand curve upward. The government could respond by letting the price rise; alternatively, it could respond by forcing a reduction in the ration that is available to the private sector. In that case, the opportunity cost of increased government expenditure is not the price but the value of the displaced consumption. If rations are allocated to those who have the highest consumer surplus, the loss is just $U'(x)$, where $U(x)$ is the social utility from consuming quantity x. The term $U'(x)$ is the *implicit* demand price, which greatly exceeds the market price. For other rationing schemes the opportunity cost will be still higher. For example, in a random rationing scheme in which each individual consumes only one unit of the commodity and all individuals for whom $v > p$, where v is the individual's utility, apply for a ration, the opportunity cost is (indexing individuals by θ, with $v'(\theta) > 0$)

$$\int_{v(p)}^{\infty} v(\theta) \, dF(\theta) \Big/ \int_{v(p)}^{\infty} dF(\theta)$$

where $F(\theta)$ is the distribution function of individuals according to the utility they derive from the commodity.

If there is rationing in the market for a certain good during this period and the next, then the relative opportunity costs will depend on the magnitude of rationing or, more importantly, on changes in the degree of rationing. Thus, if the good in question is an investment good, so that the demand functions represent demand of the input during this period and the next, the ratio of opportunity costs is equal to the ratio of the marginal productivities if the ration is allocated in order of marginal productivities. Again the rate of discount ought to be the marginal rate of transformation.

This partial-equilibrium analysis gives us some insight into the problem of how to proceed with a general-equilibrium analysis, which is vastly more complicated in that a disequilibrium in one market may make itself evident in another market. The following simple macromodel will illustrate the nature of the calculations involved.

Continuing in the spirit of the previous example, let us consider a macromodel that uses the following assumptions:

1. The goods market clears.
2. The capital market clears but the rate of interest is arbitrarily fixed at an interest rate different from that which would be market clearing at full employment. This is, we assume that the interest rate is fixed too high.
3. There are rigid money wages.
4. The money supply is homogeneous of degree one in prices and wages.

5. The demand and the supply of savings may depend on current income, but the supply of savings is more elastic.

The implication of these assumptions is that, if we let $C(Y, r)$ and $I(Y, r)$ be the consumption and the investment functions, that is, functions of current income Y and the interest rate r, then in the goods market, we have

$$Y = F(N) = C + G + I \tag{58}$$

where F is the production function, N is the level of employment, and G is public expenditure. Output is equal to consumption plus investment plus government expenditure.

Equilibrium in the product market requires that the real wage be equal to the marginal productivity of labor

$$w = pF'(N)$$

where w is the money wage and p the price of output. This can be inverted to obtain the demand function for labor

$$N^d = N^d(w/p) \tag{59}$$

while the supply function for labor is found by maximizing utility ($Z(N)$ is the disutility of work)

$$\max W \equiv U(C) - Z(N)$$

$$\text{subject to } pC = wN$$

plus a constant if there is nonwage income. Hence

$$\frac{Z'}{U'} = \frac{w}{p} \tag{60}$$

If q is the shadow price of investment, the opportunity cost of the government's investing a unit today financed by debt is

$$\frac{dW}{dG} = U' \left[\frac{dC}{dY} + q\frac{dI}{dY} - \frac{Z'}{U'}\frac{dN}{dY} \right] \frac{dY}{dG}$$

$$= \frac{U'}{s} \left[\frac{dC}{dY} + q\frac{dI}{dY} - \frac{Z/U'}{w/p} \right] \tag{61}$$

where $1 - s = \dfrac{dC}{dY} + \dfrac{dI}{dY}$

Note that if the labor market were in equilibrium, that is, if w were set at the full employment market clearing level, and the market price of investment equaled the shadow price, then the relative price of government expenditure today and government expenditure tomorrow is just the marginal rate of substitution, which equals the marginal rate of transformation. If, however, there is unemployment, then there is a correction factor. If the unemployment gap, as measured by the ratio of Z'/U' to w/p, remains constant, then the social rate of discount is still the interest rate. But if the unemployment rate is increasing, then the social rate of discount should be less than the market rate of interest. Conversely, if the unemployment rate is decreasing, then the social rate of discount should be greater than the market rate of interest. Note that if the unemployment rate is high enough the opportunity cost may be negative.

Equation (61) gave the opportunity cost of a government investment, an input, at different dates. On the other hand, the value of outputs of the public sector at different dates may not be affected in quite the same way. Assume, for instance, that national production is a function of labor and the supply of public capital goods K^p. The supply of public capital goods is, of course, a function of previous expenditure on public investment. Thus we have

$$Y = F(N, K^p) \tag{62}$$

We then ask, How will an increase in the output of public capital goods affect welfare, keeping total government expenditure, or inputs, unchanged? First, we observe that in a demand-constrained equilibrium

$$\frac{dY}{dK^p} = 0 \tag{63}$$

so that, since Y is unchanged,[16] equation (64) requires that employment must decrease by an amount

$$\frac{dN}{dK^p} = -\frac{F_{K^p}}{F_N} \tag{64}$$

---

[16] By our assumptions, C and I do not depend on K^p.

Hence

$$\frac{dW}{dK^p} = U'F_{K_p}\frac{Z'/U'}{w/p} \tag{65}$$

Again, if $(Z'/U')/(w/p)$ remains constant, we should use the market rate of interest for public projects. But if the unemployment gap as measured by $(Z'/U')/(w/p)$ is changing, the market rate of interest and the social rate of discount differ in precisely the opposite way from which they differ in evaluating inputs.

Imperfect Risk Markets

We now come to perhaps the most important reason that market prices might differ from shadow prices: imperfect risk markets. It used to be conventional to argue that the appropriate way of treating risk is to add a "risk discount factor," but that is obviously unsatisfactory. It implies, for instance, that an increase in uncertainty about a future cost makes that cost less important as viewed today.

The best way to approach the problem is, I think, within the special context of the mean-variance model. Then, at each date, we can calculate the certainty equivalent of any risky stream of returns. Under certain circumstances entailing separability of the utility functions, an appropriate way of evaluating a risky project would be to take the present discounted value of these certainty equivalents. If the ratio of the certainty equivalent to the mean is decreasing systematically over time, then an appropriate way of evaluating a risky project is to take the present discounted value—where the discount rate is augmented by the rate at which the ratio of the certainty equivalent to the mean is decreasing—of the *expected* net benefits. The ratio of the certainty equivalent to the mean will decline systematically if the risk discount factor is increasing (for which there is no obvious argument in a static population) or if risks in the future are greater than they are now. Such would be the case if the random variable is described, say, by a Wiener process.

There are some other special cases in which risk is appropriately treated by adding a risk discount factor. One such case, in particular, is that in which people have an uncertain lifetime.

Although this provides the basic procedure, it leaves unanswered the question of the relationship between observed market rates of return and the rate of discount that ought to be used for public projects. The imperfections of the risk markets may have an effect both on the aggregate level of savings and on the allocation of savings among alternative projects.

Uncertainty does not necessarily mean that the level of savings is smaller than it would have been otherwise; it might actually be larger, but to some extent this is irrelevant. What we wish to know is how we ought to evaluate, say, a safe project with a known increment in consumption at time t, of ΔC_t. If we have a separable utility function, it follows that we should calculate $\Sigma \Delta C_t EU'_t$, where U'_t is the marginal utility of consumption at time t as viewed today. The question is, What is the relationship between EU'_t and EU'_{t+1}? If there exists a perfectly safe asset in the economy, with return r, an individual will adjust his savings–consumption profile so that

$$EU'_t = EU'_{t+1}(1 + r_t)$$

It follows immediately that the presence of imperfect risk markets does not alter the basic result of discounting safe streams of return by the "safe" rate of interest. This is true regardless of whether that rate of interest is larger or smaller than it would have been had there been a perfect risk market.

The matter becomes more complicated for risky projects. Assume we have a two-period project costing a fixed amount today, C_t, and yielding a benefit stream $\tilde{C}_{t+1}$ in the next period. We wish to calculate

$$EU'_{t+1}\tilde{C}_{t+1} - U'_t C_t$$

Assume that in the private economy there is a risky stream that is perfectly correlated with $\tilde{C}$. Let $1 + \tilde{\rho}$ be the return per dollar yielded by the risky stream. Clearly

$$EU'_{t+1}(1 + \tilde{\rho}) = U'_t$$

and it follows that we can calculate the net benefits as

$$\frac{\overline{C}_{t+1}}{1 + \tilde{\rho}} - C_t$$

by discounting at the mean rate of return for the same risk class.

This calculation does not require that the market be efficient in handling risk. It requires only that the private returns be perfectly correlated with the total social return $\tilde{C}$. We use only the private returns to estimate the attitudes toward risk.

There is one important implication of imperfect risk markets. If an individual has a considerable proportion of his or her wealth held in the assets of a particular risk class, he or she will act in a more risk-averse manner than if only an infinitesimal proportion of his or her wealth is held in that risk class. As a result, the return per dollar on that risk class, in equilibrium, will be larger. Since the government in effect spreads the risk among the entire population, a particular small risk class in which only a small proportion of the population invests considerable amounts of wealth should be discounted at a lower rate than the observed mean return. How important that is, however, is debatable. For although ownership of particular assets may be quite concentrated, what is required here is concentration of ownership of particular risk classes.

The procedure described above does not work if individuals are not identical and the project has an effect on the distribution of relative prices or if we do not calculate the total consumption flows, including indirect displacements. That is, it can be shown that the stock market does not attain even a constrained pareto optimum when individuals differ and relative prices are affected by the allocation of investment (see Hart, 1975; Stiglitz, 1975). Shadow prices must take into account the changes in the price distribution and their distributional implications not taken into account by the above calculations. This is true even when there are optimal lump-sum redistributions, so long as those redistributions are not state dependent. The conditions under which this implies a higher rate of discount or a lower rate of discount than the corresponding market rate are not known.

It is important to emphasize that the displacement effects may not be inconsiderable. If the government provides one unit of a stream of returns of a particular risk class, consumers will reallocate their portfolios to hold less of private assets of that particular risk class, lowering the demand for that risk class and thus investment in that risk class. For a constant-absolute-risk-aversion utility function, for instance, the demand for risky assets is independent of wealth and hence the provision of a risky asset publicly is exactly offset by a reduction of private holdings of the risky asset in the same risk class. This is important because if private returns are less than social returns (for example, because of bankruptcy), the social value of the displaced private holdings may exceed the value of the public project. Thus, even if we believe there is insufficient investment in risky assets, increased government expenditure on risky assets may not actually lead to an increased amount of total risk taking.

The magnitude of the displacement effect depends on one's model of investment in the stock market. Consider, for instance, a situation in which a number of firms have returns that are independently normally distributed. The firms maximize their net stock market value taking the risk discount factor k and the rate of interest r as given; that is,

$$\max \frac{\bar{x}I - k\sigma^2 I^2}{1 + r} - I$$

where $\bar{x}$ is the mean return per dollar invested and σ^2 is the variance per dollar invested.

Assume that the government supplies I_g units of the risky asset at a cost $h(I)$. Firms now

$$\max \frac{\bar{x}I_p - kI_p(I_p + I_g)\sigma^2}{1 + r} - I_p \equiv V - I_p$$

that is,

$$I_p = \frac{\bar{x} - (1 + r) - kI_g\sigma^2}{2k\sigma^2}$$

Hence

$$\frac{\partial I_p}{\partial I_g} = -\tfrac{1}{2}$$

A unit increment in the government's provision of the risky asset leads to a reduction of half a unit in the provision of that asset by private firms.

Thus, the net cost for a unit of increased output of the given type of risky assets is $2h' - 1$, and hence optimality implies that

$$V/I_p = 2h' - 1$$

where V/I_p is the market value of the private firm, per dollar invested.

Hence

$$h' = \frac{V/I_p + 1}{2}$$

The discount factor to use is between the present value of the risky stream (per dollar invested) in the private sector, V/I, and what that present value would be if firms assumed that their market value were proportional to their scale. To put it another way, h' would equal 1 if productive efficiency were desired, and h' would equal V/I if the displacement effect were ignored. In this model the correct discount factor is halfway between those values of h'. Thus, if equities sell at a 20 percent premium over the value of the assets, the discount factor for public projects ought to be approximately 1.1.

It hardly needs to be emphasized that other models of investment behavior may lead to quite different displacement effects.

Much of the discussion on the rate of discount for benefit–cost analysis seems to be motivated by a concern to obtain a lower value than the mean return observed on market assets. However, those mean returns are not risk-free. The real return observed on riskless assets, or more generally, on assets uncorrelated with the business cycle, is in fact quite small—of the order of magnitude of 1 percent to 2 percent—which seems not inconsistent with the kinds of rates of discount expected on the basis of the simple savings models discussed earlier in the section on savings constraints.

For one important class of projects in natural resources it is probably the case that a still smaller discount rate ought to be used. The payoff to an invention of a substitute will be high when the price of the resource, in the absence of the discovery, would have been high. If $V(p, y)$ is the indirect utility function giving utility as a function of the price of the resource and income, then if $V_{py} > 0$, the returns to the invention are positively correlated with marginal utility of income.

In this section, I have argued that imperfect risk markets provide less reason for lowering the rate of discount from the observed market rates of return for risky assets than has sometimes been supposed. The extent to which the discount rate should be lowered depends on how well the stock market performs its function of risk sharing and the extent to which investment in risky assets is restricted below its pareto optimum level.

Conclusion

The question of the appropriate rate of discount to use for public projects has been a subject of extensive controversy. The reason for this controversy is that the number of projects for which there is an acceptable benefit–cost ratio is critically dependent on the value of this rate. The object of this paper has been to present a framework within which the scope of such controversies may be limited. We can at least hope to identify whether the disagreements are due to (1) differences in views about the structure of the economy; (2) differences in views about the relevant constraints; or (3) differences in values, for example, attitudes toward intergenerational distribution.

We have identified some of the more important constraints on the economy, which lead market prices—in particular, market rates of interest—not to reflect social values. There are some important constraints that we have not discussed: those arising from imperfections of information and imperfections of competition. For the most part, we have treated one constraint at a time, ignoring the possible important interaction among constraints. I have argued throughout that a careful specification of the nature of the constraints and the structure of the economy is required in order to obtain the correct rate at which to discount public projects. Although for several specifications we obtained a "weighted average" formula of the traditional kind, in several other important instances we obtained the result that the marginal rate of transformation ought to be used as the social rate of discount. In still other instances, the appropriate rate of discount did not even lie between the marginal rate of substitution and the marginal rate of transformation.

The value of the social rate of discount depends on a number of factors, and indeed I have argued it might vary from project to project depending, for instance, on the distributional consequences of the project. These results may be frustrating for those who seek simple answers, but such are not to be found. The decision on the appropriate rate of discount thus inevitably will entail judgments concerning what are the relevant constraints. I have suggested, for instance, that the savings constraint is probably not important but that the distortionary consequences of taxation and the implications of imperfect risk markets are significant. Both lead to social rates of discount that normally exceed the consumer rate of interest. Indeed, under not unreasonable circumstances, they may exceed the producer rate of interest.

References

Arrow, K. J. 1966. "Discounting and Public Investment Criteria," in A. V. Kneese and S. C. Smith, eds., *Water Research* (Baltimore, Johns Hopkins University Press for Resources for the Future) pp. 13–32.

———, and M. Kurz. 1970. *Public Investment, the Rate of Return and Optimal Fiscal Policy* (Baltimore, Johns Hopkins University Press for Resources for the Future).

Atkinson, A., and J. E. Stiglitz. 1980. *Lectures on Public Finance* (London, New York, McGraw–Hill).

Bevan, D. and J. E. Stiglitz. 1979. "Intergenerational Transfers and Inequality," *Greek Economic Review* vol. 1, no 1, pp. 8–26.

Blitzer, C., P. Dasgupta, and J. E. Stiglitz. 1981. "Project Evaluation and the Foreign Exchange Constraint," *Economic Journal* vol. 91, pp. 58–74.

Boiteux, M. 1956. "Sur la Gestion des Monopoles Publics Astreints a l'Équilibre Budgétaire," *Econometrica* vol. 24, pp. 22–40.

Dasgupta, P., and J. E. Stiglitz. 1974. "Benefit–Cost Analysis and Trade Policies," *Journal of Political Economy* vol. 82 (January–February) pp. 1–33.

Diamond, P. 1974. "Taxation and Public Production in a Growth Model," in J. A. Mirrlees and N. H. Stern, eds., *Models of Economic Growth* (presented at the International Economic Association Conference on the Essence of a Growth Model, 1970).

———, and J. A. Mirrlees. 1971. "Optimal Taxation and Public Production I and II," *American Economic Review* vol. 61, pp. 8–27 and 261–278.

Flemming, J. S. 1976. In Selected Evidence Submitted for Report No. 1. Royal Commission on the Distribution of Income and Wealth. London, HMSO.

Hart, O. P. 1975. "On the Optimality of Equilibrium When the Market Structure Is Incomplete," *Journal of Economic Theory* vol. 11, pp. 418–443.

Little, I. M. D., and J. A. Mirrlees. 1968. *Manual of Industrial Project Analysis, Vol. II* (Paris, OECD Development Centre).

Pestieau, P. M. 1974. "Optimal Taxation and Discount Rate for Public Investment in a Growth Setting," *Journal of Public Economics* vol. 3, pp. 217–235.

Rothschild, M., and J. E. Stiglitz. 1976. "Equilibrium in Competitive Insurance Markets: The Economics of Markets with Imperfect Information," *Quarterly Journal of Economics Symposium* vol. XC, pp. 629–649.

Solow, R. M. 1974. "The Economics of Resources or the Resources of Economics," *American Economic Review* Papers and Proceedings (May) pp. 1–14.

Stern, N. H. 1977. "The Marginal Valuation of Income," in M. J. Artis and A. R. Nobay, eds., *Studies in Modern Economic Analysis* (Oxford, Basil Blackwell) Proceedings of 1976 AUTE Conference in Edinburgh, pp. 209–258.

Stiglitz, J. E. 1970. "Factor Price Equalization in a Dynamic Economy," *Journal of Political Economy* vol. 78 (May–June) pp. 456–489.

———. 1973. "Taxation, Corporate Financial Policy, and the Cost of Capital," *Journal of Public Economics* vol. 2 (February) pp. 1–34.

———. 1974. "Wage Determination and Unemployment in L.D.C.'s. I: The Labor Turnover Model," *Quarterly Journal of Economics* vol. 88, no. 2 (May) pp. 194–227.

———. 1975. "The Efficiency of Market Prices in Long Run Allocations in the Oil Industry," in G. Brannon, ed., *Studies in Energy Tax Policy* (Cambridge, Mass., Ballinger).

———. 1976. "The Corporation Tax," *Journal of Public Economics* vol. 5, pp. 303–311.

———. 1977. "Some Further Remarks on Cost–Benefit Analysis," in H. Schwartz and R. Berney, eds., *Social and Economic Dimensions of Project Evaluation* (Proceedings of the Symposium on The Use of Socioeconomic Investment Criteria in Project Evaluation, Inter-American Development Bank, 1973).

———. 1978. "The Social Rate of Time Preference and the Rate of Discount for Cost–Benefit Analysis" (Oxford, mimeo.).

———. 1979. "A Neoclassical Analysis of the Economics of Natural Resources," in V. K. Smith, ed., *Scarcity and Growth Reconsidered* (Baltimore, Johns Hopkins University Press).

———. 1982. "The Inefficiency of the Stock Market Equilibrium," *Review of Economic Studies* vol. XLIX, pp. 241–261.

———, and P. Dasgupta. 1971. "Differential Taxation, Public Goods, and Economic Efficiency," *The Review of Economic Studies* vol. XXXVII, no. 2, pp. 151–174.

Selected Readings

Baumol, W. J. "On the Discount Rate for Public Projects," in *The Analysis and Evaluation of Public Expenditures: The PPB System* (U.S. Congress, Joint Economic Committee, Washington, 1968).

——. "On the Social Rate of Discount," *American Economic Review* (September 1968).

Bradford, D. F. "Constraints on Government Investment Opportunities and the Choice of Discount Rate," *American Economic Review* (1975) pp. 887–899.

Cass, D., and M. Yaari. "Individual Savings, Aggregate Capital Accumulation and Efficient Growth," in K. Shell, ed., *Essays on the Theory of Optimal Economic Growth* (Cambridge, Mass., M.I.T. Press, 1967).

Diamond, P. "National Debt in a Neo-Classical Growth Model," *American Economic Review* vol. 55 (1965) pp. 1126–1150.

——. "The Role of a Stock Market in a General Equilibrium Model with Technological Uncertainty," *American Economic Review* vol. 57 (1967) pp. 759–776.

Drèze, J. H. "Discount Rates and Public Investment: A Postscriptum," *Economica* vol. 41 (1974) pp. 52–61.

Hamada, K. "Lifetime Equity and Dynamic Efficiency on the Balance Growth Path," *Journal of Public Economics* vol. 1 (1972) pp. 373–396.

Kay, J. A. "Social Discount Rates," *Journal of Public Economics* vol. 1 (1972) pp. 359–378.

Marglin, S. A. "The Opportunity Costs of Public Investment," *Quarterly Journal of Economics* vol. 77 (1963) pp. 274–289.

Pestieau, P. M., and U. M. Possen. "Optimal Growth and Distribution Policies," *Journal of Public Economics* vol. 9 (1978) pp. 357–372.

Ramsey, D. D. "On the Social Rate of Discount: Comment," *American Economic Review* vol. 59 (1969) pp. 919–924.

Ramsey, F. P. "A Contribution to the Theory of Taxation," *Economic Journal* vol. 37 (1927) pp. 74–81.

Samuelson, P. A. "An Exact Consumption-Loan Model of Interest with or without the Social Contrivance of Money," *Journal of Political Economy* vol. 66 (1958) pp. 467–482.

Sandmo, A., and J. H. Drèze. "Discount Rate for Public Investment in Closed and Open Economies," *Economica* vol. 38 (1971) pp. 395–412.

Stiglitz, J. E. "On the Optimality of the Stock Market Allocation of Investment," *Quarterly Journal of Economics* vol. 86 (February 1972) pp. 25–60.

United Nations Industrial Development Organization. *Guidelines for Project Evaluation.* Prepared by P. Dasgupta, A. Sen, and S. Marglin (New York, United Nations, 1972).

6

Robert Wilson*

Risk Measurement of Public Projects

Summary

The subject of this paper is a method of valuing public projects for which streams of benefits and costs are risky. The significant feature of the method is that it provides in a single formula an evaluation of the joint effects of time and risk. This paper also considers the effect of the sequential elimination of risk with the passage of time, and the value of early information. There are two formulations, one in which the incidence of the effects of risk among individuals is arbitrary, and one in which it is assumed that capital markets (mainly the stock market) and insurance markets are sufficient to achieve an efficient allocation of risk. The latter version of the formula requires as input data only aggregate measures of benefits and costs.

There are several important lessons to be learned from the analysis. First, capital markets and insurance markets are crucial to the attainment of an efficient allocation of risk. Also, a key factor is the rate at which the riskiness of a project is eliminated over time. A third lesson is that ordinarily it is inaccurate to use a risk-adjusted interest rate. In most cases the equation requires that from the expected present value of a project one must subtract a charge for risk. Often a risk-adjusted interest rate biases the evaluations against long-lived investments. A fourth lesson is that the major component of the risk charge often is due not to the riskiness of the project in isolation but, rather, to its correlation with other projects and with other sources of national income. In fact, if this correlation is sufficiently negative, the risk charge is actually negative; that is, a risky project that tends to pay off in adverse circumstances may be valued more highly than its expected present

---

* Graduate School of Business, Stanford University.

The preparation of this study was supported in part by the National Science Foundation, Grant SOC75-21820, at the Institute for Mathematical Studies in the Social Sciences, and in part by the Energy Research and Development Administration, contract EY-76-S-03-0326, in the Operations Research Department, Stanford University. Presented at the Conference on the Social Rate of Discount, March 3–5, 1977, sponsored by Resources for the Future and the Electric Power Research Institute.

value indicates. More generally, the lesson to be learned is that a goal of public policy is to design a well-balanced portfolio of projects. The fifth lesson is that the valuation of public projects is nearly an exact analogue of the valuation of private projects and firms' shares by the stock market, with only two main exceptions. The exceptions stem from the effects of taxes and from the consumers' surplus, which is not valued in the stock market. This parallel between the two valuations permits the use of data from the stock market as a main ingredient of the valuation equation for public projects. These lessons are illustrated in several of the examples provided in the text.

The paper has a general introduction to the problem of risk measurement followed by four main sections. The first is a survey of the principles of risk measurement in a *static* context, in which time plays no essential role. The second section is a detailed analysis of risk measurement in a *dynamic* context where the joint problem of assessing time and risk is addressed. This discussion of dynamic risk measurement includes analyses of the sequential resolution of uncertainty and of the value of early resolution. The primary goal in both cases is to obtain an equation for the risk charge. The organization of both of these discussions is in three parts. The first part derives the risk charge assessed by a representative individual. The second derives the aggregate risk charge, allowing an arbitrary incidence of risk bearing among individuals and then assuming an efficient allocation of risk bearing so that aggregate measures of benefits and costs can be used in the valuation equation. Both parts allow a fair diversity of types of probability distributions and types of risk aversion among individuals. The discussion in the third part assumes that risk aversion is independent of wealth and that benefits and costs have normal distributions. This assumption permits the derivation of similar valuation equations for the stock market and their comparison with those same equations for public projects. The third major section of the paper is a brief introduction to the use of data from the stock market to obtain inputs for the valuation equations. The fourth section provides a compendium of precautions to be observed in the application of risk measurement. The conclusion summarizes in general terms some of the implications of risk analysis for matters of public policy.

Introduction

A public project is typically an investment of various resources now to obtain benefits in the future. The ultimate aim of project evaluations is to make possible a ranking of the merits of alternative projects or combinations of projects. A comparative evaluation of several projects usually depends upon some method of measurement. The method measures the attributes of differing projects in a way that makes them commensurable, thus providing a standard of comparison.

The task of measurement arises wherever attributes differ. It may be that the benefits and costs accrue to different individuals or involve different commodities. Indeed, the commodities may differ in type, quality, location, time, and so forth. In a market economy, the measurement problem is immensely simplified by recourse to the single basic strategy that uses the prevailing market prices to evaluate benefits and costs in money units. The aim of this strategy is to assess the appropriate rates of transformation or substitution between commodities. It is necessary, therefore, to adjust these prices for the effects of taxation, wealth effects, and changes in consumers' surplus. In intertemporal comparisons, for example, the discount rate prevailing in the capital market, appropriately adjusted for the effects of taxation and inflation, may provide the means of commensuration.

The task is not so simple, however, if markets are imperfect or incomplete, as the other chapters in this volume indicate quite clearly. Also, any attempt to aggregate the net benefits of different individuals invariably imposes an ethical judgment. This is most obvious in the treatment of unborn generations. Even so, choices must be made and it is the purpose of a theory of measurement to provide a method of evaluation that is consistent with the ethical values adopted and exploits fully the available market data.

In this chapter, I develop a method of comparing benefits that differ mainly in how risky they are. In the same way that charges are assessed for *delays* in the receipt of benefits, namely, future benefits are discounted by the rate of transformation or substitution between present and future benefits (as indicated by the interest rate), charges may be assessed for *risks* in the receipt of anticipated benefits. In intertemporal comparisons the discount factor is determined by the interaction in the capital market among individuals' rates of substitution between present and future income and producers' corresponding rates of transformation; of course, the discount factor is also affected by taxes and inflation. Similarly, the risk charge for uncertain benefits (say, the earnings of a firm) is determined by the interaction of individuals' aversion to risk and firms' opportunities to pursue risky investments. In principle, therefore, it is possible to devise a method of evaluating risky benefits based on the use of market data. The likely candidate is obviously the stock market, in which the risky earnings of firms are evaluated by shareholders just as the bond market reflects the evaluation of delayed earnings by savers.

It is often thought that a simple translation of the average rates of return prevailing in the stock market wholly solves the problem of assessing the charge for risk. That is, it is argued that a public project that is "in the same risk class" as a firm earning on average 20 percent of the market value of its equity should be evaluated in terms of its expected present value using a risk-adjusted interest rate of 20 percent. We shall see, however, that matters are not nearly this simple. In particular, the fact that a firm has at some time a price/earnings ratio of 5 does not necessarily mean that investors evaluate the risky earnings stream by computing its expected present value using an interest rate of 20 percent. Some models of the stock market valuation process actually imply that a charge for risk is subtracted from the expected present value computed using the interest rate on riskless bonds. A substantial part of this paper is devoted to derivations of the appropriate valuation equations, both for public projects and for their private counterparts valued in the stock market. In some cases it is appropriate to use a risk-adjusted discount rate and in other cases it is not.

Another argument on this subject has been offered by Arrow and Lind (1970). They note that if the risky variations in benefits are divided among many individuals, so that each individual's share is negligible, then the aggregate risk charge is negligible as well. The validity of this argument depends on the variance of benefits being small relative to the number of individuals, as we shall see later. Thus, if the variance is not too large, then the government should impute a small risk charge and exhibit little, if any, noticeable risk aversion provided that the risks are shared widely. This may occur either because people are able to diversify their portfolios and share these risks through the stock market or because the benefits and costs of a government project are spread widely among the population. This argument is inapplicable, nevertheless, in two situations of great practical interest. One situation involves a project with a sufficiently large variance to affect individuals significantly. The other situation involves a project for which variations are highly correlated with other variations in national income. In this second case the variance in national income is a social risk that cannot be shared so as to affect individuals negligibly. We shall see, in fact, that it is social risk that stands as the ultimate barrier to the dissipation of risk by means of sharing and insurance. In the stock market, for example, the prominent explanation for the lower price/earnings ratios of firms with risky earnings is not so much their own variance as it is their covariance with national income. This is a principal conclusion of the capital asset pricing model developed in modern theories of finance and the economics of capital markets. A substantial part of these theories is presented in this paper for the benefit of readers who are not familiar with the subject.

An important aspect of risk is its dynamic structure. Typically as time passes, the riskiness of a project is eliminated. Of course, this occurs partly because the realized benefits in successive years become known. But another part derives from the acquisition of information. This information may be received from exogenous sources or it may stem from intertemporal correlations between the benefits in different years. In either case the variance of benefits in the later years of a project's life usually declines as these years get closer. This phenomenon, the sequential resolution of uncertainty, has a substantial impact on the assessment of the risk charge. It is the main subject of my discussion of dynamic risk measurement. One implication of this study is that the early resolution of uncertainty may have significant value. The intuitive explanation of this conclusion is that early information enables individuals and firms to plan better their intertemporal patterns of consumption and production, and it eliminates the necessity of planning savings and investments as a hedge against future risks.

It is worthwhile to note that the discussion of dynamic risk measurement, which is rather complicated, reflects the fact that no clean separation is possible between the theories of evaluating delayed benefits and risky benefits. Intertemporal aspects and risk aspects interact in an intricate way that precludes use of such a simple device as a risk-adjusted discount rate.

The topic of intertemporal risk measurement is vast, and only a small portion is represented here. For example, I have neglected price risks, which may be especially important in choice-of-technique decisions. To provide simple equations, I have assumed throughout very simple forms for utility functions, probability distributions, and the like. This is hardly adequate to describe the possibility of another oil embargo or the feasibility of fusion technology. A key assumption is that the interest rate on riskless savings and loans is available equally to all individuals, and that it is perfectly known far into the future. In view of these restrictive assumptions, it should be clear that this paper is offered mainly as an indication of the methodology of risk measurement. The equations I provide may be useful to explore the role of risk in some practical situations, but in any important practical application, it may be necessary to adapt or extend the methodology to encompass the more complex features of the realistic situation.

In reading the following discussions of static and dynamic risk measurement, one can either read straight through or first read the discussion of individual risk measurement in each part and then the discussions of aggregate risk measurement and market valuation. The third section of this paper is a brief introduction to empirical methods, and the fourth concludes with several precautions to observe in the practice of risk measurement. Some of the ramifications of risk measurement for the consideration of risk in public policy analyses are described in the conclusion.

Static Risk Measurement

The task of risk measurement can be stated simply as the measurement of the aggregate of the lump-sum payments that the affected individuals would accept in lieu of the risky streams of benefits they will actually receive. My intent is partly to develop an appropriate methodology for this measurement process and to note its various features and ramifications. In addition I want to provide some easy equations that illustrate its use in simple cases and are sufficiently well specified to permit the estimation of parameters from market data.

This discussion of static risk measurement, however, is confined to the unrealistic context in which intertemporal allocation has no essential role. It is presented mainly for pedagogical purposes to introduce the principles of analysis employed in the following section, where inclusion of the dynamic aspects of risk provides a more realistic treatment.

The following discussion of individual risk measurement describes the method of risk measurement for a single individual. The method consists of determining a riskless income that an individual would accept in lieu of a risky income. The difference between the expectation of the risky income and the equivalent riskless income is called the risk charge. Various examples illustrate the computation of the risk charge.

The discussion of aggregate risk measurement considers the aggregation of many individuals' risk charges for a public project. The main thrust of this discussion is the determination of the efficient sharing of risk so as to minimize the risk charge. Moreover, various examples show that the efficient sharing of risk allows the aggregate risk charge to be computed from aggregate quantities, ignoring the actual incidence of risk bearing. The gains from efficient risk sharing are shown to differ greatly depending on individuals' tolerances for risk and the correlation of the given risk with other risky sources of income. In particular, the risk charge may even be negative if a project's benefits are negatively correlated with aggregate income.

The discussion of market allocation of risk examines the allocation of risk in insurance and capital markets and how these markets value risky private projects. The main conclusion is that the market allocation and valuation of risk are exactly the same as the socially efficient allocations and valuations of risk, with the sole exception that the market valuation does not include the consumers' surplus.

Individual Risk Measurement in a Static Context

We consider a situation in which an individual has an income $\tilde{y}$ that is uncertain. (Here and elsewhere I use a tilde to indicate an uncertain quantity, that is, a random variable, and italic type to indicate the realized value of that random variable.) After his income is known he will trade at the market prices, represented by a vector $\boldsymbol{\pi}$, to obtain a preferred bundle of consumption goods, represented by a vector $\mathbf{x}$. Assume that the individual's preferences for consumption goods are represented by a utility function u. Then, ignoring constraints on consumption,

$$U(y; \boldsymbol{\pi}) = \max \{u(\mathbf{x}) \mid \boldsymbol{\pi}\mathbf{x} \leq y\} \tag{1}$$

is his attainable utility level when his realized income is y and prices are $\boldsymbol{\pi}$. For example, if

$$u(\mathbf{x}) = \sum_j a_j \ln (x_j - b_j) ; x_j > b_j , a_j > 0 \tag{2}$$

where j indexes the marketable commodities, then

$$U(y; \boldsymbol{\pi}) = \sum_j a_j \ln (a_j/a) - \sum_j a_j \ln \pi_j + a \ln (y - b) ; y > b \tag{3}$$

where $a = \sum_j a_j$ and $b = \sum_j \pi_j b_j$. Note that if y is derived from the sale of a commodity bundle $\mathbf{w}$, then $y = \boldsymbol{\pi}\mathbf{w}$. One possibility is that $\mathbf{w}$ represents a stream of incomes, w_j being the income obtained at date j and π_j being the price now of a unit bond payable at date j, in which case y is the present value of the income stream $\mathbf{w}$. Note, however, that in this case all uncertainty must be eliminated immediately.

A second example is provided by supposing that

$$u(\mathbf{x}) = -\hat{r} \exp \left[- \frac{\prod_j (x_j - b_j)^{a_j}}{\hat{r}} \right] ; \hat{r} > 0 ; x_j > b_j \tag{4}$$

in which case

$$U(y; \boldsymbol{\pi}) = -\hat{r} \exp \left[- \frac{(y - b)^a}{r} \right] \tag{5}$$

where $r = \hat{r}/\prod_j [(a_j/a)/\pi_j]^{a_j}$. This utility function (4) actually leads to exactly the same choice of consumption, namely,

$$x_j = b_j + \frac{a_j/a}{\pi_j} (y - b) \tag{6}$$

as does the previous utility function, equation (2). Where they differ is in the induced, or indirect, utility function U for income; compare equations (3) and (5). This difference reflects the fact that in the absence of uncertainty, only the ordinal properties matter for choice behavior. We shall see, however, that the differences in cardinal properties between these two examples are of basic importance in measuring the riskiness of income.

The indirect utility function U will be used throughout the subsequent discussion since we are interested mainly in the effects of income risk rather than price risk. Similarly, the dependence of U on the prices π will be deleted, say $U(y)$. This requires an assumption that relative prices are known beforehand, and it entails a focus on quantity risks, namely the salable bundle **w**, to the exclusion of price risks. This is a deficiency about which I will comment later in discussing the pitfalls of risk analysis.

It is worth mentioning a further caveat here. Ordinarily the utility function is not independent of the event, or "state of the world," determining an individual's income, if only because the usefulness of a commodity (for example, an umbrella) is contingent upon the event (for example, rain). However, I shall assume independence partly for the sake of simplicity and partly on the supposition that the risks inherent in public projects rarely entail significant dependencies.

With these provisos, the (indirect) utility function U for income in the two examples can be expressed as

$$U(y) = \ln (y - b) \; ; y > b \tag{7}$$

in the first case, and

$$U(y) = -r \exp \left(\frac{-y}{r} \right) ; y > b \tag{8}$$

in the second, provided that $a = 1$. These expressions take advantage of the fact that the properties of the utility function are unaltered by a positive linear transformation. It is useful to construe equation (7) as a special member of the larger family

$$U(y) = \left(\frac{c}{c - 1} \right) (y - b)^{1-1/c} \; ; c > 0 \tag{9}$$

corresponding to $c = 1$, and equation (8) as the special case corresponding to the limit in which $c \to 0$, $b \to -\infty$, and $-bc \to r$. This is because the cardinal properties of the utility function U for income are fully captured by its corresponding measure of risk tolerance

$$
\begin{aligned}
R(y) &\equiv -\frac{U'(y)}{U''(y)} \\
&= \begin{cases} y - b & \text{using equation (7)} \\ r & \text{using equation (8)} \\ c(y - b) & \text{using equation (9)} \end{cases}
\end{aligned}
\tag{10}
$$

Integration of the differential equation (10) reconstructs the original utility function in each case, provided only that the two constants of integration are chosen so that $U'(y) > 0$ and $U''(y) < 0$ to reflect the desirability of income and aversion to risk.

The measure of risk tolerance is the reciprocal of the Arrow–Pratt measure of risk aversion. It has an interpretation that is central to the measurement of risk. Suppose, for example, that the utility function is exponential, as in equation (8), or equivalently that the risk tolerance given by equation (10) is constant and that the uncertain income $\tilde{y}$ has the normal distribution with mean m and variance σ^2. Then the expected utility of income satisfies the equation

$$\mathcal{E}\{U(\tilde{y})\} = U\left(m - \frac{1}{2r}\sigma^2\right) \tag{11}$$

In other words, the individual is indifferent between the uncertain income $\tilde{y}$ and the certain income $m - (1/2r)\sigma^2$. This is often expressed by saying that r is half the variance that can be tolerated per unit of the mean.

More generally, if Y is the equivalent certain income satisfying the equation

$$\mathcal{E}\{U(\tilde{y})\} = U(Y) \tag{12}$$

then a Taylor expansion of U about m on both sides yields

$$Y \doteq m - \frac{1}{2R(m)}\sigma^2 \tag{13}$$

for any admissible utility function and probability distribution with finite mean and variance.

I shall refer to the difference between the mean $m = \mathcal{E}\{\tilde{y}\}$ and the equivalent certain income Y as the "charge" for risk, denoted by

$$\Delta(\tilde{y}) \equiv \mathcal{E}\{\tilde{y}\} - Y \tag{14}$$

For example, we have seen in the special case yielding equation (11) that

$$\Delta(\tilde{y}) = \frac{\sigma^2}{2r} \tag{15}$$

Or, in the same case, if σ^2 is itself uncertain, say σ^2 has a gamma distribution with parameters α and λ, then one finds that $\Delta(\tilde{y}) = -r[\alpha + 1] \ln [1 - 1/(2\lambda r^2)]$.

Another special case of interest is specified by the power-function utility given by equation (9) or the logarithmic utility given by equation (7) with $b = 0$ together with a lognormal distribution in which $\ln \bar{y}$ has mean m and variance σ^2. In this case,

$$\Delta(\bar{y}) = [1 - \delta(\bar{y})]\mathscr{E}\{\bar{y}\} \tag{16}$$

where the risk charge $\Delta(\bar{y})$ is expressed as a percentage $1 - \delta$ of the mean, $\mathscr{E}\{\bar{y}\} = e^{m+\sigma^2/2}$, in which the discount factor is

$$\delta(\bar{y}) \equiv \frac{Y}{\mathscr{E}\{\bar{y}\}} \tag{17}$$

$$= \exp\left(-\frac{1}{2c}\sigma^2\right)$$

and $c = 1$ if the utility is logarithmic.

One more example will suffice. If the income $\bar{y}$ has a gamma distribution with parameters α and λ, namely, the mean is $\mathscr{E}\{\bar{y}\} = \alpha/\lambda$ and the variance is $V\{\bar{y}\} = \alpha/\lambda^2$, then the exponential utility given by equation (8) implies a risk charge given by the discount factor

$$\delta(\bar{y}) = r\lambda \ln\left(1 + \frac{1}{r\lambda}\right) \tag{18}$$

whereas the power utility given by equation (9) with $b = 0$ yields

$$\delta(\bar{y}) = \frac{1}{\alpha}\left[\frac{\Gamma(d + \alpha)}{\Gamma(\alpha)}\right]^{1/d} \tag{19}$$

where $d = 1 - 1/c$ and where $\Gamma(\alpha) = (\alpha - 1)!$ is the standard complete gamma function; for example, if $\alpha > 1$ and $c = \frac{1}{2}$, then $\delta(\bar{y}) = (\alpha - 1)/\alpha$. Note that equation (18) depends only on λ and equation (19) depends only on α.

In the following exposition, I will use illustrations that are based mainly on one or another of the above examples. It may be worthwhile, therefore, for me to state why I think these examples are sufficiently robust to represent the main phenomena encountered in measuring risk charges. The three probability distributions (normal, lognormal, and gamma) need little comment since they are widely used in econometric estimation. They can be justified by appeals to central limit theorems, and having two parameters each, they permit a separation of mean and variance effects. If the variance of income is small, then the exponential utility given by equation (8) with constant risk tolerance is justified by the approximation equation (13). That is, locally (meaning for small risky variations) the behavior of a risk-averse individual can always be described to a good approximation by an exponential utility having constant risk tolerance. If the variance is relatively large, then it may be necessary to allow the risk tolerance to vary with income. Increasing risk tolerance is captured fairly well, I think, by assuming it is linear, which yields the family of power and logarithmic utilities. I have omitted decreasing linear risk tolerance both because it seems unlikely in practice and because the corresponding utility functions, for example, the quadratic, are not monotonic after the point at which the risk tolerance vanishes. The various equations for the risk charge or discount factor evidence, I think, a diversity that is quite ample.

In the discussion of dynamic risk measurement, I will return to the task of measuring an individual's risk charge, but in a dynamic context. I turn now, however, to the problem of aggregating the risk charges of all individuals affected by a project in a static context.

Aggregate Risk Measurement in a Static Context

We can begin the study of aggregate risk measurement in the simplest way by assuming that there is an aggregate income $\bar{y}$, which is divided among n individuals indexed by $i = 1, \ldots, n$. In particular, suppose for simplicity that each individual i receives an income $\bar{y}_i$, which is a linear function of the aggregate income of the form

$$\bar{y}_i = b_i + t_i[\bar{y} - b] \tag{20}$$

where $b = \sum_i b_i$, $\sum_i t_i = 1$, and $t_i > 0$. If individual i has a power or logarithmic utility

$$U_i(y_i) = \left(\frac{c_i}{c_i - 1}\right)(y_i - b_i)^{1 - 1/c_i} \tag{21}$$

as in equation (9), then we can interpret b_i as i's subsistence income and $\bar{y} - b$ as the aggregate income in excess of aggregate subsistence requirements. If the individuals all have exponential utilities with constant risk tolerance,

$$U_i(y_i) = -r_i \exp(-y_i/r_i) \tag{22}$$

as in equation (8), then it is convenient to assume in equation (20) that $b \equiv \sum_i b_i = 0$.

Consider first the case in which each individual has a power or logarithmic utility as given in equation (21) and the excess aggregate income $\tilde{y} - b$ has either a lognormal or gamma distribution. From our earlier results in the discussion of individual risk measurement it follows that each individual i is indifferent between his risky income y_i and the equivalent certain income Y_i satisfying the equation

$$Y_i - b_i = t_i \delta_i(\tilde{y} - b) \mathscr{E}\{\tilde{y} - b\} \tag{23}$$

where either

$$\delta_i(\tilde{y} - b) = e^{-\sigma^2/2c_i} \tag{24}$$

using equation (17) in the lognormal case, or

$$\delta_i(\tilde{y} - b) = \frac{1}{\alpha} \left[\frac{\Gamma(\alpha + 1 - 1/c_i)}{\Gamma(\alpha)} \right]^{c_i/(c_i - 1)} \tag{25}$$

using equation (19) in the gamma case. In the aggregate, therefore, the equivalent certain excess income is

$$Y - b \equiv \sum_i (Y_i - b_i)$$
$$= \delta(\tilde{y} - b) \mathscr{E}\{\tilde{y} - b\} \tag{26}$$

where

$$\delta(\tilde{y} - b) = \sum_i t_i \delta_i(\tilde{y} - b) \tag{27}$$

is the corresponding discount factor for risk in the aggregate.

It is worthwhile to take note of the special instance in which the individuals are all alike in evaluating excess income; that is, $c_i = c$ for all i and therefore also $\delta_i(\tilde{y} - b) = \delta(\tilde{y} - b)$ for all i. We see in this instance that the mean excess income is discounted for risk in the aggregate by exactly the same factor that any one individual uses. Observe that this result is independent of the number of individuals and independent of the proportions (t_i) in which they share the risk. It is, moreover, a result that runs counter to the intuitive notion that there is no need to discount or otherwise charge for risk when the risk is divided among a large enough number of individuals. It clearly depends on the existence of a subsistence level of income at which tolerance for risk vanishes.

Consider secondly the case in which each individual has an exponential utility given by equation (22) and the aggregate income $\tilde{y}$ has either a normal or a gamma distribution. From our results in the preceding discussion of individual risk measurement it follows that each individual i is indifferent between his risky income $\bar{y}_i$ and the equivalent certain income given by

$$Y_i = b_i + t_i \mathscr{E}\{\bar{y}\} - t_i^2 \Delta_i(\bar{y}) \tag{28}$$

where

$$\Delta_i(\bar{y}) = \frac{1}{2r_i} V\{\bar{y}\} \tag{29}$$

using equation (15) in the normal case, or

$$Y_i = b_i + t_i \delta_i(t_i \bar{y}) \mathscr{E}\{\bar{y}\} \tag{30}$$

where

$$\delta_i(t_i \bar{y}) = \left(\frac{r_i \lambda}{t_i}\right) \ln\left[1 + 1 \middle/ \left(\frac{r_i \lambda}{t_i}\right)\right] \tag{31}$$

using equation (18) in the gamma case. In the aggregate, therefore, the equivalent certain income is

$$\begin{aligned} Y &\equiv \sum_i Y_i \\ &= \mathscr{E}\{\bar{y}\} - \Delta(\bar{y}) \end{aligned} \tag{32}$$

where

$$\Delta(\bar{y}) = \sum_i t_i^2 \, \Delta_i(\bar{y}) \tag{33}$$

is the aggregate risk charge in the normal case, and

$$Y = \delta(\bar{y}) \mathscr{E}\{\bar{y}\} \tag{34}$$

where

$$\delta(\bar{y}) = \sum_i t_i \delta_i(t_i \bar{y}) \tag{35}$$

is the aggregate risk discount factor in the gamma case.

In the previous example, in which $c_i = c$ for all i, we saw that in calculating the aggregate discount factor for risk it was quite irrelevant how the risk was divided, but we see in this example that the aggregate risk charge in equation (33) and the aggregate risk discount in equation (35) depend sensitively upon the way in which the risk is spread among the individuals. It is interesting, therefore, to ascertain how the income can be divided so as to maximize the aggregate equivalent certain income Y. As it turns out, minimizing either the risk charge $\Delta(\bar{y})$ in equation (33) or maximizing the risk discount $\delta(\bar{y})$ in equation (35) by choosing (t_i) so that $\sum_i t_i = 1$ yields the same answer. Namely, it is best to choose

$$t_i = r_i/r \tag{36}$$

where

$$r = \sum_i r_i \tag{37}$$

is the aggregate measure of risk tolerance. With this specification,

$$\Delta(\bar{y}) = \frac{1}{2r}V\{\bar{y}\} \tag{38}$$

in the normal case, and

$$\delta(\bar{y}) = r\lambda \ln (1 + 1/r\lambda) \tag{39}$$

in the gamma case. Thus, in both cases the aggregate measurement of risk is accomplished in exactly the same fashion as it is for any one individual except that it is the *aggregate* measure of risk tolerance that is the relevant one to use. This result depends critically, of course, on the supposition in equation (36) that the risk is shared among the individuals in proportion to each one's risk tolerance. Observe that in this case the spreading of risk among many individuals does indeed confer benefits; in particular, as $r \to \infty$ also $\Delta(\bar{y}) \to 0$ in equation (38) and $\delta(\bar{y}) \to 1$ in equation (39). In equation (38) doubling r halves the risk charge. Values of the function $\delta(\bar{y})$ in equation (39) are tabulated below.

$r\lambda$	$r\lambda \ln (1 + 1/r\lambda)$
0.01	0.046
0.10	0.240
1.00	0.693
10.00	0.953
100.00	0.995

The feature that risk should be shared by the individuals in proportion to each one's risk tolerance is actually a general requirement for the efficiency of any system of dividing risky income among several individuals. This result stems from the necessary condition for efficiency that for any two individuals i and j, and for any two incomes $\bar{y}$ and $\hat{y}$, if $s_i(\bar{y})$ is to be i's share when $\bar{y}$ obtains, and so forth, then it must be that

$$U_i'(s_i(\bar{y}))/U_i'(s_i(\hat{y})) = U_j'(s_j(\bar{y}))/U_j'(s_j(\hat{y})) \tag{40}$$

because otherwise it would be possible to improve the welfare of both individuals by changing their shares slightly for the two incomes $\bar{y}$ and $\hat{y}$. Consequently, there exists a function of income, say $\mu(y)$, and weights $w_i > 0$ for the individuals, such that

$$w_i U_i'(s_i(y)) = \mu(y) \tag{41}$$

for each individual i and each aggregate income y. Differentiating both sides of this equation with respect to y and then dividing by the respective sides of equation (41) yields

$$s_i'(y) = R_i(s_i(y)) \left[\frac{-\mu'(y)}{\mu(y)} \right] \tag{42}$$

where

$$R_i(y_i) = -U_i'(y_i)/U_i''(y_i) \tag{43}$$

is i's measure of risk tolerance. Since $\sum_i s_i(y) = y$, and therefore also $\sum_i s_i'(y) = 1$, it follows that equation (42) can be simplified to

$$s_i'(y) = R_i(s_i(y))/R(y) \tag{44}$$

where

$$R(y) = \sum_i R_i(s_i(y)) \tag{45}$$

is the aggregate risk tolerance. Thus, for efficiency, risk should be shared at the margin in proportion to risk tolerance.

We have seen previously in the case of exponential utilities with constant risk tolerances that the enforcement of an efficient sharing of risk results in the maximization of the aggregate equivalent certain income Y, and it also implies that there are substantial benefits to be gained from sharing the risk efficiently among many individuals. The analogous result does not hold in the case of power, or logarithmic, utilities (with $c_i = c$ for all i) since in that case any sharing rule of the form of equation (20) is efficient. Moreover, the aggregate risk tolerance given by

$$
\begin{aligned}
R(y) &\equiv \sum_i R_i(y_i) \\
&= \sum_i c[b_i + t_i(y - b) - b_i] \\
&= c(y - b)
\end{aligned}
\tag{46}
$$

is unaffected by the number of individuals among whom the risk is shared.

Even in the favorable case of exponential utilities with constant risk tolerances, however, it is necessary to be cautious in assessing the gains to be had from sharing the risk among numerous individuals. Suppose, for example, that the aggregate income $\bar{y}$ is actually the sum of individually produced incomes $\tilde{z}_i$ for the various individuals $i = 1, \ldots, n$. (The difference between an individual's produced income $\tilde{z}_i$ and his received income $\bar{y}_i$ is presumably accounted for by transfer payments such as insurance, shareholdings of firms, taxation, public goods, and externalities.) Assume that the vector $\tilde{\mathbf{z}} = (\tilde{z}_1, \ldots, \tilde{z}_n)$ has a normal distribution with a mean vector $\mathbf{m}$ and a variance matrix $\mathbf{V}$. Let $\mathbf{1}$ be the vector of ones. Then $\bar{\mathbf{y}} = \tilde{\mathbf{z}}\mathbf{1}$ has a normal distribution with mean $\mathbf{m1}$ and variance $\mathbf{1'V1}$. Two extreme cases indicate the range of possibilities. In the first case the individually produced incomes are independent; for example, each has variance σ^2 so that $\bar{y}$ has variance $n\sigma^2$. In this case the aggregate risk charge is

$$
\Delta(\bar{y}) = \frac{n}{2r}\sigma^2
\tag{47}
$$

using equation (38), or somewhat more cogently

$$
\Delta(\bar{y}) = \frac{1}{2\bar{r}}\sigma^2
\tag{48}
$$

where $\bar{r} = r/n$ is the average risk tolerance among the individuals. Thus, the aggregate risk charge is merely the charge that an average individual would levy against his own produced income. In the second extreme case, the individually produced incomes are highly, say perfectly, correlated perhaps because of their mutual dependence on a key exogenous factor of production. In this case $\bar{y}$ has a variance $n^2\sigma^2$ and the aggregate risk charge is

$$\Delta(\bar{y}) = \frac{n^2}{2r} \sigma^2$$

$$= n\left(\frac{1}{2\bar{r}} \sigma^2\right)$$

(49)

Thus in this case there is little gain from increased numbers since the aggregate risk charge is the sum of the risk charges that n average individuals would each levy against their own produced incomes.

In measuring the risk of a new project, its correlation with existing sources of income is a factor of major importance. Suppose, for example, that the existing aggregate income $\bar{y}$ is to be augmented by a component $\bar{z}$ if a project is adopted. If $\bar{y}$ and $\bar{z}$ have a joint normal distribution and risk tolerances are constant, then the increment in the risk charge due to the project is

$$\Delta(\bar{y} + \bar{z}) - \Delta(\bar{y}) = \frac{1}{2r} [V\{\bar{z}\} + 2 \operatorname{cov} \{\bar{y}, \bar{z}\}]$$

$$= \frac{1}{2r} [\sigma_z^2 + 2\sigma_z\sigma_y\rho_{yz}]$$

(50)

where $V\{\bar{z}\} = \sigma_z^2$, $V\{\bar{y}\} = \sigma_y^2$, and ρ_{yz} is the coefficient of correlation between $\bar{y}$ and $\bar{z}$. The advantage of a project that is negatively correlated with existing sources of income is evident in this equation. Suppose, for instance, that there are $n = 100$ million households with an average risk tolerance of $\bar{r} = \$1,000$ and that existing aggregate income has a standard deviation of $\sigma_y = \$100$ billion; thus the existing risk charge is $\Delta(\bar{y}) = \$50$ billion. Consider a project whose standard deviation is $\sigma_z = \$100$ million. If the correlation is positive, say $\rho_{yz} = 0.1$, then the increment to the risk charge is $\$10,050,000$, whereas if the correlation is negative, say $\rho_{yz} = -0.1$, then the increment is $-\$9,950,000$, reflecting an actual decrease in the aggregate risk charge.

It should be clear as well that the incremental risk charge levied against any one project depends upon the correlation between its benefits and those of other projects adopted. Thus, a project cannot be evaluated in isolation and it is necessary in principle to evaluate all possible combinations of projects for adoption.

Market Allocation of Risk in a Static Context

I turn now to an examination of the allocation of risk in competitive markets, still in a purely static context. My aim is mainly to compare the risk charges derived in the previous discussion of aggregate risk measurement with the risk charges obtained from models of market equilibrium. It is not possible here in a brief space to consider an elaborately detailed model. Instead, I consider two extreme cases, the first being an example of diversifiable risk such as occurs in ordinary insurance markets, and the second being an example of nondiversifiable risk such as occurs in markets for corporate securities.

In the first case, suppose that each of n individuals has a probability p of suffering an accident and incurring a loss of $-\ell$. If the accidents are independent and there are many individuals, then the aggregate loss $\bar{y}$ has approximately a normal distribution with mean $m = -np\ell$ and variance $\sigma^2 = n\ell^2 p(1 - p)$. We have seen previously that if each individual i has an exponential utility for such losses with constant risk tolerance r_i, then it is necessary and sufficient for efficiency to share the aggregate loss according to a sharing rule that assigns to each individual i a portion

$$s_i(\bar{y}) = b_i + (r_i/r)[\bar{y} - b] \tag{51}$$

where $r = \sum_i r_i$ is the aggregate risk tolerance and $b = \sum_i b_i$. In the ordinary case of an insurance company or a mutual insurance association, r_i/r is individual i's share of the company's common stock. Also, if π is the price of the firm's stock and q is the insurance premium, then $b_i = -q - \pi r_i/r$. In other words, the sum of the company's capital and reserves is $\pi + nq$ and individual i's net loss is

$$-\tilde{\ell}_i = -q + (r_i/r)[\bar{y} + nq] \tag{52}$$

His equivalent certain loss is

$$-L_i = -q + (r_i/r)[-np\ell + nq] - \frac{1}{2r_i}(r_i/r)^2 n\ell^2 p(1 - p) \tag{53}$$

and the aggregate equivalent certain loss per person is

$$-L/n = -p\ell - \frac{1}{2r}\ell^2 p(1 - p) \tag{54}$$

Of course, if the number of individuals is very large, so that the aggregate risk tolerance r is large, then the average risk charge, the second term in equation (54), is negligible.

The common practice of mutual insurance companies is to include shares (that is, rights to dividends) in the provisions of the policy (that is, $\pi = 0$), apparently on the presumption that most individuals have the same risk tolerance, and then set the premium q sufficiently large so that there is little chance of depleting reserves. It is here that the independence of accidents plays a critical role, for if there were substantial correlation, not only could the aggregate variance be as large as $n^2\ell^2 p(1 - p)$, thereby eliminating most of the gains from risk sharing, but also no premium substantially less than ℓ could avoid a large chance of depleting reserves. Life insurance is amenable (in peacetime) to a system of mutual insurance companies. Automobile collision insurance is a borderline case, usually organized through stock companies with substantial capital, because of the correlation inherent in the inflation of repair costs and liability settlements.

Disaster insurance is an extreme case of inherent correlation and must often be organized publicly by means of government assistance programs in which the risk is widely shared through taxation or inflation; for example, in the United States, the federal government provides limited insurance for nuclear accidents. Even so, publicly provided insurance is often vitiated by some of the other causes of the failure of private insurance markets, namely, the problems of adverse selection and moral hazard. The standard examples of moral hazard include (1) the incentive, when flood insurance is available, for individuals to move onto a flood plain and to neglect defensive measures; and (2) the incentive, when medical insurance is available, for individuals to increase demands for medical services. Thus, public remedies for absent insurance markets in the private sector do not necessarily escape all the difficulties that afflict private enterprises.

The character of the preceding results is retained if the individuals face risks that are distributed continuously. For example, if aggregate income $\mathbf{y}$ is the sum of n independent components that are normally distributed each with variance σ^2, then the aggregate risk charge per person is $\sigma^2/2r$; if the components of income are gamma distributed with parameters α and λ, then the risk discount is $r\lambda \ln (1 + 1/r\lambda)$. If the income components are uniformly distributed over a range d, then the risk charge per person is approximately $d^2/24r$ if n is large. In each case the risk charge per person is negligible when the aggregate risk tolerance is large.

When individuals' risks are not independent, as for example in the case of floods and earthquakes, insurance is sometimes sold on a state-contingent basis. Suppose, for instance, that individual i incurs a loss of $-\ell_i(\omega)$ if one of a number of states indexed by ω occurs. Let $\pi(\omega)$ be the premium for \$1 payable in state ω, at which price each individual i can buy or sell as much insurance as he pleases, say a quantity $x_i(\omega)$. In this (static) situation, individual i will choose the quantities $x_i(\omega)$ to maximize the expected utility given by

$$\mathscr{E}_i U_i[y_i(\tilde{\omega}) - \ell_i(\tilde{\omega}) + x_i(\tilde{\omega}) - \sum_\omega \pi(\omega)x_i(\tilde{\omega})] \tag{55}$$

Here I use the expectation operator $\mathscr{E}_i$ indexed by i to indicate that the expectation is with respect to i's personal assessment of the probabilities of the various states. The unconstrained maximization requires for each state ω having probability $p_i(\omega) > 0$, that $U_i'[s_i(\omega)]p_i(\omega) = \pi(\omega)\mathscr{E}_i U_i'[s_i(\tilde{\omega})]$, where $s_i(\omega)$ is the argument of U_i in equation (55). This condition is evidently a variant of the efficiency condition given by equation (41). Each equilibrium price $\pi(\omega)$ is determined by the condition that demands and supplies of insurance in state ω are equal, namely $\sum_i x_i(\omega) = 0$. Consequently, if each individual has constant risk tolerance r_i, then one finds that

$$\pi(\omega) = ke^{-[y(\omega) - \ell(\omega)]/r} \prod_i p_i(\omega)^{r_i/r} \tag{56}$$

where r is the aggregate risk tolerance, $y(\omega) = \sum_i y_i(\omega)$, $\ell(\omega) = \sum_i \ell_i(\omega)$, and the constant k is chosen so that the price of an asset paying \$1 for certain is, in fact, just \$1. Therefore, $\sum_\omega \pi(\omega) = 1$. The "market probability" $p(\omega)$ of ω is proportional to $\prod_i p_i(\omega)^{r_i/r}$, the geometric mean of the individuals' probability assessments weighted by their risk sharing.[1] For example, if $p_i(\omega)$ is the density of a normal distribution with mean m_i and "precision" $h_i = 1/\sigma_i^2$ then $p(\omega)$ is the density of a normal distribution with precision $h = \sum_i (r_i/r)h_i \equiv 1/\sigma^2$ and mean $m = \sum_i (r_i/r)(h_i/h)m_i$. If this feature is retained as an assumption along with the proviso that $y(\tilde{\omega}) - \ell(\tilde{\omega})$ is normally distributed, say $y(\tilde{\omega}) - \ell(\tilde{\omega}) = \tilde{\omega}$ for simplicity, then it follows that $\pi(\omega)$ is the density of a normal distribution with mean $m - \sigma^2/r$ and variance σ^2. Consider now a new small project that will add a component $z(\tilde{\omega})$ to income, say $z(\tilde{\omega}) = a + b\tilde{\omega}$ in order to ensure that $z(\tilde{\omega})$ is normally distributed. Its assessed value using the current market price is

$$\int z(\omega)\pi(\omega)d\omega = a + b[m - \sigma^2/r] \tag{57}$$

The reader may be startled that this equation differs from the equation for the equivalent certain income in the special case in which $z(\tilde{\omega}) = \tilde{\omega} = y(\tilde{\omega}) - \ell(\tilde{\omega})$ is the original income. That is, we found before that the equivalent certain income is $m - \sigma^2/2r$, whereas valued at market prices the equivalent certain income is $m - \sigma^2/r$. The difference is the "consumers' surplus" term $\sigma^2/2r$. In general, market prices will undervalue the equivalent certain income because they omit the term corresponding to consumers' surplus. This phenomenon will be examined in more detail in the next paragraphs as we study the subject further.

[1] If the individuals' utilities are logarithmic, then a similar computation shows that the "market probability" is an arithmetic average.

I now take up the subject of poorly diversifiable risks, still in the context of static models of markets. Chief among such risks are variations in the national economy that have pervasive effects: developments in technology; changes in productivity, employment, output, factor supplies, or prices of imported factors; and of course inflation. Other than a few futures markets, the principal market for insurance against the risk in national income is the market for corporate securities, represented mainly by shares of the common stock of firms. In the next paragraphs I present only the rudiments of the market valuation of firms' shares in a static context.

We suppose that the risky part of aggregate income is the sum of firms' earnings. In particular, let j index the various firms and represent aggregate income as the sum of firms' incomes, say $\bar{y} = \sum_j \bar{y}_j$. For the sake of simplicity assume that the vector $\bar{\eta} = (\bar{y}_1, \bar{y}_2, \ldots)$ of firms' incomes has a joint distribution that is normal with mean vector $\mathbf{m}$ and variance matrix $\mathbf{V}$; also, assume that each individual i has a constant risk tolerance r_i. We have seen previously that in this case the aggregate income $\bar{y} = \bar{\eta}\mathbf{1}$ has a normal distribution with mean $\mathbf{m}\mathbf{1}$ and variance $\mathbf{1}'\mathbf{V}\mathbf{1}$, and that the aggregate risk charge is $\mathbf{1}'\mathbf{V}\mathbf{1}/2r$ when risk is shared efficiently according to a linear sharing rule of the form $s_i(\bar{y}) = b_i + (r_i/r)[\bar{y} - b]$, where $b = \sum_i b_i$ and $r = \sum_i r_i$.

Suppose now, however, that individuals obtain shares by means of purchases or sales of firms' shares in the stock market at competitively determined prices. In the simplest static model, we can omit consideration of individuals' budget constraints. Then each individual i chooses a portfolio $\mathbf{x}_i = (x_{ij})$ of shareholdings so as to maximize

$$\mathscr{E}U_i\left(\sum_j x_{ij}[\bar{y}_j - \pi_j] + \pi\bar{\mathbf{x}}_i\right) \tag{58}$$

given that π_j is the price of firm j's shares and $\bar{\mathbf{x}}_i$ is i's initial endowment of shares. The equivalent certain income if i chooses $\mathbf{x}_i$ is

$$Y_i(\mathbf{x}_i) = [\mathbf{m} - \pi]\mathbf{x}_i - \frac{1}{2r_i}\mathbf{x}'_i\mathbf{V}\mathbf{x}_i + \pi\bar{\mathbf{x}}_i \tag{59}$$

Consequently the optimal portfolio, achieving the unconstrained maximum of equation (59), satisfies $\mathbf{m} - \pi - (1/r_i)\mathbf{V}\mathbf{x}_i = 0$. Since the vector π of equilibrium market prices is determined by the condition that aggregate demands for shares equal supplies, namely $\sum_i \mathbf{x}_i = \sum_i \bar{\mathbf{x}}_i = \mathbf{1}$, it follows that

$$\pi = \mathbf{m} - (1/r)\mathbf{V}\mathbf{1} \tag{60}$$

If the covariance matrix V is nonsingular, then in equilibrium an individual i holds the portfolio $\mathbf{x}_i = (r_i/r)\mathbf{1}$. This indicates that the resulting sharing rule, namely,

$$
\begin{aligned}
s_i(\bar{y}) &= [\tilde{\boldsymbol{\eta}} - \boldsymbol{\pi}]'\mathbf{x}_i + \boldsymbol{\pi}'\bar{\mathbf{x}}_i \\
&= b_i + (r_i/r)[\bar{y} - b]
\end{aligned}
\tag{61}
$$

where $b_i = \boldsymbol{\pi}'(\bar{\mathbf{x}}_i - \mathbf{x}_i)$ and $b = 0$, is efficient. Also, it evidences the stronger property in this special example that each individual holds the same share of each firm and could do as well to own a share of a diversified mutual fund.

Returning to the valuation equation (60), we see that in the aggregate the firms are valued at the price given by

$$
\mathbf{1}'\boldsymbol{\pi} = \mathbf{1}'\mathbf{m} - (1/r)\mathbf{1}'\mathbf{V}\mathbf{1}
\tag{62}
$$

Again this differs from the equivalent certain income by the amount of consumers' surplus, which is $(1/2r)\mathbf{1}'\mathbf{V}\mathbf{1}$. For a particular firm j the price is

$$
\begin{aligned}
\pi_j &= m_j - (1/r)\sum_k v_{jk} \\
&= m_j - (1/r)\operatorname{cov}\{\bar{y}_j, \bar{y}\}
\end{aligned}
\tag{63}
$$

where $v_{jk} = \operatorname{cov}\{\bar{y}_j, \bar{y}_k\}$ and $v_{jj} = \sigma_j^2$ is the variance of $\bar{y}_j$. This price differs from the increment to the equivalent certain income due to firm j. In particular,

$$
\Delta(\bar{y}) - \Delta(\bar{y} - \bar{y}_j) = (1/2r)\sigma_j^2 + (1/r)\sum_{k \neq j} v_{jk}
\tag{64}
$$

whereas the corresponding incremental risk charge in equation (63) differs from this amount by the term $(1/2r)\sigma_j^2$ due to the consumers' surplus. It is possible, for instance, for the market price in equation (63) to be negative, which one might naively interpret as an indication that firm j is a liability, while at the same time equation (64) is positive, indicating that it is an asset. The key role of consumers' surplus is due, of course, to the fact that for risky firms the demand function for shares is negatively sloped; that is, $\sum_i \mathbf{x}_i = r\mathbf{V}^{-1}[\mathbf{m} - \boldsymbol{\pi}]$.

The thrust of the foregoing statements is that in both the market valuation equation (63) and equation (64) for the incremental equivalent certain income, an identical portion of the risk charge is a levy against a firm (or an analogous public project) because of its correlation with other sources of aggregate income.

The preceding equations are complicated slightly if individuals differ in their probability assessments. If each individual i assesses a mean vector $\mathbf{m}_i$ and a variance matrix $\mathbf{V}_i$, then in the various equations (60), (64), and so forth, one uses

$$\mathbf{m} = \sum_i (r_i/r)\mathbf{V}\mathbf{V}_i^{-1}\mathbf{m}_i \quad \text{and}$$

$$\mathbf{V} = (\sum_i (r_i/r)\mathbf{V}_i^{-1})^{-1} \tag{65}$$

Other sources of uninsurable income, transfers, and taxes can be included in the formulation in a straightforward way. Assume that individual i obtains, after personal income taxes assessed at a rate $1 - \lambda_i$, a risky and uninsurable income of $\lambda_i z_i$ plus, for each firm j in which he holds x_{ij} shares, a share $\lambda_i x_{ij} \lambda \bar{y}_j$ of j's income after corporate taxes assessed at a rate $1 - \lambda$. If each individual i has constant risk tolerance r_i and $[(\bar{z}_i), (\bar{y}_i)]$ has a joint normal distribution, then one verifies as before that the equilibrium price of firm j is the analogue of equation (63), namely,

$$\pi_j = \mathscr{E}\{\lambda \bar{y}_j\} - (1/r) \, \text{cov} \, \{\lambda \bar{y}_j, \bar{Z}\} \tag{63*}$$

where $r = \sum_i r_i/\lambda_i$ and $\bar{Z} = \sum_i \bar{z}_i + \lambda \sum_j \bar{y}_j$. It is important to note here that the aggregate national income Z is, in principle, independent of the personal and corporate rates of taxation since government revenues from taxes are redistributed as transfers included in the individuals' incomes $(\bar{z}_i)$. Thus the aggregate national income and the aggregate risk tolerance r can both be interpreted as before taxes. A significant difference, however, is that an individual does not hold the same share of every firm, because of the effects of correlations between his uninsurable income z_i and the incomes of the various firms. Of course this analysis of other sources of income and of taxes could equally well have been done in the previous discussion of aggregate risk measurement, with comparable results except for the consumers' surplus term.

Before concluding this discussion of market allocation of risk, it is worthwhile to draw some summary conclusions about the often-mentioned distinction between risks that are diversifiable and those that are not. In principle, any risk is diversifiable in the sense that variation can be shared among many individuals so as to lessen its impact. We have seen, however, that the gains from sharing any one risk depend sensitively on its correlation with national income. Risks that are independent of national income (and each other) can be shared to great advantage through the familiar and effective institution of insurance or indirectly through capital markets. Variations in national income, however, pose a social risk that is not insurable (in the narrow sense) and at best can be shared only by means of capital markets, taxation, and the choice of public (and private) projects. In the case of public projects, there are substantial gains to be obtained from projects that are negatively correlated with other sources of national income; that is, projects that tend to pay off in adverse circumstances. For example, if national income depends significantly on the cost and supply of energy sources, then a risk analysis may attach a premium value to the development of alternative technologies and energy sources that yield benefits only in the adverse circumstances of high costs or short supplies of conventional energy sources. One can envision, for instance, that a premium value would be assigned to the exploration for oil reserves in the frontier areas of the outer continental shelf, such as the Gulf of Alaska, and to the development of technologies for coal liquefaction, solar energy conversion, and nuclear reactors based on fusion or breeding. The other side of the coin, of course, is that public as well as private projects that depend upon ample low-cost sources of energy incur a significant charge for risk.

In the three previous sections, I have surveyed the main ideas of risk analysis in a static context. The simple equations I have emphasized in the presentation are not directly useful in practice because they omit consideration of the basic features of intertemporal allocation. In any investment project, time is an essential ingredient. In the following discussion of dynamic risk measurement, I address the intertemporal aspects of risk analysis.

Dynamic Risk Measurement

In measuring the risk of an investment project, the principal difficulty in practice is to assess the dynamic effects of intertemporal allocation when the stream of income is risky. This is the "joint time/risk problem," which has central importance in practical analyses of investment decisions, although it is often ignored in theoretical expositions. It is omitted in the theory because it is immaterial when there are complete markets for contingent futures contracts. In practice, however, such markets do not exist. For most individuals the available financial markets for intertemporal contracts are severely restricted, consisting mainly of the bond markets including the assets of financial intermediaries such as money market funds and the stock market.

The limitation of markets has pronounced effects on the measurement of risk when its dynamic aspects are considered. Individuals unable to secure complete insurance, in the absence of complete markets, must rely on bonds and stocks as a means of indirect insurance to hedge against future uncertainties. Such hedging is invariably inefficient when viewed retrospectively since it is a compromise among the plans that are optimal for the various possible contingencies. In measuring dynamic risk, therefore, it is crucially important to examine in fine detail the way in which uncertainty is resolved over time.

A project in which uncertainty is eliminated early allows less hedging and the design of an intertemporal plan that is better suited to actual circumstances. Of course, a project with a long-delayed resolution of uncertainty requires hedging practices, which are expensive. Thus, one can expect that the risk charge is less for projects where the uncertainty is resolved more quickly. The risk charge is also sensitive to the availability of market opportunities. The greater the diversity of contracts available, the more efficiently the hedging can be done.

Throughout this discussion of dynamic risk measurement, I assume that an individual's uninsurable income consists solely of his share of national income and that the available market instruments are bonds and stocks. This is in addition to the prevalent sharing of social risks through taxation. I do not consider taxation separately here since the analysis is similar to the one I presented earlier in the discussion of risk measurement in the static case.

In the following section, I consider dynamic risk measurement for a single individual. The task of risk measurement is to identify the present certain wealth that an individual would accept in lieu of a risky stream of benefits. Two main examples are pursued. One is a model of risk-adjusted discount rates, whereas the other leads to the subtraction of a separate risk charge, which depends on the riskless interest rate and the pattern of intertemporal correlations of benefits. The second example is used to illustrate the value of resolving uncertainty early by means of an exogenous acquisition of information. Many of the arguments for research on alternative technologies in the energy sector can be studied in this way.

The results of the examination of aggregate risk measurement in a dynamic context closely parallel those obtained in the static case. Again efficient risk sharing permits a derivation of the aggregate risk charge in terms of aggregate quantities.

The discussion of market allocation of risk is a brief exploration of the implications of the preceding results for the theory of market prices as a stochastic process. It is shown that the random-walk hypothesis of stock prices can be explained as following from the sequential resolution of uncertainty as time progresses.

Individual Risk Measurement in a Dynamic Context

In this section, I will assume simply that an individual has a given risky stream of income denoted by the random vector $\bar{\mathbf{y}} = (\bar{y}_0, \bar{y}_1, \ldots, \bar{y}_T)$, where T is a horizon or lifetime known with certainty. Time is indexed by $t = 0, 1, \ldots, T$. At date t the individual knows the realized income stream

$'\mathbf{y} = (y_0, \ldots, y_t)$ up to that time but he remains uncertain about the remainder, which is denoted by $\bar{\mathbf{y}}^t = (\bar{y}_{t+1}, \ldots, \bar{y}_T)$.

Note that the joint probability distribution of $\mathbf{y}$ induces a conditional probability distribution on $\bar{\mathbf{y}}^t$ given $'\bar{\mathbf{y}}$. For instance, if $\bar{\mathbf{y}}$ has a normal distribution with mean vector $\mathbf{m}$ and variance matrix $\mathbf{V}$, and $\mathbf{m}$ and the precision matrix $\mathbf{H} = \mathbf{V}^{-1}$ are partitioned conformably as

$$\mathbf{m} = ('\mathbf{m}, \mathbf{m}'), \mathbf{H} = \begin{bmatrix} {}''\mathbf{H} & ('\mathbf{H}')' \\ {}'\mathbf{H}' & \mathbf{H}'' \end{bmatrix} \tag{66}$$

then $\bar{\mathbf{y}}^t$ has a conditional distribution given $'\mathbf{y}$, which is normal with precision matrix $\mathbf{H}''$ and mean vector

$$\mathbf{m}' - (\mathbf{H}'')^{-1}('\mathbf{H}')['\mathbf{y} - '\mathbf{m}] \tag{67}$$

This formula suffices for all the examples in this discussion of individual risk measurement since I will consider only income streams that have a normal or lognormal distribution. The conditional means and variances are generally denoted by $\mathscr{E}\{\cdot \mid '\mathbf{y}\}$ and $V\{\cdot \mid '\mathbf{y}\}$, although in the case of a normal distribution $\mathbf{V}^t \equiv V\{\bar{\mathbf{y}}^t \mid '\mathbf{y}\}$ is independent of the realized value of $'\mathbf{y}$.

In this section, I consider two extreme cases of restricted intertemporal markets. In the first case an individual's option to save or to borrow against future income is confined to buying or selling shares in a diversified mutual fund. In the second case the option is to buy or sell riskless bonds. In both cases I simplify matters by assuming that an individual's utility is additively separable over time, and I use representative utility functions and probability distributions that produce easy equations.

In the first example an individual's option is to trade shares of the aggregate income. Assume that the individual's utility for consumption income has the additively separable form $U(\mathbf{x}) = \sum_{t=0}^{T} \alpha_t U_t(x_t - b_t)$, in which $\mathbf{x} = (x_0, \ldots, x_T)$, x_t is the income allocated for consumption in period t, and $\alpha_t > 0$. I will assume in particular that $U_t(x_t - b_t) = (c/c - 1) \times (x_t - b_t)^{1-1/c}$, where $c = 1$ corresponds to the logarithmic utility and b_t signifies a subsistence level of consumption income. We know from the analysis of static risk measurement that if each individual has such a utility, then every efficient allocation provides each individual his subsistence income plus a share of the aggregate excess. It may be that bond markets are used to provide subsistence income, but I will ignore this possibility here and simply assume that subsistence is provided; hence, it will suffice here to assume that $b_t = 0$ in each period and that the risky disposable income $\bar{y}_t$ in each period is a fraction of aggregate income. In particular, I will assume for simplicity that the aggregate risky income stream has a lognormal distribution so that also an individual's risky income stream $\bar{y}$ has a lognormal distribution.

It is easiest to address a two-period illustration in which $T = 1$. At date 0 the individual will know his present disposable income y_0 and will assign his risky disposable future income $\bar{y}_1$ a lognormal distribution having $\mathcal{E}\{\ln \bar{y}_1 \mid \ln y_0\} \equiv m = m_1 + \rho_{01}(\sigma_1/\sigma_0)(\ln y_0 - m_0)$ and $V\{\ln \bar{y}_1 \mid \ln y_0\} \equiv \sigma^2 = \sigma_1^2(1 - \rho_{01}^2)$. Also, let π_0 be the market price at date 0 of the individual's initially endowed share of the mutual fund providing aggregate income. The individual's intertemporal problem, therefore, is to choose the fraction q_1 of his shareholding to retain until date 1 so as to maximize his conditional expected utility

$$\alpha_0 \frac{c}{c-1}(y_0 + \pi_0[1 - q_1])^{1 - 1/c} + \alpha_1 \frac{c}{c-1}\mathcal{E}\{(q_1\bar{y}_1)^{1 - 1/c}|y_0\} \qquad (68)$$

From the previous discussion of static risk measurement we know that the equivalent certain income at date 1 is $q_1\delta_1\bar{y}_1$, where $\bar{y}_1 = e^{m + \sigma^2/2}$ is the conditional mean of $\bar{y}_1$ and $\delta_1 = e^{-\sigma^2/2c}$ is the conditional discount factor for risk. Hence, one finds that the optimal choice is

$$q_1 = \frac{1 + y_0/\pi_0}{1 + \left(\dfrac{\alpha_0}{\alpha_1}\right)^c \left(\dfrac{\delta_1\bar{y}_1}{\pi_0}\right)^{1-c}} \qquad (69)$$

and with this choice the conditional expected utility in expression (68) is

$$\left[\alpha_0 + \alpha_1 \left(\frac{\delta_1\bar{y}_1}{\pi_0}\right)^{c-1}\right] \frac{c}{c-1}(y_0 + \pi_0)^{1 - 1/c} (\gamma)^{1 - 1/c} \qquad (70)$$

where $\gamma = a/(1 + a)$ for $a = (\alpha_0/\alpha_1)^c (\delta_1\bar{y}_1/\pi_0)^{1-c}$; or if $c = 1$

$$[\alpha_0 + \alpha_1] \ln (y_0 + \pi_0) + \alpha_1 \ln (\delta_1\bar{y}_1) \qquad (71)$$

apart from an irrelevant constant term.

This result has an interesting interpretation that is worth emphasizing. Suppose that we were to define an implicit riskless rate of interest in terms of an intertemporal discount factor β satisfying $\pi_0 = \beta\delta_1\bar{y}_1$. Or, we might say that $\hat{\beta} = \beta\delta_1$ is the discount factor corresponding to the interest rate appropriate for risky income. Now if the individual were to ignore risk except to the extent that he uses the "risky" interest rate in valuing his wealth, then the individual would choose incomes x_0 and x_1 for consumption in the two periods so as to maximize the certain utility

$$\alpha_0 \frac{c}{c-1} x_0^{1-1/c} + \alpha_1 \frac{c}{c-1} x_1^{1-1/c} \tag{72}$$

subject to the wealth constraint

$$x_0 + \beta x_1 = y_0 + \hat{\beta}\bar{y}_1 \tag{73}$$

The observation to be made is that this would result in exactly the same choice of a consumption plan, namely, $x_0 = \gamma[y_0 + \hat{\beta}\bar{y}_1]$, where $\gamma = \alpha_0^c/(\alpha_0^c + \beta^{1-c}\alpha_1^c)$, and yield the same (expected) utility as before. We can say, therefore, that the quantity $y_0 + \hat{\beta}\bar{y}_1$ is a conditional equivalent certain wealth at date 0 given y_0.

It should be evident that similar results obtain in a variety of models in which the risk charge can be calculated as a percentage of the mean. For instance, with the same utilities and a conditional distribution of y_1 given y_0, which is gamma distributed, the same equations apply except that the risk discount δ_1 is calculated using equation (19). (Note, however, that if exponential utilities and a gamma distribution are used, then in equation (18) one must allow for the fact that the risk discount depends upon the choice of q_1.)

In the next example, I focus mainly on the *unconditional* measure of equivalent certain wealth. This is defined to be that certain income Y at date 0 such that the individual is indifferent between the certain income stream $(Y,0,0,\ldots,0)$ and the actual risky stream $\bar{y}$. Note that Y is not conditioned on knowledge of y_0. It is important to realize that the determination of the equivalent certain wealth depends upon the opportunities for market transactions available to the individual for intertemporal reallocations of his stream of disposable income.

I assume now that saving and borrowing opportunities are restricted to the buying or selling of riskless bonds. Because I also assume exponential utilities and normal distributions, the omission of stock market trading can be explained by the result obtained in our discussion of aggregate risk measurement in a static context; that is, in this case it is efficient for each individual to hold in each firm a share that is proportional to his risk tolerance. Thus, we can assume that earnings on shareholdings are included in the individual's risky income and his portfolio at each date is known with certainty beforehand. I will examine this problem in more detail in the following discussion of aggregate risk measurement. Saving and borrowing are both represented by the same interest rate, which is assumed to be known initially with certainty. I use β_t to represent the price at date $t - 1$ of a riskless bond paying \$1 at date t, and I use β^t to represent the price at date 0 of the same bond. Of course $\beta^t = \prod_{\tau=1}^{t} \beta_\tau$, and $\beta^0 = 1$. (I do not treat here the effects of taxation explicitly. Rather I assume that each individual evaluates all incomes and prices on an after-tax basis. In particular, therefore, the bond prices are supposed to be calculated on the basis of interest rates net of income taxes and inflation, if any.)

In this context the risk charge $\Delta(y)$ can be expressed as the difference

$$\Delta(y) = \sum_{t=0}^{T} \beta^t m_t - Y \tag{74}$$

between the present value of the mean income stream and the equivalent certain wealth. Of course, this equation for the risk charge is applicable only in this context in which there are markets for riskless bonds.

The individual's utility for consumption income will be represented in the form

$$U(\mathbf{x}) = \sum_{t=0}^{T} \beta^t U_t(x_t), \ U_t(x_t) = -r_t e^{-[\alpha_t + x_t]/r_t} \tag{75}$$

reflecting a constant risk tolerance at each date. I include the bond prices β^t in the utility function so that an individual's intertemporal preferences α_t need to be accounted for only to the extent that they differ from the corresponding market rates; also, this unconventional practice yields simpler equations. The risky income stream $\tilde{y}$ is assumed to have a normal distribution as described earlier.

In this example my ultimate aim is to derive recursive equations for the risk charge for any number of periods $T \geq 1$. It is again easiest, however, to begin with the two-period case in which $T = 1$.

At date 0 the individual knows y_0 and assesses a conditional distribution for $\tilde{y}_1$ given y_0, which is normal with mean $m = m_1 + \rho_{01}(\sigma_1/\sigma_0)(y_0 - m_0)$ and variance $\sigma^2 = \sigma_1^2(1 - \rho_{01}^2)$, where $\rho_{01} = v_{01}/\sigma_0\sigma_1$ is the correlation between $\tilde{y}_0$ and $\tilde{y}_1$. If the individual were to buy an amount b_1 of bonds payable at date 1, then the equivalent certain income at date 1 would be $m + b_1 - \sigma^2/2r_1$ since the bonds are riskless. Consequently, in deciding at date 0 on the amount of bonds to buy, the individual will choose b_1 to maximize the utility

$$\sim \quad -\beta^0 r_0 e^{-[\alpha_0 + y_0 - \beta_1 b_1]/r_0} - \beta^1 r_1 e^{-[\alpha_1 + m + b_1 - \sigma^2/2r_1]/r_1} \tag{76}$$

Thus, the individual chooses

$$\beta_1 b_1 = \left[\frac{1}{r_0}(\alpha_0 + y_0) - \frac{1}{r_1}(\alpha_1 + m - \sigma^2/2r_1) \right]/[1/r_0 + 1/\beta_1 r_1] \tag{77}$$

and the expected utility is given by

$$\overline{U}(\tilde{y}|y_0) = -\beta^0 r^0 e^{-[\alpha^0 + \hat{y}^0]/r^0} \tag{78}$$

as the value of expression (76), where

$$\begin{aligned} r^0 &= r_0 + \beta_1 r_1 \\ \alpha^0 &= \alpha_0 + \beta_1 \alpha_1 \\ \text{and } \hat{y}^0 &= y_0 + \beta_1 (m - \sigma^2/2r_1) \end{aligned} \tag{79}$$

Before $\bar{y}_0$ is known, moreover, the expected utility is

$$\overline{U}(\tilde{y}) = -\beta^0 r^0 \exp\left(-\frac{[\alpha^0 + \mathscr{E}\{\tilde{\hat{y}}^0\} - V\{\tilde{\hat{y}}^0\}/2r^0]}{r^0} \right) \tag{80}$$

since evidently in equation (78) the conditional expected utility is exponential with constant risk tolerance r^0, and $\tilde{\hat{y}}^0$ has a normal distribution with mean

$$\mathscr{E}\{\tilde{\hat{y}}^0\} = m_0 + \beta_1[m_1 - \sigma^2/2r_1] \tag{81}$$

and variance

$$\begin{aligned} V\{\tilde{\hat{y}}^0\} &= \sigma_0^2[1 + \beta^1 \rho_{01}\sigma_1/\sigma_0]^2 \\ &= [\beta^0, \beta^1 \rho_{01}] \begin{bmatrix} \sigma_0^2 & \sigma_0\sigma_1 \\ \sigma_0\sigma_1 & \sigma_1^2 \end{bmatrix} \begin{bmatrix} \beta^0 \\ \beta^1\rho_{01} \end{bmatrix} \end{aligned} \tag{82}$$

Of course, if the income stream $(Y, 0)$ is certain, then the same equations apply with the mean being Y and the variance being zero. Consequently, we see from equation (80) that the equivalent certain wealth is

$$Y = \mathscr{E}\{\tilde{\hat{y}}^0\} - V\{\tilde{\hat{y}}^0\}/2r^0 \tag{83}$$

and therefore the risk charge is

$$\Delta(\tilde{\mathbf{y}}) = V\{\tilde{y}^0\}/2r^0 + \beta_1 V\{\tilde{y}_1|y_0\}/2r_1$$

$$= [\sigma_0^2 + 2\sigma_0(\beta^1\rho_{01}\sigma_1) + (\beta^1\rho_{01}\sigma_1)^2]/2r^0 \tag{84}$$

$$+ \beta^1[1 - \rho_{01}^2]\sigma_1^2/2r_1$$

It is instructive to observe in equation (84), which gives the risk charge, the specific effects of the fact that, in this situation, uncertainty is resolved sequentially. That is, first the realized value of $\tilde{y}_0$ is revealed at date 0 and then at date 1 the realized value of $\tilde{y}_1$ is revealed. The delayed resolution of the uncertainty about $\tilde{y}_1$ is expensive for the individual because it hampers his ability at date 0 to achieve the best (as viewed in retrospect from date 1) intertemporal allocation of his or her income for consumption. In particular, if the uncertainty about $\tilde{y}_1$ were resolved early at date 0 along with knowledge of y_0, then the risk charge would be only

$$V\{\tilde{y}_0 + \beta^1\tilde{y}_1\}/2r^0 = \frac{1}{2r^0}[1, \beta^1]\mathbf{V}\begin{bmatrix} 1 \\ \beta^1 \end{bmatrix} \tag{85}$$

The difference between the risk charges given by equations (84) and (85) is the cost of delayed resolution, or the value of early resolution, namely,

$$(\beta^1)^2(1 - \rho_{01}{}^2)\sigma_1{}^2[1/2\beta^1 r_1 - 1/2r^0] \tag{86}$$

For instance, if $\beta^1 = 1$, $\rho_{01} = 0$, $\sigma_t = \$100$ billion, and $r_t = n\bar{r} = (100$ million)($\$1,000) = \$100$ billion, as in the numerical illustration in the discussion of static risk measurement, then the value of early resolution is \$25 billion, which accounts for one-third of the risk charge.

The value of early resolution is an important factor in the evaluation of public projects aimed at collecting information. For example, the accelerated exploration of the outer continental shelf has a value in part because it provides earlier information about the stock of oil and gas reserves, thereby permitting better planning of the rate of depletion of fossil fuels and the rate of research on alternative technologies. Similarly, early information about the feasibility and relative costs of the various alternative technologies (fusion and breeder nuclear reactors, coal liquefaction, solar energy conversion, geothermal extraction, etc.), even though they may not be operable for several decades, permits better planning in the interim.

The preceding analysis for the two-period case with $T = 1$ is easily generalized to any number of periods by using a process of induction. At each date t define

$$\alpha^t = \sum_{\tau=t}^{T} \beta^\tau \alpha_\tau / \beta^t$$

$$= \alpha_t + \beta_{t+1}\alpha^{t+1}$$

$$r^t = \sum_{\tau=t}^{T} \beta^\tau r_\tau / \beta^t \qquad\qquad (87)$$

$$= r_t + \beta_{t+1}r^{t+1}$$

and $\tilde{y}^t = \tilde{y}_t + \beta_{t+1}Y_{t+1}({}^t\mathbf{y})$

where $Y_{t+1}({}^t\mathbf{y})$ is the conditional equivalent certain wealth corresponding to the risky income stream $\tilde{y}^t$. We know from the foregoing analysis that

$$Y_T({}^{T-1}\mathbf{y}) = \mathcal{E}\{\tilde{y}_T|^{T-1}\mathbf{y}\} - \Delta_T(\tilde{y}_T|^{T-1}\mathbf{y}) \qquad\qquad (88)$$

where $\Delta_T(\tilde{y}_T|^{T-1}\mathbf{y}) = V\{\tilde{y}_T|^{T-1}\mathbf{y}\}/2r_T$

is the risk charge in the last period; and, we have seen in equation (83) for $t = T - 1$ that

$$Y_t({}^{t-1}\mathbf{y}) = \mathcal{E}\{\tilde{y}^t|^{t-1}\mathbf{y}\} - \Delta_t(\tilde{y}^t|^{t-1}\mathbf{y}) \qquad\qquad (89)$$

where $\Delta_t(\tilde{y}^t|^{t-1}\mathbf{y}) = V\{\tilde{y}^t|^{t-1}\mathbf{y}\}/2r^t + \beta_{t+1}\Delta_{t+1}(\tilde{y}^{t+1}|^t\mathbf{y})$

yielding in equation (80) the conditional expected utility for periods $t, \ldots, T$

$$\overline{U}(\tilde{y}^{t-1}|^{t-1}\mathbf{y}) = -\beta^t r^t e^{-[\alpha^t + Y_t({}^{t-1}\mathbf{y})]/r^t} \qquad\qquad (90)$$

Observe in equation (90) that the form of the conditional expected utility for the future periods at each date is exactly the same as it is for any one period; also $Y_t({}^{t-1}\mathbf{y})$ is a linear function of ${}^{t-1}\mathbf{y}$ and therefore it also has a normal distribution calculated using expression (67). The preceding derivations therefore verify that the recursive equations (89) and (90) are valid at any date t. In particular, the (unconditional) values of Y_0 and Δ_0 are the equivalent certain wealth Y and the risk charge $\Delta(\tilde{y})$ for the entire risky stream $\tilde{y}$ evaluated at date 0 before information about y_0 is available.

Various models of the stochastic process generating the income stream lead to simple equations for the equivalent certain wealth and the risk charge, for instance, autoregressive and Bayesian learning models. Unfortunately, their exposition would take us far afield, so I omit them here.

Among the lessons to be learned from this construction are these two: (1) the risk charge depends sensitively upon the individual's market opportunities, particularly upon the interest rate in this case; and (2) the risk charge depends sensitively upon the sequential resolution of uncertainty, and can be reduced substantially if information arrives earlier to enable better-informed saving and borrowing decisions aimed at intertemporal reallocations of income for consumption.

In the following discussion of aggregate risk measurement, I will show that efficient risk sharing justifies the omission of stock market opportunities in the above analysis.

Aggregate Risk Measurement in a Dynamic Context

The discussion here will be rather brief. My main purpose is simply to show that the principles of aggregate risk measurement developed in a static context apply with little alteration in a dynamic context. Again the decisive consideration is the efficiency of the allocation of risk.

I omit detailed consideration of aggregation in the first example in the previous discussion of individual risk measurement. There, assuming $T = 1$ and using power-function or logarithmic utilities and lognormal or gamma conditional probability distributions, we found that each individual i had a conditional equivalent certain wealth $y_{i0} + \hat{\beta}\tilde{y}_{i1}$ computed using a "risky" discount factor $\hat{\beta} = \beta\delta_1$ compounded from the riskless discount factor β and the discount factor δ_1 for risk. If individual i's risky income in excess of subsistence at date t is a fraction s_{it} of the aggregate excess, that is, if $\tilde{y}_{it} = s_{it}\tilde{y}_t$, then clearly the aggregate conditional equivalent certain wealth is $y_0 + \hat{\beta}\tilde{y}_1$. We see again that in this case, the same discount factor applies in the aggregate. Consequently, as before there are no gains to be obtained from risk sharing. I omit the demonstration that all efficient sharing rules assign to each individual his subsistence income plus a fractional share of the aggregate excess.

Let us turn now to the second example with exponential utilities and normal distributions. It will suffice to illustrate the matter by considering only the two-period case in which $T = 1$. To begin, suppose for simplicity that each individual i obtains at each date t a risky disposable income $\tilde{y}_{it}$, which is a linear function of the aggregate risky income $\tilde{y}_t$, say

$$\tilde{y}_{it} = c_{it} + s_{it}[\tilde{y}_t - c_t] \tag{91}$$

where $c_t = \sum_i c_{it}$ and $\sum_i s_{it} = 1$. Of course, each individual will use the bond market to reallocate this income stream through saving or borrowing; in particular, we have seen in equation (77) that at date 0, knowing y_0, individual i will purchase an amount

$$\beta_1 b_{i1} = [\frac{1}{r_{i0}}(\alpha_{i0} + y_{i0}) \tag{92}$$

$$- \frac{1}{r_{i1}}(\alpha_{i1} + m_i - \sigma_i^2/2r_{i1})]/[1/r_{i0} + 1/\beta_1 r_{i1}]$$

of bonds, where m_i and σ_i^2 are the conditional mean and variance of $\tilde{y}_{i1}$. Assume that the aggregate revenue $\beta_1 b_1$ from these bonds is invested in riskless enterprises that return an amount $b_1 = \sum_i b_{i1}$ of aggregate income at date 1. We see immediately from equation (92) that one consequence of uncertainty about the risky income $\tilde{y}_1$ at date 1 is to increase the demand for investment in riskless firms by an amount

$$\beta_1 \sum_i \frac{r_{i0} s_{i1}^2}{r_i^0 r_{i1}} \sigma^2/2 \tag{93}$$

where σ^2 is the conditional variance of $\tilde{y}_1$ and $r_i^0 = r_{i0} + \beta_1 r_{i1}$. It should be observed that individual i's reallocation of his income stream from (y_{i0}, y_{i1}) to $(y_{i0} - \beta_1 b_{i1}, y_{i1} + b_{i1})$ still results in a linear sharing rule for allocating the aggregate income stream $(y_0 - \beta_1 b_1, y_1 + b_1)$; consequently, a linear rule of the form of equation (91) is descriptive of the risk allocation both before and after an accounting for market transactions and investments in riskless firms, although the coefficients may vary in the two cases.

The equations (83) and (84) can be used to evaluate the equivalent certain wealth Y_i and the risk charge Δ_i from the sharing rule given by equation (91). Summing these, the aggregate equivalent certain wealth is

$$Y \equiv \sum_i Y_i \tag{94}$$

$$= m_0 + \beta_1 m_1 - \Delta$$

where the aggregate risk charge Δ is

$$\Delta \equiv \sum_i \Delta_i$$

$$= \sum_i [s_{i0}^2 \sigma_0^2 + 2 s_{i0} \sigma_0 (\beta_1 \rho_{01} s_{i1} \sigma_1) + 2(\beta_1 \rho_{01} s_{i1} \sigma_1)^2/r_i^0] \tag{95}$$

$$+ \beta_1 [1 - \rho_{01}^2] \sigma_1^2 \sum_i s_{i1}^2/2 r_{i1}$$

assuming that y_t has mean m_t and variance σ_t^2 and ρ_{01} is the correlation between y_0 and y_1.

I will not demonstrate here that every efficient sharing rule is linear as in equation (91), but taking this as given, we can derive the efficient sharing proportions (s_{it}) by minimizing the aggregate risk charge Δ in equation (95) subject to the two constraints that $\sum_i s_{it} = 1$ for $t = 0$ and 1. This yields the efficient sharing proportions

$$s_{i0} = r_i^0/r^0 + (\beta_1\rho_{01}\sigma_1/\sigma_0)[r_i^0/r^0 - r_{i1}/r_1] \quad , \quad \text{and}$$
$$s_{i1} = r_{i1}/r_1 \tag{96}$$

at the two dates. Thus, sharing is in proportion to risk tolerance at the last date and at first if the two incomes are independent. But if they are correlated, then an individual i obtains a greater share at date 0 in proportion to the correlation and in proportion to his greater risk tolerance r_i^0 over the two-period span.

With this efficient sharing rule the minimum aggregate risk charge takes the simple form

$$\Delta = (\sigma_0 + \beta_1\rho_{01}\sigma_1)^2/2r^0 + \beta_1(1 - \rho_{01}^2)\sigma_1^2/2r_1 \tag{97}$$

Note that in this equation the case $\rho_{01} = 1$ corresponds to the risk charge when there is early resolution of the uncertainty about y_1. In the general case for an arbitrary $T \geq 1$, one can use the apparent inductive generalization of equation (97), which is the recursive equation

$$\Delta_0 = \left(\sum_{t=0}^{T} \beta^t\rho_{0t}\sigma_t\right)^2 /2r^0 + \beta_1\Delta_1 \tag{98}$$

for the risk charge. Here, ρ_{0t} is the correlation between y_0 and y_t and Δ_1 is the risk charge from date 1 forward. This charge is computed using the analogous equation involving Δ_2. Note that in computing Δ_1, one must use the conditional variance matrix given y_0 as in expression (67).

The preceding equations can easily be generalized in another direction. Suppose that income at date t has the form $\bar{y}_t = \sum_{\tau \leq t} \tilde{\eta}_{\tau t}$, in which the component $\tilde{\eta}_{\tau t}$ becomes known at date τ. Thus, at date t the information that is acquired is the whole vector of components $(\tilde{\eta}_{t\tau})_{\tau \geq t}$. In this case it is easily seen that the "revealed income" at date t is the present value

$$y_t^* = \sum_{\tau \geq t} \beta^\tau\eta_{t\tau}/\beta^t$$

Therefore, one can apply the preceding equations in an analogous way to the risky income stream $\bar{y}^*$.

A key feature of the above equations is that the efficient sharing proportions are predetermined independently of the sequence of realized incomes. This justifies the omission of stock market opportunities, since an individual's portfolio can be assumed to be included in the specification of his or her risky income. This is one instance in which the omission is unjustified. If there are no riskless investments possible, then the bond purchases and sales must net zero $\left(\sum_i b_{i1} = 0 \right)$ to determine the bond price β_1. But this makes the bond price a function of y_0, contrary to our assumption, and it induces sharing proportions that are not independent of income.[2]

In measuring the increment in the aggregate risk charge due to a specific project one must take into account not only its own intertemporal correlations but also its sequential correlations with the other sources of risky income. I omit presentation of the complicated equations that ensue in such an analysis since I think the method is evident, as in equation (50).

Market Allocation of Risk in a Dynamic Context

My discussion of the allocation of risk by means of stock markets will be quite brief.[3] The main principles carry over nearly intact from the static case. The key observation to be made is again that the market prices of firms' shares undervalue the equivalent certain wealth by a term equal to the consumers' surplus (which in turn is equal to the risk charge).

I confine attention to the case in which utilities are additively separable exponentials and probability distributions are normal. It is clear that in the absence of disagreement among individuals' probability assessments, each individual will in each period hold the same share of every risky firm, or a share of a diversified mutual fund, so as to obtain the efficient shares (s_{it}) of the aggregate risky income stream that we calculated previously in the discussion of aggregate risk measurement. Moreover, these shares are independent of the sequential realizations of the income stream. It suffices, therefore, to consider only the instance of a single risky firm (that is, the mutual fund) that produces the aggregate risky income.

The same algebraic factors that affected the computations in the section on market allocation of risk in a static context, again cause the price of a share to differ from the equivalent certain wealth by the risk charge calculated in the discussion of aggregate risk measurement. The price of a unit share at date 0 (before y_0 is revealed) is therefore

$$\pi_0 = \sum_{t=0}^{T} \beta^t m_t - 2\Delta_0 \qquad (99)$$

[2] It is impossible to sum equation (77) to get $b_1 = 0$, but not if the risk tolerance is constant only locally, or there are decreasing returns to investments in riskless firms.

[3] Since the preparation of this paper, a more complete exposition has been published by Stapleton and Subrahmanyam (1978). See also the comment by Kreps and Wilson (1980).

where Δ_0 is calculated using equation (98). A basic observation to be derived from this equation is that it implies that the price of a share follows a stochastic process. That is, there is a similar equation for the share price π_t, at each date t, in which the risk charge Δ_t is certain and can be fully anticipated. However, the mean-present-value term $\sum_{\tau=t}^{T} (\beta^\tau/\beta^t)m_\tau({}^{t-1}\mathbf{y})$, which arises at date t, uses the *conditional* means $m_\tau({}^{t-1}\mathbf{y}) = \mathscr{E}\frac{\tilde{y}_\tau}{{}^{t-1}\mathbf{y}}$, which depend upon the history of realized incomes before that date. This stochastic process therefore follows the law

$$\pi_t({}^{t-1}\mathbf{y}) = m_t({}^{t-1}\mathbf{y}) + \beta_{t+1}\mathscr{E}\{\pi_{t+1}({}^t\tilde{\mathbf{y}})|{}^{t-1}\mathbf{y}\} \\ - 2[\Delta_t - \beta_{t+1}\Delta_{t+1}] \tag{100}$$

We are most familiar with the stochastic features of stock market prices, which are often emphasized in theories of capital markets. For the purpose of risk measurement in the evaluation of public projects, however, it is evident that in the above law it is the deterministic component depending on the sequence of risk charges which is of primary importance. For that purpose the stochastic law given by equation (100) is useful mainly as an econometric model to use in estimating the variance matrix for the risky income stream. With this information in hand, we can use the equation directly to find the risk charge derived in the discussion of aggregate risk measurement. For a newly proposed project, there is no easy recourse but to estimate directly its own-variance matrix (over time) and its pattern of sequential correlations with existing sources of income.

Uses of Market Data

The practical task of measuring the risk charge to be levied against a public project requires simplifying assumptions. The moderate scale of a project, for instance, may justify the omission of uncertainties about relative prices and future riskless real interest rates and justify the assumption of constant risk tolerances and normal distributions. It may also be justified to ignore the role of various peripheral markets, such as commodity futures contracts, options on stocks and foreign currencies, and inflation hedges (land, precious metals, depletable resources, and the like). In this case, one of the equations derived from the models described in the preceding discussions of static and dynamic risk measurement provides a rough estimate of the risk charge. Lacking these simplifying assumptions, one can replicate the method used in those foregoing discussions to produce more sophisticated estimates based on more elaborately detailed models.

In this section, I will concentrate on the simple model of dynamic risk measurement. We saw that insurance markets for diversifiable (that is, independent) individual risks are viable but the risk charge is so small as to be undetectable (compared with transaction costs, for example) in an econometric study. On the other hand, the "insurance" market for the poorly diversifiable risks in national income, namely the stock market for shares of firms' earnings, provides a potentially rich source of information about the key parameters needed for a project evaluation.

However, one must use stock market data with considerable caution. I cite here just a few of the difficulties. We have seen, for example, that a simple equation for the risk charge, such as equation (98), is easily destroyed by the alternative specification that utilities be logarithmic, in which case there need not be any gains from risk sharing. Another possibility is that incomplete markets for contingent futures contracts leave individuals with uninsurable risks that are correlated with national income and must be taken into account (for example, unemployment and weather affecting farm crops); indeed, there is likely a substantial portion of risky national income that is not included in the earnings of firms with publicly traded securities. Uncertainties about the future course of the riskless interest rate (in constant dollars) are inevitable, and moreover, few individuals both save and borrow at the riskless real rate. Individuals may have different probability assessments, as we have seen, which lead them to hold different portfolios rather than a mutual-fund share. More fundamentally, they may have different proprietary information, which would vitiate much of the analysis. The significance of these difficulties must ultimately be assessed on empirical grounds and cannot be decided here.

Putting these difficulties aside, the simplest equations depend fundamentally upon the supposition that the sharing of risk is efficient. This would imply that, at least locally, shares are at the margin in proportion to risk tolerance. Among the minority of individuals who invest directly in the stock market, this may indeed be a valid approximation, although I am not aware of any direct evidence on the matter. Arrow and Lind (1970), however, have offered an alternative argument that is applicable to the vast majority. We know, of course, that many individuals hold shares of firms indirectly through pension funds and the like. Moreover, a substantial part of an average individual's wealth is his entitlement in funds that are publicly managed, through Social Security and Medicare, for example, and these programs depend for their financing partly upon the government's power to tax firms' income. Similarly, the annual expenses for public goods are financed in part by the corporate income tax. One sees, therefore, that to the extent that business taxes reduce an individual's personal income taxes and pension contributions, he is a shareholder in each firm. This argument does not resolve the issue completely, of course, since the corporate income tax is only about 50 percent. Also, on the matter of efficiency, this argument depends upon the notion that individuals pay personal income taxes at marginal rates roughly in proportion to their risk tolerances. The analysis of a public project is further complicated by the fact that the argument ignores the incidence of benefits among individuals, supposing instead that those benefits that do not accrue directly to firms or to the government affect individuals in proportion to their risk tolerances after compensating market transactions.

The expedient way out of these difficulties is contained in the crude approximation asserting that individuals' risk tolerances are all roughly the same and that in the long run, all individuals share about equally. The robustness of this approximation can be measured by the difference between equation (95), which uses the actual incidence of benefits, and equation (97), which assumes the efficient incidence. Whereas some projects may require calculations of individuals' risk charges based on the actual incidence, presumably there are many projects for which the supposition of efficient incidence matters little.

I turn now to the uses of market data in estimating the key parameters required for a project evaluation based on equation (98) for the risk charge. However, the main points are illustrated well enough by the static case, so I will use equation (50) for the incremental risk charge due to a single project, and equation (62) for the stock market valuation of aggregate income for which shares are publicly traded. It will suffice to assume that there is an aggregate firm represented by a diversified mutual fund, or by a stock market price index, which is adjusted to be commensurable with the aggregate valuation of all firms.

According to equation (62), the market valuation of the aggregate income $\tilde{y}$ is $\pi = m_y - (1/r)\sigma_y^2$, where $\tilde{y}$ is normal with mean m_y and variance σ_y^2. This equation can be used directly to estimate the aggregate risk tolerance r and the standard deviation σ_y from market data, or one can use data for representative firms and employ equation (63). Another estimation technique is to suppose that the earnings of specific firms conform to a regression model

$$\tilde{y}_j = a_{j0} + \sum_k a_{jk} \tilde{I}_k + \tilde{\epsilon}_j \tag{101}$$

in which $\tilde{I}_k$ is any one of a number of aggregate indices of the economic environment indexed by k and $\tilde{\epsilon}_j$ is an independent normal variate. In this case, the aggregate income $\tilde{y} = \sum_j \tilde{y}_j$ conforms to a similar regression model, and the variance σ_y^2 can be obtained from the regression coefficients and auxiliary estimates of the variance matrix of the indices. In particular,

$$\hat{\sigma}_y^2 = V\{\bar{\epsilon}\} + \mathbf{a}'\hat{\mathbf{V}}\mathbf{a} \tag{102}$$

where $\hat{\mathbf{V}}$ is the variance matrix of the indices, $\mathbf{a} = (a_k)$, $a_k = \sum_j a_{jk}$, and $\bar{\epsilon} = \sum_j \bar{\epsilon}_j$. Given this estimate of σ_y^2, one can estimate the aggregate risk tolerance r by means of the valuation equation

$$\pi = a_0 + \mathbf{a}'\hat{\mathbf{m}} - (1/r)\hat{\sigma}_y^2 \tag{103}$$

where $\hat{\mathbf{m}}$ is the mean vector of the indices. If the entire procedure is imbedded in a single relation, say

$$\pi = a_0 + \mathbf{a}'\hat{\mathbf{m}} - (1/r)[V\{\bar{\epsilon}\} + \mathbf{a}'\hat{\mathbf{V}}\mathbf{a}] \tag{104}$$

then the estimation is evidently nonlinear.

The regression model is particularly well adapted to project evaluation if there is sufficient knowledge of the project's characteristics to develop an analogous estimate, say

$$\tilde{z} = b_0 + \sum_k b_k \tilde{I}_k + \bar{\epsilon}_z \tag{105}$$

of its benefits in terms of the indices. In this case

$$\sigma_z^2 = V\{\bar{\epsilon}_z\} + \mathbf{b}'\hat{\mathbf{V}}\mathbf{b} \tag{106}$$

and the required correlation ρ_{yz} satisfies

$$\begin{aligned}
\rho_{yz}\sigma_y\sigma_z &= \text{cov}\{\tilde{y}, \tilde{z}\} \\
&= \mathbf{a}'\hat{\mathbf{V}}\mathbf{b}
\end{aligned} \tag{107}$$

This yields the increment in the risk charge due to the project $\tilde{z}$ in the estimated form of equation (50):

$$\Delta(\tilde{y} + \tilde{z}) - \Delta(\tilde{y}) = \frac{1}{2r}[V\{\bar{\epsilon}_z\} + (2\mathbf{a} + \mathbf{b})'\hat{\mathbf{V}}\mathbf{b}] \tag{108}$$

Analogous estimates based upon regression models can be developed in the dynamic case. In this case, though, one needs projections of the intertemporal variance matrix of the indices, or their interperiod correlations, in order to use the equation (98) for the risk charge. Presumably it is safe to suppose that the aggregate risk tolerance is invariant over time.

Pitfalls of Risk Analysis

In this section, I list several of the practical difficulties encountered in risk analysis. These difficulties can, if ignored, easily erode the merits of a project evaluation. My list is not exhaustive by any means, but I hope it is at least indicative of the hazards in risk analysis.

Price Risks

As I mentioned in the discussion of dynamic risk measurement, in a general equilibrium model of a closed economy, the risks in aggregate income are mostly due to quantity variations stemming from changes in productivity, technology, and resource supplies. These variations are translated into variations in the relative prices facing individuals. In principle, small variations in quantities can be evaluated using base prices, but so far as I know, it has never been demonstrated that this procedure yields the same risk charge as one would get by summing the individuals' risk charges. One can analyze the dependence on prices in equations (3) or (5), but the results are invariably quite complicated.

The absence of complete markets at any one date results in the familiar fact that there is a sequence of markets that reopen daily. Foreknowledge of prices in subsequent markets is impossible to obtain, of course. This deficiency becomes acute when the resolution of uncertainty is likely to result in drastically altered prices. For example, if subsequent resolution of the uncertainty about future sources of energy is likely to result in drastic revisions of the relative prices of primary factors such as energy, labor, and capital goods, then any adequate analysis must address this feature directly and cannot rely solely on the simplified approach adopted here.

Risky Interest Rates

A familiar feature of capital markets is the prevalence of a range of interest rates and rates of return applied to risky securities. We have seen that the model with linear risk tolerance yields results compatible with this feature. Nevertheless, this feature arises only when there is a chance of income near the subsistence level at which the risk tolerance vanishes. Any other model with utility differentiable over the range of likely incomes must conform to the approximation given in equation (13), in which the risk charge is subtracted from the mean. This implies in a multiperiod model that the use of "risky" interest rates is likely to discount benefits too severely in later periods as compared with the risk charge given by equation (98).

Sequential Resolution of Uncertainty

In the discussion of dynamic risk measurement, I addressed directly the consequences of the sequential resolution of uncertainty. We saw that measuring the risk charge requires an explicit consideration of an individual's market opportunities because his choices at any date must be based upon incomplete information about his subsequent income stream. It is easy to ignore this consideration, but the consequence is usually a severe underestimate of the risk charge if one naively supposes that uncertainty resolves completely in an initial period. This happens, for example, if it is the risk in the present value of the income stream which is measured; compare equations (84), (85), and (86). Note too that the risk charge in equation (98) depends in a complex way on the interest rates, the risk tolerances, and the interperiod correlations of incomes.

Portfolio Effects

Under the rubric of portfolio effects, I include two considerations. The first is that an individual ordinarily suffers other sources of risk that are not insurable. When these are correlated with public projects, ignoring them will bias the estimate of the risk. In equation (75), for example, one could take α_t to be such a source of risk. It is easily seen that this affects the individual's market transactions in ways that rebound throughout the subsequent derivations, as for example in the bond purchases given by equation (77).

The second consideration concerns the portfolio of public projects. As we have seen, correlated projects must be considered in terms of the possible combinations of projects that might be adopted now and later. The complexity of the analysis escalates as one adds the further possibilities of varying the scales of the projects, delaying projects, or accelerating the resolution of uncertainty. Ultimately one is confronted with the problem of constructing an intertemporal sequential plan.

Calibration Error and Moral Hazard

Calibration error is among the many elementary errors of analysis. However they are assessed, by methods ranging from panels of experts to econometric studies, probabilities are themselves subject to uncertainty. This causes no difficulty with a single probability estimate, say $\bar{p}$, since in a simple calculation one can use $\hat{p} = \mathscr{E}\{\bar{p}\}$ as the assessed probability. The observation to be made, though, is that $\bar{p}^2$ and $\mathscr{E}\{\bar{p}^2\}$ are not the same. One cannot, therefore, routinely multiply mean assessments of probabilities. In general, one must employ sequential models based on the rules of conditional probability. For example, if one wants to obtain the probability of two events, say A followed by B, both assessed to have probability $\bar{p}$, one uses $\mathscr{E}\{\bar{p}^2\} = \mathscr{E}\{\bar{p}|A\}\mathscr{E}\{\bar{p}\}$, where the conditioning on the event A reflects the fact that the occurrence of A increases the likelihood that the mean assessment of the probability was too low. This feature is pervasive in any risk analysis relying on subjectively assessed probabilities, since nearly all probability estimators are uncertain about whether their judgments are sufficiently well calibrated that a proportion p of those events assessed to have probability p actually occur.

Evaluations of the risks in public projects are often afflicted with deficiencies due to the omission of moral hazards. Moral hazards arise whenever the adoption of a project affects individuals' incentives in undertaking related actions. Disaster insurance, for example, will in the absence of other controls weaken individuals' incentives to adopt defensive measures. Often the moral hazard is part of the reason for the failure of the private sector to undertake the project.

Strategic Risks

I mention only briefly that the risks inherent in the choices of others, say a foreign nation, are not susceptible to the mode of analysis used in this paper. To take only one extreme example, it is quite possible in a competitive situation for the value of earlier or better information to be negative, whereas this is clearly impossible in a cooperative context in which efficiency is achievable.

Conclusion: Applications to Public Policy

To conclude, I summarize here some of the implications of risk measurement for public policy.

The method of risk measurement is to determine the certain wealth that is equivalent to a risky stream of benefits. The measurement depends on the allocation of risk by means of taxation and markets; in particular, the measurement depends on the set of financial instruments available. The risk charge depends on the benefits' correlations intertemporally and with national income. These features are quite general. They imply several important lessons for the treatment of risk in analyses of public policies.

First, insurable risks, those not highly correlated with national income, can usually be handled by the private sector. Public projects of the same kind are analyzed in the same way, with little need for a significant risk charge unless subsistence levels of income are threatened.

Social risks are shared through taxation and market processes. It is important, therefore, that the joint effects of tax policy and market forces be considered. It is critical to recognize that taxation has this role and to incorporate its effects into the analysis of risk.

The efficiency of risk sharing affects the magnitude of the risk charge. In some cases the primary consideration may be how to share the risk more efficiently. This is the main motive for the formation of syndicates, consortia, and the like, to pursue private projects afflicted with great risks. The process can be aided by public policy, perhaps through direct participation by the government (for example, the Communications Satellite Corporation).

Efforts to improve the market allocation of risk may have large benefits. In some cases the private risk of bankruptcy is not a social risk and it intervenes unfavorably in the market. It is likely, for instance, that this accounts for the inability of small firms to bid competitively for exploration and development leases on the outer continental shelf or for smaller, less-diversified firms to participate in the development of new energy technologies.

There is a substantial social value to the early resolution of uncertainty. In practical terms this value is manifested in better planning of stocks of depletable resources, such as gas, oil, shale, and uranium, and of investments adapted to future technology (electric generating plants). The social value of early information is, however, often not fully appropriable in the form of profits for private enterprises. In such cases government intervention may be desirable to fund the acquisition of timely information or to pursue programs of research. An example is information about reserves of oil and gas on the outer continental shelf; present estimates for oil reserves range from 16 billion to 55 billion barrels and for gas reserves, from 140 trillion to 280 trillion cubic feet. Foreknowledge of these reserves would make possible a better intertemporal allocation of domestic supplies and would define more clearly the timetable for the introduction of alternative sources of energy. A government program to sample major geological structures in frontier areas, mainly the Atlantic coast and the Gulf of Alaska, would provide some of this information. A similar argument can be made for the social value of government funding of research on new energy technologies. An early determination of the feasibility of fusion, solar, or geothermal technologies would reduce the uncertainty about energy sources in the post-2000 decades which hinders the efficient planning of fossil and nuclear fuel reserves and adds risk to long-term private investments in such industries as electric power. Indeed, I would argue that it goes so far as to affect personal savings programs for retirement and the long-term solvency of the Social Security System.

That taxation is a mechanism for sharing social risks is often ignored in analyses of the merits of the corporate income tax. Similarly, inflation often serves as a mechanism for sharing social risks, most recently in response to the Vietnam War and the cartelization of foreign oil sources. The other side of the coin is the government's opportunity to use fiscal policy and the choice of public projects to alleviate social risks. We have seen that it is important to evaluate as a whole the portfolio of public projects. In particular, any major project must be assessed in terms of the correlations between its benefits and other sources of national income, including the portfolio of other public projects. Thus, social insurance takes two forms, one being risk sharing, and the other being the selection of a balanced collection of public projects.

References

Arrow, K. J., and R. C. Lind. 1970. "Uncertainty and the Evaluation of Public Investment Decisions," *American Economic Review* vol. 60 (June).

Kreps, D., and R. Wilson. 1980. "Temporal Resolution of Uncertainty," *Econometrica* vol. 48.

Stapleton, R. C., and M. G. Subrahmanyam. 1978. "A Multiperiod Equilibrium Asset Pricing Model," *Econometrica* vol. 46.

*Hayne E. Leland**

Comment

The evaluation of risky projects poses two principal problems: how to *measure* risk; and how to *price* or weight this measure. Robert Wilson's paper provides a cornucopia of specific techniques and results for risk evaluation. But his paper also establishes some important general principles. In this note, I will discuss some points that may aid in the implementation and interpretation of Wilson's results.

On the Measurement of Risk

Traditional studies of risk and return have focused on variance as a simple measure of risk. If a consumer receives benefits from a number of sources, the variance of total returns from all these sources is the relevant measure of his risk. In such cases, the appropriate measure of a project's risk is its incremental or *marginal* contribution to total variance, which is given by

$$\sigma_j^2 + 2 \text{ cov } (\tilde{y}_j, \tilde{y}) \tag{1}$$

where σ_j^2 is the variance of the project's return; and cov $(\tilde{y}_j, \tilde{y})$ is the covariance between the project's random returns and the random returns from other sources of benefits.

It is useful to note that

$$2 \text{ cov } (\tilde{y}_j, \tilde{y}) \tag{2}$$

is an underestimate of project risk when $\tilde{y}$ does not include the project returns $\tilde{y}_j$ as in equation (1), but is an overestimate of project risk when $\tilde{y}$ is understood to include the project's returns $\tilde{y}_j$. In the following discussion of market prices, we see that for most evaluation purposes, equation (2)

* School of Business, University of California, Berkeley.

250

represents a close approximation of true risk, regardless of whether $\bar{y}_j$ is included in $\bar{y}$.

Thus, covariance rather than variance is the relevant measure of project risk. The distinction is not merely a matter of degree. As Wilson points out, projects with negative covariance may in fact be given a premium for being risky, since their risks tend to reduce the total risk of consumers' returns.

Risk measurement by covariance raises an important problem for the practitioner: With respect to which other projects or returns should covariance be computed? A first guess might be to compute covariance of a potential project's returns with the returns of other projects managed by the same agency or firm. This will be correct only in the extreme cases in which (1) the beneficiaries of the project receive benefits only from projects managed by the agency; or (2) the returns to the agency's projects are statistically independent from all other sources of benefits to consumers. Clearly these cases are exceptional. A more suitable approach, based on the contention that members of the public are reasonably well diversified through private holdings or the tax system, argues that covariance should be computed with respect to "the market portfolio."[1]

Choosing the appropriate measure of risk highlights a possible conflict of interest between managers (public or private) and beneficiaries of the projects they manage. Rewards to managers typically depend on the performance of *their* agency or firm. The risk of managerial reward is directly linked to the risk of agency returns. But consumers or stockholders with returns from other sources look beyond the bounds of the agency or firm in computing their risks. If managers fail to do likewise, they will evaluate projects incorrectly.

On Pricing Risk

I have argued that equation (1) or its approximation, equation (2), is an appropriate measure of project risk. To compute a project's risk premium, we must weight this measure by a price per unit—the "price of risk." Wilson shows that the price of risk depends on the risk aversion of the beneficiaries and the efficient sharing of risk among the members of the economy. Because key risk-aversion parameters are not directly observable, market data must

[1] The "market portfolio" typically refers to the aggregate of all sources of returns or benefits. In most empirical studies, securities listed on the New York Stock Exchange (or some subset thereof) are used as a proxy for all sources of return. Although the stock market clearly does not contain all risky returns, the omitted returns often may be considered relatively unimportant. For a contrary view, see Roll (1977). For formal models suggesting that covariance with the market is the appropriate risk measure, see Sharpe (1964) and Lintner (1965); Rubinstein (1974) suggests some extensions.

be used to estimate the price of risk. Here, we see how rough calculations of this price can be made, when risk sharing is presumed to be efficient.

Let Π_m represent the total value of the market portfolio, for which random value $\tilde{V}_m$ at the end of the year has mean $E(\tilde{V}_m)$ and standard deviation σ_m^2. From Wilson's equation (57), the price of this random return (discounted to the present) will be given by

$$\Pi_m = \frac{1}{1 + r_f}\, [E(\tilde{V}_m) - (1/r)\sigma_m^2]$$

where r_f is the riskless rate of interest. Defining $\tilde{r}_m = \tilde{V}_m/\Pi_m$ and rearranging terms gives

$$\lambda \equiv \frac{\Pi_m}{r} = [E(\tilde{r}_m) - r_f]/\sigma_{r_m}^2$$

where $\sigma_{r_m}^2$ is the variance of $\tilde{r}_m$. The term λ can be interpreted as the price of risk per unit covariance between the market's rate of return and the rate of return on a new project.[2] Historically, $E(\tilde{r}_m) \approx 9$ percent, $r_f \approx 6$ percent, and $\sigma_{r_m}^2 \approx .0225$. Therefore

$$\lambda \approx 1.33$$

Thus, if a project offered an expected annual return of 20 percent, with predicted covariance with $\tilde{r}_m$ of .09, the certainty equivalent rate of return would be[3]

$$
\begin{aligned}
r_c &= E(\tilde{r}) - \lambda \operatorname{cov}(\tilde{r}, \tilde{r}_m) \\
&= 0.20 - (1.33)(0.09) \\
&= 0.08.
\end{aligned}
$$

---

[2] Let C_j represent the project's cost. Define $\tilde{r}_j$ by $1 + \tilde{r}_j = \tilde{y}_j/C_j$ and r_c by $1 + r_c = \pi_j/C_j$. From Wilson's equation (63), dividing both sides by C_j and subtracting 1, yields

$$
\begin{aligned}
r_c &= E(r_j) - \frac{1}{r} \operatorname{cov}(1 + \tilde{r}_j, \tilde{V}_m) \\
&= E(r_j) - (\pi_{m/r}) \operatorname{cov}(1 + \tilde{r}_j, 1 + \tilde{r}_m) \\
&= E(r_j) - \lambda \operatorname{cov}(\tilde{r}_j, \tilde{r}_m)
\end{aligned}
$$

[3] If projects of a similar nature have been previously marketed, a new project's covariance with the market can be estimated using historical data. If the project is unique, covariance can be estimated by projecting market and project returns conditional on a number of scenarios or "states of nature," which are then assigned (subjective) probabilities. For an alternative approach to project valuation that does not require specification of subjective probabilities, see Beja and Leland (1977).

Thus the project should be undertaken, since its estimated certainty equivalent rate of return of 8 percent exceeds the riskless rate.[4]

On Using Market Prices

Wilson's analysis shows that actual or predicted market prices of risky projects will not be an exact measure of their benefits, since they neglect the consumers' surplus associated with new opportunities for diversification.[5] Wilson argues that market price always underestimates a project's certainty equivalent value. Some care, however, must be used in interpreting this proposition. I shall show that, if the project is already included in the market portfolio, Wilson's contention is correct: the market value is a lower bound on the project's certainty equivalent value. But if the project is new, and therefore not currently in the market, the predicted market price will in fact overvalue the project's certainty equivalent.

Proof of these assertions can be seen immediately from Wilson's equation (63). If the vector $\bar{\mathbf{y}}$ includes $\bar{y}_j$, then the estimated market price of the project will be

$$\Pi_j = [m_j - (1/r)\sum_{k \neq j} v_{jk} - (1/r)\sigma_j^2]$$
$$< [m_j - (1/r)\sum_{k \neq j} v_{jk} - (1/2r)\sigma_j^2] = Y_j$$

where Y_j is the certainty equivalent value of the project from Wilson's equation (50). That is, the market price of a project currently included in the market is less than its certainty equivalent value by an amount $(1/2r)\sigma_j^2$. But now consider the estimated price Π_j of an *unmarketed* project, where $\bar{\mathbf{y}}$ now excludes $\bar{y}_j$. In this case,

$$\Pi_j = [m_j - (1/r)\sum_{k \neq j} v_{jk}] > Y_j$$

Since new projects typically are not in the market portfolio, predictions using present prices will generally overvalue the projects' true certainty equivalents. Viewed from the perspective of equations (1) and (2) above,

---

[4] Note that, if the returns are presumed to occur over a number of periods, a dynamic model is needed. Only under strong conditions will it be appropriate to consider a "risk discounted rate of return" in a multiperiod context. See Rubinstein (1976) for further treatment using power and logarithmic utility functions.

[5] It should be emphasized that the "consumer surplus" discussed here relates to the benefits of new opportunities for diversifying risk, and not to the usual "consumer surplus" associated with public projects. The latter figure should be included in the (random) dollar benefits or returns to the project.

the computation of market value assesses the project too much risk if it is already in the market portfolio, and too little risk if it is not.[6]

The results seem to contradict Wilson's discussion surrounding his equation (57). But the paradox can be resolved easily. If a new project *adds* a component $\bar{\omega}$ to the current portfolio return (also $\bar{\omega}$), then the appropriate certainty equivalent increment is

$$\begin{aligned}
\Delta Y &= Y(2\bar{\omega}) - Y(\bar{\omega}) \\
&= [2m - (1/2r)(4\sigma^2)] - [m - (1/2r)(\sigma^2)] \\
&= [m - (3/2r)\sigma^2] \\
&< m - (1/r)\sigma^2 = \Pi
\end{aligned}$$

using Wilson's equations (11) and (57) with $a = 0$, $b = 1$. That is, the estimated market price Π using equation (57) *overvalues* the certainty equivalent of a new or *incremental* project with returns $\bar{\omega}$. If, on the other hand, one is comparing the market value of the current return $\bar{\omega}$ with its certainty equivalent, then Wilson's statement that the market price undervalues the certainty equivalent is correct.

The remaining question is, How closely do market prices approximate true certainty equivalents? Consider the example in my previous discussion of pricing risk, in which I approximated the certainty equivalent rate of return by using the covariance of the rate of return with the market as the measure of risk. If the market rate of return includes the project's returns, then the estimate of risk is a bit large and the estimate of certainty equivalent value is a bit low. If the market excludes the project's returns, the estimate of risk is low and the estimate of value is high. Because the project was new by assumption, this latter value can be thought of as the estimated market value of the project. The true certainty equivalent value, however, will be *bounded* below and above by the calculations that respectively include and exclude the project's rate of return in the market rate of return.

For anything other than colossal projects, the market's rate of return will be affected negligibly by inclusion or exclusion of the project. Since λ is approximately 1, upper and lower bounds will be very close, and the estimated market price will be an excellent approximation of true certainty equivalent.

On the Gains to Risk Sharing

Wilson generates several results related to the gains to risk sharing. Gains are measured as the decrease in the total risk premium (or increase in the certainty equivalent value) as a project's returns are shared by an increasing

---

[6] The market price is the limiting certainty equivalent value per unit of the project undertaken, for an arbitrarily small additional unit. The under- and overvaluation occurs because the projects considered are not of arbitrarily small size, and the "demand curve" for units of the project slopes downward.

number of persons. Although Wilson shows that exponential utility results in gains to risk sharing, he offers the rather disconcerting conclusion that there are no gains to risk sharing when participants have power or logarithmic utilities; for example, see Wilson's equation (46). This is doubly disconcerting since the latter class of utility functions has more attractive properties than the exponential. And it would also seem to imply that the market price of risk could be quite high, since no reduction in its price would occur through risk sharing. But the example I introduce below suggests Wilson's conclusion is warranted only in very special cases—more generally, there *will* be advantages to risk sharing even with logarithmic or power utility functions.

Consider the following investment project. Returns $\bar{y}$ before costs are estimated to be y = \$100 million with probability 0.5, and y = \$10 million with probability 0.5, yielding an expected value of \$55 million. For simplicity, assume all participants are alike, possessing logarithmic utility functions $U(y)$ = ln y. Let W denote wealth from sources other than the project; we shall initially assume W to be nonrandom and identical for all participants. Let N represent the number of people sharing proportionally in the project's returns. The total certainty equivalent value will be NY, where Y is determined by

$$\ln (W + Y) = E[\ln (W + \bar{y}/N)]$$

Computing certainty equivalent values of the project for various combinations of W and N yields the following table:

Certainty Equivalent
(in millions of $)

N \ W	0	\$10,000	\$25,000
1	\$31.6	31.6	31.6
10^3	31.6	36.9	41.1
10^7	31.6	54.990	54.997

We see that there are substantial gains to risk sharing except when wealth from other sources is negligible, the case Wilson implicitly assumes.[7] When W is positive, the risk premium approaches zero as N becomes large. If project returns are positively correlated with (random) wealth, there will still be gains to risk sharing except in the extreme case in which project returns and wealth are exactly proportional in every state of nature. But the limiting risk premium (as N becomes large) is now strictly positive rather than zero.

[7] Alternatively, one could view Wilson's analysis as assuming that when the project is shared N ways, so also is the society's *aggregate* wealth from other sources. The key to this gains-to-diversification result is that the given risk is spread over a larger wealth base as it is shared by more persons. Wilson's analysis presumes that there is the same wealth base no matter how many persons are sharing the risk.

References

Beja, A., and H. Leland. 1977. "Direct Evaluation and Corporate Financial Theory," IBER Working Paper No. 46, School of Business Administration (Berkeley, University of California, August).

Lintner, J. 1965. "The Valuation of Risk Assets and the Selection of Risky Investments in Stock Portfolios and Capital Budgets," *Review of Economics and Statistics* vol. 47 (February) pp. 13–37.

Roll, R. 1977. "A Critique of the Asset Pricing Theories' Test," *Journal of Financial Economics* vol. 4 (March) pp. 129–176.

Rubinstein, M. 1974. "An Aggregation Theorem for Securities Markets," *Journal of Financial Economics* vol. 1 (September) pp. 225–244.

———. 1976. "The Valuation of Uncertain Income Streams and the Pricing of Options," *Bell Journal of Economics* vol. 7 (Autumn) pp. 407–425.

Sharpe, W. 1964. "Capital Asset Prices: A Theory of Market Equilibrium Under Conditions of Risk," *Journal of Finance* vol. 19 (September) pp. 425–442.

7

*J. A. Stockfisch**

Measuring the Social Rate of Return on Private Investment

Introduction

One might ask why the rate of return on private investment is relevant to discussion of the social discount rate. There are two reasons.

First, the notion of a social discount rate arises from the view that the cost of capital in the private sector is an inappropriate measure for evaluating government spending. An opposing view is that the government should employ the same measure of capital cost as its citizens do.

Acknowledging this disagreement, one might still ask whether it is not inefficient for the private and public sectors to use different discount rates. This question seems central to arguments that the government employ the private sector rate of return. Advocates of a social discount rate, however, appear to be concerned with a broader set of objectives, including the economy's rate of growth in the long run, the optimum rate of saving, and the distribution of output between social groups, particularly present and future generations. To determine the practical significance of this difference in viewpoint requires both numerical specification of a social discount rate and estimation or measurement of the private sector rate.

If there is a difference between the two rates, a method must be worked out for dealing with the problem of possible misallocation of resources. Marglin (1963) and Feldstein (1964) have presented two such methods, both of which require information about the rate of return in the private sector. In other words, to employ a social discount rate as a feature of the government's resource-allocation apparatus requires information about the profitability of private investment that will be displaced or stimulated by the government's investment behavior. This is the second reason that a measure of the prevailing private sector rate of return is relevant to discussion of the social rate of discount.

---

* American Petroleum Institute, Washington, D.C.

However, the idea of "the" rate of return on private investment is itself an abstraction. The concept follows from equilibrium theory, in which rates of return obtainable from investment in many activities are equalized. Of course, during any given period for which empirical measures are taken, such equality will not be found. This condition is inherent in real economies in which preferences, technology, and other conditions change. Moreover, taxes—particularly property and corporation profits taxes—drive a wedge between physical asset earnings and the yields of private ownership claims. Rate-of-return measures thus will be biased downward. These same measures, even when adjusted for taxes, may still have shortcomings. Financial information, at best, may provide insight only into average rates of return. Yet it is the marginal rate of return that is relevant to resource allocation. Thus, the question arises whether and the extent to which some sort of average rate can serve as a measure of its marginal counterpart. To address this question requires a theoretical model.

The Theory of the Rate of Return on Private Investment: A Neoclassical Static Model

The Model

By social rate of return on private investment, I mean a measure of such concepts as "the marginal productivity of capital," "the marginal efficiency of investment," "the marginal rate of return over cost," and so on. These concepts are adjuncts of capital theory and, as such, are both ambiguous and controversial. This condition requires that any particular version of the rate of return be specified carefully. This section attempts to lay the comparative static foundation of capital theory.

Since the subject includes the behavior of capital-theory measures in a social economy, it must be treated by a general equilibrium model. In this context, a rate-of-return measure, like the costs and prices of all physical outputs, falls out of the solution determined by preferences, technology, and physical endowments. That is, capital and rate-of-return theory—if properly stated—is simply one aspect of the general theory of price and cost.[1] What follows lays out such a general equilibrium model by, first, presenting the

---

[1] Here I use the expression "capital theory" in a very narrow and specific sense: namely, the determinates of something called "the discount rate" and, by means of the time discounting algorithm, the value of the aggregation of physical assets that make up the non-labor component of an economy's physical endowment at any instant. As such, the focus is not on the determination of capital accumulation, long-run growth, and so on. These latter subjects and, especially, speculation about the demand for and acquisition of physical assets, as illustrated by the concept of "time preference," constitute a broader and richer subject. For surveys, see Burmeister and Dobell (1970) and Harcourt (1972).

standard neoclassical two-product, two-factor compound production model in which one of the factors is the *services* of capital goods and the two products are consumer goods. Second, the model will be expanded both to handle its capital theory shortcomings and to provide a theoretical underpinning for measuring the private sector rate of return.

We assume first that each of two consumer goods industries is composed of price-taking, cost-minimizing producers and that there are no industry-scale economies. The following ten equations for the two consumer goods X and Y make up the compound production model.

$$X = X(L_x, K_x) \tag{1}$$

$$Y = Y(L_y, K_y) \tag{2}$$

$$\bar{L} = L_x + L_y \tag{3}$$

$$\bar{K} = K_x + K_y \tag{4}$$

$$\frac{P_L}{P_k} = \frac{\bar{P}_L}{\bar{P}_k} \tag{5}$$

$$P_x X + P_y Y = \overline{\text{GNP}} \tag{6}$$

$$P_k = P_x \frac{\partial X}{\partial K_y} \tag{7}$$

$$P_k = P_y \frac{\partial Y}{\partial K_y} \tag{8}$$

$$P_L = P_x \frac{\partial X}{\partial L_x} \tag{9}$$

$$P_L = P_y \frac{\partial Y}{\partial L_y} \tag{10}$$

For the two industries, these ten equations present six quantity unknowns—X, Y, L_x, L_y, K_x, and K_y. The equations also present four price unknowns—P_L, P_k (capital rental), P_x, and P_y. Equations (1) and (2) are production functions for X and Y. Equations (3) and (4) assume fixed quantities of factor services $\bar{L}$ and $\bar{K}$. When producers adhere to cost-minimizing practices and respond to spenders' demands, a unique capital rental to wage rate $\dfrac{\bar{P}_L}{\bar{P}_k}$, emerges as shown in equation (5). This earnings ratio must prevail in both industries. However, factor earning rates and output prices are not defined unless a numeraire is specified. Equation (6), which assumes a fixed *dollar* level of value-adding activity, $\overline{\text{GNP}}$, handles this requirement.

An alternative to equation (6) is to set the price of one of the commodities equal to 1. A commodity numeraire has disadvantages, principally that a change in any of the system's parameters (for example, a demand shift), which changes relative prices, will change the economy's total value-adding activity, as measured either by equation (6) or by aggregate factor earnings. The nominal price level also changes. As a result, money cost and supply price schedules of non-numeraire commodities can take on a variety of peculiar shapes. Another disadvantage of a commodity numeraire arises when a model is extended to a large number of commodities. There is no assurance that the numeraire's price will not vanish.

The ratio $\overline{P}_k/\overline{P}_L$ in equation (5), determined by the framework established by equations (1) through (6), depends on the parameters for equations (1) through (4) and the relative amount of X and Y demanded by spenders. Any given allocation of $\overline{\text{GNP}}$ between X and Y determines a unique P_k/P_L ratio. If both industries are competitive and if there are no commodity taxes or private monopoly, $\overline{\text{GNP}}$ is entirely exhausted by the exchange values of the marginal products. These exchange values times the marginal products of L_x, K_x, L_y, and K_y must satisfy the cost-minimizing conditions of equations (7) through (10), which also provide the information for determining P_x and P_y.

For certain purposes, equation (5) may be replaced by an appropriate demand equation or a utility function. An example of the latter would be

$$U = U(X, Y) \tag{5a}$$

An example of an appropriate demand equation would be a partial equilibrium demand equation like

$$Q_x = Q_x(P_x) \tag{5b}$$

However, since we wish to extend the model to capital theory, we abstain from asserting any particular behavior propositions about the money demand for new capital goods.

When the model defined by equations (1) through (10) is confined to treating only consumer goods, it contains peculiar capital theory assumptions. The K that enters as arguments in the production function equations represents the service of physical agents, like machines.[2] Since the aggregate quantity of capital services is fixed, and since the economy has no sector producing new capital goods, the physical agents providing $\overline{K}$ must not depreciate—

---

[2] It is implicit in this model that the agents that provide K are homogeneous in the sense that they can be employed in either X or Y (the same assumption applies to L). As such, the model rules out the possibility that X uses tractors whereas Y uses machine tools. Any problem that this assumption might cause can be handled by specifying additional capital-like factors of production.

that is, the capital agents have infinite lives. Hence, the model is silent on the subject of capital theory, including such concepts as a discount rate, the value of the capital stock, or wealth. Although the model can provide an exact solution for P_k (along with all other prices), P_k merely measures the earnings rate of physical capital assets. This earnings rate is the counterpart of P_L, or the wage rate.

For a compound production model to treat variables relevant to capital theory, it must possess a production function equation for an industry that produces new capital goods. By this expansion, we can drop the assumption that physical capital agents have infinite lives. With addition of a demand equation for new capital goods, a price/cost equation for new capital goods is forthcoming. Given the cost of producing new physical assets K_A, the capital earnings rate P_K, and information about the time dimension of a newly produced asset's earnings stream, a discounting algorithm provides a measure of the rate of return over cost, r, or the discount rate. With information about the age composition of old physical assets, discounting the expected earnings streams of each age class and summing them provides a measure of the present value of the physical capital stock, W, or "wealth."[3]

The system of equations (1) through (10) must thus be expanded as follows to handle a capital goods production sector:

$$K_A = K_A(L_A, K_{K_A}) \tag{11}$$

$$D_{K_A} = D_{a_K}(. \, . \, .) \tag{12}$$

$$P_K = P_{K_A} \frac{\partial K_A}{\partial K_{K_A}} \tag{13}$$

$$P_L = P_{K_A} \frac{\partial K_A}{\partial L_{K_A}} \tag{14}$$

Equation (11) is the new capital goods production function. Equation (12) expresses a demand for assets as a function of unspecified arguments. Equations (13) and (14) extend the cost-minimizing conditions to the production of physical assets.[4]

---

[3] This use of the word "wealth" is less general than its meaning in much economic literature. As it is used by many English economists, it describes elements of the set of physical and other qualities that contribute to general well-being and welfare. However, the word "endowment," as it is used in modern general equilibrium models, better captures what is meant by this older concept of wealth. The word "wealth" can then be used in a way that more closely corresponds to common usage when it is said that an individual is wealthy, as measured by the money value of his assets.

[4] It is also necessary to rewrite equations (3) and (4) as follows:

$$\bar{L} = L_X + L_Y + L_{K_A} \tag{3a}$$

$$\bar{K} = K_X + K_Y + K_{K_A} \tag{4a}$$

Determination of the rate of return over cost, or the discount rate, requires an equation

$$r = r (P_{K_A}, P_K, n) \tag{15}$$

where n represents the period of time during which a new asset's cash flow P_K is forthcoming. The rate r is the "internal" discount rate that equates the cash flow with the production cost P_{K_A} of producing a new asset. If we assume that the cash flow is constant over the asset's life, equation (15) can be replaced by the familiar exact discounting equation for a constant, finite annuity

$$P_{K_A} = \frac{P_K}{r}(1 - e^{-rn}) \tag{15a}$$

where e is the base for natural logarithms, and solving for r.[5]
The physical wealth equation is

$$W = W(P_{K_j}, r, Z) \tag{16}$$

where W is the aggregate value of *old* assets (including inventory and goods in process), r is the discount rate, P_{K_j} is the cash flow of assets in the jth age class, and Z expresses features of the age composition of old assets. Account must be taken of the fact that old assets consist of items in different age classes. Where n equals the expected life of a newly produced asset, a less general expression for equation (16) would be

$$W = \sum_{j=1}^{n} \frac{\dfrac{rP_{K_j}}{n}(n - j)}{(1 + r)^j} \tag{16a}$$

where j represents the given age class.

A Numerical Example

With a model like that defined by equations (1) through (16)— particularly equation (15)—it would be possible to estimate the social rate

---

[5] In most formulations of equation (15a), the left side is specified to be "present worth," where the discount rate r is given. In the general equilibrium context, P_{K_A} is the money cost of producing an earnings stream, and is given or determined by the solution of the system of equations (1) through (14). The term P_{K_A} is also, of course, the present worth of a newly produced asset when the system's equilibrium conditions are satisfied. Given the general equilibrium solution, derivation of the discount rate, along with the present worth of "old assets" (or wealth) then falls out.

of return on private investment with information about the system's equation parameters. Unfortunately, this kind of information is not directly available, particularly with respect to production functions and, especially, the capital goods production function. Moreover, as a practical matter, it is generally necessary to measure K in terms of its monetary value—a practice that has evoked both sharp criticism and controversy (Harcourt, 1972). When rates of return are measured in the real world, they may be ratios derived from financial accounting data and, as such, are average rates; or they may be based on market values of securities that are related to accounting measures (for example, price-earnings ratios).[6] Both kinds of measures are therefore suspect as indicators of marginal and opportunity returns or costs.

Just how troublesome this "average versus marginal" dichotomy really is, however, is unclear. It is unclear because in a competitive general equilibrium, average and marginal costs (and returns) tend to be equal insofar as factor prices and product costs mutually adjust in such a way as to bring about equality. This assertion, however, is a tautology in that it is one way of defining an equilibrium. But the tautology is worth pondering by those who might reject measures of average rates of return.

Yet it must also be acknowledged that accounting data are the result of accounting conventions, tempered if not greatly bent by the motivation to reduce income tax liabilities (or more accurately, to maximize after-tax rates of return). This condition provides cause to question the economic relevance of measures derived from financial accounting data.

Question raising of this sort does not take us very far, however. A more fruitful line of inquiry might be the following: Let us specify a set of parameters for the production function equations and other exogenous variables for the general equilibrium model as defined by equations (1) through (16). Numerical solutions for the rate-of-return equation (15) and the physical-wealth equation (16) can then be derived. Total capital earnings, $(P_K \cdot \overline{K})$, and an average rate of return can be computed. Compare these with simulated business capital accounting methods. In this fashion, it may be possible to get insight regarding the extent to which rates-of-return estimates based on accounting data might be a surrogate of the price-theoretic counterpart.

Table 7-1 presents a set of equation parameters to simulate an economy producing two consumer goods, and a capital goods sector. (Each of the three industry production functions is specified as Cobb–Douglas for reasons of computational simplicity.) The economy's resource endowment consists of 100 units of labor service and 200 units of capital goods' services. The latter are provided by 200 physical assets, each of which provides one unit

---

[6] It should be pointed out that market information about the aggregate value of claims—specifically, dividend or interest payout plus capital gain minus capital loss—could measure the marginal social rate of return on private investment if there were no asset earnings taxes and no variation in aggregate cash holdings.

Table 7-1. Parameters for a Two-Consumer-Good and Capital-Good Industry Competitive General Equilibrium Model

Industry	Spending (dollars)	Production function
X	40	$L^{0.5}K^{0.5}$
Y	40	$L^{0.8}K^{0.2}$
K_A	20	$0.52L^{0.3}K^{0.7}$
Total (GNP)	100	

Factor supplies (and capital asset characteristics)
    Labor: 100 units
    Capital: 200 units
            10-year physical life
            20 units/year annual replacement
            Constant physical productivity over each year.

of service per year over a period of ten years.[7] The assumption that 20 units of physical capital are required each year for replacement implies that the existing capital stock was acquired during the past in such a way that there is an equal number of assets in each age class. The assumption that $20 a year is spent on capital goods, along with other parameters as shown in table 7-1, are such as to provide a no-growth general equilibrium.

Table 7-2 shows the exact general equilibrium solution. A necessary condition for this solution is, of course, that the marginal rate of technical substitution (MRTS) between K and L be equal across all activities. The $1.00 supply price of a new capital asset, relative to its annual cash flow of $0.21 over ten years, provides the 17.25 percent discount rate, or "marginal rate of return over cost." Discounting the cash flow of each age class of old assets and summing them according to equation (16a) provides a physical wealth measure of $128.21. Let us now compare this exact measure with a simulated accounting measure.

---

[7] Here we make explicit a critical simplifying assumption, which was implicit in the model defined by equations (1) through (16). The assumption that each asset has a physical life of ten years has the practical effect of rendering elements of our capital stock homogeneous in ways that greatly simplify the model. At the same time, it does not require that capital be regarded as "jelly," "meccano sets," or similar constructions that suggest overly unrealistic degrees of physical homogeneity. That is, in table 7-1 industry X may use tractors; industry Y, weaving machines; and industry K_A, machine tools. The stock of each of these special capital goods may be augmented or diminished by varying their respective production rates. Thus we do not have to assume instantaneous or perfect malleability.

To the extent that these assumptions are objectionable, one answer is a moré detailed model. The extra detail might have to be such that a production function be specified for each type of capital good (for example, tractors, oil refineries, and so on). To the extent that a variety of capital goods that differ in their sophistication, cost, and durability can be used in a given production process, production functions should be written to accommodate each item as an argument. Whether such an elaborate model would provide much additional insight into capital-theoretic and related policy issues is unknown.

Table 7-2. General Equilibrium: Two Consumer Goods and Capital Goods Sectors for Table 7-1 Parameters

Industry	Spending (dollars)	Quantity	Price (dollars)
X	40	57.31	0.70
Y	40	51.23	0.78
K_A	20	20.00	1.00
Total (GNP)	100		

Factor allocation	Labor	Capital	
X	24.48	95.24	
Y	55.17	38.10	
K_A	10.34	66.66	

Marginal products and $MRTS_{K/L}$	Labor	Capital	$MRTS_{K/L}$
X	0.881	0.301	0.362
Y	0.743	0.269	0.362
K_A	0.580	0.210	0.362

Distribution of total earnings
Labor (dollars)	58
Capital (dollars)	42

Factor earnings and rate of return
Labor (dollars)	0.58
Capital (dollars)	0.21
Rate of return (annual %)	17.25
Value of physical assets (dollars)	128.21

In a no-growth general equilibrium, the requirement to produce twenty new assets annually to replace worn-out assets, at a supply price of $1.00 per asset, calls for an annual $20 capital consumption charge. Gross annual asset earnings are $42. Net earnings (and accounting profits) are $22. The ratio of the $128.25 discounted value of the "old" physical capital to the $22 profits turns out to be 17.15 percent. Thus the dichotomy between average and marginal rates of return, in principle at least, appears to be a smoke screen. This should not be surprising. It is (or should be) axiomatic in capital theory that all assets yield the opportunity rate of return because assets are capitalized to provide it.

But do accounting measures of depreciation and derived accounting book values of assets adequately measure asset values? Here the answer is less definitive. A rich variety of depreciation methods bear upon estimation of asset lives and salvage values, the method of deriving an annual depreciation charge, and the way accounts are grouped or aggregated. Combinations of these methods in conjunction with differing growth rates for the firm can produce a range of both accounting profits and asset book values. Both depreciation charges, and hence the measure of accounting profits, and asset book values will be biased relative to the correct price–theoretic measures.

The numerical solution shown in table 7-2 provides only a partial insight into the kind of bias. Recall that the $128.21 asset value figure was derived by capitalization. As a practical matter, accountants are constrained to employ historical data as the basis of their depreciation charges. If a straight-line monthly depreciation charge had been made on each asset against its $1.00 cost, accumulated depreciation would be about $90 if we assume that 1.66 assets had been acquired each month over the previous ten years. The gross book value would, of course, be $200. Hence, the net book value would be $110. Since net asset earnings are $22, the accounting rate of return would be 20 percent, compared with the correct rate of 17.25 percent. Hence, the accounting rate of return in this case is biased upward by about 12 percent.

This example suggests that accounting rates of return, based on asset book values, might have a modest upward bias relative to the correct rate. However, care should be exercised in accepting the view that more accelerated depreciation methods, including use of asset lives shorter than actual ones, will greatly exaggerate this condition. Depending on the timing of their use, these practices will also bias downward the accounting profit measure.[8] Moreover, in the real world, inventories constitute a share of total physical assets, which will mitigate the bias that follows when it is assumed that all physical assets are depreciated.

Estimates of the Rate of Return on Private-Sector Physical Investment in the United States: 1961–71

There exists no single, empirical counterpart of the theoretic concept of "the" rate of return. Economic literature includes references to a "pure" or "riskless" interest rate, and the yield on long-term Treasury bonds is often regarded as its empirical counterpart. But it is unclear what such a riskless rate means apart from the point that the government guarantees paying the future dollars specified in the Treasury contracts. A better measure of the rate of return on private investment would be some weighted average of yields on private claims against physical assets. The creation of claims against privately owned physical assets entails issuing a mix of debt and equity claims, including those of proprietorships and households with owner-

---

[8] It should be emphasized that the example based on the model described in table 7-1 assumes that assets have a constant productivity and cash flow. To the extent that these quantities decrease as a function of time (because of increasing maintenance costs, lower efficiency than that of new assets embodying improved technology, and so on), the upward bias of asset book values caused by straight-line depreciation will be reduced and even have an opposite bias.

occupied housing. However, any measure of yields on claims must be adjusted for cash holdings in asset portfolios, for taxes that reduce the earnings on old and to-be-constructed assets, and hence for discount rates. Property and corporate income taxes are the principal taxes that reduce the yields of claims relative to the earnings of physical assets.

An alternative method is to estimate the earnings and value of physical assets themselves and from these derive a measure for rate of return. This section summarizes two empirical efforts though somewhat different methods to estimate the rate of return on physical investment in the United States (Gorman, 1972; Stockfisch, 1969). Gorman treats the aggregate of nonfinancial corporations and provides yearly average inflation-adjusted rates of return for the period 1948–71. My own analysis concentrated on the period 1961–65 and presented an estimate of a private corporate-sector rate of return similar to Gorman's. However, this figure was further adjusted, using equilibrium assumptions, to estimate a rate of return for the noncorporate sector, including residential housing. A weighted average of these estimates was advanced as an overall 10.6 percent average rate of return on private investment. Gorman's data, when adjusted for property taxes and noncorporate investment, suggest an overall rate of 12.8 percent during the 1961–65 period.

Table 7-3 shows the resulting measures as applied to the nonfinancial corporate sector for the period covered by both studies. The table is designed to highlight differences between the methods and data sources employed in each study.

Gorman's study employed national income and product data. Gross corporate annual investment in constant dollars is cumulated by the perpetual-inventory method. Straight-line depreciation charges, based on 85 percent of Bulletin F asset lives, and retirement of depreciable assets as a function of a frequency distribution around these asset lives are cumulatively deducted to arrive at a net value of depreciable assets. This value plus that of inventories constitutes the asset base for a given year. Earnings are the sum of profits before corporate taxes plus interest paid. Since the calculations are adjusted to constant dollars, the ratio of net asset value to annual earnings is an inflation-adjusted rate of return.

My study employed annual company financial data, as aggregated and reported by various federal regulatory agencies (for example, the Securities and Exchange Commission and the Federal Trade Commission for manufacturing). The asset base was physical inventories, accounts receivable, and net book value of plant and equipment. The earnings figure was before-corporate-tax profits, plus interest paid, less interest and dividends received. Since the measures were current earnings and values of different vintage assets, the rate-of-return measure would be biased upward as a result of inflation. A 1.6 percent inflation rate, based on the annual increase of the

Table 7-3. Summary of Average Rates of Return on Nonfinancial Corporations from Two Studies, 1961–65
(percent)

	Gorman	Stockfisch
Computed rate of return	14.1	13.5
Plus estimated property tax rate	1.5	1.5
Less inflation adjustment		−1.6
Net corporate rate of return	15.6	13.4

Source: Gorman (1972, pp. 26–27), Stockfisch (1969, pp. 8, 15).

consumption component of the GNP deflator during 1949–65, was subtracted to yield an inflation-adjusted rate of return. In both studies, corporation earnings are before property taxes. These taxes were estimated to be 1.5 percent of asset values. Addition of this rate provides net rates of return.

The estimate derived from Gorman's data is 2.2 percentage points higher than mine mainly because my study included accounts receivable in the asset base. I believed that accounts receivable represented physical goods that were ''loaned'' to customers and that companies received a rental return on them as part of their earnings. Not to include them on the same footing as plant, equipment, and inventory would tend to bias the rate of return upward. However, my decision to include them caused a downward bias. One company's accounts receivable can be another company's physical inventory. Only if the accounts receivable were due entirely from outside the corporate sector—for example, households and government—is the above reasoning for treating them as physical assets entirely correct.

The estimates in table 7-3 treat only the corporate sector. Yet the noncorporate sector, including owner-occupied housing, absorbs the largest share of the economy's investment. In 1956, according to Goldsmith, Lipsey, and Mendelson (1963, Table 1, pp. 68–69), noncorporate physical assets (excluding consumer durables) were 62 percent of total private physical wealth. Because of corporate taxes, it can be expected that capital is allocated in such a way as to equalize after-tax rates of return between the corporate and noncorporate sectors. A way to estimate this difference is to view the corporate tax (federal and state) as an ad valorem tax on corporate physical assets. For the 1961–65 period, corporate taxes were estimated to represent about 4.7 percentage points in the total rate of return. If we subtract this amount from the corporate net rate of return, we arrive at a rate of return between 8.7 (Stockfisch) and 10.9 (Gorman) percent in the noncorporate sector during 1961–65. If the corporate and noncorporate rates of return are weighted at 40 and 60 percent respectively, the overall private sector rate of return turns out to between 10.6 (Stockfisch) and 12.8 (Gorman) percent during the 1961–65 period.

Table 7-4 uses Gorman's data to provide estimates of the behavior of this measure since 1965. The first column is the corporate rate of return after

**Table 7-4. Rates of Return: Corporate, Noncorporate,
and Weighted Average, 1961–71
(percent)**

Year	Corporate rate of return		Ad valorem corp. tax	Noncorporate return	Weighted average return
	After property tax	Before property tax			
1961–65	14.1	15.6	4.7	10.9	12.8
1966	16.2	17.7	5.9	11.8	14.2
1967	14.1	15.6	5.0	10.6	12.6
1968	13.8	15.3	6.0	9.3	11.7
1969	11.6	13.1	5.5	7.6	9.9
1970	9.4	10.9	4.2	6.7	8.4
1971	9.9	11.4	4.2	7.2	8.9

Source and method: Column 1 from Gorman (1972, p. 27). Column 2 is column 1 plus 1.5 percent property tax rate from Stockfisch (1969, p. 13). Column 3 is derived from sum of physical asset net book values (inventory, depreciable and depletable assets, and land) and federal income tax accrued liabilities as shown for all active corporate returns in the 1972 *Statistics of Income*, Table 30, pp. 188–89; plus state income tax liabilities as shown in *Economic Report of the President, 1976*, Table B-68, p. 251.

property taxes as computed by Gorman. The second column adds 1.5 percentage points for property taxes. The third column is an estimate of federal and state corporation taxes as a percentage of the values of corporate assets. Subtraction of this latter rate from the before-property-tax corporate rate of return provides an estimate of the noncorporate sector rate of return shown in column 4. The overall rate of return is derived from weighting the corporate and noncorporate rates by the 40:60 ratio based on Goldsmith's data.

Conclusions

The concept of a social rate of return on private investment can be defined by a general equilibrium model that contains demand and production function equations for new capital goods. The same model can be used to compare rate of return measures derived from financial accounting (and asset depreciation) practices with economic-theoretic concepts of a rate of return. Although no systematic comparison with respect to different capital theory parameter and financial accounting techniques has been undertaken, my analysis suggests that average rate of return measures based on accounting data—when adjusted for asset earnings taxes and financial claims in asset accounts—provide a rough measure of the social marginal rate of return on private investment. By "rough measure" I mean something within 20 percent of the "correct" rate. That is, if the weighted average rate of return is 10 percent, the social return on private investment would lie between 8 and 12 percent.

Whether this degree of accuracy is adequate in relation to the concept of a social discount rate is unknown. Advocates of a social discount rate seldom indicate a number. They generally argue, however, that it is not the private social rate of return as defined in this paper. Moreover, they usually imply that the social discount rate should be lower than the rate of return prevailing in the private sector. Thus, disagreement has arisen in economic literature and in government circles. Government officials (and agencies) periodically ask the question: "What discount rate should we use when evaluating government spending programs?" One answer is the rate of return prevailing in the private sector. A contrary answer is a social discount rate that is lower than the private rate of return.

A case can be made that this disagreement is more apparent than real. It is possible that two distinct questions are being asked. On the one hand, if the question is, What cost-of-capital measure (or discount rate) should government decision makers and analysts employ in evaluating government programs at any time? the answer that it be the private sector rate of return is intended to assure that the marginal rates of technical substitution of capital and other resources are equal between private and government resource-using activities. This answer does not address the question of what the social rate of return should be in the future.

On the other hand, if the question is, What should be the rate of return prevailing in the economy, say, some 50 or 60 years hence? then the concept of a social discount rate may be relevant. Here, the case can be made that the real question is: Given the choice we have today and in the immediate future, what should be the allocation of resources between consumption and net capital accumulation? In the model described by equations (1) through (16), per capita income at a specified future date may be $\dfrac{GNP^*}{L}$, given the parameters of the unknown arguments in equation (12), which expresses the demand for new capital assets. However, if it is felt that future per capita income should be $\dfrac{GNP^{**}}{L}$, and that $\dfrac{GNP^*}{L}$ will be less than $\dfrac{GNP^{**}}{L}$, then the future rate of return r^* will be greater than the desired rate of return r^{**} or the social discount rate.

Viewed in this fashion, concern about a social discount rate seems to boil down to concern that an economy will not be saving and investing enough or that K^* will be less than K^{**}. In certain contexts, this concern may be valid. However, if it is valid, the question remains whether the objective of achieving K^{**} is served by investing capital resources in government activities for which rates of return are lower than those prevailing in the private sector.

References

Burmeister, E. A., and R. Dobell. 1970. *Mathematical Theories of Economic Growth* (New York, Macmillan).

Council of Economic Advisors. 1976. *Economic Report of the President, 1976* (Washington, GPO).

Feldstein, M. J. 1964. "Net Social Benefit Calculation and the Public Investment Decision," *Oxford Economic Papers* (April) pp. 114–131.

Goldsmith, R. W., R. Lipsey, and M. Mendelson. 1963. *Studies in the Balance Sheet of the United States*, Vol. II (Princeton, Princeton University Press).

Gorman, J. A. 1972. "Nonfinancial Corporations: New Measures of Output and Input," *Survey of Current Business* (March) pp. 21–27, 33.

Harcourt, G. C. 1972. *Some Cambridge Controversies in the Theory of Capital* (London, Cambridge University Press).

Internal Revenue Service. 1942. *Income Tax Depreciation and Obsolescence: Estimated Useful Lives and Depreciation Rates*, Bulletin F, revised (Washington, GPO).

———. 1976. *Statistics of Income—1972, Corporation Income Tax Returns* (Washington, GPO).

Marglin, S. A. 1963. "The Opportunity Costs of Public Investment," *Quarterly Journal of Economics* (May) pp. 274–289.

Stockfisch, J. A. 1969. *Measuring the Opportunity Cost of Government Investment*, Research Paper P-490 (Arlington, Va., Institute for Defense Analysis, March).

8

*Partha Dasgupta**

Resource Depletion, Research and Development, and the Social Rate of Discount

Introduction

Imagine a planner undertaking an intertemporal optimization exercise. He is morally at ease with the objective function and he is confident that he has captured all technological and institutional constraints accurately. These institutional constraints consist of, among other things, the responses of the private sector to the planner's decisions. The extent to which the planner can exercise control in the economy can be great or small, depending on the economy in question. Assume next that there is no uncertainty. It is of course well known that if an optimum exists, then under certain circumstances (for example, the objective function is concave and the constraint sets are convex) it can be decentralized, in the sense that there exists a system of intertemporal *shadow prices* which, if used in investment decisions, can sustain the desired program.[1] Let the planner choose a good as the numeraire. The shadow own rate of return on the numeraire is usually called the *social rate of discount*. It is the percentage rate at which the present-value shadow price of the

* London School of Economics and Political Science.

Note: Because the participants of the conference were from different professions, Robert Lind, the conference chairman, instructed me to avoid appealing to control theory and to discuss the main issues in a nontechnical manner. The introduction and the presentation of my general argument are nontechnical and are concerned with the relationship between optimum aggregate planning and social benefit–cost analysis in general, and with the role of social rates of discount in particular. The discussions of resource depletion, uncertainty, and technical change are more technical and are concerned with a model of capital accumulation, resource depletion, and investment in research and development. In the concluding section, I summarize what I take to be the main morals emerging from the analysis. The presentation of the material in the discussion of resource depletion is based on chapter 10 of Dasgupta and Heal (1979). I am most grateful to Geoffery Heal, Robert Solow, and Joseph Stiglitz, who have sharpened my understanding of these matters through our conversation and correspondence over the past several years.

[1] These are often called "accounting prices" or "dual variables."

numeraire falls at any given instant. Thus, let s_t denote the present-value shadow price of the numeraire at t (that is, the amount of numeraire at $t = 0$ to be paid for a unit of the numeraire to be delivered at t along the decentralized optimal program). Then, assuming continuous time and a differentiable shadow price, $-\dot{s}_t/s_t$ is the social rate of discount at t. Its precise value will depend on the commodity chosen as the numeraire since, except for some unusual circumstances, *relative* shadow prices of goods will change over time.

The introduction of uncertainty leads to no formal difficulties. A commodity is characterized not only by its physical characteristics and the date, but also by the state of nature; that is, one now has contingent commodities (see Arrow, 1953, 1971; Debreu, 1959). The shadow prices emerging from an optimization exercise are present-value contingent prices. The social rates of discount can now be defined analogously.

In this paper, I shall analyze the structure of such intertemporal shadow prices using models that accommodate exhaustible natural resources. In doing this I shall explore the sensitivity of optimal programs to certain key parameters reflecting a planner's preferences; namely, the felicity discount rate and the elasticity of marginal felicity. The next section and the discussion of resource depletion will be concerned with a world in which there is no uncertainty. In the section on uncertainty, technical change, and innovation, I shall discuss technological innovation viewed as an uncertain event. Moreover, I shall consider expenditure on research and development (R&D) as influencing this uncertainty. From each of these exercises one will be able also to obtain criteria for social benefit–cost analysis of investment, be it investment in fixed capital or in R&D.

A General Argument

Begin by supposing time to be discrete: $t = 0, 1, \ldots$. There are compelling moral arguments to justify the inclusion of all future time in the exercise. There are also technical advantages in considering an infinite horizon. I shall therefore do so.[2] Since my idea here is to explore production possibilities in a finite earth, it is reasonable to postulate a constant population size. I assume that individuals in any given instant are treated identically, either because they are identical or, if they are not, because the planner chooses to do so. To be specific, I shall suppose that consumption at time t is divided equally among the individuals at t. Let me then normalize and set the population size at unity. Let C_t be aggregate consumption at time t, and let $\{C_t\}$ denote an infinite consumption sequence $(C_0, C_1, \ldots, C_t, \ldots)$. Denote by $\mathscr{F}$ the

[2] These arguments have been discussed at length in Koopmans (1966), Chakravarty (1969), Arrow and Kurz (1970), and Dasgupta and Heal (1979).

set of *feasible* consumption sequences. This set will be specified in detail later.

Now let $W(\{C_t\}) \equiv W(C_0, C_1, \ldots, C_t, \ldots)$ represent the objective function of the planner. It is often called the planner's *social welfare function*. For the moment I do not specify its form but instead suppose only (a) that it is a real-valued function defined over $\mathcal{F}$, and (b) that it is strictly concave and twice differentiable. The planner's problem is then:

$$\text{maximize} \quad W(\{C_t\}), \tag{1}$$
$$\{C_t\} \in \mathcal{F}$$

That is, the problem is to locate those consumption sequences from $\mathcal{F}$ that maximize W. Assume for the moment that a solution to expression (1) exists.

Let us now suppose that W is increasing in each of its arguments; that is, that W is Paretian.[3] I come now to the notion of efficient consumption sequences: $\{C_t\} \in \mathcal{F}$ is efficient if there exists no feasible sequence $\{C_t'\}$ such that $C_t' \geq C_t$ for all $t \geq 0$, and $C_t' > C_t$ for at least one t. Since W is by assumption Paretian, we know in advance that an optimum consumption sequence is efficient. Efficiency is here a necessary condition for optimality. We now need a set of conditions that, in conjunction with the requirement of efficiency, will enable us to locate an optimal consumption sequence. In undertaking this task it will be useful to define a new term.

Let $\{C_t\}$ be a feasible consumption sequence. We shall call that rate at which it is found just desirable to substitute consumption at some period t for that in the next period $(t + 1)$, *the consumption rate of interest* between t and $t + 1$. We denote that rate by ρ_t; it is a welfare term. It is useful to consider the factors that might influence the consumption rate of interest. One might argue that ρ_t should be positive if $C_{t+1} > C_t$, the argument being that an extra bit of consumption at time t is more valuable than the same extra bit at $t + 1$, since individuals will, in any case, have more consumption at $t + 1$. One might then wish to have ρ_t roughly proportional to the rate of growth of consumption, or in any case, an increasing function of it. One may feel that ρ_t ought to depend on the level of consumption at time t as well. On the other hand, it may not seem reasonable to have ρ_t depend significantly on consumption rates at times far away from t.

There is a second reason why ρ_t may be positive. We might undervalue consumption at $t + 1$ as compared with consumption at t simply because $t + 1 > t$. The point is that one may wish to take into account the possibility of extinction. This component of ρ_t is usually referred to as the *rate of pure time preference*, or alternatively, the *rate of impatience*.

---

[3] This is, of course, not the usual definition of a Paretian social welfare function, but I am sure no confusion will arise in my defining it here in this manner.

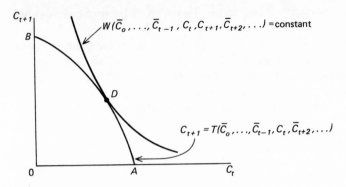

Figure 8-1

The rate ρ_t is a pure number per unit of time. In traditional terminology, it is the marginal rate of indifferent substitution between consumption at time t and consumption at $t + 1$ less unity. More formally, consider $W(\overline{C}_0, \overline{C}_1, \ldots, \overline{C}_{t-1}, C_t, C_{t+1}, \overline{C}_{t+2}, \ldots)$, where the bar denotes that these quantities are kept fixed. In figure 8-1 we can plot in the (C_t, C_{t+1}) plane the *social indifference curve,* given by

$$W(\overline{C}_0, \overline{C}_1, \ldots, \overline{C}_{t-1}, C_t, C_{t+1}, \overline{C}_{t+2}, \ldots) = \text{constant} \qquad (2)$$

If W is strictly concave, equation (2) defines a strictly convex curve. We have defined ρ_t as the negative of the slope of equation (2) minus one. Thus, from equation (2) we have

$$\frac{\partial W(\{C_t\})}{\partial C_t} dC_t + \frac{\partial W(\{C_t\})}{\partial C_{t+1}} dC_{t+1} = 0$$

yielding

$$\rho_t \equiv \frac{-dC_{t+1}}{dC_t} - 1 = \frac{\partial W(\{C_t\})/\partial C_t}{\partial W(\{C_t\})/\partial C_{t+1}} - 1 \qquad (3)$$

Notice that in general, ρ_t depends on all the arguments of W. But as we have seen, it may appear appropriate to have ρ_t depend only on C_t and C_{t+1}. This will be the case if W assumes the "utilitarian" form:

$$W(\{C_t\}) = \sum_{t=0}^{\infty} u(C_t)/(1 + \partial)^t, \quad \partial > 0 \qquad (4)$$

We are assuming here that the infinite sum exists. Then since $\partial W(\{C_t\})/\partial C_t = u'(C_t)/(1 + \partial)^t$, we have

$$\rho_t = \frac{u'(C_t) - u'(C_{t+1})/(1 + \partial)}{u'(C_{t+1})/(1 + \partial)} \tag{5}$$

When we come to discuss the utilitarian optimum in the following sections, we shall make use of equation (5). But, for the moment, I concentrate on the more general form, equation (3). Since an optimum consumption sequence is efficient, we are concerned only with efficient sequences. Thus suppose $\{C_t\} \in \mathcal{F}$ is efficient. Now suppose that consumption is reduced at time t by ϵ, where ϵ is a small positive number. Let $h(\epsilon)$ (≥ 0) be the maximum increase in consumption that is possible at $t + 1$ without lowering consumption at any other date. Suppose next that $\lim\limits_{\epsilon \to 0} \dfrac{h(\epsilon)}{\epsilon}$ exists. We now define $r_t \equiv \lim\limits_{\epsilon \to 0} \dfrac{h(\epsilon)}{\epsilon} - 1$ as the *social rate of return on investment* during $(t, t + 1)$. It will be noted that r_t depends in general on t and, in particular, on the efficient sequence along which it is being computed. Now consider a set of efficient consumption sequences expressed as

$$C_{t+1} = T(\overline{C}_0, \ldots, \overline{C}_{t-1}, C_t, \mathcal{F} \, \overline{C}_{t+2}, \ldots)$$

where, again, the bar denotes that these quantities are kept fixed. If $\mathcal{F}$ is convex, T is a concave curve. It has been drawn as AB in figure 8-1.

Figure 8-1 indicates that if consumption at all dates other than t and $t + 1$ are held fixed at their "barred" values, then in choosing between points on curve AB, we cannot do better than to choose D, the point at which $\rho_t = r_t$. The condition tells us that the marginal rate of transformation between consumption at dates t and $t + 1$ must equal the marginal rate of indifferent substitution.

Let us now generalize the above argument. First make the rather innocuous assumption that consumption along an optimal program is positive throughout (though possibly tailing off to zero in the long run). Assume that W is strictly concave. Let $\{C_t\}$ denote an efficient program, and let r_t denote the social rate of return on investment along it. Suppose $\mathcal{F}$ is convex. Then for a large class of cases a necessary and sufficient condition for this program to be optimal is that

$$r_t = \rho_t \quad \text{for all } t \tag{6}$$

It will be useful to restate condition (6) explicitly in the language of social benefit–cost analysis. Suppose that the left-hand side of equation (6) were to fall short of the right-hand side at any date. Now one marginal unit of consumption at time t can be transformed into $1 + r_t$ units at $t + 1$. But this will fall short of $1 + \rho_t$, the number of units of extra consumption at $t + 1$ that will compensate for the loss of a unit of consumption at t. It follows that social welfare could be increased by consuming somewhat more at that date and, consequently, investing just that much less. In the language of benefit–cost analysis, the rate of return r_t on marginal investment being less than the rate ρ_t at which it is socially desirable to discount the next period's consumption makes this alteration an improvement. When this marginal adjustment is made (that is, a neighboring program is chosen), presumably r_t is increased (since $\mathscr{F}$ is convex) and ρ_t is reduced (since W is concave). These marginal adjustments are made until the two rates are equal. Similarly, if the left-hand side of equation (6) exceeds its right-hand side at any date along an efficient program, a reverse argument comes into play and social welfare could be improved by consuming somewhat less at that date. In terms of benefit–cost analysis this marginal investment is worth carrying out, since the return on the investment exceeds the rate at which it is judged desirable to discount the next period's consumption. If this marginal investment is made (that is, a neighboring program is chosen), r_t decreases and ρ_t increases. These marginal adjustments are made until the two rates are equal.

The necessity of condition (6) for a program (consumption sequence) to be optimal is, therefore, clear. The sufficiency of condition (6) for an efficient program to be optimal can be proved for a large class of economies, of which the economies to be discussed in the following sections on resource depletion and uncertainty are special cases.

Now suppose that aggregate consumption is chosen as the numeraire. Then what we have called the consumption rate of interest is the social rate of discount.

This is about as far as one can go in general terms. In the next two sections I shall specify $\mathscr{F}$ and W in more detail to analyze optimal programs in the light of different ethical beliefs.

Resource Depletion in a Utilitarian World

In the following discussion, it will prove convenient to work with continuous time. I shall suppose that the planner's preferences can be represented by the continuous-time formulation of equation (4). Thus

$$W = \int_0^\infty e^{-\delta t} u(C_t)\, dt \tag{7}$$

In addition, I suppose

$$\delta \geq 0, u'(C) > 0, u''(C) < 0, \lim_{c \to 0} u'(C) = \infty, \text{ and } \lim_{c \to \infty} u(C) = 0 \qquad (8)$$

I have qualified the term "utilitarian" advisedly. There are several distinct moral frameworks that can be appealed to in order to justify equation (7), of which classical utilitarianism is one.[4] Since I shall not wish to appeal to classical utilitarianism, it will be appropriate to refer to $u(\cdot)$ as the *felicity function*.[5] The term δ then is the felicity discount rate. The assumptions (8) need no detailed comment. The first three are standard. So is the fourth, which ensures the avoidance of zero consumption at any date along the optimum. The fifth assumption will allow one to keep the exposition tidy and to discuss an important limiting case, namely, $\delta = 0$.

Return to equation (5). In the continuous-time formulation, it reads as

$$\rho_t = -\frac{\dfrac{d}{dt}[e^{-\delta t}u'(C_t)]}{e^{-\delta t}u'(C_t)} \qquad (9)$$

or

$$\rho_t = \delta - \frac{u''(C_t)\dot{C}_t}{u'(C_t)}$$

Denote $\eta(C_t)$ as the *elasticity of marginal felicity*. That is, $\eta(C_t) = -\dfrac{u''(C_t)C_t}{u'(C_t)}, (>0)$. Then equation (9) becomes

$$\rho_t = \delta + \eta(C_t)\dot{C}_t/C_t \qquad (10)$$

The above is the consumption rate of interest at time t along the program $\{C_t\}$. Thus, suppose $\delta = 0.02$, $\eta(C_t) = 2.5$, and $\dot{C}_t/C_t = 0.04$. Then $\rho_t = 0.12$ (or 12 percent per unit time). But for my purposes here this is not a useful numerical exercise. We want to make the consumption rate of interest endogenous to the analysis. Thus the program $\{C_t\}$ cannot be given in advance of the analysis. Suppose then that $\{C_t^*\}$ is the optimum program. The consumption rate of interest along the program can then be computed from equation (10). It is the social rate of discount if consumption is the numeraire.

---

[4] These frameworks have been discussed at length in Dasgupta and Heal (1979, chapter 9). Amartya Sen has discussed more general social welfare functions in his paper in this volume, focusing attention on various informational bases on which such functions can be founded.

[5] The terminology is that of Gorman (1957). Arrow and Kurz (1970) use this terminology in their book.

If, instead, felicity is chosen as the numeraire, then δ is the social rate of discount. Unless $\dot{C}_t^*/C_t^* = 0$ the two discount rates will not be equal.

Consider a feasible perturbation of the optimal program $\{C_t^*\}$. I write it as $\{\Delta C_t\}$. It is a marginal investment project. Since the perturbation is around the optimal program, social welfare will not change. Thus, taking a first-order Taylor approximation, we have

$$\int_0^\infty e^{-\delta t} u'(C_t^*) \Delta C_t \, dt = 0 \tag{11}$$

The term $e^{-\delta t} u'(C_t^*)$ is the present-value shadow price of a unit of consumption if felicity is the numeraire. Equation (11) says that the marginal investment project has zero present value of net social benefits. But

$$\int_0^\infty e^{-\delta t} u'(C_t^*) \Delta C_t \, dt = \int_0^\infty e^{-(\delta t - \log u'(C_t^*))} \Delta C_t \, dt$$

$$= \int_0^\infty e^{-\delta t} \cdot \exp \left(\int_0^t \frac{d}{d\tau} \{\log u'(C_\tau^*)\} \, d\tau \right) \Delta C_t \, dt$$

$$= \int_0^\infty \exp \left(- \int_0^t \rho_\tau \, d\tau \right) \Delta C_t \, dt = 0 \tag{12}$$

The last expression in equation (12) is the present value of the marginal investment project computed on the understanding that aggregate consumption is the numeraire.

I turn now to a description of $\mathcal{F}$ that I shall be interested in. The model is familiar.[6] The stock of a single nondeteriorating, homogeneous commodity, K_t, in conjunction with a flow of an exhaustible resource, R_t, can reproduce itself. Let Y_t denote output of this homogeneous commodity. I assume that $Y_t = F(K_t, R_t)$, where F is strictly concave, strictly increasing, twice differentiable, and homogeneous of degree less than unity. In this section, I suppose an absence of technical progress. For ease of exposition, suppose that the exhaustible resource can be extracted costlessly. Let S_t denote the resource stock at time t. A *feasible program* $[K_t, S_t, R_t, C_t]$ is one that satisfies the following condition:

$$\dot{K}_t = F(K_t, R_t) - C_t$$

$$S_t = S_0 - \int_0^t R_\tau \, d\tau \tag{13}$$

$K_t, S_t, R_t, C_t \geq 0$ and S_0 and K_0 given.

[6] See, for example, Dasgupta and Heal (1974, 1979), Solow (1974), and Stiglitz (1974).

This condition defines the set of feasible consumption programs, $\mathcal{F}$. Since I am trying to focus attention on the impact of exhaustible resources on production and consumption possibilities, I have kept my feasible set very large. Condition (13) provides that any program that is technologically feasible is institutionally feasible. Joseph Stiglitz, in his paper in this volume, analyzes various plausible institutional constraints and their implications for the social rate of discount. By contrast, I am considering, in this and the following section, an untarnished economy. I shall be looking at what is called the "first best."

Since the optimum program is efficient, it will be useful to characterize efficient programs first. Let $[K_t, S_t, R_t, C_t]$ be an efficient program, and for simplicity of exposition, suppose that $R_t > 0$ for all t along it. As in the previous section, let r_t denote the social rate of return along it. It is then well known that the program must satisfy the following two conditions:[7]

$$\dot{F}_{R_t}/F_{R_t} = r_t \tag{14}$$

and

$$\lim_{t \to \infty} S_t = 0 \tag{15}$$

Condition (14) is referred to as the Hotelling rule (1931) in honor of the man who noted it first. If output (consumption) is the numeraire, F_{R_t} is the spot shadow price of the exhaustible resource along the efficient program under consideration. The left hand side of equation (14) is then the shadow rate of return on holding the resource as an asset. This must equal the shadow rate of return on holding the homogeneous consumption good. But it is possible to satisfy equation (14) and at the same time throw away a part of the resource stock. This cannot be efficient, and condition (15) ensures that this does not happen.

Now, for the economy described in condition (13), it is simple to show that $r_t = F_{K_t}$.[8] Thus equation (14) can be written as

$$\dot{F}_{R_t}/F_{R_t} = F_{K_t} \tag{16}$$

Equations (15) and (16) are conditions that an efficient program (with $R_t > 0$ for all t) must satisfy. They are not, in general, sufficient. But it can be shown that they form a pair of necessary *and* sufficient conditions if the

---

[7] Here $F_R = \partial F/\partial R$, $F_k = \partial F/\partial K$, and so forth. For a proof, see, for example, Dasgupta and Heal (1974, 1979), Solow (1974), and Stiglitz (1974).

[8] See, for example, Dasgupta and Heal (1979, chapter 7).

production function is of the Cobb–Douglas form, that is, $F(K, R) = K^{\alpha_1}R^{\alpha_2}$; $(\alpha_1, \alpha_2, 1 - \alpha_1 - \alpha_2 > 0)$.[9]

Certain special forms of F deserve scrutiny now. Consider the class of *constant-elasticity-of-substitution* (CES) production functions, which can be written as

$$F(K, R) = [\alpha_1 K^{(\sigma - 1)\sigma} + \alpha_2 R^{(\sigma - 1)\sigma} + (1 - \alpha_1 - \alpha_2)]^{\sigma(\sigma - 1)}$$
$$\text{with } 0 < \sigma < \infty \text{ and } \sigma \neq 1 \tag{17}$$

The case $\sigma = 1$ corresponds to the Cobb–Douglas form.

The question arises whether feasible consumption can be bounded away from zero or whether it must tend to zero in the long run. Notice that if $\sigma < 1$, then average output per unit of resource flow is a declining function of resource flow and is bounded above. Hence, feasible consumption must tend to zero. The economy must decay in the long run. It is doomed. If $\sigma > 1$, then $F(K, 0) > 0$ for $K > 0$; that is, resource flow is not even necessary for production. The resource enters into production in an interesting way if F is of the Cobb–Douglas form. It can be shown that if $\alpha_2 \geq \alpha_1$, then feasible consumption must tend to zero, but that if $\alpha_1 > \alpha_2$, it is feasible to have consumption bounded away from zero and, in particular, that it is possible to have unbounded consumption by allowing capital accumulation to take place at a stiff rate in initial years.[10] Since this last point will be demonstrated later in this section, I shall not go into it now. But these considerations suggest that analytically exhaustible resources pose an interesting problem for the Cobb–Douglas economy. It is for this reason that I shall concentrate on such an economy later on. Optimal planning in a more general CES world has been discussed in Dasgupta and Heal (1974).[11]

[9] See Stiglitz (1974) and Mitra (1975). Technically, the point is that the present value of the capital stock tends to zero along any path that satisfies condition (16). Capital overaccumulation cannot then take place if condition (16) is obeyed. What can happen is an underutilization of the resource and this is ruled out by condition (15).

[10] See also Solow (1974), Stiglitz (1974), and Dasgupta and Heal (1979). Recall that I have been supposing fixed capital to be nondeteriorating, and the question arises how depreciation affects this result. It is easy to show that feasible consumption must tend to zero in the Cobb–Douglas economy (with no technical change) in the presence of exponential decay. This form of depreciation is therefore embarrassing for the discussion that follows, but it is highly unrealistic as well. Economists continually postulate it in growth models for the analytical advantages it affords. There is little else to commend it. On the other hand, if fixed capital depreciates linearly in time, our claims in the text regarding the Cobb–Douglas economy go through. Likewise, if depreciation of fixed capital is proportional to gross output, our claims obviously go through. But such considerations rather complicate the notation. Depreciation will therefore be ignored here. I am grateful to Robert Dorfman for pointing out in his discussion of this paper the need for considering the question of depreciation.

[11] In his discussion of this paper, Tjalling Koopmans expresses doubts about the legitimacy of using CES production functions for the problem at hand. My own justification for concentrating attention on CES functions is not that I think they are a good approximation for the resource

But for the moment let me return to the more general world defined by condition (13). The planning problem consists of obtaining the feasible program that will maximize equation (7). The situation may be regarded as one in which the government chooses two functions, C_t and R_t. The rates of consumption and resource extraction could then be regarded as the *control variables*. The time profiles of the stocks of the composite commodity and the exhaustible resource would then follow from equations (13). The terms K_t and S_t are usually referred to as *state variables* in this formulation. At this stage we shall not inquire into the conditions under which an optimum program exists. It will become clearer later that we shall need further assumptions to ensure that the planning problem we have posed has an answer.

Assume then that an optimum program exists. A question of interest is whether along an optimum the resource is exhausted in finite time or whether it is spread out thinly over the indefinite future. It is not desirable to exhaust the resource in finite time if either (a) the resource is necessary for production (that is, $F(K, 0) = 0$) or (b) the marginal product of the resource (or equivalently, its average product) is unbounded for vanishing resource use (that is, $\lim_{R \to 0} F_R(K, R) = \infty$).[12] To economists, condition (b) would be rather obvious. If the resource at the margin is infinitely valuable for zero rate of use, it would clearly be suboptimal to exhaust it in finite time and have no resource left for use after the exhaustion date. It would prove desirable to spread the resource thinly over the indefinite future. However, if condition (a) is satisfied, but not (b), the result is not that obvious, though perhaps to observers who are not economists it is the more transparent condition. But recall that by assumption the durable capital good can be eaten into. By assumption, gross investment in fixed capital can be negative. Therefore, one can have positive consumption at all times despite an absence of the resource. This is why condition (a) on its own is not readily transparent. But one can see why the result comes out the way it does. Suppose (a) holds. If the resource is exhausted in finite time, there is no production after the date of exhaustion. Subsequent generations will be

---

problem, but that they expose in an illuminating manner the nature of the problem. Patently, what is of interest in a world with no technical advance is the asymptotic property of the elasticity of substitution, σ, as the capital/resources flow ratio tends to infinity. Thus, suppose $\sigma = \sigma(K/R)$. Then if $\lim_{(K/R) \to \infty} \inf \sigma(K/R) > 1$ the resource is inessential. It is essential if $\lim_{(K/R) \to \infty} \sup \sigma(K/R) < 1$. For analytical purposes, restriction to CES functions is therefore not misleading.

[12] This is proved in Dasgupta and Heal (1974) under somewhat different technological conditions.

forced to consume out of the remaining stock of the durable commodity. It would be a cake-eating economy, the social rate of return on investment would be nil, and savings would have no productivity. It is this feature that could be avoided were the resource not to be exhausted in finite time. By assumption, investment is productive ($F_K > 0$) so long as production continues. But if condition (a) holds, one can have production only if $R > 0$.

If, however, neither (a) nor (b) holds, it can be shown that along an optimum program the resource is exhausted in finite time (Dasgupta and Heal, 1974). The resource is neither necessary for production nor infinitely valuable at the margin at vanishing rates of use. The idea roughly is to use up the resource early in the planning horizon to raise the levels of consumption during the initial years while fixed capital is accumulated. Production is then maintained even after the resource is exhausted.

We have now a necessary and sufficient condition under which it is desirable to spread the resource over the indefinite future. Along an optimal program $R_t > 0$ if, and only if, either condition (a) or condition (b) holds. Since this is obviously the interesting case, we shall assume in what follows that the production function satisfies either condition (a) or condition (b).

Since an optimum program is intertemporally efficient, it must satisfy the conditions (14) and (15). We know that along an efficient program $r_t = F_{K_t}$. Using this fact and equation (9) in the optimality condition (6) yields

$$\frac{\eta(C_t)\dot{C}_t}{C_t} + \delta = F_{K_t} \tag{18}$$

Equation (18) is widely referred to in the literature as the Ramsey rule.[13] It is a special case of the rather general optimality condition (6). Its virtue lies in its simplicity. The condition brings out in the simplest manner possible the various considerations that may appear morally relevant in deciding on the optimum rate of accumulation. We now analyze the set of conditions that have been obtained.

Equations (16) and (18) together imply

$$F_{K_t} + \frac{u''(C_t)C_t}{u'(C_t)}\left(\frac{\dot{C}_t}{C_t}\right) - \delta = \dot{F}_{R_t}/F_{R_t} + \frac{u''(C_t)C_t}{u'(C_t)}\left(\frac{\dot{C}_t}{C_t}\right) - \delta = 0$$

Integrating this yields

$$e^{-\delta t}u'(C_t)F_{R_t} = \lambda(>0), \ldots \tag{19}$$

[13] Frank Ramsey (1928) pioneered the theory of optimum intertemporal planning.

where λ is a constant.[14] The economy being discussed in this section possesses three commodities—felicity, aggregate output, and the exhaustible resource. Let felicity be the numeraire. Then in the language of shadow prices, $u'(C_t)$ is the spot price of output (consumption). Consequently $u'(C_t)F_{R_t}$ is the spot price of the resource. It follows that $e^{-\delta t}u'(C_t)F_{R_t}$ is the present-value price of the resource. The term δ is the own rate of interest on felicity. It should be obvious that this must be constant along an optimum program. But the shadow spot price of the resource in terms of output is F_R, and this rises to infinity at the rate F_K.

As I have mentioned earlier, equation (16) holds throughout an optimal program if, and only if, either condition (a) or condition (b) holds. At least one of these conditions is met by the class of all CES production functions so long as the elasticity of substitution is finite (see equation (17)). If $\sigma >$ 1, the resource is not necessary for production (that is, condition (a) is not satisfied) but condition (b) is met.[15] If $0 < \sigma < 1$, then while condition (b) is not satisfied, the resource is necessary for production (that is, condition (a) is met). For the Cobb–Douglas case ($\sigma = 1$), both (a) and (b) are satisfied. In what follows, we shall work with the Cobb–Douglas form because, as I have argued earlier, this provides the most interesting possibilities for the resource problem.

Necessary and sufficient conditions for a feasible program to be optimal are that it be efficient and that it satisfy the Ramsey rule. For a program to be efficient, it is necessary that conditions (14) and (15) are satisfied. Moreover, we have noted that if the production function is of the Cobb–Douglas form, conditions (14) and (15) are together also sufficient for a program to be intertemporally efficient. It follows that in a world with a Cobb–Douglas technology, equations (14), (15), and (18) form a set of necessary and sufficient conditions for a feasible program to be optimal. If an optimal program exists, it will be characterized by these equations. If an optimal program does not exist, no feasible program will satisfy them all at the same time. The three equations will be inconsistent with the requirement that the program be feasible.

It will prove immensely helpful to specialize further and suppose that η, the elasticity of marginal felicity, is a constant. The greater the value of η, the more concave the felicity function. This will imply in turn what could be termed a more egalitarian intertemporal consumption policy.

---

[14] As one would imagine, the numerical value of λ is chosen so as to satisfy the resource constraint,

$$\int_0^\infty R_t\, dt = S_0$$

[15] The resource is infinitely valuable at the margin for a vanishing rate of utilization.

Let $F(K_t, R_t) = K_t^{\alpha_1} R_t^{\alpha_2}$, and assume that $\alpha_1 > \alpha_2 > 0$. Naturally, $1 - \alpha_1 - \alpha_2 > 0$. By assumption, $\lim_{C \to \infty} u(C) = 0$. Consequently $\eta > 1$, and so

$$u(C) = -C^{-(\eta-1)}$$

Recall that I have claimed that if $\alpha_1 > \alpha_2$, it is feasible to have consumption bounded away from zero. This means that it is possible to have constant positive consumption. In what follows, I shall denote by $\overline{C}_{max}$ the maximum constant consumption level the economy is capable of providing.

Positive Felicity Discounting: $\delta > 0$

One might expect that an optimal program would exist if $\delta > 0$. This is in fact the case (Dasgupta and Heal, 1974). Here we shall characterize it in broad terms.

Rewrite equation (18) for the present model as

$$\dot{C}_t/C_t = \frac{\alpha_1 K_t^{\alpha_1 - 1} R_t^{\alpha_2} - \delta}{\eta} \tag{20}$$

Feasibility dictates that $R_t \to 0$. Since $\delta > 0$, the only way one can ensure that $\dot{C}_t/C_t$ is nonnegative in the long run is that $K_t \to 0$ as well. But if $K_t \to 0$, then $Y_t \to 0$, and hence $C_t \to 0$. Consequently equation (20) implies that $C_t \to 0$. A positive rate of impatience, no matter how small, implies that it is judged optimal to allow the economy to decay in the long run, even though it is feasible to avoid decay. This is true no matter how large a value of η we choose to express our values. A positive rate of pure time preference tilts the balance overwhelmingly against generations in the distant future. This alone is a powerful result; it indicates that utilitarianism, with a positive rate of impatience, can recommend what can be regarded as ethically questionable policies. The welfare criterion does not recommend sufficient capital accumulation in the early years to offset the declining resource use inevitable in later years. Since the optimum is efficient, consumption at some interval must exceed $\overline{C}_{max}$. It can be shown that the consumption profile will have at most one peak; the lower the value of δ, the further away in the future is the peak. In figure 8-2 a typical optimum consumption path (with $\delta > 0$) is contrasted with the intergenerational max-min consumption policy, $C_0 = \overline{C}_{max}$.

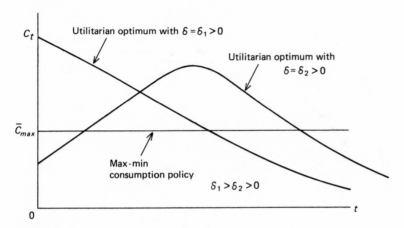

Figure 8-2

Of course, later generations (should they exist) suffer incredibly as a result of the initial profligacy under the utilitarian program. They are far worse off than they would be under the max-min policy.[16]

The Ramsey rule (20) suggests that the effect of a large value of η is to flatten the consumption path somewhat, the dive toward zero consumption being that much postponed. It is interesting to note that the two parameters reflecting ethical values, η and δ, play somewhat dissimilar roles. In a loose sense, the larger the value of η, the more egalitarian the distribution of consumption (and felicities) across generations.[17] This makes sense if one recollects that the effect of a large η on the felicity function is to impose more curvature on it, as figure 8-3 shows. There are benefits to be had in keeping consumption for a long while within the region in which the felicity

---

[16] To put the matter rather dramatically, notice that $u(C_t) \rightarrow -\infty$ as $C_t \rightarrow 0$. Nevertheless, the implication of $\delta > 0$ is that, viewed from the present instant (that is, $t = 0$), this is not only not disastrous, but desirable. But if δ reflects the possibility of future extinction, the probability that generations in the distant future will exist will also tend to zero.

In his comments on this paper, James Sweeney noted that this result depends crucially on the assumption that there is no technical change. Indeed, this will be confirmed in the following discussion of uncertainty, technical change, and innovation. But suppose the more conventional form of continuous technical progress. To be specific, suppose that

$$Y_t = e^{\beta t} K_t{}^{\alpha_1} R_t{}^{\alpha_2} \text{ (with } \beta, \alpha_1, \alpha_2, 1 - \alpha_1 - \alpha_2 > 0)$$

Then as Stiglitz (1974) and Garg and Sweeney (1977) have shown, the optimal program has the property that $C_t \rightarrow 0$ if $\delta > \beta/\alpha_2$ and $C_t \rightarrow \infty$ if $\delta < \beta/\alpha_2$. The point is that the "origin" shifts. But the moral remains that δ is a crucial parameter. At any event, it is difficult to entertain the idea of continuous technical progress (see Tjalling Koopmans' discussion, in this volume, on the probability of continuous technical progress).

[17] The precise sense in which this is true has been discussed well in Atkinson (1970).

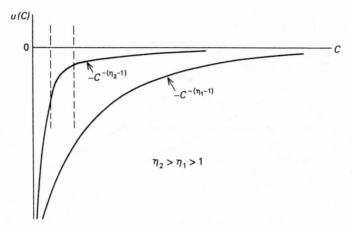

Figure 8-3

function makes a sharp turn. The effect of δ is quite different and its consequence is a discrimination against future felicities. A positive δ results in generations of the distant future receiving very little capital. Their consumption rates are nearly zero.

Much of our attention has been focused on the substitution of augmentable capital for exhaustible resources in production. With this in mind, we can write condition (16) in a simple form. It will enable us to interpret the manner in which fixed capital ought to substitute for resource use along optimal programs in general. Define $\bar{R}_t$ as $\bar{R}_t = R_t^{(1-\alpha_2)/\alpha_1}$. One is then measuring the resource use in a new system of units ($\bar{R}_t$ is a monotonically increasing function of R, and $\bar{R} = 0$ when $R = 0$; $\bar{R} = \infty$ when $R = \infty$). Now $F_R = \alpha_2 K^{\alpha_1} R^{\alpha_2 - 1} = \alpha_2 K^{\alpha_1} \bar{R}^{-\alpha_1}$. Moreover, $F_K = \alpha_1 \times K^{\alpha_1 - 1} R^{\alpha_2} = \alpha_1 \dfrac{Y}{K}$. Using this term in equation (16) yields

$$\alpha_1 \left(\dot{K}_t/K_t - \dot{\bar{R}}_t/\bar{R}_t \right) = \alpha_1 \frac{Y}{K}$$

Let $Z_t = K_t/\bar{R}_t$, and let $x_t = Y_t/K_t$ denote the output capital ratio. Then the above equation reduces to

$$\dot{Z}_t/Z_t = x_t \tag{21}$$

This is an appealing condition. It says that the greater the output capital ratio, the greater the percentage rate at which it is desirable to substitute fixed capital for the resource in use. Stating it another way, the more valuable is fixed capital in production (at the margin or on average; it does not matter), the greater is the speed with which fixed capital ought to substitute for the resource in use. It ought to be emphasized that equation (21) is a condition that efficient paths must satisfy. Its validity does not rest on the utilitarian formulation of the optimality criterion that we have been analyzing in this section.[18]

We are interested in the optimum rate of resource depletion. Return once again to our general optimality condition (19). (It is that $e^{-\delta t} u'(C_t) F_{R_t} = \lambda > 0$.) For the special case at hand (that is, isoelastic felicity function $u(C_t) = - C_t^{-(\eta-1)}$, $\eta > 1$, and Cobb–Douglas production function) this becomes

$$(\eta - 1)\, \alpha_2\, e^{-\delta t}\, C_t^{-\eta}\, R_t^{-(1-\alpha_2)}\, K_t^{\alpha_1} = \lambda$$

for $u'(C_t) = (\eta - 1)\, C_t^{-\eta}$ and $F_R = \alpha_2\, K^{\alpha_1} R^{\alpha_2 - 1}$

This is written more conveniently as

$$C_t/K_t = e^{-(\delta/\eta)t}\, ((\eta - 1)\, \alpha_2/\lambda)^{1/\eta}\, K_t^{-(1-\alpha_1/\eta)}\, R_t^{-(1-\alpha_2)/\eta} \tag{22}$$

But observe that equation (21) and the fact that $\tilde{R}_t = R_t^{(1-\alpha_2/\eta)/\alpha_1}$ imply[19]

$$\dot{C}_t/K_t = Y_t/K_t - \dot{K}_t/K_t = - \frac{(1-\alpha_2)\, \dot{R}_t}{\alpha_1\, R_t} \tag{23}$$

From equations (22) and (23) we now obtain

$$\left(\frac{1-\alpha_2}{\alpha_1}\right) \dot{R}_t/R_t = - [(\eta-1)\alpha_2/\lambda]^{1/\eta} (e^{-(\delta/\eta)t})\, K_t^{(\alpha_1/\eta - 1)}\, R_t^{-(1-\alpha_2)/\eta} < 0 \tag{24}$$

It follows that R_t declines monotonically along the optimal program.

Equation (24) is an equation in $\dot{R}_t$. We can now express the equation for capital accumulation, condition (13), as

$$\dot{K}_t = K_t^{\alpha_1} R_t^{\alpha_2} - C_t$$

Now use equation (22) to obtain

$$\dot{K}_t = K_t^{\alpha_1} R_t^{\alpha_2} - e^{-(\delta/\eta)t} [(\eta - 1)\, \alpha_2/\lambda]^{1/\eta}\, K_t^{\alpha_1/\eta}\, R_t^{-(1-\alpha_2)/\eta} \tag{25}$$

---

[18] One can in fact cast equation (16) in a form similar to equation (21) for the class of CES production functions in general. The elasticity of substitution plays a key role in such an equation. For details, see Dasgupta and Heal (1974).

[19] Equation (21) says that $\dot{K}_t/K_t - \dot{\tilde{R}}_t/\tilde{R}_t = Y_t/K_t$. But $\dot{\tilde{R}}_t/\tilde{R}_t = \dfrac{(1-\alpha_2)}{\alpha_1} \dot{R}_t/R_t$ and $C_t = Y_t - K_t$. These yield equation (23).

Equations (24) and (25) are equations in $\dot{K}_t$ and $\dot{R}_t$. With $\delta > 0$, the pair is nonautonomous in time. We have argued that both $C_t \to 0$ and $K_t \to 0$ in the long run. And of course $R_t \to 0$. Consequently $Y_t \to 0$. The economy is allowed to decay in the long run. It can be shown that $F_K \to \delta \, \alpha_2/(1-\alpha_1 + \alpha_2(\eta-1)) < \delta$. Consequently, $g_C \equiv \dot{C}_t/C_t \to \dfrac{-\delta}{\eta} (1-\alpha_2)/(1-\alpha_1-\alpha_2 + \eta \, \alpha_2) < 0$. It is also possible to demonstrate that $g_S \equiv \dot{S}_t/S_t \to -\delta(1-\alpha_1)/(1-\alpha_1 + \alpha_2 (\eta-1))$.[20] Consequently, $R_t/S_t \to \delta(1-\alpha_1)/[1-\alpha_1 + \alpha_2 (\eta-1)]$. Suppose that $\eta = 2$, $\delta = 0.02$, $\alpha_1 = 0.25$, and $\alpha_2 = 0.05$. Then $R_t/S_t \to 0.02$; about 2 percent of the then existing stock ought to be extracted in the long run. In other words, about 50 years of resource supply at the then current rates of extraction ought to be available in the long run. Moreover, with those parameters the optimum rate of consumption will be declining in the long run at about 1.2 percent per annum; while the consumption rate of interest will approach a figure of about 1.2 percent per annum.

No Felicity Discounting: $\delta = 0$

The interesting special case is $\delta = 0$. Equations (24) and (25) are then autonomous differential equations. Figure 8-4 depicts their phase paths. Path GH is the locus of points at which $\dot{K}_t = 0$. It is obtained from equation (25) by setting $\delta = 0$ and $\dot{K}_t = 0$. The equation for path GH is

$$K = ((\eta-1)\alpha_2/\eta)^{1/\alpha_1(\eta-1)} R^{-(1 + \alpha_2(\eta-1))/\alpha_1(\eta-1)} \tag{26}$$

Anywhere to the right of GH, $\dot{K}_t > 0$, and anywhere to the left of GH, $\dot{K}_t < 0$. As equation (24) makes clear, there is no corresponding locus along which $\dot{R}_t = 0$. $\dot{R}_t < 0$ at all points. Now recall that K_0 and S_0 are given as initial conditions; but R_0 has to be chosen optimally. If R_0 is chosen too low (say the initial point chosen lies to the left of GH), both $\dot{K}_t < 0$ and $\dot{R}_t < 0$. Capital will be decumulated at a rate that increases as R_t decreases (see equation (25)). The entire stock of fixed capital will be consumed in finite time, and the program will not be feasible. Indeed, as figure 8-4 makes clear, if the initial point chosen lies slightly to the right of path GH (say, the path $A'B'$), the corresponding trajectory $A'B'$ will reach a maximum value for the capital stock and will then turn down. Capital will be consumed from then on, and, as R_t decreases, the rate of consumption increases. Fixed capital will be consumed in finite time. There is then a critical phase path AB that approaches path GH asymptotically as $R \to 0$. Any path to the left of AB eventually turns down and runs out of capital in finite time. But along path

---

[20] For proofs of these assertions, see Dasgupta and Heal (1974) and Stiglitz (1974).

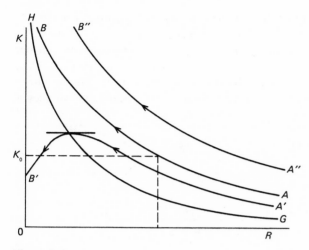

Figure 8-4

AB, $K_t \rightarrow \infty$. If an optimum exists one suspects it is this path.[21] If R_0 is chosen too high (that is, the initial point chosen lies to the northeast of path AB, say on path $A''B''$), R_t remains too large in the sense that the integral of resource use will exceed the initial stock. Such a path is infeasible.

It remains to confirm that AB is the optimal path. To do this, it would be convenient if we were able to obtain the equation representing path AB in an explicit form. For very low values of R, path AB has the same functional form as path GH since it approaches GH asymptotically. Let us suppose that path AB has the functional form

$$K = \Pi R^{-(1 + \alpha_2(\eta-1))/\alpha_1(\eta-1)}, \text{ with } \Pi > 0 \qquad (27)$$

We now need to verify that this equation satisfies the optimality conditions for some value of Π. If it does, it will yield the value of Π as well. Differentiate equation (27) with respect to time. This yields

$$\dot{K}_t = \frac{-\Pi(1 + \alpha_2(\eta-1))}{\alpha_1(\eta-1)} R_t^{-(1 + (\alpha_1 + \alpha_2)(\eta-1))/\alpha_1(\eta-1)} \dot{R}_t \qquad (28)$$

Now use equations (27) and (28) to eliminate K_t and $\dot{K}_t$ from equation (25). This gives us an equation in $\dot{R}_t$. Now eliminate $\dot{R}_t$ between this and equation (24). This yields

$$\Pi = (\eta/(\eta-1)(1-\alpha_2))^{\eta/\alpha_1(\eta-1)}((\eta-1)\alpha_2/\lambda)^{1/\alpha_1(\eta-1)} \qquad (29)$$

[21] We say "if" because we are now considering the case $\delta = 0$.

We have thus shown that the trajectory defined by equations (27) and (29) satisfies the optimality conditions. Our hunch was correct. Equation (27) does indeed denote path AB, with the value of Π being given by equation (29). We can now use equation (27) in equation (24) to eliminate K_t and reduce it to a differential equation depending solely on R_t. This in turn is readily integrable. I omit details here, but it can be checked that the integral is

$$R_t = (R_0^{1-\mu} + Mt)^{1/1-\mu} \tag{30}$$

where $M > 0$ and

$$\mu = \frac{(\alpha_1 + \alpha_2)(\eta - 1)^2 + (1 + \alpha_2)(\eta - 1) + (1 - \alpha_1)}{\alpha_1(\eta - 1)\eta} > 1 \tag{31}$$

Simple manipulation shows that $\mu > 1$ if and only if $(\alpha_1 - \alpha_2) + (1 - \alpha_1 - \alpha_2)\eta + \alpha_2 \eta^2 > 0$, which is true by assumption.

From this it follows that

$$\frac{1}{1 - \mu} = -\frac{\alpha_1(\eta - 1)\eta}{\alpha_2(\eta - 1)^2 + (\eta - 1)(1 + \alpha_2 - \alpha_1) + (1 - \alpha_1)} < 0$$

If the integral of the extraction function (30) is to converge, it is necessary and sufficient that $\dfrac{1}{1 - \mu} < -1$; or $\mu < 2$. From equation (31) it follows that this is so if and only if $\eta > \dfrac{1 - \alpha_2}{\alpha_1 - \alpha_2}$ (>1). We have therefore demonstrated by construction that if $\eta > \dfrac{1 - \alpha_2}{\alpha_1 - \alpha_2}$, there is a feasible program that satisfies the optimality conditions (15), (16), and (18), even though $\delta = 0$. Therefore this program is optimal. We have yet to describe the movement of consumption along the optimum. Using equation (27) in equation (22) yields

$$C_t = \Pi^{\alpha_1/\eta} R_t^{-1/(\eta - 1)}((\eta - 1)\alpha_2/\lambda)^{1/\eta} \tag{32}$$

Since R_t is monotonically declining (equation (30)), consumption along the optimal path is monotonically increasing. Moreover, since $R_t \to 0$, it follows that $C_t \to \infty$. As a final check, notice that $C_t^{-(\eta-1)}$ is proportional to R_t (equation (32)). Therefore, the felicity integral along this program does indeed converge. Notice further that since $K_t \to \infty$, $F_K \to 0$. It follows that the consumption rate of interest tends to zero in the long run along the optimum program. If the consumption good is chosen as the numeraire, this means that the social rate of discount, while positive throughout, declines to zero in the long run.

Now, it follows from equation (30) that $\dot{C}_t/C_t \to 0$, (that is, while consumption increases to infinity, its long-run rate of growth declines to zero). We shall presently confirm that optimum consumption is a fixed proportion of optimum gross national product. Therefore, the long-run rate of growth of optimum GNP is also zero. The behavior of the long-run resource utilization ratio is simple to work out, because equation (30) implies that R_t/S_t is proportional to $(R_0^{1-\eta} + Mt)^{-1}$. Consequently $R_t/S_t \to 0$. A vanishing fraction of a vanishing resource stock is all that is required to sustain the unbounded increase in output and consumption. When $\alpha_1 > \alpha_2$, exhaustible resources pose no threat whatsoever.

We can describe the optimal program also in terms of the savings ratio required to sustain it. Using equation (27) in the production function implies that aggregate output (GNP) along the optimum is given by

$$Y_t = \Pi^{\alpha_1} R_t^{-1/(\eta-1)}$$

and, consequently, using equation (32) implies that

$$C_t/Y_t = \left(\frac{(\eta-1)\alpha_2}{\lambda}\right)^{1/\eta} \Pi^{-(\eta-1)\alpha_1/\eta} = \frac{(\eta-1)(1-\alpha_2)}{\eta} < 1 - \alpha_2$$

or, to state it another way,

$$s_t = \dot{K}_t/Y_t = 1 - C_t/Y_t = \frac{1 + \alpha_2(\eta-1)}{\eta} > \alpha_2 \tag{33}$$

The savings ratio along the optimal program is constant and exceeds α_2.

To see what orders of magnitude may be involved, let $\alpha_1 = 0.25$ and $\alpha_2 = 0.05$. Then we need $\eta > \dfrac{95}{20}$. Suppose that $\eta = 5$, in which case s_t = 24 percent. This is a high rate of savings, though not unduly high.

We can characterize fully the optimal program for different values of η. We have argued that for $\delta = 0$ it is required that

$$\eta > \frac{1 - \alpha_2}{\alpha_1 - \alpha_2}$$

Now

$$\frac{d}{d\eta}\{1 + \alpha_2(\eta - 1)\}/\eta) < 0, \lim_{\eta \to \infty} \left(\frac{1 + \alpha_2(\eta - 1)}{\eta} \right) = \alpha_2$$

$$\lim_{\eta \to (1 - \alpha_2)/(\alpha_1 - \alpha_2)} \left(\frac{1 + \alpha_2(\eta - 1)}{\eta} \right) = \alpha_1$$

Equation (33) tells us then that if we ignore the case $\eta = \dfrac{1 - \alpha_2}{\alpha_1 - \alpha_2}$, the

optimal savings ratio falls from α_1 to α_2 as η rises from $\dfrac{1 - \alpha_2}{\alpha_1 - \alpha_2}$ to ∞. All

this squares with one's intuition and merges beautifully with the max-min consumption policy. The point is that the larger η is, the more egalitarian is the underlying preference ordering. One knows in advance that the limiting case of $\eta \to \infty$ will yield the max-min consumption policy; that is, the maximum constant consumption program $C_t = \overline{C}_{max}$. (See Hardy, Littlewood, and Polya (1934), and Arrow (1973).) A crude method of confirming this is to let η go to infinity in equation (32). In this case, the equation says that C_t is constant along the optimum program and, since the optimum is efficient, this constant level must be $\overline{C}_{max}$. In fact, $\overline{C}_{max}$ can be computed explicitly in terms of the technological coefficients α_1 and α_2 and the initial stocks K_0 and S_0. This was one of the tasks undertaken by Robert Solow (1974) in his important contribution on the question of Rawlsian savings in a world such as I have been discussing here. As one would expect, the larger α_1, K_0, and S_0 are, the larger $\overline{C}_{max}$ is. Here I am approaching the max-min policy as a limiting case of utilitarianism. Thus if $(1 - \alpha_2)/(\alpha_1 - \alpha_2) < \eta < \infty$, the utilitarian optimum is characterized by unbounded consumption in the long run, while the consumption rate of interest falls monotonically to zero (since $\dot{K}_t > 0$, and $\dot{R}_t < 0$, and therefore $\dot{F}_K < 0$ and $F_K \to 0$). But the larger is η, the more delayed is the rise in consumption to infinity. Earlier generations consume less than $\overline{C}_{max}$ (so that later generations may benefit from the higher rate of capital accumulation); but the greater is η, the closer are the initial rates of consumption to $\overline{C}_{max}$, and consequently the further delayed is the date at which consumption under utilitarianism reaches the level $\overline{C}_{max}$. That is, the utilitarian optimum consumption path becomes flatter as η is raised in value (see figure 8-5). In the limiting case, $\eta = \infty$, the utilitarian solution merges with the max-min program.

The arguments leading to the characterization of the utilitarian optimum suggest strongly that for $\delta = 0$, an optimum does not exist if $\eta < (1 - \alpha_2)/(\alpha_1 - \alpha_2)$. This is indeed the case. The point is that even though the economy is capable of unbounded consumption, it is not productive enough to allow consumption to rise to infinity at a rate fast enough for the felicity integral to converge to a finite number. All feasible programs yield con-

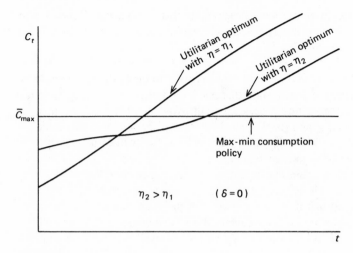

Figure 8-5

sumption paths that lead the felicity integral to diverge to $-\infty$. No optimum policy exists. That is, no feasible program satisfies the three optimality conditions (15), (16), and (18) simultaneously.

Let me summarize the results obtained in this section. If $\delta > 0$ and $\eta > 1$, a utilitarian optimum exists. Consumption and output along the optimum decline to zero in the long run. The larger the value of η (or, correspondingly, the smaller the value of δ), the more delay there is before consumption is allowed to approach zero. The optimum consumption path can have at most one peak in the future. If δ is large, optimum consumption is monotonically declining; there is no peak in the future. If δ is small, consumption rises initially, attains a peak, and then declines to zero in the long run. If $\delta = 0$, a utilitarian optimum exists only if $\eta > (1 - \alpha_2)/(\alpha_1 - \alpha_2)$. Output and consumption increase monotonically without bound along the optimum program. Earlier generations consume less than $\overline{C}_{max}$ with a view to allowing later generations to enjoy high rates of consumption. The savings ratio along the optimum is constant throughout. The larger the value of η, the flatter the optimum consumption path. In the limiting case, $\eta = \infty$, the utilitarian optimum coincides with the max-min (constant consumption) program. If $\eta \leq (1 - \alpha_2)/(\alpha_1 - \alpha_2)$ and $\delta = 0$, no utilitarian optimum exists. (See figures 8-2 and 8-5.)

Uncertainty, Technical Change, and Optimum Innovative Activity

The previous section was designed to highlight the roles that are played by the felicity discount rate δ and the elasticity of marginal felicity, η, in the characterization of an optimum program. In this section, I shall move away from the earlier, moderately pessimistic world and allow technical advance to be a distinct possibility.[22]

It is tempting to suppose technical progress is made more or less independently by many firms and then to appeal to the law of large numbers. This is typically the justification that one would offer in regarding technical progress as a continuous process. I shall avoid this here. I have in mind events that could appropriately be called major technological innovations, or what would be called technological breakthroughs, such as a clean breeder reactor or controlled nuclear fusion.[23]

I want to imagine that scientists in this construction know what they are looking for (it is very much goal-oriented research that they are undertaking) but that there are a number of problems that need to be solved before the goal is attained. Of course, there is no certainty that they will be able to solve all the problems. Research may well prove to be fruitless. Moreover, research involves the expenditure of resources. Thus we are faced with a question that is often asked: What is the optimal level of investment in such an uncertain innovative activity and, more generally, what principles should guide such a decision? We are therefore in the realm of social benefit–cost analysis of R&D.

As in the previous section, I shall generate the criterion from an overall optimization exercise. Thus, for example, "social rates of discount," appropriately defined, will emerge from the model. They will not be given before the exercise.

For simplicity I suppose a single innovation. Suppose that the innovation occurs at date $T(\geq 0)$, and let K_T and S_T denote the stocks of the reproducible homogeneous commodity and the exhaustible resource at date T. In what follows, I shall not make precise the technological possibilities open to the economy in the postinnovation era. For vividness one might wish to imagine that the innovation releases the economy from the constraint imposed by exhaustible resources. Thus, for example, thermodynamic considerations tell us that in order to produce a given level of output, Y, a given minimum flow of energy is required. This minimum is positive and no amount of substitution of other factors of production can allow Y to be produced with less energy.

---

[22] The construction that follows originated in Dasgupta and Heal (1975), Dasgupta, Heal, and Majumdar (1977), and Kamien and Schwartz (1978).

[23] Notice that I am talking of a "clean" fast breeder, suitably defined. Innovations that do not pass the test are, by assumption, prohibited from operation. This is usually justified by the observation that otherwise the present generation would be encroaching on future generations' inviolable right to a clean atmosphere. I emphasize this because it may be thought that the utilitarian formulation of the problem of optimum depletion that I am pursuing here is incapable of accommodating such considerations as rights—other than, of course, the right to utility or happiness. The route I am following here is one of removing from consideration the class of feasible programs that violate such rights. For a general discussion of rights, see the paper by Amartya Sen in this volume.

Now suppose that in the notation of the last section, R denotes a flow of energy and in particular suppose that the exhaustible resource provides us with the only source of energy. It follows then that the elasticity of substitution between K and R must be less than unity as $K/R \to \infty$.[24] The economy is then doomed (that is, feasible consumption must tend to zero in the long run) unless a new (inexhaustible) source of energy is found. The innovation I am thinking of is of this type.

Assume then that the innovation occurs at date T. For simplicity of exposition, suppose that there is no further uncertainty for the economy. At T the following problem is solved by the planners:

$$\text{maximize} \int_T^\infty u(C_t) \, e^{-\delta(t-T)} \, dt \tag{34}$$

subject to whatever constraints are operative from date T onward. Presumably the remaining stocks K_T and S_T will be of use in the postinnovation era. Then let us denote the maximized value of the integral (35) as $W(K_T, S_T)$. Viewed from the vantage point of T, this is the present discounted value of the flow of felicity from T onward generated by the optimum policy from T. I shall assume that W is strictly concave and continuously differentiable. Both of these assumptions can be justified under certain specifications. Since I am not specifying the postinnovation technology, I need to postulate them here. As I did in the previous section, I shall suppose that $u(\cdot)$ is bounded above by zero. Therefore, so is W.

Return now to the initial instant $t = 0$. We are in the preinnovation era. The economy is much like that described in the previous section, except that investment can now be allocated in R&D as well. I introduce a real variable V_t to denote the "stock of knowledge" at t. Knowledge accumulates if research is actively pursued, not otherwise. Let M_t denote the rate of expenditure at time t in the innovative activity. A simple form of the "production function" of knowledge is then $h(M_t)$, where

$$\dot{V}_t = h(M_t), \text{ with } h(0) = 0, \, h'(\cdot) > 0 \text{ and } h''(\cdot) < 0 \tag{35}$$

We can, without any loss in generality, set $V_0 = 0$, which is merely a normalization device. Suppose that the planner possesses a subjective probability density function $w(V)$ that the innovation will occur at the state of knowledge V. In particular this means that, viewed from $t = 0$, the

[24] Thus, in supposing a Cobb–Douglas production function in the previous section, I have tacitly assumed that if R denotes a flow of energy, it is not the only source, and that another source continually provides the economy with energy as well.

probability density that the innovation will occur at time t is $w(V_t)\dot{V}_t = w(V_t)h(M_t)$. Choice of an R&D expenditure program fixes this density function. Thus, for example, if no R&D expenditure is planned during an interval (t_1, t_2), then it is known in advance that the innovation cannot occur during (t_1, t_2).

Thus, there are three control variables for the planner, namely, C_t, R_t, and M_t. The planning problem at $t = 0$ is to choose intertemporal paths of C_t, R_t, and M_t with a view to maximizing

$$E\left[\int_0^T \{u(C_t)e^{-\delta t}\, dt + e^{-\delta T}W(K_T, S_T)\}\right] \tag{36}$$

subject to the constraints that the preinnovation economy faces. In integral (36), E denotes the expectation operator. Let us now describe the preinnovation economy as satisfying the following conditions:

$$\dot{K}_t = F(K_t, R_t) - C_t - M_t$$

$$\int_0^\infty R_t\, dt \le S_0 \tag{37}$$

$$\dot{V}_t = h(M_t)$$

with C_t, M_t, R_t, K_t, $S_t \ge 0$ and K_0, S_0 given; ($V_0 = 0$)

The next step is to reduce integral (36) into a transparent form. Thus suppose a feasible policy (C_t, R_t, M_t) is planned, conditional on the innovation's not having occurred. Consider a sample path in which the innovation occurs at time t. Accordingly, viewed from the present, social welfare is

$$\int_0^t u(C_\tau)e^{-\delta \tau}\, d\tau + e^{-\delta t}W(K_t, S_t)$$

Expected social welfare is then

$$\int_0^\infty w(V_t)\dot{V}_t\left\{\int_0^t u(C_\tau)e^{-\delta \tau}\, d\tau + e^{-\delta t}W(K_t, S_t)\right\} dt$$

$$+ \Omega(V_\infty)\int_0^\infty u(C_t)e^{-\delta t}\, dt \tag{38}$$

(where $\Omega(V) \equiv \int_v^\infty w(V') \, dV'$ and therefore $\Omega(V_\infty)$ represents the probability that the innovation will never occur). Integrating the integral (38) by parts yields expected social welfare as

$$\int_0^\infty e^{-\delta t} \left[u(C_t)\Omega(V_t) + w(V_t)h(M_t)W(K_t, S_t) \right] dt \tag{39}$$

The planning problem is to choose the control variables (C_t, R_t, M_t) with a view to maximizing integral (39), subject to conditions (37). The idea is to pursue this optimum policy until the innovation occurs, if ever. It is therefore a policy conditional on the innovation's not having occurred. The instant it does occur, the economy moves on to a new regime. The optimal policy from that date (say T) is the maximization of integral (34).

Let us assume that there is a policy that maximizes integral (39). This assumption can be justified under certain specifications of $w(V)$ and the postinnovation technological possibilities. In this case, I express the Hamiltonian of the problem as

$$H = e^{-\delta t}[\Omega(V_t)u(C_t) + w(V_t)h(M_t)W(K_t, S_t)]$$
$$+ e^{-\delta t}p_t[F(K_t, R_t) - C_t - M_t] - \lambda R_t + e^{-\delta t}q_t h(M_t) + \mu_t e^{-\delta t}M_t \tag{40}$$

where $e^{-\delta t}p_t$, λ, and $e^{-\delta t}q_t$ are the co-state variables of the three conditions (37), and $\mu_t \geq 0$ with $\mu_t M_t = 0$. I have consciously avoided writing down the nonnegativity constraints associated with C_t and R_t since I suppose (without further justification) that they are never binding.

We can now conclude that for a program to be optimal in the preinnovation era, we must have

$$\Omega(V_t)u'(C_t) = p_t \tag{41}$$

$$e^{-\delta t}p_t F_{R_t} = \lambda > 0 \tag{42}$$

and

$$\left.\begin{array}{r} (w(V_t)W(K_t, S_t) + q_t)h'(M_t) \leq p_t \\ M_t \geq 0 \end{array}\right\} \text{(complementary slackness)} \tag{43}$$

These three statements tell us a good deal about the structure of intertemporal shadow prices that sustain the optimum program. It should be noted that $e^{-\delta t}p_t$ is the present-value contingent price of output (consumption) with felicity at $t = 0$ as numeraire. Thus $e^{-\delta t}p_t$ is the price to be paid at $t = 0$ for delivery of a unit of output at time t if and only if the innovation has not occurred by then. Equations (41) and (42) then are self-explanatory. So is equation (42), which is the generalization of the Hotelling rule for the present construction. The rule that is not so familiar is inequality (43). Suppose that for some time t (conditional on the innovation's not having occurred), it is optimal to set $M_t > 0$. Then the first part of inequality (43) is a strict equality at time t. Along the optimum, the planner is indifferent at the margin between consumption, investment in fixed capital, and investment in R&D. Thus, $e^{-\delta t}p_t$ is the present-value contingent price of R&D investment, using felicity as numeraire. The left-hand side of the first part of inequality (43) denotes the worthwhileness of marginal investment in R&D at t. Stepping up research at time t increases the probability that the innovation will occur at time t. Its expected present value is $e^{-\delta t}w(V_t)W(K_t, S_t)h'(M_t)$. But even if the innovation does not occur, knowledge will have been increased, and this has value for the future. This value is $e^{-\delta t}q_t h'(M_t)$; note that $e^{-\delta t}q_t$ is the present-value contingent price of "knowledge" (contingent on the innovation's not having occurred by time t). If the left-hand side of inequality (43) falls short of its right-hand side, it is optimal to set $M_t = 0$. The opportunity cost of R&D investment is too high in this case, and it is not worthwhile undertaking R&D.

It is, of course, possible that the conditional optimum strategy consists of an initial period during which no R&D is undertaken (that is, $M_t = 0$) followed by a period in which R&D is actively pursued; this latter period may well be finite.[25] Since by definition

$$\int_0^\infty w(V)\,dV = 1 \quad \text{and} \quad w(V) \geq 0$$

the point is that one must have $w'(V) < 0$ for large V and $\lim_{V \to \infty} w(V) = 0$. What inequality (43) tells us is that it is the probability rate of success that is important.

It may well be optimal to have a period of intense research followed by closure of R&D because failure of the R&D could cause pessimism about future success. This can be seen most vividly if we define $\Omega(V) = \int_V^\infty w(V')\,dV'$ as the probability that the breakthrough will occur beyond the state of knowledge V. Then rewrite inequality (43) as

$$\left[\frac{w(V_t)}{\Omega(V_t)}W(K_t, S_t) + \frac{q_t}{\Omega(v_t)}\right]h'(M_t) \leq \frac{p_t}{\Omega(V_t)} \tag{44}$$

(I am supposing, of course, that $\Omega(V_t) > 0$.)

---

[25] These points have been elaborated in Dasgupta and Heal (1974), Dasgupta, Heal, and Majumdar (1977), and Kamien and Schwartz (1978).

This operation allows us to interpret the inequality from the vantage point of time t, conditional on the innovation's not having occurred. The variable of interest now is $w(V_t)/\Omega(V_t)$, and much depends on its shape. Typically, one would expect it to be single-peaked, as would be the case if $w(V)$ were lognormal. Now suppose for ease of exposition that $w(V) > 0$. Then a condition that would be sufficient to ensure that $M_t > 0$ for all t along the conditional optimum program is that $\lim_{M \to 0} h'(M) = \infty$. The "productivity" of research is so high at low rates of expenditure that it always pays to undertake R&D. But I do not know if such a production function is plausible.

What is the relationship of all this to the social rate of discount? On looking at the Hamiltonian (40), we know that the shadow price $e^{-\delta t}p_t$ must change according to the rule

$$\frac{d}{dt}(e^{-\delta t}p_t) = -\frac{\partial H}{\partial K_t} = -e^{-\delta t}h(M_t)w(V_t)W_K - e^{-\delta t}p_t F_{K_t}$$

which can be written as

$$\delta - \dot{p}_t/p_t = \frac{w(V_t)h(M_t)W_{K_t}}{p_t} + F_{K_t} \tag{45}$$

If aggregate consumption is the numeraire, then the left-hand side is—by the definition stated in the introduction—the social rate of discount. It is the percentage rate of fall of the present-value contingent price of consumption. The right-hand side of equation (45) is what is of interest, since the equation tells us that, unlike the model in the previous section, the social rate of discount is not equal to the marginal product of capital F_K. It exceeds it, so long as $M_t > 0$. The first term in the right-hand side of equation (45) can be interpreted as a *risk premium* to be added to the marginal product of capital.

An equivalent way of looking at this is to analyze the optimum consumption plan directly. Differentiate equation (41) with respect to time and, bearing in mind that $w(V) = -\Omega'(V)$, reduce equation (45) to the form

$$\eta(C_t)\dot{C}_t/C_t = F_K - \left[\delta + \frac{w(V_t)h(M_t)}{\Omega(V_t)}(1 - W_{K_t}/u'(C_t))\right] \tag{46}$$

Notice that $w(V_t)h(M_t)/\Omega(V_t) = w(V_t)\dot{V}_t/\Omega(V_t)$ is the probability density that the innovation will occur at time t conditional on its not having occurred earlier. We know in advance that $u'(C_t) > W_{K_t}$. Thus

$$\frac{w(V_t)h(M_t)}{\Omega(V_t)}(1 - W_{K_t}/u'(C_t)) > 0 \tag{47}$$

Now compare equations (45) and (46). One way of interpreting equation (46) is to have the planner pretend that the innovation will never occur and then to raise the felicity discount rate by an amount given in expression (47). This expression is bounded above by $w(V_t)h(M_t)/\Omega(V_t)$. Thus, equation (46) provides bounds within which the felicity discount rate must lie in this certainty–equivalent problem. The bounds are provided by δ and $\delta + w(V_t)h(M_t)/\Omega(V_t)$. It is only when the capital stock remaining at the date of innovation has negligible value (that is, $W_{K_t} = 0$) that this upper bound should be used.

I shall not tabulate here the general characteristics of the optimal program under specific parameterizations that have already been undertaken in Dasgupta, Heal, and Majumdar (1977). I have alluded to some of them earlier. Instead I want to explore the consequences of extreme risk aversion on the part of the planner. Suppose the preinnovation technology is characterized by the Cobb–Douglas production function, $F(K, R) = K^{\alpha_1}R^{\alpha_2}$, $(\alpha_1, \alpha_2, 1 - \alpha_1 - \alpha_2 > 0)$. For reasons discussed in the previous section, I take it that $\alpha_1 > \alpha_2$. Assume also that $h'(M) \rightarrow \infty$ as $M \rightarrow 0$ and that $w(V) > 0$. Thus $M_t > 0$ along the optimal program (see inequality (43)). Now consider the class of isoelastic felicity functions discussed earlier. An inspection of equation (46) suggests that as $\eta \rightarrow \infty$, $\dot{C}_t/C_t \rightarrow 0$ for all t along the optimum. The equation suggests strongly that the optimum along the limiting case of $\eta \rightarrow \infty$ will be characterized by constant consumption (until the date of innovation, that is). But if, as the equations suggest, $M_t > 0$ along the optimum even for this limiting case, then this constant consumption level falls short of the maximum feasible constant consumption level the preinnovation economy is capable of providing. I have been unable to provide a rigorous analysis of this limiting case with a view to settling the issue. But if in fact $M_t > 0$ even for this limiting case, then it suggests that extreme risk aversion is not in itself an argument for not undertaking R&D, even when there is a probability of failure. If the physical productivity of research ($h'(M)$) is high enough, it is worth investing in R&D even though this entails that the maximum sure level of consumption is reduced.

A special case of this model was analyzed in Dasgupta and Heal (1974). The special case consisted of supposing that $h(M_t) = 1$, which is to say that R&D is being undertaken by some other country at a rate not influenced by the decisions taken in the economy in question. Thus the probability that the innovation will occur is exogenously given. The intuition underlying the certainty–equivalent result is clearest in this case. Obviously, it is optimal to set $M_t = 0$. The problem is much simpler since the planner now needs only to control C_t and R_t. If $W_{K_t} = 0$, the case for discounting felicity at the highest rate is compelling, since "terminal capital" is of no value. Indeed, it is this special case that is analogous to the problem of an individual planning over an uncertain lifespan, a case analyzed by Yaari (1965).

Conclusions

Quite apart from any of the details that one might find interesting, the main morals that have emerged from the foregoing analysis would seem to me as follows.

A sentence such as, "It is wrong to use positive discount rates in investment decisions, since this biases against the claims of future generations," is based on a misunderstanding. First, one has to make clear what good has been chosen as the numeraire, and second, optimum discount rates are arrived at from an optimization exercise, and one's appraisal of intergenerational equity ought to be caught in the formulation of the objective function. In general, the latter may be too opaque in that the implications of a seemingly innocuous objective function may be unpalatable. This can happen because the set of feasible actions often is not well understood, as I noted in the discussion of resource depletion in a utilitarian world. It is here that exercises in optimum planning play such a useful role. They illuminate the implications of differing ethical beliefs. But the point remains that as a primitive concept, the social rate of discount is not very useful. Working with an additive, separable form of the social welfare function (equation (7)), we noted that in a model of capital accumulation and resource depletion, the optimal long-run rate of consumption depends very sensitively on whether one discounts future felicity. If the felicity discount rate is positive (no matter how small), consumption in the long run tends to zero along the optimal path, even when it is feasible to avoid decay in consumption. If, on the other hand, the felicity discount rate is nil, then when an optimum exists, it is characterized by an ever-growing rate of consumption with unbounded consumption in the long run. But in either case, the consumption rate of interest (that is, the social rate of discount, when consumption is chosen as the numeraire) is positive throughout and, for the model discussed in the section on resource depletion in a utilitarian world, equals the marginal product of capital.

Working with the class of isoelastic felicity functions, the sensitivity of the optimum consumption profile to the choice of the elasticity of marginal felicity was analyzed in the section on resource depletion in a utilitarian world. With a zero discount rate on future felicity, the effect of a larger value of this elasticity was found to be a flatter consumption profile, implying a more egalitarian distribution of consumption. In the limit, as the elasticity tends to infinity, the optimum consumption profile merges with the maximum constant consumption the economy is capable of providing. This last result is precisely what intuition would suggest.

The last section presented a model of endogenous technical change under uncertainty. The model was aimed at capturing the kinds of argument that one feels are relevant when debating on programs designed to increase the probability of major technological innovations, such as the arrival of a clean breeder reactor or controlled nuclear fusion. Rules for social benefit–cost analysis in such a world were derived, and it was found that the Ramsey rule of the previous section (equation (18)) is modified to the extent of having an additional term, which can be interpreted as a risk premium (see equations (45) and (46)). This term contains, among other things, the conditional probability of success. It is as though one pretends that the innovation will never occur and then proceeds to set the consumption rate of interest at a level exceeding the sure rate of return on investment, the difference being this risk premium. I discussed the limiting case of an infinite elasticity of marginal felicity and concluded with the conjecture that under certain parametric specifications of the R&D process, infinite risk aversion is not an argument for not undertaking R&D. If the conjecture is correct, then the intuition behind it must be that in not undertaking R&D, one is ensuring that the innovation will not be made, and an extreme risk averter will not wish to accept that.

References

Arrow, K. J. 1953. "Le Role des Valeurs Boursieres pour le Repartition la Meilleur des Risques," *Econometrie* (Paris).
——. 1971. *Theory of Risk Bearing* (Chicago, Markham).
——. 1973. "Some Ordinalist–Utilitarian Notes on Rowls' Theory of Justice," (Harvard University, mimeo.).
——, and M. Kurz. 1970. *Public Investment, the Rate of Return and Optimal Fiscal Policy* (Baltimore, Johns Hopkins University Press for Resources for the Future).
Atkinson, A. B. 1970. "On the Measurement of Inequality," *Journal of Economic Theory*.
Chakravarty, S. 1969. *Capital and Development Planning* (Cambridge, M.I.T. Press).
Dasgupta, P., and G. M. Heal. 1974. "The Optimal Depletion of Exhaustible Resources," *Review of Economic Studies,* Symposium.
——, and ——. 1975. "Resource Depletion and Research and Development," (London School of Economics, mimeo.).
——, and ——. 1979. *Economic Theory and Exhaustible Resources* (James Nisbet and Cambridge University Press).
——, ——, and M. K. Majumdar. 1977. "Resource Depletion and Research and Development," in M. Intrilligator, ed., *Frontiers of Quantitative Economics* (North–Holland).
Debreu, G. 1959. *Theory of Value* (New York, Wiley).

Garg, P., and J. Sweeney. 1977. "Optimal Growth with Depletable Resources," (Stanford University, mimeo.).

Gorman, W. M. 1957. "Convex Indifference Curves and Diminishing Marginal Utility," *Journal of Political Economy.*

Hardy, G. H., Littlewood, and Polya. 1934. *Inequalities* (Cambridge, Cambridge University Press).

Hotelling, H. 1931. "The Economics of Exhaustible Resources," *Journal of Political Economy.*

Kamien, M., and N. Schwartz. 1978. "Resource Depletion and Optimal Innovation," *Review of Economic Studies.*

Koopmans, T. C. 1966. "On the Concept of Optimal Economic Growth," in *Econometric Approach to Development* (Illinois, Rand McNally).

Mitra, T. 1975. "Efficient Growth with Exhaustible Resources in an Open Neoclassical Model," (University of Illinois at Chicago Circle, mimeo.).

Ramsey, F. 1928. "A Mathematical Theory of Saving," *Economic Journal.*

Solow, R. M. 1974. "Intergenerational Equity and Exhaustible Resources," *Review of Economic Studies,* Symposium.

Stiglitz, J. E. 1974. "Growth with Exhaustible Resources: Efficient and Optimal Paths," *Review of Economic Studies,* Symposium.

Yaari, M. 1965. "Uncertain Lifetime, Insurance, and the Theory of the Consumer," *Review of Economic Studies* vol. 32, pp. 137–150.

*James L. Sweeney**

Comment

Partha Dasgupta skillfully draws a set of striking conclusions about optimal investments in a world of depletable resources. In this paper, I address, extend, and reinterpret some of Dasgupta's conclusions, while using his basic framework. Three issues are examined. How does continual technical progress influence the optimal growth trajectory when resources are depletable? What are some empirical caveats that may substantially alter the conclusions presented? What discount rate should be used to make investment decisions under uncertainty in a world of depletable resources and endogenous research and development? These issues are addressed in the following three sections.

Optimal Growth with Depletable Resources: Continuous Technical Progress

The Dasgupta paper examines trajectories of optimal economic growth in a Cobb–Douglas economy characterized by the use of depletable resources. In this economy the resource is essential to production, yet is available only in finite quantities for allocation over all time. The explicit assumption of no technical progress is maintained throughout. Therefore, the economy is doomed unless it invests sufficiently to increase the capital stock so that the growing capital stock can be substituted for the declining rate of resource use to produce nondeclining output. Technological advance plays no role in allowing a constant output to be produced using progressively smaller quantities of capital and resource inputs. Within this world, the Dasgupta paper develops a set of striking conclusions. However, these conclusions may not be valid if there is continual technical progress in the economy.

The conclusions I present here can be drawn from a model similar to that presented by Dasgupta if two modifications are introduced: continual

* Department of Engineering–Economic Systems, Stanford University.

technical progress and continuous depreciation of capital. The justification and formal derivation of the results appear in Garg and Sweeney (1978) or in Garg (1974).

Let the economy be described by a Cobb–Douglas production function with inputs of capital K, labor L, and the exhaustible resource use R, and characterized by neutral technical progress at the rate τ:

$$Y = Ae^{\tau t}K^{\alpha}R^{\beta}L^{1-\alpha-\beta} \tag{1}$$

Following the Dasgupta assumption, this production function can be normalized so that L equals unity, and so that population is constant over time. This normalization will not be critical for the discussion that follows.

Output can be consumed or invested according to the following equation:

$$Y = C + \dot{K} + \mu K \tag{2}$$

where C is consumption and μ is the rate of exponential depreciation of capital. The total stock of the depletable resource is known with certainty initially. The welfare function will be identical to that presented by Dasgupta:

$$W = \int_0^{\infty} \left(\frac{1}{1-\eta}\right) C^{1-\eta}e^{-\delta t}\, dt \tag{3}$$

where δ represents the discount rate on felicity and η represents the elasticity of marginal felicity.

Within this model, it can be shown that, for a large enough discount rate on future felicity, there exists a locus of initial balanced endowments from which the balanced endowments trajectory is characterized by exponentially growing or decaying levels of output, consumption, and capital stock, and by exponentially declining resource base and rate of resource use. The first three exponential decline rates are equal to one another and the latter two are equal. The growth rates in the balanced endowments trajectory are:

$$\gamma_K = \gamma_C = \gamma_Y = \frac{-\delta\beta + \tau}{1 - \alpha - \beta + \eta\beta} \tag{4}$$

$$\gamma_R = \gamma_X = \frac{-(1-\alpha)\delta + \tau(1-\eta)}{1 - \alpha - \beta + \eta\beta} \tag{5}$$

where γ_K, γ_C, γ_Y, γ_R, and γ_X represent instantaneous growth rates of the capital, consumption, output, resource use, and resource stock, respectively.

Such a balanced endowments trajectory will exist as long as γ_R is negative. For δ equal to zero, if η is greater than unity, this will occur. For η smaller than unity, the balanced endowments trajectory will exist for a large enough discount rate on felicity.

An arbitrary initial endowment of capital and resource will not be consistent with the balanced endowments trajectory. However, for any initial capital stock, a resource stock can be defined such that, from the initial conditions, the optimal trajectory of the economy will always be on the balanced endowments trajectory. The relationship for balanced endowments is as follows:

$$X_* = \frac{1}{-\gamma_X} \left[\frac{\eta\gamma_K + \mu + \delta}{A\alpha} \right]^{1/\beta} K_*^{(1-\alpha)/\beta} \tag{6}$$

where X_* and K_* are values of resource stock and capital stock, respectively, on the balanced endowments trajectory.

The balanced endowments resource stock is an increasing function of the capital stock, varying between zero and infinity as capital stock varies throughout this range.

Although not all initial conditions are consistent with a balanced endowments trajectory, if such a trajectory exists, then the optimal path from arbitrary initial capital and resource stocks must converge monotonically to a balanced endowments trajectory: the ratio of an optimal variable to its value along the appropriate balanced endowments trajectory must monotonically converge to unity. Therefore, even for endowments that are not balanced, the balanced endowments trajectory is relevant for describing the long-run behavior of the economy.

The growth rate equations (4) and (5) can be used to examine the basic issues raised by Dasgupta. From equation (4) we see that whether it is optimal for the economy to grow or decline in the long run depends on three parameters, τ, β, and δ. If the rate of technical progress, τ, is greater than the product of the discount rate on felicity, δ, and the resource share of output, β, (that is, $\tau > \delta\beta$), then the economy will grow over time. If $\tau = \delta\beta$, capital, consumption, and output will remain constant in time along the balanced endowments trajectory, and with a lower rate of technical progress, the three factors will decline exponentially toward zero, with more rapid decline occurring with lower rates of technical progress. Whether the economy grows or declines is not dependent upon the depreciation rate for capital, nor is the question dependent upon the elasticity of marginal felicity. However, the rate of change will depend upon the elasticity of marginal felicity, with higher values of this elasticity leading to flatter paths in the economy. The rate of depreciation of capital influences the levels of consumption and capital along a balanced endowments trajectory but does not influence the growth rates of these variables along the trajectory.

Only a relatively small rate of technical progress is needed to insure against doom in the economy. For example, if β were 0.07 (roughly energy's share of the U.S. net national product in 1976) and δ were 0.03, then a growing economy would be assured along the balanced endowments trajectory, as long as the rate of technical progress is greater than 0.21 percent per year.

Dasgupta draws the following conclusion: "A positive rate of impatience, no matter how small, implies it is judged optimal to allow the economy to decay in the long run, even though it is feasible to avoid decay." The results shown above are in sharp contrast to the emphasis of this statement. I have shown that, with even a small rate of continual technical progress, some positive rates of impatience will be consistent with growing consumption over all time.

Dasgupta examines the limiting case of a zero discount rate on future felicity, and in which consumption along the optimal path is monotonically increasing. He concludes that for this case "it follows that the consumption rate of interest tends to zero in the long run along the optimum program." The framework presented above leads to a positive rate of interest whenever the economy is growing. Letting r represent the consumption rate of interest (or equivalently, the marginal productivity of capital net of depreciation) gives the following expressions, with equation (7) holding for all time and equation (8) holding in a balanced endowments growth path:

$$r = \delta + \eta \frac{\dot{C}}{C} \tag{7}$$

$$r = \frac{\delta(1 - \alpha - \beta) + \eta\tau}{1 - \alpha - \beta + \eta\beta} \tag{8}$$

If either the rate of discount on utility or the rate of technical progress were positive (with the other variable nonnegative), then on a balanced endowments path, the social rate of discount would be positive for all time and would converge to a positive number. For $\delta = 0$, the interest rate is proportional to the rate of technical progress.

While the characterization of technical progress discussed above is simple and unrealistic, it is reasonable to expect the historical pattern of technical progress to continue at least throughout the period during which nonrenewable energy sources are extensively used to satisfy energy demands. Thus, conclusions derived from a model that does not allow for technical progress must be viewed with suspicion if those conclusions are no longer valid when technical progress is introduced.

Caveats

An important caveat that should be attached to the analysis above and to that in the Dasgupta paper relates to the possibility of alternative sources of resource supply. In both analyses, the resource is assumed to be available only from the depletable stock, and there is no backstop technology such as has been postulated by Nordhaus (1972) and others.[1]

Currently, many technologies are available that can produce usable energy but at a high cost. At a high enough cost, uranium could be extracted from seawater to provide electricity for many hundreds of years. Backstop solar energy technologies are currently economical for some applications and could provide large amounts of energy for many other applications at a high enough price for energy. Biomass technologies are currently feasible sources of energy. While these technologies do have a high cost, their existence provides a rough upper limit on energy price and a lower limit on the available supply of energy. Thus, even with no technical progress, the flow of energy need not decline to zero, but may remain above some level over all time. Therefore, as an empirical matter, the applicability of the Dasgupta model to the U.S. or the world situation is questionable.

The nonexistence of technical progress and the nonexistence of an alternative source of energy make the Dasgupta results quite pessimistic. On the other hand, another assumption—the Cobb–Douglas technology—embedded in the two analyses is far more optimistic than seems appropriate. The Cobb–Douglas function incorporates a fundamental assumption that the elasticity of substitution between the depletable resource and all other inputs equals unity. An elasticity of substitution equal to unity applied to energy is questionable in light of the existing empirical studies.

There have been a number of studies that cast light on the issue of the appropriate elasticity of substitution between energy and other inputs. The report of the Energy Modeling Forum (1977), *Energy and the Economy,* documents the elasticity of substitution between energy and other inputs, which is implicit in the energy–economy models examined by the Forum working group. In no case was there an elasticity of substitution as large as 0.6 in any of the models.

The elasticity of substitution can be related to the elasticity of demand for primary energy. For small value shares of energy, the elasticity of substitution and the price elasticity of demand for primary energy are essentially identical. Most studies estimate the elasticity of demand for primary energy to be considerably smaller than unity, with perhaps an

---

[1] In the final sections of the Dasgupta paper, a backstop technology does exist, but it will become feasible only if sufficient monies are spent for research and development, and it may never become feasible.

elasticity of substitution of between 0.2 and 0.6 being most consistent with the existing studies.

The empirical evidence suggests that the elasticity of substitution between energy and other inputs in the U.S. economy is smaller than that implied by a Cobb–Douglas technology. In this regard, then, the analysis presented above and that of the Dasgupta paper are over optimistic.

Although its use can be criticized, the Cobb–Douglas function has been widely used in the literature on economic growth. The value of this function lies in its mathematical tractability. Solutions to Cobb–Douglas models generate insights that are valuable in analyzing models that include more realistic assumptions. This is the spirit of the analysis presented above and, presumably, of the Dasgupta work. However, in that spirit, many of the specific conclusions may be reversed when a more realistic production function is examined.

Technical Progress, Uncertainty, and the Social Rate of Return

The Dasgupta paper presents a useful, insightful model of research and development (R&D) expenditures designed to find a new technology, in this specific case a technology that releases the economy from the constraint of exhaustible resources. Within the overall optimization is an analysis of optimal investment in capital equipment.

This section provides an alternative development of and interpretation of the conditions required for optimal capital investment under uncertainty about the results of R&D. It will be shown that optimal capital investments in this economy maximize the discounted sum of expected value of output, with a discount rate equal to the consumption interest rate, $r = \delta + \eta \dfrac{\dot{C}}{C}$, the identical expression of equation (7). Thus, introducing R&D and technological uncertainty will *not* change the method of evaluating the social discount rate in this economy.

To establish the basic result, a discrete time period model will be constructed; each time period will be of length Δt. Then, in order to reconcile the results with Dasgupta's equation (46), a continuous time result will be established by examining the limiting case as $\Delta t \to 0$.

Consider a decision to decrease the total consumption at some period of time, say time zero, by one unit. In the first time period the additional output and capital will be consumed if the innovation has not occurred by that time. If the innovation has occurred by that time, there is simply an increased value to the capital stock. At the optimal level of investment, the expected value of the welfare function must remain unchanged in response to this small change in investment.

Under a discrete-time version of Dasgupta's welfare function, the change in welfare associated with the reduction in the total consumption by one unit at time zero is $-u_0'$. This deterministic change must be balanced against the uncertain changes in time period 1.

In the next time period (time period 1) the available capital stock will be increased by one unit and the innovation may or may not occur. The first state of the world—innovation does occur—will be denoted by state *I*, and the second state—innovation does not occur—will be denoted by state *NI*. If the innovation does not occur (state *NI*), then the total consumption during period 1 can be increased by one unit (the increase in capital stock) plus the increased output producible by the additional capital stock:

$$F_K \Delta t$$

Thus, the increase in welfare deriving from the increase in capital at time period 1 equals the following if no innovation occurs (state *NI*):

$$u_1' \, e^{-\delta \Delta t} (1 + F_K \Delta t)$$

The probability that an innovation will occur equals $(hw/\Omega)\Delta t$.[2] Thus, the probability of state *NI* is equal to:

$$\left(1 - \frac{hw}{\Omega}\Delta t\right)$$

In state *I*, the change in welfare deriving from the increase in capital at time period 1 is simply:

$$W_K \, e^{-\delta \Delta t}$$

with a probability of occurrence given by $(hw/\Omega)\Delta t$.

Optimality implies that the expected value of welfare increase deriving from the increase in capital stock in time period 1 equals the known welfare decrease deriving from the decrease in consumption in time period zero. Manipulation of the expressions derived above yields the following equation:

$$\frac{1}{1 + r\Delta t}\left\{(1 + F_K \Delta t)\left(1 - \frac{hw}{\Omega}\Delta t\right) + \frac{W_K}{u_1'}\left(\frac{hw}{\Omega}\right)\Delta t\right\} = 1 \qquad (9)$$

---

[2] The notation is taken from the Dasgupta paper. However, arguments of all functions have been suppressed for notational simplicity.

where

$$\frac{1}{1 + r\Delta t} = \frac{u_1'}{u_0'} e^{-\delta \Delta t} \tag{10}$$

Equation (9) can be interpreted simply. The term $(1 + F_K \Delta t)$ is the change in total consumption during time period 1 in state NI attributable to the increased capital stock, while $(1 - \frac{hw}{\Omega} \Delta t)$ is the probability that state NI will occur. The term (W_K/u_1') is the change in total consumption in time period 1 in state NI which would give the same welfare increase as a unit increase in capital stock in state I. Thus, this term is the marginal value of capital in state I, using consumption in state NI as the numeraire. The term $(hw/\Omega)\Delta t$ is the probability that state I will occur. Thus, the expression in brackets is simply the expected value of the additional capital in time period 1. This expected value is discounted at interest rate r, defined by equation (10). On the right hand side of equation (9) is the known unit reduction in consumption in time period zero. Thus, equation (9) simply states that at the margin, optimality requires the discounted expected value of the additional capital stock in time period 1 to equal the reduction in consumption in time period zero.

Equation (10) reduces to equation (7) for a continuous-time version of the analysis—for $\Delta t \to 0$. Thus, the instantaneous interest rate for discounting is simply $\delta + \eta(\dot{C}/C)$, the same rate that was found for the deterministic growth model presented earlier. Contrary to the Dasgupta conclusion, no risk premium is included in this discount rate.

How does equation (9) reconcile with Dasgupta's equation (46)? In the limiting case, as Δt becomes small—the continuous-time formulation in the Dasgupta paper—these equations are identical. To see this, expand equation (9), noting that the terms that are quadratic in Δt disappear in the limit, leaving only terms that are linear in Δt. Equation (9) thus gives:

$$r = F_K - \frac{hw}{\Omega}\left(1 - \frac{W_K}{u_1'}\right) \tag{11}$$

which, along with equation (10), gives Dasgupta's equation (46). The alternative derivation and interpretation presented here are thus consistent with Dasgupta's formal results, but not his interpretation.

The results presented above and by Dasgupta imply that the social rate of discount does not equal the rate of return on capital contingent on the occurrence of one state of the world. If there is a significant probability that other states of the world will occur, and if capital is worth less in the other states, then for projects to be acceptable, the rate of return contingent on the occurrence of that one state must be higher than the social rate of return. One must look at expected value of benefits, rather than only at the benefits that would occur with one particular state of the world.

References

Energy Modeling Forum. 1977. *Energy and the Economy,* EMF Report No. 1, (Stanford University, September).

Garg, P. 1974. *Optimal Growth with Exhaustible Resources,* unpublished Ph.D. dissertation, Department of Engineering–Economic Systems (Stanford University).

————, and J. L. Sweeney. 1978. "Optimal Growth with Depletable Resources," *Resources and Energy* vol. 1, no. 1.

Nordhaus, W. 1972. "The Allocation of Energy Resources," *Brookings Papers on Economic Activity,* pp. 493–545.

*Robert Dorfman**

Comment

I am an arithmetic teacher at heart and from that point of view, I came away impressed with Partha Dasgupta's extraordinary computational skill so long as he was dealing with letters, although he proved fallible when he confronted numbers. But a more important skill, vividly displayed in this paper, is his ability to construct highly stylized models representing hard and practical problems and to extract from them highly suggestive implications for social policy.

One might ask whether demonstrations such as this contribute to our understanding of what to do about the Alaska pipeline. I am persuaded that we cannot give reliable advice about any such practical problem involving nonrenewable resources until we have gotten to the bottom of the issues that Dasgupta deals with. Is a positive "pure rate of impatience" morally defensible? What are its consequences? Whatever the rate of impatience, what principles are there to determine the efficient rate of use of nonrenewable resources? As long as such questions are obscure, there will be no sound, generally accepted criteria for discussing the pros and cons of practical decisions or resolving practical debates.

Work such as this, then, establishes the foundations for practical decisions. Having granted that, however, I mean to complain.

My first complaint concerns the neglect of depreciation. The central analysis of the paper deals with a world in which there is a "stock of a single nondeteriorating, homogeneous commodity." The insights, however, are to be applied to a world in which steel rusts and even aluminum is subject to fatigue. That seems to make a difference, which can be seen as follows. Imagine that the capital good does deteriorate in the simple, exponential way favored by growth theorists. Then the analysis in the text goes through, word for word, except that whenever δ (the rate of impatience) occurs it has to be replaced by δ + the rate of deterioration. In due course we come to equation (20) and its interpretation, in which the same substitution has to be made. The conclusion then has to be amended to read as follows: "A positive rate

* Department of Economics, Harvard University.

315

of pure time preference *or of deterioration* tilts the balance overwhelmingly against generations in the distant future. This alone is a powerful result; it indicates that utilitarianism, with a positive rate of impatience *or of deterioration,* can recommend what can be regarded as ethically questionable policies.''

This is an even more powerful result than Dasgupta alleges. Barely conceivably, by an act of will, the current generation can abjure its pure rate of time preference. There is no way for it to obliterate deterioration without devoting any resources to the task. If it is ethically unacceptable to doom some sufficiently remote generation to life without resources or production, there is no way to avoid it within the confines of this model. In that world the best thing to do would be to indulge the pure rate of time preference, whatever that rate may be, maximize the utilitarian integral, and bear the knowledge of eventual extinction as cheerfully as possible.

I take my second complaint more seriously, though its implications are more obscure to me. Dasgupta assumes ''that the exhaustible resource can be extracted costlessly.'' That assumption is far from innocuous, and, indeed, is bound up with a misleading image of the problem of nonrenewable resources. The image is that of the world as a vast storehouse with definite (though perhaps unknown) inventories of raw materials on the shelves, to be withdrawn as desired but never restocked. It isn't like that at all, which is why I prefer to talk about nonrenewable resources rather than exhaustible resources. We never exhaust any resource, and never shall. To be sure, oil wells have been shut down and mines have been closed. But when that occurs it is always the case that a great deal of the resource originally in place is still there—typically well over half. What has happened is that extraction costs, never zero, have risen to the point at which it is unprofitable to operate the mine or well at the current level of prices for the extracted material. If the price should rise, the abandoned works may be reopened, and this too has happened often. Extraction costs are of the essence, and so is their dependence on the cumulative amount of material already extracted. The specter to fear is not that the oil or chrome will run out, but that we shall have to devote ever-increasing amounts of resources to extracting them.

The difference that this makes can be explored, incompletely, within Dasgupta's framework. He postulates that gross output, $F(K,R)$, is divided between consumption and gross investment. We can add a third claimant: extraction of the nonrenewable resource. To be explicit, I assume that the amount of the product or commodity required to extract the nonrenewable resource at a rate of R per unit of time is

$$q = A(\overline{Q} - Q)^{-\beta}R^{\gamma}$$

where $\overline{Q}$ is some positive number, Q is the amount of the resource previously extracted, and the other symbols on the right are positive parameters. This specification imposes that as Q approaches $\overline{Q}$, the cost of any given rate of extraction approaches infinity.

I shall not present the detailed analysis; it is straightforward. Up to a point it confirms Dasgupta's conclusions. With this specification, it is clear that

$$\int_0^\infty R \, dt < \overline{Q}$$

so that, just as in the exhaustibility case, $R \to 0$. The same gloomy conclusions follow, and for the same reasons. The further analysis of the optimal path of resource use on our way to inevitable doom does not appear to follow. I judge that that analysis would be substantially more complicated and, perhaps, not worth working out in detail.

My conclusion is that if the progressive depletion of nonrenewable resources drives extraction costs upward without limit, then social concern is fully as justified as in the conventional finite exhaustible quantity case analyzed by Dasgupta. The parameters on which the optimal path of extraction depends, however, are quite different.

I have one additional problem with the paper. The final substantive section is devoted to a strikingly ingenious and promising analysis of the question of the optimal time path of research and development efforts designed to relieve the stresses from inroads on the inherited stock of a nonrenewable resource. My problem is that I have great difficulty with the particular probability model that forms the basis of the analysis.

The key concept is $w(V)$, defined as the "subjective probability density function . . . that the innovation will occur at the state of knowledge V." It's a little hard to see what that means, but the way that the concept is used in the subsequent analysis appears to bear out the following interpretation. The planner is supposed to pose to himself, or his advisers, the following question: At the time, now unknown, at which the innovation is made, we are going to check and see what the contemporary state of knowledge is. What is the probability density that it will turn out to be V? The answer, as a function of V, is $w(V)$. For instance, suppose that the innovation at issue is a practicable fusion reactor and that the state of knowledge is measured by the number of relevant patents that have been granted. The planner might ask: What is the probability density that at the time we get that gadget the number of patents granted will be 100,000?

One difficulty with that formulation is that it presupposes that $w(V)$ is independent of M, the time path of research and development. But it can't be. If the planner is quite sure that there never will be as many as 100,000 relevant patents, he will answer, $w(100,000) = 0$, irrespective of his subjective probability that if there were 100,000 patents success would be at hand.

The clearest way I can state the basic source of my discomfort with this model is by appealing to an analogy. Let $p(X)$ be the probability density function of the total number of cigarettes a man has smoked at the time he dies. Very likely $p(X)$ has a peak at $X = 0$ and is comparatively large for small values of X. However that may be, $p(X)$ does not contain the kind of information one would need to ascertain the optimal time path of smoking. In the same way, the relevant probability for Dasgupta's problem is not the probability that the stock of knowledge will be V at the instant when the innovation is made, but the probability that the innovation will occur when the stock of knowledge is V (and not before). These two probabilities are connected, but not in a simple way, and not in a way that is independent of the time path of research effort.

There is a nice symmetry between the problem of resource depletion and that of knowledge cumulation. As a nonrenewable resource is extracted, the real unit cost of further extraction increases. Just so, as the stock of knowledge cumulates, the real unit cost of further learning declines, and the probability that a unit of effort will produce a critical innovation increases. The same formal model, with a change of sign, will serve for both problems.

Thus the problem of the section on uncertainty, technical change, and innovation can be explored by the same methods used so elegantly in the preceding section. I hope that Dasgupta will have occasion to study his research and development problem from that point of view.

*Mark Sharefkin**

Comment

Introduction

That there are significant depletable resources in a finite world is uncontroversial; that technological progress has, in the past century, in part offset the impact of resource depletion upon real costs is fairly well established. Whether technological progress, now a highly organized activity, will continue to play this role depends, in part, upon how that activity is directed and organized.

Thus, the proper overall level of energy-related research and development, and the allocation of those resources among alternative energy sources, including conservation, have become major questions of public policy. As with most such issues, profound differences of opinion arise—both from the different values that are held and from the lack of any good way of identifying a "best" research and development program.

Partha Dasgupta's paper is an ambitious attempt to set out, in highly idealized models, ways of choosing an optimum program. Dasgupta tries to clarify the roles of "the" discount rate, and of the presence of some exhaustible resource in the model, as determinants of that optimum program. Clarification is badly needed, because many staples of the energy debate— "discounting is unfair to future generations," for example—are based in part upon simple and remediable confusion. But only in part. Although Dasgupta's paper dispels some of that confusion, it is less successful at identifying the substantive questions posed by a more sympathetic reading of such statements. What follows is an amplification of this remark.

Facts and Stylizations: The Certainty Cases

Dasgupta works in models he characterizes as "first-best." In his certainty-case models, a planner chooses a time path for the economy by maximizing

* Resources for the Future, Washington, D.C.

319

an intergenerational social welfare function—for some purposes generally specified as Paretian, but for most of the practical applications of the paper, specialized to utilitarian form. In the latter cases the planner's utility function is taken to be additively separable, a sum, over generations of intragenerational utilities $U(C_t)$; and in these cases the same utility function represents each generation. For Dasgupta's purposes these assumptions buy considerable expositional simplicity at almost no cost in generality; but we will see that, for other purposes, they are less innocuous.

Within this framework a few additional assumptions ensure the existence of discount rates, appropriately interpreted as intertemporal shadow prices supporting an optimum program. Not wanting to discount is, in a sense, like a government not wanting to have a fiscal policy—a logical impossibility given the weak and noncontroversial commitment to Pareto-undominated programs. So much for the naive interpretation of the statement "discounting is unfair to future generations." We are left with the feeling that the distinction, familiar to all of us from elementary equilibrium theory, between efficiency (assuring that the chosen program is not Pareto-dominated) and equity (principles for the choice among Pareto-undominated programs) is equally transparent and persuasive here.

I am somewhat unwilling to let it go at that. In the last analysis, an ethical planner charged with choosing a fair program will, if the choice is to be anything but whimsical, necessarily be guided by some underlying definition of fairness. Several of these have been propounded and rather thoroughly examined in the last few years. Unfortunately the class of fairness concepts most relevant to the intertemporal problem—definitions based upon fairness as the absence of envy—lead, in entirely nonpathological production economy contexts, to the conclusion that Pareto efficiency and fairness can be incompatible. Specifically, where tastes differ and productive resources are less than fully transferable, ethical planners interested in fair plans face a tradeoff between efficiency and equity. Returning to Dasgupta's certainty case, we see that if the production model is extended to two or more commodities, if tastes are allowed to differ between generations, and if factor endowments are less than fully transferable between generations, the same difficulties will arise.

The moral of this sad tale reaffirms Dasgupta's assertion of the logical impossibility of not discounting in some guise or other, but further insists that Pareto efficiency may be an inappropriate restriction in computing discount rates appropriate to fair intertemporal plans.

Facts and Stylizations: The Uncertainty Case

To talk about R&D planning requires that uncertainty be introduced, since R&D investments with certain outcomes are easily subsumed into the definition of the intertemporal production set. In Dasgupta's stylization, a planner chooses a time path characterized in each period (or generation) by consumption, use of exhaustible resources, and R&D expenditure. The optimum program is the program maximizing the expected value of an intertemporal social welfare function in which the identically specified utilities of preinnovation and postinnovation generations are aggregated. R&D investments are assumed to bear a certain and monotonic increasing relationship to a scalar variable characterizing the "stock of knowledge"; uncertainty is introduced into the model through the planner's subjective probability estimates of the relationship between the stock of knowledge and successful completion of the intended innovation.

Two features of this stylization command attention. Note first that the things we have said about Dasgupta's treatment of the certainty case apply here. If generations differ in their attitudes toward risk, it is not necessarily true that an ethical planner, bent upon making an intertemporal allocation of uncertain consumption streams that is "fair" by some explicitly defensible criterion, can insist upon choosing among Pareto-undominated programs. Second, and perhaps more important in contemplating application of Dasgupta's results to energy R&D allocation problems, the specification of a stylization of the relationship between a stock of knowledge, cumulated by R&D, and success in the pursuit of a particular innovation is suggestive of basic research rather than developmental, or specific and targeted research. The use of a planner's subjective success probabilities, if compatible with rational behavior under uncertainty, is thus somewhat contrived. But decision rules for choice under ignorance can be, and have been, consistently formulated. In general, those rules differ in their implications from rules associated with expected utility maximization, and, in my opinion, are more relevant to the basic problem of allocation of resources for energy-related research and development.

Tjalling C. Koopmans[*]

Comment

The paper by Dasgupta is one in a category of papers that deal with optimal growth problems and that attempt to formulate them in such a way that they have implications for policy decisions. The study of optimization is useful even though we are not living in an optimizing world. It explores the best you can do, and if your representation of realistic possibilities of production and of consumers' preferences is reasonably accurate, then it provides a benchmark of the best feasible path with which to compare actual performance. Also the choice of an objective function inevitably, I believe, involves ethical speculation. We live in a society that is not necessarily ethical in its practice, but fortunately it has ethical concerns included in the ideas that affect motivations and discussions. So the availability of analytical tools to discuss various alternative ethical formulations can be regarded as constructive.

On the other hand, I feel that the work not only in this paper, but in similar literature of the last ten years is rather lacking in the realistic representation of technological feasibility, and of the possibilities of consumption—where consumption gratifies and enhances felicity, and where it does not. This leads me to make some general observations that go beyond the work in optimal growth theory, but concern some built-in risks in mathematical parameterization of production functions. To do this rigorously one must specify a production function in a well-defined domain. If the production function is in terms of capital and resources as inputs, the domain will have points on its boundary at which resource inputs have gone down to zero, although before that happens in some future path, society can have built up its capital stock very substantially. I submit that there is no practical experience pertaining to a situation in which the ratio of resource use to capital is very low. I question whether the Cobb–Douglas function or the more general constant-elasticity-of-substitution function or its variants and refinements can tell us anything about what will happen to an economy that reaches the proximity of these boundaries.

[*] Department of Economics, Yale University.

What is the statistical basis for these functions? They came in originally because of their simple parametric form. They gave us an ability to fit these functions to data that reflected past experience. They also allowed the type of reasoning that, as I have said, is a fruitful guide to the imagination. The case of easily overlooked irrelevance, I think, is reached when we get close to these boundaries of the domain in which we have no data—thus preventing us from testing the realism of the chosen form of the production function in that part of the domain.

Fortunately, with regard to production possibilities in the future, there are other lines of collecting pertinent information and bringing it to bear on the questions posed, but these have not for the most part been drawn upon in the work on optimal growth. I refer, for instance, to the book by Barnett and Morse, *Scarcity and Growth* (1963). It looks at the future course of resource scarcity as a race between depletion and technical change. In fact, technical change may also counteract the increase in cost of resource extraction.

In any case, according to the record until their book went to press—the latest year included in their time series is 1957—by and large technology had it over depletion, and resource prices were still declining in real terms. More recently, particularly with regard to energy resources, the factor of market power has entered strongly with the success of the OPEC cartel, and so the picture is blurred. The basic question still remains: On the production side, which of the two factors, depletion or technical improvements, will remain ahead, and for how long?

There is also the question of technical change in general or in specifics. I had the opportunity to ask a leading physicist whether he thought technical change could go on indefinitely. He thought that was not so; there would be some point beyond which we would have explored and unveiled all the pertinent secrets of nature. I do not think so. I think that increasingly, as we do not want to drive around in more cars or turn on more hi-fi sets, we will turn into ourselves and with increased leisure we may get to work on our genes, and we may work on our biological system more in general. There may be ways of self-stimulation less damaging and addictive than those that now are a risk to society. In any case, if we include what I shall call biotechnology, I see no end to technical change. But, in the longer run, I would expect more of it to come in consumption, while in the nearer term there is still room for much more of it along traditional lines in production and services.

For that nearer term, I would say that mathematical economists and econometricians could be particularly useful by developing tools that help us to make some sensible projections or recommendations that look forty years ahead. They should stay away from projections into corners of the domain and from other extrapolations for which an empirical basis is not available.

They should also seek to find ways in which to express in some plausible way the terminal state of the system at some arbitrarily defined horizon that is selected for the analysis. I suggest that in such an orientation of modeling and of theory, whether optimizing or descriptive, we keep in mind both acceptable and flexible prospects for beyond the end of the horizon. That is, the form of the utility function should be such that it leaves open further choices to be made at a later time and does not define alternative options in terms of specific paths of consumption out to time infinity.

While I have made several points about an entire literature, let me illustrate some of them with a quote from Dasgupta's paper. He finds that "a vanishing fraction of a vanishing resource stock is all that is required to sustain the unbounded increase in output and consumption." I would like to know what that vanishing resource is. Is it uranium? Is it perhaps a resource needed to tap temperature differences in the ocean, or what? I would like to see us use a process model that can absorb such particulars rather than a production function with aggregate inputs. There is a great deal of pertinent technological information around. With regard to the future, it is of a speculative kind. But, at its best, it can be informed speculation based in large part on laws of nature already known to engineers and scientists. I would regard that as an important avenue for applications of science, engineering, economic theory, econometrics, and mathematical programming to energy prospects that I would hope we would develop.

In reply to a question put to me in the discussion, I don't mean to imply by my remarks that we are close to any doom. I think we can still be on the upgrade in the world at least for the next forty, fifty, or sixty years if we don't do something foolish. But all during that period I would like us to size up the situation ahead in specific technological terms and ask: What sources of energy do we expect to count on or to choose from? The pressing problems will be, what combination of potential future processes may be economically viable and perhaps competitive? It is likely to be more helpful to pursue such questions than to explore what happens in the boundary of a region on which an aggregative production function has been defined because it leads to simple reasoning and is not contradicted by available data.

Reference

Barnett, H. J., and C. Morse. 1963. *Scarcity and Growth* (Baltimore, Johns Hopkins University Press for Resources for the Future).

9

*Amartya K. Sen**

Approaches to the Choice of Discount Rates for Social Benefit–Cost Analysis

In commenting on an earlier version of this paper, Bob Dorfman remarked to me that I had presented two papers concealed as one. He is, of course, quite right. The second paper begins with section 5.

The first four sections deal with some standard issues in the choice of discount rates for social benefit–cost analysis. They closely relate to earlier debates on the subject, and involve developments on well-trodden grounds. These sections explore the relation of social vis-à-vis private rates of discount under assumptions of symmetry and asymmetry, and go on to discuss also the relation of social vis-à-vis market rates of discount, which is a distinct problem with which the former is sometimes confused. The relevant parameters in each case are identified and analyzed (sections 3 and 4).

In contrast, the last four sections attempt to reinterpret the problem in explicitly ethical terms, using the formal structure of "social welfare functionals." This permits the introduction and analysis of some important ethical issues that have tended to get obscured by rather mechanical formulations of the relation between private and social rates of discount. In this discussion the information relevant to the utilitarian approach is supplemented with that required for the "Rawlsian" lexicographic maximin rule, but without necessarily accepting either utilitarianism or Rawls' "Difference Principle" (section 6). This combined information set also proves to be inadequate when issues of rights and liberty are analyzed, requiring us to go beyond what has been called "welfarism" (section 7). The relevance of these complex considerations for the choice of social discount rates in general and for discount rates for planning in particular is also discussed.

* Oxford University

Author's note. In revising the paper I have benefited from the helpful comments of Kenneth Arrow, Thomas Cotton, Robert Dorfman, Robert Lind, Talbot Page, Mark Sharefkin, and other participants.

325

1. Interpretation

Controversies on the choice of the appropriate rate of discount often include ambiguities as to precisely what is being debated, and it may be useful to begin with some preliminary issues of interpretation. In general, the discount rate specifies the rate at which additional benefits in period $t + 1$ are converted into equivalent amounts of benefits in period t. The conversion takes the form of division by $(1 + r)$, when r is the rate of discount between these two periods. But clearly the discount rate between any two periods depends on:

1. the measurement of "benefits" (in particular, the units in which the benefits of each period are measured); and
2. the concept of equivalence.

In a private profitability exercise in terms of discounted cash flows (a common exercise), the benefits have an obvious measure, namely, cash receipts (and payments). Not so in social benefit–cost analysis, no matter whether applied to public investment or to private investment evaluated from the point of view of public interest. Benefits or costs may occur *without* cash transactions (for example, skill formation, pollution, and other externalities). Even when the occurrence is accompanied by cash transactions, the social value of the benefits may not be reflected by the size of the cash transactions and may vary with a variety of factors, in particular with the commodities and persons involved in the transaction. Of course, the benefits in each period could be converted into units expressed in terms of cash, but the specification will depend on the interpretation of units of cash, for example, a dollar of commodity j going to person i may not be treated in the same way as a dollar of commodity h going to person g. It will be shown later (see section 2) that some much-argued differences between social and private rates of discount arise entirely from differences in definition of units in which benefits are measured.

A relatively unambiguous, if austere, system of accounting is provided by the choice of the benefit unit in period t as a unit of a particular commodity j going to a particular person i in that year, $x_{ij}{}^t$. The units then are dated "named goods" (see Hahn, 1971; Sen, 1976b). In the context of the exercises that will be undertaken in this paper, much use will be made of the specification of dating and naming, even though the intercommodity differences will typically receive less attention (see, however, section 7).

Even in the context of aggregated units, differences exist in the literature. The discount rate (or "discount factor") has been variously expressed in aggregate units of consumption (see Dasgupta, Marglin, and Sen, 1972), investment (see Little and Mirrlees, 1974), and "utility" or "felicity" (see Arrow and Kurz, 1970).

The other source of ambiguity is the conception of "equivalence." There are at least two alternative interpretations of equivalence, namely, in terms of (1) welfare and (2) possibility. In the first interpretation, a discount rate of r involves the judgment that one additional unit of benefit in year t would exactly compensate for the welfare loss of $(1 + r)$ units of benefit in year $t + 1$. The second interpretation involves the knowledge that one additional unit of benefit can be produced in year t by a minimal reduction of the benefit in year $t + 1$ by $(1 + r)$ units.

The difference between the two corresponds to what Hicks (1958) calls the "utility interpretation" and the "cost interpretation" of the social product, and each interpretation is possible without assuming anything about the other. Under certain general assumptions, it is necessary for social optimality that the welfare discount rates r_w equal the possibility rates of return r_p, respectively, but when these equalities do not hold, one would in general need both types of information for intertemporal decisions (see Marglin 1963b, 1976; Arrow and Kurz, 1970).

The information about welfare weights and production possibilities can be collapsed into a single term r if and only if the two happen to coincide, that is, $r_w = r_p$. If they do not, any averaging formula (see, for example, Harberger, 1968) must involve loss of relevant information (see Feldstein, 1972), since the same average can correspond to a large (in fact, uncountable) set of alternative combinations of welfare and possibility information (r_w, r_p).

In this paper, the term rate of *discount* will be reserved for the welfare interpretation, while rate of *return* will refer to the possibility interpretation. Further, unless otherwise stated, the unit of account will be consumption, typically that of a specified person at a specified point in time.

2. Private and Social Rates of Discount

The appropriateness of using the private rates of discount for social benefit–cost analysis was debated vigorously in the late 1950s and 1960s by such writers as Eckstein (1957), Sen (1957, 1961, 1967, 1968), Dobb (1960), Marglin (1963a, 1976), Feldstein (1964), Harberger (1964, 1968, 1973), Lind (1964), Tullock (1964), Usher (1964), Phelps (1965), Arrow (1966), and Baumol (1968a, 1968b). The case for using a social rate of discount lower than the private rate was argued on several grounds, of which the following received much of the attention:

1. *The super-responsibility argument:* The government has responsibility not merely to the current generation but also to future generations (over and above the concern for future generations already reflected in the preferences of the present generation).

2. *The dual-role argument:* The members of the present generation in their political or public role may be more concerned about the welfare of the future generations than they are in their day-to-day market activities.

3. *The isolation argument:* Even with a *given* set of consistent preferences, members of the present generation may be willing to join in a collective contract of more savings by all, though unwilling to save more in isolation.

Although the first two arguments raise much deeper issues—concerned as they are with the nature of state and the integrity of human personality— it was the isolation argument (Sen, 1961; Marglin, 1963) that caused most of the heated debate by, among others, Harberger (1964, 1973), Feldstein (1964), Lind (1964), Tullock (1964), Usher (1964), Phelps (1965), and Sen (1967). While a blow-by-blow account of the controversy will be devastatingly boring, the issue of interpretation discussed in the last section permits us to reassess the question in a somewhat different light.

When the private rates of discount differ among the individuals in the present generation, there will be, of course, nothing remarkable in the chosen social rate differing from any particular private rate, or even from all of them. But in the isolation argument such differences are not assumed, and all individuals are treated as identical (although of course the argument can be extended to the nonidentical cases as well). Furthermore, the only principle of group aggregation used to arrive at a social rate of discount less than the private was the weak Pareto principle based on complete unanimity: If everyone in the present generation prefers x to y, then x must be judged to be socially superior to y for the present generation. This raises the fundamental question as to how social and private rates of discount can differ if the used concept of social preference is one of unanimous individual preference. Both must reflect exactly the same welfare valuations.

Indeed, no argument for differences between individual and social rates of discount in the *named good space* (or the named income space) emerges from the isolation argument. The argument runs thus. With a weight of unity on one's own consumption, each person attaches a weight β on a unit of consumption by others in the present generation, γ on a unit of consumption by his descendants in the future generation, and α on a unit of consumption by others in the future generation. It is assumed that β, γ, and α are all less than one. If a private act of saving today yields a point return that is enjoyed by the future generation and shared by one's descendants and others in the ratio λ to $(1 - \lambda)$, then the private rate of discount is taken to be:

$$\pi = \frac{1}{\lambda\gamma + (1 - \lambda)\alpha} - 1 \tag{1}$$

If, on the other hand, a collective saving contract of one additional unit of saving each by all n persons in the present generation yields a point return enjoyed by the future generation and shared by one's descendants and others in the ratio 1 to $(n - 1)$, then the social rate of discount is taken to be given by:

$$\rho = \frac{1 + (n - 1)\beta}{\gamma + (n - 1)\alpha} - 1 \tag{2}$$

There is clearly a family of values of λ, γ, and $\frac{\alpha}{\beta}$ that make the private rate of discount, π, and social rate of discount, ρ, equal. Lind (1964) identified the case in which $\lambda = 1$ and $\gamma = \frac{\alpha}{\beta}$, which, together, do just this. The interpretation of the condition $\lambda = 1$ is that one can capture for one's own descendants the *entire* return to one's private investment. The interpretation of the second condition is that one's relative weighting of reward to one's own descendants (γ) vis-à-vis that to oneself (1) is in exactly the same proportion as one's weighting of reward to others in the future generation (α) vis-à-vis that to others in the present generation (β).[1]

On the other hand, given $\gamma = \frac{\alpha}{\beta}$, if one fails to capture the entire reward for one's own descendants because of, say, income tax, inheritance tax, or job creation for people in the unemployment pool, then clearly $\rho < \pi$, and the social rate will fall short of the private rate of discount. Similarly, given $\lambda = 1$, if one's selfishness vis-à-vis others today is stronger than one's concern for one's descendants vis-à-vis others in the future generation, then again the social rate will be less than the private rate. And, of course, a mixture of $\lambda < 1$ and $\gamma < \frac{\alpha}{\beta}$ will also have the same effect. Given the personal quality of selfishness that is not necessarily fully translated in the relative weights on one's descendants, and given the existence of taxes and unemployment, it is possibly reasonable to expect that the social rate will lie below the private rate.

So much for a quick recount. It is clear that the social and private rates here do not refer to the same units of benefits in the future and at present. The social rate refers to the weighting of an aggregate bundle of consumption at this moment vis-à-vis that of the future; the share of oneself in the present bundle is $\frac{1}{n}$ and so is the share of one's descendants in the future bundle. In

[1] The same case was identified by Dennis Robertson in a personal communication to me, dated April 4, 1962, commenting on Sen (1961).

contrast, the private rate refers to the weighting of a unit of one's own consumption today vis-à-vis an aggregate bundle in the future with a share λ of one's descendants in the latter. The difference does not lie in the private vis-à-vis social nature of the weighting, but in the *bundles* that are being weighted. Indeed, in terms of *named* consumption, the rates of discount are the same for all persons with an appropriate translation of one's identity and that of one's descendants. The social rate of discount is, in fact, a common *individual* rate of discount of equally distributed bundles of consumption for each generation.

This question of "interpretation" of the two discount rates in the isolation problem also makes clear that it may be somewhat misleading to think of the problem as arising from externalities of consumption.[2] Of course, "externalities" *are* involved in the sense that any concern for the consumption of people other than oneself and one's descendants is put under the broad heading of consumption externalities, and obviously the argument has much to do with such concerns. But whether or not there are externalities of consumption in this sense, private and social rates of discount in this exercise *may or may not* differ depending on how the units of rewards and sacrifices are defined. For example, even with externalities—no matter how strong— satisfying Lind's condition, $\gamma = \dfrac{\alpha}{\beta}$, the private and social rates must coincide if $\lambda = 1$. More important, even with no externalities of consumption at all, that is, with $\alpha = \beta = 0$, if $\lambda < 1$, the social rate of discount ρ will still be below the private rate π, as is readily checked from equations (1) and (2). The crucial question is *what* is being discounted vis-à-vis what, and not *whether* consumption externalities are present.

3. Private, Social, and Market Rates: The Symmetric Case

The issue of composition of benefits is especially important in translating the lessons from this model of the isolation problem to the question of the relation between the market rate of interest and the appropriate rate of discount for social benefit–cost analysis of public and private investment (for example, investment in energy-related research and development). First, note that the "private" rate of discount may not correspond to the market rate interest or profit. The market rate m refers to the part of the reward that goes to the investor or his heirs by the rules of property rights, and while the part of the benefits going to others through taxation is included in m, the part going to others through the creation of employment or through externalities

---

[2] See the otherwise excellent contribution of Phelps (1965), which incidentally provides a good critical survey also of other arguments concerning possible divergence between private and social rates of discounts and returns.

of production is not. If m is the market rate and e the rate of reward to others through sources other than taxation and transfer, then it is $(m + e)$ that would be equated to the private rate of discount π, as defined in the previous exercise, interpreting λ as the share going to one's own descendants in the *total* consumption generated in the future. Thus:

$$m = \pi - e \tag{3}$$

where π is as defined in equation (1). Whenever e is positive, the market rate of interest will lie below the private rate of discount, and this opens up the possibility that the social rate of discount, even when below the private rate, may well exceed the market rate.

The social rate of discount will also depend on how the sacrifices and rewards are shared. In the symmetric case of identical individuals and identical sharing (as in the old isolation model), each person's relative weighting of the average unit of consumption sacrificed today vis-à-vis the average unit of consumption generated in the future will be given by the ratio of $1 + (n - 1)\beta$ to $\gamma + (n - 1)\alpha$, and the universally accepted social rate of discount ρ will be that expressed in equation (2). It is with this ρ that the market rate m must be compared.

Let A be the amount of total consumption generated in the future by the sacrifice of a unit of consumption today. It is the sharing of A that is in the proportions λ and $(1 - \lambda)$ when the investment is *privately* undertaken by a person, and in the ratio of 1 to $(n - 1)$ when it is undertaken by a *social* contract with equal sharing, as defined in the context of deriving (1) and (2). Let the proportion of A that is covered by the gross market return $(1 + m)$ be expressed as θ:[3]

$$1 + m = \theta A \tag{4}$$

Private investment is in equilibrium when

$$\frac{A}{1 + \pi} = 1 \tag{5}$$

Putting these relations together, it is clear that $m \{\gtreqless\} \rho$ according as $(1 + \pi)\theta \{\gtreqless\} 1 + \rho$; therefore from equations (1) and (2)

$$m \{\gtreqless\} \rho \text{ according as } \frac{\theta}{\lambda + (1 - \gamma)\dfrac{\alpha}{\gamma}} \{\gtreqless\} \frac{1 + (n - 1)\beta}{1 + (n - 1)\dfrac{\alpha}{\gamma}} \tag{6}$$

[3] Note that e defined earlier is given by $A(1 - \theta)$ and that A is $(1 + r)$ when r is the rate of return in consumption units (see section 1).

With Lind's assumption of "balanced emotions," $\gamma = \dfrac{\alpha}{\beta}$, this reduces to

$$m\{\gtreqless\} \rho \text{ according as } \frac{\theta - \lambda}{1 - \lambda}\{\gtreqless\} \beta \tag{6*}$$

In using equation (6) or (6*), note must be taken of the restrictions that the various parameters must satisfy. They are: $1 \geqslant \theta \geqslant \lambda$; $1 > \beta$; $1 > \gamma$; and $1 > \alpha$. A few special cases are easy to identify.

Case 1: The condition $1 = \theta > \lambda$ implies that the social rate of discount must *lie below* the market rate of interest. This is the case in which the benefits accruing to others arise solely from taxation and other transfers, if any, out of the market return, and not from such things as externalities, or the employment of the otherwise unemployed.

Case 2: The condition $1 > \theta = \lambda$ implies that the social rate of discount must *exceed* the market rate of interest. This is the case in which *all* transfers to others take place through externalities, additional employment, and so forth, *outside* the market return rather than through taxation of, and transfers from, the market return.

Case 3: The condition $1 = \theta = \lambda$ implies that $\rho = \pi = m$. (This has to be checked from equation (6) rather than (6*) and from equations (4) and (5).) This was, in fact, the case discussed originally by Lind (1964), and there is no transfer to "others" at all (that is, no taxation, no unemployed to be absorbed with benefit accruing to them, and no externalities).

Leaving out these special cases, the general relationship between the social rate of discount and the market rate of interest is given by equations (6) and (6*) subject to the restrictions mentioned above. To interpret equation (6*), note that $(1 - \lambda)$ is the total proportionate share of others (that is, those other than one's own descendants) in the total future consumption generated A, while $(\theta - \lambda)$ is the part of the proportionate share going to others that comes from taxation (and other transfers, if any) out of the market return. Condition (6*) states that the social rate of discount will lie below the market rate of interest m if and only if the share going to others *through* taxation (and other transfers) out of the market return as a proportion of the total share going to them exceeds the *relative* weight that is put on the consumption of others (others today in comparison with oneself β, and others in the future in comparison with one's own descendants $\dfrac{\alpha}{\gamma}$).

4. Private, Social, and Market Rates with Asymmetries

The comparisons of social and market rates were facilitated in the last section by the assumption of symmetry among the persons: (1) the members of the same generation were all identical in every way, including welfare characteristics and opulence, and (2) the social contract to save more involved equal participation by all members of the present generation. But both assumptions are quite limiting. Aside from personal differences among the people involved, some are rich and some are poor. Also investment programs do not typically involve equal participation by all.

The absence of symmetry does, however, make the analysis much more complicated. In fact, even the definition of the social rate of discount becomes problematic once the reliance on the Pareto principle (to define "social preference" in terms of unanimity) becomes unavailable. More demanding ethical principles now have to be invoked.

The social rate of discount to be used for benefit–cost analysis of a public investment, or of a private investment from the public point of view, will depend both on some *descriptive* features of the investment as well as on *evaluative* weights on benefits accruing to different people. The latter— no longer obtainable from unanimity—must presumably reflect some kind of a compromise over the views of different groups in the present generation. I shall have a little bit to say on the choice of these weights in sections 5– 7, but for the moment I simply take these weights as given. Let the present community be divided into k groups: $g = 1, \ldots , k$. Let the evaluative weight on each unit of current consumption of group g be β_g, and that on each unit of its "future consumption" (that is, the consumption of its heirs) be α_g.

Regarding the descriptive features of this investment, the proportion of consumption benefit in the future that goes to group g (in fact, their heirs) is denoted by σ_g, and the proportion of current consumption sacrifice that falls on this group is σ'_g. Note that each σ_g and each σ'_g is non-negative, and

$$\sum_{g=1}^{k} \sigma_g = 1, \text{ and } \sum_{g=1}^{k} \sigma'_g = 1$$

The social rate of discount ρ for this system of weighting is, clearly, given by the following equation.[4]

---

[4] It can be easily checked that equation (7) reduces to equation (2) of the symmetric case if symmetric assumptions are added. With symmetric concerns for others and with $\sigma_g = \sigma'_g =$

$$\rho = \frac{\sum\limits_{g=1}^{k} \sigma'_g \beta_g}{\sum\limits_{g=1}^{k} \sigma_g \alpha_g} - 1 \tag{7}$$

Consider now a private investment I^j undertaken by group j. Let the share of the additional future consumption accruing to each group g (in fact, to its heirs) be σ_g^j. The weight attached by group j to the future consumption of each group g is denoted by α_g^j. The weight on the current consumption of group g is β_g^j. The unit is taken to be the weight on one unit of *current* consumption of group j itself: $\beta_j^j = 1$.

The private rate of discount of group j for this investment is given by

$$\pi^j = \frac{1}{\sum\limits_{g=1}^{k} \sigma_g^j \alpha_g^j} - 1 \tag{8}$$

The market rate of interest m is related to each private rate of discount π^j in the way specified by equations (4) and (5). Denoting the relevant θ for the investment in question as θ^j yields

$$m = \theta^j (1 + \pi^j) - 1 \tag{9}$$

Equations (8) and (9) together characterize, with the usual assumptions of smoothness, an equilibrium of divisible private investment for each group j. Thus the market interest rate m can be seen in terms of θ^j, $\{\sigma_g^j\}$, and $\{\alpha_g^j\}$ for any group j in an equilibrium of undertaken investment.

There is not a great deal that can be said about the relative magnitudes of private, social, and market rates without making more specific assumptions. Two assumptions of particular interest that we now explore are:

1. The social weight on the consumption of each group g shifts in the same ratio γ as we move from the group to its descendants:

$$\alpha_g = \gamma \beta_g, \text{ for all } g \tag{10}$$

2. The private weight by group j on the consumption of each group g shifts in the same ratio γ as we move from the group g to its descendants:

$$\alpha_g^j = \gamma \beta_g^j, \text{ for all } j \text{ and } g \tag{11}$$

$1/n$ for all g, each person j's evaluation of ρ is the same and is, in fact, that given by equation (2), when we put $\beta_j = 1$ (choice of unit), $\alpha_j = \gamma$, $\beta_g = \beta$ and $\alpha_g = \alpha$ for $g \neq j$ (choice of notation).

If the relative opulence of the different groups does not change much over this period, then equation (10) may be a reasonable assumption under "welfarism" (see sections 5–7), but whether a similar argument can be constructed in particular nonwelfaristic contexts as well is not clear. Assumption (11) is rather like Lind's (1964) case of "balanced emotions," but most obviously involves restrictions on the stationarity of the *relative* opulence of different groups, since the weighting—as in Lind's case—is of consumption rather than of utility. The requirement that the *relative* rate of change is the *same* for social and private weights is also restrictive, even though this does not at all imply that the private weights of different persons must be close to each other, or close to the social weights.

Consider now the assumption that the sharing of consumption sacrifices and the sharing of consumption gains be in the same proportions for each group in the "social" investment:

$$\sigma_g = \sigma_g', \text{ for each } g \tag{12}$$

This could be regarded as an unreasonable assumption for public investment projects, since the relatively rich could be expected to bear a higher share of the costs than of the benefits in such projects. But whether this type of "progressive" bias is typically the case even with public investments is far from clear. In any case, assumption (12) will be used tentatively, and the directional correction needed to incorporate the "progressive" hypothesis will be analyzed later.

The effect of assumptions (10) and (12) on the social rate of discount is a drastic simplification

$$\rho = \frac{1}{\gamma} - 1 \tag{13}$$

The result is not surprising: what (12) does is to permit the incremental analysis to be done in terms of a "composite" consumption bundle with an unchanging breakdown, and the characteristic of the same intertemporal relative movement (γ) of the social weights, embodied in assumption (10), reduces equation (7) to equation (13).

Given assumption (12), if assumption (10) is dropped and different relative rates of intertemporal changes in the evaluative weights are admitted, then equation (13) will hold only under the interpretation of γ standing for the $\sigma_g'\alpha_g$-weighted average of the group-specific intertemporal ratios $\{\gamma_g\}$ of the evaluative weights.

A more fundamental difference is made when assumption (12) is dropped since the composite-bundle approach is no longer usable. The "progressive" case discussed earlier is particularly worth considering since such redistribution is a frequently articulated aspect of public investments of various types. On utilitarian or equity grounds (see sections 5 and 6), the evaluative weights on the consumption of the richer groups can be taken to be less than those on the consumption of the poorer groups. The effect of this change is to raise the value of the denominator of the first term on the right-hand side of equation (7). Clearly, that must have the consequence of *lowering* the social rate of discount ρ.

Thus, it is easy to establish that when assumption (10) holds, but assumption (12) is dropped in favor of the "progressive" assumption, then

$$\rho < \frac{1}{\gamma} - 1 \tag{13*}$$

In this sense, equation (13) gives an upper bound of the value of the social rate of discount.

When the dropping of (12) for the "progressive" assumption is *combined with* the eschewing of (10), inequality (13*) can hold with γ interpreted as the $\sigma'_g \alpha_g$ = weighted average of the respective values of γ_g.

Turning now to the private rate of discount π^j for group j, it is given by the following equation in the presence of restriction (11).

$$\pi^j = \frac{1}{\gamma \sum_{g=1}^{k} \sigma_g^j \beta_g^j} - 1 \tag{14}$$

Regarding the values of the weights β_g^j, we have already defined $\beta_g^g = 1$. Given the dominance of self-seeking over sympathy,[5] it may be reasonable to assume that for all $g \neq j$: $\beta_g^j < 1$. Thus unless $\sigma_g^j = 0$ for all $g \neq j$, the denominator of the first term on the right-hand side of equation (14) must fall short of γ. Thus, leaving out the case of no taxation, no external benefits, no employment creation, and so forth (corresponding to $\lambda = 1$ in the symmetric model in sections 2 and 3, we must have

$$\pi^j > \frac{1}{\gamma} - 1 \tag{14*}$$

Thus, it would appear from statements (13), (13*), (14), and (14*) that under the specified assumptions the social rate of discount will tend to lie below the private rate of discount of each investing group j even in the asymmetric case.

[5] Note, however, that since the weighting is of consumption rather than utility, this will involve quite a strong dominance of self-seeking when one is much richer than some other groups.

But even with these assumptions, it is not certain that the social rate must lie below the *market* rate of interest m, since m itself lies below the private rate π^j whenever θ^j is less than unity (that is, when the share of "others" in private investment comes partly from *outside* the market return—through externalities, job creation, and so forth). The assertion that the social rate of discount must be chosen to be lower than the market rate of interest must, therefore, be based on some additional assumption. One such assumption is, of course, that of $\theta^j = 1$, that is, the share of "others" comes *entirely* from *within* the market return through taxation and other transfers. This will make the market rate equal the private rate of discount, thus exceeding the social discount rate to be used. An alternative set of assumptions that is sufficient for this purpose is a lack of concern for "others": $\beta_g{}^j = 0$, for $g \neq j$, combined with *some part* of the share of others coming from *within* the market return: $\theta^j > \sigma_j{}^j$.

But these are very special assumptions, and there is little reason to be sure that the social rate must be pegged at a level below the *market* rate of interest, even when one is persuaded that the social rate does lie below the *private* rate of discount of the investing groups.

5. Social Welfare Functionals and Discounting

I turn now to the question of the determination of social weights. Let X be the set of alternative "social states" including the current period, 0, and the next, 1. There are m people in the present generation (indexed $1, \ldots, m$), and $(n - m)$ in the next (indexed $m + 1, \ldots, n$), making a community of a total of n people whose interests have to be considered. For any social state x in X, let $x_i{}^0$ stand for the consumption of person i in period 0 for $i = 1, \ldots, m$, and $x_i{}^1$ for the consumption of person i in period 1 for $i = m + 1, \ldots, n$. Each individual i's personal welfare function W_i is defined over X, and while people live in exactly one period or the other, their personal welfare values may take note of any sympathy that people have for others, including for those living at another period.

Let R be any social ordering ("at least as good as") with P and I its asymmetric and symmetric factors, respectively. A *social welfare functional* (SWFL) is a functional relation that specifies exactly one social ordering R over X for any n-tuple of individual welfare functions (one for each person):

$$R = F(\{W_i\}) \tag{15}$$

The assumptions of measurability and interpersonal comparability of welfare are expressed through *invariance restrictions* on transformations of the n-tuples $\{W_i\}$ that preserve the welfare information, being "permitted" transformations (see Sen, 1970, 1977a). For example, given "ordinal" measurability of personal welfare and the complete absence of interpersonal comparability, if $\{W_i\}$ is transformed into $\{\hat{W}_i\}$ through the operation of any n-tuple of positive, monotonic transformations ϕ_i in the form: $\hat{W}_i = \phi_i(W_i)$ for all i, then $F(\{W_i\}) = F(\{\hat{W}_i\})$. This would make a social welfare functional SWFL a "social welfare function" SWF in the sense of Arrow (1951). To take another example, if cardinal measurability is combined with full interpersonal comparability, then the invariance requirement is weakened exactly to the following: If $\{W_i\}$ is transformed into $\{\hat{W}_i\}$ through the operation of any positive, affine transformation ϕ in the form $\hat{W}_i = \phi(W_i)$ for all i, then $F(\{W_i\}) = F(\{\hat{W}_i\})$. Note that the change of the permitted type of individual transformations reflects a shift in the measurability assumption (from "ordinal" to "cardinal"), while the change from a distinct transformation ϕ_i for each person to one common transformation ϕ applied to all reflects a shift in the assumption of interpersonal comparability (from none to full). Various other distinguished cases and continuums in between have been discussed elsewhere by Sen (1970, 1977a), Blackorby (1975), Fine (1975), d'Aspremont and Gevers (1977), Hammond (1977), Deschamps and Gevers (1978) and Roberts (1980a).

The relevant social rates of discount reflect a part of the content of a social ordering R. In particular, consider the choice between social state x including the social investment in question and social state y *without* it, and let this involve a reduction in the consumption in period 0 by one unit and an increase in the consumption in period 1 by $1 + q$ units. (The judgment on the relative social merits of x and y will not, in general, be independent of the interpersonal distributions of consumption gain and loss.) If xPy, then the social rate of discount relevant for this investment is less than q, and if yPx, then it exceeds q. If xIy, then the social rate of discount is exactly q.

The conditions that Arrow imposed on SWFs for his general possibility theorem correspond to the following conditions imposed on SWFLs.

Unrestricted domain (U): The domain of F includes all logically possible n-tuples of welfare functions $\{W_i\}$.

Weak Pareto principle (P): For any $\{W_i\}$, and any pair x,y, if $W_i(x) > W_i(y)$ for all i, then xPy.

Independence of irrelevant alternatives (I): For any two n-tuples $\{W_i\}$ and $\{\hat{W}_i\}$, if for some pair x,y: $W_i(x) = \hat{W}_i(x)$ and $W_i(y) = \hat{W}_i(y)$, for all i, then $xF(\{W_i\})y$ if and only if $xF(\{\hat{W}_i\})y$.

Nondictatorship (D): There is no person i such that for any $\{W_i\}$ in the domain of F and any pair x,y, if $W_i(x) > W_i(y)$, then xPy.

Arrow's theorem translates in this framework into the proposition that there is no SWFL satisfying conditions $U, P, I,$ and D and the invariance restriction for ordinal noncomparability.

The same impossibility holds even when the informational base is enriched to *cardinal* noncomparability with the invariance requirement covering $\{\hat{W}_i\}$ obtained from $\{W_i\}$ by an n-tuple of positive affine transformations ϕ_i (see Sen, 1970, Theorem 8*2). To gain any advantage with the imposed conditions, the informational base has to be enriched in the direction of introducing interpersonal comparability. The same applies to the determination of social rates of discount, which, as we have seen, is a problem embedded in the derivation of a SWFL.

If cardinal full comparability is admitted, a variety of rules can be used, and the Arrow conditions can also be strengthened in various ways.

Pareto indifference rule (P°): For any $\{W_i\}$, and any pair x,y, if $W_i(x) = W_i(y)$ for all i, then xIy.

Strong Pareto principle (P*): $P°$ holds, and also if for any $\{W_i\}$ and any pair x,y: $W_i(x) \geq W_i(y)$ for all i, and $W_i(x) > W_i(y)$ for some i, then xPy.

Anonymity (A): If $\{\hat{W}_i\}$ is a reordering of $\{W_i\}$, then $F(\{\hat{W}_i\}) = F(\{W_i\})$.

Strong neutrality (SN): For any two n-tuples $\{W_i\}$ and $\{\hat{W}_i\}$, if for social states x,y,a,b: $W_i(x) = \hat{W}_i(a)$ and $W_i(y) = \hat{W}_i(b)$ for all i, then $xF(\{W_i\})y$ if and only if $aF(\{\hat{W}_i\})b$.

It should be noted that strong Pareto principle (*P**), strong neutrality (*SN*), and anonymity (*A*) imply, respectively, Arrow's weak Pareto principle (*P*), independence of irrelevant alternatives (*I*), and nondictatorship (*D*), but each is in fact a strict strengthening of the corresponding condition.

Among the class of SWFLs satisfying *U*, *P**, *SN*, and *A*, the utilitarian rule and Rawlsian lexicographic maximin rule (derived from Rawls' "Difference Principle") have been much discussed.[6] Denote the jth worst off person in state x as $j(x)$, breaking ties when necessary in any arbitrary strict order.

Utilitarianism: xRy if and only if $\sum_{i=1}^{n} (W_i(x) - W_i(y)) \geq 0$.

Rawlsian lexicographic maximin (leximin): xIy if and only if $W_{j(x)}(x) = W_{j(y)}(y)$ for all $j = 1, \ldots, n$. And xPy if and only if there is some r: $1 \leq r \leq n$, such that $W_{r(x)}(x) > W_{r(y)}(y)$, and for all $j < r$: $W_{j(x)}(x) = W_{j(y)}(y)$.

Utilitarianism and leximin can both be derived axiomatically starting from cardinal full comparability and *U*, *P**, *I*, and *A* by additional requirements (see Hammond, 1976; Strasnick, 1976; d'Aspremont and Gevers, 1977; Deschamps and Gevers, 1978; Gevers, 1979; Maskin, 1978, 1979; Roberts, 1980a, 1980b; Arrow, 1976; and Sen, 1977a). As the formulations of utilitarianism and leximin make clear, the focus of the former is on gains and losses of personal welfare (without any concern about welfare levels as

---

[6] See Rawls (1971), Sen (1970, 1974b), Arrow (1973), Dasgupta (1974), Page (1977), and Phelps (1976), among many other contributors.

such), whereas the focus of the latter is on comparisons of welfare levels (without any concern about the exact sizes of welfare gains and losses). The dichotomy of ethical principles leads, therefore, to a dichotomy of information sets that are made "inadmissible" in the sense of making the social ordering invariant with respect to information of that type (see Sen, 1973). A less wasteful and more sensitive social welfare approach should take note of *both* types of information sets, namely, welfare *levels* as well as welfare *gains and losses* (see Sen, 1974a, 1974b, 1977a).

In determining the social rate of discount relevant for a particular investment project through the formula given by equation (7), we need, of course, the factual information about the breakdown of consumption gains and losses, $\{\sigma_g\}$ and $\{\sigma_g'\}$, respectively. In addition we need the information on which the evaluative weights $\{\alpha_g\}$ and $\{\beta_g\}$ are to be based. For utilitarianism this information is supplied by the respective *marginal utilities* of consumption, while for leximin this information is provided by values of personal welfare *levels*. Indeed, for a suitably small investment project, the vector of marginal utilities $\mathbf{W'}$ and the vector of welfare levels $\mathbf{W^*}$ in the social state without the investment are adequate for determining the relative evaluative weights under the two approaches respectively. In what follows we shall be concerned with *both* $\mathbf{W'}$ and $\mathbf{W^*}$.

Some of the underlying ethical conflicts may be easier to explain in terms of a model in which the current generation and the future generation are treated as two persons p and f, respectively, though there is not much difficulty in capturing the same conflicts also in terms of a more elaborate model. The social rate of discount can then be seen as a function of the two types of information specified:

$$\rho = D(\mathbf{W}_p^*, \mathbf{W}_f^*, \mathbf{W}_p', \mathbf{W}_f') \tag{16}$$

Let the respective partial derivatives—assuming differentiability—be D_p^*, D_f^*, D_p', and D_f'. What can we say about the signs of these derivatives? It is readily checked that under utilitarianism:

$$D_p' > 0, D_f' < 0, D_p^* = D_f^* = 0 \tag{17}$$

The Rawlsian approach is, of course, less sensitive since it gives absolute priority to the worse off, but the underlying ethical consideration is captured in a broader framework if—subject to $W_p' > 0$ and $W_f' > 0$—we require that:

$$D_p^* < 0, D_f^* > 0 \tag{18}$$

Putting the two types of sensitivity together, we may require that:[7]

$$D_p^* < 0, D_f^* > 0, D_p' > 0, D_f' < 0 \tag{19}$$

In the next section, equation (16) is explored subject to equation (19).

6. Welfare Levels and Differences: Directional Regularities

First, consider the impact of a higher growth between now and the future on the discount rate ρ. With an unchanged initial situation given by the welfare level W_p^* and marginal utility W_p', the result of the higher growth will be to raise the future welfare level W_f^* and to reduce the future marginal utility W_f', given strict concavity of the welfare function in the future. Since $D_f^* > 0$ and $D_f' < 0$ from (19), both the changes will induce the social discount rate ρ to rise. There is, thus, no ambiguity in this case about the direction of the movement of ρ, and the standard utilitarian result is reinforced.

Consider, next, an unchanged initial situation and unchanged growth rate between now and the future, but an increase of the degree of concavity of the shared welfare function relating personal welfare to own personal consumption: $W_i = W(C_i)$. Normalizing in such a way that W_p and W_p' remain unchanged, the result of such a uniform increase in concavity will be to reduce *both* W_f^* and W_f'. It follows from equation (19) that the decrease in W_f' will tend to reduce the social rate of discount; this is the standard utilitarian result. On the other hand, the decrease of W_f^* will have exactly the opposite effect. Thus the two influences will counteract each other, and the net result is no longer unambiguous.

The conflict can be illustrated in terms of the familiar utility function with a constant elasticity of marginal utility:

$$W_i = A + \frac{1}{\eta}(C_i)^\eta, \text{ with } \eta < 1 \tag{20}$$

Marginal utility of consumption is given by:

$$W_i' = (C_i)^{\eta-1} \tag{21}$$

A diminution of η, corresponding to a uniform increase in the degree of concavity, will reduce the welfare level as well as the marginal utility of consumption, for given C_i. Although the latter would shift us in the direction

---

[7] The class of rules satisfying these restrictions has a nonempty intersection with the class of rules based on adding strictly concave transformations of individual welfares (proposed by Mirrlees, 1971). But neither set is wholly contained in the other.

of giving less weight to the future consumption on "efficiency" grounds concerning the "total" (the familiar utilitarian argument), the former would shift us in the direction of *raising* the weight on future consumption on grounds of "equity" (the strength of one's claim being inversely related to one's relative prosperity). The net results will depend on the respective magnitude of the two effects, and that, of course, would depend on the particular specification of equation (16).

Therefore, the view that one does not become so much better off after all from an increased level of consumption cuts both ways. The constant-elasticity case is, of course, special in the sense that marginal and total utility are very closely related, and once a wider family of utility functions is considered, there is a greater scope for parametric variations in the relation between the marginal and the total.

Consider now a third type of variation, namely, that of a shift of the utility function over time. The impact on the discount rate ρ will depend on the nature of the shift, in particular on the respective influences on the welfare level and the marginal utility of consumption. For example, if the personal welfare function shifts in such a way that the marginal utility falls more sharply between now and the future while the rise of the overall welfare level is not changed, then clearly such a shift will kick up the social rate of discount. On the other hand, if the decline in marginal utility is not enhanced by the shift while the rise of welfare level is reduced, clearly ρ will be pulled down. An interesting case to consider in this context is a fall of A over time in equation (20):

$$W_i^t = A(t) + \frac{1}{\eta}(C_i^t)^\eta, \text{ with } \eta < 1, \text{ and } \frac{dA(t)}{dt} < 0 \qquad (22)$$

A faster rate of decline of $A(t)$ over time will have the effect of reducing W_f^*, keeping W_f' unchanged, and this will make the social discount rate ρ go down.

Is there a plausible interpretation of equation (22)? I would like to suggest two. First, increased pollution over time may cut down the general quality of life without necessarily affecting the marginal utility of consumption.[8] Even today the lack of fresh air in a city makes one feel that much worse off in general, but the usefulness of an additional unit of consumption may not be reduced (and may, in fact, even be increased if the consumer good in question is aimed at freshening the air or compensating for the ill effects of polluted air). If this characterization of increasing

---

[8] See Dasgupta's (1971) use of a utility function of the form given by equation (22), interpreting the shift as arising from population "congestion" (pp. 311–313). However, since his maximand is simply the sum total of individual utilities, the "equity" consequences of this shift have no role in his model.

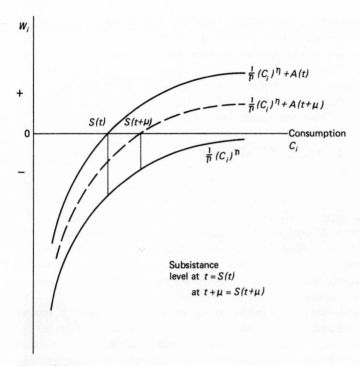

Figure 9-1

pollution is accepted, the result will be to make the discount rate less than otherwise, since the reduced welfare level will pull ρ down, while unchanged (and possibly enhanced) marginal utility of consumption will not counteract it (and will possibly reinforce it).

A second interpretation concerns the changing notion of the subsistence level. If $\eta < 0$, then the personal welfare function is bounded on top (as with Ramsey, 1928), but the value of $\frac{1}{\eta}(C_i)^\eta$ is negative for all consumption levels. If significance is attached not merely to marginal utility, but also to the value of the welfare level, then on A falls the task of pulling up the welfare schedule above the zero value for consumption levels exceeding a certain minimum, say $\overline{C}$ (see figure 9-1). The value $\overline{C}$ of consumption level for which W_i is zero may be interpreted—not without reason—as the subsistence level. An increasing subsistence requirement over time is not contrary to the actual history of social ideas, and there may be good reason to think that in the future the concept of "basic needs" will go on becoming more demanding. But this does not necessarily affect the notion of marginal utility of consumption. A downward shift of A, as in equation (22), will raise the subsistence level, pulling down total welfare values but without affecting the marginal utility schedule (see figure 9-1).

In choosing an appropriate social discount rate, therefore, one has to consider not merely the rate of growth of consumption, but also the relative roles of marginal utility vis-à-vis total welfare level, the nature and extent of concavity of the personal welfare function, as well as the characteristics of the shifts of the welfare function over time.

7. The Inadequacy of Welfarism

Utilitarianism, leximin, and the class of social welfare functionals satisfying condition (16) have the common feature of making the relative merits of the social states depend only on the personal welfare characteristics of the respective states. If any factor has to have an influence on the social ordering R, this can be only *through* its influence on the personal welfare vectors. Note that this is not a necessary characteristic of a social welfare functional, since that merely requires that the social ordering over X be a function of the n-tuple of individual welfare *functions* $\{W_i\}$.

Welfarism can be defined as making the social ordering of X depend only on the placing of each social state in the n-dimensional space of individual welfare values (ignoring the description of the states in other respects). If two states—however different—generate the same personal welfare values for each person, then under welfarism, they must be treated exactly in the same way.[9] Formally, this corresponds to the property of neutrality, which was defined in a strong form (incorporating independence of irrelevant alternatives) as condition SN in section 4. The weaker version of "neutrality," which characterizes welfarism, is the following (see also Arrow, 1963, p. 101).

Neutrality (N): If for some permutation function $\tau(\cdot)$ over X, $W_i(x) = \hat{W}_i(\tau(x))$ for all i and all x, and if $\hat{R}$ is the ordering of X obtained by replacing x by $\tau(x)$ in R for all x, then $R = F(\{W_i\})$ implies that $\hat{R} = F(\{\hat{W}_i\})$.

It can be shown that any SWFL satisfying unrestricted domain (U), independence (I), and the Pareto indifference rule (P^o) must satisfy strong neutrality SN (see d'Aspremont and Gevers, 1977; Sen, 1977a).[10] Since SN implies neutrality, any approach that leads to a social welfare functional which fulfills U, P^o, and I must satisfy welfarism.

[9] Note, however, that while this is a characteristic of the Rawlsian lexicographic maximin rule as typically formulated in economic discussions, Rawls (1971) himself applied the difference principle to the problem of distribution of "primary goods" only. Furthermore, Rawls's "two principles" taken together depart substantially from welfarism because of the principle of liberty, which indeed has priority.

[10] Guha (1972) and Blau (1976) have similar results for social decision functions (transforming each n-tuple of individual orderings to a quasi-transitive R). See also Blau and Deb (1977).

It is because of this result that in the axiomatic derivation of utilitarianism or leximin, neutrality does not have to be required as a condition on its own if U, I, and P^o (or, of course, P^*) are postulated. In fact, even in Arrow's own framework, neutrality is "nearly" present, even though he held that "the principle of neutrality is not intuitively basic" (Arrow, 1963, p. 101). Arrow combines conditions U and I with the weak Pareto principle P (dealing with unanimous strict preference) rather than the Pareto indifference rule P^o (dealing with unanimous indifference), and this leads to the neutrality of *winning* coalitions over all pairs of social states, but leaves open the question when the winning coalition is indifferent over a particular pair. (This is, in fact, the basic "lemma" in Arrow's General Possibility theorem, the proof of the theorem being completed by the demonstration that the winning coalition must consist of only one person.)

How acceptable is welfarism and related forms of neutrality? We can readily note what it denies. First, it leaves out considerations of liberty defined in the form of a person's right to have his way in choices over *specific* pairs where the choice is thought to be legitimately his "concern" only (see Sen, 1970, 1976a). Second, it leaves out "rights" and "claims" that arise from some particular action now or in the past (for example, in the concepts of "value" and "exploitation" in Marx (1887), or of "entitlements" in Nozick (1974)). Third, it leaves out all judgments arising from concepts of "desert," which—unlike "needs"—cannot be readily captured in a welfaristic framework.

Are any of these considerations relevant to the choices involved in the social rate of discount? It is possible to argue that they may be. First, there is the question whether future generations have a *right* to enjoy natural resources that the present generation is depleting rapidly. Second, there is also the question whether the liberty of the future generations can be seen as being unacceptably compromised by certain activities of the present generation—failure to control pollution, for example.

One has to be careful to avoid double-counting. If the future generation's "right" to the use of natural resources is related to their "right" to have a decent standard of living, then this can—without undue strain—be accommodated within welfarism. On the other hand, if the right to natural resources is based on some innate concept of "entitlement," irrespective of whether the future generation is going to be well off, or badly off, then clearly this is an *additional* consideration. If so, the discount rate relevant to investments for better utilization of natural resources cannot be derived only from welfaristic considerations (W_p^*, W_f^*, W_p', W_f' and so on). The choice of evaluative weights has to reflect these rights as well.

It is fair to say that the recent increase in interest in "entitlement theories" has not led to much discussion of this intergenerational issue. Many relevant questions have remained unanalyzed. Are we free to blow natural resources as we like as long as we can justify it on grounds of our low welfare level, high marginal utility, and so forth, as compared with future generations? For example, even if our marginal utility from this resource use is greater than that of the future generation and even if we remain poorer in terms of welfare level than the future generation, can the future generation still legitimately claim that we are grabbing something to which we are not entitled (capitalizing on the arbitrary fact that we could get at the resources before the future generation could)? It is far from clear how one might go about answering these questions, but one can scarcely maintain that such questions simply do not arise. And the choice of social rates of discount for investments in the development of natural resources (including energy) is certainly not independent of these issues.

On the issue of pollution perhaps a bit more can be said. The analogy with torture is not absurd. While an isolated incident like Seveso can be an accident, the broad general development of pollution is typically the result of deliberate action. Lasting pollution is a kind of calculable oppression of the future generation. It may, therefore, be quite appropriate in this context to examine whether welfarism is adequate for a normative analysis of torture.

Let i be the "inquisitor" and h the "heretic." I take it that it is unnecessary to specify who is in a position to torture whom. The social state t with torture will make h worse off and i better off than the social state s will without torture: $W_h(t) < W_h(s)$ and $W_i(t) > W_i(s)$. The utilitarian will be opposed to the torture if and only if $W_i(t) - W_i(s) < W_h(s) - W_h(t)$; that is, the torturer gains less than the tortured loses. Suppose this is not the case. The lexicographic maximin rule will be opposed to torture only if the minimal welfare level of the four possible "positions" is that of being person h in social state t: $W_i(s) \geq W_h(t)$.[11] Suppose that is not the case either: the inquisitor suffers from depression, and he is worse off in the absence of torture than the heretic is with torture: $W_i(s) < W_h(t)$. In fact, to make the welfaristic picture even more definitive on equity grounds, let us also assume that also $W_i(t) < W_h(t)$. So the miserable inquisitor is worse off than the resilient heretic whether or not the torture takes place, and his personal welfare gain from the torture is conceded to be greater than the welfare loss of the heretic.

Must we then support the torture? It is not easy to construct a welfaristic argument against torture in this case.[12] But it is legitimate to argue that the personal welfare data are inherently inadequate in deciding on an issue like this. We may wish to concede to person h his right to personal liberty, which

[11] This is a necessary condition, becoming sufficient only if $\geq$ is replaced by $>$, or supplemented by $W_i(t) > W_h(s)$.

[12] Appeals to "rule utilitarianism" and other non-act-evaluation arguments also raise problems that are well known; we can even make the situation quite unique. On this general question, see Sen (1979).

cannot be violated on grounds of net gain of the utility sum or on grounds of the torturer being in general worse off. The choice is a particular one between *t* and *s* involving an act, namely, torture, and this descriptive feature of the social states has to be noted *directly*. Person *h*'s right not to be tortured against his will cannot be captured in terms of arguments based on personal welfare information only. The same personal welfare numbers when holding for two social states *t* and *s* of *different* description (for example, *t* involving a tax on rich *h* for poor *i*'s benefit, and *s* no such tax), may require us to judge the choice differently. This distinction violates neutrality and cannot be captured within welfarism.

If the similarity between torture and calculated pollution is accepted, then it can be argued that in deciding on social rates of discount for investment projects that have a bearing on pollution, the welfaristic models of sections 5 and 6 (and in fact, virtually all models proposed so far in the literature) are quite inadequate. The evaluative weights considered in sections 2–4 cannot be made functions *only* of personal welfare information, and the analysis requires supplementation by nonwelfaristic considerations of liberty.

Suppose the investment project in question will eliminate some pollution that the present generation will otherwise impose on the future. Even if the future generation may be richer and may enjoy a higher welfare level, *and* even if its marginal utility from the consumption gain is accepted to be less than the marginal welfare loss of the present generation, this may still not be accepted to be decisive for rejecting the investment when the alternative implies long-term effects of environmental pollution. The avoidance of oppression of the future generations has to be given a value of its own.

If, on the other hand, the investment project is itself a *polluting* one, then exactly the opposite kind of a case could possibly exist even when the investment seems justified on welfaristic grounds. The evaluation of investments and the choice of relevant social rates of discount cannot, therefore, be reduced simply to considerations involving personal welfare data relating to the present and the future.

These issues are relevant to the current controversy over investment in nuclear energy, particularly fast breeder reactors. These investments are not merely capital-intensive and sensitive to the discount rates. They also involve considerable risks of environmental pollution.[13] Despite safeguards against accidents, one cannot assume the probability of accidents to be zero; over time, accidents are difficult to rule out. The accidents that have occurred illustrate that not all possibilities are foreseen. In fact, in fast breeder reactors

[13] One reason why a fast breeder program is capital-intensive is that fast breeders require a large initial inventory of plutonium, specifically, four tons of plutonium per gigawatt (10^6 kilowatts) of electric output. To start a fast breeder of a given capacity, the required plutonium inventory would amount to seven years' output of a thermal Magnox reactor of equivalent output (see Royal Commission on Environmental Pollution, 1976, p. 46).

the possibility of the failure of normal control mechanisms opens up the eventuality of "what is technically a nuclear explosion, though the growth of the chain reaction would be slow compared with that which occurs in a nuclear bomb and the energy released will be correspondingly less." If the reactor containment fails to cope with such a contingency, "then not only iodine and caesium, but substantial quantities of non-volatile fission products such as strontium, as well as plutonium, would be released" (Royal Commission on Environmental Pollution, 1976, pp. 46–47).

In addition to such accidents, the normal dangers of a plutonium economy are themselves quite worth considering, especially in the context of storage and reprocessing of radioactive wastes. There is also the not yet fully settled issue of the alleged special danger from "hot" particles (see Tamplin and Cochran, 1976; Dolphin and coauthors, 1974; Lovins and Patterson, 1975; and U.K. Medical Research Council, 1975), which *if* true, will—according to some—"effectively preclude the use of nuclear power" (Royal Commission on Environmental Pollution, 1976, p. 24).

The complexity of nuclear power issues arises from a variety of economic and ethical considerations. The returns from a nuclear energy program in general and a program of fast breeders in particular will, of course, depend on the alternative cost of energy production, for example, from sun, wind, and wave, and also from fusion. One cannot give an a priori judgment on any of these matters. But what is worth emphasizing in the context of the preceding discussion is that in addition to these relative cost considerations, there are issues in this choice involving "welfaristic" questions of relative prosperity as well as "nonwelfaristic" factors involving rights of particular groups of people whose liberty may be violated by a calculated program of nuclear energy development involving fast breeders. The cost-and-utility calculus cannot begin to convey the complexity of choices surrounding investment in nuclear power.

8. Concluding Remarks

We have investigated two departures from the utilitarian approach to the determination of social rates of discount. The first, concerned chiefly with "equity," involves a systematic attempt to supplement considerations of marginal gains and losses of personal welfare by a concern about aggregate welfare levels (section 5). Although the focus was not principally on the Rawlsian "Difference Principle," the information set for maximin (concerned with welfare *levels*) was used to supplement the utilitarian information set (concerned with welfare *differences*). A general characterization of the respective influences permitted some directional conclusions to be drawn dealing with variations in the growth rate, in the pattern of concavity of personal welfare functions, and shifts in welfare functions due to growing pollution, changing conceptions of "subsistence," and so forth (section 6).

The other departure, involved chiefly with "liberty," includes a rejection of "welfarism," which judges social states exclusively by their personal welfare characteristics.[14] Related to an earlier argument that a concern for liberty requires us to go beyond welfarism (Sen, 1970, chapter 6), the question of pollution was examined in the context of the liberty of future generations, and the need to go beyond personal welfare data was outlined (section 7). Other possible "rights" that may take us beyond welfarism (for example, the right to the use of natural resources) were touched on more briefly, noting some inherent ambiguities.

The format in which these ethical considerations were introduced is that of social welfare functionals (SWFL), which is an extension of Arrow's (1951) framework of social welfare functions (sections 5–7). The differences from Arrow consist of (i) a wider informational base of personal welfares admitted into the analysis, and (ii) the avoidance of elements of "neutrality," which push us toward welfarism and which are logically implied by combining unrestricted domain (U) and independence of irrelevant alternatives (I) with any version of the Pareto principle. (Given U and I, Arrow's weak version P implies neutrality partially, while the strong Pareto principle P^* or even the Pareto indifference rule P^o implies it fully.)

While these ethical considerations enter the problem of evaluative weighting on which the determination of *social* rates of discount depends (sections 3 and 4), the question has to be posed as to whether they do not equally enter the market determination of rates of interest through their influence on individual behavior. The inadequacy of utilitarianism has no *necessary* implication regarding the inoptimality of the market interest structure.

However, it is unlikely that these ethical considerations play a sufficiently important role in people's market behavior. First of all, they involve a fair amount of universalized moral analysis and deliberation about distant implications. Although I have tried to argue elsewhere (Sen 1977b) that the assumption that people maximize their personal welfare in their actual behavior is quite inadequate, the "nonselfish" considerations have their own biases (concerning class, community, visibility and immediacy of effects, and so forth).

Second, the information on which the choice of social rates of discount is based (in the light of these ethical analyses) may not be widely available, and some of it may in fact require new investigation. The parsimonious informational structure on which the market operates (the adequacy of which under certain circumstances has been shown for the attainment of certain

---

[14] Note that a rejection of welfarism does not necessarily imply a rejection of the so-called end-state approach, or of "consequentialism." I have explored these issues in Sen (1979, 1982).

efficiency results, for example, Pareto optimality *or* being in the core) is in fact quite inadequate to sustain ethical analysis involving equity or liberty, or even utilitarianism.

Third, even if everyone had all the information and based their market actions on exactly the same ethical analyses as their political or public activities, the interpersonal weighting implicit in the market equilibria may be quite different from the weighting that is chosen for public decisions, or for social benefit–cost analysis. The problem is present whenever personal moralities differ even when all actions (including market actions) are assumed to be fully determined by the respective personal moralities.

Fourth, the interpersonal distributions of sacrifices and benefits are not the same in different types of investment. Indeed, the difference between private and social rates of discount under the "isolation" argument can be reduced entirely to this contrast of "composition" (section 2). Even with the same evaluative weights on "named goods" (or "named consumption"), the private and social rates of discount will differ depending on the interpersonal compositions of present consumption sacrifices and future consumption gains in the two types of investment. (It was also shown that it is quite misleading to attribute this difference to externalities of consumption.) The market rates are based on a *third* type of composition, corresponding neither necessarily to the composition underlying the "social" discount rate, nor necessarily to that implicit in the "private" discount rate (sections 3 and 4). Indeed, the conclusion that the social rate may lie below the private rate in the usual simple models did not, in fact, imply that the social rate must lie below the *market* rate, and different conclusions can emerge depending on the relevant parameters (see sections 3 and 4).

There is, in fact, very little scope for avoiding a deliberate ethical exercise in choosing appropriate rates of discount for social benefit–cost analysis. The problem can be split into (1) investigation of compositions and (2) selection of evaluative weights on each element in the composite structure. The former category includes both the question of interpersonal composition of gains and losses (sections 2–4) and the identification of those descriptive features (for example, generating or counteracting pollution, preserving natural resources) that may require us to go beyond welfarist considerations (section 7). The relevance of the latter to investments in energy and related research and development can hardly be ignored.

The second category includes the use of utilitarian reasoning (based on identification of *gains and losses* of personal welfare), equity considerations (needing supplementation by considerations of personal welfare *levels*), and the analyses of the right to liberty and other rights that the future generations may be acknowledged to have (needing supplementation by nonwelfare, descriptive information).

I do not doubt that different compromises can be reached about the relative importance to be attached to these various considerations. But the least we should require is that attention be paid to the competing claims of these different influences and that the *process* of choosing discount rates for social benefit–cost analysis be made more reasoned and more explicit. The search has to be more than an intellectual blindman's buff.

References

Arrow, K. J. 1951. *Social Choice and Individual Values* (New York, Wiley).
———. 1963. *Social Choice and Individual Values* (New York, Wiley), second edition.
———. 1966. "Discounting and Public Investment Criteria," in A. V. Kneese and S. C. Smith, eds. *Water Research* (Baltimore, Johns Hopkins University Press for Resources for the Future).
———. 1973. "Some Ordinalist–Utilitarian Notes on Rawls' Theory of Justice," *Journal of Philosophy* vol. 70.
———. 1976. "Extended Sympathy and the Possibility of Social Choice," *American Economic Review* vol. 67; Discussion Paper No. 484 (Harvard Institute of Economic Research).
———, and M. Kurz. 1970. *Public Investment, the Rate of Return, and Optimal Fiscal Policy* (Baltimore, Johns Hopkins University Press for Resources for the Future).
Baumol, W. J. 1968a. "On the Appropriate Discount Rate for Evaluation of Public Projects," in Hearings before the Subcommittee on Economy of Government of the Joint Economic Committee, U.S. Congress (Washington, GPO).
———. 1968b. "On the Social Rate of Discount," *American Economic Review* vol. 58.
Blackorby, C. 1975. "Degrees of Cardinality and Aggregate Partial Ordering," *Econometrica* vol. 43.
Blau, J. H. 1976. "Neutrality, Monotonicity and the Right of Veto: A Comment," *Econometrica* vol. 44.
———, and R. Deb. 1977. "Social Decision Functions and the Veto," *Econometrica* vol. 45.
Dasgupta, P. 1971. "On the Concept of Optimum Population," *Review of Economic Studies* vol. 38.
———. 1974. "On Some Alternative Criteria for Justice between Generations," *Journal of Public Economics* vol. 3.
———, S. A. Marglin, and A. K. Sen. 1972. *Guidelines for Project Evaluation,* UNIDO, New York: United Nations.
d'Aspremont, C., and L. Gevers. 1977. "Equity and the Informational Basis of Collective Choice," *Review of Economic Studies* vol. 44.
Deschamps, R., and L. Gevers. 1978. "Leximin and Utilitarian Rules: A Joint Characterization," *Journal of Economic Theory* vol. 17.
Dobb, M. H. 1960. *An Essay on Economic Growth and Planning* (London, Routledge).

Dolphin, G. W., and coauthors. 1974. *Radiological Problems in the Protection of Persons Exposed to Plutonium* (United Kingdom, National Radiological Protection Board).

Eckstein, O. 1957. "Investment Criteria for Economic Development and the Theory of Intertemporal Welfare Economics," *Quarterly Journal of Economics* vol. 71.

Feldstein, M. S. 1964. "The Social Time Preference Discount Rate in Cost–Benefit Analysis," *Economic Journal* vol. 74.

———. 1972. "The Inadequacy of Weighted Discount Rates," in R. Layard, ed., *Cost–Benefit Analysis* (Harmondsworth and Baltimore, Penguin).

Fine, B. 1975. "A Note on Interpersonal Comparisons and Comparability," *Econometrica* vol. 43.

Gevers, L. 1979. "On Interpersonal Comparability and Social Welfare Orderings," *Econometrica* vol. 47.

Guha, A. S. 1972. "Neutrality, Monotonicity and the Right of Veto," *Econometrica* vol. 40.

Hahn, F. H. 1971. "Equilibrium with Transaction Costs," *Econometrica* vol. 39.

Hammond, P. J. 1976. "Equity, Arrow's Conditions and Rawls' Difference Principle," *Econometrica* vol. 44.

———. 1977. "Dual Interpersonal Comparisons of Utility and the Welfare Economics of Income Distribution," *Journal of Public Economics* vol. 6.

Harberger, A. C. 1964. "Techniques of Project Appraisal," Universities National Bureau of Economic Research Conference on Economic Planning (November 27–28, 1964).

———. 1968. "On Measuring the Social Opportunity Cost of Public Funds," in *The Discount Rate in Public Investment Evaluation,* Report No. 17, Conference Proceedings from the Committee on the Economics of Water Resources Development of the Western Agricultural Economics Research Council (Denver, Colorado, December 17–18, 1968).

———. 1973. *Project Evaluation: Collected Papers* (Chicago, Markham).

Hicks, J. R. 1958. "Measurement of Real Income," *Oxford Economic Papers* vol. 10.

Lind, R. C. 1964. "The Social Rate of Discount and the Optimal Rate of Investment: Further Comment," *Quarterly Journal of Economics* vol. 78.

Little, I. M. D., and J. A. Mirrlees. 1974. *Project Appraisal and Planning for Developing Countries* (London, Hutchinson).

Lovins, A. B., and W. C. Patterson. 1975. "Plutonium Particles: Some Like Them Hot," *Nature* vol. 254 (March 27) pp. 278–280.

Marglin, S. A. 1963a. "The Opportunity Cost of Investment," *Quarterly Journal of Investment* vol. 77.

———. 1963b. "The Social Rate of Discount and the Optimal Rate of Investment," *Quarterly Journal of Economics* vol. 77.

———. 1976. *Value and Price in the Labour-Surplus Economy* (Oxford, Clarendon Press).

Marx, K. 1887. *Capital: A Critical Analysis of Capitalist Production,* vol. I (London, Sonnenschein; republished, Allen & Unwin, 1938).

Maskin, E. 1978. "A Theorem on Utilitarianism," *Review of Economic Studies* vol. 45.

———. 1979. "Decision-Making Under Ignorance with Implications for Social Choice," *Theory and Decision* vol. 11.

Medical Research Council. 1975. *The Toxicity of Plutonium* (London, HMSO).

Mirrlees, J. A. 1971. "An Exploration in the Theory of Optimal Income Taxation," *Review of Economic Studies* vol. 38.

Nozick, R. 1974. *Anarchy, State and Utopia* (Oxford, Blackwell).

Page, T. 1977. *Conservation and Economic Efficiency* (Baltimore, Johns Hopkins University Press for Resources for the Future).

Phelps, E. S. 1965. *Fiscal Neutrality Toward Economic Growth* (New York, McGraw–Hill).

———. 1976. "Recent Developments in Welfare Economics: Justice et Équité," Discussion Paper No. 75–7617, Economics Workshop, Columbia University.

Ramsey, F. P. 1928. "A Mathematical Theory of Saving," *Economic Journal* vol. 38.

Rawls, J. 1971. *A Theory of Justice* (Oxford, Clarendon Press).

Roberts, K.W.S. 1980a. "Interpersonal Comparability and Social Choice Theory," *Review of Economic Studies* vol. 47.

———. 1980b. "Possibility Theorems with Interpersonally Comparable Welfare Levels," *Review of Economic Studies* vol. 47.

Royal Commission on Environmental Pollution. 1976. *Sixth Report* (London, HMSO).

Sen, A. K. 1957. "A Note on Tinbergen on the Optimum Rate of Saving," *Economic Journal* vol. 67.

———. 1960. *Choice of Techniques* (Oxford, Blackwell). [Sen (1968), third edition.]

———. 1961. "On Optimizing the Rate of Saving," *Economic Journal* vol. 71.

———. 1967. "Isolation, Assurance and the Social Rate of Discount," *Quarterly Journal of Economics* vol. 81.

———. 1968. *Choice of Techniques* (Oxford, Blackwell), third edition.

———. 1970. *Collective Choice and Social Welfare* (Edinburgh, Oliver & Boyd; San Francisco, Holden–Day).

———. 1973. *On Economic Inequality* (Oxford, Clarendon Press; New York, Norton).

———. 1974a. "Informational Bases of Alternative Welfare Approaches," *Journal of Public Economics* vol. 3.

———. 1974b. "Rawls vs. Bentham: An Axiomatic Examination of the Pure Distribution Problem," *Theory and Decision* vol. 4; reprinted in N. Daniels, ed., *Reading Rawls* (Oxford, Blackwell, 1975).

———. 1976a. "Liberty, Unanimity and Rights," *Economica* vol. 43.

———. 1976b. "Real National Income," *Review of Economic Studies* vol. 43.

———. 1977a. "On Weights and Measures: Informational Constraints in Social Welfare Analysis," Walras–Bowley Lecture, Econometric Society, *Econometrica* vol. 45.

———. 1977b. "Rational Fools: A Critique of the Behavioural Foundations of Economic Theory," *Philosophy and Public Affairs* vol. 6.

———. 1979. "Utilitarianism and Welfarism," *Journal of Philosophy* vol. 76.

———. 1982. "Rights and Agency," *Philosophy and Public Affairs* vol. 11.

Strasnick, S. 1976. "Social Choice Theory and the Derivation of Rawls' Difference Principle," *Journal of Philosophy* vol. 73.

Tamplin, A. R., and T. B. Cochran. 1976. *Radiation Standards for Hot Particles,* petition to the Atomic Energy Commission and the Environmental Protection Agency (Washington, Natural Resources Defense Council).

Tullock, G. 1964. "The Social Rate of Discount and the Optimal Rate of Investment: Comment," *Quarterly Journal of Economics* vol. 78.

Usher, D. 1964. "The Social Rate of Discount and the Optimal Rate of Investment: Comment," *Quarterly Journal of Economics* vol. 78.

*Robert Dorfman**

Comment

Sen has presented a very thoughtful and provocative analysis of the philosophical and ethical foundations of social discounting. His paper consists of two distinct parts, the first of which is a development of his work on the isolation argument for social saving decisions. The second part, to which I shall devote my attention almost exclusively, explores the implications of the theory of social welfare functions for the discount rates to be used in social decision making.

Sen's point of departure is the social welfare functional (SWFL), denoted by $F(\{W_i\})$. This functional is a rule for ranking alternative social states, and its arguments, W_i, $i = 1, \ldots, n$, are the welfares of the n individuals in the states being compared. Superficially it appears to be highly individualistic; nothing can affect the ranking except individual welfares. No points are awarded for contribution to the community as a whole. The considerations that really determine the ranking depend on what influences the individual welfares, and although Sen is not explicit about this, he gives us a good enough hint. He says that the individuals' "personal welfare values may take note of any sympathy that people have for others, including for those living at another period." From this I infer that they may also take note of animosity, envy, concern for their country's honor and prestige, dedication to civil liberties, devotion to justice and entitlements, esteem for democratic procedures, and all other such values.

On this interpretation, the SWFL is immune to the criticisms that Sen levels at it in his section on "the inadequacy of welfarism." There is some force, though, in his contentions. I shall come to their merits later, but for the present, notice that none of the high values I have mentioned can affect the SWFL's ranking of alternative states except to the extent that those values are held by individuals. If it should be true that for all i, $i = 1, \ldots, n$, in this generation and later, i does not care about the extent of civil liberties, then the SWFL will not rank x above y if x affords much greater civil liberty

* Department of Economics, Harvard University.

but is not superior to y in any other respect. To take a less loaded example, I presume that there is nobody in the United States who takes totemism seriously. Accordingly, one of the considerations that is never raised when a dam is being contemplated is the possible effects of that dam on the members of the beaver clan. A Melanesian would find this shocking. I find it quite appropriate. On what grounds should a society allow a value to affect its rankings—respect for civil liberties or totems or the nobility or whatever— if no one in the society holds that value?

Under this broad construction, the SWFL cannot be charged with ignoring significant social values. But that broad construction is inadmissible not only on Arrow's famous grounds, but because it presupposes that all the moral dilemmas that have beset humanity since before Plato have been resolved. The purpose of the SWFL is to assist in making social decisions, and the decisions cannot wait until the philosophers have returned successful from their quest for the good, the true, and the beautiful. For practical purposes we need something a good deal less ambitious.

Furthermore, Sen provides us with it. Almost immediately after the SWFL is defined in this very inclusive way, it turns out that for practical purposes the W_i in the SWFL depend entirely on consumption. Several variants occur at different places in the argument. The simplest can be denoted $W_i(C_i)$. Another version can be symbolized as $W_i (C_1, \ldots , C_n)$. A more complicated version is

$$W_i(W_i'(C_1), \ldots , W_{i-1}'(C_{i-1}), C_i, W_{i+1}'(C_{i+1}), \ldots , W_n'(C_n)),$$

where W_j' is i's perception of j's welfare, which depends only on j's consumption. All of these versions can be reduced, by elimination, to $W_i (C_1, \ldots , C_n)$. By further elimination, the SWFL itself can be reduced to $F'(\{C_i\})$. In that form it begins to be practical, and that is the form that Sen uses when he wants to deduce some conclusions.

But also it is true that that form is vulnerable to Sen's strictures against welfarism. It seems to me, though, that his animus is misplaced. Sen should be attacking "consumptionism" or "commodity fetishism" rather than welfarism, since, in the interest of practicality, the assumption has crept in that welfare depends only on one's own or others' consumption (which may include the consumption of certain quantifiable public goods and externalities).

I do not criticize this simplification; it is unavoidable. I do criticize Sen's continuing to think of the result as a *social* welfare functional. It is an *economic* welfare functional, at best, and so regarded can serve us well as a tool for ranking alternative social states that differ only in the levels of consumption that they afford. To rank alternatives that differ in the attainment of other social values, one would, I think, have to adopt the dichotomy proposed by Rawls. One would somehow have to take account of their economic welfare rankings along with their performances in other respects. Rawls advocates a lexicographic procedure. I find that unacceptable because of the well-known pathological consequences of lexicographic preferences.

Fortunately, there is a wide and important class of social decisions in which the alternatives differ only in their economic consequences. For them, the EWFL (to coin a phrase) is adequate and necessary. Those problems are hard enough for us economists, and we should be well advised to decline the challenge to solve problems that have defied all efforts since the memory of man began.

The next task for Sen and us is to learn what the EWFL implies for the social rate of discount. In approaching this task, Sen is very careful and artful. In at least two of his applications he is careful to say, "the social rate of discount relevant for this investment is . . ." This opens the possibility that different social rates of discount may be appropriate for different investments or in different circumstances. I approve of that. We have a large body of theory, some of it invented by Sen, to justify using positive rates of discount when the social states differ only in their time paths of consumption of private goods. How far this theory extends to other kinds of consequence, even in the economic realm, is still problematic. If state x increases the average life expectancy of the present generation by L person-years but reduces that of the next generation by $(1 + q)L$ person-years as compared with state y, does available theory justify ranking state x above state y so long as q is at all positive? I have to leave that question dangling.

In order to discuss the social rate of discount within the context of the EWFL, it is necessary to provide some additional structure. To that end, let us write the individual welfare functions in the form W_i $(C_{11}, \ldots, C_{1m}, C_{21}, \ldots, C_{2m})$, in which the first subscript distinguishes time periods and the second, individuals. The C_{kj} may be vectors, but that is of only technical consequence for present purposes.

It may be the case that

$$\frac{\partial W_i}{\partial C_{1j}} = (1 + \rho_i)\frac{\partial W_i}{\partial C_{2j}}$$

for all or a large class of values of j. If so, the individual's welfare function can be written in the more economical form $W_i'(C_{11} + C_{21}/(1 + \rho_i), \ldots, C_{1m''} + C_{2m''}/(1 + \rho_i))$ where m'' is the number of individuals who consume in either of the two time periods. Now the individual's welfare is seen to depend on the present value of the consumption of all individuals, computed at his personal rate of discount, ρ_i. If, on top of all other assumptions, all individuals have the same personal rate of discount, that clearly is the social rate of discount to be used in the EWFL. I should not want to make such a strong assumption. Though I cannot claim to have studied the more significant case in which the individual discount rates differ, it seems plausible that there exists an acceptable set of assumptions under which there will be some single discount rate that can be used to discount all second-year consumption and yield the correct ranking in the EWFL. That rate will, of course, be the social rate of discount. The resulting equation, in spite of the highly abstract notation, is very close to the discounting equations used in practical benefit–cost evaluations.

I have just sketched one formulation by which a social rate of discount can emerge from an EWFL. There are others and, in fact, Sen chose one of them. His approach, which is an extension of his model of saving-in-isolation versus saving-in-concert, amounts to writing the individual welfare function as W_i $(C_i, W_{op}$ $(C_{op}), W_d(C_d), W_{of}$ $(C_{of}))$ in which i stands for the individual, op for other persons in his generation, d for his descendants, and of for other future persons. He then eliminates the Ws in the parentheses, and carries through a reduction very similar to the one sketched in order to obtain a social rate of discount.

There is still another important route. Introduce F to stand for felicity, or instantaneous rate of enjoyment of consumption. Then it might be that we can write

$$W_i (F_{11} + F_{21}/(1 + \rho_i), \ldots, F_{1m} + F_{2m}/(1 + \rho_i))$$

A social rate of discount arises from this kind of welfare function also, but it has a different significance because the discount factor is applied to dated levels of felicity instead of to dated levels of consumption, as in the earlier discussion. This difference is a version of Arrow's well-known distinction between the consumption rate of discount and the utility rate. (See Partha Dasgupta's discussion of this distinction in chapter 8 of this volume.) They should never be confused, and it would be well if we had some notational conventions that distinguished them, since both rates appear frequently in the literature.

However the rates are distinguished, the distinction always depends on the same structural feature—that there is a common marginal rate of substitution between arguments pertaining to the first period and corresponding arguments pertaining to the second. This is what makes discounting possible and useful. We do not have to compare laboriously apples now with apples later, oranges now with oranges later, and so on and on. One common rate of discounting will do for all, or, at least, for many.

The concept of C used in these formulations needs some explanation, and is, indeed, bound up with the concept of a social state and even some of the philosophic issues raised at the outset. How detailed does the description of a social state have to be? Must it specify the complete bundle of commodities consumed by every individual, or contain only some measure of the collection of bundles open to him (for example, his income)? The meaning of the whole analysis, Sen's or mine, is different depending on the alternative chosen in this regard. I prefer the second—that the state specify the opportunity set open to the individuals and not their detailed consumption vectors. Then it becomes very natural to write $W_i\ (C_{1i} + C_{2i}/(1 + \rho_i))$. Furthermore, some scope for individual freedom of choice is preserved: social states are then ranked according to the opportunities they provide individuals and not according to the choices that individuals make.

In the end, Sen concludes, regretfully I happen to know, that an appropriate social discount rate can be ascertained only by a "deliberate ethical exercise." My discussion has led me to agree with that and, in fact, to feel even more comprehensive doubts. In the first place, even to construct an SWFL requires a deliberate ethical exercise that appears to be too vigorous for anyone on record. Even the more modest task of constructing an EWFL, involving, as it does, the adjudication of distributional claims, appears too arduous for most persons. That latter task must be performed nevertheless (or, more likely, fudged) to derive a defensible discount rate when individual discount rates differ. Second, we have to make some pretty strong assumptions about the structure of individual welfare functions in order to make discounting meaningful or appropriate. And finally we must always keep in mind that there is not necessarily a single discount rate to be used for all social decisions that affect present and future. Difficult ethical exercises can certainly not be avoided in making difficult social choices. The gymnasts need all the assistance that the analysts, like Sen, can give them. And he has given them some deep, clear, and illuminating insights into the nature of the problem they confront.

*Mark Sharefkin**

Comment

Introduction

Amartya Sen takes the high road, casting the discount rate argument within the framework of social choice theory. Because several of the very difficult issues facing modern societies—management policies for exhaustible and renewable resources and the valuation of long-term environmental effects—are at once foci of the discount rate debate and, necessarily, the proper subjects of a theory of intertemporal social choice, this is a brave and lonely undertaking.

Sen's results—in the strict sense of established conclusions—are meager, a tribute to the intrinsic difficulty of these problems. Nevertheless, it is a tribute to Sen that implicit in his paper are constructs and arguments which, sharpened and developed, may yet help lead us out of the morass. In this comment, all I can do is point to those constructs and arguments and suggest ways to do the sharpening.

Isolation Reconsidered

Sen's use of a recapitulation of the isolation argument debate of the 1960s is masterful, particularly in clarifying the terminological confusions that have long bedeviled analysts in this field. But the force of his demonstration suffers from not being cast in modern dress; and traditional garb hides the inadequacy of vintage isolation-argument models to deal with questions of more current interest.

Briefly, an updated isolation argument can be cast in the following way, using this notation:

N individuals in each generation
$i = 1, 2, \ldots, N$
two generations $t = 1, 2$

* Resources for the Future, Washington, D.C.

E_t aggregate initial endowment in each generation
C_t^i consumption of ith individual of tth generation
C_t aggregate consumption of tth generation
S_t^i saving of ith individual of tth generation
S_1 aggregate saving of first generation
U_1^i utility of ith individual of first generation

The generalized two-period isolation game $G(a^1, a^2, \ldots, a^N(E_t^i); g)$ is specified by naming utilities, intertemporal production sets, and—herein the novelty of isolation-type arguments—appropriability patterns and constraints: patterns indicating which agents are which agents' heirs, and constraints on intergenerational wealth transfers (beyond those imposed by the production set). Here we define G by writing, for the utility of the ith member of the first generation,

$$U_1^i(C_1^i, C_2^1, \ldots, C_2^N) \tag{1}$$

or, a simpler special case,

$$U_1^i(C_1^i, C_2^i, \sum_{j \neq i} C_2^j) \tag{2}$$

We interpret $(i, 2)$ as $(i, 1)$'s heir. An allocation is a set of $2N$ numbers (C_t^i) defining all agents' consumptions; the aggregate intertemporal production set is related to individual consumption and savings decisions by the relationship in equations (3) through (6).

$$C_t = \sum_i C_t^i \tag{3}$$

$$S_1 = \sum_i S_1^i \tag{4}$$

$$C_1 = E_1 - S_1 \tag{5}$$

$$C_2 = E_2 + (1 + g)S_1 \tag{6}$$

The appropriability assumptions underlying the model are described by

$$C_2^i = E_2^i + (1 + g)S_1 a^i(S_1^i, S_1^2, \ldots, S_1^N) \tag{7}$$

for which the special case

$$a^i(S_1^1, S_1^2, \ldots, S_1^N) = a^i(S_1^i, \sum_{j \neq i} S_1^j) \tag{8}$$

is frequently used. Note that, in general, appropriability is described by N functions that need only satisfy the two relationships

$$0 \le a^i(S_1^1, S_1^2, \ldots, S_1^N) \le 1 \tag{9}$$

$$\sum_i a^i(S_1^1, S_1^2, \ldots, S_1^N) = 1 \tag{10}$$

The social welfare problem is then

$$\max \sum_i b_i U_1^i(C_1^i, C_2^i, \sum_{j \ne i} C_2^j) \tag{11}$$

subject to equations (3), (5), (6), and (7), where the $b_1, \ldots, b_N$ are N positive numbers associated with any specified initial endowment set (E_t^i). But the isolated individual faces the problem

$$U_1^i(C_1^i, C_2^i, \sum_{j \ne i} C_2^j) \tag{12}$$

over S_1^i subject to equation (7) or (8).

So much for one way of generalizing the isolation problem. The debate centered upon a special case of this general problem, a specialization that narrowed the substantive possibilities of the debate even while providing a clear illustrative parable. The special case can be called "identical individuals and intragenerational equity." Hereafter we refer to this case as $G(h^i, l^i; (E_t)/N; g)$. It is characterized by

$$U_1^i = U_1 \tag{13}$$

$$C_t^i = C_t/N \tag{14}$$

with the appropriation functions characterized by two positive constants (h^i, ℓ^i):

$$a^i(S_1^1, S_1^2, \ldots, S_1^N) = h^i S_1^1 + \ell^i \sum_{j \ne i} S_1^j \quad \text{etc.} \tag{15}$$

Given this basis, "discount rates" can be defined. The quotation marks indicate that Sen has convinced me that, like classical notation in the calculus and "block" in game theory, a decision to abandon ambiguous and nondescriptive terminology will go far toward dispelling the confusion in this area of analysis. Suppose we begin from $2N$ commodity prices in what Sen calls the "named, dated" commodity space. We write these p_1^i, p_2^i and define them as those prices sustaining isolated decisions subject to an individual wealth constraint:

$$\max U_1^i(C_1^i, C_2^i, \sum_{j \neq i} C_2^j) \tag{16}$$

subject to

$$p_1^i C_1^i + p_2^i C_2^i = p_1^i E_1^i + p_2^i (E_2^i + S_1^i a^i(\cdot)) \tag{17}$$

Call these *private commodity prices*. Similarly define *social commodity prices* p_1^i, p_2^i as the price vector sustaining the optimum associated with the problem of equation (11). The end of the definitional argument is in sight. For if we introduce assumptions of additive separability into the specification of the individual utilities—for example, in equation (1), by writing

$$U^i(C_1^i, C_2^i, \ldots, C_2^N) = u^i(C_1^i) + \sum_j w^j(C_2^j) \tag{18}$$

then, we can define individual utility "prices" (q_t^i). Some other word than prices should be used, however, reserving prices for commodities. The assumption of additive separability is necessary for the definition of the utility "prices." It is not in general, and in the isolation argument it definitely is not, an aggregation over generations, since in the isolation argument only the first generation's preferences (however altruistic) are considered. Similarly we can define Q_ts.

In this more general framework, and in the special case in which most of the argument was couched, the analytical core of the argument can be stated succinctly: What is the relationship between the ps and the Ps, or, equivalently, between the qs and the Qs? Within the special-case context of equations (13) through (15), the answer is transparent from the specification— individuals will save too little. Sen's insistence that more than externalities in consumption are at stake is quite to the point. The "more" is presumably the way in which these externalities are specified through appropriability constraints. Still, after all these years, the general case has some claim on our attention. Are there interesting results available for richer classes of appropriation functions? If the general case is broadened even further to include portfolio choice, in what form does the problem persist? In the wake of the second question come others. Though the original intent of the isolation parable was normative, that is, a demonstration of the irrelevance of market rates of return to social benefit–cost calculations, the power of the special case has been such as to drive from the field alternative positive hypotheses about the relationship between the empirically observed and the "correct" intergenerational prices. Generational structures are far richer than the simple nonoverlapping structure of the special case. As the structure of generational overlap becomes richer, and as the markets in which present and future commodities trade are more realistically specified, what becomes of isolation-type arguments?

Social Choice Theory and the Discount Rate

The second major section of Sen's paper is a reconnaissance of the intersection of two concepts generally thought of as distinct but nevertheless intimately interrelated. The two concepts are the social discount rate (SDR) and social orderings, that is, orderings defined over "social states," or "allocations." The rough logic of the second section is that societies choose a complete specification of all commodities taken by all individuals over all time, in somehow selecting an allocation, or social state, in the sense of social choice theory. If the social discount rate is interpreted as mediating intergenerational transfers of capital, and therefore of potential welfare, the choice of SDR is a kind of choice among allocations. Thus, the two concepts, SDR and social ordering, must be closely related.

This intuitively appealing argument is partially formalized when Sen suggests defining the SDR in a manner reminiscent of revealed preference theory. Suppose for the purpose of this argument that we have a social ordering R. Sen proposes to define the relationship between the social discount rate and utility prices as follows:

Definition 1: Select two social states x, y differing in the aggregate consumption vector $(-1, 1 + q)$. Then the SDR is less than, equal to, equal to or greater than q, respectively, if xPy, xIy, yPx.

Does this definition make sense? Minimally, it must provide a unique definition of the SDR, which leads us to ask for a characterization theorem.

Problem 1: Characterize the class of social orderings R for which the definition above uniquely determines the SDR.

Two things are immediately apparent: (1) the inconsistency of this definition with Sen's own earlier terminological convention ("discount rates" for utilities, "rates of return" for commodities), indicating just how pernicious the conventional labels are, and (2) that the Rs will minimally be characterized by the property of not discriminating between social states in which income has been redistributed intratemporally. That is, if x and y differ only by intratemporal reallocations of consumption, then xIy.

That this is a very strong requirement, perhaps too strong to allow much in the way of interesting social choice rules, is recognized when Sen speaks of determining the social discount rate appropriate to a particular project from the interpersonal distribution of gains and losses associated with the project. How much light does this line of reasoning shed on the possibility of simplifying social orderings R into numbers for the purpose of social choice? Again, a little reflection leads us to pessimistic conclusions. Moreover, these conclusions follow from consideration of even that restrictive class of social orderings that can be represented by weightings of individual welfare levels and differentials. Consider a situation in which an initial allocation x_0 can be altered by selection of any project j of a class of projects J, giving us the new social state (or allocation) $x(j)$. Sen would define the project-associated social discount rate SDR(j) along the following lines:

Definition 2: If the two allocations x and y differ by the weighted aggregate consumption vector $(-1, 1 + q)$, the weights being those relevant to $R(W)$, then the project-related SDR (j) is less than, equal to, or greater than q (respectively, if $xP(W)y$, $xI(W)y$, $yP(W)x$).

Again it is clear that, in general, there may be as many project-specific SDRs as there are projects, and that the SDR(j) may be, like the proverbial 1:1 scale map, of no more help than a numerical representation of the social ordering R. Nevertheless, we can ask under what conditions will project-specific SDRs be more "informationally efficient" than R. To be more precise, we first introduce a further definition and then pose the problem formally.

Definition 3: A project-related set of discount rates SDR(j) for a set of projects and a status quo point x_0 is ℓ-efficient if $\#(\text{SDR})/\#(J)$ $= \ell$

Problem 2: Characterize either the (x_0, P) or the $R(W)$ or both for which SDR(p) is ℓ-efficient.

From this point on Sen abandons the problem of determining a social discount rate from a given social ordering R, assumes that it somehow makes sense to use a social discount rate as a kind of surrogate for a social ordering R, and, in the context of two transparent models, examines the implications of that assumption.

Because the practical implications of Sen's paper rest heavily on these sections, they warrant scrutiny. But the incomplete specification of the two models complicates this task. Consequently I have not hesitated to complete those specifications so as to allow an evaluation of the models in a way that may do injustice to Sen's intentions.

In both models there is an underlying technology capable of producing a single consumption good for both periods; there are two generations,

$t = 1, 2$, with welfare given by a constant-elasticity-of-marginal-utility function, which, for model j ($j = 1, 2$) is

$$W_t^j(C_t^j) = A_t^j + \eta(C_t)^\eta$$

The two models differ only in that, in the first model, the additive constant is taken to be independent of time: $A_1^1 = A_2^1$. Sen does not specify the particular functional form for the social discount rate as surrogate social ordering from which he reasons in this section, but all his conclusions follow from the general form, in which an intertemporally (Pareto) efficient point is selected by maximizing a Bergson social intertemporal social welfare function $F(W_1^j, W_2^j)$, the latter being only a computational device here. Trivially, if the intertemporal consumption set is convex, then any point on that set will be sustained by commodity prices; from the definition of the "social discount rate" as a "price," the SDR for these models will depend upon both the constants A and η, so that we can write SDR(A, η). The conclusions Sen draws from this model do not extend beyond this evident functional dependence: "In choosing an appropriate social discount rate, therefore, one has to consider not merely the rate of growth of consumption, but also the relative roles of marginal utility vis-à-vis total welfare. . . ."

The role played in Sen's first model by the (constant) welfare level A is key to the novel conclusions flowing from that model. That constant looks suspiciously like a nonaugmentable commodity: that is, a commodity outside the production and price systems, and one has the uneasy feeling that this is the source of the problem. That feeling is even stronger in the context of Sen's second model, in which welfare levels are allowed to vary over time: $A_1^2 \neq A_2^2$. There, "discount rates" are called upon to play a role that is too much for them, decentralizing an intertemporal "two commodity" optimum with only one relative price. This becomes close to explicit in Sen's illustrative interpretation of A^2 as the general level of pollution in model 2. Clearly, unpriced externalities lead to problems. Equally clearly, those problems can be circumvented only in particular cases by adjusting the equilibrium prices of some, but not all, commodities.

Final Comment and Conclusions

I have had little to say about Sen's frequent appeal to results in the axiomatic characterization of social choice mechanisms. In part this is because much of what I know of those results comes from Sen's illuminating work, so that he needs no lectures from me. But this stems from two judgments of my own, one rather simple-minded and the other perhaps rash, on the relevance of the literature on axiomatic characterization to the kinds of practical problems of intertemporal decisions that are the backdrop to the stylizations of Sen's paper.

Axiomatic characterizations have come long after discovery and implementation of the arrangements for decision themselves. For example, it takes nothing away from Hugo Sonnenschein's ingenious axiomatic characterizations of the price system to be grateful that use of the system came first. More importantly, perhaps, the results of social choice theory done in the axiomatic vein have typically been impossibility results—statements of the sort that "there are no good ways to aggregate preferences." Otherwise interpreted, they have been results that indicate that reasonable requirements imposed upon social choice rules imply rather chilling allocations of power.

But one central feature of the intertemporal problem is the skewed distribution of initial endowment. Future generations simply are not here. The reasoned and explicit search for ways of representing, or at least not riding roughshod over, the preferences of future generations, which Sen calls for, may be better conducted from the vantage point of concepts of fairness than from an analysis of individual orderings over full allocations. The former, which do not require the specification of preferences over full allocations, demand less and therefore allow the construction of possibility results.

•

Talbot Page*

Comment

Sen's use of the isolation paradox to define a social rate of discount suggests an interpretation in which the social rate of discount is intertemporally inefficient. I begin by interpreting λ as a distribution rule under the control of the second generation and not the first. The first generation optimizes around λ as given. In Sen's first case a collective savings rule is unavailable and the corresponding private rate of discount is defined by

$$1 + \pi = \frac{\text{change in future consumption}}{\text{change in present consumption}} \quad \begin{array}{l} \text{utility } i \text{ constant;} \\ \text{no collective savings} \\ \text{rule; given } \lambda \end{array}$$

In Sen's second case a collective savings rule is available and the corresponding social rate of discount is defined by

$$1 + \rho = \frac{\text{change in future consumption}}{\text{change in present consumption}} \quad \begin{array}{l} \text{utility } i \text{ constant;} \\ \text{collective savings} \\ \text{rule; given } \lambda \end{array}$$

We note next that one of the effects of the collective savings rule is to neutralize the λ rule of distribution, over which the first generation has no direct control. Consider a unit saved by i in the present generation, without a collective savings rule. The fraction λ of it goes to his heirs, and $\lambda/(n - 1)$ goes to each of the others in the second generation. As long as α is less than γ (i values his heirs' consumption above others' in the future) individual i will prefer larger λ to smaller λ (and he prefers most of all that $\lambda = 1$, in which case his whole unit effort goes to his heirs). Under the collective rule of savings, λ of his unit goes to his heirs directly and $\lambda/(n - 1)$ to each other individual in the second generation. However, under the collective rule

---

* Environmental Quality Laboratory, California Institute of Technology.

Author's note. I wish to thank the Rockefeller Foundation, which partially supported this research.

of savings, i's act of saving is tied to all others' saving in the first generation. For each of these others, $(1 - \lambda)/(n - 1)$ goes to i's heirs. There are $(n - 1)$ others in the first generation saving, hence i's heirs pick up a total of $(n - 1)(1 - \lambda)/(n - 1)$, or $1 - \lambda$ from savings other than i's. So the total effect of i's unit saving, under the collective rule, is $\lambda + (1 - \lambda)$ going to his heirs. In other words, the collective rule of savings guarantees that a unit saving from i in the present generation results in a unit going to i's heirs no matter what the λ rule of distribution. The situation is symmetric for all the individuals in the present. As far as each member of the first generation is concerned, his unit of saving is translated by the collective savings rule into a unit of consumption for his heirs. The λ rule of distribution is defeated.

The results of the first five sections of Sen's paper do not depend upon complete specification of utility functions. To bring out the potential intertemporal inefficiency, we specify the following identical utility functions for each of the n individuals in the present generation:

$$U_i = C_i + \beta \cdot \sum_{j \neq i} C_j + \gamma \cdot \sum_j C_{ij} + \alpha \cdot \sum_{j \neq i} \sum_k C_{jk} \tag{1}$$

where C_i is individual i's own consumption, in the present

       C_j is individual j's own consumption, in the present

       C_{ij} is the consumption of i's heirs coming from individual j's investment

β, γ, α have the same interpretation as in Sen's paper. This preference structure leads to the same concepts of private and social rates of discount as in Sen's paper.

To close the model explicitly, we further specify an equal initial endowment K for each individual i in the present, and we specify an investment function:

$$K_i = f(S_i)$$

where K_i is the investment product available for consumption in the second generation, from i's saving in the present generation

       S_i is the savings of individual i in the present generation

       $S_i + C_i = K$, for all i.

Without a collective savings rule, individual i acts to

$$\max_{C_i} U_i = C_i + \beta \cdot \sum_{j \neq i} C_j + \gamma \sum_j C_{ij} + \alpha \sum_{j \neq i} \sum_k C_{jk}$$

subject to:

$$C_{ii} = \lambda f(K - C_i)$$
$$C_{ji} = (1 - \lambda)f(K - C_i)/(n - 1), j \neq i$$

Thus each person i in the present generation sets

$$\frac{1}{\lambda\gamma + (1 - \lambda)\alpha} = f'$$

that is, sets the marginal efficiency of capital equal to the private rate of discount, as in Sen's equation (1).

With a collective savings rule, individual i acts to maximize the same utility function, again over C_i, but over different, institutionally determined constraints, namely

$$\sum_j C_{ij} = f(K - C_i) \quad \text{(defeat of } \lambda \text{ rule)}$$
$$\sum_{j \neq i} \sum_k C_{jk} = (n - 1)f(K - C_i)$$
$$\sum_{j \neq i} C_j = (n - 1)C_i$$

Thus each i in the present generation sets

$$\frac{1 + (n - 1)\beta}{\gamma + \alpha(n - 1)} = f'$$

that is, sets the marginal efficiency of capital equal to the social rate of discount, as in Sen's equation (2).

The difference between the two cases is purely in the institutionally determined constraints. The valuation coefficients α, β, and γ are all in terms of i's utility (measured in consumption units); γ is the value to i in i's contemplation of his heirs' consumption of an extra unit; α is the value to i in i's contemplation of others in the future consuming of an extra unit; and β is the value to i in i's contemplation of others in the present generation consuming an extra unit.

The framework of the isolation paradox is strangely incomplete. We are dealing with a society of $2n$ people, n in the present generation and n in the future. Pareto optimality depends upon two institutional constraints, the presence or absence of a collective savings rule and a λ rule of distribution, one constraint under the control of the present generation and the other under the control of the next. But in the traditional framework of the isolation paradox, Pareto optimality is not defined over the entire set of $2n$ people; instead it is defined over only the set of n living at the present time. The other n people are mere shadows. We have specified nothing about their preferences. Concepts of both private and social rates of discount are entirely paternalistic; they are defined in terms of preferences of members of the present generation only. These observations lead us to ask what happens if we adopt an atemporal point of view, considering Pareto optimality over the entire society of $2n$ people. From this enlarged perspective, there can be potential conflicts of interest between generations and potential gains from trade, if trade were possible.

In Sen's example the λ rule of distribution is defeated costlessly, from the point of view of the first generation because each i in the first generation does not care whether his heirs consume his investment product or the product of savings of his contemporaries. In evaluating his heirs' consumption, all i cares about is the total consumption independent of source. Suppose instead that i's consumption good is different from j's, and hence the investment product of i's saving is different from that of j. Suppose further that i derives more satisfaction from contemplating his heirs consuming a unit of his consumption good than a unit of some other consumption good. With this modification, the collective rule of saving no longer costlessly defeats the λ rule of distribution.

To keep the notation down to a bare minimum, suppose that each i of the present generation values only his own consumption and the consumption of his heirs, in the following way:

$$U_i^1 = C_i + \gamma C_{ii} + \gamma \delta \sum_{j \neq i} C_{ij} \qquad \text{where } 0 \leq \delta \leq 1 \tag{2}$$

Because the preferences of members of the second generation have so far been left unspecified, we have complete freedom in defining their preferences in such a way that might generate a conflict of interest between generations and consequently intertemporal inefficiency. Such a conflict can arise in a very simple manner. Suppose that members of the second generation have a weak preference toward egalitarianism. If they were completely egalitarian they would insist on $\lambda = 1/n$, but all we need is a weak preference for λ to be less than 1. As a second divergence of preference, each individual of the second generation does not care whether he consumes one type of consumption good or another; the sum total of the consumption goods is all that matters to him. We can specify the utility function of each member of the second generation as follows:

$$U_i^2 = \sum_j C_{ij} - (\lambda - 0.5)^2/1000 \tag{3}$$

Members of generation one control the saving–investment decision and the institutional constraint of whether or not there is collective saving. Members of generation two control the institutional constraint defined by the λ rule of distribution. Now we are ready to reconsider the question of Pareto optimality, this time in the larger context of $2n$ rather than n people and taking into account the preferences of all the people involved rather than just the first generation. We can identify three cases.

Case 1—no collective savings rule available to generation one, generation two controls λ. (If $\delta = 1$, this case reduces to Sen's example leading to a private rate of discount, with $\alpha = \beta = 0$.) In case 1 each i of the first generation maximizes equation (2) over C_i subject to

$$C_{ii} = \lambda f(K - C_i)$$

leading to the first-order condition

$$f' = \frac{1}{\lambda \gamma} \tag{4}$$

And the representative individual in generation two maximizes over λ with the result that generation two unanimously chooses $\lambda = 0.5$.

Case 2—collective savings rule available, generation two controls λ. (If $\delta = 1$, this case reduces to Sen's example leading to a social rate of discount, with $\alpha = \beta = 0$.) In case 2 each i of the first generation maximizes equation (2) over C_i subject to

$$C_{ii} = \lambda f(K - C_i)$$
$$C_{ij} = (1 - \lambda)f(K - C_j)/(n - 1)$$
$$C_j = C_i$$

leading to the first-order condition

$$f' = \frac{1}{\gamma\lambda + (1 - \lambda)\gamma\delta} \tag{5}$$

and again generation two chooses $\lambda = 0.5$.

Case 3—generation two gives up the λ rule of distribution and sets $\lambda = 1$. In this case there is no advantage to either generation one or two, whether or not the collective rule of saving is available. Individual i of the first generation maximizes equation (2) over C_i subject to

$$C_{ii} = f(K - C_i)$$

with the resulting first-order condition

$$f' = \frac{1}{\gamma} \tag{6}$$

We can call condition (6) an intertemporal rate of discount because it is based upon the preferences of both generations, taken together. With $0 \leq \lambda \leq 1$ and $0 \leq \delta \leq 1$, we have

private rate of discount	$\geq$	social rate of discount	$\geq$	intertemporal rate of discount

It is easy to demonstrate that the intertemporal rate of discount can lead to allocations that Pareto dominate both the private rate of discount and the social rate of discount. To see this we can take the following numerical example:

$$f(S) = 7S - (1/2)S^2$$

$$\gamma = 1/2$$

$$K = 21$$

$$\delta = 1/3$$

(and $\lambda = 1/2$, case 1 and case 2; $\lambda = 1$, case 3)

	Case 1 Private	Case 2 Social	Case 3 Intertemporal
f' (to be equated with the discount rate)	4	3	2
Saving by i in present generation	3	4	5
Utility, each i in present generation	23.5	23.67	27.25
Utility, each i in future generation	16.5	20.0	22.49975

In the numerical example, the social rate of discount $(3 - 1 = 2)$ is smaller than the private rate of discount $(4 - 1 = 3)$, and the allocation, for the entire community of the present and the future, under the social rate of discount (associated with collective savings) Pareto dominates the allocation under the private rate of discount (without collective savings). However, the intertemporal rate of discount $(2 - 1 = 1)$ is in turn smaller than the social rate, and its implied allocation Pareto dominates the one under the social rate.

This example demonstrates that the social rate of discount, defined in terms of the isolation paradox and a collective saving rule, is a concept of intratemporal efficiency only. The example further suggests that intertemporal institutions may be of some efficiency value. There may be, and often are, customs established in societies whereby the present generation honors preferences of the past and in turn establishes traditions for future generations to follow. In this simple example, we have two types of institutions: a collective saving rule, which is an intratemporal institution, and the possibility of linking intertemporally institutions that allow virtual bargaining across generational lines. It may be possible to do better with such intergenerationally linked institutions than without them. The rights discussion at the end of Sen's paper may be viewed partially in this light but probably more in terms of intergenerational equity.

Consider the slightly more general form of i's utility function, where i belongs to any generation t:

$$U_i^t = \gamma C_i^t + C_{ii}^{t+1} + \gamma\delta \sum_{j \neq i} C_{ij}^{t+1} - (\lambda^t - 0.5)^2$$

and there are n identical i's in each generation. For this last example, we would find that the private rate of discount and the social rate of discount lead to intertemporal collapse of the economy, while the intertemporal rate of discount leads to a sustainable and growing economy. Intertemporal equity means different things to different people, but many people may find a social rate of discount that leads to social collapse unsatisfactory. This is not to say that the intertemporal rate of discount always guarantees the future will have at least the same chance of survival as we do. Besides this possible weakness, the intertemporal rate of discount was not defined in a general way. Its main purpose in this comment is to illustrate that the social rate of discount, defined in terms of the present's preferences only, has little to say about intertemporal equity, nor does it guarantee intertemporal efficiency.

The above example interprets the isolation paradox approach to the social rate of discount as an efficiency approach, in which efficiency is defined only over the set of n people in the present. This being so, there appears to be no reason why the divergence between social and private rates of discount cannot be reduced to a matter of externalities, where externality is viewed as a direct nonmarket transfer. Note that in Sen's section 2, if $\gamma = 0$ along with α and β, then there would be no altruism at all, no nonmarket transfers, and the private and social rates of discount would be equal, both being infinite. Furthermore, it is clear that when there are externalities they do not necessarily lead to inefficiency, because there is the chance they will cancel out, as in the case of balanced emotions. Viewing the matter this way, the important thing to consider is how the externalities are generated or eliminated through institutions, such as the collective rule of savings or the λ rule of distribution.

It is important for the reader not to forget that in Sen's section 3 the three cases are all defined upon the condition of balanced emotions. If for example, $\beta = 0$ and $\gamma = \alpha$, then $m > \rho$ as long as $\theta > 1/n$, the natural case for large n, and the social rate is lower than the market rate, for any specific positive values of θ and λ. Also we have implicitly the assumption that $e > 0$, because θ is assumed less than one. However, if the externalities are negative, for example, involving external costs of radiation from nuclear power or mutation from coal combustion, then $e < 0$, $\theta > 1$, and the social rate is all the more likely to be less than the market rate.

In the framework of the isolation paradox, the welfare weights are well defined (in terms of the present generation's degree of paternalism) but of little normative use from an intertemporal point of view. It makes sense then, to shift as Sen does (in his section 5) from a viewpoint of the present n people to the intertemporal community of $2n$ people. Beginning at that point, Sen brings into account the preferences of the future as well as the present. Unfortunately when all generations are brought into the social choice mechanism, there is the strong possibility of an intertemporal conflict of interest as we have seen in my example. So there is no unanimous way of defining the intertemporal welfare weights as Sen notes. Thus some principles of intertemporal equity (or other principles) must be brought into the discussion in order to select an intertemporal social choice rule that will in turn imply an intertemporal social rate of discount. From the moral general perspective of intertemporal social choice, to consider the preferences of the present only would be to subscribe to a dictatorship of the present with each generation viewed as a single agent.

The welfarist approach, as discussed in Sen's sections 5 and 6, is an ingenious way of bringing equity principles into a definition of an intertemporal social rate of discount. It does seem, however, that there is a slight circularity in that zero rate of discount appears to be embedded into the utilitarian rule.

The combined utilitarian and modified maximum rules may be viewed as an approach appropriate to ordinary economic goods for which marginal rates of substitution can be defined. But for primary goods, marginal rates of substitution cannot be defined and a rights approach may be more appropriate for them. Rawls has stressed liberty as a primary good, but health and survival may be other candidates in the intertemporal setting, as Sen suggests. In this light the right to a livable environment might be considered an important intertemporal primary good.

Sen's paper brings us a long way from a simple definition of a social rate of discount. Indeed his paper suggests to me that it would be a vain attempt to try to define a single number, called the social rate of discount, that would incorporate satisfactory notions of both intertemporal efficiency and intertemporal equity.

It is easy to see the appeal of a social rate of discount for the energy planner. He is dealing with a distribution of costs so far into the future that discounting at normal market rates will count these costs as negligible. People sensibly object to such discounting on grounds of intertemporal fairness. At first glance it might seem that a concept of a social rate of discount offers a way of meeting the criticism. Being a socially chosen rate, the social rate of discount has an aura of fairness to it. By adjusting a market rate of discount, presumably downward, into a social rate, the idea of intertemporal fairness might be incorporated into the social rate. But such adjustment, as can be seen in the example with the isolation paradox, may have essentially nothing to do with intertemporal fairness. Moreover, we are dealing with costs distributed so far into the future that any "social" discount rate above zero will also count the very long-term costs as negligible. Are we then to abandon discounting, or to discount these long-term costs at a zero rate?

Sen shows us some of the fundamental problems with traditional concepts of the social rate of discount. That by itself is a service. But Sen goes further and suggests a constructive way of dealing with the problems of intertemporal equity and very long-term costs. The alternatives clearly are not limited to discounting at some social rate, presumably but not necessarily lower than market rates, and discounting at a zero rate. The framework of intertemporal social choice is much richer than these two alternatives. Sen's suggestion of a rights approach is, I think, a fruitful one. If we could define environmental rights for future generations and if our energy and other long-term planning were designed to protect these rights, then I think the criticism of discounting, on the grounds of intertemporal equity, would largely disappear. In this context the social rate of discount would be the opportunity cost of capital. A rights approach does not mean that we abandon discounting; it simply means that we have a place for both.

In "The Social Rate of Discount and the Optimal Rate of Investment," Marglin criticizes Pigou for viewing social welfare as "a function not only of the utilities of the individuals who are members of society at present, but of the utilities of all future members of society as well." Such a view, thought Marglin, would be authoritarian. Instead Marglin (1963, p. 97) argued for the "government's social welfare function to reflect only the preferences of present individuals." In Sen's paper we can see a development that begins with Marglin's point of view that only the preferences of the present count and ends with the Pigovian position that the preferences of the future should count as well. But the return to the Pigovian point of view is at a more sophisticated level than recommending that the government be an authoritarian guardian of future interests. If the present wishes to be fair to future generations, it may wish to play a mental game in which the preferences of the future are viewed atemporally, in an intertemporal social choice context. The purpose of the game is to define concepts of intertemporal equity to which the present might subscribe voluntarily.

Reference

Marglin, S. A., 1963. "The Social Rate of Discount and the Optimal Rate of Investment," *Quarterly Journal of Economics* vol. 77.

10

*Gordon R. Corey**

Plant Investment Decision Making in the Electric Power Industry

Introduction and Summary

The purpose of this paper is to discuss how U.S. electric power firms and other regulated public utilities make plant investment decisions. Although the discussion touches upon corporate decision making in general, the paper concerns principally the practices of public and private utilities, as determined by a 1977 sampling of the utility industry. The results of the survey were supplemented by personal observation of utility practices and corroborated by two earlier surveys that were limited to the investor-owned sector of the electric power industry.

The 1977 sampling was conducted in the preparation of this paper in order to broaden the scope of the earlier investigations. Accordingly, we queried public as well as private electric power firms and the regulated gas and telephone industries.[1] In the private sector, responses were obtained from thirty-three medium-to-large electric power firms, fifteen of which also supply gas service, nine utilities—pipeline as well as distribution companies—that supply gas only, and three telephone companies, two inside and one outside the American Telephone and Telegraph (AT&T) system. In the public sector, information was obtained from two large federal power supply systems, five local electric systems owned by municipalities or public utility districts, and twelve rural electric cooperatives. In addition, responses were received from ten consulting firms that provide architectural, engineering, and other services to electric utilities in both the private and public sectors.

The electric power firms responding to the survey directly or through their consultants are responsible for approximately 60 percent of the total output of the U.S. electric power industry. The results of the 1977 survey

---

* Commonwealth Edison Company, Chicago, Illinois.
[1] Our 1977 sampling is described in detail in the appendix, which reports the results for each industry section and compares these with the two earlier surveys, when applicable.

correspond closely to the more limited data obtained by the two earlier surveys, namely, a 1976 Edison Electric Institute (EEI) survey that covered most of the investor-owned sector of the industry and more than 80 percent of the output of the entire U.S. electric power industry[2] and an informal survey of twenty-two investor-owned firms, conducted by the Intercompany Comparison Group in 1975. Although some of the samples in the Commonwealth Edison survey are small, the responses are reasonably representative of each industry or sector. For example, two of the telephone companies queried were AT&T subsidiaries, so most of the telephone industry was well represented in the sample. Even the gas industry sample, though small, appears quite representative of the industry as a whole; it has good geographic diversity and includes both large and small systems operating as pipeline companies, distribution companies, or both. The relatively sparse returns from the smaller municipal and cooperative systems appear to have been adequately supplemented by the good responses from the consulting firms, which frequently advise such smaller systems.[3]

The highlights of the survey findings are set forth below, while the bases for these findings can be found in the following sections and the appendix.

Generally accepted practices. At the time of this writing, shortly after the survey, there is a high degree of uniformity in the plant investment decision-making practices followed by U.S. electric power firms, both public and private, as well as other regulated utilities. Virtually all the firms that do any mathematical analysis follow conventional discounted cash flow (DCF) procedures, customarily selecting the investment strategy that is expected to provide the smallest present value of future revenue requirements.

Impact of discount rates on the capital base. The plant investment decision-making practices of most U.S. electric power firms (public and private) reflect a reluctance to expand the capital base. This reluctance is reflected in tendencies—

1. to use rate-of-return objectives somewhat higher than the current marginal cost of capital;
2. to use a present-value discount rate higher than the marginal rate of disadvantage; and
3. to emphasize the costs and benefits associated with the early years of a project's life.

Although such anticapital bias is most readily recognized in the private sector,

---

[2] The survey was based upon responses obtained from 125 investor-owned electric power companies, representing nearly 96 percent of the total operating revenues of U.S. investor-owned electric power firms in 1975.

[3] See the appendix for a discussion of the statistical reliability of our sample.

it is also present to a moderate degree in the public sector. For example, the discount rates used by the large federal power supply systems exceed the current marginal cost of money to these systems. Moreover, municipal as well as federal electric systems have on occasion had to hold back on plant expansion because of budgetary restrictions.

Effect of taxes. In the private sector, the corporate income taxes on the order of 40 percent at the margin, notwithstanding the investment tax credit and other special considerations, place a significant penalty against capital-intensive alternatives. This contrasts, however, with the tendency of electric systems in the public sector to overlook the cost of taxes forgone or payments in lieu of taxes.

Inflation. Allowances in the decision-making calculations for future inflation appear to be straightforward, with no significant bias one way or the other.

Financing risks. There appears to be a growing perception that costly, long-lived plant investments are risky. This perception arises perhaps from environmental restrictions, licensing difficulties, regulatory delays, and changing political environment; the risk was evidenced in 1974 and 1975 by delays in new generating plant orders and in the construction schedules of electric utilities. In 1977 the risk is reflected in the failure of new orders for plant construction to keep pace with increases in the use of electricity. These phenomena do not seem to be directly related to analyses of estimated future costs and benefits, although annual money cost rates used for DCF analysis by investor-owned electric firms surveyed rose 2.5 percentage points between 1971 and 1977, a period during which interest rates on high-grade long-term debt showed little overall change. Reductions of credit ratings and the deteriorating quality of electric utility earnings may well account for some of this rise, thus contributing to managements' general concern over the financial outlook.

Specific project risks. There is a growing use of sophisticated evaluations of risk to determine how much anticipated results might vary without changing the decision. Moreover, the widespread perception of risk referred to above probably influences decision making beyond the consideration of explicit mathematical analysis of risk factors.

Generally Accepted Practices

The discounted cash flow (DCF) procedure is that most widely used by U.S. industry for analyzing and comparing the costs and benefits of alternative plant investment programs. Under this procedure, the present value of a stream of future expenditures is related to the present value of a stream of future revenues.[4] The term "DCF" applies to a specific group of procedures for analyzing cash flows. Although these procedures are frequently used to seek out the highest rate of return on an investment, this objective is by no means an essential DCF characteristic.[5]

Plant modernization projects, for example, are often justified by determining that the probable payback period is satisfactorily short, and where the question is close, the determination is properly based upon DCF calculations that reflect the time value of money. On the other hand, the DCF objectives used to justify or reject major plant expansion projects are usually different for regulated than for unregulated firms. The latter typically try to maximize the rate of return; most regulated utilities, both public and private, try to minimize the present value of future revenue requirements. This is because profit maximization would be inappropriate for a firm whose profit levels are limited by regulation (Grant and Ireson, 1970, pp. 485–509; Corey, 1976, pp. 554–567). The following discussion may help clarify this point.

A rate-of-return goal is normally inappropriate for use in public utility plant-investment decisions for two main reasons. First, a rate-of-return goal would commonly signal the adoption of a strategy that is inappropriate or illegal for a regulated public utility. For example, such a goal might suggest that needed capacity not be installed if it did not appear to be profitable. A possible result of such an action is that profitable industrial loads might be served whereas expensive and hard-to-serve urban redevelopment projects might not. Such actions are available and generally acceptable to unregulated industries, but they are neither available nor appropriate for a regulated public utility. Industrial firms ordinarily enjoy rather wide freedom of choice to expand or not to expand, to enter a new market or withdraw from an old market, to take a large step or none at all. Such choices are generally

---

[4] Customary DCF procedure is to relate the sum of the expenditure stream I to the sum of the revenue stream R, using the following general formula

$$\sum_{n=0}^{N} I_n \left(\frac{1}{1+r} \right)^n = \sum_{n=0}^{N} R_n \left(\frac{1}{1+r} \right)^n$$

In the above formula, r is the annual discount rate; n is the number of years before each expenditure is made or recovery obtained; N is either the total project life or the pay-back period in years; the term $\frac{1}{1+r}$ represents the present-value discount factor; and the entire right-hand side of the equation represents the present value of the revenues required to sustain the project in question. The equation is sometimes solved for the rate of return r, sometimes for the pay-back period N, and often, in the case of regulated utilities, for the present value of the revenue requirements.

[5] "The phrase 'discounted cash flow' is properly applied to any calculation to find the present worth of cash flow whether or not the calculation is used in computing the rate of return" (Grant and Ireson, 1970, p. 113).

unavailable to public utilities because they are not free *not* to expand when expansion is indicated, and they are not free to refuse service.

Second, a rate-of-return goal would involve circular reasoning for regulated firms. They are required by law to provide all customers with adequate service at reasonable rates, and the reasonableness of these rates is normally based upon predetermined rate-of-return goals.

For these reasons, regulated public utilities do not base plant expansion or retirement strategy upon a rate-of-return, or "profitability rate," goal. Minimization of payback time presents a similar objection in that a short payback time is equivalent to a high profitability rate. Consequently, the only remaining DCF goal—minimization of future revenue requirements— is generally accepted as most appropriate for making plant expansion decisions in regulated public utilities.[6]

The 1977 survey confirms the broad use of DCF procedures by utilities throughout the United States and the utilities' general acceptance of the goal of minimizing revenue requirements.

In 1971, the Federal Power Commission reported the following:

> The electric power industry in the contiguous U.S. includes nearly 3,500 systems which vary greatly in size, type of ownership and range of functions. It is made up of four distinct ownership segments—investor-owned companies, non-federal public agencies, cooperatives, and federal agencies—and is unique among world systems in the diversity and complexity of its organization (Federal Power Commission, 1971, p. I-2-1).

In spite of this wide diversity, the U.S. electric power industry in 1977 shows a high degree of uniformity in making plant investment decisions, perhaps because of a common regulatory environment. This uniformity extends to the regulated gas and telephone companies as well. Most utilities that responded to the 1977 survey reported using DCF procedures, customarily solving for the present value of revenue requirements.[7]

For decisions about generating capacity, DCF procedures are often supplemented by comparisons of the levelized costs per kilowatt hour yielding the same results where DCF procedures are used to reflect the time value of money. Also, as observed earlier, modernization projects are frequently justified by rate-of-return or payback-period computations.[8]

---

[6] This discussion does not apply to "cost saving" projects, like the upgrading of a load-dispatch computer to save fuel or obtain other benefits. Here the costs and benefits can be compared directly and the "revenue requirements" can be virtually ignored by setting the right-hand side of the DCF equation for each strategy at zero. Selection of a strategy that minimizes the pay-back period or, on occasion, maximizes rate of return can then be made without encountering regulatory opposition.

[7] All medium-to-large electric systems surveyed use DCF techniques for plant expansion decision making. Although some of the smaller municipal and cooperatively owned systems do not use DCF techniques, many rely upon consultants who do (see the appendix).

[8] See footnote 6.

Of course, decisions concerning plant expansion, retirement, and modernization are rarely based upon DCF calculations alone. Comments received in the survey from a municipally owned system indicate strong sensitivity to the effect that a proposal for plant expansion could have upon a city's budget or the utility's popularity with the electorate. Similar considerations necessarily play an important part among investor-owned utilities, federal systems, and cooperatives.

The results of the survey are summarized in the appendix. A discussion of money rates, time periods, and the problems introduced by taxes, inflation, and risk are discussed in the following sections.

Cost-of-Money and Discount Rates

A unique characteristic of the revenue requirement objective of DCF analysis is that cost-of-money and discount rates must be determined in advance. Once this is done, we can readily determine which strategy requires the minimum amount of future revenues.

Cost of Money

The 1976 Edison Electric Institute study referred to earlier reported annual cost-of-money rates averaging 11.2 percent, with individual rates mostly concentrated between 10 and 12 percent but ranging all the way from 8 to 14 percent.[9]

The 1977 Commonwealth Edison Company investigation shows roughly the same cost of money, 10.5 percent per annum, on a weighted average basis for all firms surveyed. However, the sample included investor-owned electric power firms, government-owned electric firms, electric cooperatives, telephone companies, and gas utilities, whereas the 1976 EEI survey was limited to investor-owned electric power entities.

The investor-owned electric firms in the Commonwealth Edison survey reported cost-of-money rates averaging 11.0 percent, compared with 11.2 percent for the EEI survey. The regulated gas and telephone companies responding to the 1977 inquiry used annual rates averaging 11.8 percent and 12.0 percent, respectively. Most government-owned electric systems generally used rates of 8 percent or less, although one large federal entity used an 11 percent rate.

[9] It should be noted that the rates used for decision making are significantly higher than those allowed for rate-making purposes. According to the EEI survey, for seventy-seven firms subject to original cost regulation, the returns allowed in the most recent regulatory proceedings averaged only 9.3 percent a year while actual earnings averaged only 7.4 percent in 1975, both significantly below the rates used for discounting. This indicates a likelihood that these firms are induced by the regulatory constraint to favor the least rather than the most capital-intensive alternatives, exactly opposite to the so-called Averch–Johnson proposition. See Corey (1971, pp. 358–373).

For municipalities and cooperatives, 1977 cost-of-money rates vary between 6.5 and 8 percent. Although lower than the rates used by private firms, these rates appear to approximate or exceed the marginal cost of new money for these firms.

Regulations of the Water Resources Council provide that the average (embedded) rate on outstanding federal debt securities should be used for evaluating water power projects. In 1977, this rate stood at 6.375 percent per annum, about 1.5 percentage points below the then-current market rates on long-term federal U.S. securities.[10] Additionally, regulations of the U.S. Office of Management and Budget require that a discount rate of 10 percent per annum be similarly used, except where otherwise prescribed by law or regulation.[11]

Notwithstanding these requirements, and quite understandably, the two federal power supply agencies queried in 1977 used different rates, seemingly based upon their own unique circumstances. One federal agency, which obtains its new money needs in the open market, reported using an annual discount rate of 11 percent, corresponding to that used in the private sector, derived on the basis of an 8.5 percent component for debt and a 13.25 percent component for internally generated funds. The other federal agency, which obtains its new money needs from the U.S. Treasury, reported a DCF rate of 8.25 percent per year, comparable to the debt component of the other agency's rate.

In each case, the rate in use was moderately higher than the marginal cost of new federal funds, possibly to provide a margin for error. This subject will be dealt with in greater detail in the section on risk.

Moreover, as observed earlier, considerations other than money rates often inhibit project expenditures by investor-owned as well as government-owned systems. For example, during the federal budgetary squeeze of the late 1960s and early 1970s, several federal power systems in the Pacific Northwest suffered severe capital shortages, which for a time restricted their ability to respond to anticipated transmission needs of the area.[12]

Discount Rates

The discount rate used for present valuing is not always the same as the cost-of-money rate. For example, at the time of this writing, Commonwealth Edison uses a discount rate slightly below the cost-of-money rate; the discount rate is a "rate of disadvantage" (sometimes referred to as a "rate

---

[10] Federal Register (September 10, 1973) pp. 86–87; Water Resources Council, "Info Memo" (October 27, 1976).

[11] OMB Circular No. A-94 (March 27, 1972). "The prescribed discount rate of 10 percent represents an estimate of the average rate of return on private investment before taxes and after inflation."

[12] For substantiation of this point, I rely upon comments made to me by government representatives from the Pacific Northwest.

of indifference"), which is determined by reducing the total money cost rate by the corporate income tax savings on the interest component thereof. Commonwealth Edison's discount rate in 1977 was 10.37 percent a year, 2.38 percentage points less than the marginal cost of new money, which was then estimated at 12.75 percent.[13]

Justification for using the rate of disadvantage for discounting purposes is twofold.

First, this is the only discount rate that will provide the same present value of a stream of future revenues irrespective of accounting practice. No matter what book depreciation rate is used, no matter whether the taxes deferred by accelerated depreciation or the investment credit are normalized or not, in short, no matter how the books are kept, if the rate of disadvantage is used for discounting, the present value of future revenue streams will be constant, provided cash considerations remain constant. The rate of disadvantage is the only discount rate for which this is true.

Second, the rate of disadvantage is the only discount rate that makes the timing of equivalent cash receipts a matter of indifference. For example, suppose that $100 of net (after-tax) cash received today is adequate for a particular strategy. Then what amount of cash received a year from now would be equally adequate but not excessive—$112.75, using the 12.75 percent cost-of-money rate shown in footnote 13? or $110.37, using the 10.37 percent rate of disadvantage shown in the same footnote? If $112.75 were to be provided a year hence, postponement would benefit the stockholders because $112.75 of cash provided a year hence would be more than needed to meet the $10.37 "disadvantage" of postponing the receipt for a year. However, the receipt of only $110.37 a year hence would just keep things equal. Waiting or not waiting would be a matter of indifference. Hence, the 10.37 percent rate makes the most sense.

[13] Commonwealth Edison's estimates of new money costs, based upon the 1977 market, but increased moderately to reflect secondary long-run financing risk (as discussed below in the section on risk) are as follows:

   (i) Interest on long-term debt at 9.5 percent per annum
                 × 50 percent of the capital structure =   4.75 percent*
   (ii) Earnings on equity at 16 percent per annum
                 × 50 percent of the capital structure =   8.00 percent
                 Total annual cost of money (estimated) = 12.75 percent
   (iii) Less federal and state of Illinois income taxes computed
              at 50.08 percent applied to item (i) above** =   2.38 percent
              Annual discount rate (rate of disadvantage) = 10.37 percent
  *Short-term financing costs (commercial paper and bank loans) are ignored as being devoted entirely to construction financing and thus fully embedded in project costs through the capitalization of the allowance for funds used during construction.
  **The corporate federal tax rate in 1977 was 48 percent; the Illinois rate was 4 percent. Illinois taxes are deductible for federal tax purposes. Thus the net federal tax rate is 48 percent of 96 percent, or 46.08 percent. The sum of 46.08 percent and 4.00 percent is 50.08 percent.

Notwithstanding the foregoing, only 26 percent of those investor-owned electric firms queried in the 1977 Commonwealth Edison Survey used the rate of disadvantage for discounting purposes. Sixty-five percent of the firms queried used the gross money cost for discounting, and the rest used some other rate, for example, the pretax rate of return. The number of gas systems that reported using the cost-of-money rate equaled the number using the rate of disadvantage, whereas all telephone companies surveyed used gross money cost rates for discounting.[14] For further details, see table 10-A-2 in the appendix.

When this paper was presented in preliminary form, on March 3, 1977, at a Washington, D.C., conference sponsored by Resources for the Future, several attendees suggested that before-tax rates should be used for discounting. Although a small minority of investor-owned electric firms in the sample did use such pretax rates for discounting, and such an approach can perhaps be rationalized for the macrocosm, it is difficult to see how an individual manager could give so little thought to the future of his customers or shareholders as an annual pretax discount rate of 20 percent or more would imply.[15]

Taxes

Now let us examine how taxes, especially corporate income taxes, affect plant investment decision making.

Corporate Income Taxes

All investor-owned electric power systems reflect the gross effects of corporate income taxes in the stream of estimated future costs. In addition, estimates of the special tax effects of the investment tax credit, accelerated depreciation, guideline (CLS) lives, and asset depreciation range (ADR) depreciation are normally reflected in the decision-making calculations, notwithstanding their accounting treatment. For details, see appendix table 10-A-7.

Difficult problems arise when special tax provisions, such as the investment tax credit, are scheduled by law to change before they would

[14] In general, the government-owned electric systems and rural electric cooperatives are not faced with the question of how to reflect the effect of income tax savings on the discount rate because, in general, these systems are not subject to income taxes. Consequently, for them, the rate of disadvantage is normally identical to the cost-of money rate. However, there are other tax considerations affecting the public entities, namely, "payments in lieu of taxes" and estimates of "taxes forgone." These are discussed in the following section on taxes.

[15] See table 10-A-2 in the appendix. It may be that we misunderstood some of our respondents or that they misunderstood our questions.

accrue under a proposed plan of action, but where this change may well be postponed or modified by interim legislative action. The estimation of future income tax liability also is often difficult for firms not currently paying such taxes. Such problems are normally resolved on the basis of the best information available at the time of decision. However, most utility managers assume (perhaps with unjustified optimism) that future earnings for their firms will again be sufficient to subject them to corporate income taxes. Consequently, investment tax credits (at present levels and maximum ceilings) and corporate income taxes (at current statutory rates) are generally accepted as marginal costs and credits throughout the future life of long-lived construction projects, even by firms now reporting tax losses.

Ad Valorem *Taxes and Revenue Taxes*

Although the written questionnaire for the 1977 survey did not cover *ad valorem* and revenue taxes, subsequent telephone discussions revealed that all investor-owned firms reflected current percentage levels of *ad valorem* real estate and personal property taxes as well as revenue taxes in their DCF analyses.

Inherent Bias

The added costs of government services resulting from a given project are rarely as great as the additional tax burdens associated therewith. This is true with respect to both local *ad valorem* and revenue taxes and also with respect to federal and state corporate income taxes. From the standpoint of society as a whole, therefore, most additional tax costs should probably be ignored, or their effects substantially modified, in plant investment decision making. However, the individual manager cannot ignore taxes because, for his firm, they are very real. Consequently, taxes normally appear as factors in the decision-making process—factors that, from the standpoint of optimal decision making, unduly discourage the use of capital. Although investment tax credits, accelerated depreciation, and other special benefits tend to reduce the total carrying charges, by no means do they eliminate the corporate income tax penalty against capital investment.

For example, the 12.75 percent annual cost-of-money rate referred to in footnote 13 includes 8 percentage points for equity return—but corporate income taxes are levied thereon. If we assume a 50 percent rate, but reduce the total burden by 2 or 3 percentage points to reflect the levelized value of special tax credits, the tax burden applicable to the 8 percent equity return is at least 5 percent. Therefore, the total carrying charge rate is not 12.75 percent but more like 18 percent per annum, exclusive of *ad valorem* taxes and insurance. Thus, total annual carrying charges of about 18 percent are a minimum—the real costs to most firms range between 20 and 22 percent. These are included in the stream of future costs associated with each alternative strategy, regardless of the discount rate used; and their very size (reflecting the inclusion of corporate income taxes as well as local taxes) tends to penalize the capital-intensive alternative.

Government Entities—"Taxes Forgone" and "Payments in Lieu of Taxes"

In 1958, the Water Resources Council specified that benefit–cost analyses for all federal water power projects should include estimates of the amount of federal income taxes that would be forgone if the proposed federal project were substituted for a similar private project. This requirement was withdrawn in 1961. Since then, federal water power projects have not been so burdened. According to the Commonwealth Edison survey, no government entity—federal, state, or local—now recognizes "taxes forgone" as a component of project cost.

Some government-owned power systems make payments in support of local government services; such payments are referred to occasionally as "payments in lieu of taxes." However, government electric power systems do not generally regard such payments as functions of plant investment. Hence, these payments are seldom reflected in economic analyses of the feasibility of proposals for plant expansion.[16]

Although neither taxes forgone nor payments in lieu of taxes are normally reflected in DCF analyses in the public sector, local government systems are frequently sensitive to the budget needs of their parent entities as well as to the public acceptability of projects under consideration, as observed earlier.

Inflation

Virtually all utility systems using DCF techniques try to anticipate the effect of future inflation upon their plant investment decisions. Estimates of inflation in construction costs in 1977 were in the general area of 7.5 percent per annum for the near term and in the 6.5 percent range for the longer term. These allowances are significantly below the 10 to 15 percent figures experienced in 1977 and years just before then.

Provision for escalation in the costs of fuel and operating labor similarly tended to be somewhat below actual 1977 experience, generally in the area

[16] Only one out of seven non-tax-paying utilities responding to the survey questionnaire reflected payments in lieu of taxes as a cost of capital in making investment decisions. However, the Tennessee Valley Authority makes repayments of capital to the U.S. Treasury and reflects such payments in its DCF decisions.

of 6.5 to 7.5 percent per annum. Although some firms made no provision for future escalation of operating expenses, they were in the minority.

In summary, most utilities using DCF analysis do provide for future inflation, but such provisions appear optimistic by comparison with the recent past. However, the degree of optimism does not vary significantly from one cost factor to another. Hence, the treatment of future inflation does not appear to introduce a significant bias into the selection of capital-intensive projects versus fuel- or labor-intensive projects.[17]

A detailed summary of escalation rates used in 1977 for DCF analyses is set forth in tables 10-A-10, 10-A-11, and 10-A-12 of the appendix.[18]

Risk

Plant investment decision making is often thought of as a simple matter of selecting the strategy that will provide the smallest value of future revenue requirement streams, the maximum rate of return, or the shortest payback period. However, long-term financing problems may swing the final decision against the more capital-intensive alternative. Concern over a specific technology (such as stack gas scrubbing) that has a greater than average risk may swing a decision from coal to nuclear generation or vice versa.

Many high capital-cost generation projects were canceled or deferred in 1974 and 1975 in part because of the financing problems then facing many electric utilities. These construction delays affected more than 200,000 megawatts (MW) of U.S. generating capacity (much of it nuclear) and reduced construction expenditures expected for the second half of the 1970s by more than $20 billion (Federal Power Commission, 1974, p. 9). Although

---

[17] To better understand the circumstances leading to the rather widespread practice of providing a somewhat lower rate of future inflation than that experienced in the recent past, a discussion of the practice at Commonwealth Edison Company may be helpful. We use construction cost estimates for two purposes—first, to help select the appropriate plant investment strategy and second, thereafter, to provide a construction budget for that project. For the same purpose, we endeavor to set our construction budgets on the low side in order to establish a tight goal and thereby to help hold construction costs to a minimum. One of the ways we do this is by limiting the allowance for future inflation to something less than that recently experienced. In order for this not to bias the DCF decision making in favor of the capital-intensive alternative, however, our future fuel and labor cost escalation rates are similarly set on the low side.

[18] It is occasionally suggested that inflation should be dealt with in the DCF analyses by using inflation-free discount rates and stating all estimates of future costs, benefits, and revenue requirements in current dollars. Although this may be an acceptable method of dealing with broad-brush policy for society as a whole (and even here there is some question), it is not an appropriate method to use in selecting individual construction projects because rates of inflation often vary widely among different cost components. If no attempt were made to estimate future inflation rates and all future costs were stated in current dollars, there would be no way to deal with such anticipated variations in future escalation rates. For example, if construction cost escalation is expected to be less than fuel cost escalation in the future, DCF analyses made only in current dollars would tend to favor improperly the fuel-intensive strategy rather than the capital-intensive strategy.

these delays and cutbacks reflected reduced load projections, there is no doubt that financing difficulties influenced both their extent and character. The bulk of the project cancellations affected were relatively high capital-cost nuclear generation, which accounted for 125,000 MW of the 200,000 plus MW referred to earlier.

However, uncertainties with respect to nuclear power have prevented the reinstatement of nuclear projects formerly canceled. Here we have a good example of risk evaluation. Every DCF analysis the Commonwealth Edison Company has made comparing nuclear and coal-fired generation has shown the nuclear alternative to be substantially cheaper than coal, although the Commonwealth Edison system is located in a region of relatively plentiful coal supply. Nevertheless, in 1977, Commonwealth Edison was almost alone among U.S. electric power firms in talking about ordering more nuclear capacity. This suggests that factors other than DCF cost analysis were holding sway over decision making with respect to nuclear power.

In surveying the electric power industry, Commonwealth Edison attempted to determine how long-run financing risks and specific project risks are treated with respect to plant investment decision making. Admittedly, this is a relatively new area, but there is growing recognition of the need to deal with it mathematically as well as subjectively.

Long-Run Financing Uncertainties

Long-run financing risks, as perceived by utility managers, are especially great today because of the difficulty of predicting the ability of a firm to finance its long-run future capital needs. Long-term financing uncertainties are affected by the following considerations:

1. The electric power business is the most capital-intensive of all industries. It must raise nearly $400 billion of new capital funds by 1990. This is about a third of total new money needs of all U.S. industry (Federal Power Commission, 1974, p. 11; Corey, 1977).
2. It is by no means certain that investors will be willing to provide the funds needed in the years ahead to meet these capital needs, either for the electric power business or for the capital-intensive energy business in general.
3. This uncertainty results, in part, from growing objections to the necessary increases in electric rates and the cost of other forms of energy.
4. Most U.S. investor-owned electric power companies are now earning less than the marginal cost of new money.
5. Considering that disparities between rates of return allowed, rates of return actually earned, and marginal costs of new funds in 1977 were about 4 percentage points a year for many investor-owned electric firms,

it is difficult to predict when or whether our regulatory processes will allow recovery of the capital costs now being committed for.[19]

6. It is also becoming increasingly difficult to predict long-term future load growth, particularly ten years ahead, which is the time required to plan for, license, and build a new power plant. Clearly, it is impossible to predict with certainty what the social and regulatory climate will be over the life of a generating plant investment, not to mention the difficulty of predicting even near-term technological changes.

7. The combination of these and other factors adds up to a growing perception that the long-run future may bring increased financing difficulties for electric utilities.

In view of these considerations, there is a tendency for utility managers to add percentage points to current money market rates for the analysis of future projects. This does not mean that they think they are smarter than the market or can predict future risk better than the average investor. Investors and managers are making use of similar perceptions, but they are appraising different things. The individual investor must evaluate the investment risks and returns associated with securities currently available for purchase or sale, while the utility manager must predict the effect of current plant expansion decisions upon his future financing costs. Investors are continually altering their portfolios and hedging against future possibilities, adjusting toward a new equilibrium portfolio and thus gradually altering market rates of return. The utility manager must assess this "path of adjustment" and predict what market rates will be when the new projects under consideration are ultimately financed, and how such financing of the projects now under consideration (and their near-term successors) will affect the firm's credit standing thereafter and hence the firm's ability to finance still later projects. To reflect such long-run adverse effects of our current construction program, Commonwealth Edison Company uses a percentage point add-on. In doing so, the company is trying, in a sense, to predict the future course of its own financing costs, a practice which is essentially no different than forecasting prices of fuel, labor, or any other input.

Surveys indicate that rate-of-return objectives have risen much faster than money market rates.[20] Moreover, the cost-of-money and discount rates used in 1977 in both the private and the public sectors appear to reflect a moderate built-in bias against the long-lived capital-intensive strategies, as follows:

1. Sixty-five percent of the investor-owned electric and combination (electric and gas) firms and all the telephone companies surveyed in 1977 used

---

[19] See footnote 9.

[20] The 1976 EEI survey referred to earlier showed that average annual cost-of-money rates used by investor-owned electric power firms for DCF analysis rose to 11.2 percent in 1976 from 8.8 percent in 1970, although marginal capital costs were little changed between these two years. Commonwealth Edison's 1977 sampling did not show a significant change from 1976.

the gross cost-of-money rate instead of the rate of disadvantage for present-value discounting, a practice which tends to penalize the long-lived capital-intensive strategies.[21]

2. Although Commonwealth Edison uses a slightly lower discount rate, the rate of disadvantage referred to earlier, its money-cost rates in 1977 were 1 or 2 percentage points higher than the bare-bones rates would have been, based upon 1977 money market conditions.[22] This addition is intended to reflect Commonwealth Edison's best estimate of future market conditions, that is, the growing probability that regulatory actions may restrict the future supply of capital funds available to the firm.[23]

3. Six percent of the investor-owned electric and combination firms surveyed in 1977 reported using before-tax money rates for discounting. If true (and they may have misunderstood the questionnaire), this would produce a significant bias against the capital-intensive strategies.

4. According to the survey, firms in the public sector appeared to be using money-cost rates that were somewhat closer to the 1977 money market rates. Nevertheless, the money-cost rates tended to be somewhat higher than the market, and two large federal systems surveyed reported using rates well above the current market.

Individual Project Risks

Selection of a specific plant expansion plan is always influenced by the management's subjective perception of the relative riskiness of individual strategies. There appears to be a growing trend to perform special risk evaluations to aid in making decisions. At Commonwealth Edison this trend is influenced by increasing concern over the effect of environmental, regulatory, and social uncertainties.

Two responses to these uncertainties were observed in the 1977 survey. They are as follows:

Short-period analysis. Uncertainty about future environmental regulations, the likelihood of wide variations in the future cost and availability of fuels, and even the possibility of changes in the institutional character of the electric power industry itself suggest that considerable weight be given to the stream of costs and benefits anticipated during the early years of a project's life. The survey indicated that most firms normally require long-

[21] See table 10-A-2 in the appendix.

[22] See footnote 13.

[23] This deliberate upward biasing of money-cost rates reflects the fact that conventional procedures for regulating utility rates tend to restrict the supply of capital funds available to the enterprise and that, as a result, the long-run marginal cost of such funds is likely to be higher than the current spot money market would indicate. This line of reasoning was set forth in a series of lectures I gave at MIT between 1968 and 1975. See also Corey (1971).

lived projects to be proven economical within considerably less time than their anticipated useful lives. The survey indicated that 40 percent of all firms that do DCF analysis, both public and private, regularly analyze the expected performance of a proposed project over the early years of its life. In most cases they emphasize the first five or ten years of the project's life. Nearly all such firms surveyed can make such "short-life" analyses.[24]

Specific risk evaluation. The survey did not deal directly with the matter of evaluating risk for specific projects. Consequently, the following comments are based upon personal observations.

The favored way to deal with specific project risks appears to be to calculate the range of variation likely to occur with respect to the major cost and revenue components of each strategy under consideration and to evaluate the range of probabilities associated with each such variation. The degree of sophistication associated with risk evaluation depends upon the size and importance of the project in question and the closeness of the decision involved. There is no cut-and-dried formula for risk evaluation but many firms use it for analysis of major plant expansion projects for which the decision is close. What is used are sensitivity analyses whereby the analyst varies one factor (for example, the investment tax credit) and holds all other factors constant. It is informative to determine how much each factor in question could vary without changing the ranking of the various alternatives.

Appendix

Commonwealth Edison Survey of Engineering Economics Practices of Electric and Gas Utilities, Telephone Companies, and Power Industry Consultants in the United States—1977

This survey was based upon written questionnaires and telephone conversations during the first half of 1977. The results are tabulated on the following pages. Comments on the statistical reliability are set forth after table 10-A-13.

[24] See table 10-A-5 in the appendix. For a decade or so, Commonwealth Edison has routinely given the greatest weight to the first ten years of a project's life.

Some of the responses were incomplete. On the following pages, the number of responses to a question and the total number of questionnaires received for a particular class of respondent are shown in parentheses after the class identification. Percentages shown are based upon the number of responses to the specific question. For example, if seven out of twelve respondents answered a question, the percentage breakdown is based upon those seven responses.

Where appropriate, these results have been compared with those from the 1976 survey by the Edison Electric Institute (see footnote 2 above) and the 1975 survey by the Intercompany Comparison Group (see Introduction and Summary, above).

Table 10-A-1. Number of Firms Surveyed and Responses Received

Type of firm	1977 Survey		Responses to the 1976 EEI survey[a,c]	Responses to the 1975 inter-company survey[b,c]
	Firms surveyed	Responses received		
Investor-owned electric and combination (electric and gas) systems	38	33	125	22
Investor-owned gas systems	12	9	—	—
Investor-owned telephone companies	3	3	—	—
Government-owned electric power systems	9	7	—	—
Rural electric cooperatives	12	12	—	—
Electric power consultants (primarily architect-engineers)	20	10	—	—
Total	94	74	125	22

[a] Edison Electric Institute Finance Comm., *Cost of Capital Used for Internal Economic Evaluations,* September 1976.

[b] Survey on engineering economics methodology, June 3, 1975, made by the Intercompany Comparison Group.

[c] The two surveys referred to in notes *a* and *b* were somewhat limited. Hence their results are reported in the following pages only where applicable.

Table 10-A-2. Discount Rates Used for Determining the Present Value of Future Cash Flows[a]

Type of firm	Cost of capital (after-tax rate of return) (%)	Pretax rate of return (%)	Rate of disadvantage (%)	Other (%)
Investor-owned electric and combination (electric and gas) systems—				
Based upon 1977 survey (31/33)[b]	65	6	26	6
Based upon 1975 survey (22/22)[c]	64	9	23	4
Investor-owned gas systems (9/9)	44	12	44	—
Investor-owned telephone companies (3/3)	100	—	—	—
Government-owned electric power systems (7/7)	71	—	—	29
Rural electric cooperatives (6/12)	100	—	—	—
Consultants (9/10)[b]	78	11	22	—
All firms surveyed in 1977 (65/74)[b]	69	6	22	6

[a] Based upon 1977 survey except where otherwise indicated.

[b] Totals exceed 100 percent because of multiple responses.

[c] See note b, Table 10-A-1.

Table 10-A-3. Solution Most Often Sought[a]

Type of firm	Revenue re-quirements (%)	Rate of return (%)	Payback period (%)	Other (%)
Investor-owned electric and combination (electric and gas) systems—				
Per 1977 survey (33/33)	91	3	—	9
Per 1975 survey[b]	100	—	—	—
Investor-owned gas systems (9/9)	67	44	—	11
Investor-owned telephone companies (3/3)	100	66	66	33
Government-owned electric power systems (7/7)	86	14	14	29
Rural electric cooperatives (6/12)	100	16	16	—
Consultants (10/10)	90	20	—	—
All firms surveyed in 1977 (68/74)	88	16	6	10

[a] Based upon 1977 survey except where otherwise indicated. In most cases, totals exceed 100 percent because of multiple responses.

[b] See note b, Table 10-A-1.

Table 10-A-4. Cost of Capital in Engineering Economic Studies[a] (Based on 1977 Survey Except Where Otherwise Stated)

Type of firm	Cost of common equity		Cost of debt		Cost of preferred		Weighted average cost of capital	
	Mean (%)	Std. dev.	Mean (%)	Std. dev.	Mean (%)	Std. dev.	Mean (%)	Std. dev.
All investor-owned companies								
Investor-owned electric and combination (electric and gas) systems								
Based upon 1977 survey (32/33)	14.69	0.98	8.74	0.76	8.94	0.80	11.03	0.85
Based upon 1976 EEI survey (125/125)[b]	14.4[c]	—	9.3	—	—[c]	—	11.2	0.64
Investor-owned gas systems (8/9)	14.93	0.56	9.00	0.69	9.23	1.50	11.79	0.53
Investor-owned telephone companies (3/3)	14.50	0.50	9.25	0.43	5.00	—	12.03	0.05
Total of firms surveyed in 1977 (43/45)	14.72	0.89	8.81	0.74	8.75	1.11	11.22	0.85
All investor-owned companies excluding these that use embedded interest costs								
Investor-owned electric and combination (electric and gas) systems								
Based upon 1977 survey (25/33)	14.74	1.06	9.0	0.51	9.18	1.50	11.30	0.73
Based upon 1976 EEI survey (105/123)[b]	14.4[c]	—	9.6	—	—[c]	—	11.4	—
Investor-owned gas systems (6/9)	14.91	0.61	9.20	0.54	9.54	1.54	11.85	0.58
Investor-owned telephone companies (3/3)	14.50	0.50	9.25	0.43	5.00	—	12.03	0.05
Total of firms surveyed in 1977 (34/45)	14.75	0.94	9.07	0.5	9.08	1.10	11.45	0.71
Government-owned electric power systems (7/7)	—	—	—	—	—	—	7.94	1.46
Rural electric cooperatives	—	—	—	—	—	—	7.88	1.09

[a] The numbers in parentheses after each sector indicate the general response ratio. There were some cases, however, where the participant partially answered the question, thus the response ratio might vary by a small amount between columns for the same sector.
[b] See note a, Table 10-A-1.
[c] Question asked for the "cost of equity" without the distinction between common and preferred.

Table 10-A-5. Period of Analysis[a]

Type of firm	Full life (%)	Less than full life (%)[b]	Infinite analysis (%)
Investor-owned electric and combination (electric and gas) systems (33/33)	97	24	24
Investor-owned gas systems (9/9)	89	56	—
Investor-owned telephone companies (3/3)	67	67	33
Government-owned electric power systems (7/7)	86	57	14
Rural electric cooperatives (6/12)	67	67	—
Consultants (10/10)	90	40	10
All firms surveyed (68/74)	90	40	16

[a] Based upon 1977 survey. Totals exceed 100 percent because of multiple responses.

[b] Where projects are evaluated over periods less than full life, the time periods analyzed are distributed as follows:

First 5 years	11%
First 10 years	44
First 15 years	7
First 20 years	19
Unspecified	19
	100%

Table 10-A-6. Capability for Computing Year-by-Year Carrying Charges[a]

Type of firm	Have capability (%)	Do not have capability (%)	No response (%)
Investor-owned electric and combination (electric and gas) systems (33/33)	85	12	3
Investor-owned gas systems (9/9)	89	11	—
Investor-owned telephone companies (3/3)	100	—	—
Government-owned electric power systems (7/7)	71	29	—
Rural electric cooperatives (6/12)	100	—	—
Consultants (10/10)	100	—	—
All firms surveyed (68/74)	88	10	2

[a] Based upon 1977 survey.

Table 10-A-7. Special Federal Income Tax Effects Included in Economic Analyses[a]

Type of firm	Investment tax credit (%)	Accelerated tax depreciation (%)	Shortened class lives (CLS-ADR tax lives) (%)
Investor-owned electric and combination (electric and gas) systems (33/33)	91	88	82
Investor-owned gas systems (9/9)	100	100	67
Investor-owned telephone companies (3/3)	100	100	100
Government-owned electric power systems	NA[b]	NA	NA
Rural electric cooperatives	NA	NA	NA
Consultants (10/10)	80	80	50
All firms surveyed (55/55)	91	89	75

[a] Based upon 1977 survey. The questionnaire also inquired whether provisions for deferred income taxes were reflected in the economic analyses. Those responding in the affirmative included 70 percent of the electric and combination companies, 67 percent of the gas companies, 100 percent of the telephone companies, and 80 percent of the cooperatives.

[b] NA, Not applicable.

Table 10-A-8. Treatment of Retirement Dispersion[a]

Type of firm	Normally included in analysis (%)	Not normally included in analysis (%)
Investor-owned electric and combination (electric and gas) systems (32/33)	47	53
Investor-owned gas systems (9/9)	—	100
Investor-owned telephone companies (3/3)	67	33
Government-owned electric power systems (6/7)	—	100
Rural electric cooperatives (6/12)	16	84
Consultants (9/10)	—	100
All firms surveyed (65/74)	28	72

[a] Based upon 1977 survey.

Table 10-A-9. Are Consultants Routinely Used to Perform Engineering Economic Analyses?[a]

Type of firm	Yes (%)	No (%)
Investor-owned electric and combination (electric and gas) systems (33/33)	24	76
Investor-owned gas systems (9/9)	22	78
Investor-owned telephone companies (3/3)	—	100
Government-owned electric power systems (7/7)	71	29
Rural electric cooperatives (12/12)	75	25
Consultants	NA[b]	NA
All firms surveyed (64/64)	37	63

[a] Based upon 1977 survey.
[b] NA, Not applicable.

Table 10-A-10. Inflation Allowances[a]

	Is an allowance for future cost escalation normally included in the economic analyses?	
Type of firm	Yes (%)	No (%)
Investor-owned electric and combination (electric and gas) systems (33/33)	94	6
Investor-owned gas systems (9/9)	56	44
Investor-owned telephone companies (3/3)	100	—
Government-owned electric power systems (7/7)	100	—
Rural electric cooperatives (6/12)	100	—
Consultants (10/10)	100	—
All firms surveyed (68/74)	91	9

[a] Based upon 1977 survey.

Table 10-A-11. Inflation Allowances Short-Term Annual Cost Escalation Rates[a]

Type of firm	Construction material		Construction labor		Operation and maintenance expenses		Coal		Oil		Nuclear fuel	
	Mean (%)	Std. dev.	Mean (%)	Std. dev.	Mean (%)	Std. dev.	Mean (%)	Std. dev.	Mean (%)	Std. dev.	Mean (%)	Std. dev.
Investor-owned electric and combination (electric and gas) systems (29/33)	7.58	1.23	7.88	1.32	7.11	1.18	7.67	1.66	7.19	1.76	7.49	1.90
Investor-owned gas systems (5/9)	6.40	1.82	6.90	1.34	6.32	1.11	NA[b]	NA	NA	NA	NA	NA
Investor-owned telephone companies (2/3)	6.00	1.41	7.50	0.71	6.00	1.41	NA	NA	NA	NA	NA	NA
Government-owned electric power systems (7/7)	6.61	1.00	6.89	1.35	6.43	1.27	6.00	2.10	7.10	1.02	11.25	6.85
Rural electric cooperatives (5/12)	7.40	0.89	7.40	0.89	6.63	1.25	7.00	1.46	7.50	2.18	7.50	1.30
Consultants (9/10)	7.33	2.00	8.50	1.27	6.25	1.04	6.89	1.27	8.00	0.89	6.93	1.69
All firms surveyed (57/74)	7.24	1.42	7.70	1.33	6.72	1.19	7.18	1.70	7.35	1.55	7.89	3.11

[a] Based upon 1977 survey. Standard deviations are shown in percentage points.
[b] NA, Not applicable.

Table 10-A-12. Inflation Allowances Long-Term Annual Cost Escalation Rates[a]

Type of firm	Construction material		Construction labor		Operation and maintenance expenses		Coal		Oil		Nuclear fuel	
	Mean (%)	Std. dev.	Mean (%)	Std. dev.	Mean (%)	Std. dev.	Mean (%)	Std. dev.	Mean (%)	Std. dev.	Mean (%)	Std. dev.
Investor-owned electric and combination (electric and gas) systems (29/33)	6.50	0.94	6.81	1.00	6.72	1.59	6.89	1.60	7.09	2.32	6.75	1.09
Investor-owned gas systems (5/9)	5.76	1.97	6.20	0.84	5.70	0.97	NA[b]	NA	NA	NA	NA	NA
Investor-owned telephone companies (2/3)	5.50	0.50	7.00	1.41	6.67	1.53	NA	NA	NA	NA	NA	NA
Government-owned electric power systems (7/7)	6.18	1.25	6.18	1.25	5.93	1.48	5.83	1.72	6.70	1.57	8.80	3.49
Rural electric cooperatives (5/12)	7.40	0.89	7.40	0.89	6.63	1.25	7.00	1.46	7.50	2.18	7.50	1.00
Consultants (9/10)	6.83	2.57	7.47	1.54	6.00	1.07	6.54	0.87	7.17	1.17	6.93	1.69
All firms surveyed (57/74)	6.48	1.45	6.84	1.16	6.39	1.42	6.68	1.50	7.08	1.99	7.18	1.83

a Based upon 1977 survey. Standard deviations are shown in percentage points.
b NA, Not applicable.

Table 10-A-13. General Questions[a]

Type of firm	Is some form of standard methodology used in analyses?		Is a manual or textbook used to aid analyses?		Do you have a formalized instruction course?	
	Yes (%)	No (%)	Yes (%)	No (%)	Yes (%)	No (%)
Investor-owned electric and combination (electric and gas) systems (33/33)	67	33	33	67	52	48
Investor-owned gas systems (9/9)	44	56	13	87	13	87
Investor-owned telephone companies (3/3)	100	—	100	—	100	—
Government-owned electric power systems (7/7)	29	71	—	100	—	100
Rural electric cooperatives (12/12)	8	92	—	100	—	100
Consultants (10/10)	30	70	30	70	30	70
All firms surveyed (74/74)	47	53	24	76	32	68

[a] Based upon 1977 survey. No response was assumed to be a *No* answer.

Comments on the Statistical Reliability of the 1977 Engineering Economics Survey

Investor-Owned Electric Power and Combination (Electric and Gas) Systems

Thirty-three investor-owned electric power and combination systems responded to the survey. While these are less than 10 percent of all U.S. investor-owned electric power systems by number, they accounted for approximately 50 percent of the kilowatt hour sales of the investor-owned sector of the electric power industry in 1975. They range in geographic location from California to New York and from Minnesota to Florida. While most responses were from medium-sized firms, the responses included some from nearly every size level. We feel that our sample adequately covers the investor-owned segment of the electric power industry.

Investor-Owned Gas Systems

The nine investor-owned gas systems responding to our survey are classified as follows:

5 Combined pipeline-distribution systems
3 Distribution only
1 Pipeline only

Although the sample is small, it includes firms involved in the exploration, production, transmission, storage, and distribution of natural gas for sale to consumers. The sample is geographically diversified. We feel that justifiable conclusions with respect to the gas utility industry in general can be reached from the data received from this sample.

Investor-Owned Telephone Companies

Three responses were received from telephone companies. One response was from a subsidiary of American Telephone & Telegraph Company (AT&T), one from a non-AT&T company, and one response from AT&T itself with the stipulation that it represented a response for their entire system. This single response received from AT&T represents approximately 80 percent of all telephones in service in the United States. Consequently, we feel that our sample provides a fair picture of the practices followed by the regulated telephone industry.

Government-Owned Electric Power Systems

The seven government-owned systems responding to our survey are classified as follows:

2 Federal power supply projects
2 Public utility districts
3 Municipal utilities

These systems account for approximately 43 percent of the total kilowatt hour sales by government-owned electric power systems in the United States. They range in size from relatively small municipalities to two large federal power supply projects. They are located in the South, Midwest, and West, where most government-owned systems are concentrated.

Rural Electric Cooperatives

During 1975, 933 rural electric cooperatives had kilowatt hour sales of approximately 110 billion kWh. Our survey included only 1.3 percent of the cooperatives operating in 1975, but these accounted for approximately 34 percent of all electricity sold by the cooperative sector in 1975. It is our belief that those cooperatives that we included in our survey represent an adequate cross section of the rural electric cooperative sector.

Electric Power Consultants

Ten electric power consultants responded to our written questionnaire and are included in the results of our survey. They range from medium-sized national firms to large, diversified international concerns. They are located from San Francisco to New York and serve as consultants to rural cooperatives, municipally owned systems, and large investor-owned firms.

References

Corey, G. R. 1971. "The Averch–Johnson Proposition: A Critical Analysis," *Bell Journal of Economics and Management Science* (New York).

———. 1976. "Planning for Plant: How Big, When, Where and How to Finance," in Glover and Simon, *Chief Executive's Handbook* (New York, Dow Jones–Irwin).

———. 1977. An untitled article in *Capital and Job Formation: Our Nation's 3rd Century Challenge*. American Telephone and Telegraph Co. (Homewood, Ill., Irwin Press).

Edison Electric Institute Finance Comm. 1976. *Cost of Capital Used for Internal Economic Evaluations* (September).

Federal Power Commission. 1971. *The 1970 National Power Survey, Part I* (Washington, GPO, December 21).

———. 1974. *The Financial Outlook for the Electric Power Industry*, a report by the Technical Advisory Committee, Gordon R. Corey, chairman (Washington, D.C., December).

Grant, E. L., and W. G. Ireson. 1970. *Principles of Engineering Economy*, 6th edition (New York, Ronald Press).

U.S. Water Resources Council. 1958. Water Supply Act of 1958 (40 FR 3200).

Robert Smiley*

Comment

The corporate finance literature produced by academics in the last twenty-five years can be seen as having three phases. The first began in 1958, when finance theorists began concentrating on the question of whether capital structure matters. In a paper that characterized this phase, Modigliani and Miller (1958) argued that the value of a firm is independent of its capital structure. The second phase began in the early 1960s, when academic interest shifted to the specification of risk and the construction of diversified portfolios. The questions involving capital structure were not ignored, but the finance journals became inundated with articles discussing risk and return tradeoffs. Corporate finance's third and current phase began with an article by Black and Scholes (1973) showing how, under certain conditions, options should be valued. Finance journals now seem full of variations on the Black–Scholes theme and articles explaining how every conceivable contract can be viewed as an option and thus susceptible to Black–Scholes pricing theorems.

Gorden Corey's paper provides some information on a topic that has received surprisingly little attention from academic finance researchers: just what do corporate financial officers do? The three phases of recent research history have by no means been devoid of empirical research, but the research has preponderantly used securities market data. Relatively little use has been made of corporate officers' investment objectives or of survey research techniques. Our understanding of the operation of organizations could certainly benefit from further studies of the type Corey has provided.

The paper begins with an inquiry into the objectives of the respondents in making investment decisions. Before turning to the empirical results, some discussion of the theoretical predictions is in order. When discussing regulated firms, Corey rejects what he feels to be the predominant investment objective of unregulated firms, the maximization of the rate of return. Since regulated firms are required by law to undertake certain investments (in order to meet the legal requirement to provide service to all who demand it), they are not free to pursue the same rate-of-return objectives that unregulated firms pursue.

* Graduate School of Business and Public Administration, Cornell University.

404

Corey argues that regulated firms should and do pursue the objective of minimizing the present value of future revenue requirements subject to the constraint of achieving a fair rate of return on capital.

In modeling the behavior of unregulated firms, economists rarely assume that the firm is attempting to maximize its rate of return. Pursuit of such a rate-of-return objective would lead to absurd results, with the firm choosing the one investment that has the highest rate of return and ignoring all others. Undertaking any other project would lower the rate of return available to the firm below that offered by the single most profitable investment.

The financial objective assumed by most economists is the maximization of the market value of the firm. Entrepreneurs are assumed to undertake an investment only if it will increase the value of the firm (or leave it unchanged) over what it would have been were the investment not undertaken. This objective of maximizing market value leads to a very simple investment rule. A firm attempting to maximize its share value will undertake an investment only if the present value of the after-tax cash flows resulting from the investment is positive when these cash flows are discounted at the after-tax cost of capital.

To predict, a priori, the objective followed by regulated utilities, we should first consider the difference between regulated and unregulated firms. There are two basic differences. First, regulated utilities are legally required to meet all demands for service (at the regulated prices) except in emergencies. The second difference is that regulated firms are not as free to set prices as their unregulated counterparts are. Although it is not clear what effect, if any, regulatory commissions have on prices, there is at least the added expense of the regulatory proceedings that differentiates regulated from unregulated firms. Considering these two differences, the most appropriate objective would seem to be the maximization of the market value of the firm subject to an added constraint (the requirement to provide adequate service), and subject either to an additional cost of regulatory proceedings or an additional set of constraints relating to the maximum rate of return that can be earned on the rate base, depending on whether you believe regulation is effective in controlling prices.

What then are we to make of Corey's finding that the solution most often sought in utility investment analysis is the minimization of revenue requirements? What this says is simply that when two mutually exclusive investment alternatives are considered, the firm chooses the one with the least cost. The investment alternative with the least present-value cost will, of course, result in the least revenue requirement. This sort of investment analysis is the kind commonly undertaken at the requirement of state regulatory commissions before regulated utilities may make major investments, in nuclear power plants, for example. Although this analysis probably is carried out in good faith, it does not imply that the overall objective of the firm should necessarily be characterized as the minimization of revenue requirements for its customers. The choice of the less costly of two mutually exclusive investment opportunities is consistent with the objective of maximizing the value of the firm subject to the "requirement to serve" and a constraint on rate of return. Corey's evidence simply provides us with no basis for choosing between his characterization of objectives and the traditional one.

The treatment of the Averch–Johnson proposition requires some clarification. Corey correctly states that an allowed rate of return less than the cost of capital will induce firms to favor less capital-intensive alternatives than they would if the allowed rate of return were equal to the cost of capital. But he then goes on to say this is exactly opposite to the so-called Averch–Johnson proposition; this is not true. The bias described *is* the Averch–Johnson proposition, although the proposition is more frequently stated in terms of an allowed rate of return greater than the cost of capital inducing a bias toward a capital–labor ratio in excess of what is socially optimal.

Corey's most interesting finding concerns the choice of discount rate by the firms in his sample. The respondents were asked how they determine the discount rate used in taking present values of cash flows. The three possible responses, illustrated by an example, are the pre-tax cost of capital, the after-tax cost of capital, and a hybrid of the two. The after-tax rate takes account of the fact that interest costs are tax deductible, and it is the rate almost universally recommended in modern corporate finance texts (see Van Horne, 1977, pp. 207–208). A startling finding is that a large proportion of the firms in Corey's sample used the pre-tax cost of capital, a procedure for evaluating investment alternatives that is at variance with widely accepted practice in corporate finance.

There are several possible reasons for this discrepancy. Two uninteresting explanations are that the respondent did not understand the question or does not know what procedures are used in his firm. It is likely, however, that a large proportion of electric utilities are indeed using a pre-tax cost of capital to discount cash flows. A useful follow-up to this survey would be to attempt to determine why the nation's business schools have had so little effect on investment practices in an industry that will use so much of the nation's capital in the future.

Should the utility manager use the cost of capital determined by the market in discounting future cash flows from an investment? Corey argues that although the capital market is incorporating risk in the determination of the cost of capital, the manager should increase the discount rate above this cost of capital. He states that managers should add a percentage point or two to current money market rates because managers must "predict the effect of current plant expansion decisions upon his future financing costs." But that is precisely what investors themselves are doing when they decide the terms on which they will lend money to, or invest in the equity of, a utility.

Investors have already accounted for the risk of the firm in their decisions to lend or invest, and a further increase in the cost of capital for investment comparison would seem inappropriate. Corey assumes that investors will be ignorant of the effect of a firm's current operations and investment strategies upon its future cost of capital and credit standing. This assumption is almost certainly invalid. Any procedure that deviates from the market assessed cost of capital for the choice of discount rate needs far more justification than is provided here.

Corey's statement that the very existence of corporate income taxes penalizes capital-intensive alternatives merits discussion. Whether the corporate income tax affects business behavior at all depends on the incidence of the tax. If the tax is borne entirely by consumers through higher prices, then the tax would have no effect on corporate behavior, as shown by Hall and Jorgenson (1971). Since the incidence of the corporate income tax is uncertain, it is not clear whether business behavior is affected by the corporate income tax.

Let us assume, however, that business behavior is affected by corporate income taxes, that is, that the incidence of the tax is borne in part by the shareholders. The effect of this tax will be to raise the investment hurdle rate, and thus less investment will be undertaken. But firms can invest in both capital and labor. A firm can invest in its labor force through training, education, and other means, and its decision to do so will be affected just as much by the corporate tax rate as will its decision to invest in a new plant. So it is not clear whether the presence of corporate taxes biases the capital intensiveness of a firm, if by "capital intensiveness" is meant physical capital intensiveness.

But since public utilities are among the most capital-intensive industries, it is probably true that the investment opportunities available in physical capital far outweigh the investment opportunities available in its labor force, especially when compared with less capital-intensive industries. Therefore, since the corporate income tax biases all investment downward, it probably also biases the capital-to-labor ratio downward. While this evidence suggests that Corey is correct, this issue is extremely complex.

Project Risk Assessment

How should a firm choose between two large, mutually exclusive investments such as a nuclear plant and a coal plant of equal capacity? Corey touches on the prevalent practice, which is to calculate the expected present value of future revenue requirements. Sensitivity analysis is sometimes used in assessing risk for individual projects. For example, in the comparison of a nuclear plant and a coal plant, a utility might ask what the effect on the total present value of revenue requirements would be if the cost of uranium were to double. Alternatively, a utility might ask what increase in nuclear construction cost would be required to make the present value of future revenue requirements for the nuclear plant exactly equal to the expected cost of the coal plant.

Although this procedure is preferable to a simple comparison of expected costs, it also has serious flaws. First, no probabilities are attached to the various cost estimate deviations; for example, how likely is the hypothetical doubling of nuclear fuel costs? Also, the sensitivity testing usually undertaken is incapable of a simultaneous variation in many different costs from their expected values. Monte Carlo simulation is capable of accommodating both of these problems. Although Monte Carlo simulation makes significantly greater information demands on the analyst, the resulting assessment of uncertainty for individual projects is superior to simple sensitivity analysis.

Monte Carlo analysis begins with a disaggregation of the total cost figure. A typical analysis uses five to fifteen categories of costs, for example, fuel, maintenance, construction costs, capital costs. One then needs to estimate the probability distribution for each of these costs. Although this is clearly difficult and probably a novel procedure for most cost engineers, it has been done successfully in the past. The engineer is asked a question of this sort: What is your best estimate of the fuel costs, and what is a low and a high estimate? A low estimate is taken to mean a value that has a 90 percent probability of being exceeded, and a high estimate is one that will be exceeded with a probability of 10 percent. Then a probability distribution must be chosen for these cost estimates; common choices are the triangular and the normal distributions. After distributions are obtained for each of the individual cost estimates, the simulation is run with draws being taken from each of the cost categories in accordance with their individual probability distributions. A total cost distribution is then constructed based on thousands of these simulations.

Monte Carlo simulation allows the utility manager to see a simple display of the risk associated with each of the alternatives for power generation, and the display is in a probability distribution form that is easily understood. The simulation can also tell the utility manager such information as the probability that the total cost of a coal plant will be less than the total cost of a nuclear plant, even though the expected value of the nuclear plant is lower. Alternatively, the distributions can be used to determine which alternative has a higher probability of exceeding a certain value.

Replacement of Obsolete Facilities

The increase in oil prices in 1973 and 1974 left many oil-fired electricity plants obsolete. If a utility were to compare the average variable cost of the oil facility with the expected average total cost of a new coal or nuclear plant, replacement would be the least costly alternative. But, because of the fuel-adjustment clause, many of these obsolete plants are not likely to be replaced soon.

The reason for this anti-investment bias lies in the asymmetrical uncertainty of the two alternatives. If the manager decides to replace the facility, as a comparison of the expected costs would dictate, he faces a lead time of six to twelve years before any electricity will be produced by the new plant. During this lead time (about half of which is caused by licensing hearings) many things can happen to affect the firm adversely. Events that could lead to cancellation of the application include a decrease in the growth of demand for electricity, an unfavorable license ruling, a nationwide moratorium on construction of nuclear power plants, changes in regulatory proceedings, and so on. Even if the plant is built, there is considerable uncertainty whether the utility will ever fully recover the costs involved. Commissions have begun to balk at automatically passing along rapidly escalating construction costs to consumers. Furthermore, utilities have, in many cases, not been able to earn their allowed rate of return in recent years. For all these reasons, the uncertainty surrounding the construction of a new plant is considerable, especially for the heretofore sheltered utility executive.

The alternative to constructing a new plant is, of course, to continue operating the obsolete one and to pass the higher fuel costs along to consumers through the fuel-adjustment clause. This clause, in force in every state in the union, allows all fuel-cost increases to be passed on to consumers without regulatory review or regulatory lag.[1] Unlike building a new billion-dollar nuclear plant, there is little or no uncertainty about cost recovery facing the executive who decides to continue operating his obsolete oil-fired plant. In the face of this asymmetry of uncertainty, the large number of planned nuclear plants canceled in the last five years should come as no surprise.

Considering the precarious position of the United States with respect to oil imports, any set of factors inhibiting the replacement of obsolete oil-fired electricity plants should be of concern. Several policies are available to speed the replacement of obsolete facilities. First, public utility commissions could simply order them scrapped or mothballed. Although regulatory agencies can legally order utilities to construct new facilities to meet demand, it is not clear that they can dictate the decision to replace obsolete facilities. Further, the actual running cost of the possibly obsolete facilities now in service is a classic case of what Oliver Williamson (1975) calls impacted information. Commissions do not know what these operating costs are, nor are the utilities likely to report them truthfully if doing so means being forced

---

[1] Several states pass along only 80–90 percent of fuel cost increases, allowing the utility to recover the difference through base rates. A minimal lag (but no review) of one to two months is usually involved with fuel-adjustment clauses.

to close existing plants against the utility's wishes. How will the commission know which plant to close?

Alternatively, action could be taken to reduce the asymmetry of uncertainty. The National Energy Plan issued in April 1977 proposed a review of the licensing process and proposed using a standardized nuclear power plant design to shorten the licensing and construction lead time. Streamlining regulatory processes, problematical though that may be, could induce more utilities to replace obsolete oil-fired facilities. The existing asymmetry of uncertainty could, of course, be modified in another way by reducing the certainty that all fuel costs will in fact be recovered, that is, by modifying or eliminating the fuel-adjustment clause.

The Fuel-Adjustment Clause

To understand why the fuel-adjustment clause exists, we should consider how utility rates would be set were it not in effect. Public utility commissions would then have to forecast fuel costs in addition to all other costs for the test year in order to set rates that would allow the firm to recover all reasonable (forecast) costs. If the commission adopted a forecast that turned out to be too low, the utility would, other things being equal, earn a return below the cost of capital. If the forecast was too high, the return would be above the cost of capital.

In the absence of fuel-adjustment clauses, the shareholder absorbs the risk of error in forecasting fuel prices. How significant are these risks? A simple comparison of fuel costs, dividends, and earnings for a large eastern utility, Consolidated Edison, will be sufficient to show the importance of fuel costs.

In 1975, Con Ed's fuel oil and gas purchases were $628,000,000. If the fuel-adjustment clause had not been in operation, and barring a rate increase, a 12 percent increase in oil prices would have wiped out Con Ed's 1975 dividend. Alternatively, a 33 percent increase in fuel prices would eliminate all earnings. The likelihood of increases of this magnitude is by no means trivial, so the importance of the fuel-adjustment clause as a risk-reducing device is evident.

Shareholder risk reduction for its own sake is, of course, of little consequence to the consumer. What he is concerned about is rates, or ultimately, costs. But since the fuel-adjustment clause reduces risk, it should reduce capital costs, at least if the risks eliminated are nondiversifiable (and thus of concern to the investor). Unfortunately, the evidence for these capital cost savings is difficult to gather since all utilities now operate under the fuel-adjustment clause, and risk perceptions in the period of time in which they were not all covered (before 1970) may not be typical of today's environment. The study of one utility, Public Service of New Mexico, that essentially instituted an automatic pass-through of all costs provides some peripheral evidence. Although PNM's pass-through does involve lag and is more comprehensive than the fuel-adjustment clause, the case at least provides some recent data. Herman Roseman found, in a preliminary study, that the institution of PNM's pass-through reduced the utility's cost of equity capital by one to two percentage points and its debt costs by about one-half percentage point from the period in which PNM had only a fuel-adjustment clause.[2] Thus, automatic rate adjustment clauses appear, on admittedly skimpy evidence, to reduce capital costs.

If a reduction in capital costs were the only effect of automatic adjustment clauses, we would certainly expect to find numerous advocates of clauses similar to that used in New Mexico. But, of course, there are negative aspects of both fuel-adjustment and full cost-adjustment clauses. One obvious effect is to remove both regulatory lag and regulatory review of costs. With a full cost-adjustment clause, what incentive does a utility executive have to minimize costs? Gross abuses may be prevented by the fear of losing the clause itself, but what of that extra effort expended (with no such clause in effect) by individuals whose cost savings will benefit the firm's owners, at least during the regulatory lag period? Again, empirical evaluation of the cost of eliminating regulatory lag and overview through an automatic adjustment clause that dulls incentives appears impossible. But an order-of-magnitude understanding of possible cost savings can be gained through Con Ed's experience. A one-percent savings in fuel costs to Con Ed would mean a $6.3 million savings each year to New York City's rate payers. Would the firm hire a fuel buyer capable of this type of savings if it did not have to pass the savings through to consumers immediately, that is, if it were allowed to keep them until the next rate case? To expect savings of this order of magnitude, in the absence of the fuel-adjustment clause, does not seem unreasonable.

The reduction in the risk of forecast error discussed above has another perhaps negative, effect on consumers. A major increase in the price of oil will be borne immediately by consumers through the fuel-adjustment clause. In the absence of a clause, an unexpected increase (one not forecast in the last rate case) would be absorbed by the firm as reduced earnings, at least until the conclusion of the next rate case. Thus, regulatory lag provides a sort of buffer to consumers for major price increases.[3]

An overall evaluation of the fuel-adjustment clause must balance all these factors. We have shown that the clause biases replacement decisions

[2] PNM's bond's yield to maturity decreased by 50 basis points (relative to comparable AA rated bonds) about six months after the pass-through went into effect, so it is difficult to be certain that the pass-through was the cause of the decreases (Roseman, 1976).

[3] This buffer also applies to major price decreases. If OPEC were to collapse, utilities would earn supranormal profits for a time, were the fuel-adjustment clause not in effect.

against replacing obsolete facilities and removes incentives for vigorous bargaining in fuel purchases. On the positive side, the risk of a forecast error by the regulatory commission is eliminated, with the result that capital costs are probably lowered for consumers. The other effect of this reduction in risk is that consumers will absorb the impact of unexpected changes in fuel prices more quickly than they do with the clause.

Should the clause be retained? Should it be expanded to cover all inputs, as in New Mexico? Should it be narrowed so that 10 percent of the expected fuel costs are included in base rates (invariant between rate cases) and 90 percent of all costs are subject to the clause? This would give the utility some incentive to bargain harder since it would keep 10 percent of any savings, at least between rate cases. These questions are a good example of a case in which quantitative analysis may fail us. There is no simple way of analyzing the tradeoff of incentives for cost minimization versus risk reduction and lowered capital cost.

References

Black, F., and M. Scholes. 1973. "The Pricing of Options and Corporate Liabilities," *Journal of Political Economy* vol. 81 (May–June) pp. 637–654.

Hall, R. E., and D. W. Jorgenson. 1971. "Application of the Theory of Optimum Capital Accumulation," in Gary Fromm, ed., *Tax Incentives and Capital Spending* (Washington, D.C., Brookings Institution).

Modigliani, F., and M. Miller. 1958. "The Cost of Capital, Corporation Finance, and the Theory of Investment," *American Economic Review* vol. 48 (June) pp. 261–297.

Roseman, H. 1976. "The Cost of Service Adjustment Clause and the Cost of Capital of Public Service Company of New Mexico" (National Economic Research Associates, October 1976, updated January 1978).

Van Horne, J. C. 1977. *Financial Management and Policy* (Englewood Cliffs, N.J., Prentice-Hall).

Williamson, O. 1975. *Markets and Hierarchies: Analysis and Antitrust Implications* (London, The Free Press).

11

*Thomas Stauffer**

The Social Efficiency of Electric Utility Decision Criteria

In this paper we shall investigate the social efficiency of the decision criteria used by public utilities in evaluating major capital projects. In particular, we shall focus on the question whether the utilities' decision functions, based upon their discounting procedures and selection of discount rates, are consistent with a national economic benefit–cost calculus. Are the utilities biased in favor of or against capital-intensive projects that might result in significant fuel savings? If their selection rules are not consistent with the criteria of national economic efficiency, are those inconsistencies or incongruities material when tested against the intrinsic uncertainties in project evaluations? Finally, if the inconsistencies are serious, what policy remedies might be appropriate?

One can easily marshal an array of qualitative evidence that suggests, a priori, that there must exist significant divergences between the two sets of criteria. Averch and Johnson (1962) argued that utilities are strongly biased toward capital-intensive—or fuel-nonintensive—projects, while other observers have commented on the utilities' predilection for the opposite, that is, the capital-nonintensive options. More fundamentally, the difference between the usual notion of a social rate of time preference (low) and the utilities' discount rates (higher) is sufficiently large that one might well doubt whether the two sets of decision criteria could even be close. Further, the fact that the privately owned utilities are subject to income tax liabilities, which are costs in their own project analyses, whereas income taxes are transfer payments rather than costs within the social benefit–cost calculus, should lead one to expect additional disparities in the decision functions.

We shall formulate these questions from two different but related standpoints. First, we shall measure the social economic losses or inefficiencies resulting from the utilities' use of project selection criteria that are socially suboptimal. The alternatives selected by these criteria might be either too

* Center for Middle Eastern Studies, Harvard University.

413

capital-intensive or too fuel-intensive. Second, we shall recast the relationships to examine the institutional factors that cause the two sets of criteria to diverge. In particular, we shall exhibit explicitly the effects of income taxation, especially of tax depreciation schedules, and the choice of discount rate. This second part will offer insight into the possible role of tax depreciation policy or regulatory reform in ensuring closer conformity between the utility and economic decision criteria.

In the following section on efficiency losses, we derive the investment evaluation criterion used by most electric utilities and show that it is formally equivalent to a shadow price, or scarcity value, for capital. The section on social opportunity costs summarizes a derivation of the social opportunity cost of resources (SOC) and the discounted social consumption equivalent (DSCE), which is the present value of benefit streams after allowance for partial re-investment and the creation of second- and higher-order derived benefits. In the section on comparison of utility and social criteria, we show how the generalized social opportunity costs can be combined with the utility decision criteria to derive tests for social efficiency. The final section summarizes the empirical results of applying the theory to representative U.S. electric utilities, and the appendix contains a derivation of the shadow prices for resources.

Efficiency Losses

To estimate the possible efficiency or deadweight losses resulting from the differences between the social and electric utility decision functions, we shall (1) apply the utility criteria to pairs of projects; (2) determine which project would be selected by the utility; and (3) measure the social economic costs of each. Each pair of projects produces the same amount of electricity in each time period; the projects differ only in their capital- versus fuel-intensiveness, as, for example, in the choice between a liquid metal fast breeder reactor and an oil-fired station.

The losses will be measured as the difference between the social opportunity costs of the two projects, divided by the social cost of the cheaper alternative. By specifying the losses or savings as a fraction of the optimal project cost, we avoid having to use absolute costs and we retain a useful measure of the materiality of the possible inefficiencies. The "loss" is the percentage increase in real social economic cost if the inefficient option is elected.

Two quite different metrics for "cost" will be used hereafter. For the utilities, we will discount the real (inflation-corrected) investments, fuel expenditures, and operating costs, at the inflation-corrected cost of capital as perceived by the utility for planning, using the utility's own discounting formula (investment evaluation criterion). For social costs, however, we must invoke a more general calculus, in which we consider the opportunity cost to the economy of the total economic resources consumed in each alternative.

Each dollar of expenditure by the utility will be weighted differently in the social benefit–cost calculus; capital investments will be weighted with respect to the net consumption stream that would have resulted had they been invested elsewhere. Operating outlays or savings (especially fuel) will be weighted recognizing that future outlays are discounted less heavily by society, since the social rate of time preference (SRTP) is less than the opportunity cost of capital. The weighting or shadow price to be assigned to each class of outlay will be the discounted social consumption equivalent (DSCE)—that is, the present value, discounted at the SRTP of the resources used in the project, allowing for whatever fraction of the capital is drawn from current consumption versus current capital formation, and also allowing for whatever fraction of gross project benefits might be saved and reinvested.

Let us turn to the investment criterion for an electric utility. The revenues of a regulated utility are determined as a function of its costs, both current operating costs and its investments during the previous periods. The latter are incorporated by specifying an allowable rate of return on capital, including any applicable income or real estate property taxes, plus depreciation charges. The allowable return to capital is in turn equal to the rate base (or the depreciated capital investment outstanding in each period) multiplied by the allowable return to capital. Let us introduce the following assumptions:

1. Straight-line depreciation for purposes of rate making (N years service lifetime).
2. Weighted cost of capital $\overline{R}$ equals:

$$\beta R^{\text{debt}} + (1 - \beta)R^{\text{eq}} \tag{1}$$

where R^{debt} is the utility's borrowing cost, and R^{eq} is the cost of equity capital.
3. Accelerated tax depreciation schedule is $D^{\text{tax}}(t)$.
4. Income tax rate equals T (federal and effective state tax rates).

We shall ignore the investment tax credit, construction work in progress, allowance for funds during construction, and property taxes for the moment.

The carrying charge related to the project's capital investment in any year t of the N years of the project's life is:

$$I_0 \left[\frac{1}{N(1-T)} + \overline{\overline{R}}\left\{1 - \left(\frac{t-1}{N}\right)\right\} - \left(\frac{T}{1-T}\right)D^{\text{tax}}(t) \right] \quad 1 \leq t \leq N \tag{2}$$

$$\text{where } \overline{\overline{R}} = \beta R^{\text{debt}} + \left(\frac{1-\beta}{1-T}\right)R^{\text{eq}}$$

Irrespective of the schedule of electricity production by the project, the capital-related carrying charges are highest in the first year of operation, declining linearly thereafter for the $N-1$ remaining years of service life. This follows immediately from the fact that capital charges are proportional to the rate base, which is reduced each year by the amount of the annual depreciation charge. The electricity rates charged by the utility would show the same pattern, and this somewhat idiosyncratic result means that the consumers' price for electricity would actually decline as the plant ages, even if, as assumed here, output remains constant. The pattern is the immediate consequence of using the rate base (and rate formulas as established by regulatory practice) for the calculation of electricity rates, and its implications will be pursued later.

Let us further assume that the annual operating costs, including costs of fuel, are constant over the lifetime of the facility. The only important case in which that assumption is not accurate is that in which operating costs might rise steadily—the likely prospect for fossil fuels as well as uranium. That alternative, too, will be investigated later. Under these assumptions, the annual costs as defined by the utility are:

$$I_0\left[\frac{1}{N(1-T)} + \bar{\bar{R}}\left\{1 - \left(\frac{t-1}{N}\right)\right\} - \left(\frac{T}{1-T}\right)D^{\text{tax}}(t)\right] + C \tag{3}$$

If the annual charges are discounted at the rate $\bar{r}$ we find, after extensive algebraic manipulation:

$$PVU(\bar{r}) = I_0\left[\frac{S(N,\bar{r})}{(1-T)N} + \frac{\bar{\bar{R}}}{\bar{r}}\left\{1 - \frac{S(N,\bar{r})}{N}\right\}\right]$$
$$-I_0\left(\frac{T}{1-T}\right)d^{\text{tax}}(\bar{r}) + CS(N,\bar{r}) \tag{4}$$

where $d^{\text{tax}}(\bar{r})$ is the present value of the tax depreciation schedule, $D^{\text{tax}}(t)$, discounted at rate $\bar{r}$, and:

$$\bar{\bar{R}} = \beta R^{\text{debt}} + \left(\frac{1-\beta}{1-T}\right)R^{\text{eq}} \tag{5}$$

$$S(N,x) = \frac{1}{x}\left[1 - (1+x)^{-N}\right] \tag{6}$$

The expression for the utility's cost, equation (4), can be rearranged to exhibit more explicitly the effect of capital investment:

$$PVU(\bar{r}) = \lambda^{\text{UTIL}} \cdot I_0 + CS(N,\bar{r}) \tag{7}$$

$$\text{where } \lambda^{\text{UTIL}} = \left[\frac{S(N,\bar{r})}{(1-T)N} + \frac{\bar{\bar{R}}}{\bar{r}} \left\{ 1 - \frac{S(N,\bar{r})}{N} \right\} - \left(\frac{T}{1-T} \right) d^{\text{tax}}(\bar{r}) \right] \quad (8)$$

The term λ^{UTIL} can be interpreted as the utility's scarcity value, or shadow price, for capital investment.

A special case of equation (8), which is valid for any discount rate, is of some practical relevance. Let us assume that the utility uses as its discount rate for project evaluation the tax-corrected cost of capital, R', defined below:

$$R' = (1-T)\beta R^{\text{debt}} + (1 - \beta)R^{\text{eq}} \quad (9)$$

$$= (1 - T) \cdot \bar{\bar{R}} \quad (10)$$

$$\text{since } R = \beta R^{\text{debt}} + \left(\frac{1-\beta}{1-T} \right) R^{\text{eq}} \quad (11)$$

If the expression for R' from equation (11) is substituted into equation (4), we obtain a particularly compact expression for the discounted value of the utility's cost (PVU):

$$PVU(R') = \frac{I_0}{1-T} \left\{ 1 - Td^{\text{tax}}(R') \right\} + CS(N,R') \quad (12)$$

The present discounted value of the capital charges is greater than the initial investment I_0 itself, even though we have assumed no time lags. The multiplicative factor equals the reciprocal of one minus the income tax rate T times the quantity one minus $Td^{\text{tax}}(R')$, where $d^{\text{tax}}(R')$ is the present value of the tax depreciation schedule discounted at rate R'. Since d^{tax} is always less than unity, the net scale factor is greater than unity, and the utility calculates the present value of the capital-related charges to be greater than the capital outlay itself.

Finally, it is necessary to generalize the utility decision function to include those local taxes not related to income. In addition to federal and state income taxes, the investor-owned utilities are subject to a variety of local taxes, such as property levies, franchise taxes, or gross receipts taxes. Broadly speaking, these additional imposts fall into two distinctive categories:

Investment-based: levies related to capital equipment and land, where the tax valuation might be based upon historical cost—depreciated or undepreciated—or upon some assessed figure.

Revenue-based: taxes specified as a fixed amount per kilowatt hour generated or a given percentage of gross revenues.

In the first case, the contribution of a given project to the utility's local tax burden equals the tax rate times the applicable asset base:

$$\text{Tax}_t^{\text{LOC}} = \begin{cases} T^{\text{LOC}} \cdot I_0 \left\{ 1 - \left(\dfrac{t-1}{N} \right) \right\} & \text{(depreciated base)} \quad (13) \\[3ex] T^{\text{LOC}} \cdot I_0 & \text{(undepreciated base)} \quad (14) \end{cases}$$

The impact of the taxes upon the utility's decision function is the present value of the tax, discounted at the utility's cost of capital:

$$\text{Local Tax Cost} = \begin{cases} T^{\text{LOC}} \cdot I_0 \cdot \dfrac{1}{\bar{r}} \left[1 - \dfrac{S(N,\bar{r})}{N} \right] & (15) \\[3ex] T^{\text{LOC}} \cdot I_0 \cdot S(N,\bar{r}) & (16) \end{cases}$$

If the depreciated assets are the basis for local taxes, then the effect of adding the tax cost to equation (4) for the present value of the utility's cost is to change the value of $\bar{\bar{R}}$, that is, $\bar{\bar{R}}' \rightarrow \bar{\bar{R}} + T^{\text{LOC}}$. If the undepreciated value of the assets is used for reckoning the tax, then equation (16) must be added to equation (4) and we obtain:

$$PVU(\bar{r}) \Rightarrow I_0 \left[\frac{S(N,\bar{r})}{(1-T)N} + \frac{\bar{\bar{R}}}{\bar{r}} \left\{ 1 - \frac{S(N,\bar{r})}{N} \right\} + T^{\text{LOC}} S(N,\bar{r}) \right]$$
$$- I_0 \left(\frac{T}{1-T} \right) d^{\text{tax}}(\bar{r}) + CS(N,\bar{r}) \qquad (17)$$

The effect of a receipts tax is simply to multiply the utility's cost by the factor $(1 + T^{\text{LOC}})$:

$$PVU' = (1 + T^{\text{LOC}})PVU \qquad (18)$$

and it follows from the discussion in the section on comparison of utility and social criteria that such a tax has no effect on the utility's choice of technology.

Social Opportunity Costs

Whereas the preceding section focused on determining how an electric utility would value the resources, capital versus fuel, committed to a particular energy option, we now turn to the question of the social metric for those same resources. The social opportunity cost of resources is measured as the stream of consumption, including both current and future consumption, that would be generated by the expenditure of those same resources elsewhere in the economy.

Measurement of the social opportunity cost thus necessitates distinguishing between two distinct concepts:

Productivity of Capital. This reflects the yield, including both income taxes and other levies, such as property or real estate taxes, realized in the economy on the investment dollar that is displaced by the electricity projects in question. If the source of financing for the projects is well defined, then the opportunity cost can be identified more clearly. Otherwise, if the marginal source is not known, the productivity of capital as used in this context refers to the average before-tax rate of return for the economy.

Social Rate of Time Preference. This subsumes society's intertemporal preference for consumption, indicating the discount to be applied to consumption in future periods. It is distinct from the productivity of capital, and we hereafter assume that the SRTP exists and can be defined with adequate precision.

It is shown in the appendix that the social opportunity cost of an arbitrary stream of expenditures $I(t)$ equals the product of the present value of the expenditure stream, discounted at the social rate of time preference, and the shadow price for resources, λ, which is independent of the specific projects and depends only upon the productivity of capital in the economy, a set of marginal propensities to save, and the SRTP. Stated more formally, the discounted social consumption equivalent (DSCE) of an arbitrary stream of expenditures $I(t)$, equals:

$$\text{DSCE} = i(\rho) \cdot \lambda \tag{19}$$

where $i(\rho) = \displaystyle\int_0^\infty I(t)e^{-\rho t}dt = $ present value of $I(t)$

$$\lambda = (1 - \pi)\left\{\frac{\Theta + (1 - \Theta)k(\rho)}{1 - \pi k(\rho)}\right\} \tag{20}$$

and:

$\rho = $ SRTP

$\Theta = $ fraction of expenditures that would have been consumed.

$\pi = $ fraction of benefits that is reinvested

$k(\rho) = \displaystyle\int_0^\infty K(t)e^{-\rho t}dt$, where:

$K(t) = $ cash flow generated by one dollar's investment in the economy at rate of return r, that is, $k(r) = 1.0$

The shadow price λ has an immediate economic interpretation. It is the discounted social consumption equivalent of a dollar's worth of resources. It equals the present value, discounted at the SRTP, of the net benefit stream generated by an expenditure of one dollar, if Θ of the initial dollar outlay goes directly for consumption, while $(1 - \Theta)$ is invested, and where the yield on that investment is r, the average before-tax rate of return on capital, and where a fraction π of the subsequent benefits is also reinvested.

The term λ thus represents the social opportunity cost of a unit expenditure. The social opportunity cost of an arbitrary expenditure is the product of two quite separate terms: the first is specific to the project itself—the present value of those outlays discounted at the SRTP—while the second term is specific to the economy and entirely independent of the project. The SRTP alone enters the first term, while the second depends upon the productivity of capital, r, ρ (the SRTP), and the two parameters that describe the tradeoffs between consumption and investment (Θ and π).

More generally, one can allow for different savings coefficients or different financing—values of Θ—for different categories of expenditure:

$$I(t) = \sum_j I^j(t) \tag{21}$$

$$\mathrm{DSCE} = \sum_j i^j(\rho)\, \lambda^j, \text{ where:} \tag{22}$$

$$\lambda^j = \frac{\Theta_j + (1 - \Theta_j)\, k(\rho)}{1 - \pi\, k(\rho)} \tag{23}$$

In particular we shall distinguish between two classes of expenditure:

1. Capital outlays, which compete principally with other capital projects, and for which the consumption fraction Θ is low or zero; and
2. Operating costs (fuel), which compete with consumption—that is, the propensity to consume out of any reduced costs is presumed to be high—for which the consumption fraction Θ is therefore close to unity.

The social opportunity cost (SOC) then reduces to:

$$\mathrm{SOC} = i(\rho)\lambda_0 + c(\rho)\lambda, \tag{24}$$

where $i(\rho)$ and $c(\rho)$ are the present values of the capital outlays and the operating costs (fuel), respectively, discounted at the SRTP, and λ_0 and λ_1 are the values of λ from equation (23), allowing for the appropriate values of Θ ($\Theta_0 \approx 1.0$ and $\Theta_1 \approx 0.1$). In the subsequent sections we shall assume that the investment takes place at one point, that is, $I(t) = I_0\delta(t)$, and that the operating costs are constant over time:

$$\mathrm{SOC} \rightarrow I_0\lambda_0 + CS(N,\rho) \cdot \lambda_1 \tag{25}$$

Table 11-1. **Shadow Prices**

Cash flow profile, $K(t)$	STRP ρ	Fraction of benefits reinvested π	Fraction of benefits consumed, Θ			
			0.1	0.2	0.9	1.0
Triangular	0.03	0.1	1.18	1.27	1.89	1.96
profile	0.03	0.2	1.34	1.44	2.13	2.23
	0.03	0.3	1.63	1.75	2.59	2.71
	0.05	0.1	1.11	1.17	1.55	1.60
	0.05	0.2	1.21	1.26	1.67	1.73
	0.05	0.3	1.35	1.41	1.87	1.93
Rectangular	0.03	0.1	1.31	1.45	2.47	2.62
profile	0.03	0.2	1.64	—	—	—
	0.03	0.3	2.43	2.71	4.61	4.88
	0.05	0.1	1.18	1.26	1.85	1.93
	0.05	0.2	1.33	1.43	2.09	2.19
	0.05	0.3	1.61	1.72	2.52	2.64

Source: Computations were based on equation (20) evaluated for $r = 0.1098$.

where C is the annual expenditure and $S(N,\rho)$ is the annuity formula. This simplification entails no significant loss in generality.

The shadow prices are sensitive to changes in the parameter values. A range of possible values is shown in table 11-1 for combinations of values of $\rho = 0.03$ and 0.05; $\pi = 0.1, 0.2$, and 0.3; $\Theta = 0.1, 0.2, 0.9$, and 1.0; and two possible shapes of the cash flow profile $K(t)$. Values of r are not shown, since it is amenable to rather precise measurement.

We note that the extreme range in shapes of $K(t)$ has only a modest impact on the value of λ, and we shall hereafter use only the triangular profile since a downward slope is more plausible. The sensitivity of λ to Θ and π is seen to be great; however, our results will ultimately be independent of π since only the ratio λ_1/λ_0 appears in the final equations. The fraction of benefits consumed, Θ, remains as a critical parameter, and the later results will depend intimately upon the accuracy with which one can identify the sources of finance for electricity projects, as is the case in more general applications of benefit–cost theory.

Comparison of Utility and Social Criteria

We can now proceed to a comparison of the social economic costs with the costs perceived by the utility in evaluating projects involving different technological options. The analysis focuses upon pairs of alternative projects to which the utility would be indifferent—alternatives that are equally costly as evaluated using the utility's criterion. For each such pair we then determine the difference in the social economic costs (discounted social consumption equivalents), and the difference represents the potential economic loss if the utility opts for one versus the other. The sequence of steps is:

1. Derive the cost of a project as measured by the electric utility, using its benefit–cost formula and its discount rate, including applicable taxes.
2. Equate two different projects as measured by the utility cost calculus; this is equivalent to specifying that the higher capital outlays for the one are offset by commensurately lower operating (fuel) outlays for the other.
3. Determine the DSCE cost of each of the two projects; these will in general differ, even though the two options are equal according to the utility's calculus, because of the different weights given to capital and current outlays in the social calculus, reflecting different discount rates and treatment of taxes.
4. The difference between the two DSCE costs is the loss in the present discounted value of the potential consumption benefits if the utility elects the alternative that is socially the more costly.
5. Compute the relative potential efficiency loss as the difference in DSCE costs, calculated above, divided by the DSCE cost of the cheaper alternative.

The efficiency loss (calculated here) is only potential because we cannot specify *in vacuo* which of the two equivalent projects might in fact be selected by the utility. The probability of the potential inefficiencies will be discussed later, once the relative magnitudes of the potential losses have been quantified.

Let us now consider two alternative plants that produce the same amount of electricity but differ in capital intensity; denote the investment and operating outlays for each by superscripts *1 and *2. Let us further stipulate that the utility's perceived costs for both are identical; then, from equation (4), if the utility is indifferent to the choice between alternatives *1 and *2, we have:

$$\delta PVU = PVU^{*1} - PVU^{*2} \tag{26}$$

$$= (I^{*1} - I^{*2}) \left\{ \frac{\bar{\bar{R}}}{\tilde{r}} - \frac{S(N,\tilde{r})}{N} \left[\frac{\bar{\bar{R}}}{\tilde{r}} - \left(\frac{1}{1-T} \right) \right] - \left(\frac{T}{1-T} \right) d^{\text{tax}}(\tilde{r}) \right\} \tag{27}$$
$$+ (C^{*1} - C^{*2}) S(N, \tilde{r})$$

$$\delta PVU = \delta I \cdot \lambda^{\text{UTIL}} + \delta C \cdot S(N, \tilde{r}) \tag{28}$$

where λ^{UTIL} is the utility's shadow price for capital from equation (8). But if δPVU is zero—if the utility is indifferent—we have:

$$\delta I \cdot \lambda^{\text{UTIL}} = - \delta C \, S(N, \bar{r}) \tag{29}$$

The social opportunity cost (SOC) of each alternative may be expressed in equally compact form:

$$\text{SOC}^i(\rho) = \lambda_0 I^{(i)} + \lambda_1 C^{(i)} \, S(N, \rho) \tag{30}$$

where λ_0 and λ_1 are shadow prices for investment capital and consumption outlays, and ρ is the SRTP. Let us further assume that the shadow prices here are independent of the projects. Then the difference in the social costs of the two projects becomes:

$$\begin{aligned}
\delta \text{SOC} &= \text{SOC}^{*1} - \text{SOC}^{*2} \\
&= \lambda_0 \delta I + \lambda_1 \, S(N, \rho) \delta C
\end{aligned} \tag{31}$$

From the condition that the utility be indifferent between the two choices we have a relationship, equation (29), between the difference in capital costs and the difference in the operating costs. If equation (29) is substituted into equation (31), we obtain the following expression for the deadweight economic loss that would be incurred if the utility were to select the socially more expensive option:

$$\text{Loss} = \lambda_0 \delta C \left\{ \frac{\lambda_1}{\lambda_0} S(N, \rho) - \frac{S(N, \bar{r})}{\lambda^{\text{UTIL}}} \right\} \tag{32}$$

It is useful to divide the loss as given in equation (32) by the cost of one option so that the inefficiency is measured in relative terms. It is also useful to introduce two parameters:

η = the relative operating cost (fuel cost) for the capital nonintensive option, that is, $\eta = \dfrac{C_2}{C_1}$; and

Φ = the ratio of the capital outlay for the capital-intensive option to its annual operating expense.

Then we have:

$$\text{Relative Inefficiency} = \frac{(\eta - 1) \left[\dfrac{\lambda_1}{\lambda_0} S(N, \rho) - \dfrac{S(N, \bar{r})}{\lambda^{\text{UTIL}}} \right]}{\Phi + \dfrac{\lambda_1}{\lambda_0} S(N, \rho)} \tag{33}$$

The relative inefficiency or relative deadweight loss is seen to depend upon two quite distinct sets of parameters. The terms λ_0, λ_1, ρ, $\bar{r}$, and T apply generally throughout the industry or the economy, while K^{*1}, K^{*2}, C^{*1}, C^{*2}, and N are specific to the particular projects.

Certain general properties of the deadweight loss function, equation (33) are to be noted:

1. As the utility's shadow price for capital, λ^{UTIL}, increases, the algebraic value of the loss becomes larger, that is, the utility opts increasingly for fuel-intensive alternatives. From equation (8) we observe that this directional shift can result from—

   a) an *increase* in $\bar{\bar{R}}$, caused either by property and real estate tax liabilities or an increase in the utility's cost of capital;

   b) a *reduction* in the depreciation period allowed by the regulators and used in determining rates, which causes an increase in the carrying charges;

   c) a *reduction* in the rate of depreciation for tax purposes, either through a lengthening of the tax depreciation lifetime or the choice of a slower (less accelerated) tax depreciation schedule.

   Depending upon the starting point, such a shift can offset an initial bias toward capital-intensiveness or worsen an initial bias away from fuel-conserving technologies.

2. An increase in the SRTP reduces the algebraic value of the deadweight loss under most conditions. The sensitivity of the results to the specification of a value for the SRTP, however, depends upon the empirical values of the other parameters and thus will be investigated in the following section.

3. The greater is the disparity in the operating (fuel) costs of the two alternatives (η), the greater is the possible magnitude of the deadweight efficiency loss. The converse is particularly important: the practical significance of these potential losses decreases in such measure as the alternative technologies themselves converge, so that the results depend importantly upon the specific circumstances of each case.

4. The relative magnitude of the loss decreases when Φ, the ratio of capital to annual fuel cost for the capital-intensive alternative, increases. The ratio would be in the range of 3–5 for an oil-fired station and 40–70 for a liquid metal fast breeder reactor.

Analysis of Results

Data and Parameters

To assess the relative efficiency of the investment criteria used by the electric utility industry we must derive empirical estimates of the parameters

Table 11-2. Base Case Parameters

Parameter	Real	Inflation (3%)
Social rate of time preference (SRTP)	0.03	0.06
Return on debt (R^{debt})	0.03	0.06
Return on equity (R^{eq})	0.072	0.102
Rate of disadvantage	0.0378	0.0678
Cost of money	0.0468	0.0768
Capital charge	0.0756	0.1056
Equivalent rate of return on investment in manufacturing industry (debt fraction, 30%)		
1. After-tax	0.0594	0.0894
2. Before-tax	0.1098	0.1398

used in the foregoing theoretical analysis. There are three quite distinct groups among those parameters, differing with respect to their conceptual specification and relative amenability to measurement. The most elusive parameter at this point is the social rate of time preference.

The second set is the pair of coefficients that measure the fraction of the outlays on capital equipment or fuel that substitutes for investment (Θ_0 and Θ_1, respectively). The third set is the array of before- and after-tax rates of return on equity or debt capital; these rates characterize manufacturing industry and the electric utilities in the United States.

We have elsewhere shown that the analysis is invariant with respect to the rate of inflation, provided that the regulatory authorities appropriately adjust the allowable capital charge in setting rates. Our measure of efficiency, therefore, involves only the set of rates of return or discount described above and shown in table 11-2, plus the two displacement coefficients, Θ_0 and Θ_1.

Estimates of historical real rates of return. Measures of the real rates of return within the economy are used to specify both before-tax opportunity cost of capital, r, and the rates of return on debt and equity as used by a utility in computing its carrying charges and its own discount rates. The hierarchical ranking of these several rates of return is quite independent of any measurement of either the SRTP or the displacement coefficients (Θ_0 and Θ_1), so that this set of parameters can be quantified without great difficulty.

The real (inflation-corrected) and nominal values used in the base case calculations are summarized in table 11-2. These estimates are approximate and reflect experience during the period 1952–1970, which we shall take as a proxy for normalcy, disregarding the more recent, post-1970, data on realized rates of return as nonequilibrium. The real after-tax returns on debt and equity capital are approximated as 0.03 and 0.072, respectively. For a utility in which debt constitutes 60 percent of the capital employed, this is equivalent to a weighted-average cost of capital of 0.0468, or a capital charge of 0.0756 (including 50 percent income tax on the before-tax return to equity).

The real before-tax rate of return for manufacturing industry, 0.1098, is consistent with unpublished studies that correct the observed accounting profitability figures for expensed advertising and R&D and other sources of rate-of-return bias. The figure of 0.1098 is exactly equal to the putative rate of return for a firm that realizes the same returns to both debt and equity as the utility but for which debt is 30 percent, rather than 60 percent, of the capital employed.[1]

These figures will be recomputed later; the values shown appear to be approximately correct, and the conclusions reported below would be altered only if the appropriate values were radically different. The debt–equity ratio of 60:40 is somewhat high—55:45 or 50:50 would be more representative.

Three possible discrepancies must, nonetheless, be noted:

1. The costs of debt and equity are independent of capital structure.
2. The returns to capital for utilities and manufacturing firms are uncorrected for risk.
3. The measure of the opportunity cost of investment capital within the economy is the before-tax, real rate of return on investment for manufacturing industry. More appropriate might be the weighted average of the rate of return on investment for manufacturing and the utilities.

Social rate of time preference. We have used a figure of 0.03 for the SRTP. Reflecting a current prejudice toward rather lower values of the SRTP, we chose this value equal to the cost of debt. Implicit in this choice is the notion that the market expression of time preference might be an upper bound for the SRTP.

Displacement coefficients. The results prove to be very sensitive to the estimated values for the two investment displacement coefficients, Θ_0 and Θ_1, which enter into the calculation of the shadow prices for capital and current costs, λ_0 and λ_1, respectively. We assume hereafter that the displacement coefficient for capital outlays, Θ_0, is unity; that is, that each dollar of investment by a utility substitutes for or displaces exactly one dollar of investment elsewhere in the economy.

This assumption must be scrutinized with respect to the institutional framework within which the funds for projects are raised. Nonetheless, except for the case in which projects are financed out of tax revenues, the displacement coefficient for capital outlays financed in commercial capital markets is likely to be close to unity.

---

[1] The approximate share of short- and long-term debt in total capitalization of "All Manufacturing Industry" per the IRS is 30 percent. The value 0.1098 is consistent with the assumed returns to debt and equity capital, exclusive of any risk allowances (M-M effect).

The choice of the displacement coefficient for current costs or costs of fuel is less clear—and thus the estimation of the corresponding social shadow price, λ_1, is more difficult. If we consider alternative technologies, one capital-intensive and the other fuel-intensive, the flows of funds and resources into each are indeed quite different, even if the technologies are otherwise equivalent in that the rates perceived by consumers are the same. Thus, to determine whether the current costs are financed out of savings, we must examine closely how the alternative projects perturb the flows of charges to consumers and payments to capital.

The component flows are as follows:

1. Capital investment: incremental financing.
2. Reflux of dividends, depreciation charges, and interest.
3. Electricity rates paid directly by households or indirectly as embodied in the costs of goods and services.
4. Income or property taxes paid by the utility.

The first we discussed earlier; we now must focus on the latter three. We note that the timing of rates and charges will differ among various alternatives, even if the present values of the rates are identical—that is, even if the utility is financially indifferent to the several alternatives. Since utility rates are related to the net undepreciated capital (or rate base) in each accounting period, the capital-intensive option will exhibit higher electricity rates in the earlier years, while any savings—however real—will be perceived only toward the end of the facility's service life. Compare figures 11-1a and 11-1b below.

The rates [see equation (3) above] contain subcomponents due to interest, income, and depreciation. The interest, plus a fraction of net income, is disbursed annually to the holders of bonds and shares. The shadow price applicable to the subflow is that class of recipients' marginal propensity to save.

Figure 11-1a
FUEL-INTENSIVE

Figure 11-1b
CAPITAL-INTENSIVE

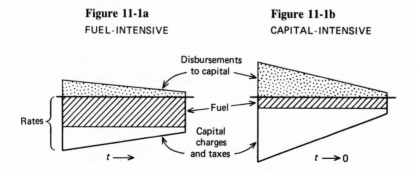

Insofar as retained earnings (including depreciation allowances) are deployed to retire sinking-fund debentures or medium-term debt, they might be viewed as income by the recipients, and only a modest fraction might be saved. However, to the extent that the utility retains cash, its demands on capital markets are commensurately reduced. Retained earnings thus substitute for savings, and the shadow price is appropriately higher.

Electricity rates are paid directly or indirectly by households,[2] and any change in savings resulting from decreased or increased electricity charges will equal the rate difference times the households' marginal propensity to save. Hence the shadow price applicable to electricity rates will involve only the lower rate of saving (investment) characterizing the economy at large.

Finally, the long-run marginal propensity of government entities to invest out of tax receipts can be taken to be quite low, so that the shadow price applicable to the tax component in the electricity rates will be close to that for interest and dividend income, or may even be less, that is, still closer to unity.

Analysis shows that the shadow price applicable to the current costs is that applicable to electricity consumers' marginal rate of saving only if the marginal rate of saving applicable to payments to capital—interest, dividends, retained earnings, and depreciation—equals that for electricity ratepayers. The propensity to save from the tax component is probably less, that for recipients of income from capital may be somewhat higher, while that on retained earnings may be much higher. Retained earnings or cash comprise approximately 20 percent of the total electricity rates, so that this effect might be equivalent to increasing the weighted-average savings rate from about 0.1 to perhaps 0.25. It will be shown below that the conclusions are affected only if the effective rate of saving out of current costs is much higher than 0.1, which we believe to be unlikely, although all these parameters will be reviewed more carefully.

Results

Using the parameters discussed above, plus the assumption that the SRTP equals 3 percent, we have proceeded to compute the efficiency of utility investment decision criteria. Since the results are so sensitive to the investment displacement coefficients, Θ, the calculations were carried out for a high value, $\Theta_1 = 0.9$, implying a low social opportunity cost ($\lambda_1 = 1.182$) for fuel. Calculations are carried out also for Θ_1 equals zero, implying that the social opportunity cost of fuel resources is as great as for capital goods.

---

[2] Government consumption is ignored, and it is further assumed that electricity charges flow through to consumers in the form of higher or lower prices for goods and services.

Table 11-3. Maximum Relative Deadweight Losses: Effects of Various Utility Decision Functions

		Fraction of operating costs that displaces investment	
		0.1	1.0
		($\Theta_1 = 0.9$)	($\Theta_1 = $ zero)
		(percentage)	
Tax-exempt utilities			
Designated cost of capital	0.03	105	0
	0.05	29	(21)
	0.08	(4)	(42)
	0.11	(30)	(55)
Taxpaying utilities			
No property taxes			
Discount rate:			
Rate of disadvantage	0.0378	17	(28)
Cost of capital	0.0468	17	(27)
Property tax @ 2.5%			
Discount rate:			
Rate of disadvantage		(1)	(40)
Cost of capital		(1)	(40)

Note: Numbers in parentheses are negative values.

Additionally, the analysis was carried out for two classes of utilities: public utilities, exempted from income and real property taxes, and private utilities, which are liable for both income and property taxes.

Case one: Tax-exempt utilities. In the case of municipal or federally owned utilities, or rural cooperatives, the question of capital structure is less important than in the case of investor-owned utilities, since most, if not all, are effectively financed with debt. We have assumed that such utilities determine their rates using their own cost of money in the capital charge and also use that same value to compute present values of alternatives in their investment decisions.

If the tax-exempt utility uses its own borrowing cost of 3 percent (real) in project evaluation, it would elect extremely capital-intensive options, compared with the socially efficient choice, for the case in which Θ equals 0.9. The social cost of the option preferred by the public utility could be twice the socially efficient value, that is, a deadweight loss of 105 percent (see table 11-3). The tax-exempt utility does indeed exhibit the Averch–Johnson phenomenon.

If the tax-exempt public utility were obligated to use a higher real discount rate in its project assessments, the bias could be reduced. At a real rate of 5 percent, two percentage points over the utility's borrowing cost, the efficiency loss is down to 29 percent. If the enforced rate of discount is raised to 8 percent, the efficiency loss is a negligible 4 percent, but the Averch–Johnson effect is reversed. At that discount rate the public utility no longer opts for a capital-intensive alternative but, instead, selects the fuel-intensive option that proves to be socially the more expensive. We note that social costs are higher if the preferred option is more capital-intensive or if it is more fuel-intensive than the optimum.

On the other hand, if the propensity to save out of reduced fuel costs is unity, the public utility's choice indeed coincides with the socially efficient choice, and there is no loss. For this case, if the displacement coefficient is so high, raising the rate of discount employed by the public utility would only force it to select increasingly inefficient fuel-intensive alternatives.

Our evaluation of public utility performance is obviously quite sensitive to specification of the marginal propensity to save out of reduced electric utility costs. A further effect must be mentioned, even though we cannot pursue the consequences. The electricity rates set by the public utility can be significantly lower than those for the taxpaying utility, since income taxes loom large in the structure of rates under most circumstances. A more comprehensive analysis should include any consumers' surplus associated with higher electricity consumption, duly recognizing the efficiency loss or subsidy implicit in the lower opportunity cost of capital perceived by the public utility.

Case two: Tax-paying utilities. We have differentiated these cases with respect to three sets of considerations:

1. Estimated marginal rate of savings from current costs: low versus high assumed rates, $(1 - \Theta) = 0.1$ and 1.0, respectively.
2. The utility's discount rate: the weighted average cost of capital versus the rate of disadvantage, which is the cost of capital corrected for the tax-deductibility of the interest component.
3. Property taxes levied on the land and equipment: zero versus a rate of 2.5 percent charged on the net depreciated value of fixed assets.

Since the local taxes seem to range between an annual charge of 2 and 4 percent of asset valuation, the result in which the utility is subject to property taxes seems most relevant and will be discussed first.

The incidence of the property tax has been approximated by assuming an annual charge of 2.5 percent of the gross cost of the plant, net of accumulated depreciation, reckoned against the beginning-of-year figure. More precisely, different rates of local taxation apply to the assessed value of land and to the gross or net historical values of various categories of plant and equipment. The figure chosen is sufficiently representative for our present purpose.

Table 11-4. Efficiency Losses—Investor-Owned Utility

(percentage)*

SRTP	No property taxes	Property taxes = 2.5%
0.03	42	−3
0.04	60	5
0.06	108	22

* Other assumptions: $\eta = 5$; $\Phi = 20$; sum-of-the-years' digits (SYD) tax depreciation with a tax lifetime of 24 years (80 percent of 30 years).

It makes little difference whether the utility uses its cost of capital or its rate of disadvantage in evaluating projects. It does make a considerable difference, however, whether the utility is subject to property taxes. The taxpaying, private utility that pays income taxes but pays no property taxes exhibits a quite weak Averch–Johnson effect, being inclined to select somewhat more capital-intensive options and thereby incurring an efficiency loss of 17 percent (see table 11-3). If a property tax of 2.5 percent is levied, as discussed above, the utility's choice quite fortuitously is almost identical to the socially efficient choice, and the deadweight loss is only 1 percent. That choice is slightly more fuel-intensive than the social optimum, which is the opposite of the Averch–Johnson conclusion, although the effect here is negligible.

If the value of the reinvestment or displacement coefficient, Θ_1, is zero, the results are quite different. In the absence of property taxes, the private utility will choose the capital-nonintensive option, thereby incurring additional social costs of about 28 percent. If the utility does pay property taxes as well as income taxes, its decision is biased even more markedly toward the fuel-intensive option and away from the Averch–Johnson response, and the efficiency loss in that case is 40 percent. For the reasons advanced earlier, we believe that $1 - \Theta_1$ is more likely to be low, less than 0.25 and closer to 0.1, but the criticality of this parameter must again be emphasized.

The numerical results are only weakly dependent upon the assumed value for the SRTP, and the conclusions are unaffected. Table 11-4 shows the calculated deadweight losses for values of the SRTP between 0.03 and 0.06 for the two cases—zero property tax and a rate of 2.5 percent levied on net fixed assets.

In the empirically uninteresting case in which the (investor-owned) utility pays income taxes but no property taxes, the estimated deadweight loss increases proportionately with the SRTP. In the much more important case in which estimated real estate and property taxes are set equal to 2.5 percent, we find that doubling the SRTP increases the calculated efficiency

**Table 11-5.   Tax Depreciation and Efficiency
Losses—Investor-Owned Utility**
(percentage)*

Tax depreciation schedule	No property taxes	Property taxes = 2.5%
SYD: 15 yrs	80	7
SYD: 24 yrs	42	−3
SYD: 30 yrs	28	−8

* Other assumptions: $\eta = 5$; $\Phi = 20$; SRTP = 3 percent.

loss from −3 percent to +22 percent. Even if the SRTP is as high as 6 percent, we find only a weak preference by the taxpaying utility for capital-intensive alternatives.

The utility's investment evaluation procedure is dominated by the regulatory rules imposed by state and local authorities, but the federal government controls income tax depreciation rules as a policy variable. In table 11-5 the effects of three different tax depreciation rules are shown.

In the absence of local property taxes, the potential efficiency loss depends strongly upon the federal tax depreciation schedule; the more rapid the depreciation, the more pronounced the utility's bias toward capital-intensive alternatives and the greater the loss. If property taxes are levied, the effect of different tax depreciation rates is very much dampened, although accelerating tax depreciation from 30 to 15 years does, at least directionally, offset a basic bias toward fuel-intensive options.

Conclusions

Our essential conclusion is that taxpaying utilities are most likely to be biased against capital-intensive alternatives, quite in contrast to the Averch–Johnson hypothesis, although over a broad range of conditions the utility decision function is efficient.

More precisely, the decision function of the taxpaying utility is essentially congruent with the social criterion; the decision function minimizes the present value of electricity rates, and the social criterion minimizes the present value of social costs, measured as the present discounted values of the consumption benefit streams that would have been generated if equivalent resources had been deployed elsewhere within the economy.

Although the two criteria involve conceptually different discount rates and structurally different objective functions, it appears that the two decision criteria for project evaluation are broadly consonant over the relevant range of the parameters. This consonance arises from an unconscious parallelism in the formulation of the two criteria. The social criterion involves the defining of a shadow price for investment resources that is greater than unity and that multiplies the capital outlays, thereby weighting them more heavily in the definition of social cost. The utility does not follow the industrial practice of discounting the capital expenditures; rather, it computes the present value of the annualized charges, including income taxes, that would enter into the rates charged to and collected from its consumers. Because these annualized charges include income and property taxes, whereas the discount rate is less than or at most equal to the after-tax return on capital, the present value of this stream of charges is greater than unity. That term enters into the utility's cost function as a factor multiplying the capital outlay, so that this procedure is formally equivalent to defining a shadow price for capital goods.

Thus, qualitatively, the empirical conclusion that the utilities' decision criteria are essentially congruent with the social criteria is equivalent to the observation that the shadow price for capital investment as perceived by society is approximately equal to the shadow price used by utilities, albeit implicitly. The congruence is only empirical, since the results are specific to the estimated parameters. The two criteria do indeed diverge for other values of the parameters. If, for example, one can assume that households reinvest a large fraction of any reduction in electricity rates, the results are quite different.

Otherwise, for the range of parameters that appear to be relevant, the agreement is surprisingly good—indeed, it is certainly within the accuracy intrinsic in the measurement of the parameters and the projections of costs over the expected service lifetimes of the alternative energy projects.

Any disparities that might arise are the opposite of the conventional argument based upon the earlier work of Averch and Johnson. Far from being inclined toward excessive capital investment, it appears the taxpaying utilities are more likely to underinvest and prefer fuel-intensive, rather than capital-intensive alternatives. This inclination is exacerbated by two effects that have not been included in the idealized analysis above:

1. Many taxpaying utilities systematically truncate the periods over which they evaluate projects, computing the costs over a period significantly shorter than the expected lifetime.

   This practice, intended to induce conservatism in project selection, understates the present value of the costs for capital-nonintensive projects and thus biases the choice toward such alternatives.

2. Utilities are also disposed to prefer more rapid depreciation schedules, which increase present values of the capital charges and therefore increase the apparent cost of the more capital-intensive option and thus bias the choice toward a less capital-intensive alternative.[3]

---

[3] In industrial project evaluation, "liberal" depreciation is normally an incentive for investment; there it increases the present value of the tax shield, thereby reducing the net corporate cost of the outlay. Here, in the case of a regulated utility, the effect is perverse because book depreciation charges enter into the utility's perceived costs and increase its shadow price.

If we allow for such modifications to the normative decision function, the utility's choices are shifted, and we could conclude that the taxpaying utilities' decision function is biased, but, if so, the nature and direction of that bias is quite the opposite of the Averch–Johnson effect.

Finally, we note that any tax-exempt status of the public utilities leads to their using artificially low costs of capital, which lead in turn to low implicit shadow prices and thus to excessive capital investment and high social costs. Only in this special subset of cases—the tax-exempt electric utilities—have we established that a significant incongruity exists, and for those cases one observes a distinct bias toward capital-intensive options.

Summary

Utility Decision Criteria

Electric utilities' project evaluation procedures differ from the rules that obtain elsewhere in the private sector in several important respects:

1. The capital outlay is translated into a stream of annual charges. The stream is then discounted, rather than the capital outlays themselves.
2. The stream of charges—the costs recognized by the utility as associated with the capital outlay—include income taxes, in contrast to the industrial procedure which evaluates after-tax receipts.
3. The discount rate is related to the utility's after-tax, target rate of return, even though part of the stream of charges being evaluated includes income or even property taxes.

These structural idiosyncrasies are related to the fact that utilities are not price takers; their revenues are prescribed by the regulators as a function of their costs as related to a presumptive level of output.

The utility assesses the cost of a project as the present value of the sum of operating costs, such as labor and fuel and the stream of carrying charges associated with the capital expenditure. The annual charges are:

$$\text{Cost}_t^{\text{UTIL}} = C + I_0 \left\{ \frac{1}{N(1-T)} + \bar{\bar{R}} \left[1 - \left(\frac{t-1}{N} \right) \right] - \left(\frac{T}{1-T} \right) D_t^{\text{tax}} \right\}$$

Within the bracketed term are components reflecting, respectively, the depreciation charge, the return allowed on the declining, unamortized asset balance, and the effect of the tax shield as a result of the depreciation schedule—D_t^{tax}. The present value of that stream of charges is:

$$\mathscr{L}[\text{Cost}^{\text{UTIL}}] = K\lambda^{\text{UTIL}} + CS(N, \bar{\bar{R}})$$

where: $\lambda^{\text{UTIL}} = \dfrac{S(N,\bar{r})}{(1-T)N} + \dfrac{\bar{\bar{R}}}{\bar{r}}\left\{1 - \dfrac{S(N,\bar{r})}{N}\right\} - \left(\dfrac{T}{1-T}\right)d^{tax}(\bar{r})$

The present value of the capital outlay, I, is multiplied by λ^{UTIL}, an implicit shadow price, where $\lambda > 1.0$.

Social Criterion

The social opportunity cost of resources is measured by the consumption stream generated if those resources were spent elsewhere in the economy, allowing for the after-tax returns to capital and the different rates of saving (investment) in different sectors of the economy.

We define a generalized shadow price as the present value of the stream of net consumption, discounted at the social rate of time preference (SRTP), arising from one dollar spent today. If one allows for the different fractions saved or consumed from the initial outlay and subsequent benefits, the shadow price is:

$$\lambda = (1 - \pi)\left\{\frac{\Theta + (1 - \Theta)k(\rho)}{1 - \pi k(\rho)}\right\}$$

This shadow price includes benefit streams over time, $K(t)$, and is a function of the fraction invested out of the initial dollar, $1 - \Theta$, as well as the fraction of benefits that is reinvested, π.

The discounted social consumption equivalent (DSCE), or social opportunity cost (SOC), for an arbitrary system of outlays over time is the product of the above shadow price and the present value of the outlays by virtue of the Separability theorem:

$$\text{SOC} = \lambda \cdot i(\text{SRTP}) = \lambda \cdot \text{PV(Outlays)}\Big|_{\text{SRTP}}$$

That social opportunity cost is equal to the product of two separate factors—the shadow price, which involves the opportunity cost of capital, and the present value of the expenditure stream, which depends only upon the SRTP.

Comparison of Utility and Social Criteria

We test the social efficiency of the utility criterion by measuring the social opportunity costs of pairs of alternative projects to which the utility is indifferent—pairs of fuel-intensive versus capital-intensive options that show equal costs under the utility's calculus.

The social opportunity costs of the options generally differ from the utility costs, and the relative potential deadweight loss is:

$$\frac{\left(\dfrac{C_2}{C_1} - 1\right)\left[\dfrac{\lambda_1}{\lambda_0} S(N,\text{SRTP}) - \dfrac{S(N,r^{\text{UTIL}})}{\lambda^{\text{UTIL}}}\right]}{\dfrac{I_1}{C_1} + \dfrac{\lambda_1}{\lambda_0} S(N,\text{SRTP})}$$

If the expression is positive, the utility's project-evaluation criterion permits it to select options that are capital-intensive compared with the social measure, and conversely.

Results

Most of the parameters—rates of return, tax rates, and so forth—are readily measurable, but two parameters are both elusive and critical: the SRTP and the marginal propensity to invest. The results will be shown for two different values of each, spanning the likely range.

The results differ markedly, depending upon whether the electric utility is subject to taxation. Again, two limiting cases have been chosen: (1) municipal utility, exempt from both property tax and income tax; and (2) an investor-owned utility, subject to both.

We have calculated the potential deadweight losses if each class of utility were to optimize its choice of technology according to its own objective function.

Maximum Deadweight Losses
(relative to socially optimal case)

	$\Theta = 0.9$	$\Theta = 0.1$
Tax-exempt utility	105%	Zero
Taxpaying utility	-1%	-40%

It is most probable that $0.80 < \Theta_1 < 0.95$, from which we conclude tentatively that the investor-owned utility will choose technologies that are essentially congruent (an efficiency loss of 1 percent) with the socially optimal criterion. The tax-exempt utility, however, exhibits the Averch–Johnson phenomenon, reflecting its low perceived cost of capital, and invests in markedly capital-intensive options. The tax-exempt utility potential would incur costs twice the optimum (deadweight loss equal to 105 percent) of the minimum.

The results are not highly sensitive to most of the assumptions, but three assumptions are critical. These are:

1. If a large fraction of fuel savings is reinvested, that is, $\Theta_1 \to 0$, the tax-exempt utility approaches the social optimum and the investor-owned utility incurs efficiency losses because of excessive fuel-intensiveness.

2. Investor-owned utilities use accelerated depreciation (shorter plant lives) and truncated cost streams in their project analyses, which bias their choices away from capital and toward fuel. This effect has not been included.

3. The results are remarkably insensitive to the actual value of the SRTP, but this has not been tested for all combinations of parameters.

Appendix

Derivation of the Shadow Price (Social Consumption Equivalent) of Energy Project Resources

We shall derive here two results that greatly facilitate the analysis in the main body of this paper:

1. Measures of the shadow price of project resources, that is, the social opportunity cost of the resources used or saved. This measure is denominated in terms of the equivalent consumption forgone if resources are used or of the equivalent consumption made possible through the realization of real savings.

2. A general theorem that the discounted consumption equivalent cost of an arbitrary stream of resources equals the product of the shadow price, defined above, and the discounted value of the investment stream itself (Separability theorem).

These two results permit a particularly compact formulation of the two analytical results as well as a direct exhibition of the key parameters that enter into the assessment of the policy issues.

Let us first determine the present value of the stream of consumption that is forgone by the diversion of one dollar at time t = zero. Let us assume that part of the dollar might have been consumed and that the remainder might have been invested. The related stream of net consumption benefits comprises several components:

1. A fraction of the initial expenditure is assumed to have been consumed directly (Θ) and thus contributes only to the initial period of the stream of consumption benefits.

2. The remaining fraction of that initial outlay $(1 - \Theta)$ is invested and yields a stream of primary benefits equal to:

$$(1 - \Theta)K(t;r) \tag{A-1}$$

where $K(t;r)$ is the time stream of net benefits generated within the economy by a one-dollar investment yielding the economy-wide pretax rate of return r.

3. Some fraction π of all the gross benefits in each year will be reinvested, thereby generating a further stream of benefits.

If we denote the total stream of gross benefits by $G(t;0)$, we obtain the following integral equation:

$$\tilde{G}(t;0) = \Theta\delta(t) + (1 - \Theta)K(t;r) + \pi\int_0^t \tilde{G}(t - \tau;0)K(\tau,r)d\tau \tag{A-2}$$

δ = Dirac delta function

The first term on the right is that due to the initial consumption of Θ dollars. The second is the stream of primary consumption benefits arising from the investment of $(1 - \Theta)$ dollars at t = zero, and the third term is the sum of all benefits generated by the reinvestment of the fraction π of the benefit streams.

No general solution to this integral equation for $G(t;0)$ exists for arbitrary forms of $K(t)$; however, we can obtain the present discounted value of $G(t;0)$ by taking the Laplace or z-transform of both sides of equation (A-2), noting that the last term on the right is a convolution integral:

$$\tilde{g}(s;0) = \Theta + (1 - \Theta)k(s) + \pi\tilde{g}(s;0)k(s) \tag{A-3}$$

Upon regrouping and multiplying through by $(1 - \pi)$—the fraction of gross benefits that is consumed (net of reinvestment)—we obtain an expression for the present discounted value of the net consumption stream:

$$g(s;0) = (1 - \pi) \left\{ \frac{\Theta + (1 - \Theta)k(s)}{1 - \pi k(s)} \right\} \tag{A-4}$$

More generally, if the one-dollar expenditure is not made at $t = $ zero but at some arbitrary point in time, τ, we find:*

$$g(s;\tau) = (1 + s)^{-\tau} g(s;0)$$

The stream of net benefits, $(1 - \pi)G(t;\tau)$ is the consumption equivalent of a unit expenditure made at time $t = \tau$, allowing for substitution between investment and consumption (Θ) and for reinvestment of a fraction π of gross benefits. If $G(t;\tau)$ is discounted at the social rate of time preference (SRTP), or ρ in our present notation, we obtain the discounted social consumption equivalent (DSCE) of that same outlay:

$$\text{DSCE} = \lambda(\tau) = (1 - \pi) \left\{ \frac{\Theta + (1 - \Theta)k(\rho)}{1 - \pi k(\rho)} \right\} (1 + \rho)^{-\tau} \tag{A-5}$$

This admits of two equivalent economic interpretations. Let a dollar be withdrawn from consumers (investors) at time τ; if Θ of that dollar would have been consumed and $(1 - \Theta)$ would have been invested, then $\lambda(\tau)$ is the present value of the net consumption stream that would have resulted if the dollar had been expended in the economy in its original use. Thus, λ represents the social opportunity cost (SOC) of one dollar at time τ.

Alternatively, λ represents the discounted value (at a rate equal to SRTP) of the net consumption streams that would have been generated if one dollar's worth of additional resources were made available to the economy at $t = \tau$. In both cases Θ describes the split between investment and current consumption for the dollar that is either conserved or expended, and we have the following theorem:

The shadow price, or social opportunity cost, or discounted social consumption equivalent, of a unit expenditure made at $t = \tau$ equals:

$$\lambda(\tau) = (1 + \rho)^{-\tau} \left\{ \frac{\Theta + (1 - \Theta)k(\rho)}{1 - \pi k(\rho)} \right\} (1 - \pi) \tag{A-6}$$

---

* For the continuous case, $(1 + s)^{-\tau}$ must be replaced by $e^{-s\tau}$.

where $(1 - \Theta)$ is the fraction of the initial dollar that is invested, π is the fraction of gross benefits reinvested, r is the long-run marginal pretax return on capital in the economy, and $K(t)$ is the weighted-average time pattern of pretax benefits thrown off by a unit investment in the economy. All of the above parameters and $K(t)$ are presumed to be invariant over time and independent of the level of investment.

The magnitude of the shadow price, or DSCE, depends intimately upon the actual values of the parameters and also, to a lesser extent, upon the form of the cash flow profile $K(t)$. Empirical estimates are discussed in the main text in the section on social opportunity costs.

. More generally, we are interested in evaluating the social opportunity cost of some arbitrary time stream of expenditures, $Y(t)$, where it is to be measured as the DSCE, after allowing for any reinvestments and discounting the stream of net benefits at the social rate of time preference.

But $G(t,\tau)$, as defined in equation (A-1), represents the stream of net benefits from a dollar (consumption plus investment) expended at time τ for all subsequent years ($t \geq \tau$). If we assume that π, Θ, ρ, and $K(t)$ are invariant—a stationary process—we can use the principle of linear super-position and assert that the net benefit stream associated with $Y(t)$ is:

$$B(t) = \int_0^t Y(\tau)G(t - \tau)d\tau \tag{A-7}$$

The present value of the net benefits, discounted at the SRTP, is:

$$b(\rho) = y(\rho)g(\rho) = y(\rho)\lambda \tag{A-8}$$

using once more the facts that equation (A-7) is a convolution integral and that the z-transform (Laplace transform) of a convolution equals the product of the z-transforms of the two integrands. This proves the Separability theorem:

> The present value of the net consumption benefits generated by an arbitrary stream of expenditures, $Y(t)$, equals the product of the present value of the expenditures, discounted at the SRTP, and the shadow price for resources, provided the processes are stationary.

This general result has several consequences:

1. Even though the benefit streams generated by alternative investments can rarely, if ever, be solved explicitly, we can measure opportunity costs as long as we know the rate of return and the approximate shape of the cash flow profile.

2. In the section on efficiency losses, where the utility capital investment was assumed to be a point function, the results can immediately be generalized to the more realistic case where outlays are spread over time, and the conclusions remain unaltered.

3. The calculation of costs and benefits can be separated into two distinct pieces; a) the analysis of the expenditure patterns, which are specific to the projects; and b) the shadow price, λ, which is independent of the given projects and relates to the economy as a whole.

The Separability theorem holds as well in the more general case where the values of Θ, the displacement coefficient, are specific to the project, or even where different values of Θ apply to different categories of expenditure, provided only that the coefficients are time-invariant.

Reference

Averch, H., and L. L. Johnson. 1962. "The Behavior of the Firm Under Regulatory Constraint," *American Economic Review* (December) pp. 1052–1069.

12

Robert C. Lind

The Rate of Discount and the Application of Social Benefit–Cost Analysis in the Context of Energy Policy Decisions

Introduction

This chapter sets forth practical procedures for applying to energy policy decisions the conceptual framework developed in chapter 2 for social benefit–cost analyses. Although much of the discussion is specific to energy policies and energy investments, the methodology and the procedures for implementing it could be applied to the analysis of any public policy or investment. In developing these procedures, and in fact in developing the entire methodological framework, I have constantly been aware of the need for simplicity.

Clearly, the simplest procedure would be to specify a single rate that could be used for discounting all public investments and would accurately reflect the opportunity cost of high-return, private investments that are displaced, the social rate of time preference, and differences in risk. For reasons that have been discussed, I believe that there is no single rate that satisfies all of these requirements for all projects. To arrive at the appropriate social evaluation of different projects, the present value of their benefits and costs would have to be evaluated using different rates of discount, depending on the nature of the financing and the nature and distribution of the costs and the benefits. Add to this the differences in riskiness, and the inescapable conclusion is that the appropriate rate of discount is project specific and depends upon a multitude of factors relating to the structure of the economy, the nature of the market imperfections, the behavior of government, and the nature of the benefits and costs themselves.

The approach I have adopted does not account for all of the effects of a public investment. Rather, it separates the question of time preference from the displacement or stimulation of private capital formation and attempts to

443

account for effects on private capital formation by using the appropriate shadow price for capital. Risk can be treated by adjusting benefits and costs or by adjusting the discount rate to produce approximately correct results when used in benefit–cost analysis. However, I will argue that, in the analysis of energy investments, a rate between the risk-free rate and the rate for the market portfolio should be used because the returns to energy investments appear to be less than perfectly correlated with the market portfolio and perhaps this correlation is even zero or negative. A negative correlation would justify using a rate below the risk-free rate.

The methodology adopted in this chapter explicitly focuses on the direct effects of public investment on private capital formation. It does not capture all of the other effects of increasing or decreasing the distortions in the economy and, therefore, does not capture all of the effects that would be captured by the series of models developed by Stiglitz in his paper for this volume. It does not capture all of the incentives and disincentives resulting from the higher or lower taxes associated with higher or lower federal budgets; these incentive or disincentive effects have been the focus of much of the debate over a major cut in federal taxes.

Rather, this approach takes as given the underlying structure of the economy, particularly the tax structure. It estimates the total effects of a public policy or project on streams of consumption and then applies the social rate of time preference as the discount rate. To do this we adjust benefits and costs that affect private capital formation and assign to them a value using the shadow price of capital. In this way the benefits and cost streams are converted to their consumption equivalents and can be discounted at the social rate. I have taken the position that the social rate should be the consumption rate of interest as measured by the after-tax rates of return based on market securities that are available to investors. In the case of energy investments, we use a rate that is between the after-tax expected rate of return on a safe asset and the after-tax expected rate of return on the market portfolio. At the same time, if one believes that the social rate of time preference should be determined politically, then whatever that rate is determined to be, this methodology would still apply if the social rate of time preference differs from the marginal rate of return on private investment.

This explicit focus of the analysis of the effects of public investments or policies on private capital formation is consistent with much of the earlier analysis that attempted to account for capital displacement by requiring that public investments earn the same rate of return as private investments or used a weighted average of the rate of return on private investment and the consumption rate of interest to reflect the fact that some of the costs of a public investment come at the expense of private investment and some at the expense of private consumption. The problem with the first approach is that it perpetuates the distortions in the private sector of the economy that cause a bias against investment in general, and against long-lived investments in particular, in the evaluation of public policy decisions.

The problem with the second approach is that we do not know how to determine the appropriate weights and in some cases the appropriate rate may lie outside of the interval determined by the consumption rate of interest and the rate of return on private investment. Moreover, the appropriate weights may well differ from project to project.

A great advantage of analyzing explicitly the impact of a public policy or investment on capital formation is that one has to consider how the investment is financed, who pays the costs and receives the benefits, and what form the benefits and costs take; for example, do benefits accrue as taxable income to individuals or as direct services to individuals which are a substitute for other consumption expenditures. All of these factors are important in determining the impact of a public policy or investment on private capital formation.

It should be emphasized that the methodology and procedures adopted here are clearly those for evaluating public policies and investments in an economy with significant market distortions, that is, in a second-best world. In this case a primary cause of these distortions is the corporate income tax and the personal income tax. Another possible contributing factor is that the managers of private firms may use a higher discount rate in evaluating projects because of their perception and attitude toward risk and because their time horizon may not be the same as that of a well-diversified stockholder. Whatever the reasons and their relative importance, the indisputable fact is that the before-tax rate of return on private investments is more than twice the after-tax rate of return that an investor has been able to earn on stocks, which are the claims through which a diversified investor can own a part of those projects, or on bonds, which were issued to finance a part of the cost of these projects. As a result there will be too little saving in the economy; perhaps as important in the case of energy policy, investment decisions will be biased against long-term capital projects with high returns well into the future. The use of the procedure adopted here corrects for this bias in public investment and policy decisions, while taking into account that these policies and projects will have effects on high-yield private investments.

Another advantage of this approach is that it focuses attention on the fact that public consumption expenditures as well as private investment expenditures influence private capital formation. To the extent that these public consumption expenditures are financed by increased taxes or increased debt, they displace private capital in just the same way as public investment. In many cases their benefits may not stimulate private investment in the same way as a public investment would. Therefore, in computing the true social opportunity cost of public expenditures, we must, generally, scale them up to reflect their negative impact on private capital formation.

Using a rate of discount above the social rate of time preference to account for the displacement of private capital distorts the decision process against public investments as compared with public consumption expenditures such as pure transfers of income. For example, it will make a program of pure income transfers incorrectly appear more desirable than a public investment in human capital through education because (1) it will neglect the true opportunity cost of the transfer, (2) it will inadequately reflect the fact that the future income generated from the investment in human capital is worth more than its dollar value because part of it will flow into increased savings and investment, and (3) it will overstate the rate of time preference, thereby undervaluing future costs and benefits relative to present ones.

Throughout this volume there has been repeated reference to the evaluation of public policies and investments or public policies and projects. The reason for this is that most public sector decisions involve investment in the private sector as well, and in many cases the preponderance of the benefits and the costs may fall on the private sector. In some cases there may be no strictly public investment or public project involved. While this is true in all fields, it is especially true of the production and use of energy. Government policies to require conversion of power plants to the use of coal, to require automobile manufacturers to make cars more energy efficient, and to set thermal efficiency standards for buildings all have the property that, except for the administrative costs of monitoring and enforcing these standards, most of the investment involved will be in the private sector. In fact, there may not be an identifiable public capital project involved.

Therefore, for energy policy analysis, we need a conceptual framework for social benefit–cost analysis and a procedure for implementing it. This procedure must be applicable to the analysis of benefits and costs that accrue to the private sector and, in particular, be able to account for the effects of these costs and benefits on private capital formation. A requirement that firms convert facilities to coal has implications for private investment and for the level of private investment in other activities. This must be appropriately accounted for in the social benefit–cost analysis of this policy option. Further, a procedure for doing this must be simple enough that it can be implemented. Most of the remainder of this chapter addresses the development of such a procedure.

The approach is to categorize benefits and costs according to who pays them or receives them, what form they take and, in the case of costs, how they are financed, and then to analyze their effect on private capital formation. Benefits and costs are then adjusted to their consumption equivalent using the shadow price of capital. The next section of this paper presents the assumptions and the parameter values that are used in this approach. The following two sections develop the appropriate shadow prices, or multipliers, for different categories of costs and benefits. They are followed by a section that provides a systhesis of this approach and comments upon the results.

The final section of the paper returns to the question of whether benefit–cost analysis as a methodology is sufficiently robust to be of use in deciding issues of intergenerational equity, such as those issues associated with the disposal of nuclear waste or with failing to undertake the research and development that will provide a clean source of energy for future generations at reasonable cost. We conclude that use of the appropriate social benefit–cost calculus will go a long way toward correcting, at least as far as public policy decisions are concerned, the distortions that bias private economic decisions in favor of consumption and against investment, particularly investments with long-run payoffs. These distortions are caused largely by government itself through the tax system and bias economic decisions against future generations. I will argue that, for practical as well as philosophical reasons, we cannot look to benefit–cost analysis alone if we are discussing present decisions about policies that may have catastrophic effects on future generations.

Framework of Analysis, Assumptions, and Parameter Values

I adopt the framework of analysis developed in chapter 2. On the basis of this analysis, I assume for purposes of this discussion that the shadow price of capital is 3.8. Again for purposes of this discussion, I assume that the marginal propensity to save out of disposable income is 0.2 and that the average marginal personal income tax rate is 20 percent and the marginal corporate income tax rate is 50 percent. Although I believe these numbers are realistic approximations, the framework of analysis and the procedures that will be developed for applying benefit–cost analysis in no way depend on these specific numbers.

In addition I believe that in most cases it will be extremely difficult to estimate the probability of benefits and costs over time and measure the covariance of the net benefits of a public policy or project with the market portfolio. Therefore, except in special cases it will be difficult to make precise adjustments in the expected value of benefits and costs to reflect the cost of risk. Similarly, it will be difficult to make fine adjustments in the discount rate even if a defensible procedure for making such adjustments is developed. As a practical alternative, I suggest that the best assumption is that returns to most government policies or projects are highly correlated with returns in the economy as a whole, unless there is a clear argument to the contrary. As a first approximation, the social rate of discount applied to such benefits and costs may be assumed to be the real after-tax rate of return on the market portfolio; I have argued that that rate is about 4.6 percent. For all the reasons set out in chapter 2, this is not a perfect procedure, but for most projects and policies, it is probably as good an approximation as can be achieved.

A strong argument can be made for using a lower rate than this approximation for certain policies and projects, such as energy investments. There are two reasons why energy investments should be discounted at a lower rate. The first is the argument that has been discussed, namely, that the return to energy investments—whether they are investments in the production of primary energy such as oil, gas, and nuclear power or investments in research and development in fusion, the breeder, synfuels, and so forth—will be negatively correlated with returns to other investments when energy prices rise. At the same time the returns to energy investments will move with the returns to the economy as a whole in those cases in which fluctuations in the level of economic activity are unrelated to movement in energy prices. On the basis of this observation and the importance of energy price shocks in our modern economy, one can tentatively conclude that the correlation between the returns to energy investments generally and those to the economy as a whole is less than one and perhaps even zero or negative. From this it follows that a rate lower than 4.6 percent would be appropriate for discounting benefits and costs.

A second reason that a lower rate would be appropriate is that energy investments generally are long lived in the sense that these benefits and costs continue to accrue many years into the future. The 4.6 percent real after-tax rate of return on the market portfolio is approximately the correct risk-adjusted rate for the average investment. As was discussed in chapter 2, however, the beta coefficient, or adjustment for risk in the discount rate, should be lower for long-lived projects than for the average project.

Because energy investments will vary in their riskiness and the degree to which they provide insurance, more analysis of this issue is clearly needed. Research and development projects may well have a greater insurance value than, say, investments in marginal oil wells. The point is that we need to think through much more carefully the insurance aspects of energy policies and programs as well as the value of information provided by the early resolution of uncertainty.

For purposes of this discussion I will assume that the real rate of discount appropriate for energy policy analysis is 3 percent. This is less than the 4.6 percent market rate and greater than the 2.0 percent rate on long-term government bonds.

The next major assumption for purposes of this discussion is that an increase in federal expenditure financed by general revenue or a decrease in federal revenues results in an increase in the federal debt. The justification for this position is set forth in chapter 2. A companion assumption, which is perhaps more controversial, is that increases in the government debt crowd out private investment dollar for dollar. This assumption and the conditions under which it holds are also discussed in chapter 2. Both of these assumptions can be modified without invalidating the general approach because, whether we believe that the marginal dollar of expenditure is financed by debt or by increased taxes or a combination of the two, and whether debt displaces investment at the time the debt is incurred on a one-to-one basis or by more or less than that, these relationships will hold for all expenditures. Once the appropriate assumptions have been established, the methodology is straight-forward. It is possible, however, that the appropriate assumptions will change over time with the state of the economy. These ideas will be illustrated with a number of examples.

My approach will be to trace the effects of a public investment on government revenues and expenses and ultimately on the level of the deficit and therefore on private investment. I will also trace the effects on the savings and investment decisions of individual firms and households. Then each benefit and cost in each of a number of categories is multiplied by the appropriate shadow price or multiplier to account for the total effect on consumption. Benefits and costs, so adjusted, are then discounted to their present value—a real rate of discount of 4.6 percent for the typical government project but 3 percent for energy investments.

Categories of Costs and Their Respective Shadow Prices

Costs that result from public policies or projects take a number of forms, affect institutions and individuals differently, and receive different tax treatment. These considerations turn out to have a critical impact on the benefits and costs of different policies and projects.

First, consider a public investment project for which all the costs are financed out of general federal revenues. Then under the assumptions we make here, this will increase the debt by an equal amount. The result is that private investment equal to the cost of the public investment will be displaced. If the shadow price of capital is 3.8, the project costs that are financed out of general federal revenues should be multiplied by 3.8.

Alternatively, we could have assumed that the marginal public expenditure would be funded by increased personal income taxes. If the marginal propensity to save is 0.2, 20 percent of the cost would be at the expense of private savings and investment, and 80 percent at the expense of private consumption. In this case the appropriate multiplier, or shadow price, for costs paid out of general revenues is $0.8 + (0.2)3.8 = 1.56$. If we assumed that the expenditure would be financed by some combination of debt and increased taxes, the appropriate multiplier could have been determined and would lie between 1.56 and 3.8.

Now consider a public investment financed by a special excise tax, such as a gasoline tax. I assume as an approximation that the tax is borne entirely by consumers through direct purchase of gasoline or through higher prices of products for which gasoline is an input, for example, taxi services. The revenue collected from the tax represents a reduction in the individual's disposable income. Therefore, the effect on savings and investment will be essentially the same as the effect of an increase in the income tax, and the multiplier should be 1.56. Note that in neither the case of the increased income tax nor the case of the gasoline tax are the effects of the price distortion caused by the tax taken into account. It is critical to remember that, given other distortions, the effect of an additional distortion may confer either a benefit or a cost on the economy in terms of increased or decreased efficiency.

In general, any federal expenditure or cost that is financed by taxes and has the effect of reducing disposable income by the amount of that cost should be multiplied by 1.56. The corporate profits tax, however, may fall on either disposable income or retained earnings or both. Does this make a difference?

Suppose that an increase in the corporate income tax raises a given amount of money, say $1,000,000. Then the effect of the tax appears to depend on what share of the earnings would have been paid out as dividends. Suppose the entire amount would have been paid as dividends. Individuals with 20 percent tax rates would have received $1,000,000 less in taxable income and would have paid $200,000 less in federal taxes and received $800,000 less of disposable income. Therefore, to gain $800,000 in net federal revenue, the government would have to generate $1,000,000 through corporate income taxes, and the result would have been to reduce private savings and investments by 20 percent and private consumption by 80 percent of the $800,000, respectively. Again the appropriate shadow price is 1.56 applied to the $800,000. However, the shadow price applied to the $1,000,000 should be (0.2)3.8, where 0.2 is the fraction of the cost that represents a reduction in income tax revenues, plus (0.8)1.56. This equals 2.01.

Now suppose that all earnings would have been retained by the corporation, which would have invested them directly or put them into the securities markets where they would have been channeled into investments. In this case the tax would raise the full $1,000,000, but an identical amount of private investment would be displaced so that costs paid by a tax that falls on retained earnings should be multiplied by 3.8. This would be true if (1) the value of the stock did not reflect the decreased value of the retained earnings that were invested, or (2) individuals did not consider the decreased value of their stock in making savings and consumption decisions. Both assumptions are improbable.

Suppose instead that a $1,000,000 decrease in retained earnings was reflected in a $1,000,000 decrease in the market value of the stock and suppose this represented a capital loss that could be written off against other income. Then individuals could, if they sold the stock, get a $1,000,000 tax deduction, which would reduce their taxes by $200,000, and they would have $800,000 less in disposable income than if the tax had not been raised. Therefore, whether the corporate income tax reduces retained earnings or dividends, the effects are the same and the multiplier should be 2.01. However, the difference in the tax treatment of capital gains and losses as compared with that of other ordinary gains or losses of income will modify this result. This of major importance for the analysis of some economic policies, but probably not for most social benefit–cost analysis.

Given the assumptions that we have adopted, we do not need to consider the effects of financing marginal projects by taxes; this analysis has been included as an alternative assumption that many analysts believe to be the correct one. The framework presented here is capable of accommodating either position or some combination of the two.

Now consider costs that fall directly on private individuals and firms, such as the costs that are reflected immediately in the higher cost of consumer goods. These costs occur when a government regulation results in higher variable production costs or higher costs for self-produced services. As a first approximation, such costs can be treated as a decrease in disposable income and therefore, like an excise tax, should be multiplied by 1.56.

Other costs take the form of investment either by the firm or by the individual, and are somewhat trickier to deal with. Consider first the case of an individual who is required by law to buy a more expensive, energy-conserving water heater. Whether the added cost comes at the expense of saving or consumption at the time of the purchase depends on the individual's perception of the benefits. Suppose first that he is aware of the savings in fuel bills that the more efficient water heater would produce and that, given his after-tax rate of return, the present value of these savings would exceed the added cost of the more efficient water heater. In this case, buying the more efficient water heater is an alternative form of saving and investment which the individual will prefer. The regulation will, therefore, have no effect on his decision and does not produce benefits for, or impose costs on, the homeowner.

Now consider the alternative situation in which the consumer perceives no benefit from the more expensive heater. From his perspective, the higher price simply removes disposable income he would have been able to save or consume without producing any offsetting benefits if the regulation had not been in effect. Therefore, the impact of the regulation will be to reduce his savings by 20 percent of the added cost and his consumption by 80 percent, so that the appropriate multiplier is again 1.56.

Now consider some intermediate situation; for example, the individual perceives that there will be savings and that the present value of these savings, using his after-tax rate of discount, is 50 percent of the added cost. Therefore,

50 percent of the cost of the regulation is like an alternative form of saving and as a result will reduce other forms of savings; the other 50 percent of the cost is like a tax on disposable income and will reduce both savings and consumption. The total effect will be a reduction in savings of $0.5 + (0.2)0.5 = 0.6$ and a reduction in consumption of 0.4. In this case the appropriate multiplier of the cost is $(0.6)3.8 + 0.4 = 2.68$.

Now consider a government policy for which the cost will take the form of additional private corporate investment that is required by law. Environmental regulations requiring that coal-fired plants be equipped with stack-gas scrubbers, or that oil-fired plants convert to coal, are government policies for which some of the cost takes the form of required private investment. If we assume that savings in the economy as a whole are fixed given its structure, including its tax structure, then these required private investments will displace other private investments and should be multiplied by 3.8.

Now consider the final category of costs associated with a project or policy, namely, external costs. Suppose that external costs fall upon the firm. To the extent that they increase the variable cost of production, they will be passed on to the consumer and can, as a first approximation, be treated as a reduction in disposable income and therefore multiplied by 1.56. To the extent that these costs require additional corporate investment, these costs should be multiplied by 3.8.

Now consider external costs borne by individuals directly. To the extent that these costs are perceived and reflected as a decrease in income or wealth, a persuasive case can be made that both consumption and savings will be affected. For example, increased noise and air pollution from a highway may decrease the value of residences near the highway, or increased smog may require that some people live farther from their places of business to avoid it. In the latter case, this cost would be reflected in the increased cost of transportation. In either of these situations the appropriate multiplier appears to be about 1.56.

Now suppose that there were an unperceived health hazard. This would not have an impact on consumption or saving until it was perceived, even though the hazard, had it been perceived, would have affected consumption and savings decisions. An array of undiscovered hazards of this type may well exist but are not especially important for benefit–cost analysis because, once the hazards are recognized, their cost will be reflected in market decisions. However, one area in which research is needed is in determining how the benefits and costs of government programs not directly reflected in an individual's disposable income—for example, free public services or the discomfort of environmental pollution—affect an individual's savings–consumption decisions.

Thus, although there is a wide variety of circumstances to be considered in analyzing costs and their shadow prices, the results can be categorized relatively simply. All costs that are reflected in increased government expenditures out of general revenues or in decreased tax revenues, for example, costs financed by tax credits, should be multiplied by 3.8. All costs that take the form of increased capital expenditure in the private sector should be multiplied by 3.8; however, investments that individuals perceive as offering no return should be multiplied by 1.56. All other costs should be multiplied by 1.56 or, in the case of a corporate tax, by 2.01. Put differently, costs are divided into two categories with one exception, those that are incurred directly at the expense of private investment and those that are treated by individuals as reductions in disposable income or wealth. The first category of costs should be multiplied by 3.8, the second, by 1.56.

Categories of Benefits and Their Respective Shadow Prices

The treatment of benefits is roughly analogous to that of costs and can be presented by using similar lines of argument. First, of all benefits that accrue to the federal government as decreased expenditures, such as fuel cost savings from the installation of energy-conserving technologies in government buildings, or as user charges, or as increased tax revenues leaving tax rates unchanged, all reduce the size of the deficit and therefore stimulate an equal amount of private investment. These benefits should be multiplied by 3.8.

Now consider the benefits that accrue to corporations as increased revenues. The component of revenue that represents depreciation is a return of capital and, at least in the aggregate, will be reinvested. Therefore, these benefits should be multiplied by 3.8. The component of revenues which represents increased corporate profits will go to corporate income taxes, which we assume to be 50 percent, and to after-tax profits. The after-tax profits will be distributed to individuals and taxed at 20 percent; the remaining 80 percent of the 50 percent of the initial benefit will become disposable income, which individuals will divide between consumption and investment. Therefore, 60 percent of the total benefit will be returned by the government through taxes, thereby reducing the deficit and correspondingly increasing private investment by the same amount. This percentage, 60 percent, of benefits should be multiplied by 3.8. Of the remaining benefits, 20 percent will be saved and 80 percent will be consumed, so that this fraction should be multiplied by 1.56. Thus, benefits that are accrued as before-tax corporate profits should be multiplied by $(0.6)3.8 + (0.4)1.56 = 2.90$.

Suppose the benefits accrue directly to individuals as increased, taxable personal income. This would include income to proprietorships and partnerships and interest income from energy investments. In this case 20 percent of these benefits would be returned to the government in higher taxes, and 80 percent would be disposable income divided between saving and consumption. The appropriate multiplier in this case is 2.01. If the marginal tax rate were higher, this multiplier would be higher.

Finally, consider benefits that accrue to individuals and are, as a first approximation, equivalent to an increase in disposable income in that they are nontaxable. Individual cost savings through conservation, reduced energy prices, and free energy-related services are examples of such benefits. In this case it is easily seen that the appropriate multiplier is 1.56.

Now consider the case of external benefits and the benefits of public goods. To the extent they are perceived as nontaxable income, or are capitalized into the value of an asset that is part of perceived wealth, they should be treated in the same way that external costs are treated; that is, they should be multiplied by 1.56 because 20 percent of these benefits will be reflected in increased savings and investment. A much trickier case is the strategic petroleum reserve, which, if successful, will deter an embargo by oil producing countries and will never be used. In this sense it is like a successful nuclear deterrent. One has to consider the expected situations with and without the reserve and the benefits will then become clear and will fit into the categories discussed above. Again we need to learn more about whether such benefits have any effect on consumption and saving.

Before summarizing the conclusions, it is instructive to consider an example that will illustrate how benefits and costs should be treated using this methodology for many of the cases cited in this section. Imagine that there is a breakthrough in fusion technology and that we are considering a major fusion research and development program that in the future would provide an inexpensive, clean, and inexhaustible supply of energy.

Assume that to have this fusion energy option in place within thirty years would require a twenty-year period of research and development to be financed entirely by the federal government and a ten-year period of constructing the capital facilities, which would be privately funded. At the end of thirty years, relatively cheap, clean electricity would become available. The net benefits would take several forms. First, there would be the net revenues to the power companies, that is, benefits equal to the sales value of the power minus operating costs. Second, because power costs would be lower, consumers would receive benefits in the form of increased consumer surplus. Third, because of the clean nature of the fusion process there would be benefits in terms of an improved environment, for example, a sharp reduction in acid rain.

How should these benefits and costs be treated within the framework presented in this paper? First, the R&D costs to the government, assuming they increased the deficit, should be multiplied by 3.8. If one assumes they were financed by increased personal income taxes, the multiplier would be 1.56. The capital costs to the private sector represent capital demands that will displace other capital investment, given our assumption of fixed savings and investment equal to total savings; therefore, these costs should also be multiplied by 3.8.

Now consider the net revenues to the power company. These have to be divided between depreciation, which is typically reinvested, and profit or the return on investment. Because depreciation will be fully reinvested, it should be multiplied by 3.8. Following our methodology, the part representing corporate profits should be multiplied by 2.9. Benefits accruing to consumers as lower energy costs should be considered as an increase in disposable income and multiplied by 1.56.

So far, this is quite simple and straightforward. However, the difficulty comes, as one might expect, with environmental benefits. To the extent that these benefits are reflected in the value of market assets—for example, resorts that are more valuable because acid rain has diminished—they probably should be treated as disposable income (at least until the assets are sold) and multiplied by 1.56. Other intangible benefits such as lower health risks or a slightly more attractive environment may not be perceived as affecting a person's wealth and therefore may not have an impact on decisions about savings and consumption. Although this is an area in need of further research, it is not a serious problem for the approach we have adopted here, because in practice we generally cannot measure these benefits, and therefore not knowing the appropriate multiplier does not pose a serious practical problem.

What is interesting about this example is that it is not as difficult as one might at first suspect to develop and apply a system of multipliers to adjust benefits and costs to their consumption equivalents.

Synthesis and Conclusions

There are a number of important conclusions one can draw from this analysis. First, if all of the costs are borne by the government in increased expenditures or decreased tax revenues and if all of the benefits accrue to the government in the form of reduced costs or increased revenues from appropriate user charges, one can use the social rate of time preference, generally 4.6 percent (3 percent in the case of energy investment), without concern about multipliers for benefits and costs. This is true whether we assume that the marginal dollar of government expenditure is financed by debt, by increased taxes, or by a combination of the two, if it is assumed to be the same for all periods in which benefits and costs occur. This is because all benefits and costs will be multiplied by the same factor. This covers all cases of cost-effectiveness analysis.

Second, if we assume that the marginal dollar of government expenditure is financed by taxation rather than deficit spending, which displaces private investment, then, except for costs that take the form of increased corporate income taxes, the multipliers associated with all categories of costs will be 1.56. For costs that represent increased corporate income taxes, the multiplier will be 2.01. Therefore, the appropriate multiple for most costs will be between 1.56 and 2.01 if a public investment is financed through increased taxation.

If we make the symmetrical assumption that increases in government revenues or decreases in costs will be passed on in lower personal income taxes, then again the multiplier to apply to benefits in virtually all categories is 1.56. Under these assumptions one would arrive at the correct answer by applying a 4.6 percent discount rate to unadjusted benefits and costs.

Third, in the case least favorable to public investment, one would multiply the costs by 3.8 and the benefits by 1.56 and discount at 4.6 percent (3 percent for energy-related investments). For almost any investment with substantial benefits well into the future, this will increase its present value over using a discount rate of 6–10 percent. This would certainly make many energy investments appear much more economical.

Fourth, the procedure of categorizing benefits and costs and then adjusting them by the use of shadow prices or multipliers is not an insurmountable task. This procedure makes it clear that the true social cost of government expenditure representing increased consumption paid for by the federal government, welfare payments, for example, are almost four times the expenditure. Therefore, the more serious displacement of private capital formation occurs not primarily as a result of public investments, which displace private capital but also stimulate future capital formation, but rather as a result of publicly financed consumption.

Finally, I have assumed a fully employed economy and a fixed saving ratio so that there is one-to-one crowding out of private investment by increased deficits. If this is not the case because there are unemployed resources that are drawn into production or because the savings rate is sensitive to the interest rate, then the crowding out of private investment by public expenditures will decrease and the appropriate multiplier will be less than 3.8 for these costs; for the case of significant unemployed resources, the multiplier will be lower still.

If this social benefit–cost calculus were applied to most energy investments, public or private, many more would appear to be economically justified even though in many cases the costs would be doubled. This is particularly true of research and development investments for which the benefits will occur well into the future. The present distortions in the private capital markets, largely due to taxes, drive a wedge between the before-tax rate of return that firms earn on capital projects and the after-tax rates of return that investors can earn on assets that represent claims against these projects. These market distortions also seriously distort the economy away from savings and investment toward consumption and, perhaps as importantly, against long-term investments. The methodology for applying social benefit–cost analysis corrects for these distortions in analyzing public policies and investments while taking account of the major effects of these distortions on private capital formation. However, it is strictly a second-best methodology designed for evaluating social choices in an economy as we now know it.

A Postscript on the Discount Rate and Intergenerational Equity

The analyses contained in this chapter and in chapter 2 make it clear that certain distortions in the economy promote consumption at the expense of investment and short-term investment at the expense of long-term investment. This is true based on the time preferences of the present generation. Certainly these distortions are biased against the interests of future generations. The framework of benefit–cost analysis developed here would help correct these distortions and biases as far as public policy decisions are concerned and could form the basis for choosing policies to correct the generational biases caused by these distortions. Perhaps the best policy would be to lessen or remove the distortions themselves by revising the tax structure.

However, benefit–cost analysis by itself has never been a tool for resolving issues of equity among members of one generation because benefits and costs are measured in terms of each individual's willingness to pay or accept compensation, and this in turn depends on his wealth. To resolve the issues of equity for individuals within a generation or for individuals in different generations, one has to make interpersonal comparisions of utility. Whether the utilitarian framework as embodied in welfare functions and economic growth models is sufficiently robust in theory to be up to this task is open to debate. However, it certainly has not been sufficiently developed to give us concrete answers concerning real decisions. It does help identify the issues we should be considering and the logical implication of certain positions. Although of great value in providing guidance about how to think about such issues, the theory itself does not decide the issues. Other rules or judgment must be evoked in deciding whether to incur the risks for the future by creating and storing nuclear waste or by not investing heavily in energy R&D. Although the choice of the discount rate has important implications for energy investment policy, these major issues of intergenerational equity should not be decided by, or buried in, the choice of the discount rate for social benefit–cost analysis.

Index